Geography
and the
Urban Environment

GEOGRAPHY AND THE URBAN ENVIRONMENT

Progress in Research and Applications

Editors

D. T. HERBERT

Professor of Geography, University College of Wales, Swansea

and

R. J. JOHNSTON

Professor of Geography, University of Sheffield

Geography and the Urban Environment

Progress in Research and Applications

Volume VI

Edited by

D. T. HERBERT
Professor of Geography
University College of Wales, Swansea

and

R. J. JOHNSTON
Professor of Geography
University of Sheffield

JOHN WILEY & SONS
Chichester · New York · Brisbane · Toronto · Singapore

Library of Congress Cataloging Card Number: 78-647093

British Library Cataloguing in Publication Data:

Geography and the urban environment.
  Vol. 6
  1. Cities and towns
  I. Herbert, David, 1935–   II. Johnston, R.J.
  910′091732   GF125
  ISBN 0 471 90417 1

Typeset by Eta Services (Typesetters) Ltd, Beccles, Suffolk
Printed by Page Brothers (Norwich) Ltd

For
David Aled and Nia Wyn Herbert
and
Chris and Lucy Johnston

List of Contributors

T. A. CLARK   *College of Design and Planning, University of Colorado, 1100 Fourteenth Street, Denver, Colorado 80202, USA*

W. A. V. CLARK   *Department of Geography, University of California, 1101 Gayley Center, Los Angeles 90024 USA*

D. M. EVANS   *Department of Geography, University of Technology, Loughborough, Leicester, LE11 3TU, UK*

R. G. GOLLEDGE   *Department of Geography, University of California, Santa Barbara, California 93106, USA*

C. HAMNETT   *Social Sciences, Open University, Walton Hall, Milton Keynes, MK7 6AA, UK*

S. HANSON   *Graduate School of Geography, Clark University, 950 Main Street, Worcester, Massachusetts 01610, USA*

A. M. HAY   *Department of Geography, University of Sheffield, Sheffield, S10 2TN, UK*

K. HOGGART   *Department of Geography, King's College, Strand, London, WC2R 2LS*

P. A. LONGLEY   *Department of Geography, University of Bristol, University Road, Bristol, BS8 1SS, UK*

M. PACIONE   *Department of Geography, University of Strathclyde, Livingstone Tower, 26 Richmond Street, Glasgow, G1 1XH, UK*

G. Rushton   *Department of Geography, University of Iowa, Iowa City, Iowa 52242, USA*

N. Wrigley   *Department of Geography, University of Bristol, University Road, Bristol, BS8 1SS, UK*

Contents

Contents

Preface

This sixth volume of *Geography and the Urban Environment* maintains the style and objectives of a series of which, unfortunately, it is the last volume. We have continued to attract manuscripts of high quality, mostly through our own initiatives as editors seeking to develop themes within the particular volumes but also occasionally by being offered finished products which fit in with our more general purposes. This continuous flow of articles and the volume of ongoing research of which it is indicative is gratifying both to us as editors of a research series and to the discipline of geography as a whole. The series ends for 'marketing' reasons, for on academic merit it has been widely acclaimed and appreciated.

Our methodological chapter on the theme of behavioural geography may seem more specific than some of its predecessors but research in the behavioural mode has had wide-ranging impact upon geographers interested in urban studies. It is also a theme subject to widely different interpretations which range from the kind of behaviouralism developing out of positivist approaches and model-building to a very different kind of research with strong humanistic meanings. Reg Golledge and Gerard Rushton belong unambiguously to the former of these positions and develop their view of behavioural geography in a rigorous and perceptive way. Neil Wrigley and Paul Longley's more technical discussion of discrete choice modelling is closely aligned to this perspective and demonstrates how human geography as a quantitative science can provide valuable tools for the measurement of some aspects of human behaviour. Susan Hanson continues the positivist analysis of behaviour with particular reference to urban travel. Her use of a behavioural perspective again relates strongly to that developed by Golledge and Rushton, using both a conceptual model and an empirical analysis, the latter based upon travel-diary data. Whilst invoking use of information levels or cognitive representations which may be less amenable to precise measurement, she does not attempt to 'unravel the causal knot' in which information and travel are intertwined. Alan Hay is also concerned with urban travel but his study of the urban public transport subsidy takes him some distance from the type of analysis followed by Susan Hanson. Subsidies for public transport are emotional and political issues which usually involve distinctive value judgements. As Hay argues, the transport (economic) and social objectives for public transport may be contradictory and there are

xi

impacts of subsidy-policies on the urban system which are not always appreciated or understood.

Thus the first four contributions in this volume provide a strong discussion around a particular interpretation of behavioural analysis and a clear link with aspects of urban travel and urban transport. Keith Hoggart's chapter provides a broad context of political urban-geography for a further series of chapters with strong legislative and judicial threads. Hoggart examines the relationship between social and geographical theory by focusing upon power relations in local communities and in doing so touches upon some of the main conceptual issues with which social geographers interested in the urban system are concerned. He rehearses the meaning of political science concepts of power and the state, scrutinizes the structural dimension and examines the roles of decision-makers at various levels in the 'hierarchy'. Capitalists, local State, local politicians, and local electorates all work within 'limits'; the extensiveness, flexibility and conditions under which such limits hold are questions which still need closer definition and measurement.

The political and legislative decision-making context is very relevant to the succeeding two chapters on suburban economic integration and judicial intervention in urban education, both of which draw upon American case studies. Both chapters draw heavily upon legal case evidence to trace changing attitudes towards the social conflicts raised by the juxtaposed needs of different socio-ethnic groups within American society. Tom Clark examines the well-known issues of exclusionary zoning and other forms of discriminatory practice which serve to perpetuate the levels of economic and residential segregation in metropolitan areas. He examines alternative strategies to reduce disparities but concludes that progress is extremely slow and judicial and legislative actions to date have only succeeded in promoting a small measure of economic integration. Bill Clark again uses judicial case histories in an extensive way to analyse the school integration process and the relationships which it holds with residential change. The conclusions which he draws hold limited optimism for those dedicated to integrated schools and the reduction of socio-ethnic barriers. Despite a couple of decades of judicial intervention and legal actions the record is patchy and inconclusive. There are at least as many changes in school integration resulting from neighbourhood transition as there are from judicial intervention, and neighbourhood or residential integration remains an elusive goal.

The remaining three chapters are concerned with urban residential areas and the processes by which they evolve. Chris Hamnett and David Evans are particularly involved with theories of residential change and their critical reviews of recent literature draw them into conflict with interpretations of those writing from a Marxist perspective. Christ Hamnett's more specific concern is with gentrification as a process by which morphological and socio-economic change occurs in the inner parts of Western cities. He traces the origin of the term, provides examples of the occurrence of gentrification and assesses the value of existing models of residential location in understanding the phenomenon. Hamnett's severest criticisms of existing attempts at explanation are aimed at Neil Smith's Marxist analysis of gentrification based upon production and transformation of residential space by capital. Among the serious flaws in Smith's approach, he claims, are the dismissal of the roles of employment and demographic change; Hamnett's argument favours an integrated theory of gentrification.

David Evans's study of suburban landscapes has a stronger empirical content with a case study of Vancouver, but he too critically reviews a range of contemporary approaches. For David Evans many of these approaches to the suburbanization process have serious deficiencies and in particular neglect the significance of 'localism' which may emerge through humanistic perspectives. A 'demystified' view of suburban space is one which grounds theoretical claims in the realities from which they spring. Michael Pacione provides the most empirically-based contribution to this volume with his analysis of local areas within Glasgow. Although he is dealing with a difficult and elusive concept, that of urban community or 'neighbourhood', his brief in this particular chapter is to use results from a detailed survey to demonstrate the existence of local community and the roles which it assumes. Classification, stability over time, cohesion and levels of satisfaction are studied in the Glasgow area and the relationships of these identified areas to various policy and decision-making functions of urban government are examined. Generally, Pacione observes that political and service-area boundaries reflect administrative convenience rather than neighbourhood or local-community feeling.

This volume of Geography and the Urban Environment contains several major themes which integrate well within the volume and relate in many ways to topics initiated in earlier volumes of the series. Principally, however, they continue to offer examples of ongoing research in full and developed discussions. Modern urban geographical research covers a wide range of topics and perspectives in what may be variously described as a 'rich diversity' on the one hand and 'eclecticism' on the other. We have consistently welcomed manuscripts which illustrate research at various points in this range of activity and those which attempt the worthwhile but unfashionable goal of academic integration. The ending of the series leaves a gap in the available outlets for research material but the six published volumes offer a collective contribution which will retain its value and relevance for some time to come.

D. T. HERBERT
R. J. JOHNSTON

Geography and the Urban Environment
Progress in Research and Applications, Volume VI
Edited by D. T. Herbert and R. J. Johnston

Chapter 1

A Review of Analytic Behavioural Research in Geography

Reginald G. Golledge and Gerard Rushton

The development of behavioural research in geography has resulted in almost as much debate as did the introduction of theory and quantitative methods. This debate has the usual structure—the setting up of senseless straw men to make useless points; misrepresentations of the somewhat varied intentions of the original behavioural researchers; volatile criticisms from those espousing alternate epistemologies, approaches and methods; and even misguided (but well-meaning) research support from those who misunderstood the nature and purpose of the approach. This paper is not designed to respond to all the above points. Rather it focuses generally on that subset of behavioural research that we label 'analytic', and specifically on two areas of this subset with which we are quite familiar—environmental cognition and spatial choice/spatial preferences.

Despite this admittedly narrow focus, the points we make are easily generalizable to other sub-areas. In particular, we stress the message that simply because a researcher examines the behaviour in space of people, plants, animals, freight flows, hazards, or industrial activities, this does *not* necessarily qualify the research as being behavioural and it may throw little light on the nature of human spatial behaviour. We cannot stress this point too much. As R. J. Johnston points out (in personal correspondence to us) 'unbridled empiricism relating to behaviour in space doesn't take you very far with regard to a general understanding of spatial behaviour'. The theme that spatial behavioural research requires an understanding of behavioural processes to achieve its goals adequately is stressed throughout the chapter. Let us then show how the theme emerged in early behavioural research, has remained a significant component of ongoing behavioural research, and has become exemplified in ongoing analytical behavioural research.

THE EMERGENCE OF BEHAVIOURAL RESEARCH IN GEOGRAPHY

Although isolated examples of behavioural research in human geography can be found in the first part of this century, it was not until the sixth decade that well-articulated behavioural research paradigms began emerging. Since many of these paradigms had their roots in other disciplines, the emergence of the behavioural movement in geography can be attributed in part to a desire to search other disciplines for 'new' models of man and environment on which to base a search for understanding and explanation. Consequent cross-disciplinary interaction saw an exchange and sharing of epistemologies, theories, methods, concepts, and models, and the development of new sub-areas within the discipline that reflected the cross-disciplinary interactions. As a result of these interactions, many scientists expanded their laboratory to include the real world, and many researchers who considered the real world their laboratory abstracted from it through processes such as simulation and model building.

While an interdisciplinary tradition had long existed in geography, it was up until this time largely characterized as the discipline interested in inventory and description of the spatial and temporal facts of existence and, where possible, representing these facts on maps. Geographic research revolved around discovering structure or order in the natural, human and built environments. In the process of recovering the form or structure of a given environment, classificatory tools (such as regions) and methods of explanation (such as areal association), were used to promote 'regional understanding'.

During the 1940s and 1950s, a series of papers appeared that are generally recognized as forerunners of widespread behavioural research in geography. These included Wright's (1947) explorations into the world of imagination, White's (1945) explorations of people's responses to intermittent hazardous occurrences, and Hagerstrand's (1952, 1954, 1957) examination of the role of information diffusion in the processes of innovation adoption and the selection of migration destinations. Each of these influenced the discipline, and, along with the rising surge of interest in theory and quantitative methods, became a major part of the discipline in the late 1950s and early 1960s.

The 1960s

The 1960s saw a rapid development of interest in behavioural research as human geographers generally focused more on spatial processes than on spatial forms. The message that behavioural researchers imparted was quite clear. Superficial descriptions of the natural, human, or built environments (whether verbal, cartographic, or mathematical) were no longer enough. What was required for both understanding and explanation was insight into why things were where they were. This theme has become known as a process-driven search for explanation and understanding.

Apart from the change in emphasis from form to process, there are a number of other stimuli that precipitated behavioural research in geography. Amongst the earliest of these was the search for alternative models of man. In particular, the omniscient economically or spatially rational beings incorporated into predictive and explanatory models during the theoretical and quantitative revolution were found to be an inadequate base for those interested in the variability of behaviour as well as its uniformity. In their articles on game theory and decision theory, Gould (1963) and Wolpert (1964) exposed the discipline to a variety of behavioural criteria other than complete rationality. Thus notions of conservative low-risk behaviour, minimum regret, Laplacian uniformity, satisficing, bounded rationality, and other more- and less-risky behaviours appeared with increasing frequency as models of human behaviour and provided a major impetus for geographic research.

Along with the search for a model of man (other than economic rationality) came an understanding that environments other than the observable external physical environment existed. Cross-disciplinary interaction prior to 1960 had clearly indicated that constraints imposed by economic, social, cultural, political, legal, and other environments were equally as real as constraints imposed by the physical environment. Researches in the 1960s show that perceptual, cognitive, ideological, philosophical, psychological, and other environments were also part of the dialectic between humanity and objective reality. These discoveries opened up brave new worlds to the geographer who had traditionally focused on the man–environment relationship as his central theme.

The development of alternate models of man and environment on which to base explanations of man's activities produced waves of new research activity in the discipline. However, for the new environments, no existing data banks were adequate. In many cases the fundamental terms, concepts and assumptions necessary for the existence of such environments were either ill-defined or poorly known. The geographer who wished to incorporate the new models of man or the new environments into his explanatory schema thus had to begin by defining a set of relevant variables so that data could be collected and used. This was, then, a time of very fundamental research into geographical primitives such as the concepts of distance (Golledge et al., 1969; Briggs, 1969; Lowrey, 1970), spatial behaviour (Rushton, 1969a; Olsson and Gale, 1968), preference (Rushton, 1965, 1969b), choice (Downs, 1970; Golledge et al., 1966), place and space (Tuan, 1974; Buttimer, 1969), landscape (Lowenthal, 1961), and so on. In most cases this fundamental research involved creating new data sets by the use of survey research or other interactive methods. The need to collect these data also encouraged the exploration of other social and behavioural sciences for appropriate collection and analysis methods. Thus it precipitated the use of non-parametric measurement procedures, complex experimental designs, and the expansion of the concept of multivariate analysis to include multidimensional analysis.

An additional focal point for behavioural researchers was the problem of scale or level of aggregation. Most of the normative models produced in the late 1950s and early 1960s focused on population aggregates and, of necessity, assumed uniform behaviours across the entire population subgroup. Behavioural researchers often rejected this level of analysis and began by focusing on the individual (a disaggregated approach) and attempted to find ways of analysing and grouping individuals on the basis of behaviours rather than *a priori* classification schemes. This change from aggregate to disaggregate scale of operation and from objective to subjective criteria for grouping produced a clear line of demarcation between behavioural and other researchers in the discipline.

Much behavioural research simply involved looking at old problems from new perspectives. However, the new perspectives often also meant that new variables and concepts had to be introduced to the discipline. Of major importance to behavioural research was the strengthening of ties to the discipline of psychology and the focusing on internal processes that resulted in human thoughts and actions—for example, learning (Golledge, 1965, 1967; Golledge and Brown, 1967; Gould, 1967a), perception (Saarinen, 1966; Sonnenfeld, 1966; Kates, 1967), attitudes (Kates, 1962), images and cognitive maps (Downs, 1970; Stea, 1969), personalities (Sonnenfeld, 1966), preferences (Gould, 1967b; Rushton, 1965, 1969a), and other human behavioural processes that were seen to be of potential use in helping to understand relations between humans and their various environments. In short, the 1960s saw the beginning of a tendency to concentrate equally on both subjective and objective environments and to become aware of the myriad individual, societal, and institutional constraints that limited human spatial behaviour.

Along with the emphasis on behaviourally oriented research activity, there came a widening of the epistemological bases of research in the discipline. While the strong positivist tradition introduced in the 1950s continued (Schaefer, 1953; Golledge and Amedeo, 1968; Harvey, 1969), interest developed in other analytic philosophies as well as various humanist and idealist philosophies (including phenomenology, existentialism, and so on). Gradually the limits of logical positivism were comprehended and a range of other scientific and analytic approaches emerged, including rationalism, empiricism, physicalism, instrumentalism, and objectivism. As part of this general concern with the constraints exerted on individual, small-group, and large-group behaviour, there also emerged an increasing level of interest in ideological bases other than those traditionally associated with Western democratic societies—particularly Marxism.

The 1960s, therefore, saw an explosion of research and a proliferation of ideas that focused attention on new epistemologies, behavioural processes, data sets, data measurement and analysis techniques, models of man, subjective environments, and an overall increasing concern for achieving satisfactory levels of explanation of spatial phenomena.

The 1970s

By the early 1970s, behavioural research was common across many sub-areas of the discipline. However, just as the 1960s had seen the development of a reaction against theoretical and quantitative work, so too in the early 1970s there emerged a reaction against behavioural research in the discipline. By the time the reaction against the quantitative revolution had gained any strength, quantitative methods were widely accepted and distributed throughout the entire discipline and the attack sputtered and faltered because of this widespread diffusion. The most vigorous attacks on behavioural research came from within: these originated to a large extent from those who labeled themselves humanists, rejected scientific and analytic behavioural research, and declared themselves to be of different ilk to other behavioural researchers. Despite this split, behavioural research became widespread throughout the discipline and began to be incorporated in a standard way in introductory textbooks (Jakle *et al.*, 1976; Porteous, 1977; Gold, 1980). In addition, books such as Downs and Stea (1973, 1977), Saarinen (1976), Moore and Golledge (1976a), and King and Golledge (1978), not only incorporated behavioural ideas into conventional geographic sub-areas, but also showed that a full understanding of many spatial problems could not ignore the behavioural dimension.

Perhaps the most significant development in the early 1970s was the forging of strong links between geography and psychology. While some of the earlier links between these two disciplines were conceptual, the 1970s saw a strengthened adaptation of measurement procedures, model building, experimental design, and other ties. The ties were expressed in two quite different ways. Lowenthal (1972), for example, pointed out that a good part of behavioural research in geography through the 1960s and early 1970s, articulated in journals such as *Environment and Behavior* and *Geographical Analysis*, was statistical in nature and model-building in orientation, and appeared tied to decision-making, choice theory, learning theories and cognitive representations of space. Other behaviourally-oriented research activities were linked to concepts of values, morals, ethics, images and subjective methods of evaluation, and found expression in journals such as the *Annals of the Association of American Geographers* and the *Geographical Review*. In particular, Lowenthal pointed out that the environmental perception literature, a bridge between these two rather disparate strands, became more and more 'metaphysical in outlook, anthropological in content, and historical and literary in ... modes of analysis and presentation' (Lowenthal, 1972, p. 252). An example of the theory/model/measurement oriented research was the volume entitled *Behavioral Problems in Geography* (Cox and Golledge, 1969), which emphasized topics such as: conceptional and measurement problems in cognitive behavioural approaches in location theory; social networks and voting models; geographical relevance of learning theories; place utility; intra-urban mobility; the definition and measurement of locational preferences; the modelling of interactions; and the measurement of mental maps. Such work emphasized understanding the processes that produced spatial behaviours as well as examining the spatial behaviours themselves. As an alternative viewpoint, the special edition of *Environment and Behavior*, edited by Lowenthal in 1972, epitomized the work on behaviour and environment in terms of personality, individual and community spaces, the significance of social interactions, and modes of apprehension.

The 1970s, then, saw a consolidation of the link between geography and psychology and an increasing awareness of what each discipline had to offer the other. This awareness was fostered in such books as *Image and Environment* (Downs and Stea, 1973), *Maps and Minds* (Downs and Stea, 1977), *Environmental Knowing* (Moore and Golledge, 1976a), *Environment and Behavior* (Porteous, 1977), *Human Behavior and Environment* (Altman and Wohlwill, 1977), *Environmental Psychology* (Proshansky *et al.*, 1970), *An Introduction to Environmental Psychology* (Ittelson *et al.*, 1974) *Cities Space and Behavior* (King and Golledge, 1978), and *Spatial Choice and Spatial Behavior*, (Golledge and Rushton, 1976). The more humanistic side was represented by offerings such as *Humanistic Geography* (Ley and Samuels, 1978); *Environmental Planning: Perception and Behavior* (Saarinen, 1976), *Experience, Environment and Human Potentials* (Leff, 1978) and *Timing Space and Spacing Time* (Carlstein *et al.*, 1978) provided links between analytical and humanist camps.

It is difficult to summarize the complete range of topics over which behavioural research spread throughout the 1970s but it appeared to infiltrate most of human geography. This emphasized the contention of the early behavioural researchers that what they were advocating was an approach rather than a development of a new subfield of the discipline (Golledge *et al.*, 1972). Along with traditional areas, however, the 1970s saw geographers entering comparatively new (for them) areas of research activity, including work with subject populations other than normal adults. Such populations included children, minority groups, and disadvantaged groups such as the aged, the infirm, the mentally handicapped, and the poor (e.g. Hart, 1978; Golledge *et al.*, 1979a,b, 1980; Golledge *et al.*, 1983). In reference to their subject populations, geographers also departed from a traditional interest in large groups of subjects and began to recognize the concepts of non-random sampling and use of small subject groups (Edgington, 1969).

The 1970s also saw the geographer and the psychologist develop a willingness to publish in journals of each other's field. This has become more common during the late 1970s and the 1980s. Papers by psychologists appeared in such journals as *Geographical Analysis* (e.g. Hubert, 1978; Baird *et al.*, 1982; Burrows and Sadalla, 1979; MacKay and Zinnes 1981), and the *Professional*

Geographer (e.g. Staplin and Sadalla, 1981; Magana *et al.*, 1981). A similar process of publishing in psychology or interdisciplinary books and journals by geographers (e.g. Louviere, 1974; Hubert and Golledge, 1981a,b; Beck and Wood, 1976; Downs, 1970, 1981; Golledge and Rayner, 1982; Blaut *et al.*, 1970; Downs and Meyer, 1978) has also become evident.

Some of the major components of behavioural research in the 1970s were methodological in nature. These included the adaptation and adoption of measurement devices such as multidimensional scaling, individual differences scaling procedures, repertory grids, environmental response inventories, measures of personality and/or emotions, thematic aperception tests, non-parametric randomization procedures, and so on. There is now in the discipline a widespread use of techniques such as semantic differential scaling, categorical measurement procedures, Markov modelling, graph-theoretic measures, and clustering techniques, as well as a range of non-parametric techniques. Use of standard psychological techniques such as block models, factorial designs, and tests of reliability and validity of survey research procedures, is now common also.

Some problems also paralleled the positive developments associated with behavioural research. For example the geographer, frequently accustomed to dealing with large data sets, often found the methods developed in psychology for use with much smaller subject and stimulus sets to be inappropriate. Consequently there has developed considerable interest in incomplete data designs, randomized block designs, and cyclical and serial designs that can be used on many normal geographic problems (Golledge and Rayner, 1982).

Perhaps another characteristic of behavioural research in geography in the 1970s has been acceptance of the notion that parallel experiments need to be undertaken in many cases so as to obtain valid and reliable interpretations of research results. Thus we see an increase in the use of multiple method experimental procedures—for example the collection of data by several different means and analysis by several different techniques, so that the interpretability and reliability of the results can be assessed.

Given this brief overview, we now turn to a more detailed treatment of two sub-areas of behavioural research that have had a considerable impact on the literature and mode of thought in geography. Both these areas have been dominated by analytic modes of research and continue a practice of early behavioural research in terms of searching for appropriate theoretical and model frameworks to serve as the bases for organizing research results. The two areas are, (a) environmental cognition and (b) spatial preference and spatial choice.

ENVIRONMENTAL COGNITION

We have seen that part of the rationale for the development of behavioural geography was an explicit recognition of the relationship between cognition and behaviour. Underlying this is a premise that argues that the mind imposes a structure on the external environment, selecting from it, ordering, grouping and simplifying the information gleaned. Such a premise inevitably leads one to a detailed examination of the process of environmental cognition and the nature of mental imagery and/or an examination of the way in which information is stored and represented in the mind.

The first primitive accepted by environmental cognition researchers is that human spatial behaviour is at least in part a function of the cognitive representation of environment. The term 'environment' includes more than the external physical environment; it is a general term covering the complete range of systems in which human action takes place. Thus, the cognitive representation of an environment includes information about the physical location and spatial relations of things and people together with a number of superimposed dimensions representing historical, cultural, political, legal, moral, and other values or significances which are inextricably related to places and associations within the physical, human and built environments. The researcher in environmental cognition accepts that there is an integral and integrated relationship between people and the various environments in which they live, and that the process of existence involves defining and solving a series of ongoing problems. In identifying and solving these problems, an initial and critical step is to construct an internal representation of the problem (i.e. a comprehension of it). The development of such comprehension clearly depends on the nature and organization of knowledge existing in memory, together with immediate sensory stimuli associated with the problem situation. The second part of the problem-solving process consists of sets of procedures which operate on this internal representation so as to allow an organism to achieve a solution or to obtain some goal. Despite the increasing quantity of research on the relationship between cognition and behaviour, it is generally accepted that the nature of the relationship between these two is not as yet fully explicated. In this section, therefore, we will comment on some of the past and current research relating to the process of environmental cognition, attempts to represent externally subsets of this information as cognitive maps, and review selected attempts to relate such cognitive maps to actual spatial behaviours.

Research on environmental cognition has not taken place in a theoretical or epistemological vacuum. Since these bases have been explicated at length elsewhere (Moore and Golledge, 1976a,b; Moore, 1979; Evans, 1980; Golledge, 1981), we will not reproduce this material here.

The nature of cognitive representations

The term cognitive representation describes a hypothetical construct referring to an individual's knowledge or thought of the world external to mind. In effect, it is a shorthand notation for an individual's knowledge structure of the various environments in which he lives, or a model of the world outside the head. Such a representation has variously been called an image, a mental map, a cognitive image, a model of reality, or one's perception of environment. Since much of the confusion associated with the use of various terms has been discussed in the literature (Downs and Stea, 1973; Downs and Stea, 1977; Moore and Golledge, 1976; Downs, 1981b; Golledge, 1981), there is no need to repeat it here. We will use the general term 'environmental cognition' to describe the process of acquiring information about external reality; 'cognitive mappings' or 'cognitive representation' will refer to the stored information about a subset of one's total knowledge structure; and the term 'cognitive map' or 'cognitive configuration' will represent an experimenter's attempt to summarize cognitive information in an external cartographic format. According to Downs and Stea (1973, p. 9), cognitive mapping is a 'process composed of a series of psychological transformations by which an individual acquires, codes, stores, recalls, and decodes information about the relative locations and attributes of phenomena in his/her everyday spatial environments'. Implicit in this definition is that this mapping process requires an understanding of spatial concepts such as proximity, closeness, dispersion, clustering, separatedness, direction, and orientation. Cognitive maps or cognitive configurations are based on an individual's interpretation of the spatial relationships among phenomena in an environment, where both the environment and the mode of representing the cognitive map is defined by the experimenter.

Within the general areas of environmental cognition and cognitive science today, controversy exists over the nature of the representation of cognitive information. This controversy relates to whether such representations are holistic images or are propositional in form (Anderson, 1978; Hayes-Roth, 1979; Kosslyn, 1981; Lloyd, 1982). Research such as that by Stevens and Coupe (1978), Byrne (1979), and Hintzman et al. (1981), asserts that cognitive mappings are propositional in nature while other research (such as that by Thorndyke, 1980, and Thorndyke and Stasz, 1980), argues that such representations consist of holograms, or pictures in the head. A third stream of researchers (Paivio, 1976; Kosslyn, 1976; Kosslyn et al., 1978) believe in a dual coding theory in which cognitive information is represented both as an interconnected propositional system and an analog memory system.

Environmental learning processes

The history of environmental cognition research has been detailed well elsewhere (Downs and Stea, 1973; Moore and Golledge, 1976a; Ittelson et al., 1974; Evans, 1980; Kaplan and Kaplan, 1982). Despite isolated examples of innovative thought in this area since the beginning of the century (e.g. Tolman, 1948), it is generally recognized that an important milestone in environmental image research was Kevin Lynch's (1960) classic book, *The Image of the City*.

Lynch linked theoretical and applied work by examining a variety of sources of subjective information about a selection of cities. He then reduced that informational mélange to five fundamental spatial components: paths, edges, districts, nodes, and landmarks. Such a categorization showed geographers (and others) how they could obtain meaningful information from people about things in the environment which could then be depicted on the geographer's favourite representational device—the two dimensional map. Building at least in part on this initial formulation, Siegel and White (1975), Golledge and Rayner (1976), and Herman and Siegel (1978), have advanced embryonic theories or conceptualizations of the environmental learning process. Since these theories have served to focus a considerable volume of research in environmental cognition in recent years, it is appropriate briefly to summarize their essence here.

Lynch (1960) hypothesized that paths serve as the initial framework for learning about an environment. Experience with the environment changes as familiarity with phenomena in the vicinity of paths increases and as the number of landmarks known by an individual grows. Navigation in an environment is based on a combination of landmark and path connections. Early experimental results of Appleyard (1970) and Devlin (1976), derived from sketch-mapping tasks, provided empirical verification of this path-node sequence of environmental learning, and Siegel and White (1975) formalized this relationship in a developmental conceptualization of the environmental learning process.

As an alternative procedure, Golledge (1978) and several of his students (Briggs, 1972; Zannaras, 1976; Rivizzigno, 1976; Spector, 1978; Richardson, 1982) have described the environmental learning process by an anchor-point theory. This is based on the initial establishment of nodes or landmarks in the environment from which path structures emerge as experience with the environment grows. Nodes are hierarchically and sequentially ordered based on a place's significance to the individual and his interactions with it. A learning sequence of node identification, path connection, and areal generalization is hypothesized. Environmental knowledge increases as a result of continued interactions and experience with the nodes, paths, and areas forming the interaction space of each individual. Recent empirical work by Evans et al. (1981) and Garling et al. (1981) supports the contention that learning about urban environments conforms to this anchor-point hypothesis.

One set of research associated with environmental learning theory focuses purely on landmark recognition. For example, early work by Appleyard (1969) examined the attributes by which buildings were known and which enhanced an individual's ability to recall and recognize them. Critical factors included frequency of use, symbolic function, peculiar form, noticeable size contrast with their immediate surrounding, and so on. However, in later work Spector (1978) found that visibly dominant cues along major pathways, even between home locations and work, need not be well known at all. In support of Appleyard's hypothesis, Pezdeck and Evans (1979) replicated his results, but indicated that semantic labels as well as physical locations were influential in the recall, recognition, and use of particular landmarks. Even given these somewhat conflicting results, the overall quantity of research on the role of landmarks in environmental cognition and learning has been scant.

Cognitive distance and way finding activities

A second major area of research in environmental cognition focused on developing route or path knowledge. Research in this area initially focused on examining subjective or cognitive distances. Such work covered a wide range of activities, ranging from examining the psychophysical relationships between subjective and objective distances (Briggs, 1972; Jones, 1972) to the practical use of the subjective distance concept in conventional models attempting to predict human spatial behaviour (for example, Thompson, 1963, 1966; Cadwallader, 1975, 1981; MacKay et al., 1975; MacKay, 1976). The bulk of research into the nature of cognitive distance found empirical evidence that a power function described the transformation from actual to judged distance (Briggs, 1972; Lowrey, 1970; Ericksen, 1975; Siegel et al., 1979; Lee, 1970; Thorndyke, 1981; Day, 1976). In particular, several of these researchers found that the distances towards the downtown of an urban area were overestimated while distances to the periphery were shortened. These results have been attributed to the increased congestion and travel time involved in journeys to the central business district (CBD), the denser packing of land uses as one approaches the centre, an increased sense of potential problems such as pollution, congestion, crime, and parking as one approaches the centre, and so on, all of which appear mentally to 'push' the CBD area further away and lengthen subjective distance estimates. As the size of the urban environment is changed, and as city form varies from multiple nuclei cities to monocentric cities, different and contradictory results are found. For example, Lee (1970), studying the monocentric city of Dundee, indicated that outward journeys from the city were overestimated to a larger degree than inward journeys. This mix of results indicates that the pure subjective/objective distance transformation is mitigated somewhat by the environmental context.

In addition to the environmental contextual effects, other researchers (Siegel et al., 1978, 1979; Siegel, 1981; Gärling and Book, 1981; Acredola, 1981; Acredola et al., 1975) also indicate that distance judgement practices vary throughout the different stages of development. Studies of both infants and children show that distance estimates are influenced by the transition from egocentric to external frames of reference, the types of landmarks used, the scale of operation, the nature of the task, and the type and number of intervening barriers. Recent work by Sadalla and Staplin (1980a,b) builds on earlier work by Briggs (1972) and Milgram (1973) and relates empirical findings in cognitive distance to a variety of information-processing models. This reflects a strong research trend in cognitive science generally in recent years (summarized in a recent paper by Smith *et al.*, 1982), which discusses various theories of knowledge acquisition and storage in an artificial intelligence-modelling framework. In this research, variables such as length of pathways, reaction times, the number of intervening landmarks, the number of intersections or turns, and the effort required to traverse a path have been used to help conceptualize and model the wayfinding task (Sadalla and Magal, 1980; MacEachren, 1980; Smith *et al.*, 1982).

Psychologists, in addition to geographers, have suggested that route knowledge has a regionalized character to it such that the knowledge structure can be envisaged as cognitively stored bits of information, with the bits representing a designated spatial segment of the route itself. Knowledge is hypothesized to be stored in an hierarchical manner, in that major nodes or major path segments dominate segments of space and other bits of information in those segments of space are directly connected to the critical anchor points. The wayfinding process, then, is conceptualized as identifying key nodes to allow positional recognition at various intervals along the path, and associating sequentially linked pieces of lower-order information with key nodes.

Metricity and error characteristics

One of the major contributions of research on cognitive distance has been built on an early hypothesis of Piaget *et al.* (1960) that as one proceeds through the development process and as cognitive capabilities mature there is a transition from topological to more fully metric knowledge structures. This is usually referred to as a transition from route to survey knowledge (Shemyakin, 1962; Stea, 1969; Thorndyke and Hayes-Roth, 1980; Richardson, 1982). The progression of knowledge from one-dimensional path sequences to a two- or three-dimensional overall frame of reference is an integral part of general theory concerning the evolution of spatial knowledge. Route knowledge is conceptualized as a set of procedural descriptions involving the recording of a starting point, intervening landmarks, and a destination. Survey knowledge is generalized to presume that a set of major anchor points provides the basis for integrated knowledge of spatial relations generally, allowing one to experiment with connections between hitherto unconnected nodes or to estimate the positional relations of previously unconnected nodes by reference to an overall known node set (Golledge, 1976, 1978). Currently there is insufficient evidence to warrant complete support of any particular one of these alternate hypotheses, but the volume of work on each of them is escalating rapidly in a variety of different disciplines. In particular, the work of Gärling *et al.* (1981), Book and Gärling (1980), and Lindberg and Gärling (1982) should be referred to in this area.

Obviously the transition from one-dimensional to two-dimensional knowledge structures incorporates the critical spatial component of direction as well as the fundamental one of distance. Direction involves some awareness of one's orientation in the environment (Howard and Templeton, 1966; Cadwallader, 1977; Hubert et al., 1983). The sense of direction implies an ability to orient oneself deliberately with respect to perceived or intuitively known landmarks or other environmental features.

As one increases the complexity of the spatial relations used in the process of environmental cognition, one must allow for error to creep into information-processing activities. Given the initial findings on the power function relation of objective to subjective distance, Baird et al. (1982) have shown that cognitive spaces are likely to be distorted from the pure Euclidean, and they refer to 'impossible' cognitive spaces based on the complexity of such spaces from a forward-looking or backward-looking point of view. Specific aspects of error and cognitive distortions have been examined by Gale (1980), who has determined two critical components of error—fuzziness and distortion. Using suggestions of Tobler (1976), Gale found that distortion could be used to describe the amount of deviation between the actual location of an environmental cue and a cognized location. The other error component, fuzziness, refers to the variability associated with cognizing landmarks; it can occur at the individual level or it can be associated with a particular cue's location by a larger subject population. On any given cognitive configuration, both distortion and fuzziness components can be summarized in terms of error ellipses, and general distortion trends, either for individuals or for groups, can thus be compiled. Currently, Golledge and Tobler (1983) are investigating the potential use of a range of indices relating to directional and distance components of error that can be used as 'add on' variables in conventional explanations of human spatial behaviour.

While much of the research on cognitive mappings has taken place in the context of an Euclidean metric, some critical papers have urged the exploration of other metrics as being potentially more suitable for the representation of cognitive information. The geometrical properties of cognitive maps was discussed in an innovative article by Tobler (1976). Cadwallader (1979) and Burrows and Sadalla (1979) found that particular properties of Euclidean spaces such as translation invariance, symmetry, and triangle inequality, were frequently violated in cognitive configurations. Richardson (1981c) suggested that a city-block method was more appropriate than a Euclidean one for representing information on cognitive maps, and Baird et al. (1982) argued that curved spaces are more appropriate than Euclidean spaces for the representation of cognitive information. Golledge and Hubert (1982) similarly suggested that a variety of curved spaces be considered as the most appropriate for representing cognitive information and for incorporating the holes, folds, or other disturbances that seem to occur in individual knowledge structures.

Recent work by Golledge *et al.* (1980) and Richardson (1981b, 1982) has focused on the use of borderline retarded individuals along with adult populations (matched by neighbourhood living area) to investigate whether route knowledge is an essential part of the early stages of cognitive development or whether it is an artefact of experimental designs. Using borderline retarded subjects with IQs ranging from 29 to 65, in two different environmental situations (Columbus, Ohio and Santa Barbara, California), these researchers showed a substantial ability by the retarded subjects to perform one-dimensional experiments satisfactorily and to participate in sequential or topological experiments related to way-finding processes. While the normal adult subjects were capable of performing both one- and two-dimensional experiments quite satisfactorily, the borderline retarded individuals uniformly failed at a series of experiments designed to elicit two-dimensional spatial knowledge. This appeared to indicate that even though the retarded subjects had reached substantial chronological ages, their capacities either for understanding two-dimensional spatial situations or for giving responses that were interpretable in a two-dimensional context were substantially lacking. All the groups tested were found to have a one-dimensional route knowledge statistically greater than one might expect to be achieved through random processes. However, the retardeds' two-dimensional results could not be differentiated from randomly-generated results, even at low levels of confidence. These very preliminary results appear to be relevant to the ongoing discussion in developmental psychology concerning whether all individuals (including the retarded) eventually pass through all stages of Piaget's development hypothesis (Piaget and Inhelder, 1967).

Environmental cognition and artificial intelligence modelling

Research and theory in cognitive science generally has begun to focus attention on the problem of representing individual knowledge structures in terms of the processes that underlie human behaviour in a wide variety of complex domains. The primitive assumption associated with this line of reasoning is that an individual's permanent knowledge structures provide the basis for interpreting all objects, actions, and events that occur in any environment external to mind. Thus, knowledge structures guide the decisions and actions of individuals in their daily activities in any given environment (Lloyd, 1982).

Of critical importance to this research effort is some controversy and discussion over the types of knowledge that exist, the way in which knowledge is represented and organized in the mind, the processes or mechanisms by which it is activated, the way that new knowledge is produced, and how inferences, evaluation, and external behaviours are related to existing knowledge structures.

It is generally accepted that a variety of knowledge types exist, including declarative, procedural, schematic, and strategic knowledge. Associated with each of these knowledge types is a domain ranging from simple or factual knowledge through action-oriented knowledge, to complex and abstract knowledge, and knowledge required for problem-solving and decision-making. This latter area, frequently called expert decision-making, has been a focus of attention in cognitive science and artificial intelligence for many years and is becoming of considerable interest to those geographers interested in spatial cognition. The overlap between behavioural geography and cognitive science has increased in recent years as researchers in both areas attempt to define the appropriate underlying conceptualizations for the acquisition and storage of knowledge and to define sets of procedural rules for solving complex problems in spatial situations. It is anticipated that research in this area will throw additional light on the question of cognitive mappings and the potential structure of cognitive configurations by adding to the knowledge of possible structural organization of spatial data. Some attempts at producing formal computational models of the acquisition of spatial knowledge exist (Kuipers, 1978; Hayes-Roth, 1977), but as yet these are not widely known or recognized in the discipline of geography.

An essential part of this link between geography and cognitive science focuses on the relation between representations of complex, large-scale environments, and human behaviour within those environments. Criticisms of behavioural research in recent years (Bunting and Guelke, 1979) have emphasized the relative lack of work linking cognitive information and actual spatial behavioural patterns. While these criticisms appear to have overlooked a steadily growing literature in this area, in general research on the relationship between knowledge and spatial behaviour has been an underdeveloped part of the total research effort. However, even without extensive proof. it has commonly been assumed by behavioural geographers that people's decisions and behaviours within any given spatial environment are some function of the cognitive representation of that environment. Behaviours include everyday spatial activities such as journey to work, to shop, to school, and so on, and episodic behaviour with greater periodicities such as recreational or entertainment behaviour, and consumer behaviour for high order shopping goods. Each behavioural activity is assumed to be integrally related to knowledge or information about both general and specific features of the particular spatial environments in which both individual and goal objects are located.

The link between knowledge structure and behaviour has been made much more explicit outside the field of geography, with researchers such as Hayes-Roth (1979); Gärling and his associates (Gärling and Book, 1981; Gärling et al., 1981; Book and Gärling, 1980); Anderson (1981); Evans et al. (1981), and others, all of whom have focused specifically on the link between cognitive representation and actual spatial behaviours. While much of this work has been related to small-scale behaviours in controlled environments, there is an

increasing emphasis on examining the relationship between knowledge structures and actual behaviour patterns in large-scale complex external environments (Smith *et al.*, 1983). Since the Smith *et al.* review of the relationship
between knowledge structures and behaviour is a current one, we will spend no
further time on that set of relationships in this paper.

SPATIAL PREFERENCE AND SPATIAL CHOICE

The early models

Early attempts to explain choices among spatial alternatives investigated the
assumptions made about such behaviour in location theories. First was the
classical assumption, reviewed by Hubbard (1978), that consumers would
choose the closest opportunity. A number of tests of this 'behavioural postulate'
indicated low levels of fit (Clark and Rushton, 1970; Fingleton, 1975; Golledge
et al., 1966; Rushton *et al.*, 1967), especially in non-rural contexts, and so better
models of how consumers make selections from alternative spatial opportunities
were sought. For a short time, the notion of a range of spatial indifference within
which random spatial choices were made appeared promising (Devletoglou,
1965; Clark and Rushton, 1970), but the evidence mounted that within this
'zone of indifference' the search among alternatives involved systematic choice
with respect to selected attributes of the alternatives rather than purely random
choice. Thomas *et al.* (1962) and Berry *et al.* (1962) showed that regression
analysis on the attributes of the spatial alternatives chosen, including distance,
was not a suitable method for identifying the choice model because the set of all
alternatives (choice set) for any person does not have an alternative from every
part of the attribute space of alternatives, and the alternative chosen cannot be
regarded as a continuous response to the attribute values (Louviere, 1981b, p.
310). Hubbard (1978, p. 12), reviewing such studies and apparently missing the
significance of the discreteness of the response space, concluded that these poor
goodness-of-fit values showed that 'the stochastic error disturbance in the
model is unusually large', or that other important variables have been omitted.
Yet it can be shown that if one simulates spatial behaviour according to a simple
preference function, which has attributes of site attraction and distance as its
arguments, a regression analysis of the alternatives selected against these two
variables will have poor goodness-of-fit values. Thus, correlation-regression
approaches on attributes of choices made from discrete alternatives will not
identify the attribute weighting function used in choice. A consensus did emerge
in geography in the 1960s that the limited set of alternatives for any person ruled
out the direct estimation of a choice function from observed behaviour outside
the context of the alternatives available.

There were some attempts to deal with this problem. Wilson (1970) suggested
entropy maximization as a principle for explaining the distribution of trips in a
system of spatial interaction. Others attempted to find a behavioural foundation

for existing models of spatial interaction (Niedercorn and Bechdolt, 1969; Smith, 1975). Nevertheless, these models had parameter values calibrated to bring model predictions as close as possible to observed flows and consequently their values were unique to each study area (Fotheringham, 1981; Sheppard, 1979, 1982; Stetzer and Phipps, 1977). Attempts to show that parameters were related to observed structural characteristics of an area (such as density) were only partially successful (Griffith, 1976; Johnston, 1976). The problem of separating the influence of 'environmental variability' from the influence of 'human choice rules' as mutual determinants of patterns of spatial interaction had not been solved (Cliff et al., 1974; Ewing, 1974; Johnston, 1976; Openshaw, 1976).

Rushton (1969a) argued that two different objectives were evident in the studies of spatial choice patterns. One objective was to describe 'the rules by which alternative locations are evaluated and choices consequently made', which he called *spatial behaviour*, and the second was 'the description of the actual spatial choices made in a particular system' which he called *behaviour in space* (Rushton, 1969a, p. 392). To him, with the exception of those studies which had tested the nearest centre or the spatial indifference hypotheses, studies at that time had the objective of describing 'behaviour in space', and they suffered from the deficiency that they were as much descriptions of the set of alternatives from which people could choose, as descriptions of the rules by which they selected from alternatives. An important impetus for the search for models of 'spatial behaviour' came from Curry (1967, p. 219), who argued that there was a need to find a postulate of spatial behaviour that did not directly describe the behaviour in a system because it was the purpose of theory to derive the distributions of alternatives as non-trivial outcomes of the theory. Rushton (1969a) argued that a preference function and associated choice model met the requirement of such a postulate because, in principle at least, it could be used to generate expected spatial behaviour patterns in any environment.

The basic spatial choice model

Behavioural geographers asked themselves how other social scientists approached this problem of interaction between choice model and problem context and they saw that, particularly in psychology, a different conceptual approach was used. There, it was common to view the choice outcome as the result of individuals applying their own internalized preference function to a unique set of opportunities and choosing that alternative in the set of opportunities (their 'choice set') which gave them the highest degree of satisfaction. The preference function of an individual is a representation of a person's expected degree of satisfaction with an alternative as a function of the values of its attributes. The key to this conceptual model was the analytical separation of preferences, opportunities and choice. Especially for problem contexts that could be characterized as involving familiar opportunity sets and repetitive behaviour patterns, this separation posed few problems and led to the development of a paradigm for studying spatial choice (Pipkin, 1981a, p. 155).

Analytical separation meant that three components of spatial choice decisions could be regarded, in the short run, as independent. The first component, 'spatial preference', involved an assumption that for the domain of alternatives with which people are familiar, they will be able, through experience with a range of environments, to order all conceivable alternatives within the domain according to the expected degree of satisfaction they would expect to gain by choosing any one of them. Notice that the only sense in which 'preferences' and 'opportunities' are linked in this conceptualization is the assumption that preferences can only be expected to exist for alternatives within a 'domain' of hypothetical alternatives. This domain was usually assumed to be defined by the range of values of each of the attributes that influenced the expected satisfaction of any alternative.

In the second component, 'spatial opportunities', it is assumed that opportunities for choice are known to each individual both as to geographical location as well as to the expected values in each case of the relevant attributes which contribute to expected satisfaction.

The third component is the decision rule by which choice is made. Early models assumed that maximization of expected satisfaction takes place in all cases. In short, the basic model assumed that people know of the existence of all alternatives that might conceivably interest them, know the values of all relevant attributes of these alternatives, have a well-defined preference function through the use of which they are able to know the expected degree of satisfaction they would receive from choosing any alternative, and, finally, that they will always choose the alternative that will give them the highest degree of expected satisfaction.

Such a conceptualization achieved two objectives: first, it set the goal as understanding individual-level human spatial behaviour and thus opened the door to the treatment of human behavioural diversity and the possibility of exploring such diversity: second, it saw the human geography of any area as the outcome of a pattern of decision-making applied to the relevant environmental conditions of the area. Thus, the geographic pattern was the product of a decision-making process applied to an environment. It was an important conceptual separation of basic human behaviour from the limited choices afforded in the short run by the environment. It was argued that such a conceptualization of the problem provided a basis from which a number of researchable questions could be pursued.

Criticisms of the model

Simple as this model was, it was not readily accepted into the literature of behavioural geography. Many apparently believed that the model simply stated that 'a person selected the object he most preferred': a view that represented the conceptual foundation of the model as a tautology and led to the conclusion that little enlightenment could result. What proof do we have that when people make spatial choices they consider their preferences? Pipkin (1981a, p. 168) concluded: 'there is little evidence that choice and preference ideas will or should be central to cognitive explanation . . .'. Ley (1981, p. 215), in asking that meaning, consciousness and subjectivity in human behaviour need to be interpreted, argued that a new form of determinism is introduced: when '. . . Rushton argues for the existence of a latent structure of preferences' his methodology produces 'a structure where none is immediately observable, a practice at odds with the necessity for objectively observable phenomena required by positivist philosophy'. In a similar vein, Cullen (1976) writes of 'the orientation to mechanical responses to spatial and social structures', and Flowerdew (1973) of his belief 'that human behaviour is far more subtle and ambiguous than can be duplicated in a mechanistic model'.

How do we know that people know about the alternatives or that they evaluate all alternatives (Pirie, 1976)? As Burnett (1981, p. 294) observed: 'the determinants may *not* be preferences and choices among alternatives as givens'. Others have argued that choice sets will, according to context, often limit severely the discretion to choose as each decision is made to fit a person's time-space schedule of interacting activities (Damm and Lerman, 1981; Forer and Kivell, 1981; Hagerstrand, 1969; Landau *et al.*, 1981; Parkes and Thrift, 1975).

Several criticisms can be traced to the view that the separation of preferences, opportunities and decision-functions in this model is not valid for many types of spatial choice. One link which received a great deal of attention was the hypothesized interaction between a person's preferences and the opportunities experienced. In the model it was assumed that a person's preference function exists externally to the opportunity set from which a choice is to be made. But from where do preferences originate? Early work noted only that preferences were presumably based on experiences, were learnt reactions to stimuli, and could presumably change with experience. If so, it was argued, a person's preferences could change as a result of changes in their opportunity set such as would occur when they moved their location. This argument, if true, undermined the validity of the premise of the structural separation of preferences and opportunities in the simple model. A person's efforts to match a set of needs which could be satisfied at different places with the need to link the places efficiently in a multi-purpose trip, led some authors to suggest that models which separated preferences and opportunities would not be adequate to model such behaviour (Burnett, 1981; Burnett and Hanson, 1979; Hanson, 1980; Hensher, 1976; Wheeler, 1972).

In addition to questioning the existence of stable preference functions, others argued that if preference functions were limited by the domain of experience, they would be ineffective in predicting a person's levels of expected satisfaction for alternatives the attribute values of which were outside the range of levels that they had experienced: '. . . changes in spatial location are likely to lead to an instability of the taste function' (MacLennan and Williams, 1980, p. 913). The conclusion was, therefore, that expected interactions between preferences and choice sets would lead to a temporal instability of preferences and that preferences could not in principle be found for combinations of attribute values that existed outside the domain of past experience (Eyles, 1971). The argument was expressed strongly by Marxist-oriented geographers who saw in this model a conceptual schema by which the poor could be seen forever to 'prefer' combinations of attributes which lay within the domain of their miserable experience in a class-oriented, capitalist society (Sheppard, 1980).

On no point has criticism been more persistent than on the fact that, in the model, space, or spatial separation, is regarded as a relevant attribute of alternatives and is treated no differently than any other attribute. The spatial properties of objects, it has been alleged, were not a part of the theory of demand and therefore when a theory of preference and choice, originally designed to meet the needs of demand theory, is adapted to explain spatial choice behaviour, some of the axioms of demand theory are unlikely to be valid: 'The existence of space is likely to complicate, or indeed make redundant the applied analysis of revealed preferences' (MacLennan and Williams, 1980, p. 912); 'studies in the spatial choice paradigm incorporate space into behavior descriptions in a particularly restrictive way' (Pipkin, 1981b, p. 319). Hubbard and Thompson (1981) pointed out that the fact that 'distance' is used as a negative good technically violates the principle of diminishing marginal rates of substitution and leads to technical difficulties in that trivial corner solutions will represent the consumer's optimal choice of store.

Finally, interaction was claimed by some to exist between a person's decision function and their choice set. It was hypothesized that where the set of alternatives and the set of values of relevant attributes were complex, frequently unknown to the chooser, and where significant costs were attached to the gaining of information, decision-makers might adopt a different decision-function (Eagle, 1980; Einhorn and Hogarth, 1981; Montgomery and Svenson, 1976; Slovic et al., 1977; Smith et al., 1982).

Responses to the criticisms

Philosophical issues

Some of the issues raised have been resolved by recent work. In the normal progress of science one might expect to find carefully-designed studies or experiments in which the points at issue would be put to the test and resolved. For example, the degree to which people, after moving to new environments, might change their preferences for objects as defined in terms of their fundamental attributes could be resolved by careful observation or experimentation (Park and Lutz, 1980). There have been few examples of such studies. Instead, the basis of so much of the criticism is the familiar shibboleth of geographical uniqueness. Yet it is most unlikely that a theory of choice, confirmed for other subject matter, would be irrelevant to spatial choice. The difficulties are more likely to lie in translating the problem so that it can be seen as a special case of the more general problem. Thus, to MacLennan and Williams (1979), it apparently was self-evident that since space implies separation and the existence of imperfect information, it is a constraint on choice, and consequently the notion of a preference structure is a construct which is not operationally identifiable. Yet all economic behaviour occurs in a world of imperfect information and models of behaviour in all fields may need to be refined to accommodate information search. Why then reject revealed preference as a mechanism for learning about people's evaluations of alternatives in situations where knowledge of alternatives is common? Where this assumption is not valid, common sense dictates the adding of an information-processing component to the model.

The conclusion of Hubbard and Thompson (1981) that consumer behaviour theory of economics could not be translated into a spatial model because the trivial corner solutions would be the consumer's best choice is no problem if one interprets the choice set space as one where discrete alternatives are found, none of which may exist at the corner 'solutions'. This interpretation is not unique to geographical problems! The problem with these criticisms appears to be the identification with the theory of conventional elements which are not a fundamental part of the theory.

Some progress has been made in resolving the issue of whether people can reveal their preferences for alternatives, the attributes of which have values outside the range of experience. A very rapidly growing field of 'direct preference estimation' has shown that in countless problem situations that are as complex as most spatial choice problems, such measurements can be made and subsequent validity tests have confirmed that such estimated preference functions are good predictors of behaviour in new problem situations (Anderson, 1981). This work has effectively answered the chorus of criticisms of preference-based choice models where the concern was to derive preference functions for novel combinations of attributes.

Are the pertinent characteristics of space represented adequately in spatial choice models? Most applications to date have employed extreme levels of simplification by representing space as distance units. Some authors have emphasized the relative location of alternatives or the ratio of distances to alternatives (Fogarty, 1977; Clark and Rushton, 1970). Pipkin (1981b) has suggested several ways in which elements of spatial context could be abstracted and incorporated in spatial choice models within existing frameworks. Weibull

(1980) has devised micro-oriented measures of opportunity, configuration and accessibility. There is scope for further work in this area.

The question of the independence of the inferred preference function from the spatial structure of the alternatives (MacLennan and Williams, 1979) is ultimately an empirical question but there are reasons for expecting such an independence to exist. Techniques for estimating preference functions are not based on the relative frequency of choice of alternatives in their settings and results are therefore insensitive to the frequencies with which any spatial alternative occurs. Efforts have been made to find the preference order as a function of the attribute values of the alternatives and to extrapolate the function beyond the points of observation (Rushton, 1976)—an approach fraught with danger but valid if used in a context where the results can be confirmed from independent observations (Timmermans, 1979). In spatial choice, a common situation is when a type of alternative is always found in the presence of another alternative that is superior to it. Providing these pairs are within the domain of alternatives studied, revealed preference analysis can predict preference between them— providing that each element of the pair has been evaluated by consumers with reference to a third (common) alternative (Girt, 1976). The case where each of the elements is related to separate elements, which themselves are related, has not yet been studied. The conclusion here is that these issues are researchable, which further work can clarify.

Though some might dispute this (Smith *et al.*, 1982), the evidence does not support the thesis that in most spatial choice situations preference structures of people are inconsistent, subject to change, and restricted to the particularities of past situations. It is possible that future studies will disprove this (Smith *et al.*, 1982). As Gould (1976, p. 85) observed, the 'most fruitful sets of assumptions in science tend to be simple and usable'.

Measurement issues

Reactions to the preference-based literature on spatial choice have rarely addressed measurement issues. Instead, the dominant reaction has been to the assumptions of the models used. Consequently, there has grown an increasing discrepancy between the level of the development of research in general in measuring preferences (see for example, Anderson, 1974, 1981; Krantz and Tversky, 1971; Levin, 1975; Rappoport and Wallsten, 1972) and those of researchers in geography. The effect is damaging to the development of behavioural studies in all aspects of urban and regional analysis.

Dimensions of alternatives

What properties of spatial alternatives are relevant to choice? How do these properties affect choice? The operationalization of the properties of alternatives and their incorporation in preference-based models of choice has proved difficult. Burnett (1973) described the problem well, though the method she employed óf interpreting the scores of alternatives on each dimension of a multidimensionally scaled space (MDS) is invalid because, as Gould (1976, p. 87) noted, 'axes in MDS space are defined by the investigator, not the attributes of the stimuli, and their location is totally arbitrary . . .'. Peterson (1967) asked subjects to make a personal preference ordering of a set of alternatives and then made several measurements of factors hypothesized to be important in a person's estimate of preference for an alternative. Regression analysis between the variable 'preference for an alternative' and measures of hypothesized relevant attributes identified the factors as well as their relative importance in explaining preference variation among alternatives. Girt (1976), Rushton (1969b), and Timmermans (1979) each hypothesized the relevant attributes and redefined the alternatives as belonging to discrete levels of attributes, including distance, hypothesized to be relevant. Rushton (1969b) argued that in using these 'locational types', alternatives were removed from their unique spatial context and people acted then to choose among the particular alternatives before them by representing them in a generalized preference-space in which all possible alternatives were present (Beavon and Hay, 1977).

Other techniques are reviewed by Burnett (1982, p. 176) and Pipkin (1981a, pp. 148–151), who concluded that there is little consensus on techniques for identifying properties of alternatives relevant to spatial choice in the work of geographers. These properties can be identified by a variety of methods prior to measuring preferences, or they can be merely hypothesized with the knowledge that preference measurement methods will eventually prove whether they were indeed relevant. The issue is merely efficiency of study design, with researchers leaning toward prior determination of relevant properties for cases where many properties are hypothesized to exist. Curiously, no research in the revealed preference tradition has yet attempted to define attractiveness of alternatives endogenously as has been successfully done in the literature of spatial interaction studies (Baxter, 1979; Cesario, 1973, 1977; Timmermans, 1981). Attractiveness of alternatives could be defined in an iterative scaling process during the calibration of the preference function. The derived attractiveness values could then be explained as a function of the attributes of the alternatives by regression procedures.

Direct assessment of preferences

Louviere (1978, 1981a,b) has described and used the 'functional measurement' approach to find the preferences of people or spatial alternatives expressed as a function of relevant attribute values (Anderson, 1970, 1974, 1981). In functional measurement it is postulated that 'utility-assignment processes of humans may be represented by some algebraic expression which is a subset of the general multi-linear form' (Louviere, 1981a, p. 386). Louviere argues that classical procedures, taken from the design and analysis of experiments in statistics, allow the researcher to control for spatial context and to distinguish between alternative functional forms in deriving statements of preferences for all conceivable alternatives within the domain of attribute values recovered by the experiment. Work in this area operationalizes a conceptualization of spatial choice decisions in which individuals assign values to levels of attributes and then combine these values into an assessment of overall worth, according to combination rules recovered by the experimenter, who uses algebraic models and analysis of variance to discriminate between alternative functional forms.

A variety of applications to spatial choice problems now exists: the decision to use public bus transportation (Norman and Louviere, 1974); travel from Australia to the United States (Louviere, 1981a); student apartment selection decisions (Louviere and Henley, 1977); shopping patterns (Louviere and Wilson, 1978); and migration decision-making (Lieber, 1979). The results strongly support the assertions that people form preferences for objects that relate to their perceptions of the attributes of the objects and to the values that they ascribe to the levels of these beliefs; that they combine these values in ways that can be accurately described by algebraic models and that their observed behaviour is consistent with the hypothesis that they make choices that are predictable from the forecast levels of individual preference, given the objective values of the attributes. If further work confirms these conclusions, such experimental approaches offer a number of advantages over more conventional revealed preference approaches. First, the researcher is no longer limited to the immediate domain of experience of the respondent, although one of the most interesting and eminently researchable questions is how far beyond the domain of experience the researcher can go and still receive valid statements of preferences which the respondent has never had the opportunity to reveal in real-world behaviour. These techniques provide an answer to Pipkin's (1981a, p. 158) concern that 'the constraint problem provides a compelling argument against a strict revealed preference orientation, since desired but unattainable choices are never observed'. Second, repetitions of situations can be built into an experiment to ensure respondent consistency. Third, the same individual can respond to different spatial contexts, thus providing the researcher with information to resolve the questions of contextual effects. Although it may be true that 'spatial context' is captured only in a primitive form in these studies, in principle it need not be so. We are shackled only by our own limited ingenuity to devise alternative forms.

There are other techniques for direct estimation of preferences (Cliff, 1973; Fishburn, 1967; Krantz and Tversky, 1971; Krantz et al., 1971; Luce and Tukey, 1964), but applications to problems of spatial choice are few. Burnett (1982), Knight and Menchik (1976), and Odland and Jakubs (1977) use conjoint measurement methods for estimating preferences from the ordering of alternatives by respondents. There has been a limited number of comparisons of the relative efficacy of alternative methods (Lieber, 1976; Louviere, 1978; Recker and Schuler, 1981).

Optimal data designs

Empirical studies of preferences and spatial choice have only recently begun to capitalize on the opportunity to resolve many of the issues described above through more innovative design of data collection and analysis. The area may develop faster with the long-delayed publication of a book devoted to this subject (Golledge and Rayner, 1982), which identifies a number of major innovations in data collection design, few examples of which are found in spatial choice studies. Incomplete experimental designs (Spence, 1982; Burnett, 1982), in which respondents reply to carefully designed subsets of alternatives, some of which can be determined, contingent on the response pattern, to force evaluation of alternatives in situations where the repondent has exhibited either inconsistency or close preferences. Computer programs have been developed for this purpose (Young and Cliff, 1972). These designs allow statistically valid overlapping of individual response patterns where the quantity of data to be evaluated is too large a task for single respondents. Tobler (1982, p. 3) likens the task to that faced by early explorers whose behaviour can be generalized as an iterative effort first to 'learn the general lay of the land, and then fill out the findings with details of increasing reliability and refinement'. The concept of interactive sampling is taken one step further by Young et al. (1982); the entire sampling design is optimized as the answers begin to appear during an experiment. There is a need to design algorithms which direct in real time the data collection effort and are sensitive to both the responses received at any point in the experiment and the hypothesis to be tested (Tobler, 1982, p. 7). Isaac's (1982) discussion of the selection of stimulus pairs to maximize the efficiency of the sample data is a step in this direction. The implication for revealed preference studies in spatial choice is that the identification of locations from which data will subsequently be collected is a major step in the study design. The design might, for example, identify a sample of respondents such that pairs of stimuli, that will not be dominated by other stimuli present, are equally likely to be present. Random samples of individuals usually result in a plethora of revealed preferences in some portions of the preference space, but few revealed preferences in other parts of the space where dominant alternatives exist. Such sampling designs are definitely inefficient for estimating preference functions that will have approximately equal degrees of confidence in all parts of the recovered preference structure.

A neglected aspect of data design in revealed preference studies is the possibility, through controlled sampling, of constructing quasi-experimental designs. Considering the controversy in the geographical literature over the effect of spatial context and the sensitivity of model parameter values to the spatial context from which data are gathered, one obvious solution is to control for spatial context by taking groups of respondents from high density areas whose location with respect to many types of spatial alternatives will therefore be essentially the same. Analysis can then proceed without the normal kinds of data contamination caused by the spatial context effect and differences in choice patterns can then be interpreted as due to differences in personal characteristics of respondents.

Spatial information search

Considerable research has been conducted in response to the criticism that people do not evaluate all spatial alternatives but rather conduct a search, often with a spatial bias, until, according to some optimal stopping rule, the search is terminated (Flowerdew, 1973). Research in this tradition emphasizes the role of different levels of information in the spatial choice decision. Brown and Holmes (1971) and Clark and Smith (1982) found that the sequence in which alternatives are examined is also ordered in space. Smith et al. (1979) developed a model of intra-urban migration in which the key concept was spatial search over the neighbourhoods ranked according to 'locational stress'. Stress was defined as the difference between the expected utility of further search in the neighbourhood and the utility of the best vacancy found to date (Clark and Smith, 1982). Their model was based on models of information search in other fields (Hanushek and Quigley, 1978), but differed from them in that it explicitly incorporated the spatial variation in stress. Clark and Smith (1979) have developed models of search behaviour, some support for which has been found in an analysis of the content of the locational information contained in the advertisements of homes in a local housing market (Smith et al., 1982). The fact that institutions and professions exist to provide decision-makers with relevant information and the fact that decision-makers are willing to pay for such information is ample proof of the importance of information in decision-making for some kinds of spatial choice decisions. Such groups (for example, realtors in housing search) mediate the search process to such a degree that an understanding of their behaviour will often be a necessary part of an understanding of the spatial choices of interest. Smith and Mertz (1980, p. 155) concluded that 'by ordering a given set of vacancies in a non-random manner, an agent may significantly affect the search time, the price and quality of the vacancy purchased, and the utility level of the vacancy purchased under conditions of information revision'.

Analytical separation of preference and opportunity

Much recent literature in this area can be characterized as a reversion to studies of behaviour in space. The principle of separation of preferences and opportunities in the observations of human spatial behaviour is forgotten (see, for example, Hubbard, 1979). Studies that classify explanation of behaviour in space and then search for socio-demographic correlates of the patterns observed have obscured this fundamental distinction. Hanson and Hanson (1981), for example, review approximately forty such studies without identifying any finding about the logic of spatial choice for which generality can be claimed. Does one income group travel more than another because they are located more disadvantageously *via-à-vis* an alternative? Unless one 'corrects for' the locations of alternatives, all findings that group X compared with group Y travel farther, more often, visit more shopping centres, undertake more social trips etc., defy useful interpretation. What should we conclude from the finding 'that those with higher social status travel to more distant activity sites than those of lower social status' (Hanson and Hanson, 1981, p. 343)? Control, however, for the location of opportunities and then show that group X travels further etc. than group Y, and some measure of generality is introduced (Rushton, 1966, p. 19). Current literature continues largely to ignore this basic need to control for spatial context when comparing travel patterns by social or economic characteristics before reaching conclusions about the socio-economic determinants of travel. Proponents of this view cannot, therefore, accept the 'logic' of Hanson and Hanson (1981, p. 334): 'Because the focus of this paper is confined to the relationship between travel and the attributes of individuals, however, the impact of spatial constraints is not considered here, but is reserved for detailed consideration elsewhere.' The essence of the problem of understanding spatial choice is the recovery of the rules by which alternatives are evaluated and choices made. Consideration of the effect of the different configuration of alternatives on the various groups cannot be reserved for 'consideration elsewhere'.

The notion that the set of alternatives available to people is a constraint on their choice is obviously true. This constraint does not make the observed behaviour less free; rather, it serves to remind us that we must never conclude that the alternative a person chooses is the alternative he or she would prefer in a world where such constraints did not exist. According to revealed preference theory, the alternative a person chooses is the one most preferred, given the unique set of alternatives before him and the associated conditions relevant to the decision. There is thus no agreeing with Gauthier and Mitchelson (1981, p. 349) that 'observed behavior may say very little concerning individual preferences'. The conclusion here is that it depends entirely on how the behaviour is observed. Observing 'behavior in space' will say nothing 'concerning individual preferences'.

If the desire is to know how changing the distribution of alternatives will affect the spatial choices of people, it is first necessary to know how any set of alternatives is evaluated and selections are made. Only then can the conclusion be reached that the pattern of urban travel can be 'viewed as conditioned more by the details of the land use system of metropolitan living environments (the

variable densities and availabilities of different activities and different populations in urban activity or action spaces) and by emotional and sociological
factors than by some utility maximizing or other rational economic calculus'
(Burnett, 1981, p. 301). The problem with concluding this before finding the
relevant preference and choice functions is that outcomes of processes (urban
travel) are confused with the inputs to the travel decision, which are the existing
opportunities for travel. The effect of the stage on performance can only be
known if first one knows how the actor reacts to the alternative possible
configurations of the stage. However unwitting, these studies represent a
retrogression to the conditions of a decade ago when studies of *behaviour in
space* dominated the field and the concept of *spatial behaviour* had only recently
emerged as a concept that, when implemented, would allow the analytical
separation of preference and opportunity in spatial choice models.

Centrifugal tendencies in spatial choice research

One image of behavioural studies of spatial choice in geography today is of
disparate groups of sholars, each apparently intent to show that their unique
view is capturing an essential component of the problem that is being missed by
other groups. Vying for our attention are considerations of access to information and spatial search; the contingencies of organizing a household activity
pattern in space-time; the role of mediators (individuals or institutions) in the
choice process; the constriction on free choice of spatial barriers or of operating
characteristics of the transport system; and the identification of all the variables
which might affect spatial choice (Burnett, 1981, p. 302). Sitting on the sidelines
are sceptics, who doubt that humans make choices by exercising their
preferences, or that they systematically examine alternatives, or that the
diversity of the spatial organization of alternatives can ever be captured in a
model. There is a richness in this kaleidoscope of views, for there is likely to be
some truth in each view. And yet, much of this work represents excursions into
territories that are far from the centre stage where progress is being made and
the potential for further advancement appears to be high. For this perspective,
the chance to advance the basic spatial choice paradigm is being passed in
favour of premature excursions into issues that are best resolved later, after the
basic model of spatial choice has been validated. Then, adapting the model to
the particular conditions of each application area will be the appropriate
question of the day. Thus, instead of a kaleidoscope of studies there exists a
cacophony of views, each vying for its place in the sun.

Abandonment of the spatial choice paradigm

Should the structure of explanation in the choice paradigm remain intact?
Pipkin (1981a, p. 162), in reviewing the impact of cognitive behavioural

geography in this area, concluded that 'the structure of explanation in the choice paradigm has remained intact. Cognitive ideas have led only to the conservative strategy of seeking psychological transformations of traditional predictors that figure as independent variables, while single trips or elicited preference rankings provide dependent variables'. This chapter is in this conservative tradition not because the complexity of human spatial behaviour is denied, nor because of any denial that, for some domains, conceptualizations will be needed that link the spatial decision with other activity decisions and predict the simultaneous resolution of both types of decisions (Damm and Lerman, 1981; Heggie and Jones, 1978). Rather, it is conservative because preference and choice are concepts slowly disappearing from the lexicon of behavioural geography. The most erudite discussions of the complexities of the 'spatial choice task' and of the 'constraints of space' cannot camouflage the fact that so much of the geographical literature on individual spatial choice has reverted once again to ever more complex descriptions of behaviour in space. Thus, under the guise of 'context dependence', Burnett (1981, p. 298) asserted that the modelling framework 'will vary from case study area to case study area and problem to problem'. She further concluded that 'conventional choice theories or demand models fail the test of consistency with known facts . . .' and that 'incipient degeneracy' is characteristic of 'conventional revealed preference, choice and utility-theoretic modelling of human decisions and behaviour' (Burnett, 1981, p. 297). This is a premature epitaph for a paradigm that has produced so much and offers more to those who hold to its principles of the separation of preferences, opportunities and choice functions. Each interacts with the other in a dynamic process that can surely be revealed if the doomsayers are ignored, if we recognize that theories of choice are central to the issues in this area and that it is likely that the problem of spatial choice will turn out to be but a special case of the general theory of choice from discrete alternatives.

CONCLUSIONS

In both the substantive sections of this paper we have stressed the need for a return to the more catholic view of behavioural research, in which behavioural processes are used to help understand various spatial behaviours. This view is somewhat in contrast to trends in the literature which seem to be emphasizing the behaviour in space paradigm once again. It is obvious to us that this latter paradigm may be stressed because it is simpler and quicker to collect and analyse objective data on overt spatial acts than it is to design and carry out research focussing on various behavioural processes. The former research is factual and to a large extent more 'form' oriented—the form being the spatial pattern of the overt acts. The *reasons* for behaviour—the forces of learning, choice, preference formation, cognition of opportunity sets and so on—have to a certain extent become somewhat neglected again. There is no doubt that research in the latter mould requires considerable time and effort spent in conceptualizing the problem, designing an experiment, collecting individual responses, possibly adapting existing methods or developing new ones—which may not bring an immediate reward. As Golledge (1981) points out, it has been almost impossible to use the notion of a 'cognitive map' freely in an analytic context because it has taken fifteen years of research to develop confidence that the cognitive maps recovered today have a meaningful structure and contain legitimately useable information! Similarly in this chapter we point to the lack of control of spatial context in preference and choice studies which has inhibited our ability to draw valid and reliable conclusions.

Behavioural research is not easy or simple. It is time-consuming; it requires more care than is often the case in geographic studies; it requires recently developed or modified analytical tools and experimental designs; it must be soundly based on epistemology and theory. Given these requirements one must expect that significant output may be slow in coming. We freely admit this. What must be guarded against, however, is the tendency to judge research on human spatial behaviour from the more narrow perspective of behaviour in space, or to move back to this latter research mode because it can quickly be accomplished. Instead, we need more researchers who are prepared to commit themselves to long-term projects that satisfy conditions of validity and reliability, who aim at making contributions to a general understanding of spatial behaviour not merely solving problems, and who aim at increasing the scope and not just the quantity of our knowledge structure.

BIBLIOGRAPHY

Acredolo, L. P. (1981). Small- and large-scale spatial concepts in infancy and childhood, in *Spatial Representations and Behavior Across the Life Span: Theory and Application* (Eds L. Liben, A. Patterson, and N. Newcombe), Academic Press, New York.

Acredolo, L. P., Pick, H. L., and Olsen, M. G. (1975). Environmental differentiation and familiarity as determinants of children's memory for spatial location, *Developmental Psychology*, **11**, 495–501.

Allen, G. L. (1981). A developmental perspective on the effects of subdividing macrospatial experience, *Journal of Experimental Psychology: Human Learning and Theory*, **7**, 120–152.

Allen, G. L., Siegel, A., and Rosinski, R. (1978). The role of perceptual context in structuring spatial knowledge, *Journal of Experimental Psychology: Human Learning and Memory*, **4**, 617–630.

Altman, I. and Wohlwill, J. F. (1977). *Human Behavior and Environment*, Vol. 2, Plenum Press, New York.

Amedeo, D. and Golledge, R. G. (1975). *An Introduction to Scientific Reasoning in Geography*, Wiley, New York.

Anderson, J. R. (1978). Arguments concerning representations for mental imagery, *Psychological Review*, **85**, 249–277.

Anderson, J. R. (Ed.) (1981). *Cognitive Skills and Their Acquisitions*. Lawrence Erlbaum Associates, Hillsdale, New Jersey.

Anderson, N. H. (1970). Functional measurement and psychological judgement, *Psychological Review*, **77**, 153–170.

Anderson, N. H. (1974). Information integration theory: A brief survey, in *Contemporary Developments in Mathematical Psychology* (Eds D. Krantz, R. C. Atkinson, R. D. Luce, and P. Suppes), Vol. 2, Freeman, San Francisco.

Anderson, N. H. (1981). *Foundations of Information Integration Theory*, Academic Press, New York.

Appleyard, D. (1969). Why buildings are known, *Environment and Behavior*, **1**, 131.

Appleyard, D. (1970). Styles and methods of structuring a city. *Environment and Behavior*, **2**, 100–118.

Baird, J., Wagner, M., and Noma, E. (1982). Impossible cognitive spaces, *Geographical Analysis*, **14**(3), 204–216.

Baxter, M. J. (1979). The interpretation of the distance and attractiveness components in models of recreational trips, *Geographical Analysis*, **11**, 311–315.

Beavon, K. and Hay, A. (1977). Consumer choice of shopping centre—a hypergeometric model, *Environment and Planning*, **9A**, 1375–1393.

Beck, R. J. and Wood, D. (1976). Cognitive transformation from urban geographic fields to mental maps, *Environment and Behavior*, **8**, 199–238.

Berry, B. J. L., Barnum, H. G., and Tennant, R. J. (1962). Retail location and consumer behavior, *Papers and Proceedings of the Regional Science Association*, **9**, 65–102.

Blaut, J. M., McCleary, G., and Blaut, A. (1970). Environmental mapping in young children. *Environment and Behavior*, **2**, 335–349.

Book, A. and Gärling, T. (1980). Processing of information about location during locomotion: Effects of concurrent task and locomotion patterns, *Scandinavian Journal of Psychology*, **21**, 185–192.

Briggs, R. (1969). Scaling of preferences for spatial locations: An example using shopping centers. Unpublished MA thesis, Department of Geography, Ohio State University, Columbus, Ohio.

Briggs, R. (1972). Cognitive distance in urban space. PhD dissertation, The Ohio State University, Columbus, Ohio.

Brown, L. A. (1968). *Diffusion Dynamics: A Review and Revision of the Quantitative Theory of the Spatial Diffusion of Innovations*, Gleerup, Lund.

Brown, L. A. and Holmes, J. (1971). Search behaviour in an intraurban migration context: A spatial perspective, *Environment and Planning*, **3**, 307–326.

Bunting, T. E. and Guelke, L. (1979). Behavioral and perceptual geography: a critical appraisal, *Annals of the Association of American Geographers*, **69**, 448–462.

Burnett, P. (1973). The dimensions of alternatives in spatial-choice processes, *Geographical Analysis*, **5**, 181–204.

Burnett, P. (1981). Theoretical advances in modelling economic and social behaviors: Applications to geographical, policy-oriented models, *Economic Geography*, **57**, 291–303.

Burnett, P. K. (1982). Data problems and the application of conjoint measurement to recurrent urban travel, in *Proximity and Preference: Problems in the Multidimensional Analysis of Large Data Sets* (Eds R. G. Golledge and J. N. Rayner), pp. 169–190, University of Minnesota Press, Minneapolis.

Burnett, P. and Hanson, S. (1979). Rationale for an alternative mathematical approach to movement as complex human behavior. *Transportation Research Record*, **723**, 11–24.

Burrows, W. J. and Sadalla, E. K. (1979). Asymmetries in distance cognition. *Geographical Analysis*, **11**, 14, 414–421.

Burton, I. and Kates, R. W. (1964). The perception of natural hazards in resource management. *Natural Resources Journal*, **3**, 412–441.

Burton, I., Kates, R. W., and White, G. F. (1968). The human ecology of extreme geophysical events, Natural Hazard Research Working Paper No. 1, Department of Geography, University of Toronto, Toronto.

Buttimer, A. (1969). Social space in interdisciplinary perspective, *Geographical Review*, **59**, 417–426.

Buttimer, A. (1974). Values in geography. Resource Paper No. 24, Association of American Geographers Commission on College Geography, Washington DC.

Byrne, R. (1979). Memory for urban geography, *Quarterly Journal of Experimental Psychology*, **31**, 147–154.

Cadwallader, M. (1975). A behavioral model of consumer spatial decision making, *Economic Geography*, **51**, 339–349.

Cadwallader, M. (1977). Frame dependency in cognitive maps: An analysis using directional statistics. *Geographical Analysis*, **9**, 284–292.

Cadwallader, M. (1979). Problems in cognitive distance and their implications for cognitive mapping, *Environment and Behavior*, **11**, 559–576.

Cadwallader, M. (1981). Towards a cognitive gravity model: The case of consumer spatial behavior, *Regional Studies*, **15**, 275–284.

Carlstein, T., Parkes, D., and Thrift, N. (1978). *Timing Space and Spacing Time*, Vol. 1–3, Edward Arnold, London.

Cesario, F. J. (1973). A generalized trip distribution model, *Journal of Regional Science*, **13**, 233–248.

Cesario, F. J. (1977). A new interpretation of the 'Normalizing' or 'Balancing' factors of gravity-type spatial models, *Socio-Economic Planning Science*, **11**, 131–136.

Clark, W. A. V. and Rushton, G. (1970). Models of intra-urban consumer behavior and their applications for central place theory, *Economic Geography*, **46**, 486–497.

Clark, W. A. V. and Smith, T. R. (1979). Modelling information use in a spatial context, *Annals of the Association of the American Geographers*, **69**, 575–588.

Clark, W. A. V. and Smith, T. R. (1982). Housing markets, search behaviour and expected utility theory. II. Processes of search, *Environment and Planning*, **14A**, 717–737.

Cliff, N. (1973). Scaling, *Annual Review of Psychology*, **24**, 473–506.

Cliff, A. D., Martin, R. L., and Ord, J. K. (1974). Evaluating the friction of distance parameters in gravity models, *Regional Studies*, **8**, 281–286.

Cox, K. R. and Golledge, R. G. (Eds). *Behavioral Problems in Geography*, Northwestern University Studies in Geography 17, Evanston.

Cullen, I. (1976). Human geography, regional science and the study of individual behaviour, *Environment and Planning*, **8A**, 397–409.

Curry, L. (1967). Central places in the random spatial economy, *Journal of Regional Science*, **7**, 217–238.

Damm, D. and Lerman, S. R. (1981). A theory of activity scheduling behaviour, *Environment and Planning*, **13A**, 703–718.

Day, R. A. (1976). Urban distance cognition: Review and contribution, *Australian Geographer*, **13**, 193–200.

Devletoglou, N. E. (1965). A dissenting view of duopoly and spatial competition, *Economica*, **32**, 140–169.

Devlin, A. (1976). The small town cognitive map: Adjusting to a new environment, in *Environmental Knowing: Theories, Research, and Methods* (Eds G. T. Moore and R. G. Golledge), Dowden, Hutchinson, and Ross, Stroudsburg, Pennsylvania.

Downs, R. M. (1970). The cognitive structure of an urban shopping center, *Environment and Behavior*, **2**, 13–39.

Downs, R. M. (1981a). Maps and metaphors, *The Professional Geographer*, **33**, 3, 287–293.

Downs, R. M. (1981b). Maps and mappings as metaphors for spatial representation, in *Spatial Representation and Behavior Across the Life Span: Theory and Applications* (Eds L. Liben, A. Patterson, and N. Newcombe), Academic Press, New York.

Downs, R. and Meyer, J. (1978). Geography and the mind: An exploration of perceptual geography, *American Behavioral Scientists*, **22**, 59–77.

Downs, R. M. and Stea, D. (Eds) (1973). *Image and Environment: Cognitive Mapping and Spatial Behavior*, Aldine, Chicago.

Downs, R. M. and Stea, D. (1977). *Maps in Minds: Reflections of Cognitive Mapping*, Harper and Row, New York.

Eagle, T. C. (1980). A review of decision rules and their role in spatial choice. Discussion Paper No. 33, Department of Geography, University of Iowa, Iowa City, Iowa.

Edgington, E. S. (1969). *Statistical Inference: The Distribution-Free Approach*, McGraw Hill, New York.

Einhorn, H. J. and Hogarth, R. M. (1981). Behavioral decision theory: Processes of judgment and choice, *Annual Review of Psychology*, **32**.

Ericksen, R. H. (1975). The effects of perceived place attributes on cognition of urban residents, Discussion Paper No. 23, Department of Geography, University of Iowa, Iowa City, Iowa.

Evans, G. W. (1980). Environmental cognition. *Psychological Bulletin*, **88**, 259–287.

Evans, G. W., Marrero, D. G., and Butler, P. A. (1981). Environmental learning and cognitive mapping, *Environment and Behavior*, **13**, 83–104.

Evans, G. W. and Pezdek, K. (1980). Cognitive mapping: Knowledge of real world distance and location information, *Journal of Experimental Psychology: Human Learning and Memory*, **6**, 3–24.

Ewing, G. (1974). Gravity and linear regression models of spatial interaction: A cautionary note, *Economic Geography*, **50**, 83–87.

Eyles, J. (1971). Pouring new sentiments into new theories: How else can we look at behavioural patterns? *Area*, **3**, 242–250.

Fingleton, B. (1975). A factorial approach to the nearest center hypothesis, *Transactions of the Institute of British Geographers*, **65**, 131–139.

Fishburn, P. C. (1967). Methods of estimating additive utilities, *Management Science*, **13**, 435–453.

Flowerdew, R. T. N. (1973). Preference rankings on several attributes: Applications in residential site selection, *Environment and Planning*, **5**, 601–609.

Fogarty, B. M. (1977). A new measurement of store attraction inferred from spatial choice data. Unpublished PhD Dissertation, Department of Geography, The University of Iowa, Iowa City, Iowa.

Forer, P. C. and Kivell, H. (1981). Space-time budgets, public transport, and spatial choice, *Environment and Planning*, **13A**, 497–509.

Fotheringham, A. S. (1981). Spatial structure and distance-decay parameters, *Annals of the Association of American Geographers*, **71**, 425–436.

Gale, N. (1980). An analysis of the distortion and fuzziness of cognitive maps by location. MA thesis, University of California, Santa Barbara, California.

Gärling, T. and Book, A. (1981). The spaciotemporal sequencing of everyday activities: How people manage to find the shortest route to travel between places in their hometown. Unpublished manuscript, University of Umea, Department of Psychology, Sweden.

Gärling, T., Book, A., Ergezen, N., and Lindberg, E. (1981). Memory for the spatial layout of the everyday physical environment: Empirical findings and their theoretical implications, in *Design Research Interactions* (Eds A. E. Osterberg, C. P. Teirman, and R. A. Findlay), Proceedings of the EDRA 12 Conference, Ames, Iowa.

Gauthier, H. L. and Mitchelson, R. L. (1981). Attribute importance and mode satisfaction in travel mode choice, *Economic Geography*, **57**, 348–361.

Girt, J. L. (1976). Some extensions to Rushton's spatial preference model, *Geographical Analysis*, **8**, 137–152.

Gold, J. R. (1980). *An Introduction to Behavioural Geography*, Oxford University Press, New York.

Golledge, R. G. (1965). A probabilistic model of market behavior—With reference to the spatial aspects of hog marketing in Eastern Iowa. Unpublished manuscript, Department of Geography, University of Iowa, Iowa City, Iowa.

Golledge, R. G. (1967). Conceptualizing the market decision process, *Journal of Regional Science*, **7**, Supplement, 239–258.

Golledge, R. G. (1969). The geographical relevance of some learning theories. In *Behavioral Problems in Geography* (Eds K. R. Cox and R. G. Golledge), Northwestern University Press, Evanston, Illinois.

Golledge, R. G. (1976). Methods and methodological issues in environmental cognition research, in *Environmental Knowing: Theories, Research, and Methods* (Eds G. Moore and R. G. Golledge), Dowden, Hutchinson and Ross, Stroudsburg, Pennsylvania.

Golledge, R. G. (1978). Learning about urban environments. In *Timing Space and Spacing Time* (Eds T. Carlstein, D. Parkes, and N. Thrift), Vol. 1, Edward Arnold, London.

Golledge, R. G. (1979). Process, reality, and the dialectical relation between man and environment, in *Philosophy in Geography* (Eds S. Gale and G. Olsson), D. Reidell, Boston.

Golledge, R. G. (1981). Misconceptions, misinterpretations, and misrepresentations of behavioural approaches in human geography, *Environment and Planning A*, **13**, 1325–1344.

Golledge, R. G. and Amedeo, D. (1968). On laws in geography, *Annals of the Association of American Geographers*, **58**, 4, 760–774.

Golledge, R. G., Briggs, R., and Demko, D. (1969). The configuration of distances in intra-urban space, *Proceedings of the Association of American Geographers*, **1**, 60–65.

Golledge, R. G. and Brown, L. A. (1967). Search, learning and the market decision process, *Geografiska Annaler*, **49**, 2, 116–124.

Golledge, R. G., Brown, L. A., and Williamson, F. (1972). Behavioural approaches in geography: An overview, *The Australian Geographer*, XII, 1, 59–79.

Golledge, R. G. and Hubert, L. J. (1982). Some comments on non-Euclidean mental maps, *Environment and Planning A*, **14**, 107–118.

Golledge, R. G., Parnicky, J. J., and Rayner, J. N. (1979a). *The Spatial Competence of Selected Populations*, Vols 1 and 2, The Ohio State University Research Foundation, Columbus, Ohio.

Golledge, R. G., Parnicky, J. J., and Rayner, J. N. (1979b). An experimental design for assessing the spatial competence of mildly retarded populations, *Social Science and Medicine*, **13**, 291–295.

Golledge, R. G., Parnicky, J. J., and Rayner, J. N. (1980). *The Spatial Competence of Selected Populations*, The Ohio State University Research Foundation, Columbus, Ohio.

Golledge, R. G. and Rayner, J. N. (1976). *Cognitive Configurations of a City*, Vol. 2, The Ohio State University Research Foundation, Columbus, Ohio.

Golledge, R. G. and Rayner, J. N. (1982). *Proximity and Preference: Problems in the Multidimensional Analysis of Large Data Sets*, University of Minnesota Press, Minneapolis.

Golledge, R. G., Richardson, G. D., Rayner, J. N., and Parnicky, J. J. (1983). The spatial competence of selected mentally retarded populations. In *Spatial Orientation and Spatial Representation* (Eds H. L. Pick and L. Acredolo), Lawrence Earlbaum, Potomac, Maryland.

Golledge, R. G. and Rushton, G. (Eds). *Spatial Choice and Spatial Behavior*, Ohio State University Press, Columbus.

Golledge, R. G., Rushton, G., and Clark, W. A. V. (1966). Some spatial characteristics of Iowa's dispersed farm population and their implications for the grouping of central place function, *Economic Geography*, **42**, 389–400.

Golledge, R. G. and Spector, A. N. (1978). Comprehending the urban environment: Theory and practice, *Geographical Analysis*, **10**, 403–426.

Golledge, R. G. and Tobler, W. R. (1983). *Spatial Variation in the Distortion and Fuzziness of Cognitive Maps*, National Science Foundation Technical Report, Department of Geography, University of California, Santa Barbara.

Golledge, R. G. and Zannaras, G. (1973). Cognitive approaches to the analysis of human spatial behavior, in *Environment and Cognition* (Ed. W. Ittelson), pp. 59–94, Seminar Press, New York.

Gould, P. (1963). Man against environment: A game theoretic framework, *Annals, Association of American Geographers*, **53**, 290–297.

Gould, P. R. (1967a). Wheat on Kilimanjaro: The perception of choice within game and learning theory frameworks, *General Systems Yearbook, 1967*, 157–166.

Gould, P. R. (1967b). Structuring information on spatio-temporal preference, *Journal of Regional Science*, **7**, 259–274.

Gould, P. R. (1969). Problems of space preference measures and relationships, *Geographical Analysis*, I, 31–44.

Gould, P. R. (1976). Cultivating the garden: a commentary and critique on some multidimensional speculations, in *Spatial Choice and Spatial Behavior* (Eds R. G. Golledge and G. Rushton), Ohio State University Press, Columbus, 83–94.

Griffith, D. A. (1976). Spatial structure and spatial interaction: A review, *Environment and Planning*, **8A**, 731–740.

Hagerstrand, T. (1952). *The Propogation of Innovation Waves*, Gleerup, Lund.

Hagerstrand, T. (1954). Migration and area, in *Migration in Sweden* (Eds D. Hanneberg, T. Hagerstrand, and B. Odeving), Gleerup, Lund.

Hagerstrand, T. (1957). *Innovation Diffusion as a Spatial Process*. University of Chicago Press, Chicago.

Hagerstrand, T. (1969). What about people in regional science? *Papers of the Regional Science Association*, **24**, 7–21.

Hanson, S. (1980). The importance of the multipurpose journey to work in urban travel behavior, *Transportation*, **9**, 229–248.

Hanson, S. and Hanson, P. (1981). The travel-activity patterns of urban residents: Dimensions and relationships to socio-demographic characteristics, *Economic Geography*, **57**, 332–347.

Hanushek, E. A. and Quigley, J. M. (1978). An explicit model of intra-metropolitan mobility, *Land Economics*, **54**, 411–429.

Hart, R. A. (1978). *Children's Experience of Place: A Developmental Study*, Halsted, New York.

Harvey, D. (1969). *Explanation in Geography*, Edward Arnold, London.

Hayes-Roth, B. (1977). Evolution of cognitive structures and processes, *Psychological Review*, **84**, 260–278.

Hayes-Roth, B. and Hayes-Roth, F. (1979). A cognitive model of planning, *Cognitive Science*, **4**, 275–318.

Hayes-Roth, F. (1979). Distinguishing theories of representation: A critique of

Anderson's 'Arguments Concerning Mental Imagery', *Psychological Review*, **86**, 376–382.

Heggie, I. and Jones, P. (1978). Defining domains for travel demand, *Transportation*, **7**, 119–125.

Hensher, D. (1976). The structure of journeys and the nature of travel patterns, *Environment and Planning*, **8**, 655–672.

Herman, J. F. and Siegel, A. W. (1978). The development of spatial representations of large-scale environments, *Journal of Experimental Child Psychology*, **26**, 389–406.

Hintzman, D. L., O'Dell, C. S., and Arndt, D. R. (1981). Orientation in cognitive maps, *Cognitive Psychology*, **13**, 149–206.

Howard, I. P. and Templeton, W. B. (1966). *Human Spatial Orientation*, Wiley, London.

Hubbard, R. (1976). The structure of journeys and the nature of travel patterns, *Environment and Planning*, **8**, 655–672.

Hubbard, R. (1978). A review of selected factors conditioning consumer travel behavior, *Journal of Consumer Research*, **5**, 1–21.

Hubbard, R. (1979). Parameter stability in cross-sectional models of ethnic shopping behaviour, *Environment and Planning*, **11A**, 977–992.

Hubbard, R. and Thompson, A. F. (1981). Preference structures and consumer spatial indifference behaviour: Some theoretical problems, *Tijdschrift voor Economische en Sociale Geografie*, **72**, 35–39.

Hubert, L. J. (1978). Nonparametric tests for pattern in geographic variation: Possible generalizations, *Geographical Analysis*, x, 1, 86–89.

Hubert, L. J. and Golledge, L. G. (1981a). A heuristic method for the comparison of related structures, *J. Math Psych*, **23**, 3, 214–226.

Hubert, L. J. and Golledge, R. G. (1981b). Matrix reorganization and dynamic programming: Applications to paired comparisons and unidimensional seriation, *Psychometrica*, **46**, 4, 429–441.

Hubert, L. J., Golledge, R. G., Costanzo, C. M., Gale, N., and Halperin, W. C. (1983). Non-parametric directional statistics. Unpublished Manuscript, Department of Geography, University of California, Santa Barbara.

Hubert, L. J. and Schultz, J. V. (1976). Quadratic assignment as a general data analysis strategy, *British Journal of Mathematical and Statistical Psychology*, **29**, 190–241.

Isaac, P. D. (1982). Considerations in the selection of stimulus pairs for data collection in multidimensional scaling, in *Proximity and Preference: Problems in the Multidimensional Analysis of Large Data Sets* (Eds R. G. Golledge and J. N. Rayner), pp. 80–89, University of Minnesota Press, Minnesota.

Ittelson, W. H., Proshansky, H. M., Rivlin, L. G., and Winkel, G. H. (1974). *An Introduction to Environmental Psychology*, Holt, Rinehart & Winston, New York.

Jakle, J. A., Brunn, S., and Roseman, C. C. (1976). *Human Spatial Behavior*, Duxbury Press, North Scituate, Massachusetts.

Johnston, R. J. (1976). On regression coefficients in comparative studies of the 'friction of distance', *Tijdschrift voor Economische en Sociale Geografie*, **67**, 51–58.

Jones, M. M. (1972). Urban path-choosing behavior: A study of environmental cues, in *Environmental Design: Research and Practice* (Ed. W. Mitchell), University of California, Los Angeles.

Kaplan, S. and Kaplan, R. (1982). *Cognition and Environment*, Praeger, New York.

Kates, R. W. (1962). Hazard and choice perception in flood plain management, Research Papers 1978, University of Chicago, Department of Geography.

Kates, R. W. (1967). The perception of storm hazard on the shores of megalopolis, in *Environmental Perception and Behavior* (Ed. D. Lowenthal), Research Paper No. 109, pp. 60–69. Chicago, Department of Geography, University of Chicago.

Kates, R. W. (1970). Human perception of the environment, *International Social Science Journal*, **22**, 648–660.

King, L. J. and Golledge, R. G. (1978). *Cities, Space and Behavior*, Prentice-Hall, Englewood Cliffs.

Knight, R. L. and Menchick, M. D. (1976). Conjoint preference estimation for residential land use policy evaluation, in *Spatial Choice and Spatial Behavior* (Eds R. G. Golledge and G. Rushton), Ohio State University Press, Columbus.

Kosslyn, S. M. (1976). Can imagery be distinguished from other forms of internal representation? Evidence from studies of information-retrieval time, *Memory and Cognition*, **4**, 291–297.

Kosslyn, S. M. (1981). The medium and the message in mental imagery: A theory, *Psychological Review*, **88**, 46–66.

Kosslyn, S. M., Pick, H. L., and Fariello, G. R. (1974). Cognitive maps in children and men, *Child Development*, **45**, 707–716.

Kosslyn, S. M., Reiser, B. J., and Ball, T. M. (1978). Visual images preserve metric spatial information: Evidence from studies of image scanning, *Journal of Experimental Psychology: Human Perception and Performance*, **4**, 47–60.

Krantz, D. H., Luce, R. D., Suppes, P., and Tversky, A. (1971). *Foundations of Measurement*, Academic Press, New York.

Krantz, D. H. and Tversky, A. (1971). Conjoint-measurement analysis of composition rules in psychology, *Psychological Review*, **78**, 151–169.

Kuipers, B. (1978). Modeling spatial knowledge, *Cognitive Science*, **2**, 129–153.

Landau, U., Prashker, J. N., and Hirsh, M. (1981). The effect of temporal constraints on household travel behaviour, *Environment and Planning*, **13A**, 435–448.

Lee, T. (1964). Psychology and living space, *Transactions of the Bartlett Society*, **2**, 11–36.

Lee, T. (1970). Perceived distance as a function of direction in the city, *Environment and Behavior*, **2**, 40–51.

Leff, H. (1978). *Experience, Environment and Human Potentials*, Oxford University Press, New York.

Levin, I. P. (1975). Information integration in numerical judgements and decision processes, *Journal of Experimental Psychology: General*, **104**, 39–53.

Ley, D. (1981). Behavioral geography and the philosophies of meaning, in *Behavioral Problems in Geography Revisited* (Eds K. R. Cox and R. G. Golledge), pp. 209–230, Methuen, New York.

Ley, D. and Samuels, M. (Eds) (1978). *Humanistic Geography: Prospects and Problems*, Maaroufa Press, Chicago.

Lieber, S. R. (1976). A comparison of metric and nonmetric scaling models in preference research, in *Spatial Choice and Spatial Behavior* (Eds R. G. Golledge and G. Rushton), Ohio State University Press, Columbus.

Lieber, S. R. (1979). An experimental approach for the migration decision process, *Tijdschrift voor Economische en Sociale Geografie*, **70**, 75–85.

Lindberg, E. and Gärling, T. (1982). Cognitive mapping: The role of central information processing. Paper presented at 20th International Congress of Applied Psychology, Edinburgh, Scotland, July 1982.

Lloyd, R. E. (1976). Cognition, preference and behavior in space: An examination of the structural linkages, *Economic Geography*, **52**, 241–253.

Lloyd, R. (1982). A look at images, *Annals of the Association of American Geographers*, **72**, 4, 532–548.

Louviere, J. J. (1974). Predicting the response to real stimulus objects from an abstract evaluation of their attributes: The case of trout streams, *Journal of Applied Psychology*, **59**, 753–758.

Louviere, J. J. (1978). Psychological measurement of travel attributes, in *Determinants of Travel Choice* (Eds D. A. Henser and Q. Dalvi), pp. 148–186, Praeger Publishers, New York.

Louviere, J. J. (1981a). On the identification of functional form of the utility expression and its relationship to discrete choice, in *Applied Discrete-Choice Modelling* (Eds D. A. Hensher and L. W. Johnson), pp. 385–415, Croom-Helm, London.

Louviere, J. J. (1981b). A conceptual and analytic framework for understanding spatial behavior and travel choices, *Economic Geography*, **57**, 304–314.

Louviere, J. J. and Henley, D. (1977). An empirical analysis of student apartment selection decisions, *Geographical Analysis*, **9**, 130–141.

Louviere, J. J. and Wilson, E. M. (1978). Predicting consumer response in travel analysis, *Transportation, Planning and Technology*, **4**, 1–9

Lowenthal, D. (1961). Geography, experience and imagination: Towards a geographic epistemology, *Annals of the Association of American Geographers*, **51**, 241–260.

Lowenthal, D. (Ed.) (1967). *Environmental Perception and Behavior*, Research Paper No. 109, Department of Geography, University of Chicago, Chicago.

Lowenthal, D. (1972). Editorial introduction; Research in environmental perception and behavior, *Environment and Behavior*, **4**, 3, 251–254 and 333–342.

Lowrey, R. A. (1970). Distance concepts of urban residents, *Environment and Behavior*, **2**, 52–73.

Luce, R. D. and Tukey, J. W. (1964). Simultaneous conjoint measurement: A new type of fundamental measurement, *Journal of Mathematical Psychology*, **1**, 1–27.

Lynch, K. (1960). *Image of the City*, MIT Press, Cambridge, Massachusetts.

MacEachren, A. M. (1980). Travel time as the basis of cognitive distance, *The Professional Geographer*, **32**, 30–36.

MacKay, D. B. (1976). The effect of spatial stimuli on the estimation of cognitive maps, *Geographical Analysis*, **8**, 439–452.

MacKay, D. B., Olshavsky, R. W., and Sentell, G. (1975). Cognitive maps and spatial behavior of consumers, *Geographical Analysis*, **7**, 19–34.

Mackay, D. G. and Zinnes, T. (1981). Probabilistic scaling of spatial distance judgements, *Geographical Analysis*, **13**, 1, 21–37.

MacLennan, D. and Williams, N. J. (1979). Revealed space preference theory—A cautionary note, *Tijdschrift voor Economische en Sociale Geografie*, **70**, 307–309.

MacLennan, D. and Williams, N. J. (1980). Revealed-preference theory and spatial choices: Some limitations, *Environment and Planning*, **12A**, 909–919.

Magana, J. R., Evans, G. W., and Romney, A. K. (1981). Scaling techniques in the analysis of environmental cognition data, *The Professional Geographer*, **33**, 3, 294–301.

Milgram, N. A. (1973). Cognition and language in mental retardation: Distinctions and implications, in *The Experimental Psychology of Mental Retardation* (Ed. D. K. Routh), Aldine, Chicago.

Milgram, S., Greenwald, J., Keesler, S., McKenna, W., and Waters, J. (1972). A psychological map of New York City, *American Scientist*, **60**, 194–200.

Milgram, S. and Jodelet, D. (1976). Psychological maps of Paris, in *Environmental Psychology* (Eds H. M. Proshansky, W. H. Ittelson and L. G. Rivlin), 2nd edn, Holt, New York.

Montgomery, H. and Svenson, O. (1976). On decision rules and information processing strategies for choice among multiattribute alternatives, *Scandinavian Journal of Psychology*, **17**, 283–291.

Moore, G. T. (1979). Knowing about environmental knowing: The current state of theory and research on environmental cognition. *Environment and Behavior*, **11**, 33–70.

Moore, G. T. and Golledge, R. G. (1976a). *Environmental Knowing: Theories, Research, and Methods*, Dowden, Hutchinson, and Ross, Stoudsburg, Pennsylvania.

Moore, G. T. and Golledge, R. G. (1976b). Environmental knowing: concepts and theories, in *Environmental Knowing: Theories, Research, and Methods*, (Eds G. T. Moore and R. G. Golledge), Dowden, Hutchinson and Ross, Stroudsburg, Pennsylvania.

Muller, Jean-Claude (1982). Non-Euclidean geographic space: Mapping functional distances, *Geographical Analysis*, **14**, 3, 189–203.

Niedercorn, J. H. and Bechdolt, B. V. (1969). An economic derivation of the 'Gravity Law' of spatial interaction, *Journal of Applied Psychology*, **59**, 753–758.

Norman, K. L. and Louviere, J. J. (1974). Integration of attributes in bus transportation: Two modelling approaches, *Journal of Applied Psychology*, **59**, 753–758.

Odland, J. and Jakubs, J. (1977). Urban travel alternatives: Models for individual and collective preferences, *Socio-Economic Planning Science*, **11**, 265–271.

Olsson, G. and Gale, S. (1968). Spatial theory and human behavior. *Papers of the Regional Science Association*, **21**.

Openshaw, S. (1976). An empirical study of some spatial interaction models, *Environment and Planning*, **8A**, 23–41.

Paivio, A. (1969). Mental imagery in associative learning and memory, *Psychological Review*, **76**, 241–263.

Park, C. W. and Lutz, R. J. (1980). Predictions of individuals choice based on a decision making net. Unpublished paper, Graduate School of Business, University of Pittsburgh, Pittsburgh.

Parkes, D. and Thrift, N. (1975). Timing space and spacing time. *Environment and Planning*, **7A**, 651–670.

Peterson, G. K. (1967). A model of preference: quantitative analysis of the visual appearance of residential neighborhoods. *Journal of Regional Science*, **7**, 19–32.

Pezdek, K. and Evans, G. W. (1979). Visual and verbal memory for objects and their spatial locations. *Journal of Experimental Psychology: Human Learning and Memory*, **5**, 360–373.

Piaget, J. and Inhelder, B. (1967). *The Child's Conception of Space*, W. W. Norton, New York.

Piaget, J., Inhelder, B., and Czeminska, A. (1960). *The Child's Conception of Geometry*, Basic Books, New York.

Pipkin, J. S. (1981a). Cognitive behavioral geography and repetitive travel, in *Behavioral Problems in Geography Revisted* (Eds K. R. Cox and R. G. Golledge), Methuen, New York.

Pipkin, J. S. (1981b). The Concept of choice and cognitive explanations of spatial behavior, *Economic Geography*, **57**, 315–331.

Pirie, G. H. (1976). Thoughts on revealed preference and spatial behavior, *Environment and Planning*, **8A**, 947–955.

Porteous, J. D. (1977). *Environment and Behavior: Planning and Everyday Urban Life*, Addison Wesley, Reading, Massachusetts.

Pred, A. (1967). Behavior and location. I, *Studies in Geography*, B, Lund University.

Proshansky, H. M., Ittelson, W. H., and Rivlin, L. G. (Eds) (1970). *Environmental Psychology*, Holt, Rinehart and Winston, New York.

Rappoport, A. and Wallsten, T. S. (1972). Individual decision behavior, *Annual Review of Psychology*, **23**, 131–176.

Recker, W. W. and Schuler, H. J. (1981). Destination choice and processing spatial information: Some empirical tests with alternative constructs, *Economic Geography*, **57**, 373–383.

Richardson, G. D. (1981a). Comparing two cognitive mapping methodologies, *Area*, **13**, 325–331.

Richardson, G. D. (1981b). Using bidimensional regression for analyzing the cognitive maps of the mentally retarded. Unpublished manuscript, Department of Geography, University of California, Santa Barbara.

Richardson, G. D. (1981c). The appropriateness of using various Minkowskian metrics for representing cognitive configurations, *Environment and Planning A*, **13**, 475–485.

Richardson, G. D. (1982). *Spatial Cognition*. PhD dissertation, Department of Geography, University of California, Santa Barbara.

Rivizzigno, V. L. (1976). Cognitive representations of an urban area. PhD Dissertation, Department of Geography, Ohio State University, Ohio.

Rushton, G. (1965). The spatial pattern of grocery purchases in Iowa. PhD Dissertation, Department of Geography, University of Iowa, Iowa City, Iowa.

Rushton, G. (1966). Spatial pattern of grocery purchases by the Iowa rural population, Study No. 9, Bureau of Business and Economic Research, University of Iowa, Iowa City, Iowa.

Rushton, G. (1969a). Analysis of spatial behavior by revealed space preference. *Annals of the Association of American Geographers*, **59**, 391–340.

Rushton, G. (1969b). The scaling of locational preferences. In *Behavioral Problems in Geography* (Eds K. R. Cox and R. G. Golledge), pp. 197–227, Northwestern University Studies in Geography, No. 17, Evanston, Illinois.

Rushton, G. (1976). Decomposition of space preference functions. In *Spatial Choice and Spatial Behavior* (Eds R. G. Golledge and G. Rushton), pp. 19–133, Ohio State University Press, Columbus.

Rushton, G., Golledge, R. G., and Clark, W. A. V. (1967). Formulation and test of a normative model for the spatial allocation of grocery expenditures for a dispersed population. *Annals of the Association of American Geographers*, **57**, 389–400.

Sadalla, E. K., Burroughs, W. J., and Staplin, L. J. (1980). Reference points in spatial cognition, *Journal of Experimental Psychology: Human Learning and Memory*, **6**, 516–528.

Sadalla, E. K. and Magel, S. G. (1980). The perception of traversed distance, *Environment and Behavior*, **12**, 65–79.

Sadalla, E. K. and Staplin, L. J. (1980a). The perception of traversed distance: Intersections, *Environment and Behavior*, **12**, 167–182.

Sadalla, E. K. and Staplin, L. J. (1980b). An information storage model for distance cognition, *Environment and Behavior*, **12**, 183–193.

Saarinen, T. (1966). Perception of the drought hazard on the Great Plains, Research Paper No. 106, University of Chicago, Department of Geography, Chicago, Illinois.

Saarinen, T. (1976). *Environmental Planning: Perception and Behavior*, Houghton Mifflin, Boston.

Schaefer, F. K. (1953). Exceptionalism in geography: A methodological examination, *Annals of the Association of American Geographers*, **43**, 3, 226–249.

Sheppard, E. S. (1979). Gravity parameter estimation. *Geographical Analysis*, **11**, 120–132.

Sheppard, E. S. (1980). The ideology of spatial choice, *Papers of the Regional Science Association*, **45**, 197–213.

Sheppard, E. S. (1982). Distance-decay parameters: A comment. *Annals of the Association of American Geographers*, **72**, 549–550.

Shemyakin, F. N. (1962). General problems of orientation in space and space representations, in *Psychological Science in the USSR* (Ed. B. G. Ananyev), US Office of Technical Reports (NTIS No. TT62-11083).

Siegel, A. (1981). The externalization of cognitive maps by children and adults: In search of ways to ask better questions. In *Spatial Representation and Behavior Across the Life Span: Theory and Application* (Eds L. Liben, A. Patterson, and N. Newcombe), Academic Press, New York.

Siegel, A. W., Allen, G. L., and Kirasic, K. C. (1979). Children's abilty to make bi-directional distance comparisons: The advantage of thinking ahead, *Developmental Psychology*, **15**, 656–665.

Siegel, A. W., Kirasic, K. C., and Kail, R. V. (1978). Stalking the elusive cognitive map: The development of children's representations of geographic space. In *Human Behavior and Environment* (Eds J. F. Wohlwill and I. Altman), Vol. 3, Plenum, New York.

Siegel, A. W. and White, S. H. (1975). The development of spatial representations of large-scale environments, in *Advances in Child Development and Behavior* (Ed. H. W. Reese), Vol. 10, Academic Press, New York.

Slovic, P., Fischoff, B., and Lichtenstein, S. C. (1977). Behavioral decision theory, *Annual Review of Psychology*, **28**, 1–39.

Smith, T. R. (1975). An axiomatic theory of spatial discounting behavior, *Papers of the Regional Science Association*, **35**, 31–44.

Smith, T. R. and Clark, W. A. V. (1982). Housing markets, search behavior and expected utility theory. I. Measuring preferences for housing. *Environment and Planning*, **14A**, 681–698.

Smith, T. R., Clark, W. A. V., Huff, J. D., and Shapiro, P. (1979). A decision making search model for intra-urban migration, *Geographical Analysis*, **11**, 1–22.

Smith, T. R., Clark, W. A. V., and Onaka, J. (1982). Information provision: An analysis of newspaper real estate advertisements. In *Modelling Housing Market Search* (Ed. W. A. V. Clark), pp. 160–186, Croom Helm, London.

Smith, T. R. and Mertz, F. (1980). An analysis of the effects of information revision on the outcome of housing market search, with special reference to the influence of realty agents, *Environment and Planning*, **12A**, 155–174.

Smith, T. R., Pellegrino J. Q., and Golledge, R. G. (1982). Computational process modeling of spatial cognition and behavior, *Geographical Analysis*, **14**, 305–325.

Sonnenfeld, J. (1966). Variable values in space and landscape: An inquiry into the nature of environmental necessity, *Journal of Social Issues*, **22**, 71–82.

Sonnenfeld, J. (1969). Equivalence and distortion of the perceptual environment, *Environment and Behavior*, **1**, 83–99.

Spector, A. N. (1978). An analysis of urban spatial imagery. PhD Dissertation, Department of Geography, Ohio State University, Columbus, Ohio.

Spence, I. (1982). Incomplete experimental designs for multidimensional scaling. In *Proximity and Preference: Problems in Multidimensional Analysis of Large Data Sets* (Eds R. G. Golledge and J. N. Rayner), pp. 29–46, University of Minnesota Press, Minneapolis.

Staplin, L. J. and Sadalla, E. K. (1981). Distance cognition in urban environments, *The Professional Geographer*, **33**, 3, 302–310.

Stetzer, F. and Phipps, A. G. (1977). Spatial choice theory and spatial indifference: A comment, *Geographical Analysis*, **9**, 400–403.

Stea, D. (1969). The measurement of mental maps: An experimental model for studying conceptual spaces, in *Behavioral Problems in Geography: A Symposium* (Eds K. R. Cox and R. G. Golledge), pp. 228–253, Northwestern University Studies in Geography No. 17, Evanston, Illinois.

Stevens, A. and Coupe, P. (1978). Distortions in judged spatial relations, *Cognitive Psychology*, **10**, 422–437.

Thomas, E. N., Mitchell, R. A., and Blome, D. A. (1962). The spatial behavior of a dispersed nonfarm population, *Papers and Proceedings of the Regional Science Association*, **9**, 107–133.

Thompson, D. L. (1963). New concept: Subjective distance, *Journal of Retailing*, **39**, 1–6.

Thompson, D. L. (1966). Future directions in retail area research, *Economic Geography*, **42**, 1–18.

Thorndyke, P. W. (1980). Performance models for spatial and locational cognition, Rand Research Report, Santa Monica, California.

Thorndyke, P. W. (1981). Distance estimation from cognitive maps, *Cognitive Psychology*, **13**, 526–550.

Thorndyke, P. W. and Hayes-Roth, B. (1980). *Differences in Spatial Knowledge Acquired from Maps and Navigation*, Rand Research Report, Santa Monica, California.

Thorndyke, P. W. and Stasz, C. (1980). *Individual Differences in Knowledge Acquisition from Maps*, Rand Research Report, Santa Monica, California.

Timmermans, H. J. P. (1979). A spatial preference model of regional shopping behavior, *Tijdschrift voor Economische en Sociale Geografie*, **70**, 45–48.

Timmermans, H. J. P. (1981). Multi-attribute shopping models and ridge regression analysis, *Environment and Planning*, **13A**, 43–56.

Tobler, W. R. (1965). Computation of the correspondence of geographical patterns, *Papers and Proceedings of the Regional Science Association*, **15**, 131–139.

Tobler, W. R. (1976). The geometry of mental maps. In *Spatial Choice and Spatial Behavior* (Eds G. Rushton and R. G. Golledge), The Ohio State University Press, Columbus, Ohio.

Tobler, W. R. (1977). Bidimensional regression. Unpublished manuscript, Department of Geography, University of California, Santa Barbara.

Tobler, W. R. (1982). Surveying multidimensional measurement. In *Proximity and Preference* (Eds R. G. Golledge and J. N. Rayner), University of Minnesota Press, Minneapolis.

Tolman, E. C. (1948). Cognitive maps in rats and men, *Psychological Review*, **55**, 189–208.

Trowbridge, C. C. (1948). *Comparative Psychology of Mental Development*, International Universities Press, New York.

Tuan, Yi-Fu (1967). Attitudes towards environment: Themes and approaches. In *Environmental Perception and Behavior* (Ed. D. Lowenthal), Chicago. Research Paper No. 109, pp. 4–17. University of Chicago, Department of Geography.

Tuan, Ti-Fu (1974). *Topophilia*, Prentice Hall, Englewood Cliffs, New Jersey.

Tuan, Yi-Fu (1975). Images and mental maps, *Annals of the Association of American Geographers*, **65**, 213.

Tuan, Yi-Fu (1977). *Space and Place: The Perspective of Experience*, University of Minnesota Press, Minneapolis.

Weibull, J. W. (1980). On the numerical measurement of accessibility, *Environment and Planning*, **12A**, 53–67.

Wheeler, J. (1972). Trip purposes and urban activity linkages, *Annals of the Association of American Geographers*, **62**, 641–654.

White, G. (1945). *Human Adjustments to Floods*, Research Paper No. 29, University of Chicago, Department of Geography, Chicago.

Wilson, A. G. (1970). *Entropy in Urban and Regional Modelling*, Pion, London.

Wolpert, J. (1964). The decision process in a spatial context, *Annals of the Association of American Geographers*, **54**, 537–558.

Wolpert, J. (1965). Behavioral aspects of the decision to migrate, *Papers of the Regional Science Association*, **15**, 159–169.

Wright, J. K. (1947). Terrai incognitae: The place of imagination in geography, *Annals of the Association of American Geographers*, **37**, 1–15.

Young, F. W. and Cliff, N. (1972). Interactive scaling with individual subjects, *Psychometrika*, **37**, 385–415.

Young, F. W., Null, C. H., Sarle, W. S., and Hoffman, D. L. (1982). Interactively ordering the similarities among a large set of stimuli. In *Proximity and Preference* (Eds R. G. Golledge and J. N. Rayner), pp. 10–28, University of Minnesota Press, Minneapolis.

Zannaras, G. (1976). The relation between cognitive structure and urban form. In *Environmental Knowing* (Eds G. T. Moore and R. G. Golledge), Dowden, Hutchinson and Ross, Stroudsburg, Pennsylvania.

Geography and the Urban Environment
Progress in Research and Applications, Volume VI
Edited by D. T. Herbert and R. J. Johnston
© 1984 John Wiley & Sons Ltd.

Chapter 2

Discrete Choice Modelling in Urban Analysis

Neil Wrigley and Paul A. Longley

Discrete choice modelling is an area of research which lies at the interface of economics, transportation science, human geography and psychology, and is a research focus which has sprung to prominence since the early 1970s. Basically, it has emerged out of a marriage of three important streams of development, (a) in micro-economic consumer theory, (b) in psychological theories of choice, and (c) of new methodologies for the statistical analysis of discrete/categorical data. Many claims have been made for the value of discrete choice models. It has been suggested that they are based upon clearly defined assumptions about human behaviour but yet remain operationally tractable, are efficient in their data requirements, are accurate in their description and prediction of many important aspects of urban choice behaviour, and are sensitive to the incorporation of policy variables. In addition, the disaggregate nature of these models is seen as producing marked advantages over traditional aggregate formulations. This is perhaps most clearly manifest in the general intuitive appeal of operational models formulated at the level of the individual decision-maker rather than abstract aggregations, but it also, more specifically, relates to the ability to provide a more coherent theory of model linkage in the disaggregate case than in the aggregate. Finally, it has often been claimed that appropriately specified discrete choice models, which capture the essence of human choice behaviour, should be transferable in both space and time.

Following the pioneering work of McFadden, Ben-Akiva and Manski at Berkeley and MIT in the early 1970s, the publication of books by Domencich and McFadden (1975) and Richards and Ben-Akiva (1975), and the subsequent research of Daganzo, Daly, Gaudry, Hensher, Horowitz, Lerman, Tardiff, and many others, discrete choice modelling has become a dominant research focus in transport planning. Likewise, in the continuing work of McFadden, Manski, Heckman, Hensher and others, it has become firmly integrated into the main stream of economic theory and econometrics (see Manski and McFadden, 1981; Hensher and Johnson, 1981a). In human geography, however, despite:

(i) the significant contributions of Williams, Louviere, Meyer and Eagle, Burnett and Hanson, and others;

(ii) the appointment by at least one major university geography department of a specialist in the field (Horowitz at the University of Iowa);

(iii) the claim by Rushton (1982), amongst others, that discrete choice theory represents one of the most significant methodological developments in behavioural geography over the past decade; and

(iv) the increasing supplementation and/or replacement of traditional Wilson-Batty type aggregate spatial interaction models with disaggregate discrete choice approaches;

the topic remains largely unknown to a surprising number of geographers and, as yet, has achieved little recognition in the standard urban geography curriculum. This is a pity as discrete choice modelling is an important component of modern urban modelling, has the potential to facilitate integration of choice/preference-oriented and constraints/allocation-oriented approaches in urban geography, and has major implications for behavioural studies in urban analysis (see Golledge and Rushton, chapter 1 this volume; Thrift, 1981; Pipkin, 1981).

As part of a wider attempt to alert geographers to the significant developments in this area of urban analysis (see also Wrigley, 1984), this chapter will review the major characteristics, the current status, and some of the potentialities and limitations of the approach. The major thrust of the chapter will be directed towards issues confronted in the application of discrete choice models in urban analysis rather than towards mathematical details of the models themselves. Nevertheless, some background description of the models is necessary and this is provided in the following section.

THE FAMILY OF DISCRETE CHOICE MODELS

Random utility maximization, probabilistic choice, and multinomial logit models

Many important decisions which an individual must take in his or her life involve selection from a limited or constrained set of discrete alternatives, as in choice of a house, neighbourhood, car, occupation, educational institution, marital status, number of children, the mode of travel on a work trip or shopping trip, the destination of a shopping or recreation trip, and so on. In these circumstances, conventional 'marginalist' micro-economic consumer theory needs modifying to allow the focusing of attention on choices at what economists term the *extensive* margin (i.e. discrete choices) rather than choices at the *intensive* margin which is treated in traditional analysis. Over the past ten years, in the work of McFadden, Manski and the other scholars noted above, significant progress has been made in this direction, and it has been shown that a logically consistent discrete choice theory can be developed based upon the hypothesis of random utility maximization.

There are two interpretations of random utility maximization which can be adopted. These have been termed the *inter-personal* and *intra-personal* interpretations respectively. The first is characteristic of most of the discrete choice modelling literature in economics, transportation science and geography (see McFadden, 1981; Manski, 1981; Williams, 1981; Wrigley, 1984). In this interpretation, the distribution of demands in the population is conceived to be the result of individual preference maximization but preferences are viewed as being influenced, in part, by variables which are unobserved by the analyst/ modeller. Because certain choice-relevant attributes are unobserved, and because the valuation of observed attributes may vary from individual to individual, a random element enters an individual's utility function and utility functions are assumed to vary over the population of decision-makers. The second interpretation (the intra-personal) is that found in the psychology literature (see Luce and Suppes, 1965). This assumes that each individual draws a utility function from a random distribution each time a decision must be made. That is to say, the individual is a classical utility maximizer given his/her state of mind, but his/her state of mind varies randomly from one choice situation to the next. The two interpretations are formally indistinguishable in their effect on the observed distribution of demand, and the random element in each implies that discrete choice problems must be handled using some form of probabilistic model.

Adopting the first (inter-personal) interpretation of random utility maximization, the conventional derivation of a probabilistic discrete model proceeds as follows:

(i) First, it is assumed that each decision-maker i is faced with a set of R available choice alternatives $\mathbf{A}_i = \{A_{li}, \ldots A_{ri}, \ldots A_{Ri}\}$. For simplicity it may be useful to make the further assumption that the same choice alternatives are available to all decision-makers, or to all decision-makers in one particular segment of the population.

(ii) Second, it is assumed that an unobservable utility value $U_{ri} = U(\mathbf{Z}_{ri}, \mathbf{S}_i)$ is associated with the choice of each alternative r by each individual i (where $\mathbf{Z}_{ri}$ is a vector of attributes of the choice alternative r faced by individual i, and $\mathbf{S}_i$ is a vector of socio-economic characteristics of individual i), and that each individual i wishes to select an alternative which yields maximum utility. That is to say, each individual is assumed to be a utility maximizer who will select choice alternative r if and only if

$$U_{ri} > U_{gi} \qquad (2.1)$$

for $g \neq r$ $g = 1, \ldots R$.

(iii) Third, it is assumed that the analyst/modeller knows the structure of the U function up to a finite parameter vector, has observed specific values of a subset of the many possible attributes Z_{ri} and socio-economic characteristics S_i, and knows up to a finite parameter vector the distribution of unobserved characteristics across the population.

In this context (and letting $x_{ri} = f(Z_{ri}, S_i)$ denote a vector of utility-relevant functions of the observed values of Z_{ri} and S_i), it is next assumed that the analyst/modeller imposes a probability distribution on the unobserved utility vector $(U_{ri}, r = 1, \ldots R)$, conditional on the known matrix $X_i = [x_{1i}, \ldots x_{ri}, \ldots x_{Ri}]$ and on an unknown parameter vector θ. The vector includes parameters of the utility function U, parameters of the distribution of unobserved socio-economic characteristics, and unknown attributes of the choice alternatives. Choice probabilities can then be derived as

$$P(r|X_i, \theta) = \text{prob}(U_{ri} > U_{gi}, g = 1, \ldots R|X_i, \theta). \qquad (2.2)$$

In this expression, $P(r|X_i, \theta)$ denotes the probability that decision-maker i faced with choice set A_i will select alternative r or, more formally, that choice alternative r will be selected by individual i conditional upon X_i and the parameters θ.

In most practical applications, the random utility function is assumed to have the linear-in-parameters additive form

$$\begin{aligned} U_{ri} &= x'_{ri}\beta + (x'_{ri}\tau_i + \eta_{ri}) \\ &= V_{ri} + \varepsilon_{ri}. \end{aligned} \qquad (2.3)$$

The first term, V_{ri}, on the right-hand side of (2.3) is referred to as the systematic or 'representative' component of utility. The second term, ε_{ri}, is the random component, which is composed of two parts. One part, η_{ri}, is a random disturbance which captures the effects of unobserved attributes of the choice alternative and unobserved socio-economic characteristics of the decision-maker. The other part represents the idiosyncratic tastes of individual i, i.e. the difference between the tastes of individual i and the average tastes of individuals with identical observed characteristics. (Notice that the 'deviation' parameters vector τ_i has an individual, i, subscript to allow this.)

The vector of random components $\varepsilon_i = [\varepsilon_{1i}, \ldots \varepsilon_{ri}, \ldots \varepsilon_{Ri}]$ has a distribution, conditioned on X_i, which lies within the parametric class $F(\varepsilon_i|X_i, \omega)$. Thus, given the expression (2.3) and the fact that $\theta = (\beta, \omega)$, the form of the choice probabilities specified in (2.2) depends on the distribution F chosen for the random components. In the early theoretical development and empirical application of discrete choice modelling it proved convenient to assume that F was the independent and identically distributed type I extreme-value (double exponential) distribution.

$$F(\varepsilon_i|X_i, \omega) = \prod_{r=1}^{R} \exp[-\exp(-\varepsilon_{ri})], \qquad (2.4)$$

and that there was no random taste variation across individuals (i.e. the elements of τ_i in equation 2.3 all equal zero and thus individuals with identical observed characteristics must have identical tastes). Under these assumptions the choice probabilities have the form

$$P(r|X_i, \beta) = \frac{\exp(x'_{ri}\beta)}{\sum_{g=1}^{R} \exp(x'_{gi}\beta)} = \frac{\exp(V_{ri})}{\sum_{g=1}^{R} \exp(V_{gi})} \qquad r = 1, \ldots R. \qquad (2.5)$$

This is the familiar multiple response category logistic model which has played such an important role in recent developments in categorical data analysis (see Wrigley, 1979, 1981, 1984) and it can readily be converted to a linear equation in which the left-hand side is the log-odds, i.e. to a linear logit model. However it has become the practice in discrete choice modelling to refer to both (2.5) and its linear logit re-expression as the *multinomial logit* (MNL) model, and this practice will be adopted here. For convenience the left-hand side of (2.5) will be simplified in the following discussion to the form $P_{r|i}$.

The reader should note that he will occasionally encounter (see Williams, 1981; Williams and Ortuzar, 1982; Hensher and Louviere, 1981) the MNL model written in the form,

$$P_{r|i} = \frac{\exp(\phi V_{ri})}{\sum_{g=1}^{R} \exp(\phi V_{gi})} \qquad r = 1, \ldots R, \qquad (2.6)$$

where ϕ (sometimes written as λ or θ) is the dispersion parameter of the extreme value distribution and takes the form,

$$\phi = \pi/\sigma\sqrt{6}. \qquad (2.7)$$

In most cases, it is not necessary to make this parameter explicit and it is normally absorbed into the utility function (see Williams, 1981, p. 57; Williams and Ortuzar, 1982, p. 174). However, the reader should note the important fact that σ in (2.7) is the common standard deviation of the random components ε_{ri} $(r = 1, \ldots R)$. It follows, therefore, that in the MNL model the variance of each of the random components is the same and equal to

$$\sigma^2 = \pi^2/6 \, \phi^2. \qquad (2.8)$$

The MNL model has significant advantages for empirical research (notably its computational tractability) and, aided by the diffusion of readily accessible package programs (see O'Brien and Wrigley, 1980, for a review), it has become very widely used over the past ten years. However, it has long been recognized that the model is based upon restrictive assumptions and that it has properties which are not always desirable. Most important in this respect is the property of the MNL known from the work of Luce (1959) as 'independence from irrelevant alternatives' (IIA). This implies that the ratio of choice probabilities for any two alternatives r and g (i.e. the odds of choosing r over g) should not depend on what other alternatives are available to the decision-maker. As a result, the IIA property implies that a new alternative entering a choice set will compete equally with each existing alternative and will obtain a share of the market by drawing from the existing alternatives in direct proportion to the original shares of the market held by these existing alternatives. In certain choice situations, where the choice alternatives are distinctly different options, this implication is reasonable. However, there are far more situations (particularly where there is distinct 'similarity' between alternatives) in which it is not. For a considerable time, beginning as far back as Debreu's (1960) review of Luce's book, examples of situations (e.g. the famous red bus/blue bus conundrum) in which the IIA property of the MNL will yield counter-intuitive behavioural forecasts have been known (see Wrigley, 1984, for illustrations). This has given rise to a search for alternative discrete choice models based upon less-demanding assumptions and with less-restrictive properties of cross-substitution embodied in their structure.

The search for less restrictive discrete choice models

It is now realised that the counter-intuitive predictions of the MNL model are not a function of the IIA property *per se*. Instead, they are common to all discrete choice models in which the random components are assumed to be independent and identically distributed, i.e. models which are assumed to have a variance-covariance matrix of the random components which takes the very simple but restrictive form,

$$\Sigma = \begin{bmatrix} \sigma^2 & 0 & \dots 0 \\ 0 & \sigma^2 & \dots 0 \\ \vdots & \vdots & \vdots \\ 0 & 0 & \dots \sigma^2 \end{bmatrix} = \sigma^2 \mathbf{I}. \tag{2.9}$$

Such models produce suspect predictions when there is distinct 'similarity' between choice alternatives because in this case the random components (e.g. ε_{ri} and ε_{gi}) are correlated but the model assumes that they are independent. To overcome such problems, models which are based upon less restrictive assumptions about the distribution of the error component are required.

The multinomial probit model

Perhaps the most general of the alternative discrete choice models is that produced when it is assumed that the vector of random components, ε_i, has a multivariate normal distribution with mean vector zero and a general variance-covariance matrix, Σ (rather than the restrictive form shown in 2.9). This assumption produces a model known as the *multinomial probit* (MNP) model, which takes the form

$$P_{r|i} = \int\limits_{-\infty}^{\infty} d\varepsilon_r \left[\prod_{g \neq r} \int\limits_{-\infty}^{V_{ri} - V_{gi} + \varepsilon_r} d\varepsilon_g \right] \phi_R(\varepsilon_1, \ldots \varepsilon_R; \Sigma), \qquad (2.10)$$

where ϕ_R is an R-dimensional normal-density function with mean vector zero and variance-covariance matrix Σ (see Horowitz, 1981b; Johnson and Hensher, 1982).

The MNP model allows the random components of the choice alternatives to be correlated and to have unequal variances. It also permits random taste variation across individuals. To achieve this, it assumes that in the random component

$$\varepsilon_{ri} = \mathbf{x}'_{ri}\tau_i + \eta_{ri} \qquad (2.11)$$

(see equation 2.3), the 'deviation' parameters τ_i are drawn from a multivariate normal distribution with mean vector zero and a $K \times K$ variance-covariance matrix Ω, and that the random disturbance η_{ri} is drawn from a multivariate normal distribution with zero means and a $R \times R$ variance-covariance matrix Δ. As a result, the general variance-covariance matrix Σ in the MNP model is an $R \times R$ matrix which takes the form

$$\Sigma = \mathbf{X}'_i \Omega \mathbf{X}_i + \Delta, \qquad (2.12)$$

where $\mathbf{X}_i$ is the $K \times R$ matrix of explanatory variables used in equation (2.2), whose rth column is $\mathbf{x}_{ri}$. The reader should contrast (2.12) to the restrictive form (2.9) used in the MNL model and note how (2.9) incorporates the assumptions of no random taste variation across individuals, and independent and identically distributed random disturbances.

Clearly, the MNP model is free from the restrictive assumptions and properties of the MNL model and these useful aspects of the MNP have been known for a considerable time. However, the MNP is extremely intractable in computational terms, and it was not until the late 1970s in the work of Hausman and Wise (1978a), Albright *et al.* (1977) and Daganzo *et al.* (1977) that any significant progress was made in developing practical estimation procedures. The most popular and cost-effective of these procedures is that suggested by Daganzo *et al.* (1977), which uses the Clark approximation (Clark, 1961) to reduce the estimation problem to one of sequential univariate integration. Daganzo (1979) has distributed a computer program called CHOMP which facilitates the application of the MNP model. However, the accuracy of the estimation procedure when the Clark approximation is adopted is still controversial, and for most users of discrete choice models the MNP model remains conceptually complex and computationally unwieldy. As a result, there has been a search for what might be termed 'half-way house' models, which lie somewhere between the generality and complexity of the MNP model and the restrictiveness but tractability of the MNL model.

The dogit model

Many possible 'half-way house' models have been suggested in recent years. The first we will consider is the *dogit* model proposed by Gaudry and Dagenais (1979), which takes the form

$$P_{r|i} = \frac{\exp(V_{ri}) + \mu_r \sum_{g=1}^{R} \exp(V_{gi})}{(1 + \sum_{g=1}^{R} \mu_g) \sum_{g=1}^{R} \exp(V_{gi})}, \tag{2.13}$$

where μ_r and $\mu_g \geqslant 0$. It gets its name because it attempts to avoid or 'dodge' the researcher's dilemma of having to choose *a priori* between a simple, computationally tractable discrete choice model (such as MNL) which commits him to restrictive assumptions and the IIA property, and a model (such as MNP) which is free from such restrictions but is conceptually and computationally complex. Essentially, the dogit model avoids the issue by allowing some pairs of choice alternatives to exhibit the IIA property but, simultaneously, allowing other pairs of choice alternatives to be free from the IIA property (i.e. the dogit model allows the MNL format to hold for some pairs of choice alternatives, but a more general format to hold for other choice pairs). It can be seen from (2.13) that if the parameters μ_g and μ_r all equal zero then the dogit model collapses to the basic MNL form. If, on the other hand, the μ parameters for just *some* pairs of choice alternatives equal zero (or if $\mu_r/\mu_g = \exp(V_{ri})/\exp(V_{gi})$ for those pairs of alternatives) then the IIA property will hold for just those particular pairs, whilst the other pairs of alternatives wil be unconstrained by the IIA property.

Following the work of Ben-Akiva (1977), the dogit model can also be given a very useful behavioural interpretation. It can be shown that the model allows for a certain degree of 'captivity' of decision-makers to particular choice alternatives. In particular, if the two elements in the numerator of (2.13) are reversed and (2.13) is reexpressed as:

$$P_{r|i} = \frac{\mu_r}{1 + \sum_g \mu_g} + \left(\frac{1}{1 + \sum_g \mu_g} \cdot \frac{\exp(V_{ri})}{\sum_g \exp(V_{gi})} \right), \tag{2.14}$$

then it can be shown that the first component on the right-hand side of (2.14) is that part of the probability of choosing alternative *r* which results from the basic need for or 'captivity' to alternative *r*, whilst the second component (shown in parentheses) is that part which results from the 'discretionary' choice of *r* out of all alternatives in the choice set. In this way, the dogit model reconciles elements of constrained choice with elements of free choice, and is compatible with Stone's (1954) approach to consumer-demand theory. However, despite this useful interpretation, empirical applications of the dogit model are, as yet, few in number (see Gaudry and Wills, 1979; Gaudry, 1980).

The nested logit model

Although the dogit model has attracted a considerable amount of attention, by far the most promising and widely adopted of these 'half-way' house models is the *nested* (structured or hierarchical) logit model. The nested logit is a special case of a model known as the *generalized extreme value* (GEV) model, the GEV being the model derived when the vector of random components is assumed to have the multivariate extreme-value distribution

$$F(\varepsilon_i|\mathbf{X}_i, \boldsymbol{\omega}) = \exp(-H\{[\exp(-\varepsilon_{li}), \ldots, \exp(-\varepsilon_{Ri})], \mathbf{X}_i\}) \qquad (2.15)$$

(see McFadden, 1981, p. 227; Manski, 1981, p. 71) rather than the type I extreme-value distribution shown in equation (2.4).

To illustrate the nested logit model, consider the simple urban shopping centre choice problem displayed in Figure 2.1 in which it is assumed that a reasonably homogeneous population of consumers in one small inner-city area has the option of shopping either in the traditional central business district of the city or in one of two purpose-built suburban shopping centres A and B. Using the MNL model this choice problem would be treated as shown in Figure 2.1a, i.e. we would treat the three shopping centres as distinctly independent alternatives and assume that each decision-maker chooses one particular shopping centre following a simultaneous evaluation of all three. In contrast, using the nested logit model we would treat the choice problem in the sequential fashion shown in Figure 2.1b and would group together the centres which show distinct similarity, i.e. the two purpose-built suburban centres. In a situation such as that shown in Figure 2.1, where there are distinct similarities between choice alternatives, the MNL model with its restrictive properties of cross-substitution is likely to provide unrealistic predictions. In contrast, the nested logit model permits correlation between the random components of the choice alternatives that is not constrained by the IIA property, and is thus able to embody more general properties of cross-substitution than the MNL model.

The nested logit model for the simple example of Figure 2.1b is a set of two

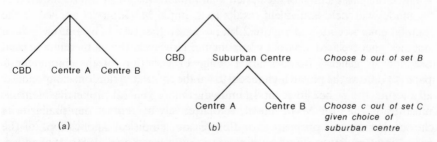

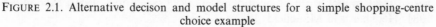

FIGURE 2.1. Alternative decison and model structures for a simple shopping-centre choice example

linked equations which (dropping the decision-maker subscript i for simplicity) can be written

$$P_{c|SUB} = \frac{\exp(V_c + V_{bc})}{\sum_{c^*=1}^{C} \exp(V_{c^*} + V_{bc^*})} \qquad c = \text{centre A or centre B}$$

(2.16)

$$P_b = \frac{\exp(V_b + \delta \tilde{U}_b)}{\sum_{b^*=1}^{B} \exp(V_{b^*} + \delta \tilde{U}_{b^*})} \qquad b = \text{CBD or suburban centre}$$

The first equation in (2.16) gives the conditional probabilities ($P_{c|SUB}$) of the choice of shopping centre A or B by individual i given that choice is constrained to a suburban centre. The second equation gives the marginal probabilities (P_b) of the choice of CBD or suburban centre. V_c and V_b denote representative components of utility which are specific to the lower and higher nest in the hierarchy, V_{bc} denotes components which relate to both nests in the hierarchy, and V_b also includes any attributes whose parameters cannot be identified in the lower nest.

In (2.16) $\tilde{U}_b$ is the so-called 'composite utility' term which in this case can be defined as:

$$\tilde{U}_b = \log_e \sum_{c^*=1}^{C} \exp(V_{c^*} + V_{bc^*}).$$

(2.17)

This term is a vital component of the nested logit model, and it acts as an hierarchical linking mechanism in equation 2.16. It allows us to assume that individuals taking decisions at the higher nest in the hierarchy will take account of the 'expected maximum utility' of decisions in the lower nest. To be consistent with random utility maximization, the parameter δ of the composite utility term must be within the range $0 < \delta \leqslant 1$, and where there are more than two levels in the hierarchy, yielding multiple composite utility terms and associated parameters δ, the values of δ should not decline when proceeding from lower to higher levels of the hierarchy (Williams, 1977; Daly and Zachary, 1978; Ben-Akiva and Lerman, 1979; McFadden, 1979).

When the parameter δ of the nested logit model equals 1, it can be shown that the model will yield equivalent results to a simple MNL model applied to the simultaneous structure in Figure 2.1a, i.e. equivalent results to a model which assumes uncorrelated random components. However, this is merely a special case and in general the permitted range of variation of the parameter δ ($0 < \delta \leqslant 1$) allows the nested logit model to handle correlated random components. As a result, the nested logit model embodies more general properties of cross-substitution than the MNL model, and effectively overcomes the 'similarity of choice alternatives' problem. For this reason, empirical applications of the nested logit model are now multiplying rapidly (see Sobel, 1980; McFadden, 1981; Hensher and Manefield, 1981).

Elimination-by-aspects models

All the models considered so far can be classified as belonging to a general set of choice models which are termed *compensatory* models. Such models assume that individuals 'trade off' attributes of the choice alternatives in the choice process. That is to say, when evaluating a choice alternative, a low (poor) value on one attribute can be compensated by a high (good) value on another (e.g. the greater distance to one particular urban shopping centre may be compensated by the lower prices that centre offers). However, another general set of choice models, termed *non-compensatory* models, can also be recognized. Such models are based upon dominance, lexicographic, conjunctive, disjunctive, lexicographic semiorder, maximin, minimax regret, and similar decision rules in which it is assumed that there is no 'trade off' of attributes in the choice process, i.e. no compensation of a low (poor) value on one attribute by a high (good) value on another (see Timmermans, 1982). Although there are many possible non-compensatory choice models, the only ones which have so far assumed significance in discrete choice modelling are the elimination-by-aspects (EBA) models proposed by Tversky (1972a,b).

In EBA models, choice is viewed as a process of elimination. At each stage in the process the individual selects a certain attribute (aspect) of the choice alternatives and eliminates all alternatives which do not possess this attribute. This process of selection and elimination then continues until only a single choice alternative remains. The MNL model can be shown to be a special case of the EBA model. However, in general the EBA model is much less restrictive than the MNL model and is able to accommodate complex patterns of cross-substitution between choice alternatives. Consequently, like the previous models in this section, it is able to overcome the 'similarity of choice alternatives' problem. Unfortunately, these useful properties of the EBA model are not achieved without cost. In particular, the EBA in its general form includes a large number of parameters which require estimation. As such, there has been a need to develop a more parsimonious form of the general EBA model. Tversky and Sattath (1979) have attempted this and have proposed an hierarchical or preference tree version of the general EBA model. This model, which is known as *pretree*, is very similar in structure and performance to the nested logit model. Both are special cases of more general formulations, and pretree bears the same relationship to the general EBA model as the nested logit does to the GEV model.

Weight-shifting models

In the basic derivation of the MNL model above, an implicit and unstated assumption was that the parameters of the representative component of utility are 'context free', i.e. the parameters remain stable as the choice set changes in composition. Although this was a useful simplifying assumption to make, it was not, however, a realistic one in all circumstances. To illustrate this, consider an individual making a three-alternative choice between shopping in either the CBD or two similar suburban centres. In this case, factors such as relative distances to the shopping centres, price levels, variety of goods available, cost and ease of car parking, etc. are likely to be the important determinants of the individual's choice. However, if the CBD is removed from the choice set, and both suburban centres which remain in the choice set are nearly identical in terms of distance, price level, variety of goods, and cost and ease of car parking, then it is reasonable to assume that the individual will tend to 'shift' his attention to those attributes on which the suburban centres do differ, e.g. factors such as opening hours, attractiveness of the shopping environment, store-to-store accessibility within the shopping centre, etc. Clearly, in this case the parameters of the utility function which represent the importance of attributes in the choice process do not remain stable as the choice set changes. The importance or 'weight' given to an attribute 'shifts' as the choice set changes, and the importance of an attribute in influencing choice covaries with the amount of variation which exists across 'other' attributes.

Although the assumption that parameters of the utility function are 'context free' and that there is no shifting in the valuation (weight) given to an attribute as the choice set changes is clearly unrealistic, it is an assumption which is not confined to the MNL model. It is also a property of other 'simultaneous' choice models, e.g. the MNP and dogit models. In contrast, the 'sequential' choice models (nested logit, pretree) explicitly acknowledge that attributes used to discriminate between choice alternatives will change between different nests (levels) of the decision hierarchy (though weight shifting is assumed not to occur within particular levels, and the need to prespecify a particular decision-tree structure can make such models, in practice, rather insensitive to the 'context dependence/weight shifting' problem).

In an attempt to incorporate context-induced parameter instability into discrete choice models, Meyer and Eagle (1981, 1982) have proposed and tested a set of adjusted logit models. These seek, simultaneously, to overcome the 'similarity of choice alternatives' problem, and the 'weight shifting/context dependent utility function' problem (see Wrigley, 1984 for further discussion). The models are still in a developmental stage; nevertheless, they do serve to focus attention on an important characteristic of decision-making and choice behaviour.

ISSUES OF EMPIRICAL APPLICATION

In the preceding discussion we have noted in a number of places the intrinsic feedback between model form and model application, e.g. the failure of the MNL model in certain circumstances (when there is distinct similarity between choice alternatives, or when the composition of the choice set changes) forces us to reconsider the appropriate form of our discrete choice model. As such, it is essentially a false dichotomy to distinguish between the form of discrete choice models and the general methodological issues confronted when the models are applied in urban analysis. Nevertheless, such a division is a useful pedagogic device which may aid the reader's transition from the theoretical to the empirical literature, and it is in this spirit that we adopt such a division below.

Variable representation and functional form

In the derivation of the basic MNL model above, we assumed that the 'representative' component of utility, V_{ri}, had the linear-in-parameters additive form

$$V_{ri} = \mathbf{x}'_{ri}\boldsymbol{\beta}$$

$$= \sum_{k=1}^{K} \beta_k X_{rik}. \tag{2.18}$$

Furthermore, we assumed that the vector of parameters, $\boldsymbol{\beta}$, has no subscript r indicating the particular choice alternative to which it refers. In other words, we assumed that the β parameters remain constant across choice alternatives (i.e. $\boldsymbol{\beta}_r = \boldsymbol{\beta}$ for all r) or, in the terminology of discrete choice modelling, that all parameters and their associated variables were 'generic'. In applications of discrete choice modelling in urban analysis both of these assumptions can readily be relaxed. The 'representative' component of utility can be specified in such a way that it is non-linear in either (or both) explanatory variables and/or parameters and, in practice, it will prove convenient in almost all applications to include what are termed 'alternative specific' variables and parameters.

The definition of 'generic' and 'alternative specific' variables and parameters, and of the difference between them, often causes considerable confusion for the researcher first encountering the literature of discrete choice modelling. Appreciation of the issue is best achieved through an extended discussion and the use of illustrative examples but, unfortunately, space limitations do not permit this here (see Wrigley, 1984, chapter 2, for the necessary elaboration). It must suffice, therefore, to state that 'generic' variables (GVs) are attributes of the choice alternatives which vary in value across all individuals and choice alternatives (e.g. travel time and travel cost in a study of urban travel mode choice) and which have associated parameters which remain constant across all choice alternatives (i.e. $\boldsymbol{\beta}_r = \boldsymbol{\beta}$ for all r). In contrast, 'alternative specific' variables (ASVs) are attributes of either the choice alternative or the choice-maker which do not vary in value across all choice alternatives and which take an assigned value of zero for certain choice alternatives. It can be said, therefore,

that ASVs have an identifiable correspondence with particular choice alternatives, and they have associated parameters which are specific to particular choice
alternatives (i.e. β_r in equation (2.18) would indicate that the vector of
parameters was specific to choice alternative r). In practice, alternative specific
variables and parameters are the means by which we include socio-economic
characteristics of the individual choice-makers into the representative utility
component (they are introduced in such a way that they are specific to $R-1$
choice alternatives where R is the total number of alternatives in the choice set).
In addition, ASVs allow us to include certain attributes which are specific to just
one or more of the choice alternatives (e.g. the number of bus transfers required
if travelling to work by bus, in a study of urban travel mode choice) and such
ASVs will often take the form of dummy variables. Finally, it should be noted
that it is usual to incorporate a set of what are referred to as 'alternative specific
constants' (ASCs) into the representative component of utility. These capture
the mean effect of unobserved factors which influence the selection of alternatives. As in the case of socio-economic variables, a set of $R-1$ ASCs will
normally be introduced, but it is not strictly necessary to include all $R-1$.

Most applications of discrete choice models in urban analysis continue to
assume that the 'generic' and 'alternative specific' variables enter the representative component of utility in a linear-in-parameters additive form. This
amounts to an assumption that the rate of change of utility with respect to
changes in each of the explanatory variables is constant. Such an assumption
offers considerable computational advantages but, in certain circumstances, it is
at variance with economic and psychological theory which suggests non-
linearity in the relationship between objective measures of variables and the
utility of choice alternatives. For example, it is widely recognized that
perceptions of time and space are non-linear in objective surrogate measures
(such as Euclidean distance) of these variables (Golledge *et al.*, 1969; Briggs,
1973) and that the relationship between perception and the surrogate measures
may be represented by logarithmic, power and other transformations.

At least three distinct methods can be used to specify non-linear forms of the
representative component of utility which more adequately represent decision-
makers' perceptions of the attributes of choice alternatives. The first of these is
the use of economic theory to derive an appropriate functional form; e.g. an
economist might derive a non-linear form of the utility function from a theory
such as the neoclassical goods/leisure trade off (see Train and McFadden, 1978).
The second possibility involves the use of functional measurement techniques
with experimental design data (see Lerman and Louviere, 1978; Louviere,
1981a) and this possibility will be considered further in a later section. The third
approach, which we will consider in more detail below, involves the use of
statistical transformations designed to 'search' for an appropriate functional
form.

The most widely-adopted example of the third approach is the use of either a

Box–Cox (1964) or the more general Box–Tukey (Gaudry and Wills, 1978) transformation of the explanatory variables to specify a more general form of the representative utility component (see, for example, Gaudry, 1980; Hensher and Johnson, 1981b; Koppelman, 1981; McCarthy, 1982). In the Box–Tukey case this takes the form

$$V_{ri} = \beta_{1r} + \sum_{k=2}^{K} \beta_{kr}(X_{rik} + \mu_k)^{\lambda_k}, \tag{2.19}$$

where

$$(X_{rik} + \mu_k)^{\lambda_k} = \frac{(X_{rik} + \mu_k)^{\lambda_k} - 1}{\lambda_k} \quad \text{if } (X_{rik} + \mu_k) > 0, \ \lambda_k \neq 0$$

$$= \log_e (X_{rik} + \mu_k) \quad \text{if } \lambda_k = 0. \tag{2.20}$$

The right-hand side of (2.19) assumes that GVs, ASVs and ASCs enter the specification, and it should be noted that the usual linear-in-parameters form of V_{ri} is merely a special case of (2.19) where the additional 'Box–Tukey' scaling parameters $\lambda_1, \ldots, \lambda_K$ equal 1 and $\mu_1, \ldots, \mu_K$ equal 0.

Using the linear-in-parameters form as a reference point, a range of alternative functional forms can be assessed by successively setting the λ and μ parameters in (2.19) to particular values and maximizing the log-likelihood function of the model with respect to the β values for that particular combination of values of the Box–Tukey λ and μ parameters. Using this search procedure, an 'optimal' combination of values of the λ and μ parameters can be found. In this way an 'optimal' functional form can be selected or, perhaps more importantly, some assessment can be made of the sensitivity of the discrete choice model to changes in the functional form of the representative component of utility. Such information can usefully inform any assessment of the predictions of the discrete choice model in the context of changes in policy variables, and can facilitate comparison of the fit of alternative types of discrete choice models. The use of the Box–Tukey transformation (or its Box–Cox specialization) provides few problems in practical urban analysis. It is a standard option in at least one (BLOGIT) of the widely used discrete choice modelling programs (see Hensher and Johnson, 1981a).

Sampling and estimation issues

Just as the majority of applications of discrete choice models assume a simple linear-in-parameters additive form for the representative component of utility, so the majority of applications also assume that parameter estimation will be conducted using standard maximum likelihood techniques on sample survey data collected from either simple or exogenously stratified random sample designs. However, just as there have been attempts to broaden the range of functional forms used in the application of discrete choice models, so there has been increased sensitivity to the implications and potential of alternative sampling designs.

The most basic sample design assumption is simple random sampling. In large samples this will yield reliable estimates of the market shares of the choice alternatives, and of the mean levels of the attributes of the choice alternatives and the socio-economic characteristics of the decision-makers. In addition, such a sample design is conventionally assumed in the derivation of the standardly-applied maximum likelihood parameter estimation techniques. In most real-world situations, however, simple random sampling can prove unnecessarily inefficient and costly. Given minimal *a priori* knowledge concerning attribute distributions within the population, considerable savings of resources and increases in efficiency can be achieved by appropriate stratification. Consequently, many applications of discrete choice modelling have emphasised sample survey procedures which embody stratification procedures of either of two types. The majority have used stratification criteria *exogenous* to the selected choice alternatives (e.g. the use of sex, age, area and occupation criteria to stratify a home interview sample survey pertaining to travel mode choice on the journey to work). In this procedure, the population is first classified into subsets on the basis of one or more exogenous variables and a random sample is then drawn from each group. However, the search for refined cost-effective sampling procedures in discrete choice modelling has frequently led to the adoption of an *endogenous* (choice-based) approach to sample stratification. In this procedure, the classification of the population into the subsets which will then be randomly sampled is based upon choices already made. That is to say, a random sample is drawn of individuals who are already committed to one particular choice alternative (e.g. in a study of travel-mode choice, we may select 500 individuals using each travel mode; bus, car, train etc., and this is referred to as 'on-board' choice-based sampling). In other words, in exogenously stratified sampling the analyst selects decision-makers and observes their choices, whilst in endogenously stratified samples the analyst selects choice alternatives and observes decision-makers choosing them.

Under certain standard regularity conditions, the maximum likelihood estimation procedures normally adopted in discrete choice modelling produce parameter estimates that are consistent, asymptotically normal and asymptotically efficient using either simple random or exogenously stratified random sampling procedures. However, endogenous (choice-based) stratified sampling presents additional estimation difficulties and, in such circumstances, the conventional maximum likelihood estimators will be inconsistent and asymptotically biased. These difficulties were neither fully acknowledged nor overcome prior to the work of Manski and Lerman (1977), Lerman and Manski (1979), Manski and McFadden (1981) and Coslett (1981).

In a recent summary of the state-of-the-art of endogenous stratification, Manski (1981, pp. 77–80) describes three alternative procedures which circumvent the associated likelihood estimation problems. The first of these assumes that the attribute density function, while not known, can *a priori* be restricted to a particular parametric family of functions prior to the maximization of the likelihood. The problem with this procedure is that the parametric restriction on the attribute density function may or may not be realistic and, in addition, computation is often costly. The second alternative does not require an assumption about the attribute density function. This is the so-called 'weighted exogenous sampling maximum likelihood' estimation procedure in which the estimators are obtained on the basis that the proportions of the population selecting each choice alternative (the aggregate market shares) are known. The third alternative is due to Cosslett (1981), and involves the use of joint maximum likelihood estimation of the choice model parameters and the attribute density function.

Although these estimation procedures can present additional computational burdens for the researcher, they do produce parameter estimators with the desirable properties of consistency and asymptotic efficiency. This is important, for once suitable estimators are available, a properly-designed, endogenously-stratified (choice-based) sample has the capacity in some circumstances to provide more precise estimates than a simple or endogenously stratified sample of the same total size. Likewise, if estimates are required to meet some prespecified level of precision, use of a properly designed, endogenously stratified (choice-based) sample can often help to reduce the size and cost of the sample required. This is particularly true where certain choice alternatives are selected only very infrequently. In these circumstances a very large simple random sample may be needed to provide useful information on the infrequently chosen alternatives, and it may not be possible by stratifying on exogenous variables to find individuals with a high probability of selecting the infrequently chosen alternatives. For this reason, it has often been found to be a valuable practice in discrete choice modelling to supplement and enrich large exogenously stratified household samples with small choice-based surveys of the alternatives which occur infrequently but are of interest in the analysis.

The work of Manski, Lerman, McFadden and Cosslett serves to stress the intrinsic and centrally important relationship between sample survey design and statistical analysis, and research continues on this same theme (e.g. Daganzo (1980) has recently considered optimal sampling strategies for discrete choice models). However, there has as yet been surprisingly little linkage with the broader, and recently rapidly developing, literature on categorical data and complex (clustered, multistage etc.) sample designs (e.g. Altham, 1979; Brier, 1980; Cohen, 1976; Fellegi, 1980; Holt *et al.*, 1980).

Panel data and dynamic modelling

As we have seen in the preceding discussion, discrete choice models are normally estimated using cross-sectional sample survey data. However, in certain circumstances the urban analyst will have access to longitudinal survey data. It is well known in the standard statistics/econometrics literature that the use of a pooled time series of cross-sectional samples (i.e. panel data) is often much more efficient, in both statistical and behavioural terms, than the estimation of separate relationships for each cross-sectional sample. It is not unreasonable, therefore, to suggest that the same is likely to be true for discrete choice models, and that specifications analogous to those adopted in standard linear modelling of a time series of cross-sectional samples will be useful.

Tardiff (1980a) adopts this approach and suggests that a useful replacement for the normal utility function (2.3) in such circumstances is

$$U_{rit} = x'_{rit}\beta + \sum_g \phi_{rg}C_{gi(t-1)} + \tilde{\varepsilon}_{ri} + \varepsilon^*_{rit}, \qquad (2.21)$$

where U_{rit} = the utility of choice alternative r to individual i at time period t,

$C_{gi(t-1)} = 1$ if individual i chooses alternative g in the previous period $(t-1)$ and 0 otherwise,

$\tilde{\varepsilon}_{ri}$ = an error component that varies among individuals but not time periods, and

ε^*_{rit} = an error component that varies among both individuals and time periods.

In addition to permitting the use of data from a time series of cross-sectional samples, the revised specification of the utility function introduces two additional elements. First, through the use of the $\sum_g C_{gi(t-1)}$ term, it allows choice in one period $(t-1)$ to influence choice in the following period. If the estimate of the associated parameter ϕ_{rg} is positive (negative), it indicates an increased (decreased) choice probability in the subsequent time period. Second, the use of a component structure for the error term (i.e. the error term ε_{ri} in equation (2.18) is decomposed into the two components $\tilde{\varepsilon}_{ri}$ and ε^*_{rit}) allows for the fact (in $\tilde{\varepsilon}_{ri}$) that some unobserved attributes may remain constant across time periods for particular individuals, but that there will also be pure random disturbance (i.e. ε^*_{rit}).

By setting various elements in (2.21) to zero, Tardiff (1980a) is able to consider three special cases of the general specification. Case 1 is where the urban analyst assumes that $\phi_{rg} = 0$ and $\tilde{\varepsilon}_{ri} = 0$ for all g, r and i. If these assumptions are valid the observations for a given individual over time can be treated as independent and the usual static discrete choice models can be applied directly to the dynamic problem. Case 2 is where the urban analyst assumes that $\tilde{\varepsilon}_{ri} = 0$ for all r and i. In this case previous choices are explicitly considered, but error terms are treated as completely random and independent across time periods and thus the usual type of discrete choice models can be applied directly. Case 3 is where the urban analyst assumes that $\phi_{rg}=0$ for all r and g. In this case previous choices are not considred but both error components are (i.e. some unobserved attributes are now assumed to remain constant across time periods for particular individuals). As a result, error terms are assumed to be correlated over time and normal estimation procedures are no longer valid. In these circumstances, Tardiff (1980a) and Heckman (1981) suggest two alternative procedures: (1) a 'fixed effects' approach, in which the $\tilde{\varepsilon}_{ri}$ terms are explicitly identified using ASCs, and then normal discrete choice models are applied directly; (2) a 'random-effects' approach, in which the more complex error variance structure is dealt with directly, in a manner analogous to the MNP model work on correlated random components among choice alternatives. If a Case 3 specification is erroneously estimated as a Case 1 type, or the 'full' specification (2.21) is erroneously estimated as a Case 2 type, further research by Tardiff (1979) suggests that exclusion of the $\tilde{\varepsilon}_{ri}$ component can result in two sources of bias in the parameter estimates: bias resulting from possible correlation between the error component and the other explanatory variables, and bias resulting from changes in the distribution of the overall error term of the utility function.

In behavioural terms, the use of panel data in discrete choice modelling and the associated utility function specification (2.21) serves to focus attention on the intertemporal nature of many choice processes. Effects of experience, time-discounted preferences, the learning process, habit persistence, and so on, become centrally important issues. In other words, many aspects of complex choice behaviour ignored in standard cross-sectional discrete choice modelling, and for which omission discrete choice modelling has been criticised in the past (see the discussion which follows), are now being incorporated (at least to a limited extent) in the theoretical and empirical studies of Heckman (1981), Tardiff (1980a), Daganzo and Sheffi (1979, 1982) and Johnson and Hensher (1982). Recently a number of panel data surveys have been undertaken in both transportation science and human geography, and there is evidence to suggest that the next few years will see considerable developments in the form, estimation, and application of discrete choice models for panel data.

Towards the incorporation of experimental design data with survey data

In certain situations in urban analysis, survey data on choice behaviour will either be non-existent or deficient in some manner. Amongst the common limitations of survey data are that: (1) they are often subject to many sources of confoundment; and (2) they are often available for only a limited range of attribute levels, a range which is often insufficient to permit extrapolation of choice predictions to the unobserved attribute mixes which are likely to define any 'new' alternatives which might enter the choice set. In these circumstances, particularly when it is necessary to forecast the choice probabilities of choice alternatives which do not currently exist, some authors (e.g. Hensher and Louviere, 1981) have suggested that simulated choice data collected on the basis of scientific principles of controlled experimental design have a particularly valuable role to play.

The chief advantage of preference data simulated in controlled experimental choice designs are that: (1) potential sources of bias can be controlled by appropriate design techniques before data are collected; (2) the researcher has the ability to make observations over repeated experimentally controlled trials and this allows the separation out of error components which become confounded in normal sample survey data; and (3) such data enable new alternatives to be described in detail so that decision-makers can respond to them and their attribute mixes. In addition, whereas in the analysis of conventional survey data choice is restricted to a subset of alternatives which are within the individual's budget constraint, in the choice experiment approach the individual's preference function is established *before* the constraining influence of the budget on the size and nature of the choice set is introduced. In other words, the spirit of the experimental approach is to acknowledge that decision-makers may well be able to formulate preferences over unattainable possibilities and that, in consequence, an attempt should be made to unconfound the probability of an alternative being in a choice set and the probability of selecting an alternative given that it is in the choice set. The implication of this is that the choice experiment approach may have the capacity to offer additional insight and leverage on the many applications of discrete choice modelling which are hierarchical and constraint-orientated in nature. It is clear that choice experiment data and the experimental design approach can play a useful complementary role in the application of discrete choice modelling in urban analysis (see Meyer and Eagle, 1981, 1982; Louviere, 1981b).

Complex and constrained behaviour

Care must be taken in any application of discrete choice modelling not to misrepresent complex choice behaviour benignly as a simple isolated event performed in an uncoordinated decision environment. This imposes two burdens upon the model-builder: (1) behaviour must be evaluated in the context of specific temporal and spatial constraints and must acknowledge the interdependence of decisions; and (2) the population of decision-makers must be segmented according to a relevant set of behavioural criteria in order to ensure greater overall model fidelity. These tasks may often be difficult but they hold the promise of improved theoretical understanding sufficient to outweigh any short-run decline in black-box forecasting success.

It became clear at an early stage that realistic discrete choice models would often require the integration of complex sets of decisions, which prior reasoning suggested might be interdependent, within a joint choice framework: thus

Lerman (1977), for example, incorporated residential location, housing, car ownership and travel mode to work within a joint-choice multinomial logit model in his study of Washington, DC, and Anas (1979) attempted a joint-choice logit formulation embracing travel demand and residential location. Subsequent studies stressed the importance of multistop and multipurpose trips within household daily activity patterns (Adler and Ben-Akiva, 1979; Hanson, 1980; Hanson and Huff, 1984) and this has stimulated some researchers to attempt to model such features using Markov and semi-Markov process models of trip-chaining behaviour (e.g. Lerman, 1979). In these models, travel is represented as a stochastic process in which trips correspond to transitions between the states of the process. However, some doubts (Horowitz, 1980c) have now been cast upon the internal consistency of such Markov models, while their depleted behavioural base, disregard for the accumulation of experience and failure to incorporate frequency, destination and mode choice simultaneously into a utility-maximizing framework convince many analysts that such models do not after all constitute a panacea for trip-chaining problems. A final, and more recent, development originates in the work of Horowitz (1980b), who incorporates trip frequency, destination, and mode choice into a joint utility-maximizing framework by dividing the day into a series of discrete time intervals which are each only long enough to begin one trip: the resulting single-trip logit models for each time interval may then be aggregated in order to yield an over-all, daily, travel-pattern formulation.

The incorporation of temporal trip-generation constraints within the Horowitz schema clearly offers one plausible framework in which to view interdependency among decisions. A much wider consideration of over-all activity constraints has been suggested by Landau et al. (1982) who, in the spirit of Hägerstrand, extend the concept of time-budgeting within over-all shopping-trip chains to encompass spatial constraints such as residential location, site of workplace and availability of public transport. Availability of spatial alternatives is also integrated into model structure through the inclusion of store locations and their opening hours. Elements in the discussion of Landau et al. (1982) are more relevant to the evaluation of the restriction of spatial choice sets upon behaviour to be discussed below: of more direct relevance to the present discussion, however, is the way in which they make allowance for the degree of flexibility in over-all activity patterns through the segmentation of trip-makers according to the relative rigidity imposed upon activity patterns by work-related travel.

This introduces the second major issue stated above—the way in which efficient population segmentation can improve model fidelity. Although in this context the existence of behaviour patterns at variance with a simple interpretation of utility maximization has long been recognized (Simon, 1957), the full implications of the way in which distinctive subgroup behaviour patterns can be handled using established modelling procedures remains largely unexplored.

Given the accelerating diversification in the range of urban applications of discrete choice modelling, the establishment of appropriate and detailed segmentation criteria is essential if the complex behaviour patterns of distinctive subgroups are not to be confounded within an over-all model framework. Indeed, Hanson and Hanson (1981) contend that: 'there has usually been an uncritical, *a priori*, acceptance of the notion that sociodemographics are strongly and causally related to human behaviour in general . . . and that some "obvious" individual/household descriptors (such as income) provide an appropriate basis for population "segmentation".' This suggests two facets to the problem: (1) that conventional segmentation criteria may not be suitable for disaggregating sub-populations at all; and (2) that even where use of conventional criteria is admissable, segmentation may need to incorporate a multitude of interrelated measures in order to draw out the latent structural dimensions of differential sub-group behaviour. With respect to the first of these points, some writers (Burnett, 1981; Burnett and Hanson, 1982) have stressed the need to develop pertinent non-traditional indices of group behaviour, such as habits, aspirations, prejudices, role-playing and avoidance behaviour. Although such indices are undoubtedly associated with distinctive complex behaviour patterns in some circumstances, it is perhaps more likely that most rapid progress will be achieved by segmentation using conventionally available individual and household criteria. To this end, Hanson and Hanson (1981) use stepwise regression procedures in order to assess how selected socio-economic variables are each related to different dimensions of travel patterns. In a similar spirit, Stapleton (1980) has suggested reformulation of the family-life-cycle concept into a form in which it is robust and meaningful enough to facilitate behavioural inference within a formal model structure. Mention should also be made of the on-going research at the Oxford University Transport Studies Unit into the development of travel-related stage-in-lifecycle segments, which incorporates the effects of socio-economic variables and which relates to the development of the Household Activity-Travel Simulator (HATS: see Jones, 1979).

The preceding discussion has, therefore, identified the ways in which the complex behaviour of individuals within urban discrete choice models may be refined and developed in accordance with the constraints faced by these individuals. However, this process can only exert maximum effect if there exists a parallel commitment to the identification of the way in which complex and constrained behaviour accords with and relates to the variable choice sets of the sampled individuals. It is towards this wider issue of choice-set generation that we now turn.

Choice-set definition and representation

Of central importance in any application of discrete choice modelling is the need for appropriate definition of the individual's choice set. This implies the need to maintain model tractability when there is a large number of 'feasible' alternatives, and the need to exclude all 'non-feasible' alternatives from the choice set.

In the case where choice alternatives are aspatial entities (modes of transport, types of car, occupations, etc.) the definition of an appropriate choice set presents far fewer problems than when choice alternatives are spatially defined (e.g. shopping centres, alternative residential locations etc.). In the latter case, the number of 'feasible' spatial choice alternatives is often much too large for practical modelling purposes. Consequently, to reduce the number to computationally manageable proportions, it is often necessary to consider limiting the number of spatial alternatives in some way. This may be achieved by considering only a sub-set common to all decision-makers or, alternatively, by defining a manageable number of alternatives on the basis of some sort of classification or spatial aggregation procedure. Tardiff (1980a) suggests that assigning spatial alternatives to broad categories is likely to be particularly useful in such circumstances. In addition he suggests that this should be accompanied by the inclusion of a corresponding set of alternative specific constants (ASCs), for ASCs have been shown (e.g. Hensher, 1981) to be important elements in the proper specification of discrete choice models and often have important effects on the predictions produced by the models.

Exclusion of 'non-feasible' choice alternatives implies the ability to divide the alternatives which face an individual into 'feasible' and 'non-feasible' sets. This not only suggests sensitivity to the household budget constraints, and to the type of spatial, temporal and contextual constraints on behaviour discussed above, but also a recognition of the institutional constraints on choice sets, particularly in societies such as Britain where there is considerable central and local government intervention in urban welfare provision. For example, most studies of the British housing market now recognize that the dwelling choice process is subject to the often rigorous restriction of individual choice sets in accordance with individual (racial, socioeconomic, income-based) and ecologically-based community (e.g. 'redlining' of selected inner-city areas) characteristics. This is not to suggest that discussion and evaluation of individual choice by restricted to the over-all ideological and socio-political origins of choice restrictions: rather it is to emphasize that the analyst has some clear obligation to supplement his model of individual decision-making strategies with a realistic assessment of the nature and magnitude of aggregate institutional constraints upon individual choice. Thus, for example, it is evident that residential location studies which seek to embrace aspects of tenure 'choice' are unrealistic when transferred from one national political system to another. Figure 2.2 identifies the various levels of a hierarchic structure which might be identified in an analysis of dwelling choice in the British context. In this example, choice is mediated by public policy interventions in the housing

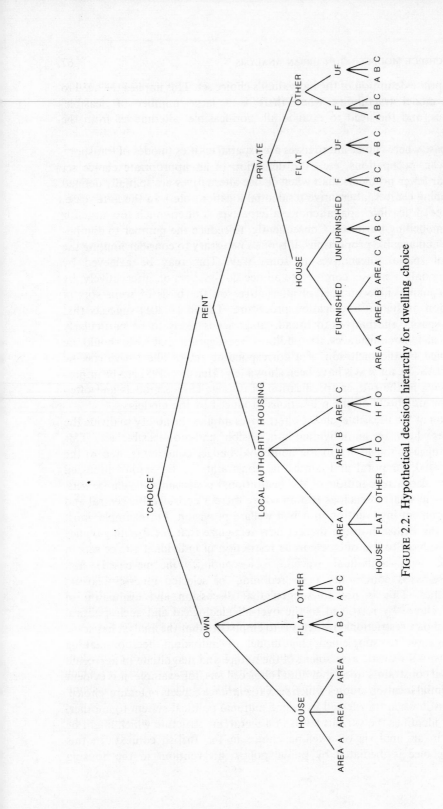

FIGURE 2.2. Hypothetical decision hierarchy for dwelling choice

market which control supply in a variety of tenure-specific ways (e.g. see Murie *et al.*, 1976; Bassett and Short, 1980 for a wider discussion). Figure 2.2 therefore illustrates a plausible sequential decison process, with different choice selection sequences within each of the three major tenure categories which reflect the differential and varied effect of public policy within each of these sub-sets. By contrast, Hensher's (1978) exposition of dwelling choice seen from an Australian viewpoint assumes much less rigid control within the major tenure categories and suggests that a simultaneous structuring of the decision process might be appropriate.

It should be fairly clear that the nested logit model described in Equation (2.16) and Figure 2.1b may usefully be adapted to consider complex decision processes in which the global choice set is divided up in accordance with different policy criteria. In this manner, all of the choice sub-sets may be restructured within an overall hierarchical decision structure which remains consistent with utility maximization and may be estimated using the tractable logit form (e.g. the schema developed by van Lierop, 1981). However, the process of imposing the choice hierarchy structure does involve the incorporation of a number of strong *a priori* assumptions concerning the sequential nature of the decision process. This remains plausible in the case shown in Figure 2.2 where many of the sub-sets correspond to discrete and clearly identifiable constraints which must be either overcome or circumvented before the choice process may proceed. However, in other cases (e.g. destination and mode choice in spatial transport models) a joint selection of all choice attributes may be made *simultaneously* from the full choice set: in such cases the decision process is most appropriately framed within a simultaneous model structure and the analyst must consciously trade off the benefits of behaviourally accurate model specification against the costs in terms of computational burden (assuming most or all attribute combinations are feasible) and possible serious behavioural mis-specification.

A related but more general issue concerns the widespread use of observed choice/revealed preference data as surrogate measures of individual preferences. In general, most researchers would agree with the assertion that revealed preferences are not independent of social structure, though support for the specific notion that analysis using such context-dependent data precludes empirical investigation is much more limited. Nevertheless, this is not to deny that such revealed preference data have been variously condemned as being inefficient in identifying individual preference transitivities or utility functions (Sheppard, 1980), failing to delimit consistently the variable extent to which individual utility functions reflect budget constraints (Maclennan and Williams, 1980), and failing to recognize how institutional constraints restrict the perceived choice sets of many respondents. Occasionally the problems associated with revealed preference data can be ameliorated by restriction of models to single-attribute choice alternatives, rather than multi-attribute alternatives such as dwellings which are complex amalgams of physical (e.g. shelter), psychological (e.g. security) and economic (e.g. the financial incentives of owner-occupation) attributes. In other cases, choice models using revealed preference data may be restricted to choice alternatives selected in relatively free-choice situations. In still other cases, the need to supplement cross-sectional revealed preference analyses with panel data, experimental designs and search/learning models should be emphasized.

However, if the modelling of complex choices is to be successful in the majority of applications where only conventional cross-sectional revealed preference data are available, then clearly alternatives must be divided into feasible and non-feasible sub-sets in accordance with the nature of the constraining criteria: within these restricted choice sets, choices can then be modelled in accordance with the central tenets of random utility theory. In this way, aggregate processes which circumscribe choice sets can be modelled alongside disaggregate choice-based processes within a single integrated methodology, a development which can only serve to hasten the fusion of choice-orientated (active) and constraint-orientated (reactive) traditions within quantitative behavioural geography (for a detailed discussion of this topic, see Thrift, 1981).

Assessing and comparing the performance of alternative discrete choice models

Given the wide range of alternative discrete choice models which are now available, there will frequently be the need in empirical urban analysis to assess and compare the performance of a set of competing models. Any such assessment will include both formal and informal components.

The informal component will involve a sensitive assessment and comparison of the models on the basis of the type of issues discussed in the six preceding sections for, ultimately, any judgement of a model's adequacy is a qualitative matter which cannot be relegated to a mechanistic procedure. Nevertheless, formal model assessment and comparison procedures can usefully serve to inform such qualitative judgements and, as a result, a number of formal procedures have been suggested and applied in discrete choice modelling. These procedures range from the use of relatively simple pseudo-$R^2(\rho^2)$ goodness-of-fit measures (Domencich and McFadden, 1975, p. 123; Tardiff, 1976; Hensher and Johnson, 1981a, p. 51), prediction success tables (McFadden, 1979; Hensher and Johnson, 1981a, p. 52; Wrigley, 1984), randomization inference strategies (Costanzo et al., 1982) and residual plots (Wrigley, 1984), to more complex disaggregate tests of the IIA property of the MNL model (McFadden et al., 1977), tests of inappropriately nested model structures (Sobel, 1980) and likelihood ratio or Langrangian multiplier tests of MNL against MNP models (Horowitz, 1980a, 1981a,b).

One very general procedure for the comparison of competing discrete choice models which is likely to be of special interest to geographers is that suggested by Halperin *et al.* (1984). This procedure is an adaptation of Hubert and Golledge's (1981; see also Golledge *et al.*, 1981) heuristic method of comparing related matrices and it utilizes the correlation statistic:

$$r_{A,(B-C)} = \frac{r_{AB} - r_{AC}}{[2(1 - r_{BC})]^{1/2}}, \tag{2.22}$$

where **A** is a proximity matrix representing actual choice data, and **B** and **C** are proximity matrices computed from the predicted probabilities for two different discrete choice models. In essence, the correlation statistic (2.22) enables the researcher to test the null hypothesis that neither model (represented by **B** or **C**) is a better representation of the choice data than the other, and the null hypothesis is evaluated using a non-parametric inference strategy in which the observed value of the correlation statistic is compared to a reference distribution constructed using a randomization model. If the observed correlation is at a suitable extreme in the reference distribution, the null hypothesis is rejected. An extreme position in the upper-tail (lower-tail) of the reference distribution implies that the model represented by **B(C)** is the better representation of the choice data.

Use of such formal model assessment and comparison procedures, together with sensitive evaluation of the competing models in terms of the general issues of model application discussed in the preceding sections, can, in most applications, enable the urban analyst to make informed judgements of the adequacy of his discrete choice models. This is particularly important, for one of the major arguments for the adoption of disaggregate discrete modelling approaches in urban analysis in place of aggregate spatial interaction approaches has centred upon the improved predictive and explanatory capabilities claimed for such models.

Spatial and temporal transferability of discrete choice models

One of the early hopes and claims for disaggregate choice models, particularly in the field of urban-travel behaviour, was that a 'well-specified' discrete choice model should be appropriate for predicting choice behaviour in other geographical locations and in other time periods, i.e. the parameter estimates of the model should be spatially and/or temporally transferable. The motivation for such model transfer was that it would allow the costs of conducting urban transportation studies to be greatly reduced, and would provide a means of 'validating' the disaggregate choice modelling approach.

Since these early claims a number of empirical studies have sought to confirm the transferability of discrete choice models but, unfortunately, their conclusions have been somewhat contradictory. The earliest studies provided optimistic conclusions on both spatial and temporal transferability. For

example, Atherton and Ben-Akiva (1976) attempted to explain travel behaviour
in Los Angeles and New Bedford, Massachusetts using the same form of work-
trip mode choice model as they had originally estimated for Washington, DC.
They found that the parameter estimates of the model were remarkably similar in
all three cities, and they took this as empirical support for the spatial
transferability of well-specified mode choice models. To aid the process of model
transferability they also suggested a set of possible updating procedures
(including a useful Bayesian procedure) which would allow a small amount of
information from the new city or region to which the model is to be transferred
to be used to improve the predictive ability of the transferred model. This study,
however, was followed by the substantially less optimistic conclusions of
Talvitie and Kirshner (1978). In a study of work-trip data sets from
Washington, DC, Minneapolis–St. Paul and the San Francisco Bay Area (both
before and after the introduction of the Bay Area Rapid Transit System),
Talvitie and Kirshner found that model parameters did not appear to be
transferable either within an urban area, between cities, or over time.

More recent studies have questioned whether such contradictory results are a
function of the use of data sets which are strictly non-comparable because of
different sample design and collection procedures, differences in questionnaire
wording and coding conventions, differences in variable definitions etc. As such,
recent studies of transferability have attempted to achieve greater consistency
across different data sets, and have been more sensitive to issues of variable
definitions, functional form etc. Despite this, results are still somewhat
contradictory. Whereas McCarthy (1982) finds evidence which supports the
short-term transferability of parameter estimates in a study of work-trip-mode
choice in the San Francisco Bay Area, Galbraith and Hensher (1982) find no
evidence to support the intra-urban spatial/temporal transferability of work-
trip-mode choice models in a study of two suburban areas in Sydney. It is clear
from these studies that the scope for transferability of the current generation of
discrete choice models is much more limited than was previously hoped. The
predictive performance of transferred models is often reasonable, and this may
be useful in terms of overall policy assessment. However, parameter estimates
are much less transferable because many of the current discrete choice model
specifications do not incorporate sufficiently well the situational and contextual
factors, plus the 'unmeasured' choice alternative attributes and socio-economic
characteristics which influence individual choice. For example, Galbraith and
Hensher (1982) note that spatial transferability has been hampered by the lack
of contextual (spatial structure) measures in many of the previous urban travel
demand models, whilst McCarthy (1982) and others have stressed the
importance of incorporating measures which reflect the interaction between
longer-term locational decisions and shorter-term travel decisions in any study
of the temporal transferability of urban-travel demand models. Galbraith and
Hensher's (1982) recommendation, therefore, is that where transferabilty is a

prime objective, the urban analyst should consider estimating a model in the base area, city (or time period) on criteria which define the new area, city (or time period).

TWO AREAS OF APPLICATION: HOUSING AND RETAILING

Many of the early empirical applications of discrete choice modelling were confined to the field of urban-travel demand (travel-mode choice, choice of destination, choice of frequency of travel and time of day of travel, parking-location decisions etc.), initially in the context of work trips and shopping trips and subsequently in the context of recreational trips. However, recent years have seen a considerable broadening of the range of applications to include studies of: the choice of residential location and housing, and studies of residential mobility (see references below); retailers' choice of location (see references below); car acquisition and type decisions (e.g. Lerman and Ben-Akiva, 1976; Lave and Train, 1979; Tardiff, 1980b; Hensher and Manefield, 1981; Manski and Sherman, 1980); selection of routes for urban freeways (McFadden, 1976); college choice and residential choice of students (Kohn et al., 1976; Punj and Staelin, 1978; Manski, 1981); labour supply, occupational choice and attainment (Boskin, 1974; Schmidt and Strauss, 1975a,b; Heckman, 1974; Ross, 1979); choice of urban child-care facilities (Robins and Spiegelman, 1978); allocation of city and region television channel licences by the Federal Communication Commission in the US (Nelson and Noll, 1978; Barton, 1979); participation of families in US urban welfare programmes (Hausman and Wise, 1978b); studies of doctors' decisions between public- and private-sector practice (Poirier, 1981); and so on. In this section we illustrate these many areas of application by considering two of the traditionally important research fields in urban analysis: housing and retailing. For each we summarize a selection of the many applications which have now been conducted and provide details of a single representative case study. These case studies also attempt to illustrate some of the important technical and empirical issues discussed above.

Housing and residential location

We first present a simple pedagogic example couched within the context of tenure choice in the British housing market in general and within the schema depicted in Figure 2.2 in particular. Of course the 'housing market' is itself an elusive concept, consisting as it does of a multitude of conflicting individual and group interests, of variable individual preferences, of spatial externality effects, and of public-policy initiatives (van Lierop, 1981). More specifically, it has been suggested above that the aggregate effect of these public-policy constraints upon dwelling choice will be to subdivide the total choice set in accordance with Figure 2.2, the first stage of which involves subdivision of the population into 'owners' and 'renters'. That this subdivision is not entirely determined by individual preferences has long been recognized, and indeed much research has been expended upon identification of the relevant criteria which are associated with the differential abilities of individuals to gain access to the owner-occupier sector. The dichotomous linear-logit model used at this stage in the process adopts the form:

$$\log_e \frac{P_{O/i}}{P_{R/i}} = \beta_1 + \beta_2(\text{HOHAGE})_i + \beta_3(\text{HHSIZE})_i + \beta_4(\text{RACE})_i + \beta_5(\text{HOH-Y})_i,$$

(2.23)

where $\log_e \dfrac{P_{O/i}}{P_{R/i}}$ = the log odds that the revealed preference of respondent i will be to choose to own (O) rather than to rent (R) a dwelling,

HOHAGE = age of head of household,

HHSIZE = number of persons in household,

RACE = a dummy variable capturing the effects of race upon choice (0 = non-white, 1 = white), and

HOH-Y = income of head of household.

Calibration of the model using some 4500 observations from the Department of the Environment's 1976 English House Condition Survey yields the parameter estimates shown in Table 2.1(a). The point should be made that the variables used in this analysis have been incorporated primarily for illustrative purposes rather than because of their individually strong *a priori* expected relationship with a specific aspect of the tenure choice process. The results shown in Table 2.1(a) do correspond with broad *a priori* expectations, however; thus the odds of owning is positively and statistically significantly related both to increasing age of head of household and increasing income of head of household, while large households are statistically more likely to be associated with renting.

Although model (2.23) is of some use in identifying the way in which the selected individual attributes relate to tenure choice patterns, it should be clear from the preceding discussion of institutional choice-set restrictions that the association between these attributes and choice could be sharpened through a segmentation of the population according to the nature and likely effects of choice-set restriction upon different groups. To this end, therefore, we next make a comparison of the attributes of respondents who have attained their preferred tenure status with those who have not. This is achieved by disaggregating renters according to their response to a question enquiring whether or not they would like to purchase their present dwelling. This produces two sub-groups of renters: those who actually prefer to rent their dwellings rather than own (RP), and those who would actually prefer to own but whose choice of a rented dwelling reflects the restriction of their choice sets by a variety of (undefined) constraints (RF). It is further assumed that all

TABLE 2.1.   Parameter estimates for the tenure choice models

	β_1	β_2 (HOHAGE)$_i$	β_3 (HHSIZE)$_i$	β_4 (RACE)$_i$	β_5 (HOH-Y)$_i$
(a) $\log_e \dfrac{P_{O/i}}{P_{R/i}}$	-1.64620	0.00924	-0.06785	-0.35281	0.00053
	(0.17871)	(0.00223)	(0.02400)	(0.21937)	(0.00003)
	$[-9.212]*$	$[4.144]*$	$[-2.827]*$	$[-1.608]$	$[19.707]*$
(b) $\log_e \dfrac{P_{OP1/i}}{P_{RP/i}}$	-1.78707	0.00791	-0.01264	-0.11400	0.00054
	(0.21903)	(0.00273)	(0.02917)	(0.25581)	(0.00003)
	$[-8.159]*$	$[2.893]*$	$[-0.433]$	$[0.446]$	$[16.507]*$
(c) $\log_e \dfrac{P_{OP2/i}}{P_{RF/i}}$	-1.33899	0.01169	-0.17932	-0.94546	0.00050
	(0.31149)	(0.00388)	(0.04286)	(0.44994)	(0.00005)
	$[-4.299]*$	$[3.015]*$	$[-4.184]*$	$[-2.101]*$	$[10.803]*$

Notes: Standard errors in parentheses.
t-Statistics in square brackets.
* Significance at the 0.05 level.

owner-occupiers have achieved their preferred tenure status. The two sub-samples of renters (RP and RF) were then each combined with stratified samples of owner-occupiers (OP1 and OP2), derived in order to maintain the original choice shares of 'owning' versus 'renting' which underlie model (2.23). Two resulting models were estimated:

$$\log_e \frac{P_{OP1/i}}{P_{RP/i}} = \beta_1 + \beta_2(HOHAGE)_i + \beta_3(HHSIZE)_i + \beta_4(RACE)_i$$
$$+ \beta_5(HOH\text{-}Y)_i \tag{2.24}$$

$$\log_e \frac{P_{OP2/i}}{P_{RF/i}} = \beta_1 + \beta_2(HOHAGE)_i + \beta_3(HHSIZE)_i + \beta_4(RACE)_i$$
$$+ \beta_5(HOH\text{-}Y)_i, \tag{2.25}$$

where HOHAGE, HHSIZE, RACE and HOH-Y are all as previously defined, and

$\log_e \dfrac{P_{OP1/i}}{P_{RP/i}} =$ the log odds that respondent i prefers to own (OP1) rather than to rent (RP) a dwelling, irrespective of whether or not owner-occupation is feasible for him

$$\log_e \frac{P_{OP2/i}}{P_{RF/i}} = \text{the log odds that respondent } i \text{ is able to realize his}$$

preference to own (OP2) rather than having to remain in the rented sector (RF).

The resulting parameter estimates are displayed in Table 2.1(b) and (c). It can be seen that as head of household's income (HOH-Y) increases, so there is an increase in the odds of preference for owner-occupation (Table 2.1(b)) and an increase in the odds of attaining the option of owner-occupation as an alternative to renting (Table 2.1(c)). The household size (HHSIZE) variable remains negatively related to the odds of home ownership in both models (2.24) and (2.25) but is rather stronger (and is statistically significant) in model (2.25). This suggests, as we would expect, that large families are more likely to be constrained to the rental sector (reflecting family-budget constraints, access to local authority housing in accordance with need criteria etc.). The ethnicity dummy (RACE) suggests a negative association between being white and the odds of owning a home: this result is in direct contrast to the findings of numerous US researchers (Struyck, 1976; Kain and Quigley, 1972) and accords more closely with studies of British conurbations (e.g. Karn, 1969, in West Yorkshire). It may on the one hand reflect the predominance in Britain of ethnic sub-groups originating in India and Pakistan who place a greater collective emphasis upon the virtues of owner-occupation, while on the other the fulfilment of length of residence criteria in order to secure access to local authority housing effectively reduces the ability of new immigrants to enter a large part of the rented sector. As might be expected because of wealth accumulation over the life cycle, and perhaps also because of an increasing desire for security, the age of head of household (HOHAGE) parameter indicates a positive relationship between the odds of homeownership and age of head of household in all three models.

It is also possible to relax the assumption of linear additivity of parameters in models (2.24) and (2.25) in accordance with the discussion of functional form above: the resulting Box–Tukey (equations 2.19–2.20) estimates each using a sample of 1485 observations are presented in Tables 2.2 and 2.3. Here a variety of λ and μ values are imposed upon HOHAGE, HHSIZE and HOH-Y to assess whether the usual specification of $\lambda = 1$ and $\mu = 0$ differs from the optimal λ and μ combination (NB whenever $\lambda = 1$, μ will not influence the log-likelihood values). It can be seen that whilst $\lambda = 1$ yields the optimum maximized log-likelihood value for model (2.24), model (2.25) reaches an optimum at $\lambda = 1.5$, $\mu = 0.001$. Although the difference in optimum maximized log-likelihood values is too small to suggest inadequacy of overall functional form at a statistically significant level, it does suggest that the functional form of perhaps just one or two of the variables might deviate more strongly from the $\lambda = 1$ form.

This two-way segmentation of the population on the basis of an attitudinal criterion therefore allows some preliminary assessment of the magnitude and

TABLE 2.2. Values of the maximized log-likelihood functions at various λ and μ combinations for model (2.24)

λ	μ				
	0.001*	10	20	30	40
0	−936.552	(−935.676)†	(−935.363)†	(−935.141)†	(−934.951)†
0.5	−926.266	(−925.708)†	(−925.595)†	(−925.531)†	(−925.483)†
1.0	−924.567	−924.567	−924.567	−924.567	−924.567
1.5	−930.036	−930.721	−930.777	−930.784	(−930.776)†
2.0	−939.954	−941.438	−941.529	−941.521	(−941.488)†

* μ must be set to an arbitrary small positive value.

† Last log-likelihood value after twenty-five iterations: approximately equal to final convergence value.

effect of overall constraints upon preference in the process of tenure-selection. It also serves systematically to reduce the variability of the utility expression of selected subgroups, aids the analyst in assessment of the effect of various policies on each segment, and reduces the danger of accentuating any multicollinearity which might be introduced into the model through incorporation of individual preferences in a dummy variable form. By more detailed population segmentation in accordance with a multitude of individually- and institutionally-defined criteria, it should then be possible to proceed through the choice hierarchy illustrated in Figure 2.2 in order to explain the nature and magnitude of individual choice constraints upon the dwelling selection process (see O'Brien (1982a) for an analysis of the lower nests of the local authority choice hierarchy shown in Figure 2.2 within the context of residential mobility in Bristol, England).

TABLE 2.3. Values of the maximized log-likelihood functions at various λ and μ combinations for model (2.25)

λ	μ				
	0.001*	10	20	30	40
0	−961.539	−957.853	(−957.379)†	(−957.126)†	(−956.938)†
0.5	−949.320	−947.669	(−947.472)†	(−947.382)†	(−947.322)†
1.0	−943.821	−943.821	−943.821	−943.821	−943.821
1.5	−943.804	−944.994	(−945.152)†	−945.206	(−945.228)†
2.0	−947.146	−949.142	−949.466	(−949.577)†	−949.622

* μ must be set to an arbitrary small positive value.

† Last log-likelihood value after twenty-five iterations: approximately equal to final convergence value.

Before moving on to consider the application of discrete choice modelling to retailing studies, we present in Table 2.4 a survey of some other selected applications concerning housing and residential location.

Table 2.4. Selected discrete choice modelling applications: Housing and residential location

Author	General area of application	Study area(s)	Objectives	Model form and special features
Anas (1979)	Transport/residential location	Simulation study	Identifying the impact of rapid-transit investment on housing values along a radial corridor	Simultaneous logit
Boehm (1982)	Dwelling choice	53 US housing markets	Relationship between selected tenurial, size and quality attributes of dwellings socio-economic attributes, attitudes and previous dwelling attributes	MNL: hierarchy structure derived by combining marginal probability of tenure choice with the subsequent conditional probabilities of size and quality choice
Cronin (1979)	Residential location/ mobility	Washington, DC	Relationship between mobility and its economic and psychological benefits and costs (including the role of previous mobility history)	Dichotomous logit
Dieleman (1982)	Residential mobility	Tilburg (the Netherlands)	Relationship between the probability of a move and selected dwelling and family attributes (family size, occupational density, birth of a new child and an interaction term)	Dichotomous logit with step-wise incorporation of variables
Friedman (1981)	Residential location	San Francisco	Assessment of the effects of public service provision etc., on residential location decisions	MNL
Kim (1981)	Residential mobility and tenure	Analysis of Michigan University panel data	Assessment of the dynamics of the joint determination of the mobility decision and tenure choice over time	Simultaneous logit structure
Lerman (1977)	Residential location/ transport mode choice	Washington, DC	Modelling joint choice of location, housing, car ownership, and mode for journey to work	MNL: simultaneous structure

Li (1977)	Tenure choice	Boston and Baltimore	Assessment of the role of socio-economic variables in the determination of tenure choice	Dichotomous linear logit: weighted least squares estimation (not set in a random utility framework)
van Lierop (1981)	Housing choice/residential mobility	The Netherlands (national survey)	Modelling of dwelling preferences and residential mobility within the Dutch housing market	Bivariate probit: 8-stage research design using a 2-period data set
Longley (1982)	Tenure choice and preference	England and Wales	Relationship between tenure 'choice' and respondent attributes: subsequent disaggregation of sample according to attitudinal criteria	MNL
Louviere (1979)	Residential preference	Wyoming	Student responses used to estimate individual utility functions, which then related to inter-personal factors	MNL: using experimental design data (separate experiments using visual and verbal stimuli)
O'Brien (1982a,b)	Public sector housing allocation	Bristol, England	Identification of spatial choice preferences as mediated by local authority allocative mechanisms	MNL and MNP (comparative analyses)
Odland and Barff (1982)	Housing deterioration	Indianapolis	Examination of the location and timing of housing condemnations in relation to a contagious diffusion process as reinforced by localized externalities	MNL (not set in a random utility framework): parameters examined for evidence of space–time interaction effects
Quigley (1976)	Estimation of short-run housing demand	Pittsburgh	Relationship between household choices and dwelling type, workplace location and intra-urban variations in house prices	MNL: stratified by 30 combinations of income and family size
Veldhuisen (1982)	Willingness to move	Western Netherlands	Relationship between desire to move and selected individual and dwelling attributes	MNL: verification of linearity assumption and use of a variable selection procedure
Weinberg (1980)	Residential mobility	Pittsburgh and Phoenix	Relationship between the probability of moving and selected household characteristics, attitudes, housing factors and policy variables	Dichotomous logit

Retailing and shopping behaviour

From the initial development of discrete choice modelling onwards, many empirical applications have been concerned with urban shopping trips and retail location. The characteristics of a representative sample of these studies are summarized in Table 2.5. Whilst the majority can be seen to be standard, cross-sectional survey applications of MNL models, a number have used less conventional sample designs and/or less restrictive discrete choice models. As an example of the latter type of application, we will consider some aspects of Miller and Lerman's (1981) use of the MNP model to study the location decisions of clothing retailers in Boston, USA.

In their study, Miller and Lerman assume that each clothing retailer will wish to choose the particular store location (l) and store size (s) combination which maximizes the marginal profitability function

$$U_{ls}^{*} = \mathbf{x}_{ls}'\boldsymbol{\beta} + \delta_1 w_l s + \delta_2 w_l s \bar{I}_l + \delta_3 w_l s \log_e(s) + \delta_4 w_l s \log_e(w_l) + \delta_5 w_l s \log_e(S_l)$$

$$+ \delta_6 w_l s \log_e(S_{tl}) + \delta_7 w_l s \log_e(M_{tl}) + \delta_8 w_l s \tau_{ls} + \eta_{ls}, \tag{2.26}$$

where $\mathbf{x}_{ls}$ is a vector of observable exogenous variables, w_l is the average wage rate paid by stores at location l, $\bar{I}_l$ is the average 'employment intensity' (number of employees per square foot of floor space) at l, S_l and S_{tl} are the total floor space of all stores and type t stores at location l, M_{tl} is the total expected sales of stores of type t at location l, and τ_{ls} and η_{ls} are error terms. In (2.26), $\delta_1, \ldots \delta_8$ are 'reduced-form' parameters and they can be used to recover the original 'structural' revenue parameters (α and $a_0, a_1, \ldots a_5$). In addition, $\delta_8 \tau_{ls}$ in the penultimate part of (2.26) can be interpreted as a type of 'taste variation' component as it describes a distribution of δ_8 across the population.

If we assume that the composite error terms

$$\varepsilon_{ls} = (\delta_8 w_l s \tau_{ls} + \eta_{ls}) \tag{2.27}$$

(see equation 2.11) are independent and identically distributed with a type I extreme-value distribution, then the choice probabilities of selecting a particular store location and size combination are given by the MNL model. Alternatively, if we assume that both τ_{ls} and η_{ls} are drawn from a multivariate normal distribution with the variance–covariance structures outlined in the earlier discussion, then the choice probabilities are given by the MNP model which allows the random components of the choice alternatives to be correlated and to have unequal variances, and also permits random taste variation across individuals.

As part of their empirical research, Miller and Lerman fitted both MNL and MNP models to a sample of 161 clothing retailers whose choice set was restricted to 7 possible locations (a mix of traditional downtown centres, planned downtown centres and suburban centres) and 2 possible store-size

TABLE 2.5. Selected discrete choice modelling applications: Retailing and shopping behaviour

Author	General area of application	Study area(s)	Objectives	Model form and special features
Adler and Ben-Akiva (1976)	Shopping trips	Washington, DC	Specification and estimation of a joint-choice model for frequency, destination and travel mode on shopping trips	MNL: 3 choices modelled simultaneously
Domencich and McFadden (1975)	Destination and mode of travel choice on shopping trips	Pittsburgh	Estimation of separate models of mode choice and destination choice on shopping trips	MNL: reporting of one of the first empirical applications
Horowitz (1980b,c)	Non-work (including shopping) travel behaviour	Washington, DC	Development and testing of a model of non-work travel behaviour that incorporates travel frequency, destination choice and mode choice for both single- and multi-destination travel. Incorporates concept that current travel decisions may depend upon past travel decisions	MNL: certain variables and special features included to capture aspects of multi-destination travel
Koppelman and Hauser (1978)	Non-grocery-shopping trips	Evanston, Illinois	Specification and estimation of a model of destination and mode choice on non-grocery-shopping trips	MNL

Table continued

Table 2.5—cont.

Author	General area of application	Study area(s)	Objectives	Model form and special features
Landau et al. (1982)	Shopping destination and mode choice	Tel Aviv	To develop and test a model which uses knowledge concerning the constraints on shopping travel to generate choice sets of retail locations	MNL as second part of a two-step procedure which begins with definition of constrained choice sets
McCarthy (1980)	Shopping-trip behaviour	San Francisco (2 separate study areas: central city and suburban)	(1) Investigation of determinants of shopping-centre choice in both study areas; (2) study of shopping-trip behaviour in central-city environment using a joint destination-mode choice model. In both cases, major focus on the influence of generalized indices (generated from attitudinal data) on choice of shopping centre	MNL (central-city model a joint-choice version): Perceptions of shopping centres elicited using Likert scales and then factor analysed. Five generalized indices/factors then used in MNL models. Elasticities calculated for component elements of generalized indices/factors
Meyer and Eagle (1982)	Grocery-store preferences	Laboratory experiment	To test binomial version of logit model adjusted to handle 'context dependence/weight shifting' problem	Linear logit

Miller and Lerman (1981)	Retailers choice of location and store size	Boston	Investigation of determinants of location and store-size decisions of clothing retailers based upon a well-developed micro-economic theory of the site selection process of retailers	MNP: 3 variants (see discussion in this chapter)
Recker and Golob (1979)	Destination choice on shopping trips	Buffalo	Development of a non-compensatory choice model. Testing of destination choice on urban shopping trips	Non-compensatory model with links to EBA and 'just noticeable differences' concepts
Recker and Kostyniuk (1978)	Choice of store and shopping-centre type on urban grocery-shopping trips	Buffalo	Evaluation of relative importance of consumer perceptions, accessibility, and number of opportunities available at destination in determining choice of store and shopping-centre type	MNL: perceptions of stores elicited using semantic differential technique then factor analysed and 4 factors retained
Richards and Ben-Akiva (1975)	Shopping destination and mode choice	Eindhoven	To develop and estimate a joint shopping destination and mode choice model as part of a wider study of disaggregate travel choice models	MNL: one of the first empirical applications of a joint destination/mode choice model
Southworth (1981)	Destination and mode of travel choice on shopping trips	West Yorkshire	Regional-level study of the determinants of travel choice on work, shopping and recreation trips	MNL: based on 7-day diary survey data, segmentation of sample by income and household structure groups

categories (under 5000 sq. ft.). The function $x'_{ls}\beta$ in (2.26) was specified as

$$x'_{ls}\beta = L_l^{dum}\beta_l + S_s^{dum}\beta_s + \beta_c COST, \qquad (2.28)$$

where L_l^{dum} is a vector of location specific dummy variables, S_s^{dum} is a vector of

TABLE 2.6. The variance–covariance structures assumed in the MNP models of Table 2.7 (adapted from Miller and Lerman, 1981)

	Location 1		Location 2		...	Location 7	
	Size 1	Size 2	Size 1	Size 2	...	Size 1	Size 2
Location 1							
Size 1	σ_1^2	$\phi\sigma_1^2$	0		...	0	
Size 2	$\phi\sigma_1^2$	σ_1^2					
Location 2							
Size 1	0		σ_2^2	$\phi\sigma_2^2$	...	0	
Size 2			$\phi\sigma_2^2$	σ_2^2			
$\vdots$	$\vdots$		$\vdots$			$\vdots$	
Location 7							
Size 1	0		0			σ_7^2	$\phi\sigma_7^2$
Size 2						$\phi\sigma_7^2$	σ_7^2

MNP model A: $\phi = 0$; $\sigma_l^2 = \sigma_{l*}^2$ for all l and l^*; $var(\tau_{ls}) = 0$
MNP model B: $\phi = 0$; $\sigma_l^2 = \sigma_{l*}^2$ for all l and l^*; $var(\tau_{ls}) \neq 0$
MNP model C: $\phi \neq 0$; $\sigma_l^2 \neq \sigma_{l*}^2$ for all l and l^*; $var(\tau_{ls}) \neq 0$

TABLE 2.7. Parameter estimates for MNL and MNP models with asymptotic 't statistics' in brackets (adapted from Tables 8 and 9 of Miller and Lerman (1981). Reproduced by permission of Pion Ltd)

	Logit	Probit		
	Model 1	Model A	Model B	Model C
*Location specific parameters (β_l)**				
Harvard Square	7.264	3.649	4.686	5.036
	(6.10)	(6.36)	(6.55)	(8.54)
Chestnut Hill	4.194	1.961	−1.320	−0.986
	(3.91)	(2.64)	(−1.47)	(−1.78)
Faneuil Hall	7.097	3.336	3.500	3.029
	(5.23)	(4.62)	(3.69)	(4.60)
Boston CBD	10.52	5.461	8.672	9.360
	(6.83)	(5.19)	(7.51)	(8.74)
Newbury/Boylston	8.905	4.862	6.485	6.541
	(6.98)	(6.34)	(7.02)	(7.65)
Prudential Center	7.277	3.480	2.968	3.386
	(4.79)	(5.44)	(3.46)	(3.46)
Small store size parameter (β_s)†	8.980	3.956	6.663	7.163
	(6.86)	(7.14)	(6.90)	(7.41)

	Logit	Probit		
	Model 1	Model A	Model B	Model C
Structural revenue parameters				
a_1	2.254	2.0778	2.4630	2.9382
	(10.97)	(8.57)	(4.08)	(3.59)
a_2	0.1459	0.1164	0.1464	0.2072
	(4.95)	(5.22)	(1.95)	(1.85)
a_3	0.2358	0.1972	0.1163	0.1723
	(5.16)	(4.43)	(1.02)	(1.37)
a_4	−0.5892	−0.4103	−0.6960	−0.9143
	(−4.73)	(−4.67)	(−3.56)	(−2.05)
a_5	0.3301	0.2661	0.7004	0.8727
	(4.01)	(3.50)	(1.65)	(2.08)
α‡	0.1300	0.0585	0.1130	0.1308
	(5.01)	(5.03)	(2.46)	(4.05)
Taste variation variance	—		0.07826	0.06805
(var τ_{ls})			(6.90)	(2.04)
Correlation between store sizes	—	—		0.04749
within a given location (ϕ)				(0.28)
Location variances (σ_l^2)				
Harvard Square		1.6449§	1.6449§	1.3061
		↑	↑	(1.70)
Chestnut Hill				2.0602
				(2.28)
Burlington Mall				0.8290
				(0.97)
Faneuil Hall				1.6255
				(2.20)
Boston CBD				1.9235
				(3.10)
Newbury/Boylston				1.3686
				(2.42)
Prudential Center		↓	↓	1.6449§

Notes:
* Burlington Mall used as base category for location specific parameters.
† Store size 2500–5000 sq. ft. used as base category for store-size parameters.
‡ Cost parameter (β_c), see equation 2.28 constrained to value of $-\alpha$.
§ Set at this value ($=\frac{1}{6}\pi^2$).

size-category dummy variables, and the COST term is simply rent at location l times store size. Table 2.7 shows the results of fitting the MNL and three variations of the MNP model.

The three versions of the MNP can be understood from an inspection of Table 2.6 which shows the variance–covariance structures assumed for the three models. Model C represents the closest version to the general MNP form outlined above. It permits random taste variation (i.e. var(τ_{ls})≠0), each location to have a different variance (i.e. $\sigma_l^2 \neq \sigma_{l^*}^2$), and correlation between store sizes within a given location (i.e. $\phi \neq 0$). Models A and B represent special forms of model C. In model B, taste variation is allowed but each location is assumed to have the same variance and no correlation is permitted between store sizes within a given location. In model A no taste variation is allowed, no correlation is permitted, and each location is assumed to have the same variance with the value $\pi^2/6$ (see equation 2.8), i.e. the composite random component ε_{ls} in (2.27) is assumed to have constant variance $\pi^2/6$. Model A is, therefore, almost identical to the MNL model and, as such, it is often given the special name *identity probit*. (The identity probit can sometimes play a useful function in the comparison of MNL and MNP models; see Horowitz, 1980a.)

For the purposes of this example, the substantive interpretation of the parameters in Table 2.7 need not concern us unduly (full details are provided by Miller and Lerman). As a brief illustration of the type of conclusions which can be drawn, however, we will simply note that the structural revenue parameter a_5 can be interpreted as the revenue elasticity of an individual store with respect to the aggregate location 'market potential' measure M_{tl}. The fact that a_5 is consistently estimated as less than 1 indicates that revenues of the small stores (under 5000 sq. ft.) considered in the estimation of Table 2.7 are inelastic with respect to aggregate shopping trips to the shopping centre in which they are located. This in turn leads Miller and Lerman to suggest two tentative hypotheses: (1) that revenues of large stores must be elastic with respect to this term, for otherwise it is unclear why agglomeration of retail activity occurs; and (2) that small changes in aggregate shopping trips caused by shifts in accessibility (as a result of say a proposed transport-system change) are not likely seriously to effect the small retailer's revenues. Conclusions of a similar type can be drawn with respect to the other parameters in the model.

Of equal importance for our purposes, however, is the fact that Table 2.7 demonstrates that:

(i) There is a family of special cases of the general MNP form discussed earlier in this chapter. The choice of which particular MNP form is used depends simply on what particular variance–covariance structure we are prepared to assume in any particular case.

(ii) The MNP appears to be a feasible model even for choice problems with a reasonably large number of alternatives in the choice set. Nevertheless, there are certain computational problems which are likely to be encountered in the estimation of large MNP models (e.g. Miller and Lerman used a modified version of the program CHOMP, and found that the likelihood function of the model was not completely 'well behaved' and that the estimation procedure was very sensitive to the parameter initialization used). This suggests that more practical empirical experience is necessary before definitive statements can be made concerning the practicality of estimating large MNP models.

CONCLUSION

Discrete choice modelling is a research field which has developed over a relatively short period of time, and it has been our objective in this chapter to provide a brief guide to its main features and to its potential in urban analysis. Nevertheless, our viewpoint is constrained to the state-of-the-art in the early 1980s. The pace of development in the field shows no signs, as yet, of flagging and the next decade is likely to see considerable methodological progress as the family of discrete choice models is expanded and refined, and as these models are linked more firmly into the wider literature on stochastic and econometric modelling. (There are already encouraging signs of the linkage of panel-data discrete choice models with more traditional stochastic consumer purchasing models, for example, and the development of general panel-data MNP models which link together both serial correlation and state-dependence phenomena.) As discrete choice modelling finds an inevitably wider role in both urban-geography teaching and research over the next decade, urban geographers can be expected to make a valuable contribution to both methodological development and empirical application. In the empirical context, urban geographers can play an extremely valuable role in undertaking the necessary empirical assessment of such models at a variety of spatial scales and in a variety of differentially constrained contexts. In this way, they will not only provide the empirical feedback necessary to refine the form and estimation of the current generation of discrete choice models, but they will also clarify the appropriate domains (see Heggie and Jones, 1978; Thrift, 1981) in which discrete choice modelling has the most effective role to play in urban analysis.

ACKNOWLEDGEMENT

The authors are indebted to the Department of the Environment for supply of data from the 1976 English House Condition Survey. The Department bears no responsibility for the views and analysis set out in this paper, which are wholly the authors' responsibility.

REFERENCES

Adler, T. J. and Ben-Akiva, M. E. (1976). Joint choice model for frequency, destination, and travel mode for shopping trips, *Transportation Research Record*, **569**, 136–150.
Adler, T. J. and Ben-Akiva, M. E. (1979). A theoretical and empirical model of trip chaining behaviour, *Transportation Research B*, **13B**, 243–257.
Albright, R. L., Lerman, S. R., and Manski, C. F. (1977). *Report on the Development of an Estimation Program for the Multinomial Probit Model*. Prepared for the Federal Highway Administration, US Department of Transportation.
Altham, P. M. E. (1979). Detecting relationships between categorical variables observed over time: a problem of deflating a chi-squared statistic, *Applied Statistics*, **28**, 115–125.

Anas, A. (1979). The impact of transit investment on housing values: a simulation experiment, *Environment and Planning A*, **11A**, 59–70.

Atherton, T. J. and Ben-Akiva, M. E. (1976). Transferability and updating of disaggregate travel demand models, *Transportation Research Record*, **610**, 12–18.

Barton, M. (1979). Conditional logit analysis of FCC decision making, *Bell Journal of Economics*, **10**, 399–411.

Bassett, K. A. and Short, J. (1980). *Housing and Residential Structure: Alternative Approaches*, Routledge and Kegan Paul, London.

Ben-Akiva, M. E. (1977). *Choice Models with Simple Choice Set Generating Processes.* Working Paper, Centre for Transportation Studies, MIT, Massachusetts, USA.

Ben-Akiva, M. E. and Lerman, S. R. (1979). Disaggregate travel and mobility choice models and measures of accessibility, in *Behavioural Travel Modelling* (Eds D. A. Hensher and P. R. Stopher), pp. 654–679, Croom Helm, London.

Boehm, T. P. (1982). A hierarchical model of housing choice, *Urban Studies*, **19**, 17–31.

Boskin, M. J. (1974). A conditional logit model of occupational choice, *Journal of Political Economy*, **82**, 389–397.

Box, G. E. P. and Cox, D. R. (1964). An analysis of transformations, *Journal of the Royal Statistical Society B*, **26**, 211–243.

Brier, S. S. (1980). Analysis of contingency tables under cluster sampling, *Biometrika*, **67**, 591–596.

Briggs, R. (1973). Urban cognitive distance, in *Image and Environment: Cognitive Mapping and Spatial Behaviour* (Eds. R. M. Downs and D. Stea), pp. 361–388, Aldine, Chicago.

Burnett, P. (1981). Theoretical advances in modeling economic and social behaviors: Applications to geographical, policy-oriented models, *Economic Geography*, **57**, 291–303.

Burnett, P. and Hanson, S. (1982). The analysis of travel as an example of complex behavior in spatially-constrained situations: Definition and measurement issues, *Transportation Research A*, **16A**, 87–102.

Clark, C. E. (1961). The greatest of a finite set of random variables, *Operations Research*, **9**, 145–162.

Cohen, J. E. (1976). The distribution of the chi-squared statistic under clustered sampling from contingency tables, *Journal of the American Statistical Association*, **71**, 665–670.

Cosslett, S. R. (1981). Efficient estimation of discrete choice models, in *Structural Analysis of Discrete Data: With Econometric Applications* (Eds. C. F. Manski and D. McFadden), pp. 51–111, MIT Press, Cambridge, Massachusetts.

Costanzo, C. M., Halperin, W. C., Gale, N. D., and Richardson, G. D. (1982). An alternative method for assessing goodness-of-fit for logit models, *Environment and Planning A*, **14A**, 963–971.

Cronin, J. (1979). *Low-income Households' Search for Housing: Preliminary Findings on Racial Differences*, The Urban Institute, Washington, DC.

Daganzo, C. F. (1979). *Multinomial Probit. The Theory and its Application to Demand Forecasting*, Academic Press, New York.

Daganzo, C. F. (1980). Optimal sampling strategies for statistical models with discrete dependent variables. *Transportation Science*, **14**, 324–345.

Daganzo, C. F., Bouthelier, F., and Sheffi, Y. (1977). Multinomial probit and qualitative choice: a computationally efficient algorithm. *Transportation Science*, **11**, 338–358.

Daganzo, C. F. and Sheffi, Y. (1979). *Estimation of Choice Models from Panel Data.* Presented at the North American Meeting of the Regional Science Association, Los Angeles, November.

Daganzo, C. F. and Sheffi, Y. (1982). Multinomial probit with time series data: unifying state dependence and serial correlation models, *Environment and Planning A*, **14A**, 1377–1388.

Daly, A. J. and Zachary, S. (1978). Improved multiple choice models, in *Determinants of Travel Choice* (Eds D. A. Hensher and M. Q. Dalvi), Teakfield, Farnborough, Hampshire.

Debreu, G. (1960). Review of R. D. Luce, *Individual Choice Behaviour*, *American Economic Review*, **50**, 186–188.

Dieleman, F. M. (1982). *Housing Adjustment of Expanding Families in Tilburg*. Paper presented at the Third European Colloquium on Theoretical and Quantitative Geography, Augsburg, September.

Domencich, T. and McFadden, D. (1975). *Urban Travel Demand: A Behavioural Analysis*, North-Holland, Amsterdam.

Fellegi, P. (1980). Approximate tests of independence and goodness of fit based on stratified multistage samples, *Journal of the American Statistical Association*, **75**, 261–275.

Friedman, J. (1981). A conditional logit model of the role of local public services in residential choice, *Urban Studies*, **18**, 347–358.

Galbraith, R. A. and Hensher, D. A. (1982). Intra-metropolitan transferability of mode choice models, *Journal of Transport Economics and Policy*, **16**, 7–29.

Gaudry, M. J. I. (1980). Dogit and logit models of travel mode choice in Montreal, *Canadian Journal of Economics*, **13**, 268–279.

Gaudry, M. J. I. and Dagenais, M. G. (1979). The dogit model. *Transportation Research B*, **13B**, 105–111.

Gaudry, M. J. I. and Wills, M. J. (1978). Estimating the functional form of travel demand models, *Transportation Research*, **12**, 257–289.

Gaudry, M. J. I. and Wills, M. J. (1979). Testing the dogit model with aggregate time-series and cross-sectional data, *Transportation Research B*, **13B**, 155–166.

Golledge, R. G., Briggs, R., and Demko, D. (1969). The configuration of distances in intra-urban space, *Proceedings of the Association of American Geographers*, **1**, 60–65.

Golledge, R. G., Hubert, L. J., and Richardson, G. D. (1981). The comparison of related data sets: examples from multidimensional scaling and cluster analysis, *Papers of the Regional Science Association*, **48**, 57–66.

Halperin, W. C., Richardson, G. D., Gale, N. D., and Costanzo, C. M. (1984). A generalised procedure for comparing models of spatial choice, *Environment and Planning A*, 16.

Hanson, S. (1980). Spatial diversification and multipurpose travel: Implications for choice theory, *Geographical Analysis*, **12**, 245–257.

Hanson, S. and Hanson, P. (1981). The travel-activity patterns of urban residents: Dimensions and relationships to sociodemographic characteristics, *Economic Geography*, **57**, 332–347.

Hanson, S. and Huff, J. O. (1984). Assessing day-to-day variability in complex travel patterns, *Transportation Research Record*.

Hausman, J. and Wise, D. A. (1978a). A conditional probit model for qualitative choice: Discrete decisions recognizing interdependence and heterogeneous preferences, *Econometrica*, **46**, 403–426.

Hausman, J. and Wise, D. (1978b). AFDC participation: measured variables or unobserved characteristics, permanent or transitory. Working Paper, Department of Economics, MIT, USA.

Heckman, J. J. (1974). Shadow prices, market wages and labour supply, *Econometrica*, **42**, 679–694.

Heckman, J. J. (1981). Statistical models for discrete panel data, in *Structural Analysis of Discrete Data: With Econometric Applications* (Eds C. F. Manski and D. McFadden, pp. 114–178, MIT Press, Cambridge, Massachusetts.
Heggie, I. G. and Jones, P. M. (1978). Defining domains for models of travel demand, *Transportation*, **7**, 119–125.
Hensher, D. A. (1978). *A Review of Individual Choice Modelling*. Report prepared for the Department of the Environment Housing and Community Development Project.
Hensher, D. A. (1981). A practical concern about the relevance of alternative-specific constants for new alternatives in simple logit models, *Transportation Research B*, **15B**, 407–410.
Hensher, D. A. and Johnson, L. W. (1981a). *Applied Discrete Choice Modelling*, Croom Helm, London.
Hensher, D. A. and Johnson, L. W. (1981b). Behavioural response and the form of the representative component of the indirect utility function in travel choice models, *Regional Science and Urban Economics*, **11**, 559–572.
Hensher, D. A. and Louviere, J. J. (1981). *An Integration of Probabilistic Discrete Choice Models and Experimental Design Data: An Application in Cultural Economics*, School of Economic and Financial Studies, Macquarie University, NSW 2113, Australia.
Hensher, D. A. and Manefield, T. (1981). *A Structured Logit Model of Automobile Acquisition and Type Choice: Some Preliminary Evidence*, School of Economic and Financial Studies, Macquarie University, NSW 2113, Australia.
Holt, D., Scott, A. J., and Ewings, P. D. (1980). Chi-squared tests with survey data, *Journal of the Royal Statistical Society A*, **143**, 303–320.
Horowitz, J. (1980a). The accuracy of the multinomial logit model as an approximation to the multinomial probit model of travel demand, *Transportation Research B*, **14B**, 331–341.
Horowitz, J. (1980b). A utility maximizing model of the demand for multidestination non-work travel, *Transportation Research B*, **14B**, 369–386.
Horowitz, J. (1980c). Random utility models of urban nonwork travel demand: A review, *Papers of the Regional Science Association*, **45**, 125–137.
Horowitz, J. (1981a). Identification and diagnosis of specification errors in the multinomial logit model, *Transportation Research B*, **15B**, 345–360.
Horowitz, J. (1981b). Testing the multinomial logit against the multinomial probit without estimating the probit parameters, *Transportation Science*, **15**, 153–163.
Hubert, L. J. and Golledge, R. G. (1981). A heuristic method for the comparison of related structures, *Journal of Mathematical Psychology*, **23**, 214–226.
Johnson, L. W. and Hensher, D. A. (1982). Application of multinomial probit to a two-period panel data set, *Transportation Research A*, **16A**, 457–464.
Jones, P. M. (1979). 'HATS': a technique for investigating household decisions, *Environment and Planning A*, **11A**, 59–70.
Kain, J. F. and Quigley, J. M. (1972). Housing market discrimination, home ownership and savings behaviour, *American Economic Review*, **62**, 263–277.
Karn, V. (1969). Property values amongst Indians and Pakistanis in a Yorkshire town, *Race*, **10**, 269–284.
Kim, H.-S. (1981). *Housing Tenure and Residential Mobility: Multi-choice Logit Approach*. PhD thesis, Princeton University.
Kohn, M. G., Manski, C. F., and Mundel, D. S. (1976). An empirical investigation of factors which influence college-going behaviour, *Annals of Economic and Social Measurement*, **5**, 391–419.
Koppelman, F. S. (1981). Non-linear functions in models of travel choice behaviour, *Transportation*, **10**, 127–146.

Koppelman, F. S. and Hauser, J. R. (1978). Estimation of choice behaviour for non-grocery shopping trips, *Transportation Research Record*, **673**, 157–165.

Landau, U., Prashker, J. N., and Alpern, B. (1982). Evaluation of activity constrained choice sets to shopping destination choice modelling, *Transportation Research A*, **16A**, 199–207.

Lave, C. A. and Train, K. (1979). A behavioural disaggregate model of automobile-type choice, *Transportation Research A*, **13A**, 1–9.

Lerman, S. R. (1977). Location, housing, automobile ownership, and mode to work: A joint choice model, *Transportation Research Record*, **610**, 6–11.

Lerman, S. R. (1979). The use of disaggregate choice models in semi-Markov process models of trip-chaining behaviour, *Transportation Science*, **13**, 273–291.

Lerman, S. R. and Ben-Akiva, M. E. (1976). A disaggregate behavioural model of auto ownership, *Transportation Research Record*, **569**, 34–51.

Lerman, S. R. and Louviere, J. J. (1978). On the use of functional measurement to identify the functional form of the utility expression in travel demand models, *Transportation Research Record*, **673**, 78–86.

Lerman, S. R. and Manski, C. F. (1979). Sample design for discrete choice: State of the art, *Transportation Research A*, **13A**, 29–44.

Li, M. M. (1977). A logit model of home ownership, *Econometrica*, **45**, 1081–1097.

Lierop, W. F. J. van (1981). Towards a new disaggregate model for the housing market, in *Locational Developments in Urban Planning* (Eds W. F. J. van Lierop and P. Nijkamp), pp. 221–243, Sijthoff and Noordhoff, The Netherlands.

Longley, P. A. (1982). *Residential Preference: A Discrete Choice Analytic Framework*. Paper presented at the Third European Colloquium on Theoretical and Quantitative Geography, Augsburg, September.

Louviere, J. J. (1979). Modelling individual residential preferences: A totally disaggregate approach, *Transportation Research A*, **13A**, 1–15.

Louviere, J. J. (1981a). On the identification of the functional form of the utility expression and its relationship to discrete choice, in *Applied Discrete Choice Modelling* (Eds D. A. Hensher and L. W. Johnson), Appendix B, Croom Helm, London.

Louviere, J. J. (1981b). A conceptual and analytical framework for understanding spatial and travel choices, *Economic Geography*, **57**, 304–314.

Luce, R. D. (1959). *Individual Choice Behaviour: A Theoretical Analysis*, John Wiley, New York.

Luce, R. D. and Suppes, P. (1965). Preference, utility and subjective probability, in *Handbook of Mathematical Psychology*, Vol. 3, (Eds R. D. Luce, R. Bush, and E. Galanter), John Wiley, New York.

Maclennan, D. and Williams, N. J. (1980). Revealed preference theory and spatial choices: some limitations, *Environment and Planning A*, **12**, 909–919.

Manski, C. F. (1981). Structural models for discrete data: the analysis of discrete choice, in *Sociological Methodology 1981* (Ed. S. Leinhardt), pp. 58–109, Jossey-Bass, San Francisco.

Manski, C. F. and Lerman, S. R. (1977). The estimation of choice probabilities from choice-based samples, *Econometrica*, **45**, 1977–1988.

Manski, C. F. and McFadden, D. (Eds) (1981). *Structural Analysis of Discrete Data: With Econometric Applications*, MIT Press, Cambridge, Massachusetts.

Manski, C. F. and McFadden, D. (1981). Alternative estimators and sample designs for discrete choice analysis, in *Structural Analysis of Discrete Data: With Econometric Applications* (Eds C. F. Manski and D. McFadden), pp. 2–50, Croom Helm, London.

Manski, C. F. and Sherman, L. (1980). An empirical analysis of household choice among motor vehicles, *Transportation Research A*, **14A**, 349–366.

McCarthy, P. S. (1980). A study of the importance of generalized attributes in shopping choice behaviour, *Environment and Planning A*, **12**, 1269–1286.

McCarthy, P. S. (1982). Further evidence of the temporal stability of disaggregate travel demand models, *Transportation Research B*, **16B**, 263–278.

McFadden, D. (1976). The revealed preferences of a government bureaucracy: Empirical evidence, *The Bell Journal of Economics*, **7**, 55–72.

McFadden, D. (1979). Quantitative methods for analysing travel behaviour of individuals: some recent developments, in *Behavioural Travel Modelling* (Eds D. A. Hensher and P. R. Stopher), Croom Helm, London.

McFadden, D. (1981). Econometric models of probabilistic choice, in *Structural Analysis of Discrete Data: With Econometric Applications* (Eds C. F. Manski and D. McFadden, pp. 198–272, Croom Helm, London.

McFadden, D., Train, D., and Tye, W. (1977). An application of diagnostic tests for the independence from irrelevant alternatives property of the multinomial logit model, *Transportation Research Record*, **637**, 39–45.

Meyer, R. J. and Eagle, T. C. (1981). *A Parsimonious Multinomial Choice Model Recognizing Alternative Interdependence and Context-Dependent Utility Functions*, Graduate School of Industrial Administration, Carnegie-Mellon University, WP 26-80-81.

Meyer, R. J. and Eagle, T. C. (1982). Context-induced parameter instability in a disaggregate-stochastic model of store choice, *Journal of Marketing Research*, **19**, 62–71.

Miller, E. J. and Lerman, S. R. (1981). Disaggregate modelling and decisions of retail firms: A case study of clothing retailers. *Environment and Planning A*, **13A**, 729–746.

Murie, A., Niner, P., and Watson, C. (1976). *Housing Policy and the Housing System*, Allen and Unwin, London.

Nelson, F. and Noll, R. (1978). In search of scientific regulation: The UHF allocation experiment. Paper presented at the Annual Meeting of the Public Choice Society. (Reported in Hensher, D. A. and Johnson, L. W. (1981a), *Applied Discrete Choice Modelling*, pp. 290–299, Croom Helm, London.)

O'Brien, L. G. (1982a). *Categorical Data Analysis for Geographical Research: With Applications to Public Sector Residential Mobility*, Unpublished PhD dissertation, University of Bristol.

O'Brien, L. G. (1982b). *Parametric Statistical Models for Categorised Data: A Comparison of Two Regression Models*. Paper presented at the Third European Colloquium on Theoretical and Quantitative Geography, Augsburg, September.

O'Brien, L. G. and Wrigley, N. (1980). Computer programs for the analysis of categorical data, *Area*, **12**, 263–268.

Odland, J. and Barff, R. (1982). A statistical model for the development of spatial patterns: applications to the spread of housing deterioration. *Geographical Analysis*, **14**, 326–339.

Pipkin, J. S. (1981). Cognitive behavioural geography and repetitive travel, in *Behavioural Problems in Geography Revisited* (Eds K. R. Cox and R. G. Golledge), pp. 145–181, Methuen, London.

Poirier, D. J. (1981). A switching simultaneous equation model of physician behaviour in Ontario, in *Structural Analysis of Discrete Data: With Econometric Applications* (Eds C. F. Manski and D. McFadden), Croom Helm, London.

Punj, G. and Staelin, R. (1978). The choice process for graduate business schools, *Journal of Marketing Research*, **15**, 588–598.

Quigley, J. M. (1976). Housing demand in the short run—an analysis of polytomous choice, *Explorations in Economic Research*, **3**, 76–102.

Recker, W. W. and Golob, T. G. (1979). A non-compensatory model of transportation behaviour based on sequential consideration of attributes, *Transportation Research B*, **13B**, 269–280.

Recker, W. W. and Kostyniuk, L. P. (1978). Factors influencing destination choice for the urban grocery shopping trip, *Transportation*, **7**, 19–33.

Richards, M. G. and Ben-Akiva, M. E. (1975). *A Disaggregate Travel Demand Model*, Saxon House, Farnborough, Hampshire.

Robins, P. K. and Spiegelman, R. C. (1978). An econometric model of the demand for child care, *Economic Enquiry*, **16**, 83–94.

Ross, R. (1979). *Disaggregate Labour Supply Function for Married Women: Preliminary Estimates for New Zealand*. Working Paper No. 37, Department of Economics, University of Sydney, Australia.

Rushton, G. (1982). Review of J. R. Gold, *An Introduction to Behavioural Geography*. *Environment and Planning A*, **14A**, 275–276.

Schmidt, P. and Strauss, R. P. (1975a). The prediction of occupation using multiple choice logit models, *International Economic Review*, **16**, 471–486.

Schmidt, P. and Strauss, R. P. (1975b). Estimation of models with jointly dependent qualitative variables: a simultaneous logit approach, *Econometrica*, **43**, 745–755.

Sheppard, E. S. (1980). The ideology of spatial choice, *Papers of the Regional Science Association*, **45**, 197–213.

Simon, H. A. (1957). *Models of Man*, John Wiley, New York.

Sobel, K. (1980). Travel demand forecasting with the nested multinomial logit model, *Transportation Research Record*, **775**, 48–55.

Southworth, F. (1981). Calibration of multinomial logit models of mode and destination choice, *Transportation Research A*, **15A**, 315–325.

Stapleton, C. M. (1980). Reformulation of the family life-cycle concept: Implications for residential mobility, *Environment and Planning A*, **12A**, 1103–1118.

Stone, R. (1954). Linear expenditure systems and demand analysis: an application to the pattern of British demand, *Economic Journal*, **64**, 511–527.

Struyck, R. J. (1976). *Urban Homeownership*, D. C. Heath, Lexington, Massachusetts.

Talvitie, A. and Kirshner, D. (1978). Specification, transferability and the effect of data outliers in modelling the choice of mode in urban travel, *Transportation*, **7**, 311–331.

Tardiff, T. J. (1976). A note on goodness-of-fit statistics for probit and logit models, *Transportation*, **5**, 377–388.

Tardiff, T. J. (1979). Specification analysis for quantal choice models, *Transportation Science*, **13**, 179–190.

Tardiff, T. J. (1980a). Definition of alternatives and representation of dynamic behaviour in spatial choice models, *Transportation Research Record*, **723**, 25–30.

Tardiff, T. J. (1980b). Vehicle choice models: Review of previous studies and directions for further research, *Transportation Research A*, **14A**, 327–336.

Thrift, N. (1981). Behavioural geography, in *Quantitative Geography: A British View* (Eds N. Wrigley and R. J. Bennett), pp. 352–365, Routledge and Kegan Paul, London.

Timmermans, H. J. P. (1982). *Individual decision models and spatial choice processes: An overview of combination rules and measurement procedures for predicting preferences among multiattribute alternatives*. Paper presented at the Third European Colloquium on Quantitative and Theoretical Geography, Augsburg, September.

Train, K. and McFadden, D. (1978). The goods/leisure trade off and disaggregate work trip mode choice models, *Transportation Research*, **12**, 349–353.

Tversky, A. (1972a). Elimination-by-aspects: A theory of choice, *Psychological Review*, **79**, 281–299.

Tversky, A. (1972b). Choice-by-elimination, *Journal of Mathematical Psychology*, **9**, 341–367.

Tversky, A. and Sattath, S. (1979). Preference trees, *Psychological Review*, **86**, 542–573.

Veldhuisen, K. J. (1982). *A Logit Model of the Willingness to Move House*. Paper presented at the Third Colloquium on Theoretical and Quantitative Geography, Augsburg, September.

Weinberg, D. H. (1980). Mobility and housing change: The Housing Allowance Demand Experiment, in *Residential Mobility and Public Policy* (Eds W. A. V. Clark and E. G. Moore), pp. 168–193, Sage, California.

Williams, H. C. W. L. (1977). On the formation of travel demand models and economic evaluation measures of user benefit, *Environment and Planning A*, **9**, 285–344.

Williams, H. W. C. L. (1981). Random utility theory and probabilistic choice models, in *Optimization in Locational and Transport Analysis* (Eds A. G. Wilson, J. D. Coelho, S. M. Macgill, and H. C. W. L. Williams), John Wiley, Chichester.

Williams, H. C. W. L. and Ortuzar, J. D. (1982). Behavioural theories of dispersion and the mis-specification of travel demand models, *Transportation Research B*, **16B**, 167–219.

Wrigley, N. (1979). Developments in the statistical analysis of categorical data, *Progress in Human Geography*, **3**, 315–355.

Wrigley, N. (1981). Categorical data analysis, in *Quantitative Geography: A British View* (Eds N. Wrigley and R. J. Bennett), pp. 111–122, London, Routledge and Kegan Paul.

Wrigley, N. (1984). *Categorical Data Analysis for Geographers and Environmental Scientists*, Longman, London.

Geography and the Urban Environment
Progress in Research and Applications, Volume VI
Edited by D. T. Herbert and R. J. Johnston
© 1984 John Wiley & Sons Ltd.

Chapter 3

Environmental Cognition and Travel Behaviour

Susan Hanson

In the 1960s that brash kid behavioural geography was born and proceeded to spend a great deal of youthful vigour attacking the fundamental character of one eminent forebear, economic man. The traits that behavioural geography found particularly offensive in economic man were complete information and complete rationality; these were assaulted for contributing substantially to the error component in models of spatial behaviour and, more importantly, for standing in the way of any real understanding of decisions underlying spatial behaviour and spatial patterns. Behavioural geography urged replacing austere economic man with more realistically human actors in the hope of providing more adequate explanations of observed patterns of behaviour and more accurate predictions of behaviour in new circumstances. As Downs (1981) has recently recalled, the original agenda for behavioural geography was based on the premise that 'in order to understand spatial structure, . . . we must know something of the antecedent decisions and behaviours which arrange phenomena over space' (Cox and Golledge, 1969, p. 2).

The looming spectre of economic man's omniscience and rigidly structured behaviour inspired many studies aimed at describing and explaining the way in which individuals make decisions that etch patterns on the landscape. Many of these studies focused upon the role of spatial or environmental cognition, or, as Downs (1981) has simply defined it, 'the comprehension of the arrangement and properties of phenomena on the earth's surface' (p. 101). Almost without exception, the stated purpose of research on environmental cognition has been to advance our understanding of spatial behaviour, but as both critics (e.g. Bunting and Guelke, 1979) and advocates (e.g. Moore, 1979; Pipkin, 1981a; Downs, 1981) of behavioural geography have not failed to note, relatively few empirical studies have actually linked cognition to behaviour.

The purpose of this chapter is threefold. First, I review research that has examined cognition in the context of one particular kind of spatial behaviour, namely urban travel; second, I sketch out a conceptual model of the role of

cognition in travel decision-making; and, third, I present the results of a study
that examines the relationship between the individual's information about
potential trip destination points within a city and the individual's observed
travel pattern over a thirty-five day period.

COGNITION AND URBAN TRAVEL: A REVIEW

A large number of researchers have either acknowledged or asserted that people's
information about locations is intimately linked to their behaviour in space (e.g.
Brown and Moore, 1970; Burnett, 1973, 1976; Chapin, 1974; Clark and Smith,
1979; Downs, 1970; Golledge, 1969, 1978a,b; Gould, 1975; Horton and
Reynolds, 1971; Huff, 1961; Kofoed, 1970; Lynch, 1960; Marble and Bowlby,
1968; Pred, 1967; Smith, 1976; Webber et al., 1975). The importance of
information stems quite naturally from the view that spatial behaviour is the
outcome of decision-making under conditions of uncertainty (e.g. Wolpert,
1964). Information, which presumably reduces uncertainty in decision-making,
is necessary if individual travellers are to be able to evaluate alternatives.
Several models of spatial behaviour have incorporated the notion that
individuals have limited information and rarely select unknown alternatives as
trip destinations (Cadwallader, 1975; Golant, 1971; Hanson, 1974; Lloyd and
Jennings, 1978). Moreover, two types of information about potential destinations have been identified as being useful to decision-makers: (1) information
on the location of a place, which is obviously needed if the traveller is to find a
given destination; and (2) information on the attributes or characteristics of a
place, which is required if the individual is to assess the likelihood that a
destination will satisfy a given need (Downs and Stea, 1973; Cox and Zanaras,
1973). These two types of information are associated with the designative rather
than the appraisive aspect of cognition (Harvey, 1969). That is, information
concerns only a person's awareness of elements in the urban environment, not
one's evaluation of such elements.

This paper focuses upon the designative aspect of cognition, and the following
review treats studies that have dealt primarily with this aspect of environmental
cognition. (Periodic assessments of the entire field of environmental cognition
have appeared with some regularity in the literature and are readily available
(e.g. Downs and Stea, 1973; Saarinen, 1976; Moore and Golledge, 1976; Gold,
1980). There is good reason, then, for restricting the focus here to studies of
cognition and urban travel.) The present review first considers different ways of
assessing individuals' cognitive representations of the urban environment, then
examines the factors identified as related to these cognitive representations, and
finally summarizes what is known about the relationships between cognition
and urban travel behaviour.

Assessing cognitive representations

Researchers have employed a variety of methods to tap individuals' cognitive representations of the urban environment. A plethora of methods is welcome because the problem of response bias is widely recognized (Golledge and Spector, 1978; Orleans, 1973; Pipkin, 1981a; Potter, 1979); that is, the measurement technique used can affect the outcome in systematic ways. Cognitive representations elicited via sketch maps, for example, are likely to be quite different from those elicited via verbal cues. There has not yet been, however, any systematic evaluation of the different available methods, and no one method is currently acknowledged as superior to others.

Although much of the work on individuals' cognitive representations of the urban environment was not originally conceived within a decision-making framework, one can interpret the results of such studies as indications of the amount of information subjects have about the city. The well-known sketch maps of Lynch (1960) and his followers (DeJong, 1962; Gulick, 1963; Orleans, 1973; Beck and Wood, 1976; Wong, 1979) have, for example, usually been interpreted as revealing something about respondents' levels of familiarity with different parts of the city. Such sketch maps were an early attempt to discover how limited was the information people relied upon for navigation in the city. The difficulties in measurement, inference, and aggregation posed by sketch maps prodded researchers to explore other ways of measuring individuals' cognition of urban environments. An alternative approach to generating cognitive configurations or cognitive maps has come from applying multidimensional scaling (MDS) techniques to respondents' estimates of the distances between pairs of places, usually buildings or stores that are identified by name to the respondent (MacKay et al., 1975; Golledge et al., 1976; Golledge and Spector, 1978; Golledge, 1978b). This technique taps primarily the individual's locational information about places in the city. In a different application of MDS, in which respondents evaluated a set of shopping centres, Burnett (1973) inferred the amount of attribute information held by the respondents. Both sketch maps and maps derived from MDS are frequently interpreted as reflecting the respondents' levels of familiarity with the urban environment in that the more detailed and accurate the sketch maps or the closer the MDS configuration to Euclidean 'reality', the more information the individual is assumed to have. The usefulness of information to a decision-maker might not, however, be a function of how closely the cognitive map conforms to some other, 'real' map based on Euclidean geometry. For this reason researchers have explored other ways of measuring familiarity levels.

In contrast to the above methods, which tap information levels indirectly, other studies have measured individuals' levels of familiarity more directly by asking them point blank how familiar they were with different parts of a city or elements in an urban environment. Such studies have measured information as either a dichotomous variable or an ordinal one. Cadwallader (1975), for example, asked consumers whether or not they were aware of each of five supermarkets, and Smith (1976) asked respondents to write down the location of 'known' grocery stores within Hamilton, Ontario. Potter (1979) also measured information as a binary variable by asking people to indicate on a base map of Stockport, England those shopping centres with which 'they were personally acquainted' (p. 22). Those who have measured individuals' information levels on an ordinal scale have asked respondents to indicate their familiarity with either areas or points within the city. Horton and Reynolds (1971) measured people's level of familiarity with different neighbourhoods in Cedar Rapids, Iowa, and Aldskogius (1977) had subjects indicate their familiarity with 5 km × 5 km cells on a map. Bowlby (1972) and Hanson (1976, 1978) used ordinal scales to measure levels of information with locations (food stores) that were conceptualized as points in space. Regardless of the method used to measure cognition, these studies, taken as a whole, have succeeded in documenting that urban residents operate with limited information and moreover that the amount of information held about the urban environment varies from person to person in systematic ways. The next section briefly summarizes the factors that have been shown to be related to individuals' cognitive representations or information levels.

Factors affecting cognitive representations

The focus of several studies has been the relationship of individuals' information levels or cognitive representations to selected socioeconomic and locational factors. Because researchers have taken different approaches, it is difficult to discern any clear consensus in the accumulated results, but three major factors have emerged as being particularly important to explaining interpersonal variation in cognitive representations: socioeconomic status, length of residence at current location, and the location of the residence and workplace *vis-à-vis* the major elements of urban spatial structure. In many cases the research design makes the impact of any one of these independent variables difficult to isolate. Horton and Reynolds (1971), for example, employed two cluster samples, each chosen to represent a different socioeconomic group and each located in a different part of the city. Similarly Orleans (1973) used cluster samples and focused on the variation in individuals' sketch maps as a function of social status and residential location. MacKay *et al.* (1975) examined the size of the difference between respondents' cognitive maps (derived from MDS) and the 'real' map as a function of certain personal characteristics and distance from home to nearest food store. In none of these studies was length of residence used as a stratification variable. Using two spatially clustered samples, however, Burnett (1973) held constant social status and stage in the life cycle and studied the destination selection criteria used by two groups who differed in their length of residence at present address. Other research designs have used a spatially random sample of individuals located throughout the city being studied and have assessed the impact of length of residence and various socioeconomic variables on cognitive configurations (Golledge and Spector, 1978), urban information fields (measured by number of places known and average distance from the respondent's home to the known places; Smith, 1976; Potter, 1979), and information levels (Aldskogius, 1977).

The results of these studies indicate that individuals' information levels, or the accuracy of their cognitive representations, are indeed related to length of residence (Burnett, 1973; Aldskogius, 1977; Golledge and Spector, 1978; Smith, 1976) and to certain socioeconomic variables, particularly automobile availability (MacKay et al., 1975; Aldskogius, 1977; Golledge and Spector, 1978), education and occupation (Smith, 1976), stage in the lifecycle (Bowlby, 1972; MacKay et al., 1975; Potter, 1979), and social class as determined by occupational category (Potter, 1979). What makes synthesis difficult here is, for example, the fact that whereas Smith (1976), working in Hamilton, Ontario, found that car ownership was not important but education was in explaining the size of the information field, Golledge and Spector (1978), working in Columbus, Ohio, reported that education was not important but automobile availability was in their respondents' ability to locate places accurately. In general, however, the studies have shown that information levels increase with socioeconomic status, with automobile ownership or availability, with length of residence, and with proximity to the choice set. These results lend support to Alcaly's (1976) contention that higher-income households should have more information because their marginal cost of travel is less than it is for lower-income households, and therefore their incentive to search is higher.

Cognition and urban travel

An inferred relationship between information and travel has been implicit in, and indeed has motivated, much of this work. Although Lynch's (1960) original study was not couched specifically in terms of people's levels of information, he pointed out that the ease with which one can travel within a city is probably related to the completeness and accuracy of one's mental representation of that city. Similarly others have stressed the expected close correspondence between one's daily activity pattern and the parts of the city with which one is familiar (Adams, 1969; Brown and Moore, 1970; Horton and Reynolds, 1971; Golledge and Spector, 1978; Potter, 1979). Moreover, although information about places can be obtained in a number of ways, including the print media and conversation with others, several researchers have suggested that the individual's own travel experience is the primary means of acquiring both locational and attribute information (Webber et al., 1975; Karlsson, 1958; Pocock, 1971). Because the process through which information levels emerge is inextricably linked to travel, and because information is in turn a necessary part of any travel decision, it is clear that information and travel are complexly intertwined in a circularly causal relationship (Jones, 1978; Adams, 1969; Webber *et al.*, 1975). I do not intend here or in the final section of the chapter to attempt to unravel that causal knot but only to examine how information levels, once formed, are related to a person's observed travel behaviour.

Only a handful of studies have even tried to tackle this question, and therefore the empirical evidence documenting any kind of a relationship between information and travel is disappointingly sparse. Webber *et al.* (1975) demonstrate that the information levels of rural residents about surrounding market towns are in large part a function of frequency of travel to those towns. At the intra-urban scale several studies have provided evidence that variables measuring respondents' cognition of destination attributes are more effective in predicting behaviour than are objective measures of such attributes (Burnett, 1973; Cadwallader, 1975; MacKay *et al.*, 1975; Lloyd and Jennings, 1978). Brög (1979) emphasizes the importance of including individuals' information about different travel modes in studies of mode choice and demonstrates the improved predictive power of mode choice models that recognize that certain modes are simply not considered by some people because these people lack sufficient information (both locational and attribute) about the modes. In another mode choice study Lerman and Manski (1982) have shown how modelling the diffusion of information about transit service change can help generate more accurate predictions of change in ridership. Potter (1977 and 1979) has demonstrated a close correspondence between consumers' information fields (defined in terms of the number of shopping centres known, the average distance from respondents' homes to known shopping centres, and the angular extent of the area encompassing the known centres) and their usage fields (defined in terms of the number of shopping centres used, the average distance from respondents' homes to visited centres, and the angular extent of the field). Similarly Aldskogius (1977) notes that there is a visual similarity between the map of known recreation places surrounding the city of Uppsala, Sweden and the map of places that are actually visited. There is evidence, too, that respondents seem able to estimate interpoint distances most accurately for those nodes or places that are close to places they report visiting regularly (Golledge and Spector, 1978). These studies do provide evidence that, at least in some general way, a link exists between information levels and travel patterns, but they provide little insight as the specific nature of this link. One study that does demonstrate more specifically the effect of information on travel is Burnett's (1973).

In an effort to identify the effects of learning on spatial choice, Burnett (1973) studied travel to women's clothing stores for two groups of women who differed in their average length of residence (2.5 years versus 9.5 years) at their present address. Store use was measured by the number of centres visited and the amount of money spent at each shopping centre by the women in each sample group during the preceding six months. Burnett found that the group with higher information levels (those who had lived at their current address for a longer time) concentrated a higher percentage of their stops and expenditure for clothing at the most preferred centre. This finding supports the widely held belief that after an initial period of spatial learning, in which many places are visited on an experimental basis, travellers settle into a habitual or stereotyped pattern of behaviour, in which a smaller number of places are visited regularly. Other studies (e.g. Louviere, 1981; Schuler, 1979; Recker and Schuler, 1981) have considered the relationship between cognitive representations and choice, but their focus has been primarily on individuals' evaluation of destination attributes rather than on the effect of information *per se*.

Existing evidence documenting the relationship between cognitive representations and overt travel behaviour is, in short, rather thin. Moreover, the studies reviewed here suffer from a number of shortcomings that make generalization difficult. Most have employed small samples and have considered behaviour with respect to only one type of destination, most often supermarkets (e.g. Cadwallader, 1975; MacKay *et al.*, 1975; Lloyd and Jennings, 1978) or shopping centres (e.g. Potter, 1977, 1979). In addition the number of supermarkets considered in the choice set has been extremely small (e.g. five in Cadwallader's study and six in the MacKay *et al.* study), and each study has examined the link between cognition and travel for only one purpose, which is usually shopping. As a result we know very little about what aspects of overall travel patterns are related to information levels. In addition, all of the studies reviewed here suffer from what I believe to be a major methodological flaw in that: (1) they measure 'observed behaviour' by means of the respondent's reported use, non-use, or frequency of use of a given destination; and (2) these data are collected at the same time at which data on information levels are also collected. When people are asked in the same interview or on the same mailed questionnaire what places they know about and what places they visit, it should come as no surprise that the two sets of places turn out to be rather similar. Moreover, the results of Massam and Bouchard's (1976) study raise the question as to how closely measures of respondents' reported behaviour conform to their actual movement patterns.

In sum, despite a long-held and active curiosity about the nature of the relationships between information and travel (or between awareness space and action space), relatively little is currently known about how the designative aspect of cognition is related to urban travel, especially to the individual's overall out-of-home travel-activity pattern, as opposed to shopping for, say, food or clothing. In the third part of this chapter I report an empirical investigation of precisely this issue. The next section sketches out a conceptual model of the role of information in travel decisions and develops, within a decision-making framework, a rationale for measuring individuals' information levels in terms of their subjectively perceived familiarity with various locations within the city.

INFORMATION IN TRAVEL DECISIONS: A CONCEPTUAL MODEL

Information helps to distinguish one object in a choice set from another and can be measured by the amount that uncertainty has been reduced (Rapoport, 1956). Marble (1967) applied Luce and Raiffa's (1957) conceptualization of decision-making under varying degrees of uncertainty to urban destination choice; he viewed travellers as making decisions under conditions of certainty, uncertainty, or risk. Individuals make decisions with *certainty* if every choice leads to a known outcome, with *uncertainty* if each choice can result in one of several possible outcomes, each of which occurs with an unknown probability, and with *risk* if each choice leads to one of a known set of outcomes, each occurring with a known probability. In this context the function of information is to increase the person's knowledge of the *a priori* distribution of probabilities associated with elements in the choice set. Information about destinations permits travellers to move from a state of uncertainty to one of risk or even, under special conditions, certainty. Note that meaning is not the same as information, and the content, value, or validity of the information is not measured—only the amount. The two concepts of choice and probability are thus closely bound up with the concept of information (Frick, 1959).

Destination selection requires travellers to acquire the two types of information mentioned earlier: information pertaining to the locations of places—their location relative to the residence, the workplace, the CBD, and to other elements in the urban environment—and information on the attributes of places; for shops, attribute information would pertain to size, product line, store layout, and other aspects associated primarily with store interiors. *Locational information* reduces uncertainty as to where to find a given place and enables the traveller to assess the expected costs of finding one place in the choice set as opposed to another. The concept of locational information can thus be linked to that of the circular probable error (see for example, Neft, 1966) where the ease and accuracy with which a place can be found is a function of how well the individual 'knows' its location. *Attribute information* increases the predictability of what the traveller will find once at the location.

The individual draws upon these two types of information when selecting one or more potential destinations from a set of opportunities, e.g. grocery stores. Each store in the opportunity set $(O_1, O_2, \ldots, O_n)$ can be described by a number of different time-dependent states of nature or prevailing conditions $(S_1, S_2, \ldots, S_m)$. In the case of food stores, S_i is a vector whose elements are store characteristics such as travel time from the residence, workplace, CBD, or other shops; proximity to parking space; prices; level of service; product line; store cleanliness; and availability of credit.

In his early work on travel as a decision process, Marble (1967) suggested that the choice situation facing a traveller could be summarized as a decision matrix of n rows, each representing a given opportunity (destination), and m columns, each corresponding to a possible state of nature. The traveller assigns a utility, u_{ij}, to each outcome, or opportunity state of nature combination. Marble assumed decision-making under conditions of risk, meaning that the decision-maker knows the probability of occurrence, P_j, for each state of nature, S_j. Under these conditions the expected payoff of visiting the ith destination is $p_j u_{ij}$.

In Marble's discussion the probability distribution that is assumed to exist over the m states of nature is assumed identical for all n opportunities. That is, the probability of occurrence of the jth state of nature does not vary from opportunity to opportunity. For the choice situation facing the urban traveller, however, the probability distribution over the states of nature is likely to vary over destinations. Hence we assume here that for each opportunity, O_i, there is some 'actual' probability distribution over the states of nature. That is, there exists P_{ij}, the probability that the ith store will take on the jth state of nature. The P_{ij} are exhaustive and mutually exclusive probabilities representing the relative frequency of each state of nature in the long run. In this case the expected payoff for the ith store is equal to $\sum_j p_j u_{ij}$.

Clearly the P_{ij} play an important role in travel decisions, but the assumption of known P_{ij}'s is valid only when the traveller has complete information. When we acknowledge that decisions are made with incomplete information, we can suppose that travellers base decisions on subjective estimates, P_{ij}^*, of the 'actual' probability distributions over the states of nature. Information on potential destinations should enable the traveller to make more accurate estimates of the probability distributions over the states of nature. The more information the individual has about a given store, the closer the subjective probability, P_{ij}^*, will be to the actual probability, P_{ij}. Information, then, helps the traveller to minimize $|P_{ij} - P_{ij}^*|$. The amount of information the decision-maker has about destination i is given by $\Delta_i = (\sum |P_{ij} - P_{ij}^*|)^{-1}$; (for convenience, the inverse is used so that Δ_i increases as the individual's information level increases).

Operationalizing this concept of information would require defining all the m possible states of nature, identifying the probability, P_{ij}, of occurrence of each state for each of the n destinations in the opportunity set, and then measuring travellers' estimated probabilities, P_{ij}^*, of these states. Clearly the concept poses formidable measurement and data-collection problems. We need to make a number of simplifying assumptions in order to operationalize it.

The first such assumption is that for each opportunity, O_i, the probability distribution over the states of nature is extremely peaked over one given state, S_{ik}. This appears reasonable inasmuch as stores do attempt to present a stable image over time in the short run. S_{ik} therefore represents the most probable state of nature for destination i, and measurements of information levels need be made only with reference to this most probable state. The information measure,

Δ_i, is thereby simplified from:

$$\Delta_i = \left(\sum_{j=1}^{m} P_{ij} - P_{ij}^* \right)^{-1} \tag{3.1}$$

to

$$\Delta_i = (|P_{ik} - P_{ik}^*|)^{-1}. \tag{3.2}$$

The second simplification stems from the observation that individuals are more likely to base travel decisions on their confidence in the subjective estimates, P_{ik}^*, than on the absolute value of Δ_i. Hence a measure of information that would seem relevant to travel decisions is

$$\Delta_i' = (P_{ik} - P_{ik}^*)^{-1}, \tag{3.3}$$

which is the individual's perceived difference between the actual probability of the most probable state and his or her own estimate of that probability. If a person places a great deal of confidence in his or her subjective estimate, P_{ik}^*, then Δ_i' will be large; if he or she thinks the subjective estimate of P_{ik} is far from the actual probability, then Δ' will be small.

A final step in deriving an appropriate measure of information about potential destinations is to decompose Δ' into the two types of information discussed earlier. The assumption is made that the two types of information are additive so that $\Delta' = a + b$, where a = locational information, and b = attribute information. To sum up, an appropriate measure of the information levels of a sample of urban residents would tap the amount of locational information and the amount of attribute information that respondents have about a given set of opportunities and would, in addition, reflect the respondents' subjective evaluation of the amount of information possessed about specific places.

This discussion sees travellers as attempting to gain information about elements in an opportunity set in order to proceed with the business of evaluation and choice. The process by which individuals accumulate spatial information over time has been admirably described elsewhere (e.g. Golledge, 1969; MacKay, 1977; Horton and Reynolds, 1971; Schneider, 1975; Burnett, 1973, 1976; Golledge and Spector, 1978) and will not be repeated here. Suffice it to say that learning occurs as the result of both accidental and deliberate search, that information can be obtained from a number of different sources (one of which is travel), and that one's information level at any one point in time can be viewed as a function not only of stage in the learning process but also, as noted above, of residential location and other characteristics of the individual and household.

It is clear, nevertheless, that vigorous search ceases before the individual has acquired complete or even abundant information (e.g. Lanzetta and Kanareff, 1962; Morlock, 1967), and the traveller, once satisfied with the limited amount of information that has been gleaned from the environment, is believed to settle into a routine of habitually visiting a relatively small number of destinations

(Golledge, 1969; Burnett, 1973; Marble and Bowlby, 1968). It is worth noting, however, that because a traveller's needs change over time in the long run and because the urban travel environment also constantly changes (with the birth and death of shops or the initiation and termination of transit services, for example), the traveller's need for acquiring new information about the city does not cease with the adoption of an 'habitual' pattern of spatial behaviour.

The following section compares the travel-activity patterns of two groups of urban residents who differ in the amount of information they hold about the urban environment. As I noted in the previous section, whereas geographers have repeatedly suggested that there should be a strong relationship between cognition and movement patterns (e.g. Marble and Bowlby, 1968; Brown and Moore, 1970; Golledge, 1978a), little previous empirical work exists to guide expectations regarding the ways in which information might be related to observed travel-activity patterns. There is the general expectation that the size of one's 'action space' (Horton and Reynolds, 1971), 'awareness space' (Brown and Moore, 1970) or 'information field' (Smith, 1976; Potter, 1979) reflects the spatial extent and intensity of one's 'activity space' or 'movement field', both of which are defined in terms of the places actually visited. More specific expectations have been suggested by Kaplan (1976), who argues that the more places about which the individual has information, the greater will be his or her potential choice in selecting a destination, the greater the ease with which a new place can be located, and the greater the individual's flexibility or ability to innovate or to solve problems in daily travel. In this regard it is worth emphasizing that information should play a critical role in enabling the individual to select that destination of a particular type (e.g. food stores) that has the highest utility, given the set of other needs to be met at any given time and the set of other places to be visited on any particular multipurpose journey (Hanson, 1980). We might expect, therefore, that the travel-activity patterns of those individuals with more information about the urban setting will exhibit a richer variety of destinations visited, will consist of more complex trip structures, and will involve travelling over greater distances than will the travel patterns of those with low information levels. If, however, those with less information are still at the early stages of the learning process and are therefore still actively engaged in search, then we would expect that they would visit more different destinations than would the group with higher information levels who could be expected to have settled into habitual behaviour patterns.

AN EMPIRICAL STUDY OF COGNITION AND TRAVEL

The empirical portion of this chapter is based upon data collected in a household travel survey carried out in Uppsala, Sweden, a city of about 100 000 people. The survey gathered detailed information on the daily travel, information levels, and socioeconomic characteristics of the members of some 300 sample households located throughout the Uppsala urbanized area. The sample households constitute a stratified random sample, drawn from the Swedish Population Register for Uppsala after the sampling frame had been stratified into six life-cycle groups. The analysis reported here is carried out on the members of 92 households (138 individuals) that were selected randomly from the larger sample in such a way as to constitute the equivalent of a simple random sample of Uppsala's households. That is, in the ninety-two-household sample each life-cycle group is represented in proportion to its occurrence in the Uppsala population.

The travel data were collected by means of a self-administered travel diary in which each individual recorded information on all out-of-home travel and activities undertaken over a period of thirty-five consecutive days. A *trip* was defined as a journey that began and ended at the person's residence, and consisted of one or more *stops*, places where the person interrupted the trip to participate in an activity, such as shopping, visiting a bank, dropping a child at day care, or seeing a film. For each stop on each trip the respondent indicated on the diary form the time of arrival at and departure from the stop, the mode of transport used (including walk and bike as well as the usual motorized modes), the type of place visited (subsequently coded to one of ninety-nine land uses such as department store, bank, day-care centre, or theatre), the nature of the activity engaged in (coded to one of seventy activities such as make a purchase, deposit or withdraw money, or jogging), the location of the stop (geocoded to point locations corresponding to the street addresses of the establishments or residences), and the amount of money spent at the destination. Additional details of the travel-diary study design are described in Hanson and Huff (1982). A large number of measures have been computed from these longitudinal travel data, each measure describing a particular aspect of the individual's travel over the thirty-five-day period.

Data on the individual's information levels and sociodemographic characteristics were collected in a personal interview at the end of the time during which respondents kept their travel diaries. (In fact there was a four-week hiatus between the end of the intensive diary-recording period and the final interview.) The sociodemographic data include motor-vehicle ownership, possession of a driver's licence, employment status (number of hours worked per week outside the home), occupation, education, marital status, age, sex, household size, household income, and length of residence.

One question asked in the final interview was: 'How many times per month do you go food shopping?' The question was motivated by curiosity about the relationship between behaviour reported in an interview and behaviour recorded in a travel diary. When the number of times reported in the interview (X_1) is compared to the number of food-store stops recorded in four weeks of the individual's diary (X_2), the sample means for the two variables are similar, but people tend to report higher stop frequencies in the interview ($\bar{X}_1 = 11.9$ and

$\bar{X}_2 = 10.0$). The correlation between the two variables is, however, not exceptionally high; $r = 0.54$. If we assume that the diary data represent a closer approximation to 'actual' behaviour, these results lend support to Massam and Bouchard's (1976) contention that there is likely to be a discrepancy between what people say they do and what they actually do.

The cognitive data measure the respondent's subjective assessment of his or her level of familiarity with each element of two opportunity sets in the city: the set of all food stores and the set of all women's clothing stores. For each element in each of the two opportunity sets, the subject was to mark on a seven-point ordinal scale his or her level of familiarity with the location of the store and on a second scale to indicate level of familiarity with the store's interior attributes. The stores were described by name, street address, and a brief description of the location—for example: Hälso Livs, St. Persgatan 3, in the centrum, just off Svartbäcksgatan. In addition, the interviewers had maps of the city on which they could point out the location of a store if the respondent was not certain which store was being described.

Food stores were chosen as stimuli for a number of reasons. First, they approximate points in urban space, and therefore a person's level of familiarity is unlikely to vary greatly with different parts of the stimulus, as is the case when large areas (e.g. neighbourhoods) are used as stimuli. Second, the ninety-four food stores in Uppsala constitute a spatially dispersed, yet functionally similar set of locations (see Figure 3.1). Food store locations are treated here as points sampled from urban space, and the familiarity levels with these locations are considered points sampled from the individual's cognitive representation of urban space. The clothing stores, by contrast, have a highly clustered spatial distribution as they are mostly in the CBD. Although the motivation is relatively low for anyone to collect detailed information on a large number of food stores (because the penalty for a suboptimal choice of store is not high; Hansen, 1972), we can expect to find interpersonal differences among the subjects in terms of the number of different grocery-store locations they have become familiar with because of what may be termed accidental search or latent learning, a result of travelling around the city for purposes other than food shopping (LaGory and Pipkin, 1981).

In two earlier studies of the cognitive levels of urban residents (Hanson, 1976; Hanson, 1978) the measurement technique described above was employed in examining the spatial characteristics of the information levels of the sample as a whole. Here the focus is on the proportion of the opportunity set known or not known by an individual and on how information, measured in this dichotomous way, is related to travel. More specifically, the present analysis addresses the question: 'How do the travel-activity patterns of those with high information levels differ from those with low information levels?'

In order to examine the nature of the relationship between cognitive levels and travel, the sample of 138 individuals has been divided into thirds on the

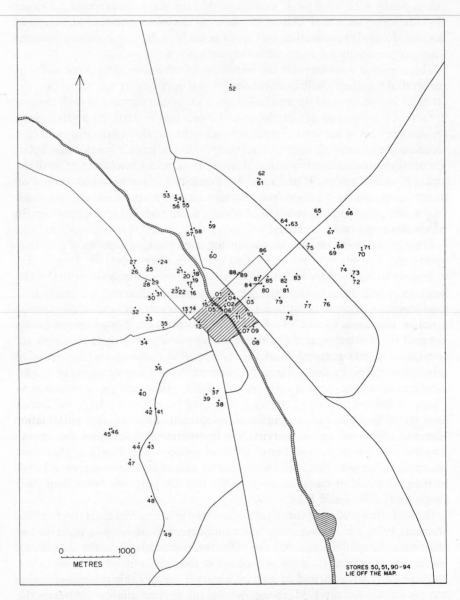

FIGURE 3.1. Food stores, Uppsala, Sweden

basis of the amount of information possessed, and the travel behaviour of the top third (those who are familiar with many places) is compared with that of the bottom third (those who are familiar with only a few places). This extreme and simple strategy is intentionally pursued for, by focusing on groups with clearly divergent information levels, we should be able to determine what aspects of travel (if any) are related to the individual's level of information about potential destinations.

Defining the groups

Because familiarity with food-store locations was considered a valid surrogate for familiarity with different places throughout the city, 'familiarity with food-store locations' was the variable used to distinguish those with high from those with low information levels. The sample was partitioned into thirds on the basis of the number of food-store locations the individual said he or she knew about; a store was considered known if the respondent placed it above category 1 on the ordinal scale measuring familiarity with store locations. (Category 1 was to be checked if a store was totally unfamiliar to the respondent; hence the seven-point ordinal scale is dichotomized here such that stores are designated as either known or unknown.) The group of respondents with the highest levels of information consists of the forty-two individuals who are at least somewhat familiar with the locations of forty-three or more stores; the group with the lowest information levels is made up of forty people who are familiar with the locations of fewer than twenty-three stores. For the sake of simplicity, henceforth these groups will be called the 'highs' and the 'lows'.

A number of tests explore the extent to which the information levels of the two groups differ significantly and the degree to which 'number of food-store locations known' is a viable indication of an individual's level of information about locations throughout the city. The first examines whether the two groups clearly differ in the *amount* of information each has about food-store locations and interior attributes. A unidimensional scaling technique (described in detail in Hanson, 1978) was used to transform each group's ordinal-scale responses to an interval scale and to compute for each stimulus (in this case each food store) a scale score (in this case a 'familiarity score') indicating the group's mean familiarity level with that store. Because the scale scores computed for two different groups in two separate runs are not comparable (Torgerson, 1958), the two groups were scaled together on a single interval scale. The input consisted of the responses of the highs to the ninety-four grocery stores and the responses of the lows to the same stores. The number of stimuli to be scaled was, then, 188. This enables direct comparison of the information levels of the highs and the lows, and as shown in the distribution of the familiarity scores in Figures 3.2 and 3.3, the highs do indeed not only know about more places, but also hold more information about these places as well.

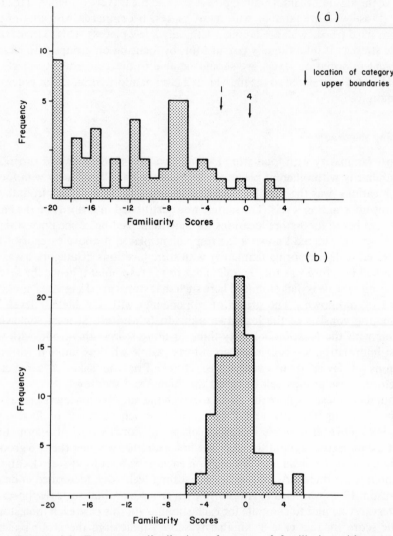

FIGURE 3.2. Frequency distribution of scores of familiarity with store location. (a) Individuals with low information levels. (b) Individuals with high information levels

A second test looked at the relationship between 'familiarity with food-store location' and the other cognitive variables for which data were collected. The results, shown in Table 3.1, demonstrate that those who are familiar with a large portion of the food-store opportunity set are also familiar with a large portion of the women's-clothing-store opportunity set (an opportunity set with a highly

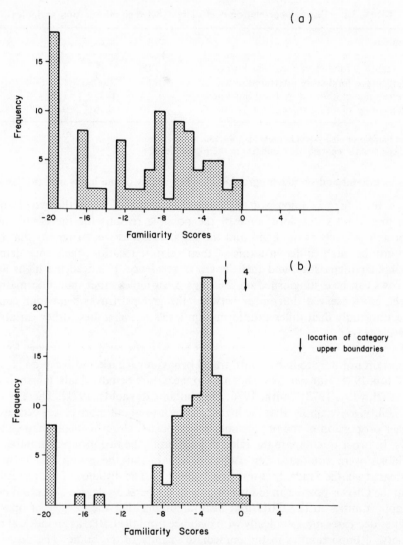

FIGURE 3.3. Frequency distribution of scores of familiarity with store interior. (a) Individuals with low information levels. (b) Individuals with high information levels.

clustered spatial distribution); moreover, there is a close correspondence between the amount of locational and the amount of attribute information one is likely to have about food stores. These checks indicate that if information levels are related to travel behaviour, we are justified in expecting that the two groups will display marked differences in their travel-activity patterns.

TABLE 3.1.   Pearson correlation coefficients* between information variables

Variables	1	2	3	4
1 Percentage food-store locations known	1.00			
2 Percentage food-store interiors known	0.63	1.00		
3 Percentage clothing-store locations known	0.54	0.38	1.00	
4 Percentage clothing-store interiors known	0.20	0.36	0.75	1.00

Note: Sample of ninety-two households, $N = 138$.
* All coefficients reported are significant at the $p < 0.05$ level.

The locational and sociodemographic characteristics of the highs and the lows

Before turning to a comparison of the travel-activity patterns of the two groups, it is important to explore some of the possible reasons for the contrasting information levels of the highs and the lows. Previous work suggests that the two groups might differ in terms of their relative location, their sociodemographic characteristics, and their length of residence. If indeed the highs and the lows can be distinguished on the basis of variables other than information levels, any observed differences between the groups' travel behaviour could reflect not only their different information levels but also these other variables as well.

The spatial distribution of activity sites *vis-à-vis* the residence has been found important not only to individuals' travel behaviour (Clark and Rushton, 1970; Rushton, 1971; Hanson, 1982) but also to the nature of individuals' information levels (Bowlby, 1972; Smith, 1976; Horton and Reynolds, 1971). There is the possibility, for example, that the highs might know about more places because a higher proportion of the opportunity set is located closer to them than to the lows. In order to compare the relative location of the two groups a number of variables were computed for each individual, and the group means were compared via the Students' t-test (see Table 3.2). The distance of the residence from the CBD is used as an index not only of the person's degree of accessibility to opportunities in the CBD, but also, assuming that the density of opportunities decreases monotonically with distance from the CBD, as an index of the density of opportunities in the immediate vicinity of the home. The distance from home to work and the distance from the workplace to the CBD are additional variables that measure the access of employed persons to activity sites over the course of the day. A number of other measures of the spatial distribution of establishments relative to the home and work location of each individual were also computed. The number of establishments within 1.0 kilometre of home is a more specific measure of the density of activity sites close to home, and the number of different land-use types within 3.5 kilometres of home measures the diversity of establishments within a middle-range distance. For those in each group who were employed outside the home, these two measures

TABLE 3.2. Measures* of relative location: Individuals with high and low information levels

	Individual's Information Level		
	High ($N=42$) x and (s)	Low ($N=40$) x and (s)	t-value
Distance from home to CBD	1.98 (0.92)	2.00 (0.90)	0.90
Distance from home to work	2.00 (1.21)	1.72 (1.14)	0.49
Distance from work to CBD	1.63 (1.26)	1.00 (0.78)	0.07
Number of establishments within 1.0 km of home	312.1 (351.0)	244.5 (311.0)	0.92
Number of different land use types† within 3.5 km of home	71.7 (3.3)	71.9 (3.6)	−0.27
Number of establishments within 1.0 km of work	483.8 (448.0)	651.6 (456.0)	−1.28
Numbers of different land use types within 3.5 km of work	70.6 (7.4)	72.9 (0.2)	−1.78

* All distance measures are airline distances in kilometres.
† The ninety-nine land-use codes identify particular types of establishments such as food store, cafe, park, doctor's office.

were also computed for the workplace. As the results in Table 3.2 indicate, in no case were the means of the distributions significantly different for the two groups. The evidence shows, therefore, that the two groups are located at similar distances from the CBD and from activity sites.

Given that the two groups are located similarly *vis-à-vis* the opportunity set, the source of the difference in their information levels is likely to be in length of residence or socioeconomic status. As outlined earlier, stage in the learning process is expected to bear a strong relationship to the amount of information accumulated, and length of residence at a particular location is the variable usually employed as a surrogate measure of stage in the learning process. Here two length-of-residence variables are used: number of years in Uppsala and number of years at present address. A comparison of the two groups in terms of their length of residence in Uppsala and at their present address reveals that there are indeed significant differences between the highs and the lows. Although most of the people in both groups are long-term residents of Uppsala, a larger proportion of the lows than of the highs has lived in the city for less than six years (31.5 per cent of the lows versus 7.9 per cent of the highs), and a larger percentage of the highs have lived in Uppsala for more than nine years (see Table 3.3). A higher proportion of the highs than of the lows have also lived at their

TABLE 3.3. Length of residence in Uppsala:
Individuals with high and low information
levels

Years in Uppsala	Individual's information level	
	High	Low
⩽1	1	3
	(2.6)*	(7.9)
2–5	2	9
	(5.3)	(23.6)
6–9	5	7
	(78.9)	(18.5)
⩾10	30	19
	(78.9)	(50.0)
Totals	38	38
	(100.0)	(100.0)

Note: $\chi^2 = 8.23$, df $= 3$, $p < 0.025$ (one-tailed test).
* Column percentages are in parentheses.

present address for more than nine years, although about one-fifth of the highs
have lived at their present address for less than two years (see Table 3.4). What
is interesting about these results is that the lows are not comprised primarily of
relative newcomers to the city, and fully half of the lows have lived in Uppsala at
least ten years. Because practically all of the members of both groups have lived
in Uppsala for at least two years, we can expect that the members of both the
highs and the lows have moved beyond the initial stage of intense search and
learning and that members of both groups will have established somewhat
stable behaviour patterns.

In addition to reflecting this difference in duration of residence, the divergent
information levels of the highs and the lows might also reflect intergroup
differences in needs, aspirations, and constraints all of which could affect one's
motivation and ability to search. These factors are usually assumed to vary as a
function of sociodemographic status. Although previous studies would lead us
to hypothesize that the highs would be characterized by higher socioeconomic
status (measured by occupation, education, and income), in fact there is very
little difference between the highs and the lows in average years of education,
average annual household income before taxes, and the occupational status of
employed persons (measured by the interval-scaled standard international
occupational prestige scale; see Lin, 1976). Similarly, although the availability
of personal transportation has been identified as important to information
levels, the two groups do not differ in terms of the number of automobiles owned

TABLE 3.4. Length of residence at present address: Individuals with high and low information levels

Years at present address	Individual's information level	
	High	Low
≤ 1	8 (21.2)*	3 (7.9)
2–5	6 (15.7)	15 (39.5)
6–9	6 (15.7)	7 (18.4)
≥ 10	18 (47.4)	13 (34.2)
Totals	38 (100.0)	38 (100.0)

Note: $\chi^2 = 7.0$, df = 3, $p < 0.05$ (one-tailed test).
* Column percentages are in parentheses.

per household, the proportion of each group holding a driver's licence, or auto availability (measured as the number of motor vehicles in the household divided by the number of people in the household with a driver's licence). One might hypothesize further that the highs are more likely to belong to larger households because they would then have a higher incentive to search, but the highs and the lows in fact come from households that are approximately the same size. Furthermore, the two groups are identical in their respective proportions of men and women. This is an important finding, for it lends credence to the notion that 'number of food-store locations known' is indeed a viable surrogate for familiarity with different places within the city and is not simply a measure tapping information acquired by one's shopping for food or by one's being a household's primary food shopper. If it were such a measure, then we could expect most of the highs to be women and most of the lows to be men, because an earlier study (Hanson and Hanson, 1980) has shown that the women in Uppsala do most of the food shopping. As it is, however, only half of the highs and fully half of the lows are women.

Despite all these similarities, there are two demographic variables that do distinguish the highs from the lows. One is age; with an average age of 39, the highs are significantly younger than the lows, whose average age is 55. The second important difference between the two groups lies in their employment status, for nearly half of the lows do not work outside the home and thirteen out of the forty in the group (32 per cent) are retired. This is in contrast to the highs, of whom only 19 per cent do not work and only 7 per cent are retired. The additional obligatory travel associated with working outside the home appears to play a role in increasing information levels.

In sum, then, the highs tend to be younger people who are active in the labour force and who have lived in Uppsala longer than the lows. The lows are generally older people, a lower percentage of whom are in the labour force and also a lower percentage of whom are long-term residents of Uppsala. These results indicate that within any urban population there will be groups with high and low information levels, but information level is not likely to be strictly a function of length of residence.

The travel activity patterns of the highs and the lows

Although information about potential destinations is unlikely to have an impact on all aspects of travel behaviour, we might expect, on the basis of the work reviewed in an earlier portion of this chapter, that the highs and lows will differ in the number and complexity of their trips, the variety of places visited, the modes used, and the spatial distribution of destinations. From each individual's thirty-five-day travel diary a number of measures have been developed, each describing behaviour over the five-week period. The following analysis uses these measures as the basis for comparing the travel-activity patterns of the highs and the lows, and employs the Student's t-test to test for a significant difference between the group means on each measure.

A number of measures describing trip generation and trip complexity are shown in Table 3.5. The picture that emerges from the material presented here is one of far greater travel activity among those with high information levels. The highs make significantly more trips and more stops than do the lows. Of perhaps greater interest is the finding that although the lows do not make significantly fewer one- and two-stop trips, they are distinctly less likely than are the highs to undertake more complex trips, that is trips with three or more stops. Moreover, this higher level of trip-making obtains not only on weekdays but also at weekends, implying that the higher level of trip generation among the highs is not simply a reflection of the fact that a larger proportion of them are employed and therefore make the journey to work. When the detailed activity codes are aggregated into the five standard trip-purpose categories (shop, social, work, recreation, and personal business), the highs are found to make more stops than the lows for every trip purpose, but the difference is statistically significant only for work (the average number of work stops is 23.4 for the highs and 15.9 for the lows; $t = 1.98$, $p = 0.05$). The evidence suggests, therefore, that although the higher level of trip-making among the highs is not attributable only to their employment status, the journey to work is the source of much of the difference. Of particular interest is that there is no difference between the two groups in the number of stops at food stores. Here is additional evidence that the method of

TABLE 3.5. Measures of trip-making over a thirty-five-day period: Individuals with high and low information levels

	Individual's Information Level		
	High $N=42$ x and (s)	Low $N=40$ x and (s)	t-value
Number of trips	51.1 (18.1)	43.2 (17.2)	2.02*
Number of stops	140.6 (44.6)	109.7 (44.6)	3.08†
Number of single-stop trips	28.5 (17.4)	25.8 (15.4)	0.75
Number of two-stop trips	14.2 (7.3)	12.2 (6.9)	1.30
Number of three-stop trips	3.7 (4.1)	2.3 (2.3)	1.88*
Number of four-stop trips	2.8 (2.6)	1.3 (1.5)	3.09†
Number of trips with five or more stops	1.7 (2.4)	0.4 (1.3)	3.07†
Number of trips on weekdays	38.4 (14.6)	31.7 (14.4)	2.08*
Number of stops on weekdays	107.6 (35.3)	85.7 (47.5)	2.37†
Number of trips on weekends	12.5 (4.7)	10.3 (4.8)	2.11*
Number of stops on weekends	32.9 (12.9)	25.9 (12.3)	2.50†
Number of stops at food stores	10.5 (8.8)	10.9 (8.9)	−0.19

* $p < 0.05$ (one-tailed test).
† $p < 0.01$ (one-tailed test).

measuring information levels does indeed reflect familiarity with different locations within the city and is not a measure of the individual's involvement in food shopping.

A second consideration in the comparison of the two groups' travel-activity patterns is the spatial distribution of the destinations visited. Much of the existing literature on mental maps and cognitive representations would lead us to expect that the lows should exhibit a destination choice pattern that is spatially more restricted than that of the highs. The measures shown in Table 3.6 indicate, however, that although the highs covered more kilometres during the five weeks, the greater distance travelled reflects this group's more intense level of trip-making, because there is no difference between the highs and the

TABLE 3.6. Spatial measures* of the thirty-five-day travel-activity pattern: Individuals with high and low information levels

	Individual's information level		
	High (N=42) $\bar{x}$ and (s)	Low (N=40) $\bar{x}$ and (s)	t-value
Total distance travelled	507.7 (374.6)	356.9 (257.8)	2.09†
Average distance from destinations visited to centroid of activity space	1.3 (0.5)	1.1 (1.0)	0.65
Average distance from home to centroid of activity space	1.4 (0.8)	1.2 (0.9)	1.09
Average distance from destinations visited to home	2.2 (0.9)	2.0 (1.1)	1.08

* Airline distance in kilometres.
† $p < 0.05$ (one-tailed test).

lows on other measures of the spatial distribution of destinations. In order to examine the spatial extent of the individual's travel-activity pattern or activity space, a number of centrographic measures were computed on the set of destinations visited by the individual over the thirty-five days. Each element in the two-dimensional point set describing a person's actual trip destinations was weighted by contact frequency. As the measures in Table 3.6 show, the points in the activity space of the highs tend to be located slightly farther from the centroid of the activity space and slightly farther from home, but the intergroup differences are not large enough to be statistically significant. Clearly there is little difference in the spatial extent of the two groups' activity spaces, and there is also no evidence that the highs regularly select destinations at greater distances than those selected by the lows. These results run counter to those reported by Potter (1977, 1979), who found a close relationship between individuals' information fields and their usage fields and found considerable spatial variation in both; it is possible, as pointed out earlier, that the close relationship uncovered in his study reflects the method of data collection.

Some researchers have argued that the travel modes used most frequently by a person should have an impact on the amount of information accumulated about the environment. Beck and Wood (1976), for example, found that automobile drivers were able to draw more accurate mental maps than were transit riders and that those who relied a great deal on foot transportation drew the poorest maps. We might expect the highs, therefore, to make a larger proportion of their stops by automobile and the lows to make a larger proportion of their stops on foot. The results show, however, that the

TABLE 3.7. Proportion of individual's movements that were made by each mode: Individuals with high and low information levels

| | Individual information level | | |
	High $N=42$ $\bar{x}$ and (s)	Low $N=40$ $\bar{x}$ and (s)	t-value
Walk	0.37 (0.25)	0.40 (0.30)	0.64
Cycle	0.13 (0.21)	0.16 (0.22)	0.64
Bus	0.14 (0.18)	0.14 (0.20)	0.99
Car driver	0.21 (0.27)	0.18 (0.29)	0.70
Car passenger	0.13 (0.13)	0.09 (0.13)	0.18

proportion of a person's travel done by one mode as opposed to another is not related to information level (Table 3.7). Although it is interesting to note (in so far as the results are congruent with expectations) that the highs drive cars more often and the lows walk more often, these differences are not large enough to be statistically signfiicant. Two groups make essentially similar use of each mode.

Perhaps the most interesting set of differences between the two groups' overall activity patterns lies in the variety of destinations visited. As Table 3.8 demonstrates, people with high information levels contacted more different (unique) locations during the study period (where a location is defined by the x,y coordinates of the destination) than did people with low information levels. The highs also visited significantly more different types of land use and engaged in a significantly greater number of out-of-home activities than did the lows. Of particular interest is that there is no difference between the two groups in number of different food stores visited. Lloyd (1977) has suggested that shopping for convenience goods such as food should be the first type of spatial behaviour to become routinized after a move. Given that very few persons from either group have lived in Uppsala for less than two years, the one function for which both groups should exhibit stereotyped behaviour is food shopping. The evidence in Table 3.8 indicates that despite their different information levels, the highs and the lows appear to be at the same stage of learning about food-shopping alternatives. The average number of food stores visited during the study period is essentially the same and members of both groups spread their patronage over several stores, with almost half of the stops for food being made at the most preferred shop.

TABLE 3.8. Measures of variety in the individual's thirty-five-day travel-activity pattern: Individuals with high and low information levels

	Individual's information level		
	High ($N=42$) $\bar{x}$ and (s)	Low ($N=40$) $\bar{x}$ and (s)	t-value
Number of unique locations (street addresses) visited	33.2 (10.4)	25.8 (9.3)	3.31§
Number of different land use types* visited	20.3 (5.6)	17.6 (6.5)	1.97‡
Number of different activities† engaged in	16.0 (4.2)	13.5 (4.1)	2.73§
Number of different food stores visited	3.6 (2.3)	3.5 (2.3)	0.28
Proportion of person's total stops at food stores that was made at the most frequently visited store	0.47 (0.26)	0.48 (0.29)	−0.11

* Land use at destination, coded to ninety-nine categories such as bank, hardware store, other person's home.
† Activity at destination, coded to seventy categories such as purchase goods or services, pay bills, visit relatives.
‡ $p < 0.05$ (one-tailed test).
§ $p < 0.01$ (one-tailed test).

The findings summarized in Table 3.8 suggest that the popular conception of the learning process as one in which the individual, through search, progressively narrows down the choice set to a few alternatives is overly simplistic. The data imply that having more information about places throughout the city does indeed enable the traveller to solve problems, as Kaplan (1976) has posited. There is evidence that the particular destination selected at any one time depends in part on whether the trip is to be single or multiple-stop and, if multiple-stop, depends on the other places to be visited on the trip (Hanson, 1980). The facts that the highs visit more locations and that they conduct more multiple-purpose trips suggests (though it does not prove) that information is useful to the traveller in planning complex trips. Necessary for proof would be measures on the number of different establishments of a certain type that were visited by each individual, especially establishments of higher-order functions. This has not been attempted here in part because a five-week period is insufficiently long to observe repetitive travel to higher-order functions.

CONCLUSION

To sum up, the comparison of the travel-activity patterns of the highs and the lows has identified a number of significant differences between the groups, but these differences are more subtle and complex than previous work had indicated they might be. Those with information about more locations within the urban environment travel more frequently and make more complex, multistop trips than do people with information about fewer locations. The highs also visit a wider variety of places, but they make essentially the same use of travel modes and they select destinations within roughly the same distances of home as do people with less information. The fact that the highs travel more frequently within activity spaces that have the same areal extent as those of the lows suggests the mutually reinforcing relationship that exists between information and travel. Because the highs and the lows differ on characteristics other than information level, however, the differences observed in their travel-activity patterns cannot be attributed solely to information. The groups' disparity in age, employment status, or length of residence could also account for the differences in travel.

The results raise some interesting issues regarding the popular hypothesis that spatial learning leads to stereotyped behaviour. It is important to note, for example, that the major difference between the two groups in their length of residence does not lie in the number who have lived in the city for a very short time (less than two years) but rather in the number who have lived there for two to ten years. The similarity in the two groups' grocery-shopping behaviour further demonstrates that the lows are not at the earliest stage of the learning process. The data suggest, therefore, the importance of the spatial learning that takes place over longer periods of time (i.e. after a person's initial two years in a new place). Moreover, the finding that the highs visit a wider variety of places raises the question as to whether stereotyped behaviour (as it is normally recognized to mean visiting a small number of places) is the end result of the learning process and indicates the importance, noted elsewhere (Hanson and Huff, 1982), of determining the amount and nature of the variability present in habitual patterns of behaviour.

Throughout this chapter, I have pointed to the importance of a number of methodological issues involved in measuring both cognition and travel-activity patterns. Although the technique used to measure information levels here is similar, though not identical, to methods used in other studies (e.g. Horton and Reynolds, 1971; Bowlby, 1972; Aldskogius, 1977), this study departs from previous work in its approach to measuring travel and in the fact that data on information levels and travel patterns were not collected at the same time. That the findings of this study differ from those of some previous work (especially in the similarity observed here in the spatial extent of the two groups' activity spaces) probably reflects to some extent the differences in the methodologies employed. There is, of course, a great deal of merit in approaching the same problem from a number of angles and in a number of different settings.

The empirical analysis reported here has described in a general way the nature of the relationship between information levels and travel-activity patterns. This study has not addressed the need, identified by both Lloyd (1982) and Pipkin (1981a,b), to scrutinize the cognitive processes involved in decision-making and to develop theory explaining the formation, storage, access, and use of cognitive images in spatial behaviour. Both Lloyd and Pipkin contend that, mainly because geographers have focused on the amount of content or cognitive information rather than on process, we lack an understanding of how cognitive processes affect spatial choice. In this regard, Pipkin has stressed the need to monitor actual choices within the detailed context of the specific choice situation facing the decision-maker. The results of this study indicate that such future work should focus particularly on complex choice situations. Whereas information about potential destinations does not appear to affect the individual's propensity to make simple one- and two-stop trips or to affect the way in which distance to destination is evaluated, such information is likely to be important to destination selection on multiple-stop trips.

REFERENCES

Adams, J. S. (1969). Directional bias in intra-urban migration, *Economic Geography*, **45**, 302–323.

Alcaly, R. E. (1976). Information and food prices, *The Bell Journal of Economics*, **1976**, 658–671.

Aldskogius, H. (1977). A conceptual framework and a Swedish case study of recreational behaviour and environmental cognition, *Economic Geography*, **53**, 163–183.

Beck, R. J. and Wood, D. (1976). Cognitive transformation of information from urban geographic fields to mental maps, *Environment and Behavior*, **8**, 199–238.

Bowlby, S. R. (1972). *Spatial Variation in Consumers' Information Levels*. Unpublished PhD Dissertation, Department of Geography, Northwestern University, Evanston, Illinois.

Brög, W. (1979). *Transport and the challenge of structural change*, ECMT, Istanbul.

Brown, L. and Moore, E. G. (1970). The intra-urban migration process: A perspective, *Geografiska Annaler*, **52B**; 1–13.

Bunting, T. and Guelke, L. (1979). Behavioural and perceptual geography: A critical appraisal, *Annals of the Association of American Geographers*, **69**, 448–462.

Burnett, P. (1973). The dimensions of alternatives in spatial choice processes, *Geographical Analysis*, **5**, 181–204.

Burnett, P. (1976). Toward dynamic models of traveller behaviour and point patterns of traveller origins, *Economic Geography*, **52**, 30–47.

Cadwallader, M. (1975). A behavioural model of consumer spatial decision-making, *Economic Geography*, **51**, 339–349.

Chapin, F. S. (1974). *Human Activity Patterns in the City*, Wiley, New York.

Clark, W. A. V. and Rushton, G. (1970). Models of intra-urban consumer behaviour and their implications for central place theory, *Economic Geography*, **46**, 486–497.

Clark, W. A. V. and Smith, T. R. (1979). Modelling information use in a spatial context, *Annals of the Association of American Geographers*, **69**, 575–588.

Cox, K. and Golledge, R. (Eds) (1969). *Behavioral Problems in Geography: A Symposium*. Studies in Geography No. 17, Northwestern University Department of Geography, Evanston, Illinois.

Cox, K. and Zanaras, G. (1973). Designative perceptions of macro-spaces: Concepts of a methodology, and applications. In *Image and Environment* (Eds R. Downs and D. Stea), pp. 162–178, Aldine Publishing Company, Chicago.

DeJonge, D. (1962). Images of urban areas: Their structures and psychological foundation, *Journal of the American Institute of Planners*, **28**, 266–276.

Downs, R. (1970). The cognitive structure of an urban shopping centre, *Environment and Behavior*, **2**, 13–39.

Downs, R. M. (1981). Cognitive mapping: A thematic analysis. In *Behavioural Problems in Geography Revisited* (Eds K. R. Cox and R. G. Golledge), pp. 95–122, Methuen, New York.

Downs, R. and Stea, D. (1973). Cognitive maps and spatial behaviour: Process and products. In *Image and Environment* (Eds Roger Downs and David Stea) pp. 8–26, Aldine Publishing Company, Chicago.

Frick, F. C. (1959). Information theory. In *Psychology: A Study of a Science*, Vol. 2 (Ed. S. Koch), pp. 611–636, McGraw-Hill, New York.

Golant, S. (1971). Adjustment process in a system: a behavioural model of human movements, *Geographical Analysis*, **3**, 203–220.

Gold, J. R. (1980). *An Introduction to Behavioural Geography*, Oxford University Press, Oxford.

Golledge, R. (1969). The geographical relevance of some learning theories. In *Behavioural Problems in Geography: A Symposium* (Eds K. R. Cox and R. Golledge), pp. 101–145, Studies in Geography No. 17. Northwestern University Department of Geography, Evanston, Illinois.

Golledge, R. (1978a). Learning about urban environments. In *Making Sense of Time* (Eds T. Carlstein, D. Parkes, and N. Thrift), pp. 76–98, Wiley, New York.

Golledge, R. G. (1978b). Representing, interpreting, and using cognized environments, *Papers of the Regional Science Association*, **41**, 169–204.

Golledge, R. (1979). Reality, process and the dialectical relation between man and environment. In *Philosophy in Geography* (Eds S. Gale and G. Olsson), pp. 109–120, Reidel, London.

Golledge, R. G., Rivizzigno, V. L., and Spector, A. (1976). Learning about a city: Analysis by multidimensional scaling. In *Spatial Choice and Spatial Behavior* (Eds R. Golledge and G. Rushton), pp. 95–118, Columbus State University Press, Columbus, Ohio.

Golledge, R. G. and Spector, A. N. (1978). Comprehending the urban environment: theory and practice, *Geographical Analysis*, **10**, 403–426.

Gould, P. (1975). Acquiring spatial information, *Economic Geography*, **51**, 87–99.

Gulick, J. (1963). Images of an Arab city, *Journal of the Institute of American Planners*, **29**, 179–198.

Hansen, F. (1972). *Consumer Choice Behaviour*, The Free Press, New York.

Hanson, S. (1974). On assessing individuals' attitudes towards potential travel destinations: A research strategy, *Transportation Research Forum*, **15**, 363–370.

Hanson, S. (1976). Spatial variation in the cognitive levels of urban residents. In *Spatial Choice and Spatial Behavior* (Eds R. Golledge and G. Rushton), pp. 157–177, Ohio State University Press, Columbus, Ohio.

Hanson, S. (1978). Measuring the cognitive levels of urban residents, *Geografiska Annaler*, **59B**, 67–81.

Hanson, S. (1980). Spatial diversification and multipurpose travel: Implications for choice theory, *Geographical Analysis*, **12**, 245–257.

Hanson, S. (1982). The determinants of daily travel-activity patterns: Relative location and sociodemographic factors, *Urban Geography*, **3**, 179–202.

Hanson, S. and Hanson, P. (1980). Gender and urban activity patterns in Uppsala, Sweden, *Geographical Review*, **70**, 291–299.

Hanson, S. and Huff, J. O. (1982). Assessing day-to-day variability in complex travel patterns, *Transportation Research Record*, 18–24.

Harvey, D. (1969). Conceptual and measurement problems in the cognitive-behavioural approach to location theory. In *Behavioral Problems in Geography: A Symposium* (Eds K. R. Cox, and R. Golledge), pp. 35–68, Studies in Geography No. 17, Northwestern University Press, Evanston, Illinois.

Horton, F. and Reynolds, D. (1971). Effects of urban spatial structure on individual behaviour, *Economic Geography*, **47**, 36–48.

Huff, D. (1961). Ecological characteristics of consumer behavior, *Papers of the Regional Science Association*, **7**, 19–28.

Jones, P. M. (1978). Destination choice and travel attributes. In *Determinants of Travel Choice* (Eds D. Hensher and M. Q. Dalvi), pp. 266–311, Saxon House, West Meade, England.

Kaplan, S. (1976). Adaptation, structure, and knowledge. In *Environmental Knowing* (Eds G. Moore and R. Golledge), pp. 32–45, Dowden Hutchinson, and Ross, Stroudsburg, Pennsylvania.

Karlsson, G. (1958). *Social Mechanisms*, Almquist and Wiksells, Uppsala, Sweden.

Kofoed, J. (1970). Person movement research: A discussion of concepts, *Papers of the Regional Science Association*, **24**, 141–156.

LaGory, M. and Pipkin, J. (1981). *Urban Social Space*. Wadsworth, Belmont, California.

Lanzetta, J. T. and Kanareff, V. (1962). Information cost, amount of payoff, and level of aspiration as determinants of information seeking in decision-making, *Behavioral Science*, **7**, 459–473.

Lerman, S. and Manski, C. F. (1982). A model of the effect of information diffusion on travel, *Transportation Science*, **16**, 171–191.

Lin, N. (1976). *Foundations of Social Research*, McGraw Hill, New York.

Lloyd, R. E. (1977). Consumer behavior after migration: A reassessment process. *Economic Geography*, **53**, 14–27.

Lloyd, R. (1982). A look at images. *Annals of the Association of American Geographers*, **72**, 532–548.

Lloyd, R. and Jennings, D. (1978). Shopping behavior and income: Comparisons in an urban environment, *Economic Geography*, **54**, 157–167.

Louviere, J. J. (1981). A conceptual and analytical framework for understanding spatial and travel choices, *Economic Geography*, **57**, 304–314.

Luce, R. D. and Raiffa, H. (1957). *Games and Decisions*, Wiley, New York.

Lynch, K. (1960). *The Image of the City*, MIT Press, Cambridge, Massachusetts.

MacKay, D. B. (1977). Cognitive mapping and processing of spatial information. In *Geographical Horizons* (Eds R. N. Taeffe and J. Odland), pp. 105–119, Kendall Hunt, Dubuque.

MacKay, D. B., Olshavsky, D. R., and Sentell, G. (1975). Cognitive maps and spatial behavior of consumers, *Geographical Analysis*, **7**, 19–34.

Marble, D. F. (1967). A theoretical exploration of individual travel behaviour. In *Quantitative Geography Part I: Economic and Cultural Topics* (Eds W. L. Garrison and D. F. Marble), pp. 33–53, Studies in Geography, No. 13, Northwestern University Department of Geography, Evanston, Illinois.

Marble, D. F. and Bowlby, S. R. (1968). Shopping alternatives and recurrent travel patterns. In *Geographic Studies of Urban Transportation and Network Analysis* (Ed. F. Horton), pp. 42–75, Studies in Geography, No. 16, Northwestern University Department of Geography, Evanston, Illinois.

Massam, B. and Bouchard, D. (1976). A comparison of observed and hypothetical choice behaviour, *Environment and Planning A*, **8**, 367–373.

Moore, G. T. (1979). Knowing about environmental knowing: The current state of theory and research on environmental cognition, *Environment and Behavior*, **11**, 33–70.

Moore, G. T. and Golledge, R. G. (1976). Environmental knowing: Concepts and theories. In *Environmental Knowing: Theories, Research and Methods* (Eds G. T. Moore and R. G. Golledge), pp. 3–24, Dowden, Hutchinson, and Ross, Stroudsburg, Pennsylvania.

Morlock, H. (1967). The effect of outcome desirability on information required for decisions, *Behavioral Science*, **12**, 296–300.

Neft, D. (1966). *Statistical Analysis for Areal Distributions*. Regional Science Research Institute Monograph Series, No. 2, Regional Science Association, Philadelphia.

Orleans, P. (1973). Differential cognition of urban residents: effects of social scale on mapping. In *Image and Environment* (Eds R. Downs and D. Stea), pp. 115–130, Aldine Publishing Company, Chicago.

Pipkin, J. S. (1981a). Cognitive behavioral geography and repetitive travel. In *Behavioral Problems in Geography Revisited* (Eds K. R. Cox and R. G. Golledge), pp. 145–181, Methuen, London.

Pipkin, J. S. (1981b). The concept of choice and cognitive explanations of spatial behavior, *Economic Geography*, **57**, 315–331.

Pocock, D. C. (1971). Urban environmental perception and behaviour, *Tijdschrift voor Economische en Sociale Geografie*, **62**, 321–326.

Potter, R. B. (1977). The nature of consumer useage fields in an urban environment: Theoretical and empirical perspectives, *Tijdschrift voor Economische en Sociale Geografie*, **68**, 168–176.

Potter, R. B. (1979). Perception of urban retailing facilities: An analysis of consumer information fields, *Geografiska Annaler*, **61B**, 19–29.

Pred, A. (1967). *Behavior and Location: Foundations for a Geographic and Dynamic Location Theory*. Lund Studies in Geography, Series B, Human Geography, Lund.

Rapoport, A. (1956). The promise and pitfalls of information theory, *Behavioral Science*, **1**, 303–309.

Recker, W. W. and Schuler, H. (1981). Destination choice and processing spatial information: Some empirical tests with alternative constructs, *Economic Geography*, **57**, 373–383.

Rushton, G. (1971). Behavioral correlates of urban spatial structure, *Economic Geography*, **47**, 49–58.

Saarinen, T. F. (1976). *Environmental Planning: Perception and Behavior*, Houghton Mifflin, Boston.

Schneider, C. (1975). Models of space searching in urban areas, *Geographical Analysis*, **7**, 173–185.

Schuler, H. J. (1979). A disaggregate store choice model of spatial decision-making, *The Professional Geographer*, **31**, 146–156.

Smith, G. (1976). The spatial information fields of urban consumers, *Transactions of the Institute of British Geographers*, **1**, 175–189.

Torgerson, W. S. (1958). *Theory and Methods of Scaling*, Wiley, New York.

Webber, M. J., Symanski, R., and Root, J. (1975). Toward a cognitive spatial theory, *Economic Geography*, **51**, 100–116.

Wolpert, J. (1964). The decision process in a spatial context, *Annals of the Association of American Geographers*, **54**, 527–538.

Wong, K. Y. (1979). Maps in minds: An empirical study, *Environment and Planning A*, **11**, 1289–1304.

Geography and the Urban Environment
Progress in Research and Applications, Volume VI
Edited by D. T. Herbert and R. J. Johnston
© 1984 John Wiley & Sons Ltd.

Chapter 4

The Subsidy of Urban Public Transport

Alan M. Hay

In many parts of the world urban public transport is in decline. This decline shows itself in a number of ways: in some places it is evident in the reduction of route density and service frequency; in other areas it is marked in terms of quality of service, cleanliness, public safety, comfort and reliability. In most cases the clearest evidence of decline is the reduction in ridership as trips are diverted to other transport modes (Webster, 1977; Meyer and Gomez-Ibanez, 1981). This decline in the physical provision and use of public transport is paralleled in many cases by a financial decline, for many public transport undertakings are failing to cover their costs (Wolman and Reigeluth, 1980: ITE, 1979). In some cases this is a failure to cover even the operating costs of the system; in many more cases the ability to cover current operating costs masks a longer-run inability to replace capital items of vehicle stock and fixed plant. In a few places financial failure has resulted in the disappearance of all public urban transport, but in most larger towns and cities such a disappearance would have been politically unacceptable for a number of reasons. In the first place the capital costs (financial and social) of solutions based mainly upon private-vehicle use have been deemed unacceptable; second, the growth of private-car use involves congestion costs, environmental hazards and energy costs which are politically unacceptable; and third, it is realized that whether for reasons of age, disability or poverty a substantial proportion of the population will never be car owners and the need to provide for them suggests that at least a skeleton public transport system (perhaps using new information technologies to make it demand responsive) is necessary (Paaswell and Recker, 1978).

The consequence of the decline in public transport, coupled with a political reluctance to see it disappear completely, has been a move towards subsidy or greater subsidy. The main purpose of this essay is to review the literature of the nature of subsidy, on the objects and implementation of subsidy, and on the results of subsidy, in each case paying special attention to the spatial implications of the evidence and arguments presented. The discussion is focused upon public transport in general (covering both urban railways and bus transport) although most of the examples cited refer to mixed systems; bus transport is the dominant partner in all but a few systems.

THE NATURE OF SUBSIDY

Types of subsidy

The subsidy of urban public transport can be conveniently summarized under three headings: revenue support, capital subsidy and financial reconstruction: these three forms are not mutually exclusive.

Revenue support is an ongoing subsidy which allows the transport undertaking to charge fares lower than those which would be needed to break even. Table 4.1 shows how widespread this practice has become. In some cases the level of support is fixed in advance and the transport management is required to budget expenditure and receipts to ensure a balance. In other cases the amount of subsidy is open-ended, the level of service and of fares being fixed and the revenue support being available to meet any consequent deficit. It is generally argued that the first type of arrangement is preferable because it limits the commitment from the subsidy source and maintains financial discipline on the management of the undertaking (Barnhart *et al.*, 1982).

The second form of subsidy is directed to the costs of major *capital* items. A transport undertaking which covers its operating costs may find itself unable to accumulate sufficient reserves to pay for major capital items which arise due to extensions of the system or obsolescence of existing equipment. Although such money can be raised by borrowing, the interest and repayments might be beyond the ability of the transport undertaking to raise in surplus. It is therefore quite usual for capital assistance to be granted for such items, even when the undertaking is required to meet its usual year-on-year operating expenses.

The third possibility is that normal financial arrangements apply to both

TABLE 4.1   Summary of the subsidy position of public transport in some European and North American cities (circa. 1980)

Subsidy as percentage of operating costs	
%	
0–15	Newcastle upon Tyne;
16–30	Toronto, Montreal, Liverpool, London;
31–45	Manchester, Cologne, Zurich, Hamburg, Munich;
46–60	Vancouver, Winnipeg, Stockholm, Oslo, Paris;
over 60	Sheffield, Vienna, Los Angeles, San Francisco.

Note: The figures used to construct this table are drawn from a variety of published and unpublished sources: they may not be exactly comparable in all cases.

recurrent costs and capital costs, but the transport operation finds itself accumulating deficits with mounting interest charges which cannot be met from operating surpluses. In such a situation the subsidizing body may write off certain accumulated deficits in the guise of *financial reconstruction*. This approach is often criticized because it gives no clear financial targets to the operator and no advance indication of the timing and magnitude of the re-financing operation.

Although they are distinct conceptually many urban transport operations have experienced a mixture of all three forms of subsidy and quite complex subsidy packages may be negotiated. From a geographical viewpoint it means that comparisons between countries and between cities within countries may be difficult to draw, a point which must be borne in mind in the discussion which follows and in reading the literature to which it refers.

Sources of subsidy

The sources of subsidy are similarly varied and often mixed, but four main types may be distinguished: subsidy from non-transport activities, from other transport activities, from central government revenue, and from local government revenue.

Subsidy from other transport activities is relatively unusual because few other transport undertakings make large operating surpluses or accumulate large reserves. In the United States, however, a number of major projects have been partially funded from such sources. In Philadelphia, for example, a commuter urban railway known as the Lindenwold line was partly funded from accumulated reserves of the Bridge and Harbour Authority, which manages harbour facilities and toll bridges. Slightly less direct was the arrangement by which San Francisco's Bay Area Rapid Transit system raised about 10 per cent of its capital cost by bonds backed by bridge tolls (Hall, 1980). In addition there has been a growth in the use of such funds to subsidize operating costs (Pucher, 1980), although the percentage subsidy from transport activities has declined.

Subsidy from non-transport activities takes two forms. In some cases the transport undertaking itself has other activities which yield a surplus. In many cases these other activities relate to land and buildings surplus to the current needs of the transport undertaking, but in one major example of such subsidy in Vancouver (Canada) the electricity utility (BC Hydro) was given the responsibility for city bus transport. In other cases the transport undertaking is managerially independent of the activities which are used in providing the subsidy: both Munich and Vienna public transport receive subsidy from publicly-owned utilities (Wolman and Reigeluth, 1980).

These solutions are not as common as subsidy from government revenue, however. Many local governments accept the need to support public transport, although in some cases the recognition that this should concern central government was more delayed. For example, in the United States the Federal government only took powers to give support to capital projects in 1964 and to operating expenses in 1974. An important issue in the United States as elsewhere was the distinction between subsidy from general taxation and subsidy from tax revenues which were ear-marked for specific purposes. So in the United States a central issue was the use for public transport of revenue raised, mainly through fuel taxes, from private motor-vehicle users which was initially intended to finance road construction and maintenance (Pikarsky and Christensen, 1976).

Non-subsidy

The literature on public transport sometimes uses the term 'subsidy' to describe various management and marketing strategies which, though not deliberate subsidy in the sense of this essay, may require deficit financing or involve a cross-subsidy between categories of user (Rock, 1976).

Some special fares are offered at off-peak periods or on low-density routes in order to maximize revenue on traffic. An economic rationale for such special fares is that they should cover their marginal costs and make some contribution to the overhead costs of the system (Lewis, 1949). The operator will try to hedge those fares with special conditions (e.g. time of day) to ensure that other traffic, which would have used the system in any case, is unable to switch to take advantage of the lower fares. Inasmuch as these fares cover their marginal costs there is no case for asserting that they are subsidized even if they contribute less than average to the overhead costs.

A similar element of cross-subsidy can occur because there are many subtle variations from time to time and from route to route in the costs of providing the service, which are ignored by operators in order to establish fare structures which are easy to operate and easily understood by the users. The most extreme case of this is where flat fares or zone fares are established regardless of time of day, length of trip, or route. The element of averaging in such a system inevitably means that some passengers pay less than the true cost of their movements while others pay in excess (Cervero, 1981b, 1982; Hodge, 1981).

In a number of places use has been made of low fare or zero-fare demonstration projects. In these, for a short period, seldom more than a few months at most a year, the attempt is made to sell public transport services to a public which may have little experience of using the system. Such demonstrations are not subsidy in the strict sense, but they may well result in deficits which must be externally funded. (They may also be important in providing evidence of short-run elasticities in demand for public transport.) As marketing strategies they have not been particularly successful but one study reported that two one-year experiments resulted in use after normal fares were reinstated remaining 'above projections based on pre-demonstration levels' but concluded that 'long term impacts . . . are probably not of sufficient magnitude to offset the revenue loss associated with the year long free fare promotion' (Doxsey and Spear, 1981, p. 47).

All these are seen as operational management issues and so not relevant to this essay except in one important respect: in their more acute forms such special arrangements may negate an intended effect of subsidy especially if the global subsidy is relatively small and the spatial and temporal cross-subsidies are relatively large (Pucher, 1982; Cervero, 1981a).

Macro-spatial issues

The existence of subsidy, especially revenue subsidy, also poses a number of spatial issues in terms of its existing distribution and its optimal allocation, and of their relation to the derivation of revenue involved. These spatial issues occur at a macro-level (which regions or towns are, or should be, recipients of the subsidy) and at a micro-level (which neighbourhoods, routes and households are, or should be, recipients). This section is devoted to the macro-level issues.

The most detailed investigation of this issue has occurred in the United States where both Federal and State governments have been involved in the financing of subsidy (Carsten *et al.*, 1976; Miller, 1979). Investigation of the methods adopted (Poitano and Keck, 1978) found twenty-two States with assistance programmes. The most common allocation criteria were related (wholly or partly) to actual deficits (twenty cases) and matching funds to Federal government assistance (ten cases). The stress on deficits is often deplored because, it is argued, such an approach removes management incentives to run an efficient service with minimal deficit. There is, therefore, a case for developing allocation criteria which represent need (by reference to population, carless households etc.), the service provided (route mileage, service frequency) or the use made (total ridership, total passenger kilometres). The ways in which these may or have been used are described by Forkenbrock and Dueker (1979) and Forkenbrock (1981). For example New York State adopted a mixed strategy based on $0.09 per vehicle mile and $0.014 per passenger carried (Miller, 1979, p. 44).

The same issue arises at a national level with the allocation of funds from Federal (central government) sources. Briggs (1980) demonstrated that in the period 1965–1977 there was no simple relationship between receipts of Federal assistance and the population or ridership of the transport systems in the forty-nine largest urbanized areas of the United States, although there is evidence that smaller cities lagged behind larger cities. An additional element in this may be that the documentation and data collection involved in successful application for subsidy is so great that only the larger undertakings are equipped to do it. Furthermore there may be a momentum effect such that successful applicants are able to repeat that success using knowledge developed in earlier programme formulation (cp. Wildavsky, 1976).

THE OBJECTIVES OF SUBSIDY

The objectives of subsidy for urban public transport are not always precisely stated and in democratic systems may represent compromises arising from coalitions of interests with varying sets of reasons for adopting the policy. It is nevertheless possible to identify two main types of objective: transport policy and social policy.

Subsidized urban public transport as a transport policy

The transport argument is that a subsidized public transport system will reduce, hold steady, or at least reduce the rate of growth of, private-car ownership and/or use. If this is achieved the subsidy will not only have financial benefits to local government (reducing traffic and therefore reducing costs of maintenance and increased provision of road space) but also have social benefits to other road users (as reduced traffic congestion reduces operating costs and journey times).

If this is the general objective of subsidizing public transport the detailed rationale for a particular policy may take several different forms. One argument (commonly associated with Meyer et al., 1965; see also Mohring, 1976), is that urban transport is characterized by increasing returns to scale, and only by a subsidy-induced greater volume of use will these returns be realized. This argument can be challenged both on theoretical grounds (Beesley, 1973) and empirical grounds (Koskal, 1970; Lee and Steedman, 1970; Williams, 1981), because there is accumulating evidence that there are few economies of scale in urban bus transport.

A second rationale is based on the claim that other transport modes do not pay their full costs so a counter-balancing subsidy is required to ensure equal or 'fair' competition between modes (Abe and Sinha, 1973), and therefore an economically efficient allocation of traffic between transport forms. There is little doubt that some forms of transport, probably private-car use, in some situations fail to pay their full costs because these are difficult to calculate, or impossible to recoup. But if counter-balancing subsidy is used as a solution to this problem it leads to a general under-pricing of transport services and therefore an inefficient allocation between transport and non-transport activities in global terms. If the premises of the argument are correct it would be better in economic terms (though difficult politically) to tax the unfairly advantaged mode than to subsidize that which is unfairly disadvantaged (Kraft and Domencich, 1972; Beesley, 1973).

A third argument which is sometimes advanced independently of those outlined above is that the subsidy will induce a change in modal shares which reduces the global cost to society of the transport system. It is difficult to see why this should be so, unless the returns-to-scale argument or the hidden costs argument hold, but even if it is accepted the argument must be further qualified: not only should the subsidy achieve the net benefit but it should also be demonstrably the highest achievable net benefit, and if some other policy yielded a higher net benefit the subsidy would not be justified (ITE, 1979).

If these transport objectives are the intended outcome from subsidy a question arises as to the most effective way of using the subsidy, because the available money may be spent on the reduction of fares or the improvement of services (Grey, 1975, chapter 3). If the first course is followed a choice must be made between different patterns of fare reduction, ranging from the blanket subsidy of all trips to subsidy which is carefully restricted to specific areas or categories of traveller. If the second course is followed a choice must be made between different types of improvement (density of routes, frequency of service, speed, comfort, standard of vehicle stock etc.).

The decision about these uses of subsidy should be based on evidence about the elasticity of demand with respect to fares and level of service for the market as a whole and for specific sectors of the market. Unfortunately there is seldom good evidence of the short-run and long-run elasticities which are relevant to specific cases (Lago et al., 1981b). A priori, many authorities argue that certain levels of service variables are probably more important than fares, because they, rather than the fare, represent the larger part of the generalized cost of trip making. The generalized cost includes not only the fare paid but also the implicit cost to the traveller of his or her time. If, for example, a trip takes one hour and costs sixty pence the generalized cost may well be five times the fare paid. This economic argument is often supported empirically by attitude surveys where users or potential users are asked which aspects of the existing service are in most need of improvement.

Subsidized urban public transport as a social policy

In some places the case for subsidy of public transport is stated purely in terms of helping the disadvantaged (the old, the disabled and the poor). Such a 'social' argument may have two facets. The first is based on the assumption that the provision of subsidized transport will greatly increase the mobility of such groups: an increase in mobility which is seen as desirable in improving the quality of life. The second approach recognizes that the demand for transport by such groups may be inelastic with respect to price, but argues that a subsidy allows the redistribution of income to deserving groups, without the barriers which often inhibit the take-up of other social-security benefits. This approach emphasizes the 'non-stigmatizing' nature of the fare subsidy.

These differences within the general argument for subsidy in social terms have considerable implications for the way in which the subsidy is used. If the first argument (mobility) is adopted the subsidy may be best used in improving services rather than in cutting fares. If fare levels are to be reduced the mobility objective can be achieved by limiting the cheap (or free) travel to specific groups whose eligibility is recognized by the issue of passes. Certainly this seems to be a more efficient method of improving mobility than a blanket subsidy which benefits all users, but it runs directly counter to the non-stigmatizing income redistributive aspect which is advocated in some quarters. On the other hand the income redistribution argument may itself be undermined if it is shown that the transport advantaged use the facilities substantially more than do the disadvantaged for whom the policy is formulated. This aspect of the argument can therefore only be resolved when the patronage pattern under a given level of fares has been established.

Conflicts in policy objectives

It will be evident that the transport and social objectives for public transport subsidy may be contradictory. A formal economic exploration of this issue is offered by Lee *et al.* (1980), who conclude that (p. 331) 'maximizing use of the public good requires a system of discriminatory prices which elevates the price paid by the poor while lowering the price paid by the more affluent'. (This paradoxical conclusion arises from the fact that in many cases public transport is an inferior good—that is one for which demand falls as income increases.) It is easy to conceive of examples of this argument; in many cities the traffic problem is caused by excessive numbers of private cars using the network at peak periods. A public-transport subsidy to reduce the traffic problem would need to reduce the fares for the higher income households in order to reduce car use. There would be no case for a similar reduction to those low-income households which, being carless, are a captive market for public transport.

THE IMPACT OF SUBSIDY ON URBAN TRANSPORT

The impact of subsidy on urban transport systems cannot easily be determined, for four reasons. First, it must not be supposed that all the subsidy will necessarily be spent on improving services or reducing fares. It is sometimes argued, though the evidence is scanty, that an unrestricted subsidy encourages greater militancy in wage bargaining from labour and greater slackness in cost control by management (Barnhart *et al.*, 1982; Pucher, 1982). Second, even when subsidy does find its way into improving services or reducing fares the exact response will vary according to the way in which the resources are used. Third, the response of individuals to the subsidy may be gradual as the presence of better or cheaper public transport leads to changes in residence, place of work and car ownership. Finally, even the observed short-run effects prove, on closer scrutiny, to be very complex.

The use of public transport

The most obvious question to ask is whether subsidy has proved to have an effect on the use of public transport. A fairly coarse approach to this problem is used by Briggs (1980). He attempted to correlate Federal assistance to public transport undertakings in the United States (1965–1977) with the changes in ridership over the same period, using cross-sectional correlation and regression. This was not the whole subsidy received by the operators in question (they also received subsidy from State and local sources) and the bulk (88 per cent) of the contribution was to capital costs. Nevertheless Briggs showed that although use of public transport had generally declined, below average rates of decline and in some cases slight increases (around 1 per cent) were associated with the Federal Assistance programme. There was a correlation (0.69 over twenty-nine cases) between Federal Assistance and change in trip-making, a correlation which was retained ($p = 0.0056$) when the influence of other variables was considered: on the other hand Briggs remarked that the size of the effect seemed small when the magnitude of the investment ($9335 millions) was considered.

There is a substantial literature on the effect of fare levels on the use of public transport (Bly, 1976; Lago et al., 1981b), evidence which is often used to indicate the probable effects of subsidy if it is used entirely to reduce fares and no other policy instruments are used in conjunction. These studies suggest, in many countries, that for small changes around existing fare levels there is a price elasticity of about -0.30. Some of this evidence is based on observations before and after a fare change (Heels and White, 1977), while other evidence comes from cross-sectional data. There is evidence that before-after data are more consistent than cross-sectional data (Lago et al., 1981a,b). There are also some studies which have produced separate elasticity estimates for different categories of traffic (peak, off-peak, short and long trips, type of route, and different modes). The published evidence suggests that elasticities are lowest for peak-period traffic on arterial routes (Fairhurst and Smith, 1977); the elasticities of different modes are also influenced by the quality of service which they offer. These studies provide sufficient information for transport operators who are seeking to maximize ridership, revenue or operating surplus. Only more detailed studies reveal whether the subsidy is achieving its objectives in terms of reducing traffic, increasing mobility and income redistribution.

Subsidies and household travel behaviour

Figures on the use of public transport or the gross operating revenue (even when broken down by time of day, type of route etc.) do not reveal where the ridership is coming from, especially whether it is generated traffic (implying improved mobility for certain sections of the population) or diverted traffic (implying a reduction in the numbers using other modes). In the longer run, too, changes in the composition of those using the public-transport system may reflect long-run changes in the population composition (age, employment, socio-economic characteristics) rather than changes in household travel behaviour.

Some studies have attempted to identify the effect of transport subsidy by cross-sectional analyses which compare the travel patterns of similar households in different public-transport environments. Such studies must, if their conclusions are to be reliable, seek to control for other variables which might also affect public-transport use. For example, in many cities the level of public-transport provision is inversely related to distance from the city centre and thus even households of similar age and socio-economic status face different geographical patterns of possible destinations which may conceal or exaggerate the effect of public-transport provision on travel patterns.

An obvious possible solution to this problem is to seek test cases where similar households lie on either side of a boundary which divides a high fare regime from a low fare regime (or a high level of provision from a lower level), Kelly (1982) carried out such an analysis for two communities which lay on either side of the boundary between South Yorkshire and North Derbyshire. Although it was possible to demonstrate that the low fare regime resulted in greater bus use the results were confused by the tendency for those living near the boundary to cross it in an attempt to benefit from the lower fares (see also Sharp, 1967).

Another element in such cross-sectional studies is the evidence (Fairhurst, 1975; Button et al., 1980a, 1980b) that the level or cost of public transport provision may be correlated with car ownership. Some authors have interpreted this as a direct causal effect with public transport contributing to a reduction in car ownership and use. Others have suggested that there is no such reduction overall, merely that long-term decisions (or preferences) on car ownership influence the choice of residential location (Fairhurst, 1975).

The second possible solution is to look at changes in household travel behaviour over time, before and after a major change in fares or service levels. A major problem here is that there will be some very short-term shock effects before a longer-term equilibrium behaviour is established, and some of the effects (for example on car ownership and residence) can only be expected to show after several years maintenance of a policy. For these reasons most researchers favour long-term comparisons of public-transport use. The counter-problem is that as the length of time between the 'before' study and the 'after' study increases so will the number of other changes (incomes, employment, land-use patterns, costs of car ownership and use) which may affect the use of public transport.

A solution to this last problem is possibly to use a hybrid approach which looks at contrasts over space and over time. A study in progress on the effects of South Yorkshire's subsidy policy involves not only a temporal comparison (1972 and 1981) for specified household types, but also a cross-sectional element in that similar temporal comparisons are being made for Manchester where no such subsidy has occurred.

REDISTRIBUTIVE ASPECTS OF SUBSIDY

It was noted that some of the support for the subsidy of public transport arises from the belief that it has a desirable effect on the redistribution of income without any stigmatization of the recipients. Research has suggested that this will not always occur and that the exact balance can depend upon quite fine details of the fare structure, travel behaviour, taxation and the way in which the subsidy is used. It is obviously best if such data can be collected in a disaggregate form (using the household and the public transport route as the unit of analysis) but it is seldom possible to collect all the necessary data at this scale and recourse is made to averages based on aggregate data relating to network costs, travel behaviour and the incidence of taxation. The fallacies which may result from such an approach are outlined by Hodge (1981). The optimal solution is clearly to use local disaggregate data, only using aggregate-based averages when no other data are available.

The incidence of contributions

Studies of the incidence of contributions to subsidy can raise a number of technical problems mainly related to the type of revenue source which is used.

The simplest case is where the unit for which travel behaviour is recorded (most often the household) is also the unit responsible for paying into the revenue according to some easily determined basis. In the United Kingdom a major source of local government income is the household rate (a property tax) which can be calculated from publicly accessible rateable values and the known charge per pound. But even this method is complicated by three other factors. First, not all the tax is collected from domestic rates, a proportion of the rate burden and thus of subsidy being paid by commercial property owners. Second, many poorer households are entitled to rate rebates and their contribution is thereby reduced. Third, although rates and similar taxes are a major source of local government revenue in many countries, a proportion of the costs of local government is met by subventions from other levels of government. The general pattern nevertheless seems to be that contributions through property taxes tend to rise absolutely with income. (It is of course these absolute figures which are relevant to the net distribution question rather than the percentage of income used in analysing regressive and progressive taxation; as for example in Pucher 1981 and Pucher and Hirschman, 1981.)

Contributions via sales taxes (purchase tax, value added tax etc.) are again the responsibility of the household or individual, but here the detailed expenditure pattern of a household is either unavailable or requires a substantial increase in the data which must be collected from respondents. Where the sales tax is local, account must be taken of the proportion of expenditure which falls outside the taxation area and this same problem occurs if expenditure patterns are estimated for national aggregates. Another complication is that some sales taxes exclude (or have a lower rate on) some essentials (including food). Where the sales tax covers all items it is usually progressive in absolute terms (in the sense that contributions rise with income) and regressive in relative terms (in the sense that contributions as a proportion of income fall with increasing income): but where basic staples are exempt the sales tax is usually progressive in both senses.

Income-tax contributions are also difficult to estimate (heads of households may not know the incomes of all members and individual members may have no clear idea of their tax payments) so here again recourse is often made to national estimates. Most studies conclude (e.g. Wickes, 1979; Pucher and Hirschman, 1982) that income taxes are absolutely and relatively progressive in their incidence, and thus in their contribution to transport subsidy.

Taxation of commercial and industrial activities (including payroll taxes and corporation tax) is more difficult to interpret. In the first place it may (where the demand for products is inelastic) be recouped entirely from consumers by increased prices, from investors by reducing distributed profits, or from the labour force by holding wage rates. The second problem concerns leakage because the consumers and investors concerned (though not usually the labour force) may well be located outside the geographic area in which the subsidy is effective. Nevertheless it appears likely that these contributions will also be progressive, both absolutely and relatively (Pucher and Hirschman, 1981, 1982).

Each source of subsidy therefore has special problems if its incidence is to be understood: the problems are compounded if, as in many cases, the subsidy is funded by a package of revenue from several different sources. Despite these problems, Pucher and Hirschman (1982) have succeeded in a comparative study of six United States cities and concluded that the total tax burden of transit is progressive (both in absolute sums contributed per household and as a proportion of household income) but that this is mainly a consequence of Federal taxation. More local taxes show a U-shaped relationship with income; the lowest income categories contribute relatively more than those with moderate incomes ($10 000 to $24 999, in 1978), although estimates of the contributions of higher income households were sensitive to the assumptions used.

The incidence of benefit from subsidy

The incidence of subsidy by broad geographical areas or by type of household is similarly difficult to calculate.

Technical problems arise because of the accounting difficulty in attributing costs and revenues to particular routes, portions of routes, times of day and geographical areas. On the cost side, variations in operating costs (influenced for example by traffic conditions) within a single system are difficult to determine (Levinson and Conrad, 1979), while on the revenue side fares paid in a specific geographic area may cover travel on quite different parts of the network, and revenue is itself spatially variable according to load factors. These issues may be resolved in case studies of specific routes but analysis of a whole system usually resorts to averaging of costs and of revenue per passenger kilometre, across the whole system or large parts of the system, in order to arrive at an average subsidy which can be used to estimate the gross receipts experienced by an individual or household with known trip-making behaviour (Neff, 1982).

Even if these accounting problems are resolved there remain two conceptual problems which have been insufficiently recognized in these analyses. The first concerns those situations in which subsidy had achieved a *diversion* of traffic to the subsidized system. In such a case the aggregate *financial subsidy* is given by the total number of trips (or passenger kilometres) multiplied by the subsidy per trip (or passenger kilometres). The aggregate benefits to users in terms of *consumer surplus* are given by the 'rule of a half' (Pearce 1971, p. 19), as the subsidy per trip multiplied by the number of pre-existing trips, plus half the subsidy per trip multiplied by the number of diverted trips. Algebraically:

$$TS = V^1 s \tag{4.1}$$

$$TB = Vs + \tfrac{1}{2}(V^1 - V)s, \tag{4.2}$$

where V = volume of traffic before subsidy
V^1 = volume of traffic after subsidy
s = subsidy per unit of travel
TS = total subsidy
TB = total benefit.

It is clear that in general $TS > TB$. The difference between the two sums can be seen as the compensation or inducement paid to the users to persuade them to use a different mode.

The second problem is almost identical: if the subsidy results in a marked *generation* of trips, which would not otherwise have been made, then the value to the travellers of the generated trips will be $\tfrac{1}{2}(V^1 - V)s$, and the total value of the subsidy for all trips will be

$$Vs + \tfrac{1}{2}(V^1 - V)s. \tag{4.3}$$

The conclusion from these two related arguments is that, even if all routes and times had similar costs and load factors, the benefit to any individual or household will range from the whole subsidy element (where no trips by public transport are attracted or generated) to approximately half the financial subsidy (where all trips by public transport are so generated or attracted). It is notable that the smallest consumer benefits (in terms of direct public transport use) occur when the policy is having the maximum effect in terms of transport. These conclusions are, of course, subject to the criticism often levelled at social cost:benefit methodology—especially in this case the assumption that the benefit of a trip to an individual should be measured by the marginal price at which he or she would be prepared to make the trip. Nevertheless this argument (recognized by Frankema, 1973) is an important query on those studies (e.g. Neff, 1982) which continue to assume that the benefit of subsidy to a user equals the financial subsidy received.

THE IMPACT OF SUBSIDY ON THE URBAN SYSTEM

The historical evolution of cities in many parts of the world, but especially in Western Europe and North America, was clearly affected by successive changes in public transport by rail, by tram, by underground railway and finally by motor bus. The period since 1930 has seen further dramatic changes with a growth in car ownership conferring new levels of mobility on many households and, it is claimed, permitting the rapid dispersal of manufacturing and service activities away from the city centres. Furthermore the private motor car has permitted the development of low-density residential areas around the peripheries of many great cities, especially in the United States (Foster, 1981). It is sometimes implied that the subsidy of urban transport will in some way halt or even reverse these trends.

There is an underlying flaw in such an implication which must be identified prior to the detailed discussion. The technical characteristics of the motor car give it such an advantage over all existing public-transport modes that even free public transport is unlikely to check the growth of, let alone reduce, levels of car ownership and use. This view underlay the *Buchanan Report* (Buchanan, 1963) and is the undergirding assumption of many recent studies (e.g. Meyer and Gomez-Ibanez, 1981). It is, therefore, unlikely that the subsidy of public transport alone will lead to any major shifts in the development of the urban system, although such shifts might result from a simultaneous improvement in public-transport technologies, decreases in fare levels and a major increase in the user costs of the private car (whether occasioned by energy cost, taxation or congestion; Meyer and Gomez-Ibanez, 1981, pp. 87–88).

Much attention should therefore focus upon the impact of subsidy (and therefore potentially increased mobility) on the behaviour of carless individuals and households. Three areas of change are identified. First, subsidized public transport may enable low-mobility consumers to patronize service centres (retail, professional, recreation etc.) at a greater distance from place of residence. Such a trend (like the mobility conferred by car ownership) will tend to lead to the decline of local shopping centres, but inasmuch as public transport services have a strongly nodal structure the patronage will be transferred to central locations. (Central locations will also benefit if low public-transport fares or improved services enable them to retain custom which might otherwise have been lost due to traffic congestion and parking problems.) Second, a number of studies have identified a correlation between transport and unemployment in that low-wage and low-mobility individuals often face limited employment opportunities within a given time and cost radius: improved (and/or cheaper) public transport may help to reduce such unemployment, but only if the unemployment is due solely to a spatial mismatch of vacant jobs and unemployed persons. A related possibility is that employers using such labour forces will be able to tap larger labour pools if public transport benefits from subsidy: again this might be expected to benefit those located at the nodes of the public-transport network, especially the city centre. The third possibility concerns the residential choices of low-mobility households. If their present residential choices are strongly influenced by access (to work, to service centres etc.) the subsidy of public transport may enable such groups to disperse. But, as Richardson (1971) notes, this argument is debatable, and even if there is some trade-off of accessibility there are many other constraints on housing choice, especially for the old and the poor (i.e. those groups most dependent upon public transport).

Any empirical investigation of the three possible effects of subsidy is difficult; too few cities have had a prolonged subsidy of public transport to provide any test cases, and too many other variables have changed over time to permit an unambiguous identification of the effects of the subsidy. It is therefore necessary to examine the implications of alternative public-transport strategies by using calibrated models of specific systems. Mackett (1980, 1981) used a model of Leeds to predict that a major increase in public-transport fares (of 237 per cent) would result (1976–1991) in an increase in the inner-city housing stock (+3.9 per cent), a decline in inner-city employment (−21.4 per cent), and a huge decline in inner-city retail sales of durable goods (−43.3 per cent). (The model also forecasts changes in residence and location with higher fares resulting in relatively more of the inner-city jobs being held by inner-city dwellers, although the absolute numbers decline.) It is difficult to extrapolate from a single case study, and the relative magnitude of the effects predicted by Mackett will not necessarily be repeated in other cities of different sizes. But the implications of the Mackett analysis for subsidy in Leeds is clear: if subsidy is used to prevent major increases in public transport fares it will help to maintain sales and retail and service employment which would otherwise be lost to the inner city.

CONCLUSIONS

The growth in subsidy for public transport in many countries over the period 1965 to 1980 was partly a result of increasing political awareness of public

transport, but also reflected a rapid escalation in the costs of providing public
transport (Pucher, 1982), which operators could not recoup because ridership
was declining. The open-ended commitment to subsidy has resulted in a
backlash (Barnhart *et al.*, 1982), which may itself be part of a broader political-
economic reaction against government intervention. The ensuing debate has
tended to assume that the implications of subsidy for transport in the city, for
income redistribution and for the evolution of urban form, are understood. The
literature reviewed in this paper permits no easy conclusions about whether
such subsidies are 'right' or 'wrong', of what degree of subsidy is 'fair', or how
subsidy should be used to achieve desired objectives.

BIBLIOGRAPHY

Abe, M. A. and Sinha, K. C. (1973). Pricing in mass transportation, *ASCE Transportation Engineering Journal*, **99**, 182–195.

Barnhart, R. A., Loftus, W., Fenello, M. J., and Teele, A. E. (1982). Changes in Federal Transportation Policy, *Transportation Quarterly*, **36**, 166–191.

Beesley, M. E. (1973). *Urban Transport: Studies in Economic Policy*, Butterworth, London.

Bly, P. H. (1976). *The Effect of Fares on Bus Patronage*, Transport and Road Research Laboratory (LR 733), Crowthorne.

Briggs, R. (1980). The impact of federal local public transportation assistance upon travel behavior, *Professional Geographer*, **32**, 316–325.

Buchanan, C. D. (1963). *Traffic in Towns*, Penguin, Harmondsworth.

Button, K. J., Pearman, A. D., and Fowkes, A. S. (1980a). Car availibility and public transport, *International Journal of Transport Economics*, **7**, 339–343.

Button, K. J., Pearman, A. D., and Fowkes, A. S. (1980b). Car ownership in West Yorkshire: The influence of public transport accessibility, *Urban Studies*, **17**, 211–215.

Carstens, R. L., Mercier, C. R., and Kannel, E. J. (1976). Status of state level support for transit, *Transportation Research Record*, **589**.

Cervero, R. (1981a). Efficiency and equity impacts of transit fare policies, *Transportation Research Record*, **799**, 7–15.

Cervero, R. (1981b). Flat versus differentiated transit pricing: What's a fair fare? *Transportation*, **10**, 211–232.

Cervero, R. (1982). Transit cross-subsidies, *Transportation Quarterly*, **36**, 377–389.

Doxsey, L. B. and Spear, B. D. (1981). Free fare transit: Some empirical findings, *Transportation Research Record*, **799**, 47–49.

Fairhurst, M. H. (1975). The influence of public transport on car ownership in London, *Journal of Transport Economics and Policy*, **9**, 193–208.

Fairhurst, M. H. and Smith, R. S. (1977). *Development and Calibration of London Transport's Scenario Model*. Economic Research Report R229, London Transport Executive, London.

Forkenbrock, D. J. (1981). Transit assistance allocation, further research findings, *Transportation Research A*, **15**, 363–366.

Forkenbrock, D. J. and Dueker, K. J. (1979). Transit assistance allocation, *Transportation Research A*, **13**, 317–327.

Foster, M. S. (1981). *From Streetcar to Superhighway*, Temple University Press, Philadelphia.

Frankema, M. (1973). Income distributional effects of urban transit subsidies, *Journal of Transport Economics and Policy*, 7, 215–230.

Grey, A. J. (1975). *Urban fares policy*, Saxon House, London.

Hall, P. (1980). *Great Planning Disasters*, Penguin, Harmondsworth.

Heels, P. and White, P. R. (1977). *Fare elasticities on Inter-urban and Rural Bus Services*, Transport Studies Group, Polytechnic of Central London, London.

Hodge, D. C. (1981). Modelling the geographic components of mass transit subsidies, *Environment and Planning A*, 13, 581–599.

ITE Informational Report (1979). Transit operating studies, *ITE Journal*, 49, 40–48.

Kelly, T. (1982). *Spatial Differential Bus Fare Pricing and Passenger Behaviour Around a Fare Boundary*. B.A. Dissertation, Department of Geography, University of Sheffield.

Koskal, R. K. (1970). Economies of scale in bus transport, *Journal of Transport Economics and Policy*, 4, 29–36.

Kraft, G. and Domencich, T. A. (1972). Free transit. In *Readings in Urban Economics* (Eds M. Edel and J. Rothenberg), pp. 468–482, Macmillan, New York.

Lago, A. M., Mayworm, P. D., and McEnroe, J. M. (1981a). Further evidence on aggregate and disaggregate transit fare elasticities, *Transportation Research Record*, 799, 42–47.

Lago, A. M., Mayworm, P. D., and McEnroe, J. M. (1981b). Transit service elasticities. Evidence from demonstrations and demand models, *Journal of Transport Economics and Policy*, 15, 99–120.

Lee, D. R., Smith, W. J., and Formby, J. P. (1980). The public provision of urban mass transit: A conflict in objectives, *International Journal of Transport Economics*, 7, 327–332.

Lee, N. and Steedman, I. (1970). Economies of scale in bus transport, *Journal of Transport Economics and Policy*, 4, 15–27.

Levinson, H. S. and Conrad, P. E. (1979). How to allocate bus route costs, *Transit Journal*, 5, 54–64.

Lewis, W. A. (1949). *Overhead Costs*, Allen and Unwin, London.

Mackett, R. L. (1980). Transport and the viability of central and inner urban areas, *Journal of Transport Economics and Policy*, 14, 267–294.

Mackett, R. L. (1981). Some issues in modelling the impact of changes in transport costs on residential and employment locations, *International Journal of Transport Economics*, 8, 59–78.

Meyer, J. R., Kain, J. F., and Wohl, M. (1965). *The Urban Transportation Problem*, Harvard University Press, Cambridge, Massachusetts.

Meyer, J. R. and Gomez-Ibanez, J. A. (1981). *Autos, Transit and Cities*, Harvard University Press, Cambridge, Massachusetts.

Miller, J. H. (1979). An evaluation of allocation methodologies for public transportation operating assistance, *Transportation Journal*, 20, 40–49.

Mohring, H. (1976). *Transportation Economics*, Ballinger, Harvard, Massachusetts.

Neff, P. J. (1982). The incidence of public bus system costs and benefits, *Transportation Quarterly*, 36, 301–316.

Paaswell, R. E. and Recker, W. W. (1978). *Problems of the Carless*, Praeger, New York.

Pearce, D. W. (1971). *Cost Benefit Analysis*, Macmillan, London.

Pikarsky, M. and Christensen, D. (1976). *Urban Transportation Policy and Management*, Heath, Lexington, Massachusetts.

Poitano, M. R. and Keck, C. A. (1978). *Operating Assistance for Public Transportation Systems: A Survey of State Level Programmes*, New York State Department of Transportation, Albany, New York.

Pucher, J. (1980). Transit financing trends in large US metropolitan areas 1973–78, *Transportation Research Record*, **759**, 6–12.

Pucher, J. (1981). Equity in transit finance, *Journal of the American Planning Association*, **4**, 387–407.

Pucher, J. (1982). Effects of subsidies on transit costs, *Transportation Quarterly*, **36**, 549–562.

Pucher, J. and Hirschman, I. (1981). Distribution of the tax burden of transit subsidies in the US, *Public Policy*, **3**, 341–367.

Pucher, J. and Hirschman, I. (1982). Distribution of the transit tax burden in five US metropolitan areas, *Transportation*, **11**, 3–28.

Richardson, H. W. (1971). *Urban Economics*, Penguin, Harmondsworth.

Rock, S. M. (1976). Redistributive effects of public transport: Framework and case study, *Transportation Research Record*, **589**, 1–7.

Rock, S. M. (1979). Income equity of two transit funding sources, *Transportation Research Record*, **791**, 10–14.

Sharp, C. H. (1967). *Problems of Urban Passenger Transport*, University Press, Leicester.

Webster, F. V. W. (1977). *Urban Passenger Transport, Trends and Prospects*, Transport and Road Research Laboratory (LR771), Crowthorne.

Wickes, R. (1979). *The Effect on Different Income Groups of Financing Public Transport by Means Other Than Fares*. Unpublished M.Eng. Thesis, University of Sheffield, Sheffield.

Wildavsky, A. B. (1976). *The Politics of the Budgetary Process*, Little, Brown, Boston.

Williams, M. (1981). The economic justification for local bus transport subsidies, *International Journal of Transport Economics*, **8**, 79–88.

Wolman, H. and Reigeluth, G. (1980). *Financing Urban Public Transportation: The U.S. and Europe*, Transaction Books, London.

Geography and the Urban Environment
Progress in Research and Applications, Volume VI
Edited by D. T. Herbert and R. J. Johnston
© 1984 John Wiley & Sons Ltd.

Chapter 5

Community Power and Local State: Britain and the United States

Keith Hoggart

Over the last dozen years, reviewers have contrasted the past, pitiful perform-ance and the future promise of political geography (Hall, 1974; Logan, 1978; Johnston, 1980). Within both damning critiques and wishful expectations about the subdiscipline is a belief that the exercise of power lies at the heart of politics and should be a central focus of political geography. If 'the ultimate answer to every geographical problem is a political question' (Dear, 1979, p. 63), the future of power analyses in geography should be secure. Yet the word 'political' in political geography has most commonly been equated with 'governmental' when the two are not synonymous (Taylor, 1980). If power relations are critical in the operation of governments, this is because they are critical to the organization of society as a whole. To emphasize that deeper understanding of power relations is needed in political geography is commendable, but does not go far enough. Analyses of power processes should not be compartmentalized into one subdiscipline, when they infiltrate every aspect of the discipline. That political geography houses researchers who emphasize the theoretical merit of power investigations in no sense makes the subdiscipline the natural 'home' for power analyses. Statements about the need to study power relations in political geography stem largely from a recognition of their importance in determining government behaviour. Yet it is equally important to inquire where government institutions themselves stand in power networks. The study of government behaviour requires not only that we examine where, when, how and with what consequences governments act, but also where, when, how and with what consequences they do not act. Embodied in both of these is the more fundamental question of why governments do and do not act, the answer for which is strongly affected by power relations within government institutions, amongst government institutions and between government institutions and non-government organizations.

Power is one of the main dimensions along which society is stratified (Weber, 1948). Consequently, an understanding of power relations should shed light on all aspects of spatial structure (whether fixed locations—with associated spatial and man-environment relations—or interconnections between locations—flows of money, information, people, goods, etc). Evidence on the effects of power relations is plentiful and available at a variety of geographical scales. The location of public facilities can be determined by the outcome of power struggles (Wolpert, 1970), as can the nature of neighbourhood change (Moore, 1978; Glassberg, 1981). The values, initiative and drive of local elites partly determines the growth or decline of settlements, perhaps due to deliberate restrictiveness (Kendall, 1963; Gaventa, 1980), inability to grasp opportunities (Chadwick et al., 1972; Lantz, 1972), or the active pursuit of economic advancement (Adams, 1969; Gold, 1975). These effects are further contained within broader intra-national power relations, which promote inter-regional variations in development (Friedmann, 1973; Graziano, 1978), and international power relations, which foster variation in both rates of national development (Hymer, 1975; Frobell et al., 1980) and national control over societal change (Kavanagh, 1974; Clement, 1977). Unfortunately, with the exception of Marxism (and perhaps corporatist forms of managerialism) comparatively little geographic research has explicitly examined connections between social and spatial structures. This paper offers a somewhat faltering step in the direction of closer integration of social and geographical theory. It does so not by confronting these links directly, but by examining power relations in local communities in order to help understand the interrelations and behaviour of key decision-makers and so provide insight into the main forces determining spatial structures (e.g. Flowerdew, 1982). The nettle that is grasped is not all encompassing. It is limited by focusing largely on two countries, Britain and the United States, and is mainly concerned with the role of locally based government institutions (i.e. the local State).* The starting assumption is that government institutions should be key foci for geographic research, as the level, quality and location of their services and expenditures, alongside direct legislative effects on others' behaviour, can be critical determinants of the social well-being of citizens and the spatial structure of their habitat. The principal issue to be addressed stems from this assumption, in that it inquires into the centrality and dominance of local State institutions in local power structures.

POWER

Power is both one of the most fundamental concepts of social research and one of its most contentious. Power is a concept whose meaning is intuitively understood, and whose exercise is readily appreciated, but whose empirical dimensions are little agreed upon. Other than at a simplistic level, social researchers disagree on what power is, how it is exercised (and can be shown

* Throughout this chapter, State as a concept is capitalized, whereas examples of particular states are not.

empirically to be exercised), who exercises it most, and with what consequences. As with so many controversies in social research, at the root of these disagreements are differences in researchers' political ideologies and academic values. Because power relations are intimately associated with basic questions about the nature, causes and desirability of social inequality, their analysis is more deeply (and, possibly, more covertly) infiltrated by researchers' basic values than analyses of most other concepts.

Power analyses have a tendency to be as notable for what they do not tell us about power as for what they do. As a corollary, critiques of power studies often inform us as much about the reviewer as about the study or its researcher(s). In the literature there are claims which state or imply that researchers are inept, narrow-minded, dogmatic and biased (e.g. Cockburn, 1977, p. 3; Polsby, 1980, pp. 233–234, at times in language that betrays a clear absence of academic candour. Thus, when commenting on the first modern community power study (Hunter's (1953) *Community Power Structure*), Peterson (1981, pp. 136–137) charged that: 'Hunter's research was conducted in a casual manner; his writings fluctuated from sociological obfuscatism to journalistic sensationalism; and inferences he drew were not warranted by the findings produced.' I know of no one who would claim Hunter's work was methodologically perfect, but few would suggest its weaknesses merit this castigation. Certainly, Hunter's book has been criticized on methodological grounds, yet it is now recognized that these critiques were partly ideological in nature, with methodological weaknesses being pounced upon to justify rejection of his substantive conclusions (Saunders, 1979, p. 336). At a city level, Hunter provided what C. Wright Mills (1956) was later to provide at a national level, namely a case for believing that American society is controlled by a small elite of non-elected individuals. Perhaps Hunter and Mills published their books too close to the McCarthy era, for 'a small American industry organised itself around proving them wrong' (Newton, 1973, p. 287). This industry thereby highlighted the crucial effects of ideology on the conclusions of power analyses. Hunter's primary questions about the origins of public policy were set aside in favour of descriptive reviews of leadership groups (Walton, 1976), while research issues and methodological requirements were judiciously selected to 'prove' that communities were governed by politicians and hence, it was argued, the public (Morriss, 1971; Domhoff, 1978). By way of wishful thinking, and some heroic assumptions, conclusions with a remarkable resemblance to Hunter's were interpreted in substantially different ways (Rosenbaum, 1967; Friedland, 1981a).

Hunter's book stimulated the development of the community power literature. Prior to the publication of *Community Power Structure*, 'the question, "Who governs?" was answered in much the same manner by both social scientists and the lay public' (Bonjean and Olson, 1964, p. 279). The book was (and is) important not primarily because of its results or the methods it introduced, but because it stimulated a mass of research on a major issue. That this research has not generated a wealth of widely accepted generalizations owes more to the nature of the subject matter (and researchers' beliefs about it) than to ineptitude, laziness, or an unwillingness to generalize. Community power structures are not 'out there' waiting to be found. What is and is not a power relationship is far from universally agreed. Even if it were, little agreement exists on how power relations can be identified empirically. This does not lessen the value of analysing power relations, for such problems are not peculiar to power studies, just more obvious in them.

Superficially community power studies appear as a single body of literature, but in fact they draw on a variety of fairly distinct research traditions, each of which incorporates material differing widely in focus, content and aims (let alone conclusions). To search for generalizations from the literature requires a preliminary identification of the research traditions it embodies. These traditions are based on both conceptual and methodological differences, but, since the former should determine the latter (rather than vice versa), variation in power conceptualizations provide the main basis of division. All community power methodologies possess clear weaknesses (Hoggart, 1981b), but these are insufficient to invalidate (or validate) their conclusions on principle (albeit this might be so for particular applications of a method). In any event the generality of research findings can be assessed by cross-checking conclusions against those obtained in other places and by alternative methodologies. To do this validly, of course, requires that comparable studies are being examined; that there is an equivalent interpretation of power.

At its simplest level, power is probably most widely understood as the ability to get what you want. An 'actor' (i.e. a person, institution, social class or nation) is powerful to the extent that his, her or its wants are satisfied. Although expressed more rigorously, the spirit of this understanding is contained in academic definitions associated with a variety of subject areas and research approaches (e.g. Peterson, 1981; Simmie, 1981; Walsh *et al.*, 1981). Where critical disagreements exist is in translating this understanding into a conceptual framework which specifies the form, content and limits of social interactions which merit the designation 'power relations'. Numerous conceptualizations of power have been published, but most present a unified view of the concept, arguing or implying that their single interpretation is superior. Two exceptions to this are Lukes' (1974) three-dimensional view of power and Domhoff's (1978) recognition of situational, structural and systematic power components. Both researchers identify three 'aspects' of power, but, as they present them, their conceptualizations are not equivalent. There are none the less notable similarities in these schemes, and with readily justifiable modifications they can be treated in a similar fashion.

Probably the most widely known of these two conceptualizations is that of Lukes (1974). His first power dimension is a behavioural dimension, where power is exerted through the 'direct' interaction of two actors ('direct' does not mean that third parties cannot be intermediaries, merely that an actor who submits to another actor's wishes, or to beliefs about those wishes, knows that he, she or it is submitting). This is the most widely acknowledged view of power. Its definition, which is derived from Max Weber (1948), is that A has power over B to the extent that A can get B to do what A wants. This definition makes Lukes' first dimension essentially equivalent to Domhoff's situation component, which can be phrased, somewhat simplistically, as who wins the most and/or the 'important' decisions. This is what I shall refer to as the *decision* dimension of power, it assumes that A and B interact, that their objectives conflict (or at least that B cannot act without A's assistance), and that the outcome of their interaction is a particular decision (or decisions), which can result in either action or inaction. This conception does not require that B must do what A wants, merely that the probability of B's behaviour taking a particular path is changed by A (Polsby, 1980). To exercise power in this way, A must possess 'resources' which can be utilized to influence the behaviour of B (e.g. money inducements, feelings of obligation, physical force). These power resources are not equivalent to power itself. Relative resource levels alone do not determine the power of A and B, for the relative efficiency of resource use and the ability to convert resources into forms useful for power exertion are also important. The resources an actor possesses should therefore be kept conceptually distinct from power itself (Clark, 1973; Laver, 1978). For this reason I do not accept that Domhoff's structural power, which he defined as the governing of society's most important institutions, is a power dimension. Major society-wide power relations are almost certainly channelled through key institutions (Dye, 1976; Turk, 1977; Higley *et al.*, 1979), and for certain investigations institutional position-holding can be a serviceable proxy for power (Friedland, 1976; Johnston, 1977). Yet it must be emphasized that the starting point for modern community power investigations was Hunter's (1953) illustration that formal positions of institutional authority are not inevitably the home of the most powerful. Institutional position is a resource, it is not power *per se*.

Lukes' second power dimension has most frequently been referred to as non-decision-making. The essence of non-decision-making was expressed by Bachrach and Baratz (1970, p. 44) as 'a means by which demands for change in the existing allocation of benefits and privileges in the community can be killed before they are even voiced'. B does not act due to a belief that A would disapprove of (or veto) the proposed action. On different counts, this conception of power has been severely criticized and researchers have suggested it be abandoned (Parry and Morriss, 1974; Debnam, 1976; Hoggart, 1981b). Two main criticisms stand out. The first is methodological and concerns the difficulty of identifying non-decision-making. The second is conceptual, in that it challenges the assertion that non-decision-making is a distinct dimension of power. Taking the latter first, the essence of this critique is that, since non-decision-making involves the suppression or thwarting of challenges to A, it either involves an actual decision, and consequently is an aspect of the decision dimension of power, or it involves structuring B's options so challenges to A are either effectively impossible or not even considered, in which case it is an aspect of Lukes' third power dimension. In essence, this second dimension 'steals' components from the first and third dimensions. Admittedly, when this concept was introduced community power researchers were concentrating on the decision dimension alone (and then only on overt, controversial issues), so it played an important part in broadening our understanding of power relations. However, since a more encompassing understanding now exists, the utility of this concept must be seriously questioned. Recognition that A can affect B covertly is essential; placing this into a concept on its own is not.

As for methodological problems, the issues raised concerning non-decision-making are equally relevant for Lukes' third power dimension. This third dimension focuses upon how the (social, economic, political and cultural) organization of society structures relations so as to favour certain actors and disadvantage others. As Lukes (1974, pp. 21–22) expressed it: 'the bias of the system is not sustained by a series of individually chosen acts, but also, most importantly, by the socially structured and culturally patterned behaviour of groups and practices of institutions'. This dimension of power can be equated in many respects with Domhoff's systematic power, which he defined as who benefits most from the social system. Where Lukes and Domhoff differ is in Lukes' more careful treatment of the direct association between social organization and societal benefits. Although power relations are one means of determining the distribution of benefits, this does not mean that they are equivalent (the distribution of power might determine the distribution of benefits, but this does not mean that the distribution of benefits identifies the distribution of power). As theorists across the political spectrum have recognized, to preserve social order and foster support for the existing social system, the more powerful 'give' benefits to the less powerful over and above those achieved through power conflicts—support for the system is enhanced if the needs of the less powerful are met 'voluntarily' and are not simply obtained through overt social conflict (Lenski, 1966; O'Connor, 1973; Greenberg, 1974). Rather than viewing this power dimension in terms of outcomes (benefits), Lukes conceptualized it in terms of structuring courses of action. Such structuring can take a variety of forms—in capitalist countries, property laws bias the distribution of benefits towards existing wealth (Peet, 1981); in less economically advanced areas, paternalistic social relationships maintain the dominance of existing elites (Newby, 1977b; Gaventa, 1980; Chubb, 1981); while the structure of occupational benefits (and promotion criteria) in both public and private bureaucracies help ensure that middle- and upper-class interests take precedence over those of working-class people (Sjoberg et al., 1966; Stone, 1980). Such 'institutions' are commonly not challenged even though they help maintain the dominance of one group over another. Existing power relations help shape beliefs about the social system, such that the more powerful are not challenged on ideological grounds (Poulantzas, 1973), or because the 'dull compulsion of economic relations' translates challenges to the 'system' into threats to one's own socioeconomic well-being (Abercrombie *et al.*, 1980).

To make allowance for this dimension of power, Lukes defined the concept such that A exercises power over B when A affects B in a manner contrary to B's interests. It is at this point that the most fundamental disagreements on this power dimension emerge. Earlier I presented a simplistic definition of power as the ability to get what you want. Lukes' third dimension suggests that many people do not know what they want, that they accept decisions which are not in their interests and do not recognize what is in their interests (their wants not necessarily being in their best interests). A major problem with evaluating this dimension is its close association with researchers' conceptions of social organization. Students of social stratification have long recognized that most theories of social organization can be placed in (or largely draw their components from) one of two camps (Dahrendorf, 1959; Allardt, 1968). Integration theory holds that social stratification (and hence the uneven distribution of benefits and power) results from a consensus of values in society, with the most 'worthy' (or functionally useful) people attaining the highest positions. Even accepting certain 'inefficiencies' in the system, if this view is accepted, then the third dimension of power adds little, since any existing biases in the social system are acceptable (given value consensus). For conflict theorists, by contrast, this third dimension is crucial, since they view society as held together by coercion and constraint. The third power dimension identifies instances where structural arrangements help maintain a state of powerlessness for some, while helping maintain the hegemony of others. This presents a very simplistic view of theories of social organization, but even in outline these theories provide a necessary context for evaluating disagreements over Lukes' third dimension.

A further point of contention concerns the identification of people's 'interests'. Specifying what someone else's interests are has been claimed to be both a highly subjective and a highly contestable operation (e.g. Martin, 1977). Yet in reality such specifications are no more contestable than the identification of social 'needs' (Bradshaw, 1974), and researchers rarely shy away from this task. 'Interests' can be utilized in an heuristic manner (Lukes, 1974), just as much as they can be assumed to be 'real' (Poulantzas, 1973); after all, the existence of 'real' interests is assumed as much in integration theory as in conflict theory. Similarly, although Lukes' third dimension undoubtedly raises serious methodological problems (Martin, 1977), these can be overcome (e.g. Gaventa, 1980). The crux of the research problem is not very different from that faced by historians (Carr, 1961), participant observers of primitive tribes (McCall and Simmons, 1969), and psychiatrists (Cooper, 1967); evidence must be carefully assembled to support a case, with consideration given to other potential explanations. The workload required for investigating Lukes' third dimension is daunting (as it is for the first dimension), and requires a greater emphasis on historical analysis than the first dimension, but these do not make the task impossible.

In essence, then, I believe that power has two principal dimensions—a *decision* dimension and a *structural* dimension (equivalent to Lukes' third dimension)—which are conceptually distinct, because patterns of power relations in one dimension can (potentially) be different from those in the other dimension. Since researchers' conceptualizations of society are translated into their acceptance of these power dimensions, they must go some way toward pre-determining the conclusions of empirical investigations. Supporting this view, Saunders (1979, pp. 30–31) has noted that if contentious issues alone are studied, with *structural* power and covert aspects of *decision* power ignored, researchers run the risk of solely considering 'what happens to the political crumbs strewn carelessly about by an elite with its hands clasped firmly around the cake'. If this particular view is correct, then the bulk of the community power literature ignores the most significant aspects of power and, not surprisingly, the majority of reviews and conceptualizations of local power structures are partial (e.g. Bonjean and Olson, 1964). In this paper it is hoped to present a more 'balanced' view of local power structures, at least in that both decision and structural power are examined.

THE STATE AND COMMUNITY POWER

To specify the structure of local power requires identification of which power relationships are most important. Clearly a vast array of power relations exists, but no unidimensional evaluation of their importance is feasible. The concentration camp inmate, the young school child, and the manual worker all exist in environments permeated by clearly specified power networks, distinguishing 'equals', 'masters' and 'subordinates'. Yet each is encompassed within a broader power system. For a Dachau inmate, critical power relations are likely with guards and kapos (Bettelheim, 1960), just as a Toxteth youth's are often with the police, yet both relationships depend on more embracing and dominant power structures for their existence. What is experienced is not necessarily most crucial. While analyses of power can legitimately start at the individual level and build up—identifying broader (or dependent) power structures as they do—such an approach runs the risk of becoming bogged down by the sheer multitude of relationships that exist. There is not simply a danger of not seeing the wood for the trees, but even of not seeing the tree due to its vast number of branches. A guiding hand is needed to identify major power relationships. This is found in theories of the State.

As a general principle, taking the State as a starting point for power analyses is possibly arbitrary, but it can be justified on two main counts. First, in layman's terms, everyday life in advanced capitalist society is surrounded, if not engulfed, by the facts and fictions of 'democratic' government, wherein government institutions are seen as the dominant power holders. Second, in academic terms there is no single theory of the State, and no single view on the actual (independent) power of government institutions, but there is agreement that such institutions are key foci around which society is organized. Even when the State is conceptualized as an instrument of 'other' interests, it is still viewed as a critical power centre.

The state

That a variety of theories of the State exists attests to a lack of agreement over its function and purpose. If we accept Cunningham's (1973) case, then objective social research exists where researchers with very different values agree with the conclusions of an empirical investigation or the propositions of a theory. Adopting this criterion, there is little hope of the State being studied 'objectively'. State theories differ greatly in purpose, content and assumptions (Laski, 1935; Hill, 1977; Service, 1978; Clark and Dear, 1981; Johnston, 1981). None is particularly coherent, for within any one theoretical tradition there is substantial variation in emphasis, style and comprehensiveness (e.g. Jessop, 1977). The lack of specificity and level of generality of State theories effectively precludes 'objective' assessment. No doubt there is some truth in all State theories. The objective herein is not to evaluate their 'truth', but to draw on insights from them, to help guide us through a patchwork of seemingly contradictory and unconnected events, about which evidence is at best very partial, and so develop propositions about the structure of community power.

For us, the importance of State theories lies in their links with conceptualizations of community power structures, for they emphasize that local power relations are an integral part of broader social processes. In generalized terms, three theoretical perspectives on the State are currently in favour (Greenberg, 1974). The first, though not foremost, is the welfare state perspective. A somewhat ambiguous and poorly articulated theory, this basically holds that the State acts almost as a technician seeking to further the general welfare of all. The State is the focal point of societal organization, being called on to provide (collective) services which can only be provided on an individual basis with difficulty, while also tempering negative externalities from others' activities. In many respects, this perspective has close similarities with the second, pluralist, perspective. The main distinction between them lies in their conceptualizations of State autonomy. In pluralist theory the State is again believed to be neutral, but this is because it responds to the interests of non-State individuals, groups and organizations. The State furthers the general welfare of all, but this is not due to innate State properties. Rather, it arises because the public articulates its interests to the State, in demands for action and votes for politicians who provide it. Given fear of electoral retribution, State politicians ensure that no groups in society are unduly favoured and that society's benefits are distributed 'fairly'. On this point, the third, Marxist, perspective offers a very different interpretation. Marxist theory proposes that the State is an instrument of the ruling class. Any semblance of 'fairness' in State actions is viewed as mystification. In many instances, Marxists do not portray the State as one component of a vast capitalist conspiracy, but contend that the structure of capitalist society is such that the State inevitably favours capitalists (Harvey, 1976).

Community power structures

These theoretical perspectives cannot be traced directly into a community power context, but their basic components exist in conceptualizations of both community power (Saunders, 1981a) and relations between localities and broader social processes (Dunleavy, 1980a). Consistent with the theme of the State as an autonomous, technical agency is managerialism (or, as Dunleavy, 1980a, has it, neopluralism). Most frequently associated with the writings of Ray Pahl and John Rex, managerialism essentially holds that (non-elected) government officers (who manipulate their elected 'overseers') are the central actors in local affairs. As with all the theoretical perspectives examined here, managerialism has taken a considerable battering over time and has been subjected to significant modifications (for a recent review, see Leonard, 1982). Warts and all, it is an impressive theoretical contribution (Saunders, 1981b) and raises a theoretical proposition for this chapter; namely, that public bureaucrats are key local power holders. Perhaps more than other community power conceptualizations, pluralism has been the object of both vitriol and acclaim in abundance. As with its societal counterpart, the community power version of pluralist theory stresses both the centrality of (elected) local State institutions and their neutrality (or responsiveness). Its key theoretical propositions are that local State institutions mediate the most significant local power relations and that their mediations are unbiased. Directly challenging this view is instrumentalism (or elitism). Although not directly derived from Marxism, instrumentalism shares with Marxism the view that the local State is biased towards non-elected, unrepresentative, property interests, which comprise the real power centres in society. What distinguishes these two is the behavioural orientation of instrumentalism, as compared with the structural orientation of Marxism. The key proposition of instrumentalism is that business leaders dominate local power structures, with local State institutions largely acting at their (often covertly expressed) directions. The key Marxist proposition is that the structure of society is such that capitalist interests are inevitably furthered, whether or not capitalists are involved in the policy-making process. The phrase 'capitalist interests' implies a monolithic conception of the capitalist class, but Marxist theorists recognize that capitalists compete (to avoid joining the proletariat, for example, competition is spurred by the quest for growth). However, this does not mean that Marxists accept a pluralistic notion of societal organization being primarily the outcome of competition amongst elites (who then represent particular interest groups). Granted that society is comprised of a multitude of 'classes' (Pareto, 1935), the division of society into elites and non-elites (or capitalists and non-capitalists) is undoubtedly simplistic. Further, even though major conflicts in society are predominantly between elites, rather than between elites and non-elites (Pareto, 1901), fundamental changes in elite rule (albeit occurring infrequently) occur when non-elites 'force' their way into elite positions, dispossessing existing elites of their status (Pareto, 1935). It is in this sense that 'capitalist interests' can be recognized—in terms of mutual interests in preserving the existing distribution of social benefits which favours property-owners in general and, more especially, given control over the means of production, large-scale capitalist enteprises (or their owners and controllers).

These exceedingly sketchy and simplistic caricatures of (State and) community power conceptualizations are intended to emphasize two main points: first, each conceptualization recognizes that society is governed by a small number of elites (as individuals or as members of a class), but different conceptualizations emphasize the dominance of different sets of elites; and second, although the others recognize some structural effects, Marxism stands alone in stressing the dominance of structural considerations. In so far as this theoretical dissimilarity coincides with the conceptual distinction between structural and decision dimensions of power, it is appropriate to examine first the structural dimension of community power relations.

THE STRUCTURAL DIMENSION

Only comparatively recently has the community power literature given much attention to structural power. One reason for this was the neglect of community studies by Marxists. With their attention directed towards class and production relationships, Marxists have not unexpectedly focused most heavily on institutions and processes at national and international levels. Research on local power relations has largely been undertaken by researchers of other persuasions. When they have addressed the local setting, Marxists have at times shown a somewhat simplistic tendency to view local as national writ small (Cockburn, 1977; Duncan and Goodwin, 1982). This undoubtedly results in some fairly basic weaknesses in Marxist theorizing on local communities (Mollenkopf, 1979; Dunleavy, 1980a; Saunders, 1982b), but these cannot detract from the substantial insights Marxism offers on structural aspects of power. In essence, what we are looking for in analysing structural power is evidence that the context in which decisions are made provides differential access to societal benefits and restricts or enhances the freedom of action of particular groups. The origins of particular structural arrangements can be obvious, single (often controversial) decisions or incremental, perhaps almost unnoticed, introductions of conventions and regulations. Structural arrangements can come about due to deliberate acts or can be unintentional; but if they are unintentional, resistance to them can be expected if they challenge the interests of very powerful members of society. Many processes can induce enduring structural power relations, but in a local State context three merit special consideration—local jurisdictions, local resources and local actors. For each of these, the crucial question derived from Marxism is the same, does the structural framework of the local State favour capitalists?

Local jurisdictions

In most capitalist nations the jurisdictions of local State institutions are (formally) determined by central government, although the latitude given to local policy-makers varies enormously. In Britain, each of changes in boundaries, functions and policy-making powers requires central approval. Under *ultra vires* every local authority action should be capable of being traced to a specific Act of Parliament—British local authorities can only act (legally) if Parliament has given them authority to do so (by contrast, in some countries, like Norway, they can undertake any activity unless specifically forbidden to do so). In unitary States like Britain, local State jurisdictions tend, with special exceptions (like Scotland), to apply over the whole nation. By contrast, in federal States, like the United States, substantial variations occur, both across states, provinces and regions and within them. Thus, in the United States, home rule provisions give some cities the ability to redraw their government charter, reorganize their government structure and extend their boundaries without the approval of a state legislature, while other states specify the boundaries, functions, party representations, electoral procedures and resources of their local governments (Harrigan, 1976). This means that generalizations about power advantages derived from local jurisdictional organization are extremely difficult to make. Even so, it is clear that different spatial, administrative and functional patterns of local State organization can potentially further sectional interests.

The spatial organization of local State institutions has a primary impact on the composition of (formal) local State leadership. Very obvious examples exist in both Britain and the United States. As the ruling national party when both London (1963) and the rest of England (1972) had their local government systems reorganized, the Conservative Party was able to adjust Royal Commission recommendations so new local-authority boundaries provided enhanced opportunities for Conservative electoral victories. That they largely succeeded is quite clear. Dunleavy (1980a), for example, has estimated that even allowing for exceptionally large swings against the party that controls a local authority, over 75 per cent of the population of England and Wales live where the most important local authority tier (London borough, metropolitan district, non-metropolitan county) will always be ruled by one party. Fifty-eight per cent live in safe Conservative areas, with only 20 per cent in safe Labour authorities. The blemish on these otherwise masterly boundary manipulations was a miscalculation over the size of Greater London. By releasing too many suburban areas to the shire counties, control over the Greater London Council (GLC) has been shared between Labour and Conservative parties, when it was hoped to place it firmly in Conservative hands (Smallwood, 1965; Young and Garside, 1982). That the Conservative Party has deliberately attempted to gain local control from reorganization is well illustrated by the petulance of party leaders once the GLC did not fall into Conservative hands. The threats of disbanding the authority which prevailed under the 1970–1974 Conservative Government (Young, 1975) remain potent in Mrs. Thatchers' brave new world, and the reduction of GLC housing functions and recent threats to reduce its transport and planning functions show that the 'traditional' Conservative desire to weaken major Labour-controlled authorities still holds sway (Young, 1975; Young and Garside, 1982). Such 'fixing' of local jurisdictions is less common in the United States, due to the lesser importance of political parties at the local level. But as shown in 1957, when the newly-elected Republican state government stripped (Democratic) New York City of important and patronage rich functions, a similar process does operate where parties are in competition (Shefter, 1976).

More commonly, the key differences between the United States and Britain arise in how boundary placements are achieved and what they are achieved for. In the United States, the most common instance of boundary placing occurs when new local governments are incorporated and special districts are established. Ease of incorporation plays a major role in determining the spatial organization of local government, but incorporation is frequently not for administrative or functional reasons (as advanced to justify change in Britain). Instead the intention is to gain control of municipal functions—the change is not from one municipality to another with different boundaries (as in Britain), but from an unincorporated area to an incorporated one. The aim of incorporation is usually not to gain party advantage—for about 60 per cent of cities with over 5000 plus inhabitants are non-partisan (Antunes and Mladenka, 1976)—but to promote 'personal' advantage. Two common causes of incorporation ably demonstrate this. The first is to increase business profits. As aptly shown by the incorporations of Estero Municipal Improvement District in the San Francisco Bay area (Harrigan, 1976) and Clear Lake City near Houston (Cox and Nartowicz, 1980), residential developers can turn 'virgin' land into incorporated municipalities simply to issue tax-free municipal bonds to finance their new residential subdivisions (see also Checkoway, 1980; Miller, 1981).

The second objective is to gain control of land-use zoning, for by placing restrictions on lot sizes and house types the socioeconomic composition of area residents can be comfortably controlled. Most commentators see the primary intention of such zoning as keeping out those who place a heavy drain on municipal funds, while contributing little in municipal revenue (the poor and children in particular). The objective is to maximize tax resources, while minimizing public expenditure (Danielson, 1976; Newton, 1978). The effectiveness and extensiveness of such practices varies, but their intensity can be marked. Thus, in northern New Jersey 82 per cent of remaining open land is zoned for houses set in more-than-half-acre lots, in south-west Connecticut 75 per cent of available land is for houses in more than one acre, as is 64 per cent of suburban Philadelphia. Also in this last area, 38 per cent of municipalities prohibit multiple family dwellings and, in an attempt to exclude children, 42 per cent restrict the number of bedrooms per flat to one (Muller, 1975). A similar situation exists for non-residential property, with some municipalities being zoned almost exclusively for commerce and industry. Among the more famous examples are Teterboro, New Jersey, with less than a dozen residents, Vernon, California, and City of Industry, California, which had to take in the 169 patients and 31 employees of a mental sanitorium to reach the 500 inhabitants it needed for incorporation (Danielson, 1976; Miller, 1981).

Both the British and the United States situations can be and have been interpreted in class terms (e.g. Cox and Nartowicz, 1980). In both nations the drawing of boundaries has emphasized the separation of social classes (Bristow, 1978; Williams and Eklund, 1978; Miller, 1981), dividing the nation into groups of affluent communities with (relatively or absolutely) few demands for local State services and poor communities with heavy service demands. For the benefit of the wealthy, the poor are kept out of sight, out of sound and out of pocket. Differences in tax income are enormous (in California, for example, taxable property per pupil varies by school district from around $100 to over $950 000; Adams and Brown, 1976), with municipal resource inequality increasing in United States metropolitan areas as the proportion of blacks and the highly paid rises (Hill, 1974). The system works against the interests of the disadvantaged and also, in some measure, against those of the middle-class; advantages predominantly accrue to the most wealthy (Schneider and Logan, 1981). Yet one must be cautious in placing too straightfoward a class interpretation on the structures that exist. Moore (1978), for example, has shown that zoning regulations can be less of a determinant of residential circumstances than a response to them. Rather than determining class segregation, incorporation and zoning might simply formalize them. Of course where local institutions are bigger this equalizes resources somewhat, but substantial disparities exist in Britain, even though local authorities are much bigger and exclusionary land-use zoning is less prevalent. Further, evidence on cooperation agreements and the merger of municipalities yields little support for a class-based interpretation of such organizational arrangements (Williams *et al.*, 1965; Lyons and Engstrom, 1973). With evidence that the more wealthy are generally most in favour of metropolitan-wide government (Scott, 1968), even though such reforms seem to redistribute resources in favour of poor areas (Gusteley, 1977), it is possible that different factions within the property-owning class derive benefits from different organizational forms. It is also possible that the organization of local State institutions provides only marginal benefits for such groups, allowing scope for considerable variety in organizational form to meet the preferences of particular factions.

The working of the capitalist land economy inevitably produces an uneven spatial distribution of classes (Scott, 1980). Consequently any spatial demarcation inevitably produces an uneven distribution of (property) resources. Just because municipal boundaries formalize (perhaps even emphasize) resource inequalities does not demonstrate that their spatial structure is geared to maintain capitalist domination. Certainly in specific instances (Estero, Clear Lake City, Lakewood) capitalists have 'exploited' boundary placements for personal profit, but the land market alone ensures that (if the *local* State exists) the wealthy will generally benefit from better resource-need ratios than the poor.

The spatial organization of Britain's local government structure can be explained more happily in terms of political party advantage and the preferences of central-government bureaucracies than in class advantage terms (given its recent loud proclamations of woe, I assume the CBI would agree that the Conservative Party is not merely a puppet of dominant capitalist interests). Similarly the United States situation fits as easily into a lifestyle (William *et al.*, 1965) or 'consumption sector' explanation (Dunleavy, 1979) as a class explanation. Specialized communities for the elderly, the childless, second-home owners, industry, farmers, Mennonites and so on can be as readily explained as a recognition of mutual consumption/lifestyle interests as a similarity of production interests. Undoubtedly some of these groups overlap with classes, and some of their consumption interests cannot be divorced from tax considerations, but due to the workings of the land economy the advantages of small authorities over large stem more from maintaining status group control of local institutions (and reducing political conflict; Newton, 1978) than from fostering class advantage. As Britain clearly shows, industrial, commercial and financial institutions, alongside wealthy householders, can readily find geographic locations that provide them with favourable resource-need ratios, even when local State institutions are large. The small size of American municipalities provides a fine-tuning that enables wealthy residents to select packages of taxes and services to best-meet their 'lifestyle'. Any class advantage fostered by such fine-tuning is marginal. More fundamental is the operation of the land market and the failure of central governments to adequately compensate for differential resource-need ratios.

The main argument of the above paragraph is of course couched in terms of the spatial organization of the local State. When functional and administrative organization are examined, the case for a Marxist interpretation stands on somewhat firmer ground, but is still not particularly strong. Some Marxist writers have suggested that the local State is distinguished from the nation State by the particular functions it performs (e.g. Cockburn, 1977; for a non-Marxist view which implies the same see Saunders, 1980, 1982a). Using O'Connor's (1973) distinction between social investment policies, which increase the productivity of labour (e.g. investment grants, highways, industrial parks), and social consumption policies, which lower the costs of and help maintain a compliant labour force (e.g. education, welfare, social housing), it has been argued that the local State is primarily characterized by a concern for consumption policy—the nation State presiding over investment policy. This conceptualization is not without shortcomings (Fincher, 1981b), but it does provide a useful heuristic device for interpreting State organization. If the State is organized so that economic functions crucial to capitalist profit-making are shielded from public overview and pressure, this is suggestive of bias in local State organization. Such bias is most obvious in the United States, where non-elected appointees govern special districts with control over crucial economic functions. Characteristically, for example, urban renewal programmes have been organized and operated by corporation-dominated special districts, which issue their own revenue bonds and operate almost wholly without reference to the mayor, the city council and the electorate (Hartman, 1974; Friedland, 1980). Organizations like Boston's Massachusetts Port Authority, the New York Port Authority, and the Triborough Bridge and Tunnel Authority operate in much the same manner, controlling institutions with (potentially) major effects on the local economy, but being impervious to electoral restraint (Friedland et al., 1978; Peterson, 1981). Given the class and power advantages such insulation provides, it is not surprising that the number of special districts continues to increase rapidly (Harrigan, 1976).

If the notion of functional distinctiveness is broadly correct, then even if non-capitalists control elected local State institutions, they only govern activities which do not challenge capitalist advantage (see also Miliband, 1977; Friedland et al., 1978). This point merits careful consideration. Since absolute separation of production and consumption functions does not exist, the relative import-ance (to capitalists) of functions handled by local and national spheres is open to interpretation and debate. In Britain, local authorities' commitment and expenditure on industrial promotion are increasing rapidly (Minns and Thornley, 1978), but they lack significant formal power over industrial policy and the government has resisted attempts to increase their powers (Scarrow, 1971; Rogers and Smith, 1977). What is more, British business leaders have themselves suggested that local govenments' lack of control over major economic functions is a reason for their lack of direct involvement in local authority affairs (Clements, 1969). Yet British council-house investments clearly affect the profits of capitalists (Dunleavy, 1981), just as the urban renewal programmes of American local institutions do (Hayes, 1972; Hartman, 1974). Moreover, such investments are British local authorities' largest capital outlays and are made with a notable degree of local discretion (Ball, 1980; Hoggart, 1984). Local State activities are also of keen interest to capitalists because local property taxes comprise a large and increasing share of their total tax payments (Jackman and Ferry, 1978).

The notion that investment and consumption policy-making is split between State levels must be further questioned given the substantial involvement of State institutions in the consumption sector. The National Health Service, national overview and statutory requirements for local education policies, and unemployment benefits are consumption oriented, but centrally controlled. Yet these examples are no more than suggestive. The manner in which functions are divided between local and national State institutions, or the degree to which non-elected appointees control policy-making, is easy to ascertain but the system is so complex that illustrations of class bias must be patched together and can be countered by a similar patchwork which casts doubt on its existence.

The crux comes down to the relative weights placed on institutions that are shielded from 'interference' from the general public. The most notable and evident examples that back the class bias case are special districts in the United States (Friedland et al., 1978); where business leaders or their agents are commonly given the authority to control government policy in their own interests. The most obvious example of this is urban renewal. Friedland, for example, has demonstrated that the policies of urban renewal agencies are more responsive to urban growth (assisting profit making) than urban decline (improving housing for the poor); similarly the distribution of US War on Poverty funds seems to owe more to corporate fears of social unrest than the needs of the poor (Friedland, 1976, 1980). Likewise at the intra-city level, evidence on independent urban renewal agencies, health authorities and even education authorities indicates that such institutions can be used to further class advantage (Phelan and Pozen, 1973; Hartman, 1974). These cases are none the less somewhat specialized and their extensiveness needs to be closely documented. There are many 'special districts' that are not concerned primarily with private profit-making (e.g. area health authorities in Britain). Further, the case for class domination can be questioned as it rests on the assumption that nation State institutions are more responsive to the requests (or perceived interests) of capitalists, and less to non-capitalist pressures, than the local State. With local government areas more likely to be inhabited by persons predominantly from one class, the distribution of local resources providing little sustenance for ruling working-class representatives, and electoral competition frequently more marked at national than local levels, it is feasible to argue the contrary; overall working-class interests are better represented at national level than at local level.

What adds further support to this suggestion is the manner in which local politico-administrative structures can further capitalist interests. Again the clearest examples are in the United States, where the absence of a socialist party can partly be explained by local administrative structures. The introduction, sometimes by state government legislation, of non-partisan and city-wide local elections has reduced representation from the working-class and minority groups on city councils (Hawley, 1973). Socialist Party control of city councils, like Oakland, California (Hayes, 1972), and Dayton, Ohio (Weinstein, 1968), was clearly thwarted by the timely introduction of such changes in electoral and administrative arrangements. Despite the rhetoric of good government and efficiency, it is clear that such changes represented deliberate attempts to restrict the control of city government to those of higher social status (Hays, 1964; Weinstein, 1968; Anderson, 1979). Reform government certainly reduced working-class representation on city councils, but it also enhanced the power of higher-status non-capitalists. Although Newton's (1978) observation that reform government minimizes public participation without disenfranchizing anyone applies for those of lower social status, evidence indicates that reform governments are more responsive to community group pressures than are non-reformed governments (Hoffman, 1976; Getter and Schumaker, 1978). The association of responsiveness to higher status community groups in reformed cities and differences in councillor attributes can legitimately be expected to result in distinctive public policies in these two city types. Yet evidence suggests that these alternative administrative structures are not associated with policy differences (Morgan and Pelissero, 1980; and Peterson, 1981, for comments on the literature). This is perhaps largely explained by non-reformed cities typically being governed by non-ideological party machines, which are commonly characterized by their very close connections with dominant business groups (Greer, 1979; Peterson, 1981). If the local State is biased in favour of capitalists this does not appear to depend fundamentally upon particular administrative forms (see Fincher, 1981b), and any biases that do exist seem to be shared in large measure with non-capitalists of higher social status.

Local resources

In the bulk of advanced capitalist countries, the most prominent local State revenue source is the property tax. As with its national counterpart, the economic vitality of the local State is directly dependent upon the health of private enterprise. More so than national counterparts, local institutions engage in competition with one another to attract new private investments and maintain old ones (Apilado, 1971; Camina, 1974). Unless boundary and zoning structures have combined to give favourable resource-need ratios, local State institutions are, for reasons of preservation, electoral gain or social responsibility, pushed towards offering tax cuts, low-interest loans, cheap services or some other financial inducements to entice private companies into their areas. Once located, authorities must attempt to keep these enterprises. Detroit City Council, for example, has offered the Chrysler Corporation a long-run tax break simply to keep the company in the city (Markusen, 1976), and numerous American communities have had to forego introducing adequate air-pollution standards because corporations have threatened to relocate their plants if they did (Phelan and Pozen, 1973; Greer, 1979). The result is fiscal mercantilism (Molotch, 1976; Cox, 1978). Poor authorities are constrained by the necessity of either maintaining and enhancing property resources or reducing expenditure burdens. Not surprisingly, 'it is no exaggeration to state ... that one of the attractions of urban renewal and highway construction programmes in central cities has been physical removal of the fiscally burdensome poor' (Cox, 1978, p. 95; also Hartman, 1974). Although higher levels of central government funding make such policies less prevalent in Britain, the deliberate exclusion of council-house dwellings by some authorities (Young and Kramer, 1978), the emphasis placed on attracting and helping establish new businesses in others (Minns and Thornley, 1978; Underwood and Stewart, 1978), and local authority reorganizations which do little to reduce disparities between needs and resources (Bristow, 1972, 1978), all indicate that fiscal mercantilism has a role to play.

Although the threats and pressures of capitalists can be resisted, where resource-need ratios are poor, there are severe restraints on how far resistance can be pursued. Even when backed by the might of Chicago's Democratic machine, Mayor Richard Daley withdrew his plan to tax stock and commodity transactions when the Midwest Stock Exchange threatened that this would make them leave the city for the suburbs (Friedland, 1981a). Similarly, given corporate flight from the city (Quante, 1970), federal discouragement of housing investment in central cities (Checkoway, 1980), high levels of centrally-imposed tax exemptions and expenditure compulsions (e.g. Talarchek and Agnew, 1979; Peterson, 1981) and an extreme imbalance between expenditure needs and tax resources (Tabb, 1977), it is hardly surprising that local financial institutions found it easy to bankrupt New York City in 1975 (Lichten, 1979). What is surprising is they needed to do so. New York financiers have previously brought the city council to heel without the drama of bankruptcy (Shefter, 1976) and city finances were subject to detailed annual checks by state government officials (Bingham *et al.*, 1978). A problem with evaluating power relations solely in terms of involvement in decision issues is clearly revealed in the New York bankruptcy case. If, prior to bankruptcy, corporate and financial institutions had few behavioural power relations with the city council, it could be concluded that political and economic decision spheres were largely independent. The bankruptcy of New York revealed that this clearly was not the case. In the aftermath of bankruptcy it was made clear that the city was beholden to major local businesses, that the city had to appease its corporate citizens to stop their emigration, and that the means of doing so was to follow markedly pro-business policies—involving mass redundancies, reduced welfare and other service expenditures, and the subjugation of municipal trade unions (Tabb, 1977; Bingham et al., 1978; David and Kantor, 1979; Lichten, 1979; Peterson, 1981). Corporations had expressed their disapproval of New York policies by withdrawal from the city; their power was revealed in that withdrawal, which reduced the freedom of action of New York political leaders and ultimately produced bankruptcy. The bankruptcy signified that there were limits to the range of local activities corporate interests would accept; as White (1976) noted, to be evaluated adequately, power needs to be assessed with an eye on what might have happened had decision-makers behaved differently.

Capitalist interests cannot be challenged too severely with impunity. New York's ultimate stumbling block was that it borrowed too heavily. With city debts neither controlled nor underwritten by the federal government (unlike in Britain), the cost and availability of credit is in private hands. Each local State institution is allocated a credit rating such that, as local policies meet disfavour in (private) financial circles, the cost of borrowing increases (Clark and Ferguson, 1981; Sbragia, 1981). City credit ratings vary markedly, with a clear tendency for northeastern cities to be increasingly penalized (Peterson, 1980; Zeigler, 1981). It can be argued that bad northeastern ratings stem from overstaffing and high wage bills resulting from militant union activity, but with local fiscal strain bearing little relationship to city expenditure levels (Clark, 1977), fiscal stress can be more realistically seen as a consequence of population and tax losses (in good measure) resulting from corporations restructuring their operations by either relocating to, or focusing new investments in, low-cost suburban, southern or western areas (Breckenfeld, 1977; Perry and Watkins, 1977; Ratcliff, 1979; Taggart and Smith, 1981). The fiscal strain of northeastern cities is greatly aided by a corporate sector that reduces investment in the name of higher profits, then penalizes cities (through the cost of borrowing) because they have lost investment. In such a tightly restrained financial environment, it matters little who formally controls northeastern cities (Preston, 1976; Salanick and Pfeffer, 1977). Whether disinvestment is for the suburbs or the South, the result for central cities is the same—few resources and substantial expenditure needs result in a 'Pariah City' (Hill, 1978).

In general, cities in the South do not fit this description and the fiscal environment of British cities is certainly somewhat different. Even so, there are clear grounds for acknowledging the crucial effects of capitalist fiscal domination in constraining local State activities. In fact, as Clark (1977) has recorded, one of the main features that distinguishes United States cities in fiscal distress from those that are not is that, in the latter, capitalists are more strongly represented in day-by-day policy-making processes; to slip through a tight structural noose seemingly results from being captured in a behavioural snare. Any changes in this situation are likely to increase capitalist control, for as elected leaders see their tax base decline and unemployment grow their ability to resist the demands of capitalists will diminish (Yates, 1979). Possibly the situation is less intense in Britain, but structural restraints are still there, as evidenced by the last Labour Government's introduction of local expenditure restraints in response to pressure (in 1976) from the International Monetary Fund.

What principally distinguishes the British and United States situations is unequal dependence on central government funding. There is nothing intrinsically class-related in the division of local revenue sources between locality and centre. Substantial inequalities in local revenue sources might work to the disadvantage of working-class areas, but this does not mean that central funding benefits these areas. Thus a principal aim of the 1973 Italian financial reforms was to shift responsibility for tax collection and distribution away from cities, which were increasingly coming under Communist Party control, in favour of Christian Democrat-controlled central and regional governments (Friedland et al., 1978). Federal and state grants in the United States show few redistributive tendencies (Dye and Hurley, 1978; Hoggart, 1981a), while recent manoeuvrings of the British Secretary of State for Environment are clearly intended to raise the grants of wealthy (Tory) authorites and penalize those of poorer (Labour) authorities (Bennett, 1982). Yet while central government can use the distribution of grants to promote its own preferences, it does not have a completely free hand in doing so. As recent British Government experience shows, government action can be thwarted by internal disagreements over both objectives and strategy, as with the attempted introduction of spending guidelines for individual local authorities (e.g. 'Grant veto clause to be dropped', The Times, February 1982, pp. 1 and 22), and if they are introduced, as in Scotland, they are difficult to enforce (Page, 1980). The situation does none the less have similarities with New York's bankruptcy, for the 'freedom' Page (1980) has identified might result from authorities staying within acceptable 'disturbance' limits. The withdrawal of £47 million from Lothian Regional Council certainly demonstrates that stepping beyond these limits can produce heavy penalties ('Lothian loses £47m rate grant after vote to defy Government', The Times, 12 August 1981, p 1).

In its current attempts to control local government expenditures, British government behaviour demonstrates not only that it has the ability to change local revenues but also that it is itself tightly constrainted by political considerations in doing so. Open conflicts bring bad publicity and bad publicity loses votes. British local authorities have become accustomed to receiving substantial central grant payments (Bennett, 1981). Placing more emphasis on local revenue sources produces fierce opposition, not only from the general public but also from capitalists, whose tax payments are increasingly directed towards the local State rather than the national State. In Britain, for example, the proportion of company profits accounted for by non-domestic rates increased from 8 per cent in 1955 to 38 per cent in 1975 (Dunleavy, 1980b, p. 63), with rates now contributing in the order of 70 per cent of the taxes paid by non-domestic taxpayers (Jackman and Ferry, 1978). Similar patterns exist in the United States, where corporate income taxes declined as a proportion of federal revenues from 30 per cent in 1954 to 15 per cent in 1974 (Greer, 1979, p. 265).

An alternative to tax increases is to cut services, but this also creates bad publicity (e.g. 'Cuts and falling pupil numbers are damaging quality of education, school inspectors say', *The Times*, 14 February 1981, p. 3). Further complications arise when the government relies on tried and trusted excuses, like local government inefficiency, to justify cuts in grant levels. The government is clearly hampered by the necessity of maintaining the electorally acceptable guise of distributing funds 'objectively', and to date, no matter how it has juggled the books, results have repeatedly shown that Conservative-controlled authorities are predominant in the 'wasteful overspender' category (e.g. 'Penalising overspenders could hit Tories', *The Times*, 11 May 1981, p. 2). Given the extra control specific grants can provide, most especially in periods of economic austerity (Levine and Posner, 1981), it is not surprising that specific grants grew in importance in Britain over the 1970s (Bennett, 1981). There are none the less limits to the extent to which it is politically feasible to use such grants in place of block grants. The ideology of local democracy and autonomy is strong and attracts considerable public support. Irrespective of the mythology involved, vast numbers of votes could possibly be lost unless the government can persuade the public that a massive central takeover is democratically necessary. The spectre of large impersonal, London-based bureaucracies replacing small, locally-based, democratically-elected councils might well be mythology, but it cannot be ignored with impunity.

Local actors

Marxist theories of the State do not rest upon class differences in the characteristics of key actors (Miliband, 1977) but, as attempts to exclude working-class and minority groups from formal positions of authority show (Hays, 1964; Weinstein, 1968), class bias in position-holding is commonly assumed to have a behavioural counterpart. Three specific aspects of the characteristics of local actors are pertinent for examining Marxist interpretations of structural power—class bias in the composition of elected officials and public bureaucrats, and the value premises of the general population.

Studies have repeatedly identified an over-representation of the upper- and middle-classes, as well as private business representatives from retail, industrial, professional and farming occupations, in the composition of local policy-makers (Newton, 1979). Admittedly, in Britain at least, such over-representations have declined over time (e.g. Morris and Newton, 1970), but this partly stems from the increased size of the largest companies and the consequent declining significance of individual localities in their affairs; the decline of 'big business' in local politics is associated with a reorientation of their involvements in government toward the national sphere. The increased presence of left-wing parties on local councils has also increased working-class representation, though parties like Britain's Labour Party, aided by inadequate financial compensation and difficulties obtaining time-off work (e.g. 'Councillors leaving because of cash loss', *The Times*, 16 May 1980, p. 3), are increasingly taking middle-class appearances. What is significant about such biases, not only in class terms but also against women, those under the age of 40 and minority groups, is councillors' overwhelming tendency to view themselves as 'trustees' (Downes, 1968; Grant, 1977; Saunders, 1979)—who believe electors give them a free hand—rather than 'delegates' (who directly represent their electors' interests). Any tendency for class background to determine policy-making behaviour is emphasized by the dominant councillor belief that they have the right to do as they think best, rather than an obligation to follow their electors' wishes.

In part, any predisposition to favour upper- and middle-class interests by councillors will be somewhat held in check by electoral considerations. This is a less potent restraint for public bureaucrats, however. Working in a stratified society, bureaucrats are predisposed toward upper-class interests for their own self-advancement (Sjoberg *et al.*, 1966; Stone, 1980). Thus, professional standards in public libraries result in 'quality' books being stocked, rather than more 'practical' and easily 'digested' materials which interest those with less education (Levy *et al.*, 1974). Planning inquiries are notorious for prefacing submissons with questions to establish the technical authority and credibility of witnesses; 'expert testimony', which can be bought by those with sufficient resources, must be kept separate from mere 'points of view', so preserving the image that planning is a technical exercise and not a political process (O'Dowd and Tomlinson, 1980; Wynne, 1980). Similarly, through the operation of 'neutral' bureaucratic decision rules, the most experienced (and given high demand 'best') American teachers commonly transfer from 'troubled' working-class city schools to 'well-behaved' middle-class schools (Levy *et al.*, 1974; Mladenka, 1980). Further, many of the important professions in public bureaucracies have their senior members in the private sector—planners, architects and accountants are examples—so professional leadership tends to place disproportionate emphasis on private sector considerations (Dunleavy, 1980b, p. 113), as well as being predominantly conservative in outlook (Downs, 1967; Eversley, 1973): 'It is often the case that the weak must struggle while the strong only have to ask' (Stone, 1980, p. 981).

It is further often the case that the weak never think to ask. As Newby (1977a) and Gaventa (1980) have ably shown, in working-class, enclosed occupational communities, most especially when reinforced by employer houses, employer police, employer stores, employer-supported schools and employer-controlled local government, formidable obstacles develop over time to the generation of political activism and consciousness. Paternalistic social relations can evolve, where subordinates not only recognize the control superordinates have over them, but also believe in their moral *right* to have such control (Newby, 1977b). Although in the twentieth century the logic of capitalist undertakings has generally restricted such social relationships to small, largely self-contained communities (Newby, 1977b), there are many other instances where dominant groups are able to further their interests without opposition (even when these work against others' interests). Fear, a sense of vulnerability, or even fatalism undoubtedly play a part here (Salamon and Van Evera, 1973; Gaventa, 1980), but these feelings are not 'natural' since they are generally derived from past experiences. It is notable, for example, that the growth of the police force in the United States seems to owe more to quelling labour or racial strife and trade union organizing than it does to limiting crime (Welch, 1975; Greer, 1979, pp. 120–122). Similarly, vigilante attacks on ordinary members, leadership deportations and widespread repression arising from the paranoia of the post-Russian Revolution and McCarthy eras have undoubtedly helped foster an aversion to socialist party representation amongst the North American-working class (Weinstein, 1967; Brown and Brown, 1973; Burbank, 1976; Green, 1978; Klehr, 1978). More generally, support for capitalism stems less from repression than either an ideological (Poulantzas, 1973) or an economic commitment to the system (via mortgages, jobs, property—Abercrombie *et al.*, 1980). 'What have the Romans done for us?', asked the 'revolutionaries' in Monty Python's *The Life of Brian*; the answer, 'for most a great deal', could have been given for capitalism, even if at the same time it has (arguably) worked against their 'best interests'.

Review

There can be no doubt that the structural framework within which decision-based power relations occur leads to some groups occupying more favourable power positions than others. The critical issue is how much autonomy decision-makers have from these structural frameworks. The crux of Marxist theorizing is that, while autonomy exists, it is slight, since power advantages, no matter what the precise form of the capitalist State, are predominantly derived from structural frameworks and processes (Miliband, 1977). There is evidence of bias in society which ideologically and behaviourally favours capitalists. Similarly, there is obvious evidence that resource contexts foster local State dependence on property-owners. When these structural effects have proved insufficient to keep local State behaviour within 'acceptable' bounds the behavioural option of a 'coup' has been resorted to (e.g. David and Kantor, 1979); not only at the local level, but also, as shown in Greece in 1967 and Chile in 1973, at a national level. These aspects of local State behaviour support the main thrust of Marxist theorizing and yet the support they provide is imprecise. Marxist theory provides very general propositions about the structure of the State, but is weak in providing specific hypotheses that can be readily tested empirically. A problem for Marxist theorizing is that structural effects are both spatially and temporally variable. Thus, in some areas key economic functions are kept apart from electorally-based institutions, whereas in others they are not. The lack of universality of particular organizational forms does not lead to a rejection of Marxist propositions, but it does require careful justification. There is every possibility that the absence of one mechanism favouring capitalists might simply result from the presence of an alternative. For such a proposition to be acceptable, however, testable hypotheses must be examined which specify where, when and why alternative mechanisms occur. At present Marxist theorists appear some way from providing so specific a set of hypotheses (Rich, 1982; Saunders, 1982b), and some Marxists believe they are not necessary (Duncan and Goodwin, 1982). No doubt variations in cultural and historical circumstances, alongside internal divisions and conflicts (resulting in spatial and temporal variation in the coincidence of organizational innovation and factional dominance), provide some answers, but so might variation in the autonomy of the State from capitalist control. There is none the less a danger of searching for Marxist explanations for all structural considerations. In general, for instance, I can find little support for a Marxist interpretation of the jurisdictional organization of the local State. I believe that any biases in the social system in favour of capitalists do not fundamentally depend on such organizational forms. The organizational framework can clearly advantage capitalist interests, but overall these advantages tend to be marginal when compared with the biases provided by economic resource restrictions. A case can justifiably be made for favouring other theoretical propositions about local State organization (political party advantage, lifestyle, bureaucratic preference) without challenging the basic Marxist premise of bias in the system as a whole. Until substantially more evidence is available, most especially concerning the limits of State autonomy (e.g. What effects do tax increases have on the flight to the suburbs?: Under what conditions do capitalists cease to rely on structural restraints and adopt a behavioural option to control State institutions?), conclusions about structural power will lack a firm empirical foundation and will be more easily discounted on the grounds of theoretical and empirical imprecision. In a community—power context, the analysis of structural power clearly suggests that there is a bias in favour of property-owners, though the evidence is at so general a level that it explains little of variation in local State organization and behaviour.

THE DECISION DIMENSION

Investigations dominated by the analysis of decision processes have identified a wide variety of community power structures. This variety is reflected in community power classification schemes, which are in some ways more suggestive in their dissimilarities than informative in their content (e.g. Rossi, 1960; Banfield and Wilson, 1967; Wirt, 1974; Burt, 1981). Classificatory problems arise not only because researchers use different methodologies and focus on dissimilar aspects of community life, but also because such studies are necessarily partial and their results are not readily amenable to simplistic classification. Nelson (1974) made this explicit when he examined the validity of classificatory schemes by asking investigators to fit their own studies into them. He found little agreement between investigators' interpretations of their own work and classifiers' interpretations. The classifiers' problems stem from power relations being both non-quantifiable and multidimensional. At least five dimensions can be recognised which distinguish community power structures: (1) the extent to which a broad or narrow section of the population comprises the 'power' elite; (2) the degree to which elites compete; (3) how responsive elites are to non-elites and whether social groups are differentially favoured in responsiveness patterns; (4) how far local elites act independently of extralocal elites; and (5) the extent to which social group separation means that groups do not need to compete within their locality (accepting that conflict can occur between localities).

It is undoubtedly a major weakness of the community power literature that for many years the complexity of power structures was insufficiently acknowledged. Ideological predispositions led researchers to demonstrate that communities were (predominantly) either elitist or pluralist. While much was learnt about the nature of decision power, insufficient was learnt about the nature of community power structures. If the intention is to further understanding of power structures, then the crux lies in identifying the intensity, extensiveness and circumstances in which decision-making 'groups' exert power. Derived from the dimensions listed above, and existing community-power conceptualizations, three main decision arenas can be distinguished for assessing power relations—local-central relations, relations within local State institutions, and relations between these institutions and other local organizations, groups and individuals.

Local-central relations

Elsewhere, I have argued that the autonomy of local State institutions from their national counterparts can be evaluated with reference to four components—the decision *issue*, the *framework* (or structure) in which decisions are made, the precise *decision-makers* involved, and the strategies and options open to decision-makers in the decision *process* (Hoggart, 1981b, pp. 17–32). In essence, this means that: first, the structural framework within which decisions are made usually sets boundaries on feasible decision outcomes and (potential) decision-maker power—*ultra vires* restrains local government behaviour, just as absence of resources does; second, the nature of local-central power relations varies across broad decision arenas and/or specific decisions—central departments and agencies develop their own ethos, which leads to variation in the intensity and extensiveness of central attempts to dominate local institutions (Griffith, 1966; Rhodes, 1981); third, certain local institutions are 'allowed' more autonomy from central overview than others—larger local authorities with more professional staff are commonly subject to less central control than smaller authorities (Weidner, 1944; Griffith, 1966); and fourth, the relative power of decision-makers is affected by the strategies they adopt in the decision-process and by the stage to which that process has advanced—the longer the sequence of negotiation and power exertion has taken, and the closer a contentious issue seems to resolution, the more committed decision-makers become to particular ('compromise') courses of action, resulting in greater constraints on their willingness to consider alternative solutions (Levin, 1972; J. Grant, 1977). These four components are by no means specific to local-central interactions, for (potentially at least) they play a part in all decision—power relations. They are listed here to stress the multidimensional (and dynamic) nature of power relations.

Structural power relations between local and central State institutions commonly suggest a pattern of tight restraints on local behaviour. The situation for decision power is both more and less clear. It is less clear in part because the study of local-central decision issues does not have so well developed a research tradition in the United States as in Britain. Impressive studies of local-central interactions exist (e.g. Pressman and Wildavsky, 1973), but perhaps as a result of the multiplicity of local, state and national institutions, and the lower levels of local State finance derived from national sources, this literature has not developed as a coherent whole. Consequently this section largely focuses on the British situation, where local-central decision relations are more clearly understood.

In Britain, the range of local *decision-making* autonomy seems substantial, for there is considerable evidence that central institutions find it difficult (at times impossible) to impose their will on their local counterparts. Indeed, if we accept that local policy-makers are not intent on challenging their constitutional position, it is clear that there is 'little evidence that local government officials and councillors feel unduly hampered by central controls' (Gyford, 1976, p. 15). One reason for this is that instructions and communications from central to local institutions are commonly ambiguous and open to wide interpretation (Shipp and Harris, 1977). Local policy-makers can utilize such communications to justify unpopular decisions they would make anyway—an example is

Westminster's privatization of housing repair jobs following District Auditor criticisms of its direct labour force (Randall, 1979; and see Dearlove, 1973)—or they can ignore them, frequently with impunity—as with Southwark's ignoring of District Auditor advice to raise council house rents (Randall, 1979). In a similar manner, central policy-makers distance themselves somewhat from local State activities so as not to be blamed (and lose votes) for local consequences of national policies (e.g. school closures). Central policy-makers have a vested interest in perpetuating an ideology of local democracy, even though it places (at times severe) restraints on their actions. Public acrimonious disputes between individual localities and central institutions are generally avoided as they generate bad publicity, which can lose prestige for the Minister and votes for the party (Griffith, 1966; Rhodes, 1981). Partly as a result, centrally imposed changes in the structural arrangements of local institutions tend to be incremental rather than revolutionary. To justify sweeping changes an ideological prop is required—the 1974 English local government reorganization was justified by the 'objectivity' of a Royal Commission report and the obvious disparity between socioeconomic activity patterns and local government boundaries, while the 1975 reorganization of New York's administration was justified by the city's bankruptcy. If such props are not available, especially where central acts foster political advantage, freedom to manoeuvre is restricted. A feature of the current British Government's attempts to restrain local authority expenditures, for example, has been the fear that severely penalizing Labour authorities for 'excessive' spending might result in a Labour Government penalizing Conservative authorities for 'underspending'. As noted earlier, in Britain at least, the chances of central government suffering electoral defeat are much higher than changes in local party control occurring. This means that if the government does not muster widespread support or ideological acceptance for major changes in local structures a change in government could well herald the revoking of changes made (as with Labour's 1974 annulment of the Tories' 1972 Housing Finance Act). Meanwhile, an authority that publicly resists not only embarrasses the government on that issue, but also reduces government willingness to embark on other (simultaneous) controversial changes.

Organization theory predicts that an organization will try to manipulate its environment to avoid uncertainty (Cyert and March, 1963; Thompson, 1967). Any tendency toward uncertainty avoidance is likely to be enhanced if agencies within local and national States are dependent on one another. The dependence of local institutions on central institutions is obvious, but the relationship is reciprocal. Central institutions need local institutions to administer (national) programmes and, through their heterogeneity and consequent policy variation, provide innovation and testing-beds for new policy development (two good examples being the provision of insulin to diabetics and the introduction of comprehensive secondary education—see, Swann, 1972; Fenwick, 1976). In managing their environment, local and national institutions seek to manipulate each other in a manner that benefits themselves. The principal means of accomplishing this is by developing mutually agreeable coalitions. This is especially so given divisions and conflicts at both local and nation State levels between politicians and bureaucrats and between State departments and agencies (a good example is the tussles between the Treasury and national spending departments over increased programme expenditures—see Heclo and Wildavsky, 1974). Given the latter, it is not surprising that the 'complaint, general throughout local government, is that the left hand of central government is urging expenditure at the same time the right hand is urging economy' (Oliver and Stanyer, 1970, p. 151). The result is the emergence of a coalition of government agencies, at different government levels, who share interests in the development of a particular policy arena (Rhodes, 1981). This is not unexpected given that local-central relations predominantly involve bureaucratic interaction and accommodation, with bureaucrats' personal advancement depending substantially on the growth of the bureaucracy itself (Downs, 1967). Since very tight central control would require a substantial increase in the size of central bureaucracies, it might at first glance seem desirable for central bureaucrats to favour greater powers of central overview. Yet such an option would be undesirable for (central) bureaucrats for two reasons: first, since large bureaucracies are electorally unpopular, their activities will likely be subject to greater and more tempestuous scrutiny; and second, as shown in France (Kesselman, 1967; Becquart-Leclercq, 1977), the more rigid the bureaucratic system, the more likely politicians by-pass it (most especially for 'key' projects) by calling on personal contacts. Either way, the end result can be reduced bureaucratic power. In these circumstances, it is not surprising that bureaucratic professions can be conceptualized as attempting to manage the distribution of decisions between central and local government to strengthen the hand of their profession (Laffin, 1980), or that analyses of decision-making processes stress the considerable latitude open to local authorities in their interactions with central institutions (Dearlove, 1973; Shipp and Harris, 1977; Ball, 1980; Webb and Wistow, 1980).

The situation for local representatives of central agencies is far less clear, largely due to the relative paucity of research on the autonomy of regional and local offices in central government bureaucracies. What evidence is available suggests that central agents lack the resources needed to check or control the behaviour of local institutions—both within their own organization and in associated organizations (LeGates, 1972; Webb and Wistow, 1980; Dunleavy, 1981)—so it is not surprising to find descriptions of such local offices which portray them either as being coopted by city governments, special districts or local interest groups (LeGates, 1972; Hartman, 1974) or being more closely associated with local authorities than with their central department (e.g. Lojkine, 1981). The situation is undoubtedly a complex one, however, for the absence of local electoral overview enhances bureaucratic power. With adequate resources, this can mean that such agencies can pursue policies which meet the preferences of bureau personnel and place the needs and demands of local citizens and policy-makers well down their priority lists (Eyles *et al.*, 1982). Further, given that the promotion of these bureaucrats and the funding (and broadly-defined tasks) of their bureaux are centrally determined, it is not unreasonable to expect these officers to be forceful advocates of central policy.

Although I have stressed the 'desirability' of maintaining 'friendly' relations between government levels, there are quite commonly instances of open conflict. These are not only between local and national institutions but also amongst local institutions themselves. Characteristic of inter-community conflicts are the resistance of outer boroughs to the Greater London Council's attempts to suburbanize council-house construction (Young and Kramer, 1978), county and district conflicts over the location of gypsy sites (Elcock, 1979) and central-city opposition conflicting with suburban support for urban motorways (Nowlan and Nowlan, 1970). Significant local-central conflicts have included opposition to the 1972 Housing Finance Act (Skinner and Langdon, 1974), Conservative authorities' opposition to comprehensive education (Fenwick, 1976), local opposition to nuclear power plants (Wynne, 1980), and central-government opposition to South Yorkshire's cheap-fares, public-transport policy. Characteristically such conflicts are specific to particular programmes or projects. They might simply indicate the range of central tolerance—although local institutions seemingly possess considerable autonomy, this autonomy might exist because their activities are not greatly at variance with the main trends of government policy preferences. But if this is so, then, as Bromley's continued resistance to council housing and South Yorkshire's long-preserved, cheap-fares policy show, local institutions are capable of sustaining prolonged onslaughts from higher government levels for long time periods. Similarly, although Preteceille (1981) has argued that the detail of overview and tightness of central control prohibits the development of truly local policy in France, other researchers have recorded clear evidence of local policy initiation and implementation (Milch, 1974; Becquart-Leclercq, 1977). Evidence is sufficiently plentiful to acknowledge that local State institutions have an independent organizational existence, even if this is within a national interorganizational network. The day-by-day decisions of local institutions are made with considerable autonomy (e.g. Dearlove, 1973; Milch, 1974), even if central institutions set broad limits and provide general long-term direction for policy development (e.g. Newton, 1976; Ball, 1980).

Internal decision processes

While the literature recognizes great variety in community power structures, much importance is attached to the focal position of locally elected political representatives. This is especially so in Britain, since researchers have principally distinguished British community power structures from those of the United States by the more dominant position of elected officials (Green, 1968; Miller, 1970; Parsons, 1972; Woodhead, 1972). This does not mean that politicians occupy strategic power positions on account of their personal properties. On the contrary, overwhelmingly the significant element of political leadership is the formal authority vested in particular elected (or appointed) positions (and resources this gives access to). Yet people do not occupy these positions by accident and, since position occupance carries with it certain expectations about behaviour, as well as specific obligations, the political attributes of persons occupying key positions is clearly of some importance.

The clearest basis for distinguishing elected representatives (or indeed appointed officials) on the basis of their obligations and power base arises from their independence from or position in a political party. For both Britain and the United States no straightforward statement can capture the precise effects of political parties as power bases. In both nations, party systems vary not only in their extensiveness, but also in form and forcefulness. The most notable national dissimilarity lies in the extensiveness of non-partisan politics. Non-partisanship in the United States is dominant in municipal government and, though less prevalent among the largest cities, is found at all levels of the settlement hierarchy. In Britain non-partisanship is largely restricted to rural areas, and is also in decline. Whereas in the United States local administrative reform has been instituted to maintain, enhance and even reintroduce non-partisanship (Hays, 1964; Weinstein, 1968; Hawley, 1973), in Britain reforms have been a catalyst for the rapid decline of 'independent' politics (Grant, W. 1977; Bealey and Sewel, 1981). Against this backcloth of differential distributional extensiveness, there is an underlying similarity of political character. The 'independence' of American politicians disguises a Republican, business-oriented flavour (Hawley, 1973), just as 'independent' British politicians are disproportionately drawn from Conservative, land-owning interests (Rhodes, 1974; Dyer, 1978). While there is certainly some evidence that non-partisanship in Britain partly reflects a 'traditional' citizen opposition to political parties (Grant, W. 1977; Bealey and Sewel, 1981), such 'traditions' can stem from deliberate policies of thwarting party development and the deliberate encouragement of political styles based on 'those you know' who are 'fit to govern' (Axford, 1978; Dyer, 1978; Newby et al., 1978). When viewed alongside the marked decline of 'independent' politics following the recent reorganizations of British local government, it is possible to equate British non-partisanship with its United States counterpart; not a democratic reflection of citizens' preferences, but an imposed organizational form which favours specific interests.

One must be somewhat careful in accepting this interpretation, for non-partisanship is commonly associated with an enhanced role for public bureaucrats (not simply greater control for a specific group of politicians). Most obviously, this is seen in the United States, where the structural arrangements of 'reformed' governments commonly mean that non-partisanship exists alongside commission or city-manager administrations. As Wirt (1974) observed for San Francisco, partyless politics can result in a lack of leadership from elected representatives, producing government by clerks. Leadership is not wholly absent, for senior bureaucrats predominantly reject a division between politics and administration and believe they should be active policy advocates (Loveridge, 1968). In Britain, the pattern is similar, but the causes are different. Non-partisanship in the United States is found in large cities with (essentially) full-time councillors, whereas in Britain it is associated more with government by local notables, whose other commitments restrict their involvement in local State activities. This is symbolized by the infrequency of council meetings (Stanyer, 1967; Rhodes, 1974) and the unequal basis on which part-time councillors can compete with full-time public bureaucrats to provide coherent, technically feasible 'solutions' to problems of service provision and planning (McAuslan and Bevan, 1977; Haywood, 1977; Blowers, 1980; Flynn, 1981). From the 'average' councillor's viewpoint, it is often necessary to defer to the views of senior politicians and councillors since the 'sheer pressure of time and work make this deference to the opinion of others essential if the work is to be completed' (Rhodes, 1974, p. 158). Yet while the 'average' councillors might, in many cases, allow bureaucrats considerable latitude in both the formulation and implementation of policy, they can keep a tight check on the level of resources allocated (e.g. Rhodes, 1974, p. 201). The non-partisan belt on Britain's political map appears more bureaucrat-dominated than its partisan counterpart, but very commonly the manoeuvrability of bureaucrats is restricted by councillor concern over the level of local property taxes.

Critical issues in partisan areas are how far politicians are free from party control and how party control affects the behaviour of public bureaucrats. A partial answer for the first issue is the ability of certain politicians to 'stand above' their party. The obvious stature of American city bosses like the late Richard Daley of Chicago and the association of certain mayors, such as New York's John Lindsay, with a possible Presidential candidacy, clearly signifies that local politicians can attain a personal stature and following over and above that of their party. Such personalities are perhaps less common in Britain, but they do exist. Gillard and Tomkinson (1980, p. 84), for instance, have described Durham County's Andrew Cunningham as 'a Chicago style political boss who ran the county as if it were his private "rotten borough"', for he 'was a virtual dictator of Durham politics . . . Cunningham's word was the one that counted' (Fitzwalter and Taylor, 1981, p. 65). When we recall names like Newcastle's T. Dan Smith, London's Herbert Morrison and Liverpool's John Braddock as well, the British 'boss' is clearly seen to have an existence of his (or her) own (Kesselman, 1967, and Machin, 1977, suggest a comparable situation for France, as does Chubb, 1980, for Italy). Even so, the truth is that 'bosses' are few and far between. The leader of council (i.e. majority party) occupies the most important British local government position, yet these people have few personal followers—the public more commonly associates council leadership with the honorary position of mayor (Birch, 1959). Changes in leadership can result in changed policies, over and above any party effects (e.g. Charles Burman's effect on housing policy in Birmingham—see Dunleavy, 1981), but personal effects are most likely minor when placed alongside institutional and party influences. This is especially seen in local election results (e.g. Green, 1972; Newton, 1976), but also finds a place in leaders' effects on policy (Jackson, 1972; Salanick and Pfeffer, 1977; Welch and Karnig, 1979). As accounts of eminent American city bosses demonstrate, leadership can confer substantial (potential) power, but the dictates of political survival place severe restraints on freedom of action (Banfield, 1961; Gittell, 1967). Although media coverage of political events is characterized by the promotion of personality cults, few local leaders attain eminent (independent) positions of power in local affairs.

There is a strong body of opinion that emphasizes essentially the same point for political parties (Karp, 1973; Fried, 1975). Specific instances can certainly be found where changes in party control induce changes in local policy (Jones, 1969; Grant, J. 1977), but counterbalancing instances exist where parties intent on forcing change have been unable to do so (Chubb, 1980; Fudge, 1981). Parties which gain control of local institutions are hampered by central regulations, resource requirements, citizen demands and expectations, bureaucratic interests, and their own internal structures, in addition to which politicians want to be re-elected. This is partly to pursue particular policy objectives, but also (in some place overwhelmingly) to rule for its own sake (Butterworth, 1966; Turner, 1978). The intensity with which 'government' is sought is evidenced by blatant attempts at ballot-rigging (as Greer, 1979, described for Gary, Indiana) and deliberate attempts to mislead the public in order to present a 'rosy' picture of an administration's performance (as illustrated by Mayor Rizzo's fixing of Philadelphia's budget figures in his re-election year—see Clark and Ferguson, 1981). Once elected, politicians seek to maintain control of government, which makes them cautious of major changes, which can bring uncertainty and the possibility of failure and public humiliation. All these factors might on their own be overcome, but in combination they are formidable restraints on innovation and change.

These restraints can be considered both from a party's viewpoint and from the viewpoint of other interests (or, with a focus on internal power structures, the public bureaucrat's viewpoint). First, it should be emphasized that parties are not unitary entities. Local parties, though carrying the same label as national counterparts, take on a 'lifestyle' of their own (Birch, 1959; Bulpitt, 1967) and are largely free from the dictates of national head offices (Birch, 1959; Jones, 1969). What is more they are commonly lax in enforcing party discipline (Bulpitt, 1967), even though, or perhaps because, their membership often lacks a clear unity of purpose. Thus, Woodhead's (1972) observation that the South Shields Labour Party was divided into an old guard, whose primary loyalty was to the town, and a younger group, who were more party and class-oriented, is part of a theme that runs throughout Britain (e.g. Peschek and Brand, 1966; Glassberg, 1981). Senior councillors expect junior councillors both to learn their place and to learn how (senior councillors believe) things should be done (Corina, 1972; Dearlove, 1973; Axford, 1978). Since senior councillors usually represent 'safe' wards (hence their seniority), whereas junior councillors are more likely from marginal wards (which, because they are marginal, might have different socioeconomic circumstances and needs), it is to be expected that the latter want to 'get things done' (to make a quick impact), even if this means changing plans already drawn up by their seniors. Those who are not drawn into the senior-councillor circle are potentially alienated from their party leaders on the grounds of age, seniority, needs of constituents and pressures for change.

This is not to imply that parties are alive with internal conflicts and widespread discontent amongst junior councillors. What generally distinguishes party leaders from their juniors is their orientation towards policy-making, as opposed to 'nursing' a ward (Corina, 1974; Grant, W. 1977). Many councillors are very happy to leave policy-making to party (or council) leaders. Perhaps not without other aids, such differences amongst councillors can conspire to orient senior councillors away from their party roots towards more stable associations with either senior bureaucrats or leaders of other parties (Olsen, 1970). Given deference to leadership, such as characterizes the British Conservatives (Rose, 1965), this problem is unlikely to be critical, but where such deference is not present, open hostility can emerge. Such open conflict is disconcerting for party leaders, both because it challenges their position and brings 'bad publicity'. To circumvent conflict, and preserve their grasp on much coveted power and patronage positions (Bulpitt, 1967; Corina, 1972), leaders can 'close down' the party, by restricting membership and working against party members who threaten to challenge its leadership (Butterworth, 1966; Baxter, 1972; Turner, 1978). At this point the party takes on a life divorced from representing interests other than those of party leaders. This is probably most explicit in the United States, where primary elections for mayoral office can produce candidates who do not meet party leaders' approval, 'forcing' them openly to support candidates from opposition parties (Karp, 1973; Greer, 1979). A comparable British example is the expulsion of 'troublesome' councillors from their party for embarrassing party leaders (e.g. Butterworth, 1966).

Obviously not all local parties can be described in such 'reactionary' terms. The observation that council leadership falls to a small number does nevertheless find strong support in the literature. Lee (1963) has coined the phrase 'ministerialist party' to describe these groups. They are commonly comprised of a few senior councillors from the majority party (in non-partisan areas, the more senior councillors), together with a restricted number of senior bureaucrats

(Olsen, 1970; Axford, 1978; Blowers, 1980; Green, 1981) and in a few localities even senior councillors from opposition parties have a role (Clements, 1976). Within councils the leadership base has become increasingly narrow, with leaders tending towards more autocratic policy-making (Cousins, 1979). Dunleavy's (1980b, p. 140) belief that 'for almost all purposes the full council is a body of less and less relevance in local politics' has been expressed more flamboyantly by T. Dan Smith—'If 95 per cent of them [councillors] never went near the council chamber it would make no difference' (Green, 1981, p. 65)—but the essential message is the same. Council leaders are moreover more isolated from the general public than junior councillors, with a clear bias in their public contacts towards more powerful local interest groups (e.g. Newton, 1973; Darke and Walker, 1977). In addition, with senior councillors sitting in safer electoral wards, changes in leadership can be slow in coming and might be largely dependent upon 'dramatic' events, like huge national electoral swings against the party or evidence of widespread corruption (Chamberlayne, 1978; Glassberg, 1981).

For the 'average' councillors, the relative insignificance of their back-bench position is reinforced by an inability to control bureaucratic behaviour. As reviews of local bureaucracies emphasize, evidence on the relative power of councillors and bureaucrats is far from unequivocal (e.g. Randall, 1981). What is noticeable is a growing tendency for analysts to stress the dominant position of bureaucrats (Gittell, 1967; Lowi, 1967; Jones, 1969; Friend and Jessop, 1977; Flynn, 1981). Generalization on such issues is none the less difficult, since contrasts are often seemingly made between 'average' councillors and senior bureaucrats, with statements about relative power being made as if the context was unidimensional, instead of multidimensional. Examples of these dimensions are indications that bureaucratic power is lower where party control is marginal (Cox and Nartowicz, 1980; Randall, 1981), where the Labour Party is in the majority (Gyford, 1976), and where the decision issue is controversial or class related (Kantor, 1976; Randall, 1981). From the bureaucratic side, the competence of chief officers enhances their power (Friend and Jessop, 1977), while the predispositions of officers themselves are various, leading some to favour caretaker-administrator roles and others more leadership-policy orien- ted roles (Headrick, 1962; David, 1977). In contrast with policy formulation, evidence very clearly indicates that bureaucrats have the most decisive effects on decision implementation. 'Field' or street-level bureaucrats are widely recog- nized to have substantial autonomy not only from their political masters but also from senior bureaucrats (Nivola, 1978; Prottas, 1977). Bureaucratic decision rules and street-level decisions have consistently been shown to have dominant effects on the distribution of services and amenities (Lineberry, 1977; Mladenka, 1980; Eyles et al., 1982). Even where politicians have clear effects on the distribution of resources, bureaucratic effects still dominate (Glassberg, 1973; Jones, 1981).

What must be clearly borne in mind when examining councillor-bureaucrat power is that while determining the distribution of resources is important, determining the level of resources that can be distributed is critical. These critical questions are not only most likely decided by the ministerialist party, because they provide leadership, but also because this 'party' excludes others from policy-making. In Halifax, for example, 'Rate Notices have been printed *prior* to the meeting at which the rate was determined' (Corina, 1972, p. 195), a practice that closely parallels Newcastle councillors being given thirty minutes to read, digest and then approve the city's annual budget (Green, 1981). The actual restraints placed on leaders by backbenchers is unclear. Cases like Liverpool (Baxter, 1972) and Newcastle (Green, 1981) suggest they can be largely ignored with impunity, but there are undoubtedly variations in leaders' styles and power (Cousins, 1979; Green, 1981). Much is still unknown, but the ministerialist group appears to set broad priorities in policy-making, though usually without dotting the i's and crossing the t's. This detail does not fall to the full council, but is decided by functional 'committees' (Lowi, 1967; Kantor, 1976)—the functional departments in the United States and the functional committees of British authorities (the local education authority, the housing committee, the planning committee and so on). In the United States, where councils are smaller, such functional committees are more dominant than in Britain (Lowi, 1967). Even so, unless (as with special districts) they have independent revenue-collecting abilities, they are subordinate to the resource-allocating ministerialist group (albeit active and powerful chairmen or senior bureaucrats, whether part of the ministerialist group or not, can induce more resources and greater policy-making autonomy for a committee—e.g. Newton, 1976). In general terms then, it appears that, even if locally-elected institutions occupy critical positions in community power structures, locally-elected representatives do not. Rather a small sub-set of such representatives do and even then they share their centrality with senior public bureaucrats.

Local state and locality

Pluralist theory predicts that local State institutions will be responsive to the electorate's wishes, with their decisions reflecting an equal regard for representations made by social groups, alongside politicians' 'natural' responsiveness to the needs of non-represented groups. Instrumentalism favours an interpretation based on business domination, where responsiveness to non-business groups largely represents an attempt to maintain the guise of democratic government as ideological camouflage for non-representative, self-interested rule. The interpretation found in managerialism portrays government institutions with more autonomy, though it is recognized that they commonly combine with business leaders to form oligopolistic power structures (Simmie, 1981). The essential differences between these are embodied in two issues—the independence of local

State institutions from business leaders and their responsiveness to the general electorate's 'demands'.

Studies of business–local State decision-making relations suggest that dominance and collusion exist in some places (Monahan, 1976; Newby et al., 1978; Bealey and Sewel, 1981; Simmie, 1981), but in others economic and political spheres seem largely independent (Green, 1968; Stinchcombe, 1968; Woodhead, 1972; Haranne, 1979). The actual value of these conclusions must nevertheless be questioned given the characteristic of community-power analysts to reinterpret other researchers' findings and argue they have misinterpreted their own results (Polsby, 1980, provides a good example). Such reinterpretations can undoubtedly enhance our understanding of power relations (as with Saunders', 1982b, comments on Simmie, 1981), but there has been an unfortunate tendency for reinterpretations to degenerate into attempts to fit one theory to all localities. Such a position is, I believe, both naive and academically dishonest. All too frequently reinterpretations are transparently ideologically motivated, with methodological critiques as pertinent for studies supporting the critic's favoured theory as for those that do not. This places reviewers in an uncertain position. To illustrate, possibly the most influential and widely respected community power study is Dahl's *Who Governs?*, in which he concluded that elected political leaders are dominant in New Haven's power structure. Dahl's work has been the object of several critiques (e.g. Rosenbaum, 1967; Morriss, 1971), the most detailed of which included fresh data collection and the conclusion that Dahl was wrong—New Haven's power structure was business-dominated (Domhoff, 1978). In rejecting these critiques, Polsby, one of Dahl's co-workers, was particularly severe on Domhoff, claiming that, 'Only a very partial, garbled, frequently inaccurate and unclear version can be found in Domhoff's book', and his 'conclusions [on New Haven's critical urban renewal programme] are certainly not sustained by the available historical evidence, of which his book gives what can charitably be called a skewed example' (1980, p. 188). Polsby's criticisms were not restricted to Dahl's challengers, for he found one 'of the most remarkable features of the progress of the community power literature since 1960 has been the explicit detachment of a goodly portion of this literature from empirical restraint' (pp. 233–234). Since Dahl himself has been criticized for allowing wishful thinking to cloud his result interpretation (Rosenbaum, 1967; Debnam, 1976), it appears that empirical evidence which supports instrumentalist, managerialist or pluralist theories can be readily interpreted in other ways. This being the case, it is not surprising that the community power literature has developed few widely-accepted generalizations on local State–locality relationships. Rather than assuming one theory fits all communities, it seems advisable to accept that since power studies are difficult to undertake 'objectively', researchers will inevitably 'overemphasize' aspects of power relations. It is very likely that aspects of instrumentalism, managerialism and pluralism exist in all communities, for none of these are all-embracing theories. If generalization is the aim, however, we should not be happy with others' descriptions of *what* relations exist (in any particular community), unless it is clear *why* they exist. It is feasible, as a hypothetical example, for pluralism to provide a very accurate description of what power relations exist in a community, but only because community boundaries have been drawn to exclude interests that would challenge the prevailing ethos. The search for generalizations must in large measure depend upon researchers' reports on communities, since their 'accuracy' can hardly be checked, but this does not mean they provide a sufficient description of power structures. Valid theoretical generalization depends not simply on how often a pattern is recorded but, more importantly, on the conditions under which and reasons why they are recorded.

In terms of relationships with the local State, the most commonly recognized behavioural distinction for business organizations is the division between national/multinational corporations and locally-owned firms; in Wirt's (1974) terminology, the Big Rich and the Little Rich. Changes in ownership from local to extralocal spheres has long been recognized to induce changes in local power structures (see Mott, 1970). As the largest firms become 'nationalized', the significance of any one location in company affairs declines. Owners and managers withdraw from local political involvements, because they no longer provide him (or her) with 'what he seemed to value most in local participation, visibility, respect and the ability to safeguard his own economic interests' (Garrard, 1977, p. 258). This enabled businessmen from smaller (local) firms to emerge as local political leaders (Birch, 1959; Bradley and Zald, 1965; Morris and Newton, 1970; Garrard, 1977) and, with major local employers releasing their grip on local political institutions, seemingly provided a clearer separation of economic and political control. Political representation of a broader spectrum of interests in local State policy-making was made easier and a more diffuse (decision-making) power structure resulted (Schulze, 1958; French, 1970; Mott, 1970). The 'withdrawal' of large-scale local employers from local politics did not signify a fall in their interest in local politics. This is particularly evident where localities house corporate headquarters or very substantial corporate investments. In such communities, in defence of their own interests, corporations are commonly active participants in local affairs (Phelan and Pozen, 1973; Greer, 1979; Gaventa, 1980). Likewise, corporations have actively responded to threats of local social unrest, providing and promoting aid programmes to dampen disquiet (Friedland, 1976; Orren, 1976). They have actively promoted the acceptance of local State policies which favour their interests (Checkoway, 1980; O'Dowd and Tomlinson, 1980; Dunleavy, 1981), as well as resisting policies that would inhibit their profit-making (Scarrow, 1971; Checkoway, 1980; Meehan, 1982). Yet in both cases corporate-power exertion is generally directed at national State institutions, as the backing of 'Government Policy' legitimizes corporate pressures on local institutions, turning 'political' acts of self-advancement into neutral 'economic' bids which help fulfil government intentions. In general, major corporations are not crucial participants in local decision processes because their national and international orientation means that it is national policies which are critical for their operations (e.g. overall tax demands, pollution legislation, employment regulations). Further, from the corporate viewpoint, national State institutions can be expected to discourage their local counterparts from straying far from the national 'average'. Even if they do, corporate involvement in local decision processes is still largely unnecessary (unless corporations have very substantial local commitments), since such 'deviance' can be punished by not investing in or withdrawing investment from a community.

By concentrating their policy initiatives at the national level, major corporations not only disguise their political impacts on the local State but also conceal their conflicts with locally-owned businesses. Characteristic of the pressure for mass-produced public housing, for instance, is a reallocation of local State housing contracts away from small, local firms towards national corporations (Dunleavy, 1981). More obviously at a local level, the development of new shopping centres, often grounded in a belief that the retail attractiveness of urban centres will be enhanced, most commonly results in the relative demise of local businesses and increased advantages for corporate retail outlets (Lojkine, 1977; Bennison and Davies, 1980; Simmie, 1981). The apparent inconsistency in local businesses supporting developments that damage their (communal) interests is reconciled when it is recognized that *some* local businesses do benefit and *all* local businesses depend upon the continued attractiveness of their urban centre for their profitability. It is no surprise that real estate, retail, professional and, in the United States, newspaper representatives are the most active business participants in local State policy-making (Banfield and Wilson, 1967; Molotch, 1976), just as it is not unexpected that their involvement can provide greater benefits for national corporations than for themselves (Saunders, 1979). Direct office holding, or indeed direct participation in local policy-making, is not an essential prerequisite for deriving power and income advantages from local State activities.

Office-holding and decision-making involvement is none the less important for local businesses. This is seen in their control of special districts whose policies are business-related (Hartman, 1974; Bealey and Sewel, 1981), their organized resistance to local politicians who represent 'anti-business' parties (e.g. 'Businessmen fund drive to fight G.L.C. in courts', *The Times*, 7 November 1981, p. 2), their direct promotion of candidates who will further the profit-making cause (Phelan and Pozen, 1973; Hartman, 1974), and their contributions to electoral campaign funds in order to elicit 'favours' (Wirt, 1974; Gottdiener, 1977). Outside the formal framework of local State institutions, business leaders have clubbed together to form alliances which present ready-made, business-supported, prestige projects, both to enhance private profitability and to induce politician support due to their vote catching appeal (Banfield and Wilson, 1967; Friedland, 1981a). On occasion they have offered organizational and financial 'aid' to help provide local services, though the seeming benevolence in such offers must be set against the greater power this gives business groups over local State policies—as seen in agricultural tied cottages, which reduce British local authorities' need to provide council housing (Newby *et al.*, 1978), the unwillingness of Wilmington community organizations to pursue policies (or employ personnel) that 'offend' the Du Pont Corporation (Phelan and Pozen, 1973), and threats to withdraw funds from Croydon's technical college unless courses were available that companies directly needed (Saunders, 1979). These represent a few specific instances, but there are cases where such practices permeate most aspects of local State activity (Edgar, 1970; Phelan and Pozen, 1973). As a very general observation on the community power literature, it is noticeable that very few studies, including those supporting pluralism, report cases where major business groups are challenged on fundamental issues and 'defeated'. Even where local economic affairs are seemingly overwhelmingly dependent upon the government sector for their prosperity (e.g. Chubb, 1981), this very dependence can result from broader economic forces (Graziano, 1978). Most descriptions which support the pluralist ideal find business interests not directly involved, rather than defeated.

This conclusion does not apply for community groups, for a dominant theme of the community-power–public participation literature is the marginal effect community groups have on local State policies. The literature does, however, suggest that cross-national differences occur. One example is the local press. In Britain local newspapers act more as mechanisms for dispersing information from councils to the public than as active or effective supporters of causes: 'If the local press is a public watchdog on the town hall, it is a singularly accommodating animal, with no bite and a rather muffled bark' (Gyford, 1976, p. 122). In combination with other groups the press can raise the level of public debate and support for particular causes, but local political leaders seem ably capable of ignoring its attentions (e.g. Christensen, 1981); it is an occasional irritant, but almost never a serious threat (Gyford, 1976). The United States provides a marked contrast, since newspapers have been identified as one of the most powerful actors in many communities (Burt, 1981). Their strong tradition of investigative reporting, which can act as a check on politician and bureaucrat behaviour, accompanied by a mutuality of interests with large retail, professional and real estate interests, can induce more responsive local government, both to local business interests (Molotch, 1976) and to public opinion (Getter and Schumaker, 1978). Another illustration of cross-national differences is provided by trade unions. Whereas British unions have commonly refused to participate in local politics, because it is not relevant to their immediate work situation, or have limited their involvement to passing resolutions (Kraushaar, 1981), American unions have involved themselves actively in local politics (in many northern cities at least) and occupy major power positions in some cities (Banfield and Wilson, 1967; Hill, 1980; Burt, 1981).

Effectively, however, such differences are more apparent than real. Evidence suggests that newspapers predominantly (though not inevitably) support the position of dominant business groups. The press is structurally dependent on other businesses for the bulk of its revenue (through advertising) and if it occupies a key position in the power structure, it appears to do so under either the 'licence' or the direction of local business leaders (Hartman, 1974; Domhoff, 1978). Likewise, in cities dominated by party machines, the press is commonly used to portray the party in good light (Guterbock, 1980), exercising its 'freedom' by ignoring the dominant party's opponents or castigating them as troublemakers (Greer, 1979). The appearance of cross-national differences most likely reflects dissimilarities in structural contexts, for with less need for fiscal mercantilism and the greater dominance of national institutions in Britain (government, business and press), dominant local power interests have less need for the local press. As for trade unions, in both countries they seek largely to gain benefits for their own members alone and are noted for their lack of socialist zeal (Cole, 1948; Miliband, 1961; Stinchcombe, 1968; Peterson, 1981). The position of American unions in local power structures seems to owe more to their cooption by dominant business groups than their ability to wield independent, substantive power (Hartman, 1974; Friedland, 1976; Hill, 1980). Even though work experience (especially in areas like South Yorkshire) can have political ramifications (e.g. Newby et al., 1978; White, 1980), unions have generally failed to associate struggles in the workplace with struggles over local State policies (unlike the situation in France—Lojkine, 1977). The apparent local power of unions in the United States comes when they merge with local capitalists to support programmes of economic growth, not from any general effects on local affairs.

This view of trade union effects is not strictly accurate if their indirect effects are considered. In association with political parties of the Left, trade unions should provide primary vehicles for representing the interests of working-class people. Given divisions by skill, employment sector (monopoly or competitive), consumption behaviour (home-owner or renter, car driver or public transport user), race, and political party affiliation, working-class interests are of course not uniform and are also more difficult to represent than those of the middle- and upper-classes (Dunleavy, 1979; Rose, 1980; Elliott and McCrone, 1981; Wattenberg, 1981). Nevertheless, trade unions can justifiably be accused of weakening the power of the working-class, as a class, through the pursuit of narrow allocational benefits (largely for their own members), which foster intra-class divisions. It would not be unfair to claim that American unions are strongly anti-socialist (Weinstein, 1967); indeed, they reveal an antagonism to redistributive government policies almost as marked as that of major business organizations, with their level of support frequently below the average for major community organizations (Williams and Zimmerman, 1981). They appear to have had little effect on general welfare programmes (Friedland, 1976), and have certainly given little sustenance to working-class political parties, even when they have been fairly successful (Bedford, 1966; Burbank, 1976). Likewise, in Britain, aided by control over party finances, trade unions have been crucial advocates of a centrist, 'pseudo-socialist' orientation for the Labour Party (Cole, 1948; Miliband, 1961; Clark, 1981), which has on occasion resulted in national party leaders being bitterly opposed to forceful pro-working-class local parties (Miliband, 1961; Branson, 1979).

Any relative failure of political parties to represent the interests of working-class people derives from a complexity of causes. On both sides of the Atlantic a clear tendency has existed for parties of the Left to be internally divided—partly over which faction accurately reflects working-class interests (Cole, 1948; Weinstein, 1967; McCormack, 1977; Miliband, 1977). These finely-tuned ideological disputes contrast with the apparent harmony and policy fuzziness of parties of the Right. As long ago as the American Civil War, American commentators were expressing some exasperation over their inability to rely on Britain's Conservative Party leaders, who 'had scarcely a distinctive principle except the traditional loyalty to the person of the sovereign' (Catton, 1965, p. 131). Expressed differently, Rose (1965) has characterized Conservative principles as extremely vague, with tendencies towards defence of the status quo, reaction and gradual reform, but sufficient flexibility to legitimize a wide variety of policy options. The objective is to rule in order to defend the status quo, not to carry through particular policies (e.g. Cornford, 1963). This flexibility has served right-wing parties extremely well, for their election manifestos have advocated almost any policy that attracts votes and in consequence have at critical times stolen the banner of left-wing parties (see Weinstein, 1967).

Such ideological flexibility is perhaps best exemplified in a local setting by political party 'machines' and patron–clientele relationships. Public stigma usually decries both of these forms of political system, for they are believed to depend largely on the exchange of votes for financial or employment benefits (Rakove, 1975; White, 1980). But recent evidence has suggested that their support derives more from good organization, the electorate's ignorance of government procedures, and general (though deliberate) policy biases in favour of key voting groups (Guterbock, 1980; Chubb, 1981). That such systems manipulate the electorate to maintain the dominance of a party elite can hardly be denied, but such manipulation is hardly restricted to these political systems. Many instances of single-party rule can be described in much the same way (Butterworth, 1966; Baxter, 1972; Dearlove, 1973; Newby et al., 1978). It must none the less be recognized that local party leaders operate within certain constraints. Whether the result of local factors alone, or a combination of local and national, the electoral system provides the electorate with the opportunity to end single-party rule. Admittedly, this occurs rarely, but as in Islington in 1968 (Chamberlayne, 1978) and Naples in 1975 (Chubb, 1980), when the electorate is 'offended' by ruling (national or local) parties it has the electoral muscle to end single-party rule. Seemingly this should give the electorate notable power over local politicians' behaviour, even where single-party rule occurs. This might seem to be so given that local State policies are strongly affected by the 'needs' of local residents (Newton, 1974). Yet the meeting of these needs, both in extent and content, reflects the views of policy-makers rather than those of the electorate (Rigby, 1980, for example, has found almost no attempts by English local authorities to identify the transport needs of their residents even though they have a statutory obligation to do so—politicians clearly interpret 'messages' from the public in a manner in keeping with their existing predispositions—see Lowi, 1964; Dearlove, 1973). Where activities have become involved at the grass-roots level to identify and seek action on local residents' needs and preferences, they have commonly been opposed by local party leaders (very likely, as Hayes, 1972, showed in Oakland, this is because the preferences and requirements of local residents—most especially the working-class—differ substantially from those local policy-makers are prepared to recognize). Some examples of this include the Poplar conflicts of the 1920s (Branson, 1979), the opposition of some Labour councillors to CDP projects (Kraushaar, 1981), councillor castigation of those Newham residents who opposed their high-rise policy as 'troublemakers' (Dunleavy, 1977) and even, in some ways, the frictions that have developed between Communist-controlled Florence City Council and the neighbourhood associations the party itself established (Seidelman, 1981). Perhaps not surprisingly, the failure of political parties adequately to represent the needs and preferences of local residents has been one of the main reasons for the growth of micro-political activity in advanced capitalist nations (Hindess, 1971; Donnison, 1973).

The image I have presented so far pictures party rule as principally concerned with self-preservation and largely unresponsive to grass-roots political pressures. I accept that this is something of an exaggeration and recognize that the form of party rule can vary substantially across localities (Bulpitt, 1967). Further, I recognize that examples exist where local politicians have actively sought grass-roots advice as a party policy (Chamberlayne, 1978; Glassberg, 1981; Seidelman, 1981). My main point is to stress that parties frequently fail to provide alternative representation for interests that are not locally powerful (Newton, 1976, for instance, concluded that the failure of Birmingham City Council to respond to the needs of ethnic minorities owes much to their not living in marginal electoral wards). This is not because politicians are generally dishonest, but follows from the structure of the local political system. Local State institutions occupy environments characterized by widespread public ignorance, where local parties have comparatively little effect on local election results (either because boundaries have been 'gerrymandered' to maintain single party rule or because elections are largely determined by national considerations). Should changes in party control occur, the new controlling party is commonly hampered by a bureaucracy committed to the previous party's (or its own) policies, alongside restrictions imposed by either higher levels of government (which themselves might very well be controlled by a different party—Chubb, 1980; Fudge, 1981), or dominant business groups (Greer, 1979). In such circumstances it is not surprising to find comparatively little evidence that party differences have had consistent (inter-community) policy effects (Newton, 1974; Fried, 1975; Sharpe, 1981). Most especially with ideological differences between parties lessening (Hindess, 1971; Thomas, 1975), the effects of parties are more likely to be fairly gentle, depending more on timing and emphasis than basic differences in orientation (Rose, 1965; Newton, 1976; Hoggart, 1984).

The lack of markedly distinct party effects is undoubtedly a partial result of resource considerations, though it is also affected by certain similarities in political orientations amongst politicians from different parties. One clear example of this is politicians' (and bureaucrats') preference for a policy-making environment which is 'closed' from public involvement. This preference is perhaps understandable given that, when voter support for policy change is required, the public reveals a tendency to overturn the plans policy-makers have prepared (e.g. Brunn et al., 1969; Wirt, 1974; Hennigh, 1978). Such items of democratic policy-making as referenda are not wholly met with favour by local policy-makers—the proportion of money raised for bond issues through referenda declined in the United States from over 50 per cent in 1968 to 10 to 15 per cent in 1975 (Friedland, 1981b). Similarly, legally-required public meetings are commonly conducted less to establish the British electorate's views than to inform them of what is going to happen.

> We held parents' meetings and all that, and some officers from the Education Office spoke to them. But this wasn't to *consult*; this was to *tell* the parents what their authority had decided to do about comprehensive schools . . . we *tell* parents what the authority has decided is best for their children. (Peterson and Kantor, 1977, p. 202)

This suggests that local policy-makers do not favour public participation. Yet while this undoubtedly applies in some situations (Monahan, 1976; Chamberlayne, 1978), in others policy-makers actively encourage participation. Most notably this is when they require public backing for their views. Saunders (1975), for example, reported that Croydon Council produced citizen complaints as justification for rejecting a comprehensive school scheme the government wished it to adopt. Others have recorded how inter-departmental disputes have led to bureaucrats seeking to strengthen their case by demonstrating public backing (Lipsky, 1970; Mason, 1978; Paris and Blackaby, 1979) or using participation to weaken community groups by divide-and-rule tactics (Hartman, 1974; Fincher, 1981a).

Where local policy-makers respond to pressure from the general public this does not so much represent public determination of public policy, as public determination of the *limits* of local policy. That limits exist is clearly illustrated by specific examples. The emergence and electoral success of ratepayers' associations in English local government owed much to huge increases in local council rate demands following the 1974 reorganization of local government (Grant, W. 1977). Where local politicians have let service levels fall substantially below citizen expectations, the response has not uncommonly been strong support for a change in political control—as indicated by support for metropolitan government reform in Jacksonville and Nashville (Harrigan, 1976) and the takeover of South Umpqua School Board by dissatisfied parents (Hennigh, 1978). Not surprisingly, local politicians are reluctant to provoke local residents unnecessarily, especially when they have the resources and organizational ability to embarrass them—this is well illustrated in Bromley Council's adoption of a 'focused development' policy, where 'unwelcome developments' are restricted to specific neighbourhoods (Glassberg, 1981), as it is in the former Middlesex County Council's unwillingness to reduce subsidies to private schools (via assisted places) since councillors feared an upper-middle-class backlash which, with a Conservative Government in office, could have induced central-government pressure on the authority (Saran, 1967; this kind of process is described by Kesselman, 1967, as common in French communes). Similarly, where marginal party control is present, there is clear evidence of local policy-makers responding to pressure from key wards—the correspondence of marginal electoral wards and route selection for London's proposed motorway system provided a key reason for the demise of the scheme for instance (Hall, 1980). What distinguishes these cases is that they involve challenges to the power of policy-makers themselves, rather than challenges to particular policies. I can find little evidence to support Dahl's notion that politicians 'are all constrained by the wide adherence to the [democratic] creed that exists through the community' (1961, p. 325). My reading of the evidence is that politicians and bureaucrats support and encourage public participation when it is in their own interests, and are responsive to the general public's requests for action when they believe this threatens their position, but generally they seek either to reduce the amount of public involvement in local State affairs or weaken its impact.

Public pressure is aided by policy-makers' inability clearly to distinguish issues that could weaken their position from those that are unlikely to. It is notable, for instance, that although there is little evidence that changes in property taxes affect election results, local politicians are cautious about raising them for fear of electoral reprisals (Antunes and Mladenka, 1976; Newton, 1976). Consequently, policy-makers do acknowledge public pressure, most especially when issues are controversial or receive widespread publicity and support. They do nevertheless try to reduce the impact of these pressures, and in doing so call on such ploys as coopting opposition-group leaders, discrediting causes, delay and fostering divisions amongst opponents (Lipsky, 1968; Gelb, 1970; Dearlove, 1974). Obviously these ploys will not always prove successful, most especially if policy-makers' opponents have the resources, organizational ability, expertise and internal cohesion to resist forcefully, possibly over a long time period. Given the distribution of these attributes in the population, it is no surprise that policy-makers seek to appease middle- and upper-class groups more than working-class groups (Schumaker and Billeaux, 1978; Elliott and McCrone, 1981). Further, lack of resources, organizational weakness and internal divisions, along with a frequent need for fast action to cure pressing problems, commonly means that the 'behaviour styles available to dis-advantaged groups are precisely those styles which the public and agency officials believe to be illegitimate' (Schumaker and Billeaux, 1978, p. 297). This is especially seen in open protests against policy-makers. It is not by chance that powerful groups in society exert their pressure 'behind the scenes' (Saunders, 1975; Newton, 1976; Stone, 1980). Public displays of opposition are a reflection of powerlessness, which is further emphasized by policy-makers discrediting the powerless because of the tactics they employ (Dearlove, 1974). Protest activity is not always ineffective, but, where it is effective, this commonly results from broader (often middle- and upper-class) support for or empathy with the protestors' cause (Clark, 1970; Lipsky, 1970; Lamb, 1975)—a recent good example is the increased government aid to British inner cities following the 1981 summer riots ('Riots that changed the cash priorities', *The Guardian*, 12 April 1982, p. 3). More commonly, protest behaviour can be made to look illegitimate and the protestors' case ignored.

Since, other things being equal, the effectiveness of protest activity is greater for middle- and upper-class groups, policy-makers not unexpectedly seek to reduce the likelihood of confrontation with such groups by drawing them into policy-making circles. The tendency for such groups to be more politically active orients them towards such involvement anyway, but policy-makers show little inclination to encourage greater working-class participation or provide a more 'balanced' representation of interests (Batley, 1972). In fact, as Seidelman (1981) has shown, where working-class representation is genuinely encouraged, the end result can be 'too hot' for policy-makers to handle. Groups invited into policy-making circles represent a biased selection, for they tend to be wealthier, with larger memberships and a middle- and upper-class composition (Cousins, 1976; Newton, 1976; Buller, 1981). Groups which are allowed into policy-making circles must 'behave' properly and show they can 'control' their members (Gilbert and Specht, 1975; King and Nugent, 1978; Mason, 1978). This commonly means they are not much different from policy-makers themselves (Peterson and Kantor, 1977; Buller and Lowe, 1982). There is little doubt that policy-makers try to 'domesticate' the leaders of incorporated groups; to bring them, and through them the public, to accept and support local State policies, rather than vice versa (Batley, 1972; Rhodes, 1974; Cousins, 1976; Glassberg, 1981). Such groups are there to provide an early warning system against public opposition, as well as advice (and possibly aid) on implementing policies more 'efficiently'. To maintain group compliance, financial and other benefits are often awarded (Gelb, 1970; Cousins, 1976). These should not be discounted, for they are often significant benefits to the groups concerned and result in a much closer affiliation between groups and policy-makers. Further, even if the aim is mainly to reconcile these groups to policy-makers' policies, their introduction into policy-making processes necessarily orients policy somewhat towards group aims. Where right-wing leadership is dominant, community and business groups find it easier to gain access, but they tend to reinforce a policy disposition that already exists. Where left-wing leadership is dominant, a more contentious political environment can arise, for divisions within the working-class, differences from (more politically active) middle- and upper-class residents, bureaucratic desires for a quiet life (of bureaucratic growth and 'efficient management'), and the constraints of poor resources and fears of capitalist repercussions following from the pursuit of left-wing policies, all make policy-making more difficult and contentious. Not surprisingly, researchers have recorded a tendency to discourage public participation and, as case studies like Buchanan's (1982) have shown, where it has been encouraged (or accepted) evidence strongly suggests that the 'consensual approach will get no more than the authorities want to give it' (Dearlove, 1974, p. 30; also Blowers, 1980).

On its own, however, this statement is too gross a simplification. To evaluate public participation in local State policy-making requires some consideration for the structural contexts of participation and the consequences of these structural arrangements (see Nowak et al., 1982). For example, in San Francisco a very open participatory structure, with 'easy' access to referenda, has fostered a lack of political leadership and greater power for community organizations (Wirt, 1974). This system bears close comparison with a frequently portrayed characteristic of (some) American cities, that of political leaders having to forge alliances of community groups to obtain sufficient support for policy innovation and implementation (Banfield, 1961; Yates, 1979). There are two important points to make about such characterizations. First, as with reformed government structures, they enhance the upper-class bias of local policies by giving business and 'prestigious' community groups an effective veto over policy initiation. A particularly clear example of this is the need to obtain business support to provide favourable publicity and sanction for municipal bond issues (e.g. Hayes, 1972). Second, in the absence of strong political leadership, the role of the local bureaucracy is enhanced (Wirt, 1974), which, not in the distribution of services provided perhaps (Lineberry, 1977) but certainly in the range and content of services provided (Mladenka, 1980), further advantages high status and business groups. Pairing these latter two groups together suggests an affinity that is not always present. Evidence is readily available demonstrating that, say, household property-owners and business leaders engage in intense political conflicts in some localities (e.g. Moore, 1978; Manyak, 1980; Simmie, 1981). Such conflicts do not contradict the main thrust of the argument presented here, for it is recognized that similarity of interests is not a universal phenomenon, merely that it is much more likely amongst the middle- and upper-classes than the working-class (Mills, 1956; Dunleavy, 1979; Elliott and McCrone, 1981).

There are then five main propositions in this section. First, political leaders are believed to place a high value on obtaining and maintaining political control. Second, in order to maintain control, public policy needs to respond in some measure to citizens' needs, hence where disadvantaged groups form a large portion of the local population policy-makers are more inclined to respond to their needs (e.g. Rossi *et al.*, 1974). Third, this reponsiveness reflects policy-makers' desire to 'manage' the political environment, for predictability and stability ease their task and lessen the chance of their position being challenged; hence where leaders have little fear of electoral defeat, responsiveness to public pressure carries less weight (e.g. Butterworth, 1966; Turner, 1978). Fourth, even given electoral security, policy-makers will respond to challenges to their position. Where local political parties are vibrant or where areas are dominated by middle- and upper-class residents, challenges to leadership are more likely, as is responsiveness to community group pressures and a disposition toward incorporating such groups into policy-making circles (in Britain, for instance, Conservative-dominated authorities run the risk of stimulating ratepayer or neighbourhood association electoral activity if they appear too unresponsive to citizen pressures). Fifth, working-class groups are less likely to threaten policy-makers. This is not simply because they cannot muster sufficient troops for battle, nor because they lack the will, organization or leadership ability to fight (though all these help in some measure), but because their lack of common interests individualizes their complaints. Whereas those of higher status can dress their preferences in universal-benefit terms—conserving the environment (Newby *et al.*, 1978; Buller and Lowe, 1982) or creating jobs and making a better city (Hartman, 1974; Molotch, 1976)—the demands of lower-status groups tend to be specific to themselves or their neighbourhood. (I am not pretending the same does not commonly apply for higher-status groups, merely that in presenting their case in more universalistic terms they encourage broader support and so weaken policy-makers' resistance.) Predispositions toward middle- and upper-class groups are further enhanced by the resource base of institutions—just where working-class groups can be expected to hold sway, where they dominate the population structure, their very dominance frequently results in a poorer tax base. If not ameliorated by external funding, this can 'force' local political leaders to orient their policies in favour of property-owners in order to enhance the local resource base (Lichten, 1979; Hill, 1980). These five propositions suggest that local State–locality relationships can be conceptualized as multidimensional; although not all dimensions or the complexity of relations along each can be identified here. What should be clear, however, is that specific combinations of conditions (say, working-class area, electoral security and inactive political parties) will very likely produce a particular pattern of local State–locality interactions. What is still unknown is which dimensions are most important and what are the conditions that determine variation along each dimension.

OVERVIEW

Throughout this paper the reader has probably wanted to add numerous qualifying caveats. The reader is not alone. Qualifying comments could be added in many places. To give a concrete example; when it was asserted that changes from locally-owned to absentee-owned firms reduces business involvement in local political affairs, it could have been added that Pellegrin and Coates (1956) found absentee-owned firms to be active participants in local politics. The reason for not noting this is that, although a different pattern is suggested, the underlying causes are the same. In Baton Rouge the involvement of absentee-owned corporations was primarily motivated by a desire to present the corporation in a favourable light to local citizens and zealously to guard corporate interests (Pellegrin and Coates, 1956), just as in other communities corporate lack of involvement is conditioned by a recognition that active involvement can have serious adverse effects on a corporation's image (Mott, 1970). Cultural differences between more paternalistic social structures in the southern United States and more contractual relations elsewhere alters the form of business involvement, but does not change the conclusion that absentee-owned firms are interested in local State behaviour. A basic characteristic of evidence on community power is that individual studies (and the body of literature as a whole) present partial insights, which are conditioned by specific historical differences between communities. The reviewers' task is not to accept described patterns at face value, but to impose an order or organizational framework within which partial, even contradictory, and at times sketchy accounts can be understood. As with Saunders (1981a), I believe the search for single theories to account for community power structures is fruitless. In placing order on scattered, uncoordinated events, the theorist inevitably confronts materials that support most of the major theoretical positions. True, the imposition of an organizational framework itself results in a tendency to emphasize some positions more than others, but, unless power is defined to exclude particular kinds of power relation, each of the main theoretical positions should have something to offer.

A major problem with placing existing evidence into an imposed organizational framework is the danger of undue simplification (or crass generalization). There are elements of this in this paper—in large measure, for example, capitalists have been treated as a single group, whereas factions clearly exist. The paucity of research on many aspects of community power and the theoretical and methodological characteristics of existing studies certainly make generalization difficult. In particular, to provide sufficient support for key arguments, researchers must devote substantial efforts to data collection, which usually results in studies being restricted to a small number of communities (often one). Comparisons of results thereby predominantly rely on analyses of individual communities, which draw on different theoretical perspectives and use alternative methodologies, over dissimilar periods of time, and at different points in time. Even so, despite distractions and what has at times seemed like aimless wanderings, substantial progress has been made over the past thirty years (Walton, 1976).

Although there is still room for considerable improvement, the limitations of the main theoretical models are better understood and the complexity of power relations and necessity to recognize their multidimensional and dynamic nature are more widely appreciated. Numerous caveats and exceptions can be recorded for most generalizations that are drawn from the literature and yet there are clear trends in local power structures that seem both dominant and enduring. From the perspective of decision power, perhaps the most notable of these are the concentration of power in the hands of few local residents, the considerable autonomy of the local State from nation State institutions, the dominance of business leaders in some communities but their relative lack of involvement in many (perhaps most), and the tendency for local policy-makers to restrict the public's access to and effects on the policy determination process. These trends must none the less be placed in the context of broad limits placed on the local State by the nation State, property-owners and the public in general. The structural framework of local State existence guarantees its heavy dependence on property-owners for its resources and, given the dominance of national corporations on the location of housing and employment, this predominantly means dependence on large-scale capitalist enterprises. With inadequate central-government compensation for resource inequalities (North West Interprofessional Group, 1974; LeGrand, 1975; Dye and Hurley, 1978; Hoggart, 1981a), property-tax inequalities alone act as fundamental determinants of local State policy (Fried, 1975; Peterson, 1981). Further restraints on local policy-makers derive from local elections, though these are declining in significance as the number of special districts and importance of local agencies of central government grows, and authorities are 'gerrymandered' to maintain single-party rule. Further, although the local State has considerable autonomy from the nation State in day-by-day decision-making, this must be seen in the light of the functions it performs. Clearly it would not be acceptable for a 'democratic' national government to enforce the residential segregation of social classes or races, yet 'democratic' local governments can do so 'legitimately'—by restricting the construction of public housing (Young and Kramer, 1978; Jackson, 1981) or zoning (Danielson, 1976; Newton, 1978), and such acts seem to find ready support in the courts (Johnston, 1982). Although it could not be claimed that capitalists do not experience 'defeats' in their interactions with local State institutions, evidence suggests that local State activity predominantly favours and works within limits set by property-owners (and so predominantly capitalists). Within these limits there is evidence of pluralist activity and in some localities instrumentalist theory finds support, but predominantly one finds a striving amongst local policy-makers to make managerialist theory a *fait accompli*.

Given the comparative basis of this paper, it is pertinent to ask if the above statements fit both countries. Certainly it would appear that pluralism is more notable in the United States than in Britain (Kantor, 1976), although Sharpe's (1973) careful discussion has illustrated that this impression is greatly over-played, especially since so many American municipalities are structured deliberately to exclude groups that might challenge dominant interests (Newton, 1978). Perhaps, though, the major question mark can be placed over the similarity of capitalist involvements in the local State. Although I recognize that there are obvious differences between the United States and British situations, their similarities are also clear, though in Britain capitalist effects are more notable at the national level. To illustrate, the fiscal mercantilism that characterizes American municipal behaviour (Molotch, 1976) finds a counter-part in British Government attempts to entice multinationals into the country and provide funds to keep them there (e.g. McDonald, 1977). The power networks which integrate capitalists in American cities (Edgar, 1970; McLaughlin, 1975; Ratcliff, 1979) are reproduced at a national level in both the United States (Domhoff, 1975; Dye, 1976) and Britain (Scott, 1979). Likewise, the pattern of close associations between local (and national) policy-makers and major corporations which is characteristic in the United States (Freitag, 1975; Domhoff, 1978) bears close comparison with the connections of national politicians and senior ('retired') bureaucrats in Britain (see Dunleavy, 1981, on Sir Keith Joseph's Bovis connections and Geoffrey Rippon's Cubitts links—also Guttsman, 1968; Newby *et al.*, 1978). As for capitalists staging 'coups' when government action meets their disfavour, Chris Mullins' fictional *A Very British Coup* merits serious consideration as the likely outcome resulting from the election of a committed socialist government in Britain. If the tame Wilson and Callaghan administrations produced capitalist rumblings aimed at over-throwing them (like Cecil King's use of the *Daily Mail* to try to bring down Wilson in 1968 and his approaches to Mountbatten to form a 'businessman's government'), genuine attempts to redistribute wealth in the nation can almost certainly be expected to meet a violent response. Britain is a small country, heavily dependent on international trade, with a 'glorious' history and a business community that has for centuries been spoon-fed on milk and honey extracted from former colonies. It is no surprise that business institutions are more national in orientation than their United States counterparts. Capitalists impose restrictions on the local State in Britain in a manner that differs little from that in the United States. The surface difference arises because many capitalist effects in Britain are filtered through nation State institutions. Certainly this means that these effects are somewhat altered, but the direction and forcefulness of their basic message is little affected.

At present we appreciate that capitalists place limits on the behaviour of local State activities, just as the local electorate does. Local politicians place limits on the behaviour of public bureaucrats and bureaucrats reciprocate. Where we still lack empirical evidence is in the identification of the extensiveness, flexibility and conditions under which such limits hold. The answers are important on theoretical grounds, because they will help clarify the validity and general applicability of the main community-power theories. They are also important on practical grounds because they tell us about the ability of local State institutions to provide leadership in the quest for improved human well-being. Evidence to date suggests that the local State has little independent capacity to improve the position of the most disadvantaged in society. If I can steal an apt analogy from Herman (1981), the likelihood of local State institutions providing leadership and aid for the advancement of the disadvantaged seems about as likely as a person in blindfold giving leadership to a herd of wild buffaloes.

ACKNOWLEDGEMENTS

I am grateful for David Green's and Henry Buller's comments on an earlier draft of this paper and wish I could have incorporated more of their suggestions more adequately.

BIBLIOGRAPHY

Abercrombie, N., Hill, S., and Turner, B. S. (1980). *The Dominant Ideology Thesis*, George Allen & Unwin, London.

Adams, B. N. (1969). The small trade centre: processes and perceptions of growth and decline. In *The Community* (Ed. R. M. French), F. E. Peacock Publishers, Itasca, Illinois.

Adams, J. S. and Brown, K. M. (1976). Public school goals and parochial school attendance in twenty American cities. In *Urban Policy-Making and Metropolitan Dynamics* (Ed. J. S. Adams), pp. 219–255, Ballinger, Cambridge, Massachusetts.

Allardt, E. (1968). Theories about social stratification. In *Social Stratification* (Ed. J. A. Jackson), pp. 14–24, Cambridge University Press, Cambridge.

Anderson, J. D. (1979). The municipal government reform movement in Western Canada, 1880–1920. In *The Usable Urban Past: Planning and Politics in the Modern*

Canadian City (Eds A. F. J. Artibise and G. A. Stelter), pp. 73–111, Macmillan, Toronto.

Antunes, G. and Mladenka, K. (1976). The politics of local services and service distribution. In *The New Urban Politics* (Eds L. H. Masotti and R. L. Lineberry), pp. 147–169, Ballinger, Cambridge, Massachusetts.

Apilado, V. P. (1971). Corporate-government interplay: The era of industrial aid finance, *Urban Affairs Quarterly*, **7**, 219–241.

Axford, B. (1978). Charles Selwyn and Mark Woodnutt, political leaders on the Isle of Wight. In *Political Leadership in Local Authorities* (Eds G. W. Jones and A. Norton), pp. 81–100, University of Birmingham, Institute of Local Government Studies, Birmingham.

Bachrach, P. and Baratz, M. S. (1970). *Power and Poverty: Theory and Practice*, Oxford University Press, New York.

Ball, I. D. (1980). Urban investment controls in Britain. In *National Resources and Urban Policy* (Ed. D. E. Ashford), pp. 115–142, Croom Helm, London.

Banfield, E. C. (1961). *Political Influence*, Free Press, New York.

Banfield, E. C. and Wilson, J. Q. (1967). *City Politics*, Harvard University Press, Cambridge, Massachusetts.

Batley, R. (1972). An explanation of non-participation in planning, *Policy and Politics*, **1** (2), 95–114.

Baxter, R. (1972). The working class and Labour politics, *Political Studies*, **20**, 97–107.

Bealey, F. and Sewel, J. (1981). *The Politics of Independence: A Study of a Scottish Town*, Aberdeen University Press, Aberdeen.

Becquart-Leclercq, J. (1977). French mayors and communal policy outputs: The case of small cities. In *Power, Paradigms and Community Research* (Eds R. J. Liebert and A. W. Imershein), pp. 79–119, Sage, Beverly Hills, California.

Bedford, H. F. (1966). *Socialism and the Workers in Massachusetts 1886–1912*, University of Massachusetts Press, Amherst.

Bennett, R. J. (1981). The rate support grant in England and Wales: A review of changing emphases and objectives. In *Geography and the Urban Environment* Vol. 4 (Eds D. T. Herbert and R. J. Johnston), Wiley, Chichester.

Bennett, R. J. (1982). A representative need index of local authority expenditure in England and Wales 1974/1975–1980/1981, *Environment and Planning*, **A14**, 933–950.

Bennison, D. J. and Davies, R. L. (1980). The impact of town centre shopping schemes in Britain, *Progress in Planning*, **14**(1), Pergamon, Oxford.

Bettelheim, B. (1960) *The Informed Heart: Autonomy in a Mass Age*, Free Press, New York.

Bingham, R., Hawkins, B. W., and Herbert, F. T. (1978). *The Politics of Raising State and Local Revenue*, Praeger, New York.

Birch, A. H. (1959). *Small-Town Politics: A Study of Political Life in Glossop*, Oxford University Press, London.

Blowers, A. (1980). *The Limits of Power: The Politics of Local Planning Policy*, Pergamon, Oxford.

Bonjean, C. M. and Olson, D. M. (1964). Community leadership: Directions of research, *Administrative Science Quarterly*, **9**, 278–300.

Bradley, D. S. and Zald, M. N. (1965). From commercial elite to political administrator: The recruitment of the mayors of Chicago, *American Journal of Sociology*, **71**, 153–167.

Bradshaw, J. (1974). The concept of social need, *Ekistics*, **37**(220), 184–187.

Branson, N. (1979). *Poplarism, 1919–1925: George Lansbury and the Councillors' Revolt*, Lawrence and Wishart, London.

Breckenfeld, G. (1977). Business loves the sunbelt (and vice versa), *Fortune*, **95**(6), 132–146.

Bristow, S. L. (1972). The criteria for local government reorganization and local authority autonomy, *Policy and Politics*, **1**, 143–162.

Bristow, S. L. (1978). Local politics after reorganization—the homogenization of local government in England and Wales, *Public Administration Bulletin*, **28**, 17–33.

Brown, L. and Brown, C. (1973). *An Unauthorized History of the RCMP*, James Lewis & Samuel, Toronto.

Brunn, S. D., Hoffman, W. L., and Romsa, G. H. (1969). The defeat of a Youngstown school levy, *Southeastern Geographer*, **39**, 67–79.

Buchanan, S. (1982), Power and planning in rural areas: Preparation of the Suffolk County Structure Plan. In *Power, Planning and People in Rural East Anglia* (Ed. M. J. Moseley), pp. 1–20, University of East Anglia, Centre for East Anglian Studies, Norwich.

Buller, H. (1981). *Pressure Groups and the Pluralist Model of Society: The Example of Local Amenity Societies*, Occasional Paper 14, Department of Geography, Kings' College London, London.

Buller, H. and Lowe, P. (1982). Politics and class in rural preservation: A study of the Suffolk Preservation Society. In *Power, Planning and People in Rural East Anglia* (Ed. M. J. Moseley), pp. 21–41, University of East Anglia, Centre for East Anglian Studies, Norwich.

Bulpitt, J. G. (1967). *Party Politics in English Local Government*, Longman, London.

Burbank, G. (1976). *When Farmers Voted Red: The Gospel of Socialism in the Oklahoma Countryside, 1910–1927*, Greenwood Press, Westport, Connecticut.

Burt, R. S. (1981). Comparative power structures in American communities, *Social Science Research*, **10**, 115–176.

Butterworth, R. (1966). Islington Borough Council: Some characteristics of single-party rule, *Politics*, **1**(1), 21–31.

Camina, M. M. (1974). Local authorities and the attraction of industry, *Progress in Planning*, **3**(2), Pergamon, London.

Carr, E. H. (1961). *What is History?*, Macmillan, London.

Catton, B. (1965). *Never Call Retreat*, Pocket Press, New York.

Chadwick, J. W., Houston, J. B., and Mason, J. R. W. (1972). *Ballina: A Local Study in Regional Economic Development*, Institute of Public Administration, Dublin.

Chamberlayne, P. (1978). The politics of participation: An enquiry into four London boroughs, 1968–1974, *The London Journal*, **4**(1), 47–68.

Checkoway, B. (1980). Large builders, federal housing programmes, and postwar suburbanization, *International Journal of Urban and Regional Research*, **4**, 21–45.

Christensen, T. (1981). The politics of redevelopment: Covent Garden. In *Geography and the Urban Environment* Vol. 4 (Eds D. T. Herbert and R. J. Johnston), pp. 115–137, Wiley, Chichester.

Chubb, J. (1980). Naples under the Left: The limits of local change, *Comparative Politics*, **13**, 53–78.

Chubb, J. (1981). The social bases of an urban political machine: the case of Palermo, *Political Science Quarterly*, **96**, 107–125.

Clark, D. (1981). *Colne Valley: Radicalism to Socialism*, Longman, London.

Clark, G. (1970). The lesson of Acklam Road, *New Statesman*, 7 August 1970, 139–140.

Clark, G. and Dear, M. (1981). The State in capitalism and the capitalist State. In *Urbanisation and Urban Planning in Capitalist Society* (Eds M. Dear and A. J. Scott), pp. 45–61, Methuen, London.

Clark, T. N. (1973). *Community Power and Policy Outputs*, Sage, Beverly Hills, California.

Clark, T. N. (1977). Fiscal management of American cities: Funds flow indicators, *Journal of Accounting Research*, **15**, 54–106.

Clark, T. N. and Ferguson, L. C. (1981). Fiscal strain and American cities: Six basic processes. In *Urban Political Economy* (Ed. K. Newton), pp. 137–155, Frances Pinter, London.

Clement, W. (1977). *Continental Corporate Power: Economic Elite Linkages Between Canada and the United States*, McClelland & Stewart, Toronto.

Clements, R. V. (1969). *Local Notables and the City Council*, Macmillan, London.

Clements, R. V. (1976). Political leadership in Bristol and Avon, *Local Government Studies*, **2**(2), 39–50.

Cockburn, C. (1977). *The Local State: Management of Cities and People*, Pluto Press, London.

Cole, G. D. H. (1948). *A History of the Labour Party from 1914*, Routledge & Kegan Paul, London.

Cooper, D. (1967). *Psychiatry and Anti-Psychiatry*, Tavistock, London.

Corina, L. (1972). The working of Halifax County Borough Council since 1945. Unpublished PhD Thesis, Department of Social Studies, University of Leeds, Leeds.

Corina, L. (1974). Elected representatives in a party system: A typology. *Policy and Politics*, **3**, 69–87.

Cornford, H. (1963). The transformation of Conservatism in the late nineteenth century, *Victorian Studies*, **7**, 35–66.

Cousins, P. F. (1976). Voluntary organizations and local government in three south London boroughs, *Public Administration*, **54**, 63–81.

Cousins, P. F. (1979). Council leaders—London's 33 Prime Ministers, *Local Government Studies*, **5**(5), 35–46.

Cox, K. R. (1978). Local interests and urban political processes in market societies. In *Urbanization and Conflict in Market Societies* (Ed. K. R. Cox), Methuen, London.

Cox, K. R. and Nartowicz, F. Z. (1980). Jurisdictional fragmentation in the American metropolis: Alternative perspectives, *International Journal of Urban and Regional Research*, **4**, 196–209.

Cunningham, F. A. (1973). *Objectivity in Social Science*, University of Toronto Press, Toronto.

Cyert, R. M. and March, J. G. (1963). *A Behavioural Theory of the Firm*, Prentice-Hall, Englewood Cliffs, New Jersey.

Dahl, R. A. (1961). *Who Governs? Democracy and Power in an American City*, Yale University Press, New Haven.

Dahrendorf, R. (1959). *Class and Conflict in Industrial Society*, Routledge & Kegan Paul, London.

Danielson, M. N. (1976). *The Politics of Exclusion*, Columbia University Press, New York.

Darke, R. and Walker, R. (1977). Attitudes towards the public. In *Local Government and the Public* (Eds R. Darke and R. Walker), pp. 70–87, Leonard Hill, London.

David, M. E. (1977). *Reform, Reaction and Resources: The Three Rs of Educational Planning*, National Foundation for Educational Research, Windsor, Berkshire.

David, S. M. and Kantor, P. (1979). Politial theory and transformations in urban budgetary arenas: The case of New York City. In *Urban Policy Making* (Ed. D. R. Marshall), Sage Yearbook in Politics and Public Policy 7, Beverly Hills, California.

Dear, M. (1979). Thirteen axioms of a geography of the public sector. In *Philosophy in Geography* (Eds S. Gale and G. Olsson), pp. 53–64, D. Reidel, Dordrecht.

Dearlove, J. (1973). *The Politics of Policy in Local Government: The Making and Maintenance of Public Policy in the Royal Borough of Kensington and Chelsea*, Cambridge University Press, Cambridge.

Dearlove, J. (1974). The control of change and regulation of community action. In *Community Work One* (Eds D. Jones and M. Mayo), pp. 22–43, Routledge & Kegan Paul, London.

Debnam, G. (1976). Nondecisions and power: The two faces of Bachrach and Baratz, *American Political Science Review*, **69**, 889–899.

Domhoff, G. W. (1975). Social clubs, policy-planning groups and corporations: A network study of ruling class cohesiveness, *The Insurgent Sociologist*, **5**(3), 173–184.

Domhoff, G. W. (1978). *Who Really Rules? New Haven and Community Power Reexamined*, Transaction Press, New Brunswick, New Jersey.

Donnison, D. (1973). Micro-politics of the city. In *London: Urban Patterns, Problems and Policies* (Eds D. Donnison and D. Eversley), pp. 383–404, Heinemann, London.

Downes, B. T. (1968). Municipal social rank and the characteristics of local political leaders. *Midwest Journal of Political Science*, **12**, 514–537.

Downs, A. (1967). *Inside Bureaucracy*, Little, Brown & Co, Boston.

Duncan, S. S. and Goodwin, M. (1982). The local state: Functionalism, autonomy and class relations in Cockburn and Saunders, *Political Geography Quarterly*, **1**, 77–96.

Dunleavy, P. (1977). Protest and quiescence in urban politics: A critique of some pluralist and structuralist myths, *International Journal of Urban and Regional Research*, **1**, 193–218.

Dunleavy, P. (1979). The urban basis of political alignment: Social class, domestic property ownership and state intervention in the consumption process, *British Journal of Political Science*, **9**, 409–443.

Dunleavy, P. (1980a). Social and political theory and the issues in central-local relations. In *New Approaches to the Study of Central-Local Government Relationships* (Ed. G. W. Jones), pp. 116–136, Gower, Farnborough, Hampshire.

Dunleavy, P. (1980b). *Urban Political Analysis: The Politics of Collective Consumption*, Macmillan, London.

Dunleavy, P. (1981). *The Politics of Mass Housing in Britain, 1945–1975: A Study of Corporate Power and Professional Influence in the Welfare State*, Clarendon, Oxford.

Dye, T. R. (1976). *Who's Ruling America: Institutional Leadership in the United States*, Prentice-Hall, Englewood Cliffs, New Jersey.

Dye, T. R. and Hurley, T. L. (1978). The responsiveness of federal and state governments to urban problems, *Journal of Politics*, **40**, 196–207.

Dyer, M. C. (1978). Leadership in a rural Scottish county. In *Political Leadership in Local Government* (Eds G. W. Jones and A. Norton), pp. 30–50, University of Birmingham, Institute of Local Government Studies, Birmingham.

Edgar, R. E. (1970). *Urban Power and Social Welfare: Corporate Influence in an American City*, Sage, Beverly Hills, California.

Elcock, H. (1979). Politicians, organisations, and the public—the provision of gypsy sites, *Local Government Studies*, **5**(3), 43–54.

Elliott, B. and McCrone, D. (1981). Power and protest in the city, in *New Perspectives in Urban Change and Conflict* (Ed. M. Harloe), pp. 63–79, Heinemann, London.

Eversley, D. (1973). *The Planner in Society: The Changing Role of a Profession*, Faber & Faber, London.

Eyles, J., Smith, D. M., and Woods, K. J. (1982) Spatial resource allocation and state practice: The case of health service planning in London, *Regional Studies*, **16**, 239–253.

Fenwick, I. G. K. (1976). *The Comprehensive School 1944–1970: The Politics of Secondary School Reorganization*, Methuen, London.

Fincher, R. (1981a). Implementation strategies in the urban built environment, *Environment and Planning*, **A13**, 1233–1252.

Fincher, R. (1981b). Analysis of the local level capitalist state, *Antipode*, **13**(2), 25–31.

Fitzwalter, R. and Taylor, D. (1981). *Web of Corruption: The Story of J. G. L. Poulson and T. Dan Smith*, Granada, London.

Flowerdew, R. (Ed.) (1982). *Institutions and Geographical Patterns*, Croom Helm, London.

Flynn, R. (1981). Managing consensus: Strategies and rationales in policy-making. In *New Perspectives in Urban Change and Conflict* (Ed. M. Harloe), pp. 50–62, Heinemann, London.

Freitag, P. J. (1975). The Cabinet and big business: A study of interlocks, *Social Problems*, **23**, 137–152.

French, R. M. (1970), Economic change and community power structure. In *The Structure of Community Power* (Eds M. Aiken and P. E. Mott), pp. 181–189, Random House, New York.

Fried, R. C. (1975). Comparative urban policy and performance. In *Policies and Policy-Making: Handbook of Political Science*, Vol. 6 (Eds F. I. Greenstein and N. W. Polsby), pp. 305–379, Addison-Wesley, Reading, Massachusetts.

Friedland, R. (1976). Class power and social control: The War on Poverty, *Politics and Society*, **6**, 459–489.

Friedland, R. (1980). Corporate power and urban growth: The case of urban renewal, *Politics and Society*, **10**, 203–224.

Friedland, R. (1981a). The local economy of political power: Participation, organization and dominance, *Pacific Sociological Review*, **24**, 139–174.

Friedland, R. (1981b). Central city fiscal strains: The public cost of private growth, *International Journal of Urban and Regional Research*, **5**, 356–375.

Friedland, R., Piven, F. F., and Alford, R. R. (1978). Political conflict, urban structure and the fiscal crisis. In *Comparing Public Policies* (Ed. D. E. Ashford), pp. 197–225, Sage, Beverly Hills, California.

Friedmann, J. (1973). The spatial organization of power in the development of urban systems, *Development and Change*, **3**(3), 12–50.

Friend, J. K. and Jessop, W. N. (1977). *Local Government and Strategic Choice* (2nd edn), Pergamon, Oxford.

Frobell, F., Heinrichs, J., and Kreye, O. (1980). *The New International Division of Labour: Structural Unemployment in Industrialized Countries and Industrialization in Developing Countries*, Cambridge University Press, Cambridge.

Fudge, C. (1981). Winning an election and gaining control: The formulation and implementation of a 'local' political manifesto. In *Policy and Action* (Eds S. Barrett and C. Fudge), pp. 123–141, Methuen, London.

Garrard, J. A. (1977). The history of local political power, *Political Studies*, **25**, 252–269.

Gaventa, J. (1980). *Power and Powerlessness: Quiescence and Rebellion in an Appalachian Valley*, Clarendon Press, Oxford.

Gelb, J. (1970). Blacks, blocs and ballots: The relevance of party politics to the Negro, *Polity*, **3**(1), 44–69.

Getter, R. W. and Schumaker, P. D. (1978). Contextual bases of responsiveness to citizen preferences and group demands, *Policy and Politics*, **6**, 249–278.

Gilbert, N. and Specht H. (1975). Socio-political correlates of community action: Conflict, political integration and citizen influence. In *The Sociology of Community Action* (Ed. P. Leonard), pp. 93–111, Sociological Review Monograph 21, Keele.

Gillard, M. and Tomkinson, M. (1980). *Nothing to Declare: The Political Corruptions of John Poulson*, John Calder, London.

Gittell, M. (1967). Professionalism and public participation in educational policy-making: New York City, a case study, *Public Administration Review*, **27**, 237–251.

Glassberg, A. (1973). The linkage between urban policy outputs and voting behaviour: New York and London, *British Journal of Political Science*, **3**, 341–361.

Glassberg, A. D. (1981). *Representation and Urban Community*, Macmillan, London.

Gold, G. L. (1975). *Saint Pascal: Changing Leadership and Social Organization in a Quebec Town*, Holt, Rinehart & Winston, Toronto.

Gottdiener, M. (1977). *Planned Sprawl: Private and Public Interests in Suburbia*, Sage, Beverly Hills, California.

Grant, J. (1977). *The Politics of Urban Transport Planning*, Earth Resources Research Ltd, London.

Grant, W. P. (1977). *Independent Local Politics in England and Wales*, Saxon House, Farnborough.

Graziano, L. (1978). Centre-periphery relations and the Italian crisis. In *Territorial Politics in Industrial Nations* (Eds S. Tarrow, P. J. Katzenstein, and L. Graziano), pp. 290–326, Praeger, New York.

Green, B. S. R. (1968). Community decision-making in Georgian city. Unpublished PhD Thesis, Bath University of Technology, Bath.

Green, D. (1981). *Power and Party in an English City: An Account of Single-Party Rule*, George Allen & Unwin, London.

Green, G. (1972). National, city and ward components of local voting, *Policy and Politics*, **1**, 45–54.

Green, J. R. (1978). *Grass-Roots Socialism: Radical Movements in the Southwest 1895–1943*, Louisiana State University Press, Baton Rouge.

Greenberg, E. S. (1974). *Serving the Few: Corporate Capitalism and the Bias of Government Policy*, Wiley, New York.

Greer, E. (1979). *Big Steel: Black Politics and Corporate Power in Gary, Indiana*, Monthly Review Press, New York.

Griffith, J. A. G. (1966). *Central Departments and Local Authorities*, George Allen & Unwin, London.

Gusteley, R. D. (1977). The allocational and distributional impacts of government consolidation: The Dade County experience, *Urban Affairs Quarterly*, **12**, 349–364.

Guterbock, T. M. (1980). *Machine Politics in Transition: Party and Community in Chicago*, University of Chicago Press, Chicago.

Guttsman, W. L. (1968). *The British Political Elite*, MacGibbon & Kee, London.

Gyford, J. (1976). *Local Politics in Britain*, Croom Helm, London.

Hall, P. (1974). A new political geography, *Transactions of the Institute of British Geographers*, **63**, 48–52.

Hall, P. (1980). *Great Planning Disasters*, Weidenfeld & Nicolson, London.

Haranne, M. (1979). *Community Power Structure Studies: An Appraisal of an Ever-Green Research Tradition with a Finnish Example*, Research Report 23, Research Group for Comparative Sociology, University of Helsinki, Helsinki.

Harrigan, J. J. (1976). *Political Change in the Metropolis*, Little, Brown & Co., Boston.

Hartman, C. (1974). *Yerba Buena: Land Grab and Community Resistance in San Francisco*, Glide Publications, San Francisco.

Harvey, D. (1976). The Marxian theory of the State, *Antipode*, **8**(2), 80–89.

Hawley, W. D. (1973). *Nonpartisan Elections and the Case for Party Politics*, Wiley, New York.

Hayes, E. C. (1972). *Power Structure and Urban Policy: Who Rules in Oakland?*, McGraw-Hill, New York.

Hays, S. P. (1964). The politics of reform in municipal government in the progressive era, *Pacific Northwest Quarterly*, **55**, 157–169.

Haywood, S. (1977). Decision-making in local government—the case of an 'Independent' council, *Local Government Studies*, **3**(4), 41–55.

Headrick, T. E. (1962). *The Town Clerk in English Local Government*, George Allen & Unwin, London.

Heclo, H. and Wildavsky, A. (1974) *The Private Government of Public Money*, Macmillan, London.

Hennigh, L. (1978). The good life and the taxpayers' revolt, *Rural Sociology*, **43**, 178–190.

Herman, E. S. (1981). *Corporate Control, Corporate Power*, Cambridge University Press, Cambridge.

Higley, J., Deacon, D., and Smart, D. (1979). *Elites in Australia*, Routledge & Kegan Paul, London.

Hill, R. C. (1974). Separate and unequal: Governmental inequality in the metropolis, *American Political Science Review*, **58**, 1557–1568.

Hill, R. C. (1977). Two divergent theories of the State, *International Journal of Urban and Regional Research*, **1**, 37–44.

Hill, R. C. (1978). Fiscal collapse and political struggle in decaying central cities in the United States. In *Marxism and the Metropolis* (Eds W. K. Tabb and L. Sawers), pp. 213–240, Oxford University Press, New York.

Hill, R. C. (1980). Race, class and the State: The metropolitan enclave system in the United States, *The Insurgent Sociologist*, **10**(2), 45–59.

Hindess, B. (1971). *The Decline of Working-Class Politics*, MacGibbon & Kee, London.

Hoffman, W. (1976). The democratic response of urban governments: An empirical test with simple spatial models, *Policy and Politics*, **4**, 51–74.

Hoggart, K. (1981a). Social needs, political representation, and federal outlays in the East North Central United States of America, *Environment and Planning*, **A13**, 531–546.

Hoggart, K. (1981b). *Local Decision-Making Autonomy: A Review of Conceptual and Methodological Issues*, Occasional Paper 13, Department of Geography, King's College London, London.

Hoggart, K. (1984). Political parties and local authority capital investment in English cities, 1966–1971, *Political Geography Quarterly*, **3**, 5–32.

Hunter, F. (1953). *Community Power Structure*, University of North Carolina Press, Chapel Hill.

Hymer, S. (1975). The multinational corporation and the law of uneven development. In *International Firms and Modern Imperialism* (Ed. H. Radice), pp. 37–62, Penguin, Harmondsworth.

Jackman, R. and Ferry, J. (1978). The burden of non-domestic rates, *CES Review*, **4**, 45–47.

Jackson, J. E. (1972). Politics and the budgetary process, *Social Science Research*, **1**, 35–60.

Jackson, K. T. (1981) The spatial dimensions of social control: Race, ethnicity and government housing policy in the United States, 1918–1968. In *Modern Industrial Cities: History, Policy and Survival* (Ed. B. M. Stave), pp. 79–128, Sage, Beverly Hills, California.

Jessop, B. (1977). Recent theories of the capitalist State, *Cambridge Journal of Economics*, **1**, 353–373.

Johnston, R. J. (1977). National sovereignity and national power in European institutions, *Environment and Planning*, **A9**, 569–577.

Johnston, R. J. (1980). Political geography without politics, *Progress in Human Geography*, **4**, 439–446.

Johnston, R. J. (1981). The State and the study of social geography. In *Social Interaction and Ethnic Segregation* (Eds P. Jackson and S. J. Smith), pp. 205–222, Academic Press, London.

Johnston, R. J. (1982). The local State and the judiciary: Institutions in American suburbia. In *Institutions and Geographical Patterns* (Ed. R. Flowerdew), pp. 255–287, Croom Helm, London.

Jones, B. D. (1981). Party and bureaucracy: The influence of intermediary groups on urban public service delivery, *American Political Science Review*, **75**, 688–700.

Jones, G. W. (1969). *Borough Politics: A Study of the Wolverhampton Town Council 1888–1964*, Macmillan, London.

Kantor, P. (1976). Elites, pluralists and policy arenas in London: Toward a comparative theory of city policy formation, *British Journal of Political Science*, **3**, 311–334.

Karp, W. (1973). *Indispensable Enemies: The Politics of Misrule in America*, Penguin, Baltimore.

Kavanagh, D. (1974). Beyond autonomy? The problems of corporations, *Government and Opposition*, **9**, 42–60.

Kendall, D. (1963). Portrait of a disappearing English village, *Sociologia Ruralis*, **3**, 157–165.

Kesselman, M. (1967). *The Ambiguous Consensus: A Study of Local Government in France*, Alfred A. Knopf, New York.

King, R. and Nugent, N. (1978). Ratepayers' associations in Newcastle and Wakefield. In *The Middle Class in Politics* (Eds J. Garrard *et al.*), pp. 229–261, Saxon House, Farnborough, Hampshire.

Klehr, H. (1978). *Communist Cadre: The Social Background of the American Communist Party Elite*, Hoover Institution Publication 198, Stanford University, Stanford, California.

Kraushaar, R. (1981). Policy without protest: The dilemma of organising for change in Britain. In *New Perspectives in Urban Change and Conflict* (Ed. M. Harloe), pp. 101–121, Heinemann, London.

Laffin, M. (1980). Professionalism in central-local relations. In *New Approaches to the Study of Central-Local Government Relationships* (Ed. G. W. Jones), pp. 18–27, Gower, Farnborough, Hampshire.

Lamb, C. (1975). *Political Power in Poor Neighbourhoods*, Wiley, New York.

Lantz, H. R. (1972). *A Community in Search of Itself: A Case History of Cairo, Illinois*, Southern Illinois University Press, Carbondale, Illinois.

Laski, H. (1935). *The State in Theory and Practice*, George Allen & Unwin, London.

Laver, M. (1978). The problems of measuring power in Europe, *Environment and Planning*, **A10**, 901–906.

LeGates, R. (1972). *Can Federal Welfare Bureaucracies Control their Programmes: The Case of H.U.D. and Urban Renewal*, Working Paper 172, Institute of Urban and Regional Development, University of California, Berkeley.

LeGrand, J. (1975). Fiscal equity and central government grants to local authorities, *Economic Journal*, **85**, 531–547.

Lee, J. M. (1963). *Social Leaders and Public Persons: A Study of County Government in Cheshire since 1888*, Clarendon, Oxford.

Lenski, G. E. (1966). *Power and Privilege: A Theory of Social Stratification*, McGraw-Hill, New York.

Leonard, S. (1982). Urban managerialism: A period of transition?, *Progress in Human Geography*, **6**, 190–215.

Levin, P. H. (1972). On decisions and decision-making, *Public Administration*, **50**, 19–44.

Levine, C. H. and Posner, P. L. (1981). The centralising effects of austerity on the intergovernmental system, *Political Science Quarterly*, **96**, 67–85.

Levy, F., Meltsner, A. J., and Wildavsky, A. (1974). *Urban Outcomes: Schools, Streets and Libraries*, University of California Press, Berkeley.

Lineberry, R. L. (1977). *Equality and Urban Policy: The Distribution of Municipal Public Services*, Sage, Beverly Hills, California.

Lipsky, M. (1968). Protest as a political resource, *American Political Science Review*, **62**, 1144–1158.

Lipsky, M. (1970). *Protest in City Politics: Rent Strikes, Housing and the Power of the Poor*, Rand McNally, Chicago.

Lichten, E. (1979). The fiscal crisis of New York City and the development of austerity, *The Insurgent Sociologist*, **9**(2, 3), 75–92.

Logan, W. S. (1978). *Post-Convergence Political Geography—Death or Transfiguration?*, Publication in Geography 18, Monash University, Melbourne.

Lojkine, J. (1977). Big firms' strategies, urban policy and urban social movements. In *Captive Cities* (Ed. M. Harloe), pp. 141–156, Wiley, London.

Lojkine, J. (1981). Urban policy and local power: Some aspects of recent research in Lille. In *City, Class and Capital* (Eds M. Harloe and E. Lebas), pp. 89–104, Edward Arnold, London.

Loveridge, R. O. (1968). The city manager in legislative politics: A collision of role conceptions, *Polity*, **1**, 213–236.

Lowi, T. J. (1964). American business, public policy, case studies and political theory, *World Politics*, **16**, 677–715.

Lowi, T. J. (1967). Machine politics—old and new, *The Public Interest*, **9**, 83–92.

Lukes, S. (1974). *Power: A Radical View*, Macmillan, London.

Lyons, W. E. and Engstrom, R. L. (1973). Life-style and fringe attitudes toward the political integration of urban governments, *American Journal of Political Science*, **17**, 182–188.

McAuslan, J. P. W. B. and Bevan, R. G. (1977). The influence of officers and councillors on procedures in planning—a case study, *Local Government Studies*, **3**(3), 7–21.

McCall, G. J. and Simmons, J. L. (Eds) (1969). *Issues in Participant Observation*, Addison-Wesley, Reading, Massachusetts.

McCormack, A. R. (1977). *Reformers, Rebels and Revolutionaries: The Western Canadian Radical Movement* 1899–1919, University of Toronto Press, Toronto.

McDonald, O. (1977). Multinationals, spatial inequalities and workers' control. In *Alternative Frameworks for Analysis* (Eds D. B. Massey and P. W. J. Batey), pp. 68–85, Pion, London.

McLaughlin, E. M. (1975). The power network in Phoenix, *The Insurgent Sociologist*, **5**(3), 185–195.

Machin, H. (1977). *The Prefect in French Public Administration*, Croom Helm, London.

Manyak, T. G. (1980). Behavioural dimensions in city council decision-making, *Urban Systems*, **5**, 115–121.

Markusen, A. R. (1976). Class and urban social expenditure, *Kapitalstate*, **4**(5), 50–65.

Martin, R. (1977). *The Sociology of Power*, Routledge & Kegan Paul, London.

Mason, T. (1978). Community action and the local authority: A study in the incorporation of protest. In *Urban Change and Conflict* (Ed. M. Harloe), pp. 89–116, Centre for Environmental Studies Conference Series 19, London.

Meehan, E. J. (1982). The rise and fall of public housing in the United States: A case study of programmed failure in policy-making. In *Urban Change and Conflict* (Eds A. Blowers *et al.*), pp. 198–209, Harper & Row, London.

Milch, J. E. (1974). Influence as power: French local government reconsidered, *British Journal of Political Science*, **4**, 139–161.

Miliband, R. (1961). *Parliamentary Socialism: A Study in the Politics of Labour*, Monthly Review Press, New York.

Miliband, R. (1977). *Marxism and Politics*, Oxford University Press, Oxford.

Miller, D. C. (1970). *International Community Power Structures*, Indiana University Press, Bloomington.

Miller, G. J. (1981). *Cities by Contract: The Politics of Municipal Incorporation*, M.I.T. Press, Cambridge, Massachusetts.

Mills, C. W. (1956). *The Power Elite*, Oxford University Press, New York.

Minns, R. and Thornley, J. (1978). *Local Government Economic Planning and the Provision of Risk Capital for Small Firms*, Centre for Environmental Studies Policy Series 6, London.

Mladenka, K. R. (1980). The urban bureaucracy and the Chicago political machine: Who gets what and the limits to political control, *American Political Science Review*, **74**, 991–998.

Mollenkopf, J. (1979). Untangling the logics of urban service bureaucracies: The strange case of the San Francisco Municipal Railway, *International Journal of Health Services*, **9**, 255–268.

Molotch, H. (1976). The city as a growth machine, *American Journal of Sociology*, **82**, 309–332.

Monahan, J. (1976). Up against the planners in Covent Garden. In *Community Politics* (Ed. P. Hain), pp. 175–192, John Calder, London.

Moore, P. W. (1978). Zoning and neighbourhood change in The Annex of Toronto 1900–1970. Unpublished PhD Thesis, Department of Geography, University of Toronto, Toronto.

Morgan, D. R. and Pelissero, J. P. (1980). Urban policy: Does political structure matter?, *American Political Science Review*, **74**, 999–1006.

Morris, D. S. and Newton, K. (1970), Profile of a local political elite: Businessmen as community decision-makers in Birmingham, 1838–1966, *New Atlantis*, **1**(2), 111–123.

Morriss, P. (1971). Power in New Haven: A reassessment of 'Who Governs'?, *British Journal of Political Science*, **2**, 457–465.

Mott, P. E. (1970). The role of the absentee-owned corporation in the changing community. In *The Structure of Community Power* (Eds M. Aiken and P. E. Mott), pp. 170–179, Random House, New York.

Muller, P. O. (1975). *The Outer City: Geographical Consequences of the Urbanization of the Suburbs*, Resource Paper 75–2, Association of American Geographers, Washington, DC.

Mullin, C. (1982). *A Very British Coup*, Hodder & Stoughton, London.

Nelson, M. D. (1974). The validity of secondary analyses of community power studies, *Social Forces*, **52**, 531–537.

Newby, H. (1977a). *The Deferential Worker*, Penguin, Harmondsworth.

Newby, H. (1977b). Paternalism and capitalism. In *Industrial Society: Class, Cleavage and Control* (Ed. R. Scase), pp. 59–73, George Allen & Unwin, London.

Newby, H., Bell, C., Rose, D., and Saunders, P. (1978). *Property, Paternalism and Power: Class and Control in Rural England*, Hutchinson, London.

Newton, K. (1973). Links between leaders and citizens in a local political system, *Policy and Politics*, **1**, 287–305.

Newton, K. (1974). Community performance in Britain, *Current Sociology*, **22**, 49–86.

Newton, K. (1976). *Second City Politics: Democratic Processes and Decision-Making in Birmingham*, Oxford University Press, Oxford.

Newton, K. (1978). Conflict avoidance and conflict suppression: The case of urban politics in the United States. In *Urbanization and Conflict in Market Societies* (Ed. K. R. Cox), pp. 76–93, Methuen, London.

Newton, K. (1979). The local political elite in England and Wales. In *Local Government in Britain and France* (Eds J. Lagroye and V. Wright), pp. 105–113, George Allen & Unwin, London.

Nivola, P. S. (1978). Distributing a municipal service: A case study of housing inspection, *Journal of Politics*, **40**, 59–81.

North West Interprofessional Group (1974). *Local Authority Needs and Resources—The Effects of the Rate Support Grant in the North West*, Centre for Environmental Studies Research Paper 12, London.

Nowak, P. J., Rickson, R. E., Ramsey, C. E., and Goudy, W. J. (1982). Community conflict and models of political participation, *Rural Sociology*, **47**, 333–348.

Nowlan, D. and Nowlan, N. (1970). *The Bad Trip: The Untold Story of the Spadina Expressway*, New Press, Toronto.

O'Connor, J. (1973). *The Fiscal Crisis of the State*, St Martin's Press, New York.

O'Dowd, L. and Tomlinson, M. (1980). Urban politics in Belfast: Two case studies, *International Journal of Urban and Regional Research*, **4**, 72–95.

Oliver, F. R. and Stanyer, J. (1970). Local government finance. In *Local Government in England 1958–1969* (Ed. H. V. Wiseman), pp. 145–176, Routledge & Kegan Paul, London.

Olsen, J. P. (1970). Local budgeting—decision-making or a ritual act?, *Scandinavian Political Studies*, **5**, 85–118.

Orren, K. (1976). Corporate power and the slums: Is big business a paper tiger?. In *Theoretical Perspectives on Urban Politics* (Ed. W. D. Hawley), pp. 45–66, Prentice-Hall, Englewood Cliffs, New Jersey.

Page, E. (1980). The measurement of central control, *Political Studies*, **28**, 117–120.

Pareto, V. (1901). *The Rise and Fall of the Elites* (1968), Bedminster Press, Totowa, New Jersey.

Pareto, V. (1935). *Mind and Society: A Treatise on General Sociology*, Jonathon Cape, London.

Paris, C. and Blackaby, R. (1979). *Not Much Improvement: Urban Renewal Policy in Birmingham*, Heinemann, London.

Parry, G. and Morriss, P. (1974). When is a decision not a decision?. In *British Political Sociology Yearbook: Elites in Western Democracy* (Ed. I. Crewe), pp. 317–336, Croom Helm, London.

Parsons, K. (1972). Attitudes, beliefs and behaviour: Elites and politics in Derby and Reading, Unpublished PhD Thesis, Department of Politics, University of Reading, Reading.

Peet, R. (1981). Historical forms of the property relation: A reconstruction of Marx's theory, *Antipode*, **13**(3), 13–25.

Pellegrin, R. J. and Coates, C. H. (1956). Absentee-owned corporations and community power structure, *American Journal of Sociology*, **61**, 413–419.

Perry, D. C. and Watkins, A. J. (1977). People, profit, and the rise of the sunbelt cities. In *The Rise of the Sunbelt Cities* (Eds D. C. Perry and A. J. Watkins), pp. 277–305, Sage Urban Affairs Annual Review 14, Beverly Hills, California.

Peschek, D. and Brand, J. (1966). *Policies and Politics in Secondary Education: Case Studies in West Ham and Reading*, Greater London Paper 11, London School of Economics, University of London, London.

Peterson, J. E. (1980). Changing fiscal structure and credit quality: Large U.S. cities. In *Fiscal Stress and Public Policy* (Eds C. H. Levine and I. Rubin) pp. 179–199, Sage Yearbook in Politics and Public Policy 9, Beverly Hills, California.

Peterson, P. E. (1981). *City Limits*, University of Chicago Press, Chicago.

Peterson, P. and Kantor, P. (1977). Political parties and citizen participation in English city politics, *Comparative Politics*, **9**, 197–217.

Phelan, J. and Pozen, R. (1973). *The Company State*, Grossman, New York.

Polsby, N. W. (1980). *Community Power and Political Theory*, (2nd edn) Yale University Press, New Haven, Connecticut.

Poulantzas, N. (1973). *Political Power and Social Classes*, New Left Books, London.

Pressman, J. and Wildavsky, A. (1973). *Implementation: How Great Expectations in Washington are Dashed in Oakland*, University of California Press, Berkeley.

Preston, M. (1976). Limitations of black urban power: the case of black mayors. In *The New Urban Politics* (Eds L. H. Masotti and R. L. Lineberry), pp. 111–132, Ballinger, Cambridge, Massachusetts.

Preteceille, E. (1981). Left wing local governments and services policy in France, *International Journal of Urban and Regional Research*, **5**, 411–424.

Prottas, J. M. (1977). *The Power of the Street-Level Bureaucrat in Public Service Bureaucracies*, Urban Planning Policy Analysis and Administration Discussion Paper D77–20, Harvard University, Cambridge, Massachusetts.

Quante, W. (1970). Flight of corporate headquarters: New York's reign as the nation's business centre has ended, *Society*, **13**(4), 37–41.

Rakove, M. L. (1975). *Don't Make No Waves, Don't Back No Losers: An Insider's Analysis of the Daley Machine*, Indiana University Press, Bloomington.

Randall, M. V. (1979). The decision-making process in three London boroughs, 1964–1972. Unpublished PhD Thesis, London School of Economics, University of London, London.

Randall, M. V. (1981). Housing policy-making in London boroughs: The role of paid officers, *The London Journal*, **7**, 161–176.

Ratcliff, R. E. (1979). Capitalist class struggle and the decline of older industrial cities, *The Insurgent Sociologist*, **9**(2, 3), 60–74.

Rhodes, R. A. W. (1974). A comparative study of the decision-making process within Oxford City and Oxfordshire County Council 1963–1968'. Unpublished BLitt Thesis, University of Oxford, Oxford.

Rhodes, R. A. W. (1981). *Control and Power in Central-Local Government Relations*, Gower, Farnborough, Hampshire.

Rich, R. C. (1980). The complex web of urban governance: Gossamer or iron?, *American Behavioural Scientist*, **24**, 277–298.

Rich, R. C. (1982). Urban development and the political economy of public production of services. In *Public Provision and Urban Politics* (Eds A. M. Kirby and S. Pinch), pp. 73–95 Geographical Paper 80, Department of Geography, University of Reading, Reading.

Rigby, J. P. (1980). *Public Transport Planning in Shire Counties*, Working Paper 46, Department of Town Planning, Oxford Polytechnic, Oxford.

Rogers, P. B. and Smith, C. R. (1977). The local authority's role in economic development: The Tyne and Wear Act 1976, *Regional Studies*, **11**, 153–163.

Rose, R. (1965). *Politics in England: An Interpretation*, Faber & Faber, London.

Rose, R. (1980). *Class Does Not Equal Party: The Decline of a Model of British Voting*, Studies in Public Policy 74, University of Strathclyde, Glasgow.

Rosenbaum, A. (1967). Community power and political theory: A case of misperception, *Berkeley Journal of Sociology*, **12**, 91–116.

Rossi, P. H. (1960). Power and community structure, *Midwest Journal of Political Science*, **4**, 390–401.

Rossi, P. H., Berk, R. A., and Eidson, B. K. (1974). *The Roots of Urban Discontent: Public Policy, Municipal Institutions, and the Ghetto*, Wiley, New York.

Salamon, L. M. and Van Evera, S. (1973). Fear, apathy and discrimination: A test of three explanations of political participation, *American Political Science Review*, **67**, 1288–1306.

Salanick, G. R. and Pfeffer, J. (1977). Constraints on administrative discretions: The limited influence of mayors on city budgets, *Urban Affairs Quarterly*, **12**, 475–498.

Saran, R. (1967). Decision-making by a local education authority, *Public Administration*, **45**, 387–402.

Saunders, P. (1975). They make the rules: Political routines and the generation of political bias, *Policy and Politics*, **4**(1), 31–58.

Saunders, P. (1979). *Urban Politics: A Sociological Interpretation*, Hutchinson, London.

Saunders, P. (1980). *Toward a Non-Spatial Urban Sociology*, Working Paper 21, Urban and Regional Studies, University of Sussex, Brighton.

Saunders, P. (1981a). Community power, urban managerialism and the 'local state'. In *New Perspectives in Urban Change and Conflict* (Ed. M. Harloe), pp. 27–49, Heinemann, London.

Saunders, P. (1981b). *Social Theory and the Urban Question*, Heinemann, London.

Saunders, P. (1982a). Urban politics, a rejoinder to Hooper and Duncan/Goodwin, *Political Geography Quarterly*, **1**, 181–187.

Saunders, P. (1982b). The relevance of Weberian sociology for urban political analysis. In *Public Provision and Urban Politics* (Eds A. M. Kirby and S. Pinch), pp. 1–24, Geographical Paper 80, Department of Geography, University of Reading, Reading.

Sbragia, A. (1981). Cities, capital and banks: The politics of debt in the United States, United Kingdom and France. In *Urban Political Economy* (Ed. K. Newton), pp. 200–220, Frances Pinter, London.

Scarrow, H. A. (1971). Policy pressures by British local government: The case of regulation in the 'Public Interest', *Comparative Politics*, **4**, 1–28.

Schneider, M. and Logan, J. R. (1981). Fiscal implications of class segregation: Inequalities in the distribution of public goods and services in suburban municipalities, *Urban Affairs Quarterly*, **17**, 23–36.

Schulze, R. O. (1958). The role of economic dominants in community power structure, *American Sociological Review*, **23**, 3–9.

Schumaker, P. D. and Billeaux, D. M. (1978). Group representation in local bureaucracies, *Administration and Society*, **10**, 285–316.

Scott, A. J. (1980). *The Urban Land Nexus and the State*, Pion, London.

Scott, J. (1979). *Corporations, Classes and Capitalism*, Hutchinson, London.

Scott, T. M. (1968). Metropolitan government reorganization proposals, *Western Political Quarterly*, **21**, 252–261.

Seidelman, R. (1981). Urban movements and Communist power in Florence, *Comparative Politics*, **13**, 437–459.

Service, E. R. (1978). Classical and modern theories of the origins of government. In *Origins of the State: The Anthropology of Political Evolution* (Eds R. Cohen and E. R. Service), pp. 21–34, Institute for the Study of Human Issues, Philadelphia.

Sharpe, L. J. (1973). American democracy reconsidered: Part I, *British Journal of Political Science*, **3**, 1–28.

Sharpe, L. J. (1981). Does politics matter?. In *Urban Political Economy* (Ed. K. Newton), pp. 1–26, Frances Pinter, London.

Shefter, M. (1976). The emergence of the political machine: An alternative view. In *Theoretical Perspectives on Urban Politics* (Ed. W. D. Hawley), pp. 14–44, Prentice-Hall, Englewood Cliffs, New Jersey.

Shipp, P. J. and Harris, R. (1977). *Communications Between Central and Local*

Government in the Management of Local Authority Expenditure, Social Science Research Council Report HR5032, London.

Simmie, J. (1981). *Power, Property and Corporatism: The Political Sociology of Planning*, Macmillan, London.

Sjoberg, G., Brymer, R. A., and Farris, B. (1966). Bureaucracy and the lower class, *Sociology and Social Research*, **50**, 325–337.

Skinner, D. and Langdon, J. (1974). *The Story of Clay Cross*, Bertrand Russell Peace Foundation (Spokesman Books), Nottingham.

Smallwood, F. (1965). *Greater London: The Politics of Metropolitan Reform*, Bobbs-Merrill, Indianapolis.

Stanyer, J. (1967). *County Government in England and Wales*, Routledge & Kegan Paul, London.

Stinchcombe, J. L. (1968). *Reform and Reaction: City Politics in Toledo*, Wadsworth, Belmont, California.

Stone, C. N. (1980). Systematic power in community decision-making: A restatement of stratification theory, *American Political Science Review*, **74**, 978–990.

Swann, B. (1972). Local initiative and central control: The insulin decision, *Policy and Politics*, **1**, 55–63.

Tabb, W. K. (1977). Blaming the victim. In *The Fiscal Crisis of American Cities* (Eds R. E. Alcaly and D. Mermelstein), pp. 315–326, Random House, New York.

Taggart, H. T. and Smith, K. W. (1981). Redlining: An assessment of the evidence of disinvestment in metropolitan Boston, *Urban Affairs Quarterly*, **17**, 91–107.

Talarchek, G. M. and Agnew, J. A. (1979). The pattern of property-tax exemptions in a metropolitan fiscal setting, *Professional Geographer*, **31**, 284–291.

Taylor, P. J. (1980). *A Materialist Framework for Political Geography*, Seminar Paper 37, Department of Geography, University of Newcastle-upon-Tyne, Newcastle-upon-Tyne.

Thomas, J. C. (1975). *The Decline of Ideology in Western Political Parties: A Study of Changing Policy Orientations*, Sage, Beverly Hills, California.

Thompson, J. D. (1967). *Organizations in Action: Social Science Bases of Administrative Theory*, McGraw-Hill, New York.

Turk, H. (1977). *Organizations in Modern Life: Cities and Other Large Networks*, Jossey-Bass, San Francisco.

Turner, J. E. (1978). *Labour's Doorstep Politics in London*, Macmillan, London.

Underwood, J. and Stewart, M. (1978). Local economic initiatives by local authorities, *The Planner*, **64**(4), 110–112.

Walsh, K., Hinings, R., Greenwood, R., and Ranson, S. (1981). Power and advantage in organizations, *Organization Studies*, **2**(2), 131–152.

Walton, J. (1976). Community power and the retreat from politics: Full circle after 20 years?, *Social Problems*, **23**, 292–303.

Wattenburg, M. P. (1981). The decline of political partisanship in the United States: Negativity or neutrality, *American Political Science Review*, **75**, 941–950.

Webb, A. and Wistow, G. (1980). Implementation, central-local relations and the personal social services. In *New Approaches to the Study of Central-Local Government Relationships* (Ed. G. W. Jones), pp. 69–83, Gower, Farnborough, Hampshire.

Weber, M. (1948). *From Max Weber* (Eds. H. H. Gerth and C. W. Mills), Routledge & Kegan Paul, London.

Weidner, E. W. (1944). State supervision of local government in Minnesota, *Public Administration Review*, **4**, 226–233.

Weinstein, J. (1967). *The Decline of Socialism in America 1912–1925*, Monthly Review Press, New York.

Weinstein, J. (1968). *The Corporate Ideal in the Liberal State: 1900–1918*, Beacon Press, Boston.

Welch, S. (1975). The impact of urban riots on urban expenditures, *American Journal of Political Science*, **19**, 741–760.

Welch, S. and Karnig, A. K. (1979). The impact of black elected officials on urban expenditures and intergovernmental revenue. In *Urban Policy Making* (Ed. D. R. Marshall), pp. 101–126, Sage Yearbook in Politics and Public Policy 7, Beverly Hills, California.

White, C. (1980). *Patrons and Partisans: A Study of Politics in Two Southern Italian Comuni*, Cambridge University Press, Cambridge.

White, L. T. (1976). Local autonomy in China during the Cultural Revolution: The theoretical uses of an atypical case, *American Political Science Review*, **70**, 479–491.

Williams, J. A. and Zimmerman, E. (1981). American business organizations and redistributive preferences, *Urban Affairs Quarterly*, **16**, 453–464.

Williams, O. P. and Eklund, K. (1978). Segregation in a fragmented context: 1950–1970. In *Urbanisation and Conflict in Market Societies* (Ed. K. R. Cox), pp. 213–228, Methuen, London.

Williams, O. P., Herman, H., Liebman, C. S., and Dye, T. R. (1965). *Suburban Differences and Metropolitan Policies: A Philadelphia Story*, University of Pennsylvania Press, Philadelphia.

Wirt, F. M. (1974). *Power in the City: Decision-Making in San Francisco*, University of California Press, Berkeley.

Wolpert, J. (1970). Departures from the usual environment in locational analysis, *Annals of the Association of American Geographers*, **60**, 220–229.

Woodhead, D. J. (1972). *Leadership and Decision-Making in the Tyneside Conurbation*, Unpublished PhD Thesis, University of Durham, Durham.

Wynne, B. (1980). Windscale: A case history of the political art of muddling through. In *Progress in Resource Management and Environmental Planning* (Vol. II) (Eds T. O'Riordan and R. K. Turner), pp. 165–204, Wiley, Chichester.

Yates, D. (1979). The mayor's eight-ring circus: The shape of urban politics in its evolving policy arenas. In *Urban Policy Making* (Ed. D. R. Marshall), pp. 41–69, Sage, Beverly Hills, California.

Young, K. (1975). The Conservative strategy for London, 1855–1975, *The London Journal*, **1**(1), 56–81.

Young, K. and Garside, P. L. (1982). *Metropolitan London: Politics and Urban Change 1837–1981*, Edward Arnold, London.

Young, K. and Kramer, J. (1978). *Strategy and Conflict in Metropolitan Housing: Suburbia Versus the Greater London Council 1965–1975*, Heinemann, London.

Zeigler, D. J. (1981). Changing regional patterns of central city credit ratings: 1960–1980, *Urban Geography*, **2**, 269–283.

Geography and the Urban Environment
Progress in Research and Applications, Volume VI
Edited by D. T. Herbert and R. J. Johnston
© 1984 John Wiley & Sons Ltd.

Chapter 6

Suburban Economic Integration: External Initiatives and Community Responses

Thomas A. Clark

Economic integration of suburban municipalities through dispersal of lower income households out of central cities and lower status suburbs is now considered to be one major strategic option in increasing the effective incomes of the poor in the United States (Downs, 1973; Clark, 1982; Mallach, 1981) and elsewhere (Cox, 1978, Ch. 10). It is one discernible facet of the diverse cluster of legislative and judicial actions which have sought, for various reasons and in varying degrees, to promote a more equitable distribution of wealth in this nation in recent decades (Frieden and Kaplan, 1975; Rubinfeld, 1979). Centremost among these actions have been efforts to employ the poor and subsidize their consumption in order to instill self-sufficiency and limit the transmission of poverty across generations. Most of these efforts have focused on metropolitan areas since these areas (SMSAs) contain nearly two-thirds of the 23 million Americans now living in poverty and many more on the fringe of poverty.

Suburban 'solutions' have won particular attention since almost two-thirds of the metropolitan poor reside in central cities (US Dept. of Commerce, 1977, 1978), but there is considerable resistance to such solutions by higher-status municipalities which are both empowered and politically inclined to deny low-income access through the exercise of instruments of exclusion (Sagar, 1978). These instruments primarily inhibit the construction of new low-income housing by denying developable land, imposing delays and inflating costs (Blumstein, 1979). Few existing dwelling units in these areas are likely to filter down to the financial reach of the poor in the absence of substantial subsidies having large opportunity costs. Non-residents are virtually powerless in obstructing the use of such tactics through local confrontation. Their success in gaining entry will therefore depend almost exclusively on external intervention. Both Federal and State initiatives to promote economic integration have been pursued during the last decade, but later discussion will demonstrate the inherent limits of these approaches and the powerbase from which they have arisen. Community responses which constrain the ultimate effectiveness of these initiatives will also be examined.

Classes and communities, in general, have evolved positions regarding dispersal which may overtly espouse the welfare of the poor, but which are clearly informed by self-interest. For the underclass and its reformist allies, however, that which is good for the poor is favoured irrespective of its social externalities, except in so far as these indirectly affect the welfare of the poor. Among advocates for the poor there is no consensus. Proponents of dispersal tend to attribute vertical 'interclass' inequities to the current horizontal pattern of socio-spatial disparities in metropolitan areas, though few maintain that spatial reorganization would wholly eliminate these inequities. They assert economic integration would improve access to favoured jobs, provide a superior environment in which to raise families, and in effect subsidize the consumption of housing, public services and some private market commodities (Clark, 1979; Inman and Rubinfeld, 1979). This subsidy would issue from the more equitable treatment of different economic classes in suburbs than in central cities as a result of taxing and spending practices and from lower land prices, not from governmental transfers (Baar, 1981; Berry and Bednarz, 1975; Inman and Rubinfeld, 1979). In the longer run, economic integration would heighten the opportunity for equity accumulation through home ownership and other investments (Lake, 1981a), and permit entry into key avenues of social advancement.

Advocates for the poor who oppose dispersal do so for a variety of reasons. Some assert that spatial strategies of any sort do not address a more fundamental conflict among economic classes which gives rise to any particular socio-spatial arrangement (Fainstein and Fainstein, 1982). Others consider dispersal to be inferior strategy. They would prefer central-city revitalization in the interest of the poor, though the poor seem to be at a distinct disadvantage in capturing the benefits of core-area redevelopment efforts currently underway. Those favouring this position note that dispersal may dilute the political voice of the poor. This position is taken despite the existence of countervailing forces. The strength of this voice is generally inverse to the resources commanded by the jurisdictions in which the poor predominate. In addition there is a clear suburban bias in State and Federal legislatures as a result of reapportionment. Further, opponents question the utility of dispersal given the possibility that new and more invidious forms of economic containment may arise following dispersal. Clearly dispersal may take many different forms, some more favourable for the poor than others. Opponents would rightly be suspicious of any set of dispersal policies primarily motivated by capital owners seeking to depopulate the central city in order to secure new investment opportunities (see Edel, 1980). Finally, opponents note that in many central cities there is an abundance of quality housing which may become increasingly available to lower income households as the wealthier population departs (Clark, 1979).

This prospect is enhanced by recent evidence suggesting such an interchange of population may not seriously diminish the capacity of central cities to fund public services (Frey, 1980; but see Schneider and Logan, 1981). Additional arguments against dispersal are provided by Rose (1979) within a 'general welfare' perspective. He notes dispersal would result in the needless duplication of facilities, inflate suburban tax rates, resegregate the central city, hamper central-city revitalization (see also LeGates and Hartman, 1981), and foster sprawl.

Against this backdrop of controversy the ensuing commentary seeks to answer these critical questions:

(i) What factors account for the current pattern of economic segregation in metropolitan areas?

(ii) What are the major legislative and judicial avenues of external intervention for promoting suburban economic integration, and are they complementary?

(iii) Is it likely that external intervention will lead to a significant measure of suburban economic integration in light of both:
   (a) the institutional and political limitations which confront such action at the State and Federal levels, and
   (b) the array of response options available to local jurisdictions and their residents—new forms of exclusion or containment, and various forms of 'exit' including outmigration and the repositioning of public services in the private sector—which may confront and ultimately negate these efforts?

(iv) A major alternative to dispersal is a strategy centred on metropolitan tax-base equalization. Such a strategy would be supported by the promotion of more equitable fiscal practices in central cities, economic revitalization of these cities and lower-status suburbs, and efforts to direct the benefits of revitalization through low-income value-capture. How would this approach compare to dispersal with respect to ease of implementation and impact on the welfare of the poor? Might these two approaches be combined?

SUBURBANIZATION AND POLITICAL FRAGMENTATION

The political fragmentation of metropolitan America was a probable though not inevitable product of growth in population and increase in its economic and ethnic heterogeneity. By the late nineteenth century a massive influx of migrants from rural regions of the United States and abroad had begun to foster selective decentralization. The industrial economy shaped this process, imposing characteristic spatial affinities and social antipathies. The wealthier gradually fled the interior for newer lower density neighbourhoods in outlying areas. Many were located within the core city or soon annexed by it. Both gained: the city sustained its 'growth' image, and residents secured needed services (Teaford, 1979). Location and the internal physical homogeneity of these upper-status neighbourhoods ensured social isolation, and city revenue requirements were small in relation to incomes. As a result there was initially relatively little incentive for these areas to isolate themselves still further through independent political incorporation, the procedure for which was established by State government (Johnston, 1981b). The wealthy, therefore, were generally accepting of State-enabling legislation which facilitated easy annexation.

In time this attitude changed. The core cities were to become still more dense and heterogeneous, and the cost of government began to rise in relation to personal income. In addition, the social isolation of higher-status neighbourhoods began to diminish. This was largely the result of transportation-cost reductions, as well as the inability of these neighbourhoods to control adjacent land development. Surrounding neighbourhoods became increasingly economically heterogeneous. Realizing that political incorporation would afford residents both fiscal autonomy and the capacity to regulate development and therefore to control social access and the tax base (but see James and Windsor, 1976), the wealthier classes came to prefer incorporation over central annexation. State legislatures responded to those pressures by tightening the rules for annexation while facilitating political fragmentation (Teaford, 1979). In the absence of centralizing legislation such as Great Britain's Municipal Corporation Act of 1863, it is difficult to envisage any other result (Teaford, 1979). Within the average SMSA there are now more than twenty municipalities (Johnston, 1981c). Of these, the preferred suburbs today tend to have superior services with low levels of per capita tax-effort. The central city and its lower-status suburbs, on the other hand, tend to offer inferior services at higher unit costs supported by higher levels of tax-effort (Inman and Rubinfeld, 1979; see also Denzan and Weingast, 1982).

Surprisingly, the role of suburban political fragmentation has generally not found its way into conventional theories of urban socio-spatial structure. Standard neoclassical economic models, for example, ignore this function within most single-class, monocentric formulations of the complex calculus which is claimed to explain gradients of land value and population density (Wheaton, 1979). A contrasting scenario is one in which selective population deconcentration leads to political fragmentation. Fragmentation enables the localization of fiscal and land-use policies. Lower suburban population densities result from the evolving capacity of suburbs generally to attract higher-income households opposed to higher-density residential development. Political incorporation subsidizes suburban residents by isolating them from central-city tax burdens and affording them control over land development. They can, therefore, exclude activities which would entail denser development or impose inordinate property-tax increases. These tax 'savings' are then used to 'subsidize' lower-density development by funding the higher infrastructure costs which lower-density development usually requires, and increasing the disposable income of households available for the purchase of lower-density housing. Incorporation also ensures that the tax payments of the wealthy will generate public expenditures within relatively closer proximity to their homes than would likely occur if they lived in a larger and economically more diverse community. They may, therefore, capture a significant portion of the 'value' which their tax payments produce. And this leads to appreciation in the value of their homes, equity accumulation and price-exclusion. Concentration of middle- and upper-income households in suburban municipalities may also make it easier to target intergovernmental transfers to their advantage, and these have begun to equal or exceed locally generated revenues in many suburban jurisdictions.

CURRENT DIMENSIONS OF ECONOMIC SEGREGATION

Not all peripheral municipalities have been equally effective in sustaining economic homogeneity. Nevertheless, even when examined in the aggregate, non-central-city municipalities in the nation's SMSAs now differ substantially from central cities regarding the distribution of income and housing costs among resident households. Nearly two-thirds of all households living in SMSAs in 1979 who had incomes of under $7000 per year, lived in central cities (Table 6.1). Further, 60 per cent of all owner-occupied dwellings in SMSAs valued at less than $30 000 in this year were located in central cities. And 73 per cent of all renter-occupied units having gross rents under $125 per month were in central cities.

Among suburban municipalities there is significant socioeconomic diversity (Lake and Cutter, 1980; Brown, 1981), including income diversity (Pack and Pack, 1977; but see Elgie, 1980), yet within single metropolitan areas their status stratification is becoming increasingly rigid. Prior to 1950, Guest (1978) finds their relative standing was in flux, as some were more successful than others in attracting new increments of valued resources and favoured populations. After 1950, however, he observes the emergence of a fairly stable rank-ordering of suburban municipalities with respect to socio-economic status. Schwartz (1980) indicates a widening of the disparity between high- and low-status suburbs, and between central cities and suburban rings as a whole, whilst Logan (1978) believes that economic disparity among competing places is a more or less inevitable product of differences in relative location, endowment, and the time at which competitive advantages are initially consolidated.

INSTITUTIONAL FOUNDATIONS FOR EXTERNAL INTERVENTION

In the United States, the same governmental arrangements which were responsible for establishing the ground rules for metropolitan fragmentation are

TABLE 6.1. Household* income by housing tenure, cost and metropolitan residence, 1979

	Income ($)		
	0–6999	7000–14 999	Over 14 999
Tenure			
Owner-occupied (27.9 million units = 100%)			
Value ($)			
Central cities	(%)	(%)	(%)
0–29 999	3	3	4
30 000–59 999	2	4	10
Over 59 999	1	1	8
Suburbs			
0–29 999	2	2	3
30 000–59 999	3	6	19
Over 59 999	1	4	25
Tenure			
Renter-occupied† (19.8 million units = 100%)			
Gross rent ($)‡			
Central cities			
0–124	7	1	—§
125–274	13	15	8
Over 274	2	5	7
Suburbs			
0–124	2	1	—§
125–274	6	10	6
Over 274	2	6	9

Source: US Department of Commerce (1981, Table A-1).
* Households include families and primary individuals.
† Excludes households in units having no cash rent.
‡ Gross rent includes monthly contract rent plus utilities.
§ Less than 0.5%. All figures rounded to nearest whole per cent.

now also the major vehicles for external intervention to promote suburban economic integration. They are so by default, and are not ideally suited to the task due to the multiplicity of interests they represent and the preponderance of power groupings in State and Federal legislatures inclined to oppose integration. To understand current integration initiatives originating in the more spatially extensive units of government it is necessary to comprehend the distribution of authority within the Federal system. Under the Tenth Amendment to the US Constitution powers not delegated to the Federal (national) government or denied the States by the Constitution are reserved for the States or the 'people' (see Johnston, 1981a).

Local governments—not recognized by the US Constitution—are creations of State action and may exercise only those powers which are expressly delegated or implicit to these powers and essential for their exercise (Frug, 1980; see also Johnston, 1982). But a State cannot delegate any power it does not first possess, and neither States nor localities may 'abridge the privileges and immunities of citizens . . .; nor . . . deprive any person of life, liberty, or property, without due process of the law; nor deny to any person . . . equal protection of the laws' (Fourteenth Amendment to the US Constitution). Under these provisions, broad ambiguous conceptualizations of 'equality' have far less efficacy than assertions of specific individual rights (Westen, 1982). In addition, Article VI of the US Constitution holds that Federal laws made 'in pursuance' of the Constitution are the 'supreme law of the land'. Finally, both Federal and State spending laws exercise considerable influence over localities both through the expenditures themselves and the local actions which may be required as a prerequisite for external funding (Dear and Clark, 1981). Each of these provisions or practices has been instrumental in the effort to promote economic integration, through legislative and judicial action.

Judicial intervention is generally initiated by low-income non-resident plaintiffs seeking entry to higher-status municipalities. They may be joined by other co-plaintiffs including lower-status suburbs, the government of the central city, and in certain instances the US Justice Department. Almost always they will allege that their exclusion is the product of non-economic (racial, ethnic or other) discrimination, perpetrated by local policies which are overtly economic (Clark, 1981). In Federal courts, these suits normally assert the denial of equal protection under the Fourteenth Amendment, or a violation of the Fair Housing Act of 1968 which is a Federal law outlawing most forms of non-economic discrimination in the sale or rental of housing. The Constitution's Supremacy Clause insures this Act will supersede any others which may conflict.

Plaintiffs may also assert violations of State constitutions and laws before State courts, and these have been the predominant arbiter of exclusionary cases until recently. The most prominent of recent State court decisions is the New Jersey Supreme Court's Mt. Laurel decision (*Southern Burlington County NAACP* v. *Township of Mt. Laurel*, 336 A.2d 713 (1975)) mandating the elimination of exclusionary barriers and the apportionment of 'fair shares' of low- and moderate-income-housing among suburban municipalities. State courts have also been sporadically engaged in cases brought to promote greater fiscal equity within central cities through the elimination of taxing and spending practices which discriminate against the poor, and among all metropolitan municipalities through tax-base equalization. These few decisions, which have not yet won US Supreme Court backing, could conceivably lessen the pressure for economic integration by transferring wealth from higher-income classes and places to lower-income classes and places. Residential integration need not be a prerequisite for economic redistribution.

Legislative action is an essential complement to judicial intervention. As already seen, the Federal Fair Housing Act of 1968 now constitutes one of two key bases for suits by non-residents. This Act is a particularly effective vehicle for such suits since under it plaintiffs need only prove local public policies have the 'effect' of fostering racial discrimination through residential exclusion. Under the Fourteenth Amendment the plaintiff must demonstrate the existence of local 'intent' to discriminate, and this is generally far more difficult (*Harvard Law Review*, 1978).

Legislation has also been instrumental in generating larger supplies of lower-income housing, and ensuring that some of this housing is constructed in suburban municipalities. The nation's major programme in recent years has been the so-called 'Section 8' programme contained within the Housing and Community Development Act of 1974. This programme subsidized low- and moderate- income housing construction. The Act also made Community Development Block Grants (CDBGs) available to suburban communities, and directed that a portion of these funds be used primarily to benefit disadvantaged households and neighbourhoods. Each potential recipient of a CDBG must submit a Housing Assistance Plan (HAP). This plan is required to estimate the number of non-resident lower-income households 'expected to reside' within the municipality in future years. It has been the basis for distributing low-income housing certificates. Suburban municipalities were thus given a strong incentive to construct some low-income housing. The programme also influenced litigation. Defendant municipalities whose HAPs indicated that 'zero' lower-income residents were expected to reside within their borders in future years occasionally found that this information would be interpreted by the courts as evidence of an intent to discriminate. In addition, the presence of such a programme made it easier for courts to mandate the actual construction of new lower-income units, though until recently few went beyond the requirement that culpable communities should eliminate passive exclusionary barriers. It is also possible that if courts were more customarily to mandate affirmative relief in the form of new housing, the legislative branches of the State and Federal governments might be led to enact laws to further subsidize lower-income housing in suburban areas.

CONFRONTING EXCLUSIONARY PRACTICES

Elimination of municipal barriers to the construction of low- and even moderate-income housing does not ensure such housing will actually be built, but it is an essential first step. Most barriers result from the exercise of the municipality's 'police power'. This power is delegated by the State, and enables the municipality to protect the health, safety, morals and general welfare of its residents. The application of this power may have the effect of increasing the cost of occupancy of new housing beyond the reach of lower-income households. Among public actions which may have this effect are subdivision ordinances, building codes, and other ordinances which control the construction of streets, sewers, water and power lines, and facilities for public use (Davidoff and Brooks, 1976; see also Goetz and Wofford, 1979). Voter referenda have also been employed to review public-housing proposals and zoning provisions (Tarlock, 1980). Of all local actions, zoning ordinances have probably had the greatest exclusionary effect. These determine permissible densities and building types, entail administrative delays, and consequently increase costs.

Landowners and non-resident lower-income households seeking to void zoning ordinances generally pursue different objectives, but both confront similar judicial hurdles. First, the power to zone land or rezone it at higher ('upzoning') or lower ('downzoning') intensities was defined expansively by the US Supreme Court in its initial decision upholding this application of police power. The Court indicated zoning would normally be upheld unless the ordinance in question is 'clearly arbitrary and unreasonable, having no substantial relation to 'legitimate police-power objectives' (*Village of Euclid* v. *Ambler Realty Co.*, 272 US 365 (1926)). Second, courts usually hold that zoning is a 'legislative' function and therefore is entitled to a presumption of validity (Williamson, 1980). Ordinances have, therefore, generally been upheld whenever they have been shown to contribute to the general welfare, but the power of plaintiffs to challenge zoning ordinances has been enhanced recently, and the courts have begun to intervene with increasing frequency.

Downzoning litigation: landowner's rights

Landowners, including those intending to construct lower-income housing, have available several judicial stances from which to pursue redress. Aside from their capacity to assert the rights of non-resident households seeking entry, they may argue that the zoning ordinance is arbitrary, unreasonable, piecemeal and therefore discriminates against single members of a broad class of landowners, or is insufficiently connected to an acceptable use of police power (*Harvard Law Review*, 1978). The ordinance's reasonableness may be called into question if the treatment of the landowner's property is inconsistent with the municipality's comprehensive plan, or with the zoning classifications assigned to similar or neighbouring parcels (Williamson, 1980). This approach offers some hope to those seeking to develop lower-income housing on their own land, especially if the comprehensive plan called for such a use of their property, or if comparable parcels have already been assigned such a use.

Landowners may seek recourse on other constitutional grounds, arguing that the zoning ordinance amounts to a *de facto* 'taking' of property for public use without just compensation. The Fifth Amendment to the US Constitution establishes such a rule, and the Fourteenth Amendment applies it to the states. All State constitutions have or imply a similar provision (Cunningham, 1981). Whether landowners will find this a useful approach in their efforts to develop lower-income housing will depend on the eventual resolution of two issues: the definition of a 'taking', and the kind of remedy to be offered when takings are found to have occurred.

Consider the taking issue first. The key issue here is whether the relevant fact is the proportion of the property's value removed through zoning, or the amount of value which remains following adoption of the ordinance. Guidelines established in recent decisions of the US Supreme Court are ambiguous. In *Penn Central Transportation Co.* v. *New York City* 438 US 104 (1978), the Court seemed to indicate that an ordinance regulating property would not constitute a taking so long as the landowner retains a 'reasonable beneficial use' of the property. But in *Agins* v. *City of Tiburon* 477 US 255 (1980) the Court clearly indicated that a 'reasonable beneficial use' may be one in which virtually all forms of development are precluded. In this instance the city zoned the plaintiff's tract composed of five acres of prime land for use in single-family residence or as open space. No more than one dwelling unit per acre was allowed, and it was possible that subsequent architectural and environmental assessments of development proposals would permit even fewer. The Court held that this local ordinance did not prevent the 'best use' of the land, and since this may imply no development whatsoever, it must be concluded that a 'reasonable beneficial use' may be one in which there is virtually no opportunity for financial gain.

The second issue confronting the courts concerns permissible remedies when takings are found to have occurred. The US Supreme Court, in the *Agins* case, let stand the prior ruling of the California Supreme Court that the only form of redress available to the landowner if he successfully demonstrated that a taking had occurred would be invalidation of the ordinance. It explicitly denied relief under the theory of 'inverse condemnation' by which the landlord had sought to transmute an excessive use of police power into a lawful taking for which compensation must be paid under eminent domain (598 P.2d 25 (California, 1979)). Underlying this denial was the fear that such a practice would exhaust the public treasury or so weaken the institution of zoning as to render it ineffective (see also Ellickson, 1973; and Krasnowiecki, 1980). Justice Brennan's dissent in *San Diego Gas and Electric Co.* v. *City of San Diego* (49 USLW 4317 (1981) however, strongly suggests the US Supreme Court will eventually be prepared to award landowners compensation for at least that period of time between the moment a taking occurs and that at which the government entity chooses to rescind or amend the offending regulation (Cunningham, 1981).

Landowners seeking to develop lower-income housing will probably find little encouragement in the judicial precedents surrounding the taking issue. If a taking is found to have occurred, the municipality will probably almost always elect to alter the ordinance to permit the landowner a 'reasonable beneficial use'. But even the revised ordinance will probably seldom enable the development of lower-income housing. The landowner will therefore have to rely far more on demonstrations of arbitrariness or on assertions regarding the rights of non-resident households seeking low-income housing within the municipality. These are considered next.

Non-residents confronting discriminatory practices

Non-resident, lower income households are in a better position than land-owners in pursuing the development of lower-income housing. Both may join in suing municipalities, however, so their legal strategies may be complementary. Landowners, for example, will benefit if it can be demonstrated that downzoning was prompted by a desire to deny racial or other minorities access, or that it had this consequence.

Challenges of exclusionary practices in Federal courts by lower-income, non-resident households have asserted the denial of rights of three types. They have claimed these practices, (1) violate the Equal Protection Clause of the Fourteenth Amendment which was enacted to ensure that States would guarantee blacks the same civil rights as whites, or (2) conflict with Federal laws and must therefore yield under the mandate of the Supremacy Clause, or (3) infringe on the constitutional right to travel defined by the Privileges and Immunities Clause of the Fourteenth Amendment. The third of these has been severely weakened as a basis for judicial action by the Supreme Court (*Village of Belle Terre* v. *Boraas*, 416 US 1 (1974)). The first and second are generally asserted simultaneously, and the Federal legislative basis for the second is almost always the Fair Housing Act of 1968.

The Fair Housing Act of 1968 constituted a significant redefinition of the geographical orientation of Federal housing policy. Prior Federal legislation had given lip-service to racial integration, but did little to disperse lower-income housing in metropolitan areas. Most public housing built under provisions of the Housing Act of 1949, for example, was located in lower-income neighbour-hoods, at least until the Civil Rights Act of 1964 declared that no activity receiving Federal aid could discriminate on the basis of race. Whether this Act will lead to a significant degree of suburban dispersal is uncertain. The Supreme Court's ambivalence was underscored in *Hills* v. *Gautreaux* 425 US 284 (1976). It ruled the Federal government should not have funded the activities of the Chicago Housing Authority because the Authority refused to build public housing in predominantly white areas. At the same time, the Court claimed its decree would not 'displace the rights and powers accorded local government entities under Federal or State housing statutes or existing land use laws' (see also Lev, 1981).

In contrast, the Fair Housing Act was apparently intended to invoke 'regional' solutions for the problems of central cities (see Vol. 114 Congressional Record 2276, 3421–2 (1968)). The Act sharpens the Fourteenth Amendment's prohibition against official discrimination by States and therefore municipalities, and extends this prohibition to encompass private-sector housing discrimination in both the sale and rental of housing. It also contains stipulations against discrimination in housing finance and brokerage services, and defines procedures by which the US Department of Housing and Urban Development is to mediate complaints. The Department, however, is given no authority to compel settlements or punish offenders (Lake, 1981a), and in 1979 almost half of all attempted conciliations were unsuccessful. Aggrieved parties may initiate civil actions when conciliation fails, and the Act empowers the US Justice Department to join in the suit when there is evidence of a clear 'pattern and practice' of discrimination within the municipality.

Non-residents who claim to have been denied entry as a result of exclusionary practices which discriminate on the basis of race are generally in a favourable position in pursuing adjudication. This is because race is a 'suspect class' since it designates a group which has been 'subjected to such a history of purposeful unequal treatment, or relegated to such a position of political powerlessness as to command extraordinary protection from the majoritarian political process' (*San Antonio Independent School District* v. *Rodriguez*, 411 US 28 (1973)). First, the 'suspectness' of the class delineated by a discriminatory policy eases the burden of demonstrating a standing to sue. Standing is necessary for adjudication to proceed. According to a recent Supreme Court decision, standing in this type of case requires evidence of injury, that this injury stemmed from the defendant's actions, and that the remedy sought will redress the injury (*Warth* v. *Seldin*, 422 US 490 (1975)). On its face, this standard seems to be a radical proscription of non-resident standing since the mere removal of exclusionary barriers does not ensure that actual construction will occur (Sager, 1978). In its subsequent decision in *Village of Arlington Heights* v. *Metropolitan Housing Development Corp.* 429 US (1977), however, the Supreme Court did allow standing even though there was no proof that elimination of the allegedly discriminatory zoning ordinance would enable the non-resident plaintiff to move into a proposed project. Second, the 'suspectness' of a class will substantially lessen the efficacy of a legal defence of exclusionary municipal policies which asserts they are motivated by a 'compelling public interest'. Such a defence is normally only successful when the public objective is legitimate, so important as to override discriminatory consequences, and cannot be achieved through other means which are less discriminatory (*Kennedy Park Homes Association* v. *City of Lackawanna*, 436 F.2d 108 (2d Cir. 1970)). Whether local land-use policies having explicit environmental or fiscal purposes can withstand non-resident challenges when their by-product is the perpetuation of racial segregation has not yet been thoroughly examined by the Supreme Court.

The ascendance of the Fair Housing Act as a vehicle for non-resident suits is primarily due to recent Supreme Court decisions which indicate that plaintiffs must demonstrate that the municipality whose actions are allegedly discriminatory, and therefore in violation of the Fourteenth Amendment, actually *intended* to discriminate. Ascertaining legislative motive is usually a prohibitively speculative undertaking, and the Court has not yet declared that proof of discriminatory *effect* would not suffice when violations of the Fair Housing Act are asserted. An early indication that the Court might be prepared to examine motivations underlying overtly 'neutral' official acts came in its decision in *James* v. *Valtierra* 402 US 137 (1971). The Court held that the California constitution's requirement that no low-income housing project could be developed by any public body without first securing approval in a local referendum did not violate the Equal Protection Clause. To reach this conclusion it first determined that, taken at face value, the law was neutral, then sought evidence of racial motivation: none was found. This result might have been anticipated since the state procedure for mandatory referenda was not restricted to proposals involving low-income housing.

Clearly, if intent, not effect, is to be the standard for judging local practices then the empirical domain to which strict scrutiny would apply is contracted. This indeed was to become the standard applied in zoning cases. In *Arlington Heights*, the Court ruled that a zoning ordinance preventing the construction of a federally subsidized low-income housing project by a non-profit corporation in an exclusive Chicago suburb was not discriminatorily motivated and therefore not in violation of the Fourteenth Amendment. Demonstration of such an intent is now thought to require evidence not only that the practice or policy has had a disproportionate impact in perpetuating segregation, but also that it, (1) reflects past discriminatory behaviour, (2) arose against a background of racial discord, and (3) was adopted soon after and in direct response to an initiative to construct low-income housing. The magnitude of the impediment posed by the intent standard was recently underscored in the Court's decision in *City of Memphis* v. *Greene* No. 79-1176, US (1981). It ruled that the closing of a city street at the junction of black and white neighbourhoods was not evidence of a racially discriminatory intent in violation of the Fourteenth Amendment. To reach this conclusion it accepted the city's argument that the sole purpose of its action was to reduce traffic and thereby increase neighbourhood safety. It dismissed as speculative or inconsequential, evidence that blacks would suffer some inconvenience, isolation, and depreciation in property value.

Non-resident plaintiffs may state a successful cause of action under the Fair Housing Act merely by demonstrating that the defendant's actions had a discriminatory effect according to most of the lower courts within the Federal judicial system. In *Kennedy Park Homes Association* v. *City of Lackawanna* the plaintiff alleged the violation of both the Fourteenth Amendment's Equal

Protection Clause and the Fair Housing Act. It brought suit to compel the city to permit construction of a specific low-income housing project. Soon after the project had been proposed the city adopted a moratorium on any new subdivisions and re-zoned the site which had been chosen for the project as open space. The Court of Appeals ruled for the plaintiff, finding the city contravened both the Fourteenth Amendment and the Fair Housing Act. But while it had no difficulty in uncovering a discriminatory motivation, the Court went on to observe that even if discrimination was merely the result of 'thoughtlessness rather than a purposeful scheme' it would still be prepared to find the city at fault for having placed blacks at a severe disadvantage which it could not justify. This decision came before the 'intent' standard had been firmly established, but the clear implication was that demonstration of a discriminatory effect would be sufficient to find the defendant to be culpable under the Fair Housing Act.

Demonstrations of discriminatory effect meant to establish liability under the Fair Housing Act are primarily though not exclusively dependent on statistical evidence of disproportionate impact. These also contribute to the demonstration of an intent to discriminate but are not sufficient to prove an invidious motivation. No single statistical standard has emerged. In *Resident Advisory Board* v. *Rizzo* 564 F.2d 126 (3rd Cir. 1977), the Court of Appeals found that in clearing a site within an older neighbourhood in preparation for the construction of new low-income public housing and then failing to build such housing, the City of Philadelphia and its co-defendants were guilty of racial discrimination. This finding was based on evidence that almost all the black households living in the neighbourhood resided on the tract which was cleared, and that while about one-third of the city's population was black, over 90 per cent of all persons on the waiting list for public housing were black.

A different standard was established in *United States* v. *City of Black Jack* 508 F.2d 1179 (8th Cir. 1974), a 'pattern and practice' suit brought by the US Justice Department. When it became known that lower-income, multiple-family housing was being planned for a predominantly white unincorporated area outside St Louis, citizens arranged to become incorporated and then adopted a zoning ordinance which prohibited any new, multiple-family dwellings. The District Court could discover no discriminatory effect, and so it found for the defendant. This conclusion was primarily based on evidence that approximately equal proportions of black and white families living within the metropolitan area would be eligible to reside in the proposed housing. The Court of Appeals reversed this decision noting that the municipality was 99 per cent white and that the zoning prohibition would ultimately deny proportionately more blacks (85 per cent) than whites (14 per cent) living in the metropolitan-area access to the city.

Whether the Fair Housing Act of 1968 will become a more potent force in the future than it has been in the past will depend on the future course of legislative action and the path of judicial response. Congress may elect to amend the Act. Any amendment produced by the current Congress or one similarly constituted would almost certainly weaken the Act, possibly by declaring that culpability under the Act requires proof of discriminatory intent. Recent efforts to strengthen the Act through amendment have failed. In 1980, for example, conservative Democrats and a majority of Republicans in the Senate rejected an amendment which would have empowered the Department of Housing and Urban Development to appoint administrative law judges to prosecute cases and levy fines. This would almost certainly have widened the impact of the Act by allowing the adjudication of more cases than is now possible within the Federal court system. Giving these judges the power to fine offending municipalities, and allowing successful plaintiffs to collect court fees would also have presumably induced some communities to eliminate exclusionary barriers in advance of adjudication. Some courts however, have already awarded plaintiffs substantial money damages under the existing law.

The Federal courts will also, of course, play a major role in shaping the future impact of the Fair Housing Act. The Supreme Court, for example, may elect to require proof of discriminatory intent under the Act, even in the absence of action by a conservative Congress, or it may instead clarify the 'effect' standard fashioned by the lower courts. Or the Court may elect to restore the full force of the *Warth* doctrine—seemingly violated in the *Arlington Heights* decision—which limited the judicial standing of potential plaintiffs to instances in which the removal of exclusionary barriers would lead directly to the construction of housing. Adjudication of cases involving alleged violations of the Fair Housing Act will also be dependent on the larger policy context in which they are heard. If Congress or the State legislatures were to vote substantial new subsidies for the construction of lower-income housing, the plaintiff's position would be considerably enhanced. Not only would judicial standing be easier to secure, even under the stringent conditions established in *Warth*, but also, a municipality's failure to pursue such subsidies could be interpreted as evidence of discriminatory intent.

Further, the courts may be more ready to find violations of the Act if it can be demonstrated to their satisfaction that housing discrimination is instrumental in maintaining segregated schools and limiting access to jobs. Increasing the perceived magnitude of the 'injury' suffered by a plaintiff would diminish the efficacy of a municipality's justification of a practice which has a discriminatory effect, based on a 'compelling public interest'. This type of linkage is asserted in two pending suits filed by the Federal government. The first, filed by the Carter Justice Department, alleges that the City of Yonkers, New York chose sites for subsidized housing which aggravated residential and therefore school segregation. Another suit, the first filed against a municipality under the Fair Housing Act by the Reagan Justice Department, alleges that the Town of Cicero, Illinois denies blacks access to housing. It further alleges that residential exclusion prevents them from securing jobs in the town's government since applicants were required to have lived within the town for at least one year.

Challenges of exclusionary practices in State courts amount to a second major opportunity for judicial intervention. These cases differ from their Federal counterparts since, (1) they involve assertions of rights under State laws or constitutions, (2) stem from a tradition of more energetic oversight of municipal practices, and (3) have produced decisions which mandate region-wide rather than site-specific solutions. The leading decision is that of the New Jersey Supreme Court in *South Burlington, County NAACP* v. *Township of Mt. Laurel* 336 A.2d 713 (1975), hereafter to be called *Mt. Laurel I* to distinguish it from a more recent decision of that Court which is discussed later. This decision set in motion a search for an acceptable formula for allocating 'fair shares' of regional low- and moderate-income housing among suburban communities. The Court held that 'developing' communities must adopt zoning ordinances which will accommodate their fair share of the regional supply of lower-income housing. 'Developing' communities were those located within the regional housing market in which lower-income households would search in the absence of exclusionary barriers. Such communities would have considerable open space, be located beyond the inner ring of older suburbs, and fall within the path of metropolitan expansion.

The crucial issue in *Mt. Laurel I* and all similar State cases is what determines that a zoning ordinance is 'exclusionary'. In New Jersey this determination has been based primarily on whether the ordinance provides 'sufficient' space for lower-income housing, but until recently the Court had provided no comprehensive institutional or statistical process for establishing fair shares (*Oakwood at Madison, Inc.* v. *Township of Madison*, 371 A.2d 1192 (1977)). New Jersey employs an 'effect' standard so no further inquiry into motivation is necessary. Few of the fair-share formulae which have been proposed merely apportion space for lower income housing according to the recipient group's proportionate presence in the region. Instead most take into account, (1) municipal capacity, (2) housing needs of existing lower-income residents, and (3) the needs of additional lower-income households expected to reside within the municipality in future years due to growth and change in the local employment base (Listokin, 1976).

TOWARDS AFFIRMATIVE RELIEF

Fifteen years of judicial intervention on behalf of non-resident plaintiffs seeking to reside in higher-status suburban municipalities has produced only minor gains, primarily because the elimination of passive barriers has been insufficient to enable construction to occur. Despite zoning revisions required by the Court in 1975 to enable construction of 515 additional lower-income dwelling units in Mt. Laurel Township, New Jersey, none has actually been built. The reason is that unsubsidized units generally do not yield a sufficient economic return; many municipalities have resisted the use of available subsidies within their borders, and the courts have tended not to mandate affirmative relief in the form of actual construction. This section addresses the impact of Federal housing legislation and the implications of Reagan's 'new Federalism', and finally reports on the current magnitude of suburban housing subsides.

Negative assessments of progress toward economic integration have led some courts to go beyond passive relief. Even the lower Federal courts have begun to explore new avenues of intervention. In *Parkview Heights Corp.* v. *City of Black Jack* 605 F.2d 1033 (8th Cir. 1979), the Court of Appeals determined that the District Court should grant remedial injunctive relief pursuant to its finding that a city zoning ordinance was in violation of the Fair Housing Act. The major factor distinguishing this case was that the plaintiff was prepared to construct lower-income housing when it was confronted by the exclusionary ordinance. But the delay during litigation, rising costs and other factors made it impossible for the developer to proceed with construction once the courts had acted. The Court therefore remanded the case to the District Court requiring it to arrange for the plaintiff class and the city to work together to identify appropriate sites and establish a workable plan to permit actual construction. If this cooperative effort were to fail, the lower court would be responsible for formulating its own decree. The Court, however, cautioned against excessive judicial intrusion into the domain of local action. Therefore it stopped short of requiring the City to enact ordinances subsidizing development (see also Cavalieri, 1979–80).

An even greater degree of judicial intervention to provide affirmative relief was sanctioned by still another lower Federal court. In *United States* v. *City of Parma* 661 F.2d (6th Cir. 1981) a Court of Appeals mandated complex affirmative relief in response to a non-resident plaintiff's successful demonstration that the City had pursued a pattern and practice of racial discrimination in violation of both the Fourteenth Amendment and the Fair Housing Act. The Court rejected the lower District Court's order setting an annual numerical quota of new low-income housing units, and requiring a 'special master' to oversee implementation. But it did explicitly require Parma to participate in both public housing and other public subsidy programmes for which it was already eligible. It also approved appointment of a 'fair housing' committee to oversee compliance, and enjoined enforcement of exclusionary ordinances. As in *Black Jack* the Court affirmed the application of the Fair Housing Act to public as well as private discrimination, encouraged a municipality to go beyond mere passive relief, but refused to declare exactly what positive steps it should pursue. Together these decisions indicate growing support for economic integration within the Federal judiciary. Together also, they suggest that a workable formula is evolving which may appreciably strengthen the role of the Federal courts without their usurping local legislative authority. In light of this emerging trend it would seem unlikely that future non-resident plaintiffs will find it

worthwhile to pursue court action based on Federal legislation other than the
Fair Housing Act. But if Congress were to foreclose this avenue, it now appears
they would be inclined to turn to assertions of rights and responsibilities
contained within Federal anti-trust law (Payne, 1981), or Section 1983 of Title
42 of the US Code (i.e. the Civil Rights Act of 1871). The latter may eventually
be interpreted to permit plaintiffs to recover damages when local officials violate
any of a plethora of Federal statutes bearing on land use which cannot now be
used to construct a private cause of action (see Payne, 1981; and Pearlman,
1982).

It now appears that both Federal and State courts are gradually becoming
more willing to specify affirmative relief of two broad categories: one requires
the municipality to pursue subsidies for the State and Federal governments; the
other, to restructure local provisions so as to induce low-income housing
construction. The New Jersey Supreme Court, for example, mandated the
elimination of passive barriers to the construction of low- and moderate-
income housing in *Mt. Laurel I* (1975), but then retreated from this stance in
Oakwood at Madison v. *Township of Madison* 371 A.2d 1192 (1977). In the latter
case the Court held the Township responsible only for adjusting its zoning
ordinance so as to accommodate the least-costly housing which private
developers could produce in light of prevailing economic conditions. In its most
recent decision, however, the Court determined in *Mt. Laurel II* (1983) that
once a municipality is found to have acted to prevent construction of its fair
share of lower income housing it will be responsible for stimulating construction
through inclusionary devices and by assisting developers with applications for
externally provided subsidies. This decision reaffirms *Mt. Laurel I*, but also
clarifies its mandate by providing an extra-judicial mechanism for determining if
the effect of local ordinances is exclusionary, and by requiring offending
municipalities to take positive steps to lower the cost of 'least-cost' housing.

There are a number of strategies for reducing construction costs through local
action, though not all may be equally effective. These strategies fall into two
broad classes. The first includes those which cut unit costs through the relaxation
of some building and zoning requirements ('override' procedures), and the
provision of 'density bonuses' which permit higher densities when lower-income
dwellings are provided. Those belonging to the second class take the form of
intra-municipal subsidies. These range from tax breaks which spread costs across
the entire community, to those which are internal to the specific housing project.
'Inclusionary zoning' ordinances, for example, require developers to include a
specified percentage of lower income units in their projects. While these
ordinances do entail a 'taking' of property rights, not all or even an appreciable
portion of a property's value is removed. Courts are, therefore, likely to find
them to be a valid use of police power, and in any case, some of this value is
frequently returned to the developer in the form of density bonuses. Ellickson,
however, argues that ordinances such as those recently enacted in California will

actually impede the attainment of economic integration because they increase the price of the upper-income units in the project while attempting integration at a spatial scale which he believes is generally unacceptable to both lower- and upper-income households. The end result, he asserts, would be to inflate the prices of the economically segregated portions of the local market (Ellickson, 1981). Tax breaks, in contrast, are not linked to any particular scale of integration, nor would their direct price effects be as large or so spatially concentrated.

Federal and, to a lesser degree, State housing programmes, have also been instrumental in dispersing lower-income housing into suburban areas. This results from three factors: the linkage between housing plans and other subsidies, the formulae by which housing subsidies are allocated among jurisdictions, and the impact of housing subsidies on adjudication—particularly regarding the existence of discrimination and the character of relief once discrimination is found to have occurred. All three arise out of the provisions of the Housing and Community Development Act which make the allocation of Community Development Block Grants (CDBGs) contingent on a municipality's submission of an acceptable Housing Assistance Plan (HAP). Such a plan

> accurately surveys the condition of the housing stock in the community and assesses the housing assistance needs of lower-income persons . . . *residing in or expected to reside* [emphasis added] in the community as a result of existing or projected employment opportunities in the community (and those elderly persons residing in or expected to reside in the community), or as estimated in a community accepted State or regional housing opportunity plan (Vol. 42 USC section 5304 (1980))

Administrative guidelines further clarify procedures for estimating three categories of households expected to reside within the municipality: households presently working in but not living in the municipality, those who would be attracted by planned new employment opportunities, and non-resident elderly households (see Vol. 24 CFR section 570.306). In requiring cognizance of non-resident, external housing demands, the Act explicitly encourages a regional perspective. Further, when a HAP exists it may also be used in allocating lower-income housing subsidies under the 'Section 8' lower-income housing programme contained within the same 1974 legislation (Vol. 42 USC section 1437F). This was the nation's major lower-income housing programme until it was allowed to expire in late 1982. None has yet been devised to replace it.

Each of the three impacts of the Housing and Community Development Act of 1974 upon lower-income dispersal is now considered. The first of these results from the linkage between the HAP requirement and the allocation of CDBGs. A suburban city having population in excess of 50 000 is eligible for entitlement funds once it submits an acceptable HAP and complies with other provisions for grant management. Allocations of entitlement funds are based on 'need' measured according to both demographic (size and extent of poverty) and housing criteria. Until recently, 75 per cent of the grant had been used principally to benefit lower-income households. These grants have been employed mainly to build infrastructure. Smaller suburban cities are eligible only for discretionary grants. They must also file an acceptable HAP. The evaluation of their proposals entails the application of a point system emphasizing criteria which favour lower-income households. Actual funding decisions, however, are not highly correlated with need. Further, discretionary allocations to smaller cities in metropolitan areas have been disproportionately small relative to need (Isserman, 1981). Nevertheless, CDBGs have been sufficiently large to entice many communities to apply for them even when doing so would mainly benefit existing lower-income neighbourhoods within their borders and possibly attract additional lower-income households to the area. The likelihood that the pursuit of a CDBG will lead to an increase in the supply of lower-income housing within the community has lessened in recent years. The most important reason for this, of course, is the elimination of the 'Section 8' Federal housing programme. Another reason is that CDBG funding is now less likely than earlier to be devoted primarily to investments benefiting existing lower-income residents. This is true of both entitlement and discretionary grants. Finally, municipalities are becoming more aware that they can rationalize lower estimates of the number of lower-income households expected to reside within their borders by constraining the development of low-wage industries.

The formulae by which housing subsidies are allocated among jurisdictions also have an impact on low-income dispersal. Under the 'Section 8' Federal housing programme, subsidies were available for lower-income families to enable them to occupy existing units or to permit rehabilitation or new construction of structures having at least some lower-income units. In the case of existing units, the US Department of Housing and Urban Development (DHUD) was empowered to enter into annual contributions contracts with local public-housing agencies to subsidize specified numbers of units. These agencies would then contract with the owners of existing units located within their service areas to provide assistance payments. If no such agency existed, DHUD could contract directly with owners. Similar provisions applied regarding rehabilitation and new construction. Qualifying tenants then seek out available units within the service area. Whenever DHUD received an application for local assistance furthermore, it was required to inform the relevant local government. If there existed a HAP and if the local government could demonstrate that approval of the application would violate the provisions of the HAP, then the application would be denied. The local government's intent under these circumstances was almost always to limit local housing assistance, while local housing agencies and developers usually used the HAP to demonstrate a market for their properties. Overall, the direct effect of the Housing and Community Development Act of 1974 on the supply of lower-income housing in exclusive suburban municipalities has been slight. This is a product not only of the small size of the total amount of resources commanded by the 'Section 8' programme, but also the allocational provisions of the Act. CDBGs have probably had far less effect in promoting the economic integration of smaller suburban cities than in opening up the larger metropolitan municipalities. And the 'Section 8' programme was not successful in generating significant new supplies of lower-income housing in the upper-status suburban communities. This was primarily because, (1) these communities were very effective in preventing the establishment of local public-housing agencies, (2) DHUD did not aggressively pursue subsidization in communities where these agencies did not exist, and (3) households were eligible for certification only by the housing agency in whose district they resided (see also, Levin, 1980; and Zarembka, 1980). These households could not transfer their certificates of participation into the higher-status suburban communities. State tax and spending limits have further reduced the nation's capacity to fund lower-income housing (Rose, 1982).

The third impact of the Housing and Community Development Act of 1974 on low-income dispersal follows from its role in the adjudication of cases involving alleged violations of the Fair Housing Act of 1968. First, the availability of both CDBG and 'Section 8' subsidies gives credence to a non-resident plaintiff's claim that the successful demonstration of housing discrimination would lead to actual relief in the form of new housing. Judicial standing, even under the severe *Warth* doctrine is therefore easier to secure. Second, courts may find that a Housing Assistance Plan indicating a negligible estimate of the number of lower-income households expected to reside within the community is evidence of discrimination in violation of the Fair Housing Act.

INTRA-METROPOLITAN HOUSING SUBSIDIES

To date government-subsidized units constitute only a small fraction of the nation's total housing stock. Just 6 per cent of all occupied units in SMSAs are subsidized directly (9 per cent in central cities, and 3 per cent in their suburbs) (US Department of Commerce, 1981, Table A-1). The vast majority of subsidized units have been in publicly owned structures, i.e. 'public housing', and even now over three-quarters of all subsidized, occupied units in SMSAs are of this type (Table 6.2). Most of these receive Federal subsidies. Despite ongoing image problems the Federal public-housing programme was at least momentarily reinvigorated in the 1960s through new design standards, a shift to more elderly tenants, and a new scheme for the private development of these units

TABLE 6.2.   Government-subsidized rental units by household income and metropolitan residence (1979)

	Units in public housing projects* (000)		Privately owned units with government subsidy† (000)	
Income ($)	Central cities	Suburbs	Central cities	Suburbs
0–6999	818 (70%)‡	214 (53%)‡	321 (73%)‡	151 (70%)‡
7000–14999	273 (23%)	146 (36%)	106 (24%)	48 (22%)
Over 14999	81 (7%)	43 (11%)	15 (3%)	18 (8%)
Column total	1172	403	442	217
Column total as percentage of all rental units in same place	9.8%	4.7%	3.7%	2.5%

Source: US Department of Commerce (1981, Table A-1).
* Structure is owned by a local housing authority or other public agency. These organizations may receive Federal or State subsidies.
† These units are not in public housing projects but the resident household pays a lower rent due to government subsidies regarding construction, financing or operations. The major Federal programmes administered by the US Department of Housing and Urban Development include moderate-income rental and co-operative interest subsidies, direct loans for housing of the elderly, and low-income rent supplements.
‡ Per cent of column total.

('turnkey' housing). The programme, however, is again in jeopardy, this time due to rising operating costs. Today, under one-quarter of all occupied, subsidized units in SMSAs are in privately owned structures, and again, most are Federally assisted. Further, well over half of all occupied, subsidized units in SMSAs are occupied by households having incomes under $7000 per year (Table 6.2).

The spatial distribution of low-income housing subsidies continues to promote the disproportionate concentration of lower-income households in central cities. Sixty-one per cent of all SMSA households having incomes under $7000 reside in central cities, and 26 per cent of these live in subsidized units. The remaining 39 per cent of households in this income range live in the suburban ring, but just 19 per cent of these occupy subsidized units. Further, 59 per cent of all SMSA households having incomes of $7000 or more reside in the suburban ring. If an identical proportion of SMSA households having incomes under $7000 lived in suburbs, then 53 per cent more such households would live there than do now.

GROWTH MANAGEMENT AS COMMUNITY RESPONSE

With the onset of the environmental movement in the United States, the judiciary seemed more prepared to find protection of the natural environment to be a laudable application of local police power. Objections that severely restrictive ordinances constituted unjust and uncompensated 'takings' of property rights, or racially exclusionary practices, weakened in the face of the environmental ethic. Since then the courts have appeared to be surprisingly receptive to comprehensive development constraints packaged as growth management schemes (Blumstein, 1979). Ellickson (1977) finds three major classes of costs for existing residents arising from new development which the municipality might seek to avoid or recover: nuisance costs, fiscal costs, and congestion costs. Nuisance costs are those leading to the decline in value of nearby parcels. Courts have been almost uniformly unwilling to support ordinances seeking to avoid such costs when their effect is demonstrably exclusionary. They have also been reluctant to uphold ordinances whose prime intent is to prevent developments having net negative fiscal impacts, or to charge new developments the full incremental cost of required public utilities and other services, when to do so would exclude lower-income housing. But when local land-use legislation is assembled into a comprehensive ordinance to control growth so as to prevent 'congestion costs' associated with despoilation of the environment or the overloading of public facilities, courts have been inclined to validate them (Blumstein, 1979; see also, Rubin, 1982). Of course, much of the development precluded by growth-control ordinances is high-value housing. Suits seeking to void such ordinances because they have this effect are not bolstered by legal safeguards against racial discrimination (Ellickson, 1977).

Some communities have coupled provisions for limiting growth with inclusionary mandates or incentives in order to strengthen their defence against charges that their control ordinances are exclusionary. Petaluma, California, for example, set a quota on annual housing starts, and allocated the quota among developers using a point system which rewarded those proposing projects which would contain lower-income units. The Circuit Court upheld the plan (*Construction Industry Association* v. *City of Petaluma*, 522 F.2d 897 (9th Cir. 1975)), claiming it stood in 'stark contrast' to the exclusionary programmes of so many other suburbs. Ellickson (1981), however, claims the inclusionary provision was really a legal cover for exclusionary practices and that this helps to explain why Petaluma's quota has not been met in most years. Not only does it inflate the costs of the high-value units beyond the reach of many households, but it also reduces the potential size of the stock available for eventual filtering.

Growth management systems such as Petaluma's are just one of several means for limiting growth or preserving farmland and open space, but all are potentially exclusionary. Freilich and David (1981) identify four major classes of development constraints: (1) regulatory (e.g. zoning, performance standards, quotas and agricultural districts), (2) spending (i.e. withholding essential utilities and services), (3) tax policy (e.g. preferential assessments, and capital gains taxes to discourage speculation), and (4) compensatory approaches (e.g. land-banking, compensatory zoning and transfers of development rights). Any of these is better able to withstand exclusionary challenges if it is a legitimate application of police power, is based on thoroughly documented analysis, and adheres to a comprehensive plan for the area's development.

Efforts to influence the racial composition of local residential areas constitute another form of growth/change management (Lake and Winslow, 1981). Because they seek to regulate housing access of blacks and whites having similar economic status through the strategic supply of market information (Lake, 1981a), and through benign racial steering or quotas (Harvard Law Review, 1980) in order to prevent resegregation, they risk judicial challenge. Racial quotas setting an upper limit on black households have been upheld when employed in public housing (*Otero* v. *New York City Housing Authority* 484 F.2d 1122 (2d Cir. 1973) but have never been applied in private housing. Informational strategies including the Department of Housing and Urban Development's affirmative marketing programmes will probably find little judicial resistance (Beaton and Sossamon, 1982). Whether benign racial steering will meet with judicial approval will ultimately depend on the willingness of courts to find 'integration' to fall within the realm of 'compelling public interest' and so important as to offset diminished housing access.

It is unlikely that racial 'integration' can be maintained if black housing demands continue to be satisfied in only those few suburban municipalities having open doors, in the absence of such policies. Even if all suburban communities were to have open doors racial segregation would probably still appear so long as blacks on average prefer to live in neighbourhoods or municipalities having a proportionate black presence which is higher than that preferred by whites (Schelling, 1971). Few have yet addressed the long-run implications of such provisions for the price/rent structure of the local housing market and the character of new construction.

FISCAL REFORM VERSUS ECONOMIC INTEGRATION

It should now be abundantly clear that suburban economic integration through low-income dispersal faces major hurdles in the face of high construction costs, the continuation of exclusionary practices, the absence of sufficient subsidies for low-income housing and a judicial reluctance to mandate broad affirmative relief in cases involving housing discrimination. Even if metropolitan-wide economic integration was to occur, the benefit to lower-income households might be diminished through new forms of exclusion *within* jurisdictions or erosion of the local resource base through the departure of or failure to attract favoured firms and higher status households. Further, even in the absence of these negative community responses the impact of economic integration on the distribution of household income within the region may be slight. It is therefore prudent to consider alternatives to economic integration as well as complementary strategies. Of these, the most important are policies for promoting local and regional fiscal equity. Their central merit is that they entail fiscal redistribution without residential relocation. Their major detriment is that pure fiscal reform may have as little impact on income distribution as would economic integration.

The impetus for fiscal reform primarily resides in the judiciary through interjurisdictional reforms such as tax-base sharing which are the products of state enabling legislature (Beaton, 1980). The judicial approach has been sporadic and piecemeal, and seldom explicitly motivated by a desire to promote income redistribution (Inman and Rubinfeld, 1979), now has the Federal judiciary generated any unequivocal national standards. Intrajurisdictional reforms fall into two classes: those seeking to equalize spending across all income classes, and those which promote equity among taxpayers by mandating uniformity in property-tax assessment practices. Both address inequities which are most pronounced in central cities and older suburbs, and in each case the effect of the reform may be negated through municipal responses or household migration (Inman and Rubinfeld, 1979). *Hawkins* v. *Town of Shaw* 461 F.2d 1171 (5th Cir. 1972) called for the town to provide equal services for all classes. Application of this standard in central cities would possibly attract additional lower-income households while inducing the rich to leave, causing a decline in the tax base and an overall reduction in the quantity of services provided. The city might, therefore, seek to offset this reduction in the fiscal advantage of the rich by gradually reducing property assessments of the rich while increasing those of the poor. However, if there were also a judicial mandate requiring uniformity of assessment practices so as to eliminate the over-assessment of those properties whose taxes are paid by the poor (see Baar, 1981), such a response would not be possible.

One precedent for such a mandate was provided in *Hellerstein* v. *Assessor of the Town of Islip* 386 NYS2d 406 (1976). Here the court's ruling led to a shift of the tax burden toward the upper-income population and away from the poor. In the absence of a companion declaration mandating equal service provision, most central cities would probably be inclined to increase the services provided for the rich to maintain their favourable standing and forestall outmigration. Even if both tax and spending equalization were to be required simultaneously, the community may still attempt to maintain the advantageous position of the rich by eliminating services which primarily benefit the poor, or introducing provisions by which the poor would have to bear most of the costs of such services through special assessments. The community might also reduce spending overall, leading to large proportionate tax savings for the rich who might then purchase equivalent services in the private sector (Inman and Rubinfeld, 1979).

Since intrajurisdictional fiscal reforms can often be negated through compensatory actions and since these address inequities found primarily in central cities, proponents of income redistribution have turned to interjurisdictional, metropolitan-wide solutions. Promotion of interjurisdictional fiscal equity now rests primarily within the purview of state supreme courts though the US Supreme Court may eventually intervene despite a reluctance voiced in its major decision in this area (*San Antonio School District* v. *Rodriguez*, 411 US 1 (1973)). In *Serrano* v. *Priest* 487 P.2d 1241 (California, 1971), the State Supreme Court held that the use of the local property tax to finance public education violated the equal protection provisions of the US Constitution and the state's constitution because the wide disparity in tax bases among municipalities led to radically differing levels of per pupil expenditure. Subsequently the court reaffirmed the decision despite the US Supreme Court's having precluded its initial interpretation of the US Constitution. Similar decisions have arisen in other States' courts, all based on State constitutional provisions: New Jersey, *Robinson* v. *Cahill* 303 A.2d 273 (1973); and Connecticut, *Horton* v. *Meskill* 376 A.2d 359 (1977). None mandated a specific legislative response, but all clearly indicate that legislative action must promote equal educational opportunity by lessening disparities among districts. Possible solutions include the redrawing of district boundaries to equalize the distribution of property wealth, or State funding of part or all of the cost of education. It is too early to determine whether State courts will extend this logic to the provision of other categories of public services.

State legislatures have also been instrumental in fostering the centralization of fiscal functions in metropolitan areas, apart from judicial mandates. Some have enabled municipalities to join together to pool a portion of recent additions to their commercial and industrial tax base (Reschovsky and Knaff, 1977). These stop short of a full-scale equalization of revenue-generating capacity, but they do tend to place few restrictions on the uses to which shared revenues may be applied. In addition, many States permit metropolitan municipalities to consolidate, or federate, or in other ways coalesce in order to manage spillovers and achieve scale economies in service provision. Few State legislatures have been inclined to coerce municipal participation or to enable forms of centralization which would seriously compromise the fiscal welfare of the higher-status suburban communities (Wilken, 1974). As a result, interjurisdictional equity tends to be fostered only indirectly, as a by-product of service efficiencies. Interclass equity, in turn, is generated even less directly if at all, as a result of the reduction of interjurisdictional disparities. This consequence will depend on the degree to which disparities of class and place are heteromorphic.

CONCLUSIONS

It has been demonstrated that rapid growth of an increasingly heterogeneous population gave way to political fragmentation in metropolitan areas in the United States. Political incorporation enabled higher-status suburban municipalities to control social access through the management of land development, and to isolate their fiscal base. As a result, the impacted poor become inordinately concentrated in central cities and older suburban communities. These places now generally lack the fiscal resources required to provide the mix and quality of services their residents require. Efforts to promote a more equitable distribution of metropolitan resources fall into two categories. These are, (1) the economic integration of suburban municipalities through the dispersal of lower-income households from central cities and the lower-status suburbs, and (2) the redistribution of fiscal resources through intermunicipal transfers. Each strategy would have to be coupled with intramunicipal approaches to ensure that the poor realize the full potential benefit. Suburban economic integration would have to be supported by efforts to guard against the substitution of non-geographic for geographic forms of exclusion. Intermunicipal fiscal transfers would have to be complemented by efforts to promote progressive tax assessment and spending practices within jurisdictions, and to direct the benefits of economic and neighbourhood revitalization to the poor.

Neither strategy has a high probability of widespread adoption in the near future. Judicial and legislative actions have been instrumental in promoting some small measure of economic integration, but despite recent judicial advances these efforts still confront major obstacles. These include efforts to weaken legislative foundations of judicial action, the minimal supply of construction subsidies for lower-income housing, and a growing judicial tolerance of local growth management practices even when they are exclusionary. Likewise, fiscal redistribution has been mandated by only a few State and lower Federal courts. Intramunicipal fiscal reforms have been found to have the least potential since socioeconomic disparities are generally larger among than within jurisdictions, and local responses can often negate the effect of the reform. Intermunicipal transfers offer much greater potential, and have been sanctioned by some States' courts to promote equal educational opportunity. Centralization of fiscal functions within metropolitan areas as a product of State-enabling legislation has so far yielded only marginal increases in intermunicipal equity and probably only a negligible reduction in interclass disparities.

Each of the two major strategies to promote a more equitable distribution of metropolitan resources has its own momentum and rationale. Neither will therefore be 'chosen' over the other as the sanctioned vehicle for generating equity. The success of either, however, may lessen the intensity with which its counterpart is pursued. Economic integration would tend to promote an equalization of tax bases and permit wider local choice regarding service mix. Fiscal redistribution through tax-base equalization would possibly reduce the incentive of lower-income households to disperse into higher-status suburbs, at least in the long-run. Such redistribution would not eliminate every form of intermunicipal difference, even if a progressive redistributional formula were applied. Most importantly, it remains uncertain to what degree or how quickly socioeconomic inequalities in metropolitan areas would be lessened even if both strategies were to be fully implemented. Interclass transfers are a far more direct and efficacious strategy for reducing class disparities than one founded on the elimination of 'place' disparities. But the elimination of place disparities through economic integration and fiscal equalization has merit in its own right as a complement to direct interclass transfers and as an expression of fairness.

REFERENCES

Articles and laws

Baar, K. (1981). Property tax discrimination against low-income neighbourhoods, *Clearinghouse Review*, **15**, 6, 467–486.
Beaton, W. P. (1980). Regional tax base sharing: a conceptual analysis, *Journal of the American Planning Association*, **46**, 3, 315–322.
Beaton, W. P. and Sossamon, L. B. (1982). Housing integration and rent supplements to existing housing, *The Professional Geographer*, **34**, 2, 147–155.
Berry, B. J. L. and Bednarz, R. S. (1975). A hedonic model of prices and assessments for single-family homes, *Land Economics*, **51**, 21–40.
Blumstein, J. F. (1979). A prolegomenon to growth management and exclusionary zoning issues, *Law and Contemporary Problems*, **43**, 2, 5–110.
Brown, M. (1981). A typology of suburbs and its public policy implications, *Urban Geography*, **2**, 4, 288–310.
Cavalieri, V. L. (1979–80). Beyond hollow victories: The affirmative obligations remedy for exclusionary zoning—*Park View Heights Corp.* v. *City of Black Jack*, *New York University Review of Law and Social Change*, IX, 3, 409–430.
Civil Rights Act of 1871, see 42 USC Section 1983 (Supp. IV 1980).
Clark, T. A. (1979). *Blacks in Suburbs: A National Perspective*, Center for Urban Policy Research, Rutgers University, New Brunswick, New Jersey.
Clark, T. A. (1981). Race, class, and suburban housing discrimination: Alternative judicial standards of proof and relief, *Urban Geography*, **2**, 4, 327–338.
Clark, T. A. (1982). Federal initiatives promoting the dispersal of low-income housing in suburbs, *The Professional Geographer*, **34**, 2, 136–146.
Cox, K. R. (Ed.) (1978). *Urbanization and Conflict in Market Societies*, Maaroufa Press, Chicago, Illinois.
Cunningham, R. A. (1981). Inverse condemnation as a remedy for 'regulatory takings'. *Hastings Constitutional Law Quarterly*, **8**, 3, 517–544.
Davidoff, P. and Brooks, M. E. (1976). Zoning out the poor. In *Suburbia: The American Dream and Dilemma* (Ed. P. C. Dolce), pp. 135–166, Anchor Books, Garden City, New York.

Dear, M. and Clark, G. L. (1981). Dimensions of local state autonomy, *Environment and Planning A*, **13**, 1277–1294.

Denzan, A. T. and Weingast, B. R. (1982). The political economy of land use regulation, *Urban Law Annual*, **23**, 385–405.

Downs, A. (1973). *Opening Up the Suburbs*, Yale University Press, New Haven.

Edel, M. (1980). 'People' versus 'places' in urban impact analysis. In *The Urban Impacts of Federal Policies* (Ed. N. J. Glickman), pp. 175–191, The Johns Hopkins University Press, Baltimore.

Elgie, R. A. (1980). Socioeconomic diversity and the balanced community, *Proceedings of the Middle States Division of the Association of American Geography*, **14**, 5–9.

Ellickson, R. C. (1973). Alternatives to zoning: Covenants, nuisance rules, and fines as land use controls, *University of Chicago Law Review*, **40**, 681–781.

Ellickson, R. C. (1977). Suburban growth controls: An economic and legal analysis, *The Yale Law Journal*, **86**, 3, 385–511.

Ellickson, R. C. (1981). The irony of 'inclusionary zoning', *Southern California Law Review*, **54**, 6, 1167–1216.

Fainstein, N. I. and Fainstein, S. S. (1982). Restructuring the American city. In *Urban Policy Under Capitalism* (Eds N. Fainstein and S. Fainstein), pp. 161–190, Croom Helm, London.

Fair Housing Act of 1968. Pub. L. No. 90-284, Title VIII (42 USC Sections 3601 to 3631).

Freilich, R. H. and David, L. K. (1981). Saving the land: The utilization of modern techniques of growth management to preserve rural and agricultural America, *The Urban Lawyer*, **13**, 1, 27–43.

Frey, W. H. (1980). Black in-migration, white flight, and the changing economic base of the central city, *American Journal of Sociology*, **85**, 6, 1396–1417.

Frieden, B. J. and Kaplan, M. (1975). *The Politics of Neglect: Urban Aid From Model Cities to Revenue Sharing*, MIT Press, Cambridge.

Frug, G. E. (1980). The city as a legal concept, *Harvard Law Review*, **93**, 1057–1154.

Goetz, M. L. and Wofford, L. E. (1979). The motivation for zoning: Efficiency or wealth redistribution? *Land Economics*, **55**, 472–485.

Guest, A. M. (1978). Suburban social status: Persistence or evolution? *American Sociological Review*, **43**, 251–264.

Harvard Law Review (1978). Developments in the law-zoning, *Harvard Law Review*, **91**, 1427–1708.

Harvard Law Review (1980). Benign steering and benign quotas: The validity of race-conscious government policies to promote residential integration, *Harvard Law Review*, **93**, 938–965.

Housing and Community Development Act of 1974. Pub. L. No. 93-383 (42 USC 1437 *et seq.*).

Inman, R. P. and Rubinfeld, D. L. (1979). The judicial pursuit of local fiscal equity, *Harvard Law Review*, **92**, 1662–1750.

Isserman, A. M. (1981). The allocation of funds to small cities under the community development block grant program, *Journal of the American Planning Association*, **47**, 1, 3–24.

James, F. J. and Windsor, O. D. (1976). Fiscal zoning, fiscal reform, and exclusionary land use controls, *Journal of the American Institute of Planners*, **42**, 2, 130–141.

Johnston, R. J. (1981a). The management and autonomy of the local state: the role of the judiciary in the US, *Environment and Planning A*, **13**, 1305–1315.

Johnston, R. J. (1981b). Local government, suburban segregation and litigation in US metropolitan areas, *American Studies*, **15**, 2, 211–230.

Johnston, R. J. (1981c). The political element in suburbia, *Geography*, **66**, 4, 286–296.
Johnston, R. J. (1982). The local state and the judiciary: Institutions in American suburbia. In *Institutions and Geographical Patterns* (Ed. R. Flowerdew), pp. 255–287, Croom Helm, London.
Krasnowiecki, J. Z. (1980). Abolish zoning, *Syracuse Law Review*, **31**, 3, 719–753.
Lake, R. W. (1981a). The Fair Housing Act in a discriminatory market: A persisting dilemma, *Journal of the American Planning Association*, **47**, 48–58.
Lake, R. W. (1981b). *The New Suburbanites: Race and Housing in the Suburbs*, Center for Urban Policy Research, Rutgers University, New Brunswick New Jersey.
Lake, R. W. and Cutter, S. C. (1980). A typology of black suburbanization in New Jersey since 1970, *Geographical Review*, **70**, 167–181.
Lake, R. W. and Winslow, J. (1981). Integration management: Municipal constraints on residential mobility, *Urban Geography*, **2**, 4, 311–326.
LeGates, R. T. and Hartman, C. (1981). Displacement, *Clearinghouse Review*, **15**, 3, 207–249.
Lev, S. (1981). HUD site and neighborhood selection standards: An easing of placement restrictions, *Urban Law Annual*, **22**, 199–225.
Levin, L. (1980). *King* v. *Harris*: Defining the 'relevant area' in section 8 site selection, *Urban Law Annual*, **19**, 303–318.
Listokin, D. (1976). *Fair Share Housing Allocation*, Center for Urban Policy Research, Rutgers University, New Brunswick, New Jersey.
Logan, J. R. (1978). Growth, politics and the stratification of places, *American Journal of Sociology*, **84**, 404–416.
Mallach, A. (1981). Exclusionary zoning litigation: Setting the record straight, *Real Estate Law Journal*, **9**, 4, 275–310.
Pack, H. and Pack, J. R. (1977). Metropolitan fragmentation and suburban homogeneity. *Urban Studies*, **14**, 191–201.
Payne, J. M. (1981). From the courts, *Real Estate Law Journal*, **10**, 76–81 and 146–153.
Pearlman, K. (1982). Section 1983 and the liability of local officials for land use decisions, *Urban Law Annual*, **23**, 57–107.
Reschovsky, A. and Knaff, E. (1977). Tax base sharing, *Journal of the American Institute of Planners*, **43**, 361–370.
Rose, J. G. (1979). Myths and misconceptions of exclusionary zoning litigation, *Real Estate Law Journal*, **8**, 99–124.
Rose, J. G. (1982). State tax and spending restraints: The implications for developers. *Real Estate Law Journal*, **10**, 210–227.
Rubin, F. A. (1982). Local growth management and regional housing needs, *Urban Law Annual*, **23**, 407–422.
Rubinfeld, D. L. (179). Judicial approaches to local public-sector equity: An economic analysis. In *Current Issues in Urban Economics* (Eds P. Mieszkowski and M. Straszheim), pp. 542–576, The Johns Hopkins University Press, Baltimore.
Sagar, L. G. (1978). Insular majorities unabated, *Harvard Law Review*, **91**, 1373–1426.
Schelling, T. C. (1971). On the ecology of micromotives, *Public Interest*, **25**, 61–98.
Schneider, M. and Logan, J. R. (1981). Fiscal implications of class segregation: Inequalities in the distribution of public goods and services in suburban municipalities, *Urban Affairs Quarterly*, **17**, 1, 23–36.
Schwartz, B. (1980). The suburban landscape, *Contemporary Sociology*, **9**, 640–650.
Tarlock, A. D. (1980). An economic analysis of direct voter participation in zoning changes, *UCLA Journal of Environmental Law and Policy*, **1**, 31–46.
Teaford, J. C. (1979). *City and Suburb: The Political Fragmentation of Metropolitan America, 1850–1970*, The Johns Hopkins University Press, Baltimore.

US Department of Commerce, Bureau of the Census (1977 and 1978). *Current population reports*, series P-60, No. 106, Table 4; and series P-20, No. 116, Table 21. Government Printing Office, Washington, DC.

US Department of Commerce, Bureau of the Census (1981). *Current housing reports*, series H-150-79, financial characteristics of the housing inventory for the US and regions: 1979, Annual Housing Survey-1979, Part C. Government Printing Office, Washington, DC.

Wheaton, W. C. (1979). Monocentric models of urban land use: Contributions and criticisms. In *Current Issues in Urban Economics* (Eds P. Mieszkowski and M. Straszheim), pp. 107–129, The Johns Hopkins University Press, Baltimore.

Westen, P. (1982). The empty idea of equality, *Harvard Law Review*, **95**, 3, 537–596.

Wilken, W. H. (1974). The impact of centralization on access and equity. In *Organizing Public Services in Metropolitan Areas* (Eds T. P. Murphy and C. R. Warren), pp. 127–137, Lexington Books, Lexington, Massachusetts.

Williamson, C. T. III (1980). Constitutional and judicial limitations on the community's power to downzone, *The Urban Lawyer*, **12**, 1, 157–182.

Zarembka, A. (1980). The regional housing mobility program: The government's 'solution' to the urban crisis, *Housing Law Bulletin*, x, 3.

Cases

Agins v. *City of Tiburon*, 598 P.2d 25 (California, 1979); 447 US 255 (1980).

City of Memphis v. *Greene*, Slip opinion No. 79-1176 of the US Supreme Court, April 20, 1981.

Construction Industry Association v. *City of Petaluma*, 522 F.2d 897 (9th Cir. 1975).

Gladstone Realtors v. *Village of Bellwood*, 441 US 91 (1979).

Hawkins v. *Town of Shaw*, 437 F.2d 1286 (5th Cir. 1971), affirmed on rehearing, 461 F.2d 1171 (5th Cir. 1972).

Hellerstein v. *Assessor of the Town of Islip*, 386 NYS2d 406 (1976).

Hills v. *Gautreaux*, 425 US 284 (1976).

Horton v. *Meskill*, 376 A.2d 359 (1977).

James v. *Valtierra*, 402 US 137 (1971).

Kennedy Park Homes Association v. *City of Lackawanna*, 318 F. Supp. 669 (WDNY 1970), affirmed, 436 F.2d 108 (2d Cir. 1970), certiorari denied, 401 US 1010 (1971).

Oakwood at Madison, Inc. v. *Township of Madison*, 371 A.2d 1192 (New Jersey, 1977).

Otero v. *New York City Housing Authority*, 484 F.2d 1122 (2d Cir. 1973).

Park View Heights Corp. v. *City of Black Jack*, 605 F.2d 1033 (8th Cir. 1979), certiorari denied, 445 US 905 (1980).

Penn Central Transportation Co. v. *New York City*, 438 US 104 (1978).

Resident Advisory Board v. *Rizzo*, 425 F. Supp. 987 (E.D. Pa. 1976); modified, 564, F.2d 126 (3rd Cir. 1977).

Robinson v. *Cahill*, 303 A.2d 273 (1973).

San Antonio School District v. *Rodriguez*, 411 US (1973).

San Diego Gas and Elec. Co. v. *City of San Diego*, 49 USLW 4317 (1981).

Serrano v. *Priest*, 487 P.2d 1241 (California, 1971), and Serrano v. Priest, 557 P.2d 929 (California, 1976).

Southern Burlington County NAACP v. *Township of Mt. Laurel*, 336 A.2d 713 (New Jersey, 1975), certiorari denied, 423 US 808 (1975).

United States v. *City of Black Jack*, 508 F.2d 1179 (8th Cir. 1974), certiorari denied, 422 US 1042 (1975).

United States v. *City of Parma*, 661 F.2d 562 (6th Cir. 1981), affirming in part 494 F.
   Supp. 1049 and 504 F. Supp. 913 (N.D. Ohio, 1980).
Village of Arlington Heights v. *Metropolitan Housing Corp.*, 429 US 252 (1977).
Village of Belle Terre v. *Boraas*, 416 US 1 (1974).
Village of Euclid v. *Ambler Realty Co.*, 272 US 365 (1926).
Warth v. *Seldin*, 422 US 490 (1975).

Geography and the Urban Environment
Progress in Research and Applications, Volume VI
Edited by D. T. Herbert and R. J. Johnston
© 1984 John Wiley & Sons Ltd.

Chapter 7

Judicial Intervention, Busing and Local Residential Change

William A. V. Clark

Within the United States there is a widely held view that if schools are integrated, the experience of the minority children and their parents in the neighbourhoods to which the children are bused, will lead to residential relocation and residential integration. Both Orfield (1978, p. 97) in a general discussion of the links between housing integration and school integration and Taeuber in court testimony (*Armstrong* v. *O'Connell*, 1978) suggest that if all neighbourhoods had integrated schools and the movement of black families into a neighbourhood made no difference to the local school, the continuing cycle of neighbourhood transition would be broken and that inter-racial busing would have had the effect of enhancing residential mobility on non-racial lines. Both authors wished to establish that the school integration process would lead to the desirable social goal of residential integration. The same view is reflected in more general court testimony cited by Wolf (1981, p. 142). But not all scholars are so sanguine. In particular, Lowry argues that any integration programme 'will require either much more draconian measures than so far have been applied or a much longer time than its enthusiasts care to acknowledge' (Lowry, 1980, p. 30).

There is little empirical evidence for either position and documentation for the position that school integration will lead to neighbourhood integration would be a powerful positive argument for continuing mandatory busing despite the considerable public opposition. But a study of this topic requires an analysis of school and neighbourhood changes at the individual level, whereas most studies of school and housing links have been at the aggregate district level. To provide some evidence on the nature of the school–neighbourhood links, this chapter examines a small sample of schools and neighbourhoods in Los Angeles.

Two kinds of studies are employed. First, actual enrolment changes in a sample of schools are used to determine the variation in school enrolment and composition changes in response to court-ordered busing. This first analysis is also a test of the adequacy of district-wide aggregate analysis of enrolment change. The second approach is focused on the relationship between school enrolment changes and changes in the neighbourhood. What is the interplay of changes in schools and changes in neighbourhoods? Are there reciprocal impacts or are the impacts unidirectional? The central question, of course, is whether or not schools do have the power to affect neighbourhood change. The second theme raises the issue of the relative role of judges versus demographic processes (the aging of the population, changing family composition, changing household size, population relocation etc.) on changes in the urban structure.

Earlier papers (Clark, 1980, 1982) reviewed the literature which addressed the interrelated issues of residential mobility, neighbourhood change and racial residential segregation, but provided only limited empirical documentation of specific effects of the impacts of court orders. The present chapter is designed to extend those earlier papers by reference to case studies but begins with an outline of the legal and demographic contexts and the broadly relevant literature.

THE HISTORICAL AND LEGAL CONTEXT

The debate about school desegregation and the means to achieve it has been prolonged and often acrimonious. In fact this debate has been more spirited than on other topics of similar significance because public schools in the United States have (traditionally) been supported by local taxes (usually a property tax) and subject to local control with minimal state and federal intervention. In particular the neighbourhood school has been a central concern amongst those opposed to busing children to other school attendance zones.

Up until the initial court cases which moved to eliminate the separation of the races in the school systems there was *de jure* segregation of the races in Southern schools (the so-called dual school system) and *de facto* separation of the races in northern school systems. The initial thrust of the desegregation rulings by the US Supreme Court after the initial *Brown* v. *Board of Education* ruling was addressed to dismantling *de jure* segregation in the Southern States. The 1964 Civil Rights Act gave some impetus to this process but it was *Green* in 1969 which ushered in a new phase of desegregation, a phase which emphasized a more active role by the courts and the department of Health, Education and Welfare (HEW) in pushing actively for the elimination of school desegregation (Table 7.1). A review of the history of court and government intervention and responses, both by state and individuals, is provided in a detailed study of school changes in Mississippi (Lowry, 1973).

The principal national legal cases which served as the context for intervention in the school systems have been analysed elsewhere (Read, 1975; Lord, 1977; Farley, 1978a and b; and Clark, 1980), but for those readers who may not be familiar with the structure of court decisions on school desegregation in the

TABLE 7.1. Selected court decisions on school desegregation

Year	Case	Descriptive comments
1954	*Brown* v. *Board of Education* (Topeka, Kansas)	Initial school desegregation case.
1968	*Green* v. *County School Board* (New Kent County, Virginia)	Emphasized that school desegregation must proceed immediately.
1971	*Swann* v. *Charlotte Mecklenberg Board of Education* (North Carolina)	Established the principle of pupil busing for desegregation.
1973	*Keyes* v. *School District No. 1* (Parkhill, Denver, Colorado)	First northern desegregation case. Non-statutory actions found to be violations and identified school boards as a factor in segregation.
1974	*Milliken* v. *Bradley* (Detroit, Michigan)	First major 'metro' case. The Supreme Court decision held that unless there were violations by suburban school boards, busing across city–county lines was not required to eliminate racial segregation.
1976	*Pasadena City Board of Education* v. *Spangler* (Pasadena, California)	First case which Supreme Court found in favour of a school board. School board does not have to continually alter school attendance districts to match changes in demographic patterns.
1977	*Dayton Board of Education* v. *Brinkman*, (Dayton, Ohio)	The remedy for segregated patterns was required to match the amount of segregative action on the part of the school board.
1979	*Columbus Board of Education* v. *Penick* (Columbus, Ohio)	A violation in part of the school system requires that the whole school district must be involved in desegregation remedies.
1980	*Armour* v. *Nix* (Atlanta, Georgia)	Reiterated the Detroit decision that busing across county lines requires evidence of inter-district violations by defendant school boards.

United States, the major cases are listed (Table 7.1). The most significant cases within that structure are the initial decision in 1954 by the US Supreme Court in *Brown* v. *The Board of Education* which moved to eliminate school segregation as a violation of the Constitution, the 1971 Supreme Court decision in *Swann* v. *Charlotte Mecklenberg Board of Education*, which established the principle of school busing, and *Milliken* v. *Bradley* in 1974, which allowed a continuing distinction between city and suburban school systems, and set up the context for the debate about central city versus metropolitan school desegregation. As argued elsewhere, these cases formed a structure which allowed individual judges at the local level (as a result of plaintiff requests) to intervene in school systems, ordering desegregation remedies which involved large-scale mandatory busing (Clark, 1982).

While the Supreme Court decisions have set a national context for intervention, in each local case there have been considerable local variations in the way in which the legal decision-making has occurred. In the present analysis of Los Angeles, the legal history has only in part paralleled the national structure. And, although the concern is principally with the outcomes of judicial intervention, it is important to have a firm understanding of the context of local intervention and the particular legal situations which have evolved over the past twenty years. Certainly, the Los Angeles Unified School District is not unique in being the target of a desegregation suit. Most school districts in metropolitan areas have been faced with such suits, usually in the federal courts, but the Los Angeles case is different from many other big-city desegregation cases in the fact of its size, the fact that the desegregation litigation has been pursued in the state courts, not in the federal courts, and the fact that the school system is tri-ethnic rather than a single-minority school system.

The history of the Los Angeles schools desegregation case stretches over twenty years and involves a tangle of State and Federal courts at every level (Table 7.2). In addition to being a legal battle, it has been a political battle, in which a judge lost his seat (State Court judges are subject to confirmation by the voters) and a school-board president was recalled and defeated. (Under California law a school-board member can be required to run again for office prior to the expiration of his official term when a sufficient number of voters petition the registrar of voters.) This brief discussion does not intend to chronicle the full legal battle nor the political history. What follows is a short chronology of events in the Los Angeles schools desegregation suit which provides the minimum necessary historical background to the analysis of judicial intervention. Glenn (1979) provides a good survey of the legal developments in the Los Angeles desegregation cases.

The Crawford case

The Los Angeles case began in August, 1963, when the American Civil Liberties Union (ACLU) filed suit in a State superior court petitioning for desegregation of two severely racially imbalanced Los Angeles high schools: *Crawford* v. *The Board of Education of the City of Los Angeles* (all succeeding references will be to Crawford and the date). The suit was filed nine years after the original *Brown* decision against racial discrimination in schools.

In 1963, desegregation suits were focused on the statutory segregated school districts of the South, not in the residentially segregated cities of the North. Moreover, even 'successful' desegregation meant freedom-of-choice plans in

TABLE 7.2. Court decisions and responses in the Los Angeles desegregation case

Year	Case/Event	Descriptive comments
1963	*Crawford* v. *Board of Education of the City of Los Angeles*	Case filed by ACLU against two schools.
1963	*Jackson* v. *Pasadena School District*	Held that the State has an obligation to alleviate racial segregation in the public schools regardless of the cause.
1966	*Crawford* v. *Board of Education*	Amended suit included all schools in the Los Angeles Unified School District.
1970	*Crawford* v. *Board of Education*	Judge Gitelson found *de facto* and *de jure* segregation, violating State and Federal Constitutions.
1975	*Crawford* v. *Board of Education*	State Appeals Court reversed Gitelson.
1976	*Crawford* v. *Board of Education*	State Supreme Court reversed the Appeals Court ruling. Used Jackson as basis for the ruling.
1979	Proposition 1	Proposition 1, a Constitutional amendment was passed by the voters and required California courts to follow Federal law with respect to rights to equal opportunity.
1980	*Crawford* v. *Board of Education*	Appellate Court held that Proposition 1 is applicable to desegregation rulings in California.
1981	Appeal to California Supreme Court	California's Supreme Court declined to hear an appeal of the 1980 ruling.
1982	*Crawford* v. *Board of Education*	US Supreme Court affirmed Proposition 1.

which school officials could not forbid black children from otherwise 'white' schools. State courts generally had shown themselves unsympathetic to desegregation efforts, especially in the South, where Federal courts invoked federal supremacy clauses against claims of State's rights. However, California courts, already noted for their 'liberal' rulings, adopted the view that the constitutional evil lay in the *de facto* segregation, the mere condition of segregation itself (*Jackson* v. *Pasadena School District*, 1963).

In 1966, the ACLU expanded the suit to include the entire Los Angeles Unified School District. It required two more years for the case to reach trial before Judge Alfred Gitelson of the California State Superior Court. By this time, the approach to school desegregation in Federal courts had drastically altered under the impetus of the US Supreme Court demand in *Green* that delays cease and desegregation take place at once. After two years of hearings, Judge Gitelson found both *de facto* segregation as well as intentional, *de jure* acts of segregation by the Los Angeles School Board which constituted a violation of both Federal and State constitutions. Judge Gitelson issued his findings in February, 1970, and directed the school board to implement a desegregation plan.

The school board appealed the decision to a State appeals court, which stayed Judge Gitelson's order for five years while the appeal was heard. In 1975, the State appeals court reversed Judge Gitelson's order, and found that the Los Angeles school district had not committed *de jure* segregation. It followed the lead of Federal decisions (*Swann* and *Keyes*) which stated that only *de jure* segregation was remediable, and vacated Judge Gitelson's desegregation order because it found only *de facto*, not *de jure*, segregation in Los Angeles. The ACLU appealed to the California Supreme Court.

In *Crawford* v. *the Board of Education* (1976), the State Supreme Court reversed the appeals court ruling and ordered the Los Angeles school board to prepare a desegregation plan for presentation to the Los Angeles Superior Court. This decision elaborated the broad right to equal education under the California Constitution, a right considerably broader than that construed by Federal courts under the equal protection clause (the Fourteenth Amendment to the Constitution). The State Supreme Court held that, in California, education is a special State concern, and that it does not matter how segregated schools arose, because they interfere with the broad California right to equal education (Glenn, 1979). Thus, the California Supreme Court eliminated the *de jure* requirement outlined by Federal courts and used by the appellate court against the Gitelson ruling. Some quite limited voluntary busing had been initiated in 1972 under the permit to attend a certain school with transportation provided (PWT) and it was expanded in 1976.

In 1977, Judge Paul Egly was appointed to oversee the desegregation of Los Angeles schools according to the principles outlined in *Crawford* (1976). The school board submitted a plan calling for the busing of some elementary school students to integrated 'learning centres' for nine weeks of the year, and also expanding voluntary desegregation efforts. Judge Egly rejected the plan as unconstitutional under *Crawford* and demanded a new plan. In response, the school board prepared a plan calling for mandatory busing of students in the fourth to eighth grades. Judge Egly accepted this as a first, albeit inadequate, step toward real integration.

The mandatory busing programme of grades four to eight began in September, 1978, without major disruption in the community. (Grades four, five, and six are the last three years of elementary school, grades seven and eight the first two years of junior high or high school.) A wave of anti-busing sentiment, especially from the San Fernando Valley (a largely white, suburban part of the City of Los Angeles) provided support for new elections to the School Board, and by 1980, anti-busing forces controlled the school board. Directed by the new school board, attorneys for the Los Angeles school system argued that mandatory busing in Los Angeles was not producing increased integration.

During the same period, Proposition 1, an anti-busing measure was being placed on the November 1979 ballot. Proposition 1 was a constitutional amendment changing the State Constitution to reflect only the Federal right to equal education and restricting busing remedies to those permissible under Federal decision and law. In other words, Proposition 1 overruled the broadened right to education found in 1976 in *Crawford*, and restricted California courts to remedying *de jure*, not *de facto*, segregation. Proposition 1 was passed by the voters in November, 1979, and thus became an amendment to the California State Constitution. The constitutionality of the amendment was challenged in appellate court in 1980. The appellate court held the amendment constitutional, vacated the mandatory busing orders, and reversed Judge Gitelson's 1970 finding of *de jure* segregation in Los Angeles. The appellate court order was stayed pending appeal to the State Supreme Court.

On March 11, 1981, the California Supreme Court declined to hear the appeal of pro-busing advocates against Proposition 1. This denial was surprising to the extent that in the past, the Supreme Court had never hesitated to support desegregation. Technically, the court had not ruled on the constitutionality of the amendment, but the denial allowed the Los Angeles school district to end mandatory busing in the spring of 1981. The final appeal of the constitutionality of Proposition 1 to the US Supreme Court affirmed Proposition 1 in the spring of 1982. The tortuous legal proceedings yielded a busing experiment which was voluntary between 1976 and 1978, mandatory between 1978 and 1981, and has continued on a voluntary basis since 1981.

While the history of the Los Angeles experience seems different, the issues are the same as those which have had an impact on other school districts across the country during the past twenty years. Los Angeles is undeniably a heavily segregated school system, and has become more segregated as whites leave the system and the minority population increases. Advocates of integration view busing as the only feasible way to implement large- or even moderate-scale desegregation, and as in other cities, busing has met with widespread anger amongst large segments of the city population. As in many other big-city desegregation cases, the community has become fragmented in its response to court orders, and the courts themselves have become alienated from the community as they attempt to mandate remedies against the desires of a large segment of the population. As in other Northern school desegregation cases too, the litigation has been painfully slow, single step at a time, and seemingly without end.*

---

* At the time of writing, there is some sense that *Crawford* will be relitigated in the Federal courts.

THE DEMOGRAPHIC AND SCHOOL CONTEXT

The legal history provides part of the context. The other part of the context is the changing demography of the Los Angeles metropolitan area over the period of the desegregation suit. The Los Angeles Unified School District is approximately coterminous with the city of Los Angeles (Figure 7.1). The school district is somewhat larger than the city itself, and, in 1980, included approximately 3.5 million people, whereas the city itself is approximately 2.9 million people.

Los Angeles grew rapidly in the 1950s and 1960s, but during the 1970s the total population growth in the city and county slowed considerably (Table 7.3). The rapid growth of the black population up to 1970 has been overtaken by the significant growth in the Hispanic population. Now, in 1980, the majority of the residents of the city are minorities (Hispanics and blacks, predominantly, although Asians are also a significant element of the population composition). Table 7.3 captures the three important elements of population structure and change in the Los Angeles city and metropolitan areas over the thirty-year period between 1950 and 1980. First, the significant growth of the black population between 1950 and 1960, second, the significant suburban growth in Los Angeles County during the 1950s (compare city and county populations), and third, the growth of the Hispanic population in the late 1960s and through the 1970s.

Clearly, the growth of the Hispanic population in both the City and County of Los Angeles is one of the most remarkable population composition changes in the past century. The numbers are even more remarkable in that they do not reflect a sizeable illegal migrant population. The growth of the Hispanic population is related to the economic opportunities within the Southern California region, the willingness of recent legal and illegal migrants to work at

TABLE 7.3. Population estimates by race for Los Angeles city and county, 1950–1980

City of Los Angeles	1950	1960	1970	1980
Total	1 970 358	2 481 456	2 816 061	2 966 850
Black	175 361	342 441	498 443	495 723
White	1 594 019	1 784 167	1 661 476	1 317 281
Hispanic	157 629	265 516	515 339	816 076
County of Los Angeles				
Total	4 151 687	6 042 431	7 032 075	7 444 521
Black	220 039	531 734	843 849	944 099
White	3 582 906	4 773 521	4 634 137	3 677 593
Hispanic	286 466	598 201	1 272 806	2 144 022

Source: US Bureau of the Census

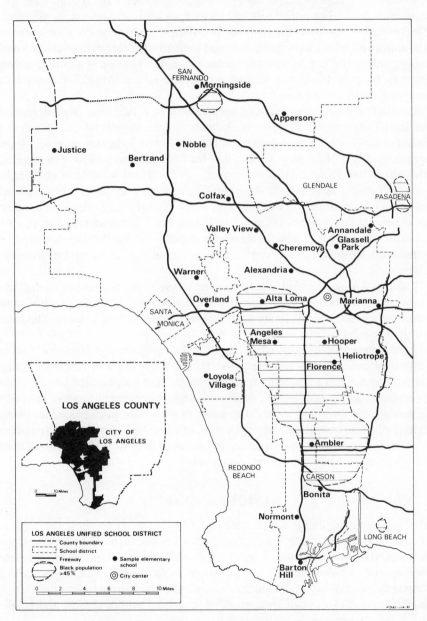

FIGURE 7.1. The Los Angeles school district

low wages, the ease of access between Mexico and the United States and the increasing cultural opportunities in a city which is rapidly becoming bilingual. Unlike black households the Hispanic population, apart from concentrations in Alhambra and East Los Angeles, is broadly distributed throughout the city and county and in the last decade has spread throughout formerly white suburban areas in the San Fernando Valley and outside of Los Angeles County into Orange County to the South.

Like other major metropolitan areas, there is a relatively high degree of residential segregation of black households in Los Angeles. A comparison of dissimilarity indices* across large cities for 1970 indicates a range from approximately 0.74 for New York to 0.91 for Chicago, and 0.89 for Los Angeles, Milwaukee and Detroit (Van Valey et al., 1977). There have been only slight changes (usually declines) in desegregation indices over time. The extent of residential segregation varies by group. Black households are concentrated in south-central Los Angeles and in several other small communities (Figure 7.1). However, as we noted above, there is a significant distribution of Hispanic population throughout the city, including suburban areas of Los Angeles County.

The Los Angeles Unified School District is one of the largest school districts in the nation. There are approximately 575 high school, junior high school and elementary grade schools in the Los Angeles Unified School District. The total enrolled population was approximately 500 000 pupils in 1980. Of these schools, 427 are elementary schools, educating children up to the age of twelve, and in 1980, they enrolled approximately 280 000 students. The Los Angeles Unified School District has a declining total enrolment, and a significant loss of white students. At an aggregate level, much of this white enrolment loss has been due to general demographic trends: the aging of the white population, declining fertility of white households, the relocation of white households to surrounding suburban areas, and the decision by in-migrating households to choose suburban rather than central-city locations.

PREVIOUS RESEARCH

The major general area in which there have been attempts to assess the impacts of court intervention have involved analyses of 'white flight'. These studies can be subdivided into three categories, (1) studies which have attempted to estimate the amount of 'white flight', (2) the attempts to assess 'white flight' in the context of central-city and suburban population change, including the role of migration, and (3) specific disaggregated studies of school change and neighbourhood change.

---

* The dissimilarity indices are calculated for black–white separation and do not reflect the Hispanic composition.

Estimating the amount of white flight

The initial 'white flight' studies by Coleman et al. (1975) and the responses by Farley (1975), Rossell (1975), and Pettigrew and Green (1976), focused on the extent of white loss and the degree to which that white loss was related to desegregation. Later studies by Farley et al. (1980), Rossell (1978), and Armor (1978, 1980) concluded that there were white enrolment losses related to specific desegregation plans. There is now general agreement that white enrolment loss is greatest in the year of desegregation and when there are accessible white suburbs around a central city with a large minority population. However, white loss also varies with type of desegregation programme. A re-analysis of the Coleman et al. (1975) data by Clotfelter (1979) has once again reiterated that there is little room for argument over the fact that 'white flight' does occur. The research issue is now the variation in loss rates within a school district.

'White flight', migration and suburbanization

As studies of the 'white flight' issue proliferated it became clear that white enrolment losses in central cities of metropolitan areas of the United States had to be seen in the context of the overall population decline of those central cities. A series of papers (Frey, 1979ab, 1980) set the 'white flight' issue in the larger context of demographic change, specifically the migration of white households from central cities to the suburbran rings of metropolitan areas. Frey notes that this relocation of the white population to suburban rings is not a new phenomenon and it has been going on since the Second World War. He argues that white enrolment losses in the schools do not appear to be explained by desegregation programmes. His conclusions are consistent with much of what we know about housing and locational choice. Households tend to make relocation decisions based on a complex set of needs and it is very unlikely that a household would move only because of schooling issues. A recent attempt to cast schools in a more central role in the residential decision-making process is unconvincing (Pearce, 1981). Indeed, housing choice is a complicated issue, occurs at varying points in the life cycle, and is clearly related to changes in the life cycle (Clark and Onaka, 1983). Given that relocation is going to occur, it is *destination choice* that is critical in creating a black central city and white suburban ring with the consequent effects on school systems.

Even though at the aggregate level there is evidence for desgregation impacts on population relocation, it is the evidence from individual school districts which suggests that inter- and intra-urban migration does occur in response to desegregation. Studies by Lord and Catau (1976, 1977) and by Estabrook (cited in Rossell et al., 1981, p. 18) offer tentative evidence that white enrolment losses include the relocation of households. In the study of Charlotte-

Mecklenburg (Lord and Catau, 1976, 1977) they indicate that relocation behaviour has to be seen in the context of residential mobility in general. They point out that busing was variable within the district and some divisions of the school district had much greater busing than other districts. This allowed households to relocate within the district to minimize the number of years that their children would be bused. To the extent that change occurred it confirmed, (1) general movement to school zones which had little or no busing, and (2) a continuation of the suburban trend.

Estabrook reports that of a panel study of white residents in Boston neighbourhoods that withdrew their children from public schools, almost half moved to the suburbs during the two-year implementation period of desegregation. This is greater than, but similar to, figures that have been calculated and reported in the Los Angeles Metropolitan School District desegregation case (Clark, 1982). Conway and Graham (1982) suggest that court orders in Louisville have not only promoted a decision to move, but have influenced search behaviour as well. However, another study in Louisville (Cunningham and Husk, 1980) found only minor residential relocation. These results suggest that we must treat with caution Rossell's generalization that 'most flight from desegregation is to private schools within the district rather than residential relocation outside the district' (Rossell et al., 1981, p. 46).

Within-district studies and neighbourhood effects

Only two studies have focused on within-district variations in white enrolment loss. This is notable to the extent that it is the differential impact of 'white flight' as it affects particular schools in particular districts that I believe is critical in understanding the outcomes of desegregation implementation. There are case studies of individual schools by Lord (1977), Lord and Catau (1976), Levine and Mayer (1977), and Wegmann (1975), but the only broad-based within-district comparative analyses are by Armor (1978) and Rossell (1978). Although they examine white enrolment loss in detail, they do not analyse the variation across cities and in comparison with aggregate district-wide losses or the relationship of these losses to the neighbourhood context.

One study which does attempt to link changes in individual school segregation to school attendance zones (neighbourhoods) suggests that there are significant correlations between school segregation and neighbourhood segregation (Wilson and Taeuber, 1978, p. 58). Unfortunately, they focus only on segregation indices, address only a cross-sectional analysis (1970 data) and note that the small number of districts (p. 59) precludes any conclusive results. However, the notion of relating school characteristics (and change) to neighbourhood characteristics and change, is fundamental to the empirical section of this chapter.

DATA AND METHODOLOGY

The data used in this study consist of a sample of 24 elementary schools chosen from the 427 elementary schools within the Los Angeles Unified School District (LAUSD). These twenty-four schools were randomly selected to represent geographic areas of the city, varying proportions of black, Hispanic and white students, and varying rates of population change. The LAUSD was partitioned into eight approximately equal-sized geographic units (these were variations of the seven administrative districts used by the LAUSD). Three schools were chosen from each of these eight areas. In each area, the schools were stratified into those schools which had declining, stable, or increasing enrolments. One school was chosen from each type. The stratification procedure was designed to provide the maximum variation in enrolment trends and variations in the relationship of those trends to changes in neighbourhood structure.

For each of these schools, data on total enrolment and ethnic breakdown were collected for the period for which figures were available—1966–1980. The school attendance boundaries were identified from attendance maps in the offices of the Los Angeles Unified School District, and those boundaries transferred to census tract maps. The appropriate census tracts which included the administrative boundaries of the school district were identified. Figure 7.2 indicates that this process required overbounding school districts—that is, the group of census tracts which contained the school district was always somewhat larger than the school district itself. Data for racial composition, population age

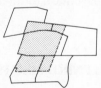

Alta Loma

Annandale

Colfax

Marianna

Noble

Overland

FIGURE 7.2. Examples of school-neighbourhood spatial overlap

and housing stock characteristics by census tract were collected from the 1960, 1970, and 1980 Censuses.

The first analytical issue in the research is the identification of within-district variation in enrolment trends and the relative impact of white enrolment loss on individual schools. Ordinary least squares regression analysis is used to estimate trends in enrolment over time. Although both linear and cohort extrapolation methods have been used for estimating the degree of district-wide 'white flight', there have been disagreements about the methodologies. Rossell is critical of the Armor cohort method and other studies have been critical of linear and curvilinear regression approaches (Rossell *et al.*, p. 26). However, over short intervals, the linear methods seem to be quite adequate in capturing the rate of enrolment loss and the relative year to year change in enrolment. Moreover, the main interest is in the relationship of enrolment loss/or gain to aggregate loss/or gain of population in the school districts as a whole.

The second theme is the analysis of school enrolment changes in relationship to changes in the neighbourhood (the aggregate of census tracts) to determine the extent to which proportional change in one can be related to proportional change in the neighbourhood population and its composition. Again, OLS techniques are used to evaluate demographic, housing, and ethnic composition changes in neighbourhoods. A linear analysis with only three points (the census years) can only be a general trend analysis of the change in the neighbourhood. On the other hand, it does allow an assessment of the degree to which change in the neighbourhood is proportional to changes in the schools. It is this linked nature of change in the school and change in the neighbourhood which has been overlooked in studies of 'white flight' up to the present time, and it is the change in the local school enrolment, with or without a neighbourhood population change, which is central to the analysis in this paper and critical for the survival of the school as a viable educational unit.

AN ANALYSIS OF CHANGING SCHOOL ENROLMENTS

Changes in enrolment levels and in ethnic composition across the sample of elementary schools are compared with system-wide changes. The analysis of enrolment change is divided into two parts. The first part focuses on compositional changes, the second part deals with a linear prediction from the data for 1966–1975 for enrolment after 1976. The linear trend prior to mandatory busing in 1978 captures the school population loss which arises from ongoing demographic processes. The regression line naturally includes the continuing losses due to the aging of the baby boom through the school system. However, the regression analysis also builds in those losses which are unrelated to demographic events, including white losses because of dissatisfaction with school quality or because of increasing minority enrolments.

Changing school composition

The analysis of composition changes in the school system as a whole and in the sample of twenty-four schools shows that the school district has undergone considerable change in the period from 1966 to 1980 (Figure 7.3). In 1966, the school district was approximately 53 per cent white, 23 per cent black, and 20 per cent Hispanic. The remainder, approximately 4 per cent in 1966, is accounted for by the Asian population in the school system. By the end of the period, the school-district enrolment was 55 per cent Hispanic, about 18 per cent white and 20 per cent black. This significant change in ethnic structure has changed a school district which had a composition which reflected the city population to a system that is now predominantly minority, and within that minority, predominantly Hispanic. The school composition does not reflect the general population composition of the city (28 per cent Hispanic, 44 per cent, white, 17 per cent black).

One of the reasons for the legal intervention was to integrate a system, which was largely segregated, on a school-by-school basis. There has been considerable discussion in the court cases over *definitions* of integrated school systems. There are at least three different definitions which have been used to classify schools as integrated. One view of integration argues that there should be no racially identifiable schools within a district. This has been interpreted to mean that all schools within the district should have about the same racial composition as the entire district. Thus, none of them can be identified as schools designated for blacks or whites (Farley, 1978b). A second view of integration suggests that minorities be assigned to schools which have large white enrolments, preferably majority white enrolments. This reflects the principles initially enunciated in *Brown*. That is, a school will be integrated only

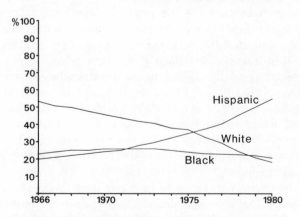

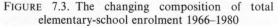

FIGURE 7.3. The changing composition of total elementary-school enrolment 1966–1980

if it has a majority of white students. A third definition suggests that a school is integrated if the white enrolment is numerically larger than any single minority. That is, a school is integrated if it has a plurality of white students (Farley, 1978b).

Using the graphs (Figure 7.4a–d) and the percentage of the total school-district population, which was black, Hispanic and white in 1966, it is possible to classify schools as predominantly black, Hispanic or white or integrated. Schools which had at least 80 per cent of one race and no other minority (black or Hispanic) of more than 20 per cent, were identified as white, black or Hispanic schools. Two exceptions should be noted; Ambler which was 72 per cent black in 1966 was identified as a black school and Glassel Park which was 60 per cent Hispanic and 38 per cent white was identified as Hispanic. Both decisions are based on the observation that Glassel Park and Ambler have more than three times the district enrolment in a racial minority. The remaining schools were identified as integrated. These schools vary from those like Alexandria and Annandale with approximately 70 per cent white and 20 per cent Hispanic enrolment to Barton Hill and Normont with somewhat equal numbers of whites, blacks and Hispanics. It is not possible to provide a more strict definition of integrated, but the definition used in this analysis of composition change fits most closely with the first of the definitions discussed earlier. When the proportion of white and Hispanic or white and black, or white, black, and Hispanic are approximately equal to the proportions in the city as a whole, the school is identified as integrated. This definition yields the largest number of integrated schools (in the sample) and is therefore the broadest interpretation of integration Table 7.4. It is likely that more schools will be identified as integrated under this definition than under definitions 2 and 3. The actual compositional changes are clear in the graphs (Figure 7.4), so that the 1966 classification can be recovered.

The question to be raised is the extent to which the schools have been integrated in their composition by the use of limited voluntary integration from 1976 to 1978, and mandatory integration from 1978 to 1980. Table 7.5 summarizes this information. Clearly, the ten white schools have been integrated, in all cases by significant intra-district busing (note the compositional changes after 1978 in Justice, Warner, and Bertrand) three of the four black schools have remained as identifiably black, one of the black schools can be considered integrated if integration is defined as approximately equal proportions of blacks and Hispanics. The three Hispanic schools have remained Hispanic, and five of the seven integrated schools are now clearly Hispanic. Two have remained integrated.

The most interesting conclusion to be drawn from this simple graphical and tabular analysis is that although almost half of the schools in the sample have been integrated by busing, the actual number of integrated schools has increased by only five. It appears that demographic processes have changed six formerly

TABLE 7.4.   Classification of schools by proportions of blacks, whites, and Hispanics in 1966–1970

White	Black	Hispanic	Integrated
Apperson	Alta Loma	Florence	Alexandria
Bertrand	Ambler	Glassell Park	Annandale
Cheremoya	Angeles Mesa	Marianna	Barton Hill
Colfax	Hooper		Bonita
Justice			Heliotrope
Loyola Village			Morningside
Noble			Normont
Overland			
Valley View			
Warner			

TABLE 7.5.   Transitions between racial classifications by school enrolment, 1966–1970 to 1980

	White 1980	Black 1980	Hispanic 1980	Integrated 1980
White 1966–1970			Noble	Apperson Bertrand Cheremoya Colfax Justice Loyola Village Overland Valley View Warner
Black 1966–1970		Alta Loma Ambler Angeles Mesa		Hooper
Hispanic 1966–1970			Florence Glassell Park Marianna	
Integrated 1966–1970			Annandale Barton Hill Heliotrope Morningside Normont	Alexandria Bonita

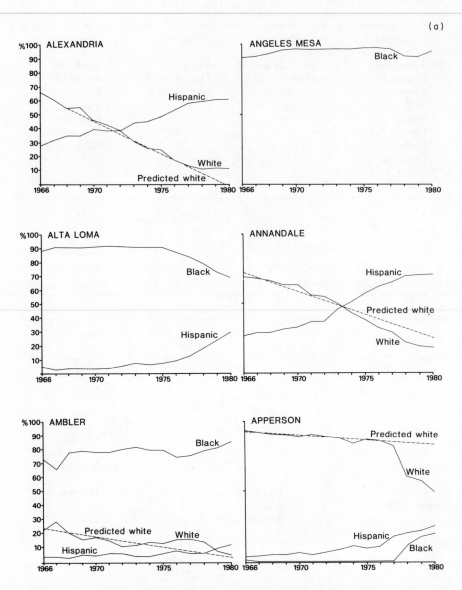

FIGURE 7.4a–d. Composition changes by individual schools 1966–1980

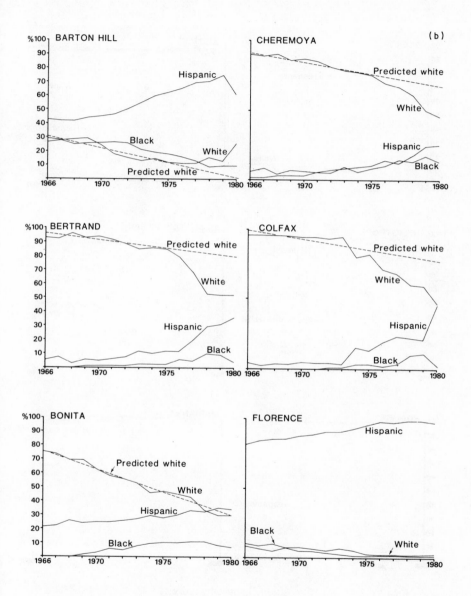

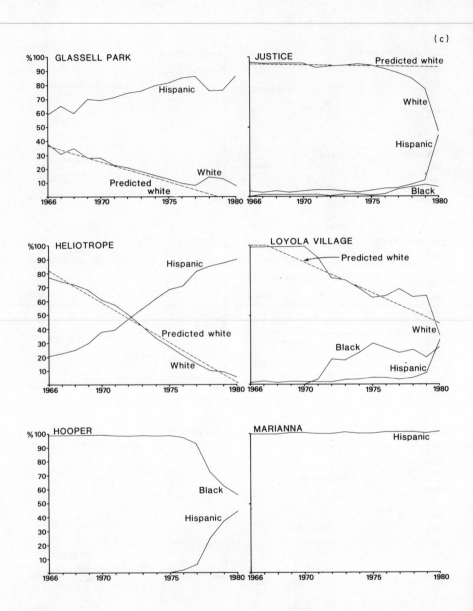

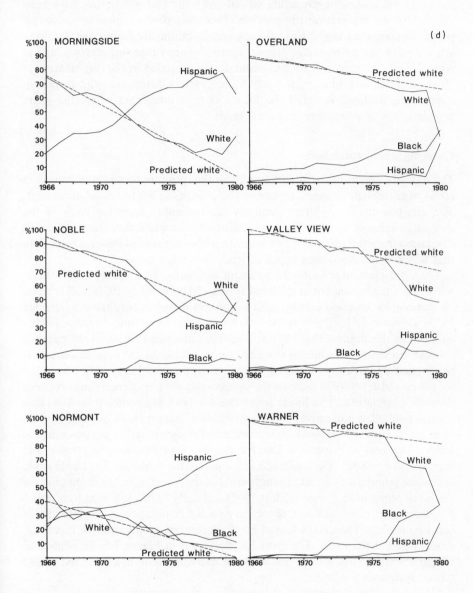

integrated schools to single ethnic composition schools. There was no change in
the other six schools. Only white schools with in- and out-busing have been
affected by the integration programme. There has been no change under this
programme in schools which are already heavily ethnically dominated. Only ten
schools have whites in greater proportion to any one other single group, and in
several cases, the percentage white population is exceeded by the combination of
Hispanic and black minorities. Only Valley View, Cheremoya, and Apperson
might be considered to fulfill the *Brown* view of integrated where the white
population is in a majority (Figure 7.4a–d).

Changing school enrolments

The second element of the analysis concerns the response to this intervention in
terms of enrolment changes, especially the changes in white school enrolment.
The analysis involved fitting ordinary least squares lines for each of the
individual schools for both total enrolment and for white enrolment. Negative
deviations from the regression line indicate school enrolment losses greater than
that which could have been expected from enrolment trends.

The total elementary-school enrolment fluctuated in a rather flat S-curve,
with increasing enrolment in the late 1960s, a dip in the early 1970s, followed by
an increase in the middle 1970s, and significant drops in enrolment in the late
1970s (Figure 7.5). The analysis of these data by ethnic breakdown re-
emphasizes the changes that have already been identified earlier in the paper—
massive decreases in white enrolment, rather stable black population enrolments, and significantly increasing Hispanic enrolments. Regression lines fitted
for the period 1966–1975 indicate the significantly greater decrease in enrolment
in white population. The linear trend line for both Hispanics ($r^2 = 0.94$) and
white ($r^2 = 0.98$) is a relatively good fit to the data, but for black populations, the
fit is much lower ($r^2 = 0.44$). It is presented for comparative purposes in the
figure. The best-fit regression line for the black populations is a quadratic
regression ($r^2 = 0.98$). The quadratic fit is equal to the linear fits for the Hispanic
and white populations over the same period of time, and reflects a slight bulge in
the black population during the late 1960s and early 1970s, followed by a rather
flat decrease in the black and elementary school population in the later 1970s
(see Figure 7.5). The excess loss of black elementary population is, therefore,
more apparent than real. The cross-hatched areas in Figure 7.5, for white and
Hispanic enrolments, clearly indicate the exchange that has occurred in the
school system as a whole.

One of the stated themes of the paper is a clearer grasp of the variation in
white enrolment loss across different schools, and the extent of white enrolment
loss in specific schools that have gone through the process of integration (by
mandatory busing) during the period 1978–1980. The graphs in Figure 7.6a–d
show the total enrolment by school and the white enrolment for schools (in

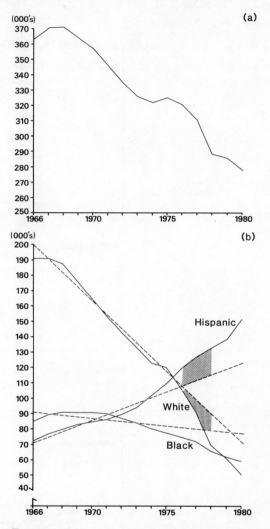

FIGURE 7.5. (a) Total elementary-school enrolment. (b) Total and predicted enrolment of Hispanic, white, and black elementary-school students

schools with greater than 100 white students enrolled in the initial period). Regression lines fitted for the period 1966–1975 are projected through 1980. The levels of fit for individual schools is summarized in Table 7.6.

There is considerable variation in the response of individual schools to the integration programme. Of the ten white schools which were integrated by busing, Colfax, Loyola, and Overland had stable enrolments or modest

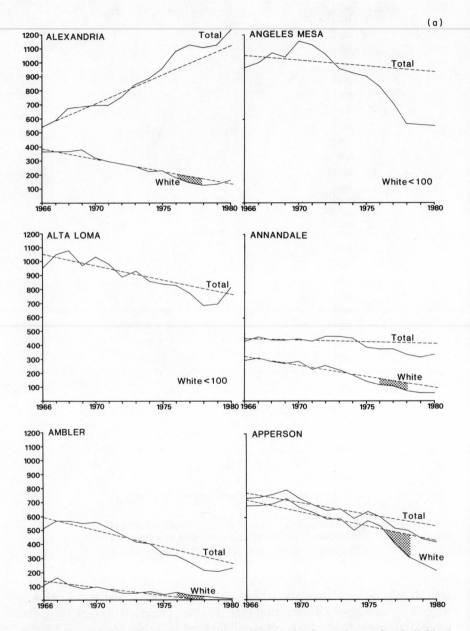

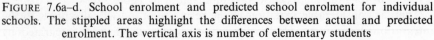

FIGURE 7.6a–d. School enrolment and predicted school enrolment for individual schools. The stippled areas highlight the differences between actual and predicted enrolment. The vertical axis is number of elementary students

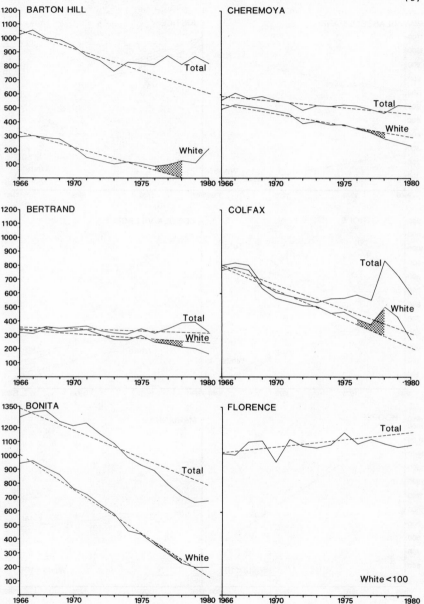

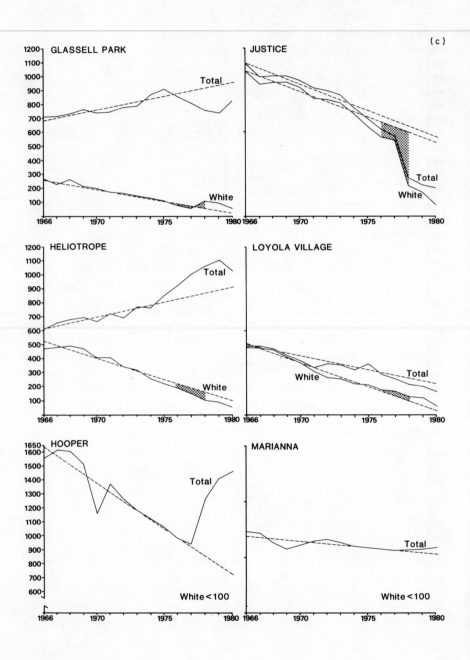

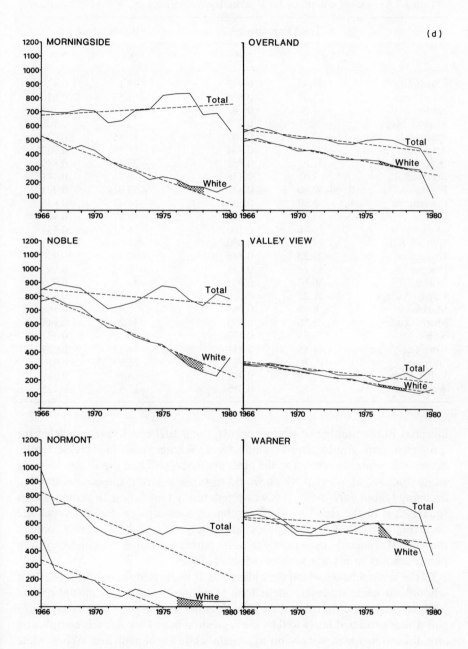

TABLE 7.6.   Linear equations for total and white enrolment 1966–1975 by school

	Total Enrolment		White Enrolment	
	b	r^2	b	r^2
Alexandria	41.45	0.943	−17.12	0.879
Alta Loma	−21.02	0.608	− 1.57	0.656
Ambler	−23.50	0.742	−10.81	0.762
Angeles Mesa	− 7.87	0.073	− 3.04	0.705
Annandale	− 2.41	0.107	−15.85	0.871
Apperson	−17.90	0.701	−21.16	0.762
Barton Hill	−31.03	0.853	−27.68	0.889
Bertrand	− 2.65	0.178	− 6.22	0.441
Bonita	−40.60	0.845	−63.01	0.971
Cheremoya	− 8.80	0.593	−16.47	0.846
Colfax	−33.45	0.802	−40.87	0.908
Florence	10.46	0.260	− 6.57	0.836
Glassell Park	19.36	0.800	−16.48	0.943
Heliotrope	21.58	0.846	−30.10	0.905
Hooper	−63.74	0.821	− 0.12	0.013
Justice	−36.84	0.903	−37.18	0.920
Loyola Village	−19.25	0.816	−33.98	0.962
Marianna	− 8.26	0.364	− 0.42	0.368
Morningside	5.56	0.109	−34.2	0.948
Noble	− 7.65	0.132	−40.15	0.961
Normont	−44.55	0.711	−34.52	0.673
Overland	−10.30	0.783	−16.97	0.948
Valley View	− 9.98	0.903	−14.61	0.949
Warner	− 5.12	0.085	−12.82	0.425

increases in the number of white students, the actual enrolment paralleled the 'projected demographic trend'. One school, Warner, had an increase then a decrease in white students, and the other six schools all had significant losses of white students, above that which would be projected from the general trend of declining school enrolment. It is worth reiterating that fitting an ordinary least squares line to the trend in white enrolment does capture declines which are occurring because of demographic change, but may well be capturing some of the general tendency, over time, for white parents to move their children from public schools to private schools (Maeroff, 1982).

Of the seven schools which were identified as integrated schools in 1966, three schools lost white students, one school, Morningside, had a significant gain of white students, and the other three schools either had very few white students or had whites predicted fairly well by the regression line. This analysis complicates any discussion based simply on aggregate white enrolment loss. While white enrolment loss is most likely to occur in formerly all-white schools which are integrated by mandatory busing, in 40 per cent of the cases, there were increases or only minor losses of white students over that period of time. This suggests that white enrolment loss in response to mandatory busing is more complicated than suggested by a simple district-wide analysis. Moreover, it appears that even in those formerly integrated schools, there is also significant white loss in at least half of the cases. In the other half of the cases, there is an indication of increasing enrolment. This variability suggests that we require more information than simple data on white enrolment loss to understand the complex interaction process between schools, mandatory integration programmes, neighbourhood change, and the potential for change in school enrolment over time.

Analysis of neighbourhood change and changes in school enrolment composition

The third part of the analysis focuses on the interrelationships between school enrolment change and neighbourhood change. It is also concerned with the explanations for the nature of white enrolment loss across schools.

To analyse neighbourhood racial change versus school enrolment composition change this preliminary analysis uses census data on racial composition in neighbourhoods (Table 7.7). Because we are interested in the nature of aggregate compositional changes in the schools and any similar aggregate change in the neighbourhood the census is an appropriate data context. Future detailed studies which will attempt to measure the dynamics of change, the actual relocation behaviour of the populations in these neighbourhoods, will require survey data. The neighbourhoods are the combination of census tracts

TABLE 7.7. Transitions between racial classifications by neighbourhood composition 1960 to 1980

	White 1980	Black 1980	Hispanic 1980	Integrated 1980
White 1960	Apperson Bertrand Colfax Justice Loyola Village Overland Valley View Warner		Heliotrope Morningside	Alexandria Ambler Annandale† Bonita Cheremoya Noble
Black 1960				Hooper†
Hispanic 1960			Marianna	
Integrated 1960		Alta Loma* Angeles Mesa*	Florence* Glassell Park	Barton Hill Normont

* Major transition between 1960–1970
† Major transition between 1970–1980

which overbounded the school (school names are used to identify the neighbourhoods). The neighbourhoods are defined as white, black, Hispanic, the dominant racial composition, or integrated, if they had a racial composition which approximately reflected the city racial composition in 1960 and 1980. Asterisks or † indicate if the transition was primarily between 1960 and 1970 or 1970 and 1980. The neighbourhood Cheremoya was classified as a white to integrated change although the neighbourhood was over 70 per cent white in 1980. Of the initial neighbourhoods which were white in 1960, seven of those neighbourhoods have remained more than 90 per cent white, and two others over 80 per cent white. Two neighbourhoods have made the transition from white to Hispanic, and a further six neighbourhoods have gone from being white to integrated. One black neighbourhood has changed from being black to integrated (with Hispanic), and one Hispanic neighbourhood has remained Hispanic. Four integrated neighbourhoods have changed to black or Hispanic. Two neighbourhoods began and remained integrated (Table 7.7).

A comparison of Table 7.7 with the table for school change (Table 7.5) shows that there is little relationship, at least in the short run, between change in the neighbourhood and change in the school system. The school enrolment changes do not have a comparable racial change especially in white neighbourhoods. While this limited integration experience took place in voluntary and mandatory form for only five years, 1976–1981, and rapid change in the neighbourhood as a result of this limited busing experiment would not be expected, it is clear that there is a real distinction between the integration of the school and the integration of the neighbourhood. The continuing and major differences between ethnic structures for the school and the neighbourhood suggest that it would be misleading to suggest that rapid and significant neighbourhood integration will follow school integration. These results cast doubt on the views of those social scientists who believe that school desegregation will lead to neighbourhood integration.

A specific analysis of changes in Tables 7.5 and 7.7 offers further insights on the complexity of the relationship between neighbourhood change and school enrolment change. Of those schools which changed from white to integrated only Cheremoya could be described as having a neighbourhood change. Neighbourhoods which changed from white to Hispanic had schools which changed from integrated to Hispanic suggesting that the change in the school composition is being driven by the change in neighbourhood composition. But, in at least two cases, Alexandria and Bonita, schools which were integrated throughout the period, had neighbourhoods which changed from white to integrated. The test will be whether the neighbourhoods remain integrated or change to Hispanic. Two other neighbourhoods Barton Hill and Normont were integrated throughout but the schools changed from integrated to Hispanic. Clearly, in this case, it is not possible to argue that the schools have influenced neighbourhood integration. At the present the conclusion must be that neighbourhood transition precedes the transition in the schools (excepting mandatory reassignment) and it is the neighbourhood transition which is the main mechanism for school enrolment change.

To further analyse the relationship of neighbourhood transition and to explain what may be occurring within these neighbourhoods, an analysis of the change in population, racial composition, in the proportion of the population under 18 years of age and over 64 years of age, and the proportion of single-family and owner-occupied dwellings was carried out. Other data on socio-economic characteristics has not yet been released for the 1980 census. Neighbourhoods were analysed by fitting linear regression lines over the 1960, 1970, and 1980 census data for total population, percentage black, percentage white, percentage Hispanic, percentage of the population under 18, percentage of the population over 64, percentage of the housing in single family units, and percentage of the housing occupied by owners. The slope coefficients and the regression coefficients are reported in detail in Table 7.8 and in summary form in

TABLE 7.8. b values from OLS regressions on census tract characteristics (1960, 1970, 1980) by neighbourhood

	Black (%)	Hispanic (%)	White (%)	Age < 18 (%)	Age > 64 (%)	Single-family Housing (%)	Owner-occupied Housing (%)
Alexandria	0.20	1.93	−2.13	0.61	−0.52	0.58	−0.31
Alta Loma	1.32	0.83	−2.15	0.15	−0.18	0.93	−0.35
Ambler	1.25	0.52	−1.77	−0.71	0.23	−1.28	0.68
Angeles Mesa	2.63	−0.10	−2.52	0.12	−0.29	0.43	−0.18
Annandale	0.06	1.81	−1.87	−0.39	−0.01	0.03	−0.04
Apperson	0.06	0.31	−0.38	−0.53	−0.10	−0.42	−0.14
Barton Hill	−0.21	0.05	0.16	−0.37	0.02	0.82	0.72
Bertrand	0.08	0.51	−0.58	−1.21	0.33	−2.43	−2.61
Bonita	0.39	0.97	−1.36	−0.85	0.24	0.44	1.51
Cheremoya	0.29	0.42	−0.72	−0.04	−0.22	0.56	0.11
Colfax	0.07	0.26	−0.33	−0.50	0.34	0.10	−0.39
Florence	−0.32	2.32	−2.00	0.25	−0.22	−0.14	0.77
Glassell Park	0.05	1.78	−1.83	0.11	−0.15	−0.33	−0.35
Heliotrope	0.01	2.59	−2.60	0.04	0.06	−0.59	−0.29
Hooper	−1.14	1.30	−0.16	0.28	0.07	−0.32	−0.15
Justice	0.08	0.20	−0.28	−0.92	0.20	−1.87	−0.99
Loyola Village	0.12	0.31	−0.43	−1.32	0.19	−1.53	−1.66
Marianna	−0.01	1.40	−1.39	−0.39	0.11	−0.57	−0.04
Morningside	0.04	2.51	−2.55	−1.40	−0.10	−0.41	−0.28
Noble	0.28	1.29	−1.57	−0.54	0.34	−1.54	−1.39
Normont	0.54	0.89	−1.43	−0.86	0.25	−1.26	−0.19
Overland	0.09	0.26	−0.35	−0.46	0.29	−0.00	−0.37
Valley View	0.10	0.11	−0.20	−0.51	0.22	−0.20	−0.21
Warner	0.01	0.11	−0.11	−0.21	0.21	0.82	1.01

TABLE 7.9.   The characteristics of neighbourhood change

	Total Pop.	Black	Hispanic	White	Age < 18	Age > 64	Single-family housing	Owner-occupied housing
Alexandria	+	0	+	−	0	0	0	0
Alta Loma	0	+	+	−	0	0	+	0
Ambler	0	+	0	−	0	0	−	0
Angeles Mesa	0	+	0	−	0	0	0	0
Annandale	0	0	+	−	0	0	0	0
Apperson	−	0	0	0	0	0	0	0
Barton Hill	+	0	0	0	0	0	−	−
Bertrand	+	0	0	0	−	0	−	−
Bonita	0	0	+	−	−	0	0	0
Cheremoya	0	0	+	−	0	0	0	0
Colfax	−	0	0	0	0	0	0	0
Florence	+	0	+	−	0	0	−	0
Glassell Park	+	0	+	−	0	0	0	0
Heliotrope	0	0	+	−	0	0	0	0
Hooper	0	−	+	0	0	0	0	0
Justice	+	0	0	0	−	0	−	−
Loyola Village	+	0	0	0	−	0	−	−
Marianna	−	0	+	−	0	0	0	0
Morningside	+	0	+	−	−	0	0	0
Noble	+	0	+	−	0	0	0	0
Normont	−	+	+	−	−	0	−	0
Overland	−	0	0	0	0	0	0	0
Valley View	+	0	0	0	0	0	0	0
Warner	−	0	0	0	0	0	+	+

0 = little change; + = significant increase; − = significant decrease.

Table 7.9. From the analysis it is possible to determine those neighbourhoods which have had significant negative or positive changes in the various measures.

From Tables 7.7, 7.8 and 7.9 it is possible to develop an analysis of the type of neighbourhood change, population composition change and associated changes in age structure and tenure status. Neighbourhoods are grouped into those with no change, those with transition to integrated populations, those with neighbourhood transitions to black or Hispanic populations, and those with neighbourhood transitions from white to Hispanic populations (Table 7.10).

Of the neighbourhoods which showed no change in composition, the neighbourhoods in several cases had significant declines in population, associated declines in the percentage of the population under 18, and compositional changes in the housing. These were the districts with all-white schools at the beginning of the period, which had integrated schools via mandatory busing at the end of the period, but little neighbourhood change. They are classic cases of neighbourhoods which would be described as 'white-flight' neighbourhoods, and the data from the decreasing percentage under 18 in the neighbourhood, and the compositional change with decreasing percentages in owner-occupied housing (indicating increasing percentages of renters), suggests some actual population relocation out of the district. In most

TABLE 7.10   The relationship between neighbourhood change and school enrolment/composition change

Type of neighbourhood change (from Table 7.7)	Population composition change	Type of school change
No change		
Apperson	No change	Integrated, varying levels of white loss
Bertrand	No change	Integrated, varying levels of white loss
Colfax	No change	Integrated, varying levels of white loss
Justice	No change	Integrated, varying levels of white loss
Loyola Village	No change	Integrated, varying levels of white loss
Overland	No change	Integrated, varying levels of white loss
Valley View	No change	Integrated, varying levels of white loss
Warner	No change	Integrated, varying levels of white loss
Barton Hill	No change	Integrated and remained so
Marianna	Including Hispanic/white loss	Hispanic and remained so
Normont	Including black and Hispanic/white loss	Integrated to Hispanic
Neighbourhood transition to integrated		
Alexandria	Including Hispanic/white loss	Integrated and remained so
Ambler	Including black/white loss	Black and remained so
Annandale	Including Hispanic/white loss	Integrated to Hispanic
Bonita	Including Hispanic/white loss	Integrated and remained so
Cheremoya	Including Hispanic/white loss	White to integrated
Hooper	Including Hispanic	Black to integrated
Noble	Including Hispanic	White to integrated
Neighbourhood transition integrated to black or Hispanic		
Alta Loma	Including black and Hispanic/white loss	Black and remained so
Angeles Mesa	Including black/white loss	Black and remained so
Florence	Including Hispanic/white loss	Hispanic and remained so
Glassell Park	Including Hispanic/white loss	Hispanic and remained so
Neighbourhood transition white to Hispanic		
Heliotrope	Including Hispanic/white loss	Integrated to Hispanic
Morningside	Including Hispanic/white loss	Integrated to Hispanic

neighbourhoods, however, the declines in enrolment reflect increased private-school enrolment.

The second group of neighbourhoods had schools with increasing Hispanic enrolments (Noble and Cheremoya, for example). They are classic cases of neighbourhoods which are in transition from white to presently integrated neighbourhoods. But, they are probably neighbourhoods in transition from white to Hispanic, and the schools which are presently integrated are integrated as a function of the neighbourhood transition which is occurring. The third group are those neighbourhoods which have had significant losses of white population and increasing proportions of minorities, either blacks or Hispanics. The neighbourhoods continue their transition, the schools are already minority. The final group has significant increases in the Hispanic population and associated changes in the school system. In general for the eleven schools with increasing Hispanic populations, the neighbourhoods are all losing white populations. However, four of the schools have little change in composition, four others, Annandale, Heliotrope, Morningside and Normont are clearly neighbourhoods in transition from integrated to Hispanic, and the other three schools are already Hispanic.

What can we conclude from this analysis of neighbourhood change? Thirteen of the twenty-four neighbourhoods underwent important neighbourhood transition during the period 1960–1980. This neighbourhood transition drove associated school change and is evidence of the power of the demographic processes. It is the link between the neighbourhood change and the school change so clearly documented in this detailed study which reiterates the points made earlier by Farley (1978b) and Glenn (1979) in his review of the Los Angeles case. Without embedding the intervention by the judicial process in the on-going demographic profile at the neighbourhood level within the city, little will be accomplished with respect to the effect of desegregation of the school system.

CONCLUSION: IMPLICATIONS OF INTERVENTION

What can we conclude from this small sample analysis of school enrolment change and neighbourhood composition change on a school-by-school, neighbourhood-by-neighbourhood basis? First, the nature of enrolment change and associated composition changes in the schools is far more complex than can be suggested by an aggregate district-wide analysis. The analysis shows that not all white schools lose population equally, and that while some schools have dramatic losses of white students (Justice) other schools have stable or increasing white enrolments. At the same time, the long-term impact for all white schools seems to be that there will be fewer and fewer white students, and that the elusive goal of integration may well not be achieved by any form of mandatory or voluntary busing.

Second, with respect to the impact of intervention on the integration of schools, the results are at best mixed. It is correct that the judicial system has been able to integrate a subset of schools—those schools which were initially white and have been temporarily integrated. But even within the short time period of this study, it is clear that this is a limited gain. Already the busing has changed the composition of schools to the point where few schools can be considered to be integrated in terms of the original *Brown* decision. Therefore, a successful programme designed to integrate a society is probably not best implemented through the school system; more severe measures may be necessary to achieve integration on a national basis.

Third, there are at least as many changes in school integration as a result of neighbourhood transition as there are from judicial intervention. It is neighbourhood transition which underlies so much of the school-level change. And, to the extent that the judges have influenced school composition, they have exacerbated rather than ameliorated the effects of these ongoing demographic processes.

Finally, there is little evidence of neighbourhood integration as a result of school integration. Unfortunately, from an experimental point of view, busing was halted in 1981, and thus the longer-term effects of school integration on neighbourhood integration cannot be tested. For now it appears that the larger impacts of school integration on the urban fabric itself are limited. At the same time, we must recognize that if the intent is only to provide an integrative educational experience, at least for those whites who remain in the school system, the process of integration may have been a positive experience. But in general the evidence of this paper offers no strong support for the notion that real advances in societal integration will come from a process which relies solely on school integration.

REFERENCES

Articles

Armor, D. (1978). White flight, demographic transition, and the future of school desegregation, *The Rand Paper Series*, P5931, The Rand Corporation, Santa Monica, California.

Armor, D. (1980). White flight and the future of school desegregation. In *School Desegregation* (Eds W. G. Stephen and J. R. Feagin), Plenum, New York.

Armstrong v. O'Connell (1978). Reporter's daily transcript, July 11, 261ff.

Clark, W. A. V. (1980). Residential mobility and neighborhood change: Some implications for racial residential segregation, *Urban Geography*, 1, 95–117.

Clark, W. A. V. (1982). Judicial intervention as policy: Impacts on population distribution and redistribution in urban areas in the United States, *Population Research and Policy Review*, 1, 79–100.

Clark, W. A. V. and Onaka, J. (1983). A review and interpretation of reasons for moving, *Urban Studies*, 20, 47–58.

Conway, D. and Graham, M. (1982). Court ordered busing and housing searches, *Environment and Behavior*, 14, 45–71.

Clotfelter, C. T. (1976). School desegregation, 'tipping,' and private school enrolment, *Journal of Human Resources*, 11, 28–50.

Clotfelter, C. T. (1979). Urban school desegregation and declines in white enrolment: A re-examination, *Journal of Urban Economics*, 5, 352–370.

Coleman, J. S., Kelley, S., and Moore, J. (1975). Trends in school desegregation, 1968–1975, *Paper, UI 722-03-91*. The Urban Institute, Washington, DC.

Cunningham, G. and Husk, W. (1980). White flight, a closer look at the assumptions, *The Urban Review*, 12, 23–29.

Farley, R. (1975). *School Integration and White Flight*, University of Michigan, Population Studies Center, Ann Arbor, Michigan.

Farley, R. (1978a). Social integration in the U.S. In *The Demography of Racial and Ethnic Groups* (Eds F. D. Bean and W. P. Frisbie), Academic Press, New York.

Farley, R. (1978b). Report to the Honorable Judge Paul Egly in response to Minute Order Number C 822 854, Population Studies Center, University of Michigan, Ann Arbor, Michigan.

Farley, R. (1979). Supplemental report to the Honorable Judge Paul Egly, in response to Minute Order C 822 854, Population Studies Center, University of Michigan, Ann Arbor, Michigan.

Farley, R., Richards, T., and Wurdock, C. (1980). School desegregation and white flight: An investigation of competing models and their discrepant findings, *Sociology of Education*, **53**, 129–139.

Frey, W. H. (1979a). Central city white flight: Racial and non-racial causes, *American Sociological Review*, **44**, 425–448.

Frey, W. H. (1979b). White flight and central city loss: Application of an analytic migration framework, *Environment and Planning A*, **11**, 129–147.

Frey, W. H. (1980). Black in-migration, white flight, and the changing economic base of the central city, *American Journal of Sociology*, **85**, 1396–1417.

Glenn, A. S. (1979). State court desegregation orders: Multi-district busing, Supreme Court Review, and the Los Angeles school case, *UCLA Law Review*, **26**, 1183–1230.

Johnston, R. J. (1981). The management and autonomy of the local state: The role of the judiciary in the United States, *Environment and Planning A*, **13**, 1183–1230.

Levine, D. U. and Meyer, J. K. (1977). Desegregation and white enrolment decline in a big city school district. In *The Future of Big City Schools* (Eds D. U. Levine and R. J. Havinghurst), McCutchan, Berkeley.

Lord, J. D. (1977). *Spatial Perspectives on School Desegregation and Busing*. Resource Papers 77–3, Association of American Geographers, Washington, DC.

Lord, J. D. and Catau, J. (1976). School desegregation, busing and suburban migration, *Urban Education*, **11**, 275–294.

Lord, J. D. and Catau, J. D. (1977). School desegregation policy and intra-school district migration, *Social Science Quarterly*, **57**, 784–796.

Lord, J. D. and Catau, J. (1981). The school desegregation-resegregation scenario: Charlotte-Mecklenburg's experience. *Urban Affairs Quarterly*, **16**, 346–376.

Lowry, I (1980). Bringing mobility research to bear on public policy. In *Residential Mobility and Public Policy* (Eds W. A. V. Clark and E. Moore), pp. 29–33, Sage, Beverly Hills.

Lowry, M. (1973). Schools in transition, *Annals of the Association of American Geographers*, **63**, 167–180.

Maeroff, G. I. (1982). Enrollment drop: Growing threat to public schools, *New York Times*, September 7.

Noblit, G. W. and Collins, T. W. (1978). School flight and social policy: Desegregation and resegregation in the Memphis city schools, *The Urban Review*, **10**, 203–212.

Orfield, G. (1978). *Must we bus*, The Brookings Institution, Washington, DC.

Pearce, D. (1981). Deciphering the dynamics of segregation: The role of schools in the housing choice process, *The Urban Review*, **13**, 85–101.

Pettigrew, T. F. and Green, R. (1976). School desegregation in large cities: A critique of the Coleman white flight thesis, *Harvard Educational Review*, **46**, 1–53.

Read, F. (1975). Judicial evolution of the law of school integration since *Brown* v. *Board of Education*, *Law and Contemporary Problems*, **39**, 7–45.

Rossell, C. H. (1975). School desegregation and white flight, *Political Science Quarterly*, **90**, 675–695.

Rossell, C. H. (1978). *The unintended impacts of public policy: School desegregation and resegregation*, Institute of Policy Sciences, Duke University.

Rossell, C. H. *et al.* (1981). A review of the empirical research on desegregation: Community response, race relations, academic achievement and resegregation. In *Assessment of Current Knowledge About the Effectiveness of School Desegregation Strategies* (Eds C. H. Rossell *et al.*), Center for Education and Human Development Policy, Institute for Public Policy Studies, Vanderbilt University.

Taeuber, K. (1979). Housing, schools, and incremental segregative effects, *Annals*, *AAPSS*, **441**, 157–167.

Van Valey, T., Roof, W. C., and Wilcox, J. E. (1977). Trends in residential segregation 1960–1970, *American Journal of Sociology*, **82**, 826–844.
Wegmann, R. G. (1975). Neighborhood and schools in racial transition, *Growth and Change*, **6**, 6–8.
Wilson, F. D. and Taeuber, K. E. (1978). Residential and school segregation: Some tests of their association. In *The Demography of Racial and Ethnic Groups*, (Eds F. D. Bean and W. P. Frisbie), Academic Press, New York.
Wolf, E. P. (1981). *Trial and Error: The Detroit School Desegregation Case*, Wayne State University Press, Detroit.

Cases

Brown v. *Board of Education of Topeka Kansas*, 367 U.S. 483 (1954).
Crawford v. *Board of Education of the City of Los Angeles*, 17 Cal.3d 280 (1963).
Jackson v. *Pasadena City School District*, 59 Cal.2d 876 (1963).
Green v. *County School Board of New Kent County*, 391 U.S. 430 (1968).
Swann v. *Charlotte-Mecklenberg Board of Education*, 402 U.S. 1 (1971).
Keyes v. *School District No. 1, Parkhill Denver*, 413 U.S. 189 (1973).
Milliken v. *Bradley*, 418 U.S. 717 (1974).
Pasadena City Board of Education v. *Spangler*, 427 U.S. 424 (1976).
Crawford v. *Board of Education of the City of Los Angeles*, 130 Cal. Rptr. 724 (1976).
Dayton Board of Education v. *Brinkman*, 433 U.S. 406 (1977).
Columbus Board of Education v. *Penick*, 443 U.S. 449 (1979).
Armor v. *Nix* (1979).
Crawford v. *Board of Education of the City of Los Angeles*, 113 Cal. App.3d 633 (1980).
Crawford v. *Board of Education of the City of Los Angeles*, 170 Cal. Rptr. 495 (1982).

Geography and the Urban Environment
Progress in Research and Applications, Volume VI
Edited by D. T. Herbert and R. J. Johnston
© 1984 John Wiley & Sons Ltd.

Chapter 8

Gentrification and Residential Location Theory: A Review and Assessment

C. Hamnett

INTRODUCTION

The late 1960s and 1970s have seen the rise to prominence in a number of large Western cities of a phenomenon known variously as gentrification (Glass, 1963, 1973; Hamnett, 1973; Hamnett and Williams, 1980), private-market housing renovation (Black, 1977), 'neighbourhood reinvestment' (Clay, 1980), 'neighbourhood renewal' (Clay, 1979), 'urban re-invasion' (London, 1980), 'middle-class resettlement' (Gale, 1979), 'central-city revival' (Lipton, 1977), 'private urban renewal' (Zeitz, 1979), 'inner-city revitalization' (London *et al.*, 1980), 'private-market inner-city rehabilitation' (Berry, 1980), 'residential revitalization' (Holcomb and Beauregard, 1981) or just plain 'revitalization' (Berry, 1980).

Despite the great variety of different labels the nature of the phenomenon remains essentially the same and we shall refer to it here by its original name of *gentrification*. First identified in London by Ruth Glass in 1973, she described the process as follows:

> One by one, many of the working class quarters of London have been invaded by the middle-class-upper and lower-shabby modest mews and cottages . . . have been taken over when their leases expired, and have become elegant, expensive residences. Larger Victorian houses, downgraded in an earlier or recent period—which were used as lodging houses or were otherwise in multiple occupation—have been upgraded once again. . . . Once this process of 'gentrification' starts in a district it goes on rapidly until all or most of the original working class occupiers are displaced and the whole social character of the district is changed. (Glass, 1963, p. xviii)

Despite the ungainly and inelegant nature of the ephithet, and the ironic connotations of a new 'gentry', contained in the label 'gentrification', Glass's description of the process embodies all the vital ingredients of what is simultaneously a physical, economic, social and cultural phenomenon. Gentrification commonly involves the invasion by middle-class or higher-income groups (Gale, 1979) of what were previously working-class neighbourhoods or multi-occupied 'twilight areas' (Hamnett, 1973) and the replacement or displacement of many of their original occupants (McCarthy, 1975; Grier and Grier, 1980; Cybriwsky, 1978). It involves the physical renovation or rehabilitation of what was frequently a highly deteriorated housing stock (Smith, 1979a) and its upgrading to meet the requirements of its new owners. In the process, housing in the areas affected, both renovated and unrenovated, undergoes a significant price appreciation (Nield, 1974; Williams, 1976; Cybriwsky and Meyer, 1977). Such a process of neighbourhood transition commonly involves a degree of tenure transformation from renting to owning (Williams, 1976; Hamnett and Williams, 1979) and, in certain North American cities (Cybriwsky, 1978; Zeitz, 1979) an ethnic transition from black to white. As a result the process of gentrification often involves a high degree of social, cultural and ethnic conflict, the lifestyle, colour, class and tenure of the new in-migrants differing radically from those of the existing residents (Cybriwsky, 1978; Auger, 1979; Zeitz, 1979). As early as 1965 the Milner–Holland Report on Housing in Greater London identified the four consequences of the process as, the remarkable rise in prices, the progressive transfers of housing stock from renting to owner-occupancy, the reduction in net occupancy rate and density as individual households replace multiple occupation, and the alteration in socio-economic structure as the population changes from mainly working class to mainly upper-middle class.

Finally, as Glass's reference to 'larger Victorian houses, downgraded in an earlier or recent period' implies, the process often takes place in areas that were originally built for and occupied by the middle or upper classes but which were subsequently abandoned to lower-class and lower-income groups in the classic process of downward filtering or 'invasion and succession'. Hence London's (1980) description of the process of 'urban reinvasion'. This process took place in Philadelphia (Rapkin and Grigsby, 1960) and much of inner London. As Raban rather graphically put it:

> A combination of class fear and railway engineering turned a vast stretch of residential London into a no-man's land. . . . Camden Town, Holloway, Islington, were abandoned to the hopelessly entrenched working class. Its only in the last decade or so that a new middle class, trendy and pioneer, have replaced these buffer areas, between the nobs and the mob of N1 and NW1. (Raban, 1974).

Gentrification is not, however, a 'back to the city' movement, if by that it is construed that the gentrifiers have returned from the suburbs. As Gale (1976,

1977), Smith (1979a), and Chambers (1974) amongst others have shown, gentrification commonly involves migration within the inner city itself as small, youthful households, commonly in the prechildbearing or early child rearing stages of the family life cycle have moved from rented accommodation to single-family owner occupation in the inner city, rather than seeking a suburban home. As Clay (1980, p. 14) put it: 'What is commonly referred to as back to the city is fundamentally a resettlement in and a renewal of older neighbourhoods mainly by middle-class people who are presently residents in the city in other neighbourhoods as renters.' As this makes clear it is important to distinguish gentrification from both the intensification of existing high-status areas and from the process of neighbourhood revitalization involving 'incumbent upgrading' (Clay, 1979) where upwards social change may occur without spatial mobility. As London (1980) points out, it is not uncommon in stable working class or ethnic neighbourhoods in American cities:

> for second or third generation inhabitants of a house, many of whom have been upwardly mobile inter-generationally, to inherit the dwelling from their parents, upgrade the physical structure, and remain as adults in the neighbourhood they grew up in. (London, 1980, p. 78).

As the burgeoning literature indicates, the late 1970s has seen the discovery of gentrification in a number of large North American cities. The reaction to it has been equally varied. It has been hailed as the saviour of declining inner-city areas and, more commonly, reviled as an agent of working-class displacement. Some reference has already been made to the literature on displacement, and the conflicting interpretation as to its scale, extent and importance are clearly seen in the exchange between Sumka (1979) and Hartman (1979). That gentrification is resulting in some degree of displacement is not doubted and this is indicative of the weak position of the poor in the housing market; whereas they were once concentrated in the inner city because of their limited purchasing power, they are now being displaced from it for the same reason. As Ley (1981, p. 144) has observed: 'The market, which has failed the disadvantaged in the industrial inner city through under-investment, is penalizing the same group in the post-industrial city through over-investment.' The remainder of this paper will address four aspects of gentrification: its scale, extent, and characteristics; its implications for traditional models of residential location and neighbourhood change; the nature of the explanations and theories which have been advanced; and its future prospects.

SCALE, EXTENT AND CHARACTERISTICS

Gentrification has been observed in many of the larger European and North American cities under a variety of different labels, some such as 'brownstoning' in the older brownstone town houses of New York or, 'white painting' in Toronto (Dynes, 1974; Rebizant and Whitaker, 1975) highly evocative of the cultural and physical nature of the process. Apart from a limited amount of early research on London (Hamnett, 1973, 1976; Williams, 1976; Hamnett and Williams, 1979, 1980) and Paris (Bentham and Moseley, 1980; Moseley, 1980) most of the recent research has been conducted in North America where gentrification has been found to be occurring, among other places, in Washington (Zeitz, 1979; Gale, 1979), New Orleans (Laska and Spain, 1980a; O'Loughlin and Munski, 1979), Philadelphia (Cybriwsky, 1978; Smith, 1979b), New York (Winters, 1979), Columbus, Ohio (Harris, 1976; Ford and Fusch, 1976; Fusch, 1980), Vancouver (Stobie, 1979; Fujii, 1981; Ley, 1981), Toronto (Maher, 1974), Seattle (Hodge, 1980, 1981) and Boston (Pattison, 1977). It has also been identified in Australia in Adelaide (Badcock and Urlich Cloher, 1981), and Melbourne (Maher, 1979). Although these well-documented studies are collectively highly significant, they are almost all studies of individual cities (see Gale, 1979) and for a wider perspective on the scale and extent of gentrification we have to turn to three other more general but far less detailed American studies.

On the basis of research conducted between 1976 and 1979, Clay (1979) found evidence of private residential reinvestment in all thirty of America's largest cities. The pace and extent of this renewal varied considerably, however, with only one or two relatively small neighbourhoods being involved and no more than 50 per cent and sometimes as little as 20 per cent of the houses in these neighbourhoods having been physically rehabilitated. Clay found Washington to have perhaps the most extensive neighbourhood renewal with 'several reinvestment neighbourhoods almost completely surrounding the central business and government area'. San Francisco and Seattle also had extensive private renewal. Clay also found at the other extreme cities like Detroit, Newark and Cleveland with small-scale and very limited reinvestment. Finally, Clay found a middle range of older cities such as St Louis, Baltimore, Philadelphia, New Orleans and Boston where significant private renewal was associated with wider economic decline and population loss.

Whilst illustrative, it must be said that Clay's methodology was not particularly rigorous, consisting as it did of no more than a survey of expert informants in the thirty largest cities, field visits to half of them and examination of secondary materials. Much the same can be said of the second general survey by the Urban Land Institute reported in Black et al. (1977) and Black (1980). A mail and telephone survey in 1975 of 260 central cities with populations of 50 000 and over resulted in 143 useable responses—a 55 per cent response rate; a response from at least one of three city offices or departments being judged acceptable. The response rate was virtually 100 per cent with cities over 250 000 but only 66 per cent in cities of 100 000–250 000 and only 30 per cent in cities of 50 000–100 000. On the basis of the survey results it was estimated that 124 of the central cities were experiencing 'some degree of private-market, non subsidized housing renovation in older, deteriorated areas'. The incidence of renovation varied directly with city size—with 19 or 73 per cent of the 26 cities over 500 000 experiencing some renovation activity, compared to 63 per cent of the 30 cities from 250 000–500 000, 58 per cent of those from 100 000–250 000, and 32 per cent of those from 50 000–100 000. It should be noted that these figures were produced by the rather dubious procedure of assuming no bias in the responses for the two lower-size classes and applying the percentage of positive responses for each size class to the total number of cities in each class. So too, the precise degree of renovation remained unspecified. In January 1979 the Urban Land Institute undertook a further national survey of central-city investment activity in 88 central cities with a population of 150 000 or more. On the basis of responses from 64 cities, it was found that renovation activity was reported in 86 per cent of cities with more than 150 000 people compared to 65 per cent in 1975. The number of units renovated was also found to be several times greater on average for the period 1975–1978 than in the period 1968–1975 covered by the earlier survey. For the 42 cities providing estimates, the average for the two time periods was 1200 in 1975–1978 compared to 440 in 1968–1975.

Of the three general surveys conducted, that by Lipton (1977) is perhaps the most rigorous though his methodology can also be criticized. Focusing on the core areas (rather problematically defined as those areas within two miles of the central business district (CBD)) of the twenty largest SMSAs in the United States, Lipton used Census tract data for 1960 and 1970 to compare the number of tracts with median family incomes and median educational attainments greater than or equal to that for the SMSA as a whole in each time period. This rather crude aggregate measure is of course biased towards higher-status tracts and excludes the possibility of significant gentrification in lower-status tracts which does not bring them up to the SMSA median. It also excludes the possibility of significant gentrification occurring in a limited number of tracts which are already of median or higher status. It is, therefore, quite possible for gentrification to have occurred in certain tracts whilst the number of tracts at or above the median level remains constant or even falls over time if deterioration is still occurring in some of them. Lipton in fact admitted that census tracts could contain both rich and poor and that this would distort his findings. Lipton's analysis was also carried out for the period 1960–1970 whereas it is commonly believed that gentrification only really got under way in any scale in many cities during the 1970s (Spain, 1980, p. 27). This is a problem which bedevils all attempts to study gentrification using census data and it is only when the detailed small area results of the 1980 censuses of Canada and the United States and the 1981 Census of population in Britain are published that it will be possible to assess systematically the scale and extent of gentrification. These major methodological caveats aside, Lipton sought to address the highly pertinent questions as to whether:

phenomena such as Georgetown in Washington D.C. and the brownstone revival in New York City are simply minor exceptions to the basic structural changes and population shifts . . . or are they early indicators of still another new pattern of population change in American cities? Is it possible that *some* American cities are beginning to experience a rebirth in the desirability of central-city locations for middle and upper-income residential use or is this phenomenon so rare and unique as to be largely lost in the continuation of the earlier pattern of outward flight by any population segments with sufficient wealthier social status to allow them access to more suburban locations? (Lipton, 1977, p. 137, emphasis added).

Lipton found three distinct trends. First, there were three cities (New York, Washington, and Boston) in which the number of tracts at or above the median increased over the 1960s. A second group (Philadelphia, Seattle, Minneapolis, Pittsburgh, Milwaukee, Los Angeles, and Baltimore), showed a decline in the number of tracts at or above the median within the two-mile radius of the CBD but showed an increase within or directly adjacent to the CBD. The third group of cities (San Francisco, Dallas, Houston, Atlanta, Cleveland, St Paul, and Newark) showed deteriorating or stagnant cores during the 1960s. On the basis of his analysis Lipton (1977, p. 57–58) concluded that 'while not all cities examined showed . . . signs (of gentrification), enough did to call into question the universal acceptance of the inappropriateness of central-city locations as residential sites for those who have the financial ability to make a choice'.

Taken collectively these studies highlight a number of important points, not the least of which is that evidence of a significant degree of gentrification has so far been confined to only a relatively small number of large metropolitan cities. As will be argued, the city-specific nature of gentrification has important theoretical implications. It is clearly not a general or universal phenomenon within all Western capitalist cities and its concentration requires explanation.

TRADITIONAL MODELS OF RESIDENTIAL LOCATION AND NEIGHBOURHOOD CHANGE

The traditional models of residential location, namely those of Burgess (1925), Hoyt (1939) and Alonso (1960, 1964) all point in the same direction. Higher-status groups live on or towards the periphery of the urban area. There is a positive correlation between distance from the city centre and higher social status. Whilst Johnston (1966, 1969, 1970, 1971, 1972) has pointed to the existence of numerous empirical discrepancies, these models still exert a powerful influence as does the related idea of the one-way process of downwards filtering of both houses and neighbourhoods. As Evans (1973, p. 139) put it: 'The high-income households who locate, at, or near, the centre provide one of the most interesting problems in the analysis of patterns of residential location.

For one thing, many American authors seem to imply that no such households exist or that, if they do, they are at a sub-optimal location.' In so far as gentrification would seem partially to confound these traditional conceptions it is useful to examine them in detail with a view to highlighting the historically and culturally specific nature of the assumptions on which they are based.

Burgess and Hoyt

Turning first to Burgess, perhaps the most important point to be made regarding his concentric zone theory was that it was a theory of residential differentiation through outwards growth. In what must be one of the classic physical reifications of a socio-spatial process, Burgess (1925) declared that: 'The typical process of the expansion of the city can best be illustrated, perhaps, by a series of concentric circles which may be numbered to designate both the successive zones of urban extension and the types of areas differentiated in the process of expansion.' The zones themselves are too well known to merit description here, suffice to note that they illustrated what Burgess (1925) referred to as: 'the main fact of expansion, namely the tendency of each inner core to extend its area by the invasion of the next outer zone. This aspect of expansion may be called *succession*.' Burgess was quite explicit that the *pattern* of concentric zonation be identified was an ideal-type model, noting that: 'it hardly needs to be added that neither Chicago nor any other city fits perfectly into this ideal scheme'. He did not make this qualification of the process of invasion and succession, however, and it would appear that he viewed the downward transition of neighbourhoods as a general if not a universal characteristic of urban growth, irrespective of the precise form taken by the pattern of concentric zonation.

Robson (1969, p. 13) described the Burgess model as 'the logical, spatial expression of human ecological concepts' but this is far from being the case as the model can only be derived from these by making very strong assumptions regarding the locational preferences of the high-income groups. Burgess though did not in fact make the explicit assumption of a preference for suburban living on the part of the affluent and hence identify the high income 'Gold Coast' sector along the lakeshore. On the contrary, his conception of the process of outwards growth and differentiation was very much one of the outwards push of invasion and succession and Johnston (1969) rightly describes this as a special case of filtering. This is clearly seen in Burgess's reference to the invasion of cities like Chicago and New York by tens of thousands of immigrants annually. This, as Burgess argues, has the effect of a tidal wave inundating first the immigrant colonies, the ports of first entry, dislodging thousands of inhabitants who overflow into the next zone, and so on and on until the momentum of the wave has spent its force on the last urban zone. The whole effect is to speed up the process of expansion, to speed up industry, to speed up the '*junking*' process in the area of deterioration (Burgess, 1925, p. 58). Downward neighbourhood change in Burgess's eyes was then very much a product of pressure of numbers working outwards from the centre and as a historical description of Chicago in the early years of this century it was no doubt very accurate. As is now commonly recognized, however, it was based on a highly historically and culturally specific set of conditions that are no longer operative (Freedman 1967; Robson, 1969; Lipton, 1979).

Unfortunately this simple yet central point is all too often neglected or forgotten. European immigration was largely halted by the late 1920s and the subsequent black immigration into the northern cities is now also much reduced though partly replaced by the immigration of Hispanic groups. Most of the larger older central cities are now losing population and have been throughout the 1960s and 1970s (Barabba, 1980). A marked change has also occurred in the nature of the labour market and the occupational structure of many of the larger cities over the last twenty years as industry has decentralized or disappeared to be replaced by an increasing amount of white-collar office employment. Quite clearly, Burgess's model was based on a set of historical assumptions which, although still just valid at the time he wrote, were to change rapidly during the course of the next fifty years.

Hoyt (1939) was led to stress the sectoral organization of cities as a result of his work on movement of high rent areas in twenty-five American cities from 1900 to 1935. More importantly, Hoyt identified three dynamic factors working for the growth and outwards expansion of the city and of the high rent areas within it. The first, as with Burgess, was the continual flow of in-migrants. Second, there was the steady deterioration of existing structures which caused existing high-rent areas to become less desirable, and third, there was obsolescence. In Hoyt's words: 'The constant competition of new areas is itself a cause of neighbourhood shifts. Every building boom with its new crop of structures equipped with the latest modern devices pushes all existing structures a notch down in the scale of desirability.'

However, as Hoyt noted, it is not the movement of the buildings, but the changing character of their occupants that produces neighbourhood change. Hoyt termed such changes 'filtering' as opposed to the classical ecological concepts of invasion and succession utilized by Burgess and the mechanism, if not the result, was viewed very differently: 'The new houses constructed for the occupancy of the higher rental groups are situated on the outward edge of the high rent area. As these areas grow outwards the lower and intermediate rental groups filter into the homes *given up* by the higher income groups' (Hoyt, 1939, p. 122).

The motive force of downward filtering as Hoyt saw it was clearly the provision of desirable new peripheral structures. How far the expansionary pressures of the lower and intermediate rental groups exercised an influence on this remains unclear. The point, however, is that neighbourhood change was viewed by both Hoyt and Burgess as a one-way *downwards* process. Whilst Hoyt noted that luxury apartments were frequently replacing older tenements and sub-standard housing in the centre of New York, he remained of the view that the movement of the high-rent area in any direction but outwards was generally impossible since 'the wealthy seldom reverse their steps and move backwards into the obsolete housing which they are giving up' (p. 118).

Whereas this view may have been generally valid in the context of its time it embodies a very specific set of assumptions regarding both the rate of urban growth and the desirability of newer structures which gentrification calls into question. Gentrification also challenges the central assumption of much of the filtering literature which is that filtering is a uni-directional downwards process. Thus, Grigsby (1963, p. 17) states that 'filtering occurs only when values *decline* more rapidly than quality, so that families can obtain either higher quality or more space at the same price, or the same quality and space at a lower price than formerly' (my emphasis). Ratcliff (1949, p. 32) similarly defined filtering as: 'the changing of occupancy as the housing that is occupied by one income group becomes available to the next *lower* income group as a result of a *decline* in market prices' (my emphasis). Only Smith's (1964, p. 14) definition of filtering as 'the occupancy of particular houses or neighbourhoods by some different class of households . . . in response to any change in the conditions of supply and demand' is sufficiently flexible to accommodate the possibility of both upwards and downwards filtering, and hence the existence of gentrification which Maher (1974) identified in a price-based study of filtering in Toronto over the period 1953–1971.

Alonso and space preference

When we turn to Alonso's (1960) theory of the urban land market and his subsequent (1964) comparison of the 'historical theory' of Burgess and his own 'structural' theory, we find a similar set of assumptions. Again, the general nature and outcome of Alonso's bid rent model are too well known to warrant repetition here. It should merely be noted that the seeming paradox that 'the poor will tend to central locations on expensive land and the rich to cheaper land on the periphery' which is explained by Alonso as a result of accessibility behaving as an inferior good for higher income groups, rests on a clearly expressed preference by both groups to live at lower densities. Indeed, Alonso clearly states that 'the structural forces depend on tastes' (Alonso, 1964, p. 230). Although he goes on to accept that 'there is in the United States a substantial minority of the well-to-do that does prefer accessibility to space and this minority lives in luxury apartments or town houses in the central area', he firmly adheres to the strength of the preference for space and lower densities. As he puts it:

Taste and preference for space are possibly words too weak to denote what is really meant by this key variable of the structural theory. Rather, the nature of the demand for space in this country seems to be a deeply engrained cultural value, associated not only with such functional needs as play space for children, but also with basic attitudes towards nature, privacy and the meaning of the family. (Alonso, 1964, p. 230)

Leaving aside the dubious analytical validity of consumer taste and preference as the main or sole determinant of urban residential structure, a view strongly criticized by Form (1954), Gray (1975), Boddy (1975), Smith (1979a,b) and others, a change in such preferences could clearly have a profound impact, as Alonso himself recognized. This possibility has also been noted by Lave (1970) and Simmons (1968) who observed that: 'A shift in middle-class norms regarding the value of access to downtown could be more significant than all the urban renewal to date.' Indeed, Alonso himself argues in relation to those cities where the rich apparently place no great value on space and tend instead to live near the centre that: 'This is in agreement with the structural theory because, as there is no attraction in the substitution of space for accessibility, greater purchasing power is used to buy greater accessibility' (Alonso, 1964, p. 230). The problem of course with this type of analysis is that the basis of the seeming difference in preferences is not examined and nor, indeed, is the structure of the housing market.

Bid-rent theory is capable of being applied, after the fact, to any given pattern of residential distribution and the structure of preferences allegedly embodied therein. This criticism applies not just to Alonso's justification of the validity of his theory to cities where the rich are centrally located but also to Evans's (1973) extension and elaboration of Alonso's basic model to incorporate the existence of different sets of preferences on the part of the rich. Although Evans's analysis clearly represents a major step forward in terms of formal marginalist economic theory, the variation in the income elasticities for space on the part of the rich which he incorporates are taken as given and remain unexamined and unexplained. When Evans sets about explaining the consequences of an increase in the size of the high-income group wishing to locate near the centre, the antecedent causes are referred to merely as 'some reason'. Thus, although Evans's theory is capable of 'explaining' any given pattern *post hoc*, it is dependent upon the parameters of choice and preference being specified indirectly through location. It thus suffers all the defects of the 'revealed preference' approach (Rushton, 1969, 1971) in which the existence of supposed preference structures are inferred from aggregate outcomes. Even on the assumption that residential location is solely a product of preferences, the origin and basis of different changing preference remain a black box.

The residential structure of cities is not, however, purely a product of residential preferences, nor, as Harvey (1973) and others have pointed out, is it the product of an instantaneous equilibrium solution. It is the product of a specific process of historical development and to ignore this is to fall into the trap of ahistorical abstraction. Indeed, as Kirby (1976) has pointed out, Alonso's model is actually a model of land rather than housing consumption. In consequence, it ignores the tenure-specific nature of the historical process of urban development, by which the inner areas are dominated more by rental than owner-occupied housing. This is clearly completely unrealistic.

In consequence, Bassett and Short's (1980, p. 24) criticism of the ecological approach applies equally to bid-rent theory. As they noted:

> The ecological approach, by considering the nature of housing supply and allocation in early twentieth century North America as a constant, given and often 'natural' variable, is unable to say anything meaningful about the structure of the housing market and consequently has little explanation to offer for the patterns of residential differentiation which it describes.

Alonso's critique of 'historical' theory

If the *post hoc* flexibility of bid-rent theory stems from its ahistorical abstraction, the contemporary validity of the classical ecological modes of Burgess and Hoyt can be questioned precisely because of the highly cultural and historical specific manner in which they were formulated. It is singularly ironic, therefore, that the only attempt to reformulate them in a more generalized and less historically specific fashion should have been made by one of their sternest critics in the context of a paper assessing the relative validity of the two approaches and their implications for urban renewal.

The crucial point made by Alonso, and the focus of his attack on what he terms the 'historical theory', is that, whereas both the historical and the 'structural' theories tended in practice to have the same outcome in terms of urban structure up until the early 1960s, the residential urban renewal programmes for the inner urban areas assume that the provision of land and new structures will attract the rich back. In effect says Alonso:

> It makes land available in the center for high income housing, while still endorsing the trickle-down view of the housing market. If correct, this means that Americans will no longer follow each other like lemmings from the center to the suburbs and then to the exurbs as population grows and buildings age. Rather, this centrifugal expansion will now be turned inwards and the *growth ring will be near the centre*. The suburbs, as time goes by, and buildings age, will become available to those of lower income. But of course the new central housing built by urban renewal will in time age also and the wealthy will again be on the move. . . . Following this reasoning, *urban renewal in the long run will be a ring expending outwards*, through the urban mass, leaving behind a gradient of housing that ages toward the center and pushing against the

oldest housing of the urban area until the center is once again the oldest and the process starts again. *Thus, the simple movement outward of high income to the suburbs will be replaced by a convection flow like that of boiling water in a pot.* (Alonso, 1964, p. 228) (my emphasis)

As Alonso recognizes, this is a highly simplified view of the implications of historical theory for urban renewal. For the process to work 'there must be a balance of the rates of population growth, new construction, aging of buildings, and the structure of demand, according to income, age and type of families' (Alonso, 1964, p. 228). Alonso of course challenged this formulation on the grounds that higher-income groups are not attracted to new or rehabilitated housing *per se*, be it central or peripheral but to the space to be found on the periphery. As he put it:

Structural theory represents the working out of tastes, costs and income in the structure of the market, It does not rely on the historical process although this process is undeniable and has been a strong influence reinforcing the structural forces. To put it another way, the structural theory says that a city which developed so quickly that the structure had no time to age would still show the same basic urban form: low income near the centre and high income further out. (Alonso, 1964, p. 229)

The point of this discussion, however, is not so much whether structural or historical theory provides the more valid historical explanation, but that Alonso inadvertently opened up the possibility of a more general historical theory which incorporates the temporal dynamics of change in urban areas as a central element.

This alone of course is inadequate, for as I argue in the following section, a purely mechanical model or urban residential location based solely or even largely on the historical aging process of buildings and not also on the changing occupational and demographic structure of the population and the changing nature of housing supply cannot explain a great deal. It does, however, represent a step in the right direction away from a largely static, pattern-dominated conception of urban residential structure and towards a conception based more on the processes of change which produce urban residential patterns. Again somewhat ironically, Alonso made precisely this point in attacking urban renewal schemes based on what he saw as a simplified conception of the historical theory. Arguing that current renewal projects were in danger of 'skimming a narrow and specialized sector of demand which will soon dry up' (p. 231), Alonso outlined an essentially demographic explanation for the increase in apartment construction in the centre of some American cities in the late 1950s and early 1960s. Referring to the convection-flow life cycle of the American middle class family, Alonso argued that:

The young and the old need apartments while it is those in their thirties that power the demand for single-family houses. Those reaching the age of thirty these days are those who were born in the Great Depression when the birth rate fell dramatically. Thus, in the 1960–70 decade there is less demand for single-family houses because there are 9 per cent fewer people coming into their thirties than in the 1950 to 1960 decade. But this situation will change sharply in 1970: there will be an increase of almost 40 per cent among those reaching their thirties in the 1970–80 decade over the 1960–70 decade. Thus we may attribute much of the shift from single to multiple dwellings to temporary changes in the age composition of the population rather than to fundamental change in taste and we may expect that these changes will be short-lived. (Alonso, 1964, p. 230)

The argument made here by Alonso is a highly important one and, demographic changes have a considerable part to play in explaining not only the rise of gentrification in the inner areas of certain large cities in the 1970s but also its likely future. We cannot however, as Alonso seems to do, view both the decrease in the birthrate in the 1930s and the increase immediately post-war as aberrations from some long-term trend which, when running smoothly, results in a continuing demand for peripheral-suburban, single-family housing from those middle-class households entering their thirties. On the contrary, it would appear that Alonso is attempting to both have his cake and eat it by attributing the likely fall in demand for single-family housing in both the 1950s and the 1970s to, on the one hand the result of an earlier fall in the birth rate and, on the other, to the result of a rise in the birth-rate. The point that needs to be made is that, just as in the early years of this century when, high immigration into American cities resulted in rapid outward growth and downwards filtering, all changes in urban residential structure are historically specific and contingent. There is no universal pattern.

STAGE MODELS OF URBAN RESIDENTIAL CHANGE

The need to modify traditional theories of residential location had been apparent long before gentrification. In what remains by far and away the most systematic and comprehensive summary of research on the residential patterning of cities, Johnston (1971) highlighted the fact that the elite areas of many cities are not peripheral, even within the high status sector(s) tending instead towards an intermediate or even central position. The stability of such areas over time has also been remarked by Firey (1947), Davis (1965), Johnston (1971) and others and Schnore (1965, p. 84) referred to 'the persistence of elite areas near the centre of many cities'.

From the finding that high-status areas are not necessarily susceptible to inevitable downwards filtering it is but a short step to the idea that under the appropriate market conditions they may even expand into adjacent lower-status areas. The historically specific context of Burgess and Hoyt's work has already been alluded to and it is significant that on the basis of his analysis of the 1940 Chicago census data, Freedman (1967) cast doubt on one of the central assumptions of both models, namely that city growth proceeds outwards from the centre propelled by a high rate of in-migration into the central areas.

It would seem, therefore, that the traditional ecological theories of Burgess and Hoyt constitute no more than historically and culturally specific generalizations based on assumptions related to the conditions prevailing at the time they were formulated. They may have accurately described the structure and process of neighbourhood change characteristic of early twentieth century American industrial cities but their contemporary relevance and applicability is open to doubt.

It is important to note in this context that both Burgess and Hoyt may well have stood too close to their subject matter historically speaking to be able to place the downward transition of inner-city neighbourhoods in a wider historical context. Both authors were writing of cities which had only begun to grow rapidly in the last quarter of the nineteenth century and had not existed long enough for any longer-term changes to become apparent. Thus, it is interesting that Hoover and Vernon (1959), Birch (1971) and Hartshorn (1971) have all postulated the existence of a general cycle of growth, decline and (potential) revitalization and renewal. Hoover and Vernon identified a five-stage cycle of neighbourhood change on the basis of their work in New York, the fifth and final stage of which was one of residential upgrading, especially in neighbourhoods close to the city centre. Whilst it should be borne in mind that they saw no inevitability in the sequence, neighbourhoods remaining at any stage almost indefinitely, they believed that if change occurred it was likely to be in the direction of neighbourhood deterioration, residential upgrading being limited to only a few areas. Similarly, Hartshorn (1971, p. 95) concluded on the basis of a detailed empirical analysis of neighbourhood change in Cedar Rapids, Iowa during the period 1940–1960 'significant renewal occurs only after severe downgrading has taken place ... decline and expansion, improvement and contraction of housing quality are apparently instances of the same basic process of residential change'. A more systematic theoretical explanation of this process in terms of the continuing search for profitability by capital is provided by Smith (1979a) in the subsequent section of this paper. Meanwhile, it should be borne in mind that both Hoover and Vernon and Hartshorn were writing on the 1940s and 1950s. The occurrence of gentrification in the 1970s puts the concept of a cycle of neighbourhood growth, decline and renewal in a fresh light.

More generally, Schnore (1965) has suggested that both the pre-industrial pattern in which social status decreased with distance from the city centre and the Burgess-type pattern in which social status increased with distance from the city centre are 'both special cases more adequately subscribed under a more general theory of residential land-uses in urban areas' (Schnore, 1965, p. 324). Schnore went on to suggest that whereas it had been previously generally assumed that two separate patterns existed which had evolved under distinct and separate conditions, they could instead be seen as 'separate stages of a single evolutionary sequence, whose basic independent variable is a society's level of modernization' (Johnston, 1972, p. 86).

The deployment of evolutionary models of any kind, but particularly of a cross-cultural nature, is a dangerous exercise fraught with difficulties, not the least of which is the idea that the stages are necessary and inevitable rather than historically and culturally contingent. Johnston (1972) rejected Schnore's model as an over-simplification and suggested instead an alternative formulation which focused on the 'development of the middle classes and their attendant housing choice behaviour'. On the basis of a wide-ranging empirical summary, Johnston went on to advance a three-stage model which attempted to explain the development of occupational and class differentiation from the pre-industrial city onwards in terms of the development of occupational differentiation and class stratification. Whilst a variety of detailed objections can be made to the highly schematic nature of Johnston's formulation, it remains the case that it represents virtually the sole attempt to relate the changing pattern of residential differentiation to the evolving class structure. Johnston also stressed the tentative and non-definitive nature of his model, arguing rightly that whereas a great deal of effort has been expended attacking Burgess and Hoyt's models on the basis of specific empirical studies, few attempts have been made to work towards any more general conception. This said, however, Johnston's attempt to sketch out a historical sequence of the development of urban residential structure is marred by his depiction of the third stage as the final one. Given Johnston's attempt to formulate a historical stage model this is a remarkably ahistorical conception as the widespread occurrence of gentrification in certain large Western capitalist cities clearly indicates. At the very least, therefore, gentrification serves to point up Schnore's view that the traditional models of urban residential patterning must be seen as special cases of a more general theory. Indeed, it is suggested that 'with the revitalization process of the past decade, sections of the post-industrial inner city have begun a transformation from the home of the labouring classes toward a zone of privilege reminiscent of the innermost residential ring in Sjoberg's model of the pre-industrial city' (Ley, 1981, p. 145).

How far such a transformation will proceed remains to be seen, but what is clear is that any attempt to theorize and explain the rise of gentrification must go considerably beyond the ecological models specifying the nature of the processes involved. As Robson (1969, p. 131) has observed, the work of the Chicago school of social ecology tended to foster a concern 'with the isolation of models *per se*, rather than the isolation of these forces which operate within urban areas to produce residential patterns'.

Indeed, apart from the vague passing reference to the process of distribution which 'sifts and sorts and relocates individuals and groups by residence and occupation' in the expansion of the city, Burgess's analysis is remarkable for the virtual absence of any reference to process. Although subsequent attempts have been made to rectify this situation (see Johnston, 1980). Firey's (1947) comment that 'nowhere in this theory is there a definite statement of the *modus operandi* by which people are propelled to their appointed niches in space' remains a valid assessment of the initial formulations.

TOWARDS AN INTEGRATED THEORY OF GENTRIFICATION

The rapid growth of gentrification in the late 1960s and early 1970s was followed by an equally rapid expansion of the literature on gentrification in the late 1970s. Perhaps predictably, most of this literature consisted of empirical case studies, more concerned with the description of the phenomenon, its incidence, scale and effects, than with any attempt at systematic explanation.

Such 'explanations' as have been preferred have generally consisted of little more than tentative explanation sketches, commonly drawing on a taken-for-granted model of changing lifestyles and consumer preferences. Not until 1979 were the first attempts made to systematically identify and critically examine the various types of explanation which had been advanced (Hamnett and Williams, 1979; Smith, 1979a). Both papers pointed to the dominance of demand-orientated explanations to date and both, to varying degrees attempted to rectify the situation by developing institutional, supply-side political economy explanations. Smith's analysis is by far the most sophisticated theoretically developed explanation available to date and any attempt to develop a systematic explanation of gentrification must take his work as a major point of departure. Accordingly, Smith's analysis will be the subject of a detailed individual critique later in this review. First, however, it is necessary to outline the major conventional explanations to which Smith's analysis represents a response and a reaction.

Gentrification is very much a product of the late 1960s and 1970s and it is only found on any significant scale in the inner areas of major Western cities such as London, Paris, Washington, San Francisco, Toronto and Vancouver. The explanatory problem, therefore, is to account for the marked temporal and spatial incidence of gentrification. Why has gentrification occurred when and where it has? There are perhaps five main conventional explanations or explanatory factors which are by no means mutually exclusive and have been advanced by different authors in a variety of combinations. They are, in order, first, the impact of increasing city size and changes in the trade-off between the preference for space and accessibility, second, changes in the demographic and household structure of the population, third, lifestyle and preference shifts, fourth, changes in relative house price inflation and investment, and fifth, changes in the employment base and occupational structure of certain large cities.

Space and accessibility

In terms of the trade-off models of Alonso (1960), Muth (1969) and others, residential location is viewed as a trade-off between preference for space and accessibility. As was indicated earlier, Alonso (1964) recognized the possibility of a small number of high-income residents living in city-centre apartments but argued that this was very much a minority taste. Evans (1973) subsequently elaborated and extended Alonso's basic model by incorporating a number of different bid-rent curves, thereby allowing the existence of a high-income, central residential area in terms of the theory. Even in terms of bid-rent theory this does not explain why gentrification has recently come to prominence: it is very much a static, cross-sectional explanation. It is, however, possible to introduce a shift of preference (and bid-rent curves) into the model, and the notion that the increasing size of metropolitan areas may lead to increased commuting journeys and commuting costs, and thus to (re)centralization, has quite a long history. Alonso (1964, p. 230) comments that 'as metropolitan areas have grown bigger and roads more congested it may be that some have come to feel that the commuting trip is too long and have returned to central locations'. Similarly, Richards (1963) suggested that:

> one would anticipate that accessibility desires would vary over time in large, growing, urban areas. As the population increases and the city grows outwards by accretion, the problem of accessibility becomes more important to urban inhabitants ... certain individuals become willing to substitute amenities on the outer fringe to satisfy their desire for accessibility to the inner core.

The Milner-Holland report (1965) related this thesis specifically to London: 'The sum of the waste of time and effort and money and discomfort attendant upon this arrangement (commuting) is immeasurable, and it has had its own reaction. There are some who have bought old houses in the inner parts of London rather than face such a daily journey' (p. 20).

There is no doubt some truth in this thesis but it is not without major defects. First, and perhaps most importantly, it leaves out of account those elements of residential (re)centralization which are related to factors other than increased commuting costs. It ignores the increased attractiveness of central residential locations for some groups. Second, there is the related assumption which is made explicit by Alonso that increased commuting times are related solely to *re*centralization. By ignoring the fact that many new young households originate in the inner city, it excludes the equal if not stronger possibility that gentrification may represent continuing centralization, young households deciding against a move out to the suburbs. Herein lies the origins of the myth which views gentrification as a return or back to the city movement; a myth convincingly scotched by the findings of Chambers (1974), Gale (1979) and Smith (1979a). Third, there is the inbuilt assumption of trade-off models that a space/amenity—accessibility continuum exists where more of one implies less of the other. This is a direct product of the ahistorical nature of trade-off models and it ignores the fact that generally speaking people do not compete for land but for houses (Kirby, 1976). The overwhelming majority of the housing stock is not new and many inner-city areas contain substantial period houses, many of which are considerably larger and more spacious than a good deal of the newer inter-war and post-war suburban housing. In Britain at least, the increasing cost of land and construction has tended to lead to a decline rather than an increase in average house size over the last 30–40 years (Ball and Kirwan, 1977). Finally, notwithstanding the weakness of trade-off arguments in general, the commuting cost/accessibility thesis fails both to distinguish these individuals or groups who decide to opt for more accessible locations from those who do not and to explain why the balance of space-versus-accessibility should have shifted so markedly in the late 1960s and 1970s. If we are adequately to explain this we must turn to a consideration of the second explanatory factor, that of demographic change.

Demographic change

A number of commentators, notably Clay (1980), Long (1980), and Berry (1980), have pointed to the changing demographic situation as a key factor underpinning gentrification. As Clay (1980, p. 15) put it: 'The question of why reinvestment is occurring now rather than in the 1960s and early 1970s . . . can be answered partially by examining the maturation of the post-war baby boom cohort.' There is a number of aspects which are common to the post-war demographic changes experienced in both Britain and the United States as well as in other advanced Western industrial economies. First, as the earlier discussion of Alonso (1964) indicated, both Britain and America experienced a substantial increase in the birth rate between 1946 and 1955, followed by a more or less continual decline. In consequence the early 1970s saw the beginning of a rapid increase in the birth cohorts aged 20–24 years which, as is well known, had previously placed considerable demands on the educational systems and which is likely, other things being equal, to place similar demands on care for the elderly in the early decade of the next century. This group is of major importance in determining the rate of new household formation, and Gilg (1977) has argued that they played a major part in the house-price explosion of the early 1970s in Britain where they increased by 30 per cent between 1968 and 1972. In the United States Grebler and Mittelbach (1979) have shown that the 25–30 age group increased from 22 millions or 11.5 per cent of the total population in 1965 to 33 million or nearly 15 per cent of the population in 1976. Alonso (1977) has also shown that between 1970 and 1985 the 25–35 age group will have increased by no less than 58 per cent.

An important related factor has been the increase in the number and type of separate households. Thus, whilst the number of households in the United States increased by 15 per cent from 1970 to 1976, their average size has steadily declined from 3.67 persons in 1940 to 2.89 in 1976 (Alonso, 1977). This reduction in the average size of households is a product not just of the increase in the young-adult age groups already referred to but to life-style changes which have resulted in a falling proportion of traditional nuclear families. Households headed by single women increased by 33 per cent from 1970 to 1976 and households comprised or two or more unrelated individuals increased by 67 per cent (Alonso, 1977) and, as a result by 1978 over half of all American households were comprised of either one or two adults.

The implications of these changes for housing demand will clearly have been considerable and the spatial expression of that demand is likely to have been highly unequal given the traditional over-representation of young-adult households in the inner city (see Stapleton, 1980). As Long has put it:

A life cycle effect (person's in their 20s traditionally being attracted to cities) may be interacting with an age cohort effect (more persons in their 20s) to boost city populations at this age group, while other trends (smaller households, more two owner-households), and rising prices of single family homes may be keeping more of them in cities. It is certainly *not* a back to the city movement as some have suggested. (Long, 1980, p. 66)

What is equally clear is that whilst these demographic changes provide a strong demographic underpinning for emergence of gentrification on a major scale in the 1970s they do not, of themselves constitute an explanation of where and why it occurred. Demographic changes alone are not a sufficient condition for the occurrence of gentrification but, as will be shown, they have important implications for the continuation of gentrification on a major scale.

Lifestyle and preference shifts

The changing demographic structure of the population is frequently held to have been associated with life-style changes which have had important consequences for residential preferences. Thus it has been suggested that: 'There have been significant changes in lifestyle that decrease the relative desirability of single-family, suburban homes compared to central-city multiple-family dwellings. Decreasing family size has reduced the portion of adult's lives in which they must consider amenities that are child-related when choosing housing' (Lipton, 1977, p. 58).

Whilst decreasing family size may well be important, as Lipton suggests, it is arguable that it is the much greater number of childless households created by later marriage or deferred childbearing which is of primary importance. Berry (1980) and Lipton also suggest that the increase in the proportion of working women especially in professional, managerial and administration jobs will have a similar effect, especially in households where both husband and wife work centrally. Berry (1980, p. 22) argues that as a result of life-style shifts consequent upon greater economic opportunities for women, the rising direct and opportunity cost of child-rearing and the improvement of birth-control techniques, there has been a proliferation of new two-worker, professional, higher-income, childless home-owners, seeking inner-city neighbourhoods with good-quality housing, a wide variety of amenities within safe walking distance, and a range of high-quality retail and entertainment facilities.

Clearly, a high degree of accessibility is likely to prove highly desirable for young childless households working downtown for both employment and social reasons as Abu-Lughod (1961) argued more than twenty years ago (see also Stapleton, 1980). It would be naive, however, to attribute such shifts in residential location solely to shifts in the structure of residential preferences unconstrained by financial factors. Thus, Clay (1980, p. 16) suggests that: 'The rediscovery of city neighbourhoods is part of the way . . . young households are coping with the high cost of suburban housing that increasingly small proportions of them can afford.'

Housing supply and demand

Smith's 1979 analysis apart, the links between housing supply, house prices and gentrification have been most clearly articulated by Berry (1980). Starting from the premise that the crucial variable in understanding the rate of housing abandonment or rehabilitation in individual housing markets is the replacement supply—a product of the relationship between the rate of new housing construction and the rate of household growth, Berry argued that new housing construction and rehabilitation tend to be inversely related (see also Hay, 1981). Historically, says Berry, high rates of new suburban construction have resulted in faster abandonment of older inner-city housing as the existing housing stock in the oldest areas is devalued.

New housing construction increased rapidly during the building boom of the early 1970s, and the numbers of building permits taken out in central cities for residential alterations and additions slumped. After 1974, as the housing industry entered a period of combined inflation and recession, new housing construction lagged and private market revitalization of the inner city began to take hold. (Berry, 1980, p. 20)

Berry went on to argue that whilst part of reason for revitalization is the decline in new housing construction since 1974, the most rapid rate of house-price inflation and the most substantial degree of neighbourhood revitalization has been experienced in those metropolitan areas where the rate of replacement supply is least—in other words where the gap between new household creation and new housing construction is greatest. When this is combined with the marked increase in owner-occupation between 1970 and 1975, particularly among the younger age groups, the result, says Berry, is a strong demand for inner-city housing in superior neighbourhoods in those metropolitan areas with the lowest rates of replacement supply. Significantly, Berry goes on to link this to changes in employment structure, arguing that these metropolitan areas are precisely the ones in which:

There is a sufficient cluster of professional jobs to support the youthful college-educated labour force most likely to evidence supportive life-style shifts. An implication is that significant revitalization may be limited to the metropolitan centres with clusters of post-industrial management, control and information processing activities (Berry, 1980, p. 23)

especially to those with rapidly growing downtown office complexes. *This job base has permitted the emergence of a new life-style and community type: that of the new urban gentry.* (Berry, 1981, p. 68)

This is a crucial point and it leads us to a consideration of the last factor—that of employment structure.

Employment structure

Berry is not alone in stressing the key role of employment structure in providing, as it were, the occupational raw material for gentrification. The concentration of gentrification in cities with a highly developed, 'post-industrial' employment structure has also been given prominence by Ley (1980), who suggests that the growing service categories of quaternary office employment tend to be concentrated in the largest metropoitan centres. The quaternary sector says Ley, bears out Jefferson's dictum that 'the most skilled workers in every science and art' are to be found in primate cities, these groups being characterized by extreme geographic concentration at the national and intra-urban scales. Ley points out that Paris contains the headquarters offices of 90 per cent of France's major corporations and half its national civil-service jobs. Using figures from Daniels (1977) Ley shows that in 1971 London's quaternary employment (administrators and professionals) was *four times* as great as combined total for the remaining 5 British conurbations and its quaternary employment growth of 35 000 from 1966 to 1971 was *twelve times* greater than the total for the other 5 conurbations combined (see also Hamnett and Williams, 1979).

Looking specifically at Vancouver, Ley (1981) points out that the city is heavily dominated by the fast-growing tertiary and quaternary occupations, having some 70 per cent of its work-force in white-collar jobs in 1971. Ley also notes that some 75 per cent of the city's 7000 new jobs each year from 1971 to 1980, were generated by new office construction, some three-quarters of which is contained in the rapidly growing downtown area which doubled its office floor space in ten years. The importance of these changes, says Ley, is the fact that:

> It is possible to follow the transmission of large scale adjustments in the economy to the pattern of job creation in Vancouver, with trends favouring white-collar job growth in the central business district. These contextual factors lie behind demographic changes in the metropolitan area and the housing demand pressures that accompanied them (Ley, 1981, p. 128).

Thus, whilst Ley is also at pains to stress the relevance of the amenity and culture rich nature of inner city life to the explanation of gentrification, arguing that 'these desiderata of the culture of consumption should not be underestimated in interpreting the revitalization of the inner city', it is also clear that Ley accepts the importance of underlying structural changes.

The most explicit attempt systematically to assess on an empirical basis the impact of employment structure on the distribution and incidence of gentrification has been made by Lipton (1977). He postulated that gentrification would only be likely to occur where high-status, white-collar jobs were concentrated in and around the CBD and where commuting distances were high. In order to test this statistically, Lipton carried out regression and correlation analyses on the largest twenty SMSAs in the United States in an attempt to determine the extent to which gentrification was positively associated with these factors and negatively associated with manufacturing employment. Whilst criticisms can be made of aspects of Lipton's methodology, his analyses generally supported his thesis and he concluded that 'those cities that have administrative CBD's without heavy industry, and with significant commuting distance to the suburbs from the core were likely to contain middle class and upper class neighbourhoods near the centre' (Lipton, 1977, p. 146).

What then can we conclude thus far regarding the causes of gentrification? The problem is to distinguish and separate out the contribution of a number of inter-related factors. Clearly, city size and increasing commuting costs and distances are of some importance but of themselves these factors do not take us very far. Nor does the idea of some autonomous change in preferences away from new suburban housing and towards older period housing. Clearly, changing life styles and preferences have played a considerable role in the process, not least because of the frequent association between gentrification and areas of architecturally attractive housing and the oft-mentioned occupational characteristics of the gentrifiers themselves. As we have seen, however, there have been wider forces at work and to the extent that the 'new brahmins' of North London and elsewhere are mostly intellectual and artistic entrepreneurs, as Raban (1974) rather maliciously categorizes them, this is a consequence not so much of a change of tastes as of the fact that the changes in the demographic, educational, and employment structure has meant that there are far more of them. Equally, whilst it may be true to say, as Raban (1974) does, that gentrifiers choose their environment as 'a social and architectural complement to their scrupulous . . . sense of their own identity', it is equally clear that the spatial expression of such tastes and preferences are made manifest in the residential location achievable under the constraint of financial availability.

To the extent that it is possible to synthesize the various explanatory factors identified thus far, it would appear that changes in the demographic and employment structure have led simultaneously to a growing concentration in certain large cities of young, relatively affluent and highly educated childless households, frequently with one or more city-centre workers with a strong preference for accessibility. They have faced (and partly created) a structure of housing supply and rapidly rising house prices which, if it has not actually necessitated inner-city residence, has certainly pointed strongly in that direction. An understanding of the role played by the housing market is clearly crucial for any explanation of gentrification as the analyses of Berry (1980) and others make clear and it is to a critique of Smith's work in this area that the next section is addressed.

SMITH'S THEORY OF GENTRIFICATION

A satisfactory analysis of the changing role and structure of the housing market is obviously a key element in the explanation of gentrification as the pioneering work of Williams (1976) clearly shows. Unfortunately, the early concentration on choice and preference-based explanations of gentrification has tended to play down, if not actually ignore, this vital element. Whilst an attempt was made by Hamnett and Williams (1979) to analyse the growth of gentrification in terms of the political economy of the housing market, the work of Smith (1979a, 1982) constitutes by far the most sophisticated, theoretically developed, explanation available to date and any attempt to develop a systematic and integrated explanation of gentrification must take his work as a major point of departure. As I shall seek to show, however, Smith's attempt to develop a Marxist analysis of gentrification based on the production and transformation of residential space by capital is severely flawed as a direct consequence of his marked antipathy towards all other forms of explanation which he erroneously relegates to the explanatory dustbin of preference. This severely constrains the potential explanatory power of his own approach which is focused exclusively on the structure and operation of the urban land and housing markets under capitalism to the almost total neglect of the other factors discussed above. It is, in consequence, both partial and one-sided. This is all the more regrettable because Smith's approach is of considerable value when it is integrated with some of the other approaches he so cavalierly dismisses. Given the undoubted importance of Smith's analysis and the fact that, at present, it constitutes virtually the *only* attempt to explain theoretically the occurrence and the process by which gentrification is brought about within certain areas of the city, it demands a detailed critique.

Smith's approach to the analysis of gentrification is predicated on the assumption that it must be explained, as the sub-title of his 1979a paper makes clear, as 'A back to the city movement by capital not people'. Whereas conventional consumer sovereignty explanations took for granted the availability of areas ripe for gentrification, this, says Smith, is precisely what had to be explained. Thus, according to Smith, a theory of gentrification must, therefore, explain why some neighbourhoods are profitable to redevelop while others are not. Smith's analysis focuses on the relationship between capital depreciation and re-investment. As he put it:

> A theory of gentrification will need to explain the detailed historical mechanisms of capital depreciation in the inner city and the precise way in which this depreciation produces the possibility of profitable re-investment (Smith, 1979a, p. 542).

Smith then elaborates the changing relationship between land value and property value, arguing that: 'The physical deterioration and economic depreciation of inner city neighbourhoods is a strictly logical "rational" outcome of the operation of the land and housing market' (p. 543). It is this depreciation and devaluation of capital invested in inner-city residential neighbourhoods which 'produces the objective economic conditions that make capital *revaluation* (gentrification) a rational market response'. Smith sees the disparity between the potential ground-rent level and the actual ground rent capitalized under the present land use, the 'rent gap' as he terms it, of crucial importance in that:

> Only when this gap emerges can redevelopment be expected since, if the present use succeeded in capitalizing all or most of the ground rent, little economic benefit could be derived from redevelopment. As filtering and neighbourhood decline proceed, the rent gap widens. Gentrification occurs when the gap is wide enough.... Once the rent gap is wide enough, gentrification *may* be initiated in a given neighbourhood by several different actors in the land and housing market. (Smith, 1979a, p. 545) (my emphasis)

In a subsequent theoretical paper, Smith (1982) locates this cycle of the valorization, devalorization, and revalorization of capital invested in the built environment within the wider framework of uneven development under capitalism. Arguing that the main pattern of uneven development at the urban scale is to be found in the relationship between the inner city and the suburbs, Smith asserts that the crucial economic force mediating this relation at the urban scale is ground rent, the equalization and differentiation of ground-rent levels within different areas of the metropolitan region determining the unevenness of development. It is significant, however, that whilst Smith attributes the 'pivotal role' in his process to ground rent, he notes that:

> While managing or mediating this differentiation of urban space, ground rent is not in itself the origin of differentiation. Rather, the ground rent surface translates into a quantitative measure the actual forces tending towards differentiation in the urban landscape (Smith, 1982, p. 145).

Smith goes on to argue that there are two major sources for these differentiating forces in contemporary capitalist cities. The first, which he describes as functional, he defines extremely vaguely as the difference between different types and scales of land uses. The second force, which he sees as applying mainly to residential land use is 'differentiation according to class and race'. These two sources of social and functional differentiation are, says Smith, 'translated into a geographical differentiation mainly through the ground rent structure' (Smith, 1982, p. 145).

This further elaboration of Smith's theory is extremely important in two respects. First, Smith clearly recognizes and acknowledges that ground rent is not in itself the origin of differentiation. Instead, it is a mediating mechanism which translates the actual forces of differentiation. Second, whilst Smith's paper contains a valuable general treatment of the theory of uneven development and its application to the city, it is extremely unspecific as to both the nature of the forces of differentiation themselves and the precise incidence and timing of gentrification. Thus, although Smith argues that gentrification has clearly illustrated the limitations of conventional neo-classical urban theory his own highly generalized explanation does not, of itself, take us very far. As he himself later comments: 'Whether a residential neighbourhood experiences the devalorization cycle . . . depends on many things' (Smith 1982, p. 147).

This is the rub; although, in general theoretical terms, a strong case can be made for the existence of a cycle of valorization, devalorization, and revalorization in the production of the built environments, the extent to which this cycle manifests itself either in whole or in part is contingent on a variety of other factors external to the housing and land markets, none of which Smith attempts to detail, let alone explain. Indeed, Smith is dismissively contemptuous of such low level empirical trivia. Discussing the restructuring of urban space, he states that: 'While this restructuring certainly involves such "factors" as the baby boom, energy prices and the cost of new housing units, its roots and momentum derive from a deeper and very specific [sic] process of uneven development' (Smith, 1982, p. 142). The explanatory weakness of this kind of abstract theoreticism is made abundantly clear when we turn back to Smith's (1979a) paper. As we saw earlier, Smith argued that 'depreciation produces the profitable reinvestment' (1979a, p. 542) and later he argued that: 'Once the rent gap is wide enough, gentrification *may* be initiated in a given neighbourhood' (1979a, p. 545).

It is important to note here Smith's use of the word 'may'. There is no necessity invoked. Yet, only a page later Smith argues that:

> Viewed in this way, gentrification is not a chance occurrence or an inexplicable reversal of some inevitable filtering process. On the contrary, it is to be *expected*. The depreciation of capital in nineteenth century inner city neighbourhoods, together with continued urban growth during the first half of the twentieth century, have combined to produce conditions in which profitable reinvestment is *possible* (Smith, 1979a, p. 546) (my emphases).

Leaving aside the superficial similarities between Smith's analysis of potential and actual ground rents and the traditional neo-classical formulations of the economics of redevelopment and the stage theories of neighbourhood change, the argument begs almost as many questions as it answers. Taking them in order, Smith first of all fails to explain why some inner-city neighbourhoods fail to deteriorate and depreciate at all. Second, when discussing the relationship between gentrification and the rent gap he fails to answer the question of how wide is 'wide enough'. Third, he fails to explain why reinvestment should take the form of gentrification rather than redevelopment. Fourth, Smith is inconsistent as to the extent to which gentrification is seen as a necessary rather than a possible or probable outcome of the rent gap. Whilst, on balance, Smith seems to opt for the probabilistic rather than a deterministic explanation of gentrification, this still requires him to explain *why* gentrification began to occur *when* and *where* it did. Smith makes no attempt to explain the timing of gentrification unless we are to somehow accept that conditions for profitable reinvestment came to fruition in the late 1960s and early 1970s. This is a major deficiency of his analysis which could have been considerably strengthened had he not relegated demographic and other changes into the discredited consumer sovereignty approach.

As to the locational question, Smith argues that:

> If the rent gap theory of gentrification is correct it would be expected that rehabilitation began where the gap was greatest and the highest returns available, i.e. in neighbourhoods particularly close to the city centre and in neighbourhoods where the sequence of declining values had pretty much run

its course. Empirically, this seems to have been the case. The theory also suggests that as these first areas are recycled, other areas offering lower but still substantial returns would be sought out by developers. This would involve areas further from the city centre and areas where decline was less advanced (Smith, 1979a, p. 546).

Whilst the evidence broadly supports Smith's analysis on this point, it is quite clear that in London and Paris (Hamnett and Williams, 1980; Moseley, 1980) at least gentrification has not been simply related to the age of the district and proximity to the city centre but to the existing pattern of high-status areas which have tended to expand outwards into surrounding lower-status areas. More importantly, however, Smith's analysis offers no explanation of why gentrification tends to be confined to a relatively small number of major cities possessing similar employment structures.

Viewed overall, the major contribution made by Smith's analysis is to the explanation of why gentrification occurred where it did within cities. The profitable reinvestment implicit in gentrification cannot occur without some prior depreciation. This insight is not unique to political economy, however. Traditional land economists pointed this out long ago. When it comes to explaining both the scale of gentrification and its temporal specificity, however, Smith's analysis is much weaker and it entirely fails to address the related question as to why gentrification has occurred in some cities but not in others. Presumably the rent gap is a phenomenon common to all nineteenth-century residential areas and yet gentrification has occurred extensively in Paris and London but not to any significant extent in Leeds, Liverpool or Newark, New Jersey. Indeed, in a number of large, east-coast cities residential decline and abandonment have proceeded largely unchecked (Dear 1976).

The problems associated with Smith's exclusive focus on the role of the rent gap as *the* explanation of gentrification are more clearly revealed by a brief consideration of the realist distinction between the internal, necessary relations between phenomena and their contingent, external relations (see Sayer, 1982). In essence, Smith's analysis of gentrification appears to operate exclusively at the level of the necessary, internal relations between depreciation, the rent gap and capital revaluation in the urban land and housing market. External relations are dismissed as mere 'factors' of little or no consequence. As Sayer has pointed out however:

The problem with universalizing internal relations at the expense of external relations is that the power of the former concept is thereby nullified. If everything is internally related to everything else then the concept does not help us say anything particular about specific structures, apart from countering the equally absurd extreme of atomism which makes all relations external (Sayer, 1982, p. 70).

Given that every concrete situation is a combination of internal and external, necessary and contingent relations, the extent to which and the way in which the 'necessary' relationship between devaluation and revaluation embodied in the rent gap will manifest itself depends entirely upon the existence of a variety of contingent factors. Put another way, the existence of some abstract tendency towards the production of a rent gap does not necessarily imply that such a gap will be produced or that it will be closed. This is a contingent empirical question which no amount of theorizing can resolve. Indeed, as Sayer has argued:

> If there is one major lesson to be drawn from empirical research in economic geography, it is that areas are constituted by a diverse range of activities, some internally related, some externally related: they are 'conjunctures' whose content cannot be known 'in advance' on the basis of theoretical knowledge of necessary relations alone (Sayer, 1982, p. 79).

It is perhaps possible to go even further and suggest that the relationship between 'the potential ground rent level and the actual ground rent capitalized under the present land use' which constitutes the rent gap, comprises only one element of the necessary internal relations of gentrification. The demographic and employment factors which I have categorized here as contingent external relations for the purposes of discussion could themselves constitute internal relations of gentrification, Smith, however, merely dismisses them as inconsequential, his argument being consequently characterized by a functional 'capital logic'.

It is my contention here that in order to explain satisfactorily the central questions of why gentrification occurred where and when it did, it is necessary to explain first its concentration in a limited number of large cities, second its rapid growth in the late 1960s and early 1970s, and third its specific areas of occurrence in cities. Smith's theory helps explain only the third of these. In order to explain the first two questions it is necessary to resort to a consideration of employment and demographic changes both of which Smith (1979a) resolutely dismisses as either mere 'factors' or forms of preference-based 'taken for granted' explanation. Smith reaches this grotesque conclusion via a form of Procrustean categorization. He identifies just two categories of explanation, the cultural and the economic, the label economic being applied to the rising commuting cost and the proximity to workplace theses and to the view that inner-city rehabilitation becomes more viable as the cost of new housing rises. Under the heading 'cultural' Smith groups together three radically different explanations, namely the lifestyle and the demographic explanations which he erroneously conflates, and the arguments made by Ley, Berry, Lipton and others regarding the impact of the changing employment and occupational structure in these cities with a strongly developed downtown office core and a large tertiary and quaternary 'white-collar' labour force.

Smith then proceeds to the next and equally untenable step in his process of conceptual conflation. Referring to both the cultural and the economic explanatory categories, Smith asserts that: 'These conventional hypotheses are by no means mutually exclusive. They are often invoked jointly and share in one vital respect a common perspective—an emphasis on *consumer preference*' (Smith, 1979, p. 539). This is quite simply incorrect. Although the changing demographic and employment structure of the population are frequently employed as necessary underpinning for arguments relating to shifts in lifestyle preference they do not, of themselves, emphasize consumer preference. Nor does Berry's (1980) analysis of the changing balance between new construction and rehabilitation. Indeed, Berry's (1980, p. 16) argument that

no invisible hand neatly excises substandard units from the housing stock. Rather, substandard units are retrieved only when they are judged sub- standard in the market-place, i.e. when they are not worth anything in cash terms, and are abandoned by their owners. Thus, large-scale retirement means the devaluation of an entire stock of existing housing concentrated in the inner-most of the historical growth rings

bears close resemblance to parts of Smith's own analysis of the process of the devalorization of capital in the built environment.

Admittedly, Ley's (1978) argument that the replacement in contemporary 'post-industrial' cities of blue-collar production, with white-collar service occupations, brings with it an emphasis on consumption and amenity rather than work, is open to question, and his assertion that 'the values of consumption rather than production guide central city land-use decisions' (Ley, 1978, p. 11) is equally debatable. None the less, the changing occupational and employment structure of cities such as Paris, London, Washington and Vancouver is of demonstrable importance and for Smith to simply categorize and write off such crucial *material* changes as the changing occupational and demographic structure of the populations as 'cultural' factors is as untenable as it is erroneous. Braverman (1974) and Kumar (1978) have both clearly and convincingly made the case that changes in occupational structure are a central element of the capitalist mode of production and it can be argued that the rapid post-war growth of the female labour force and the two-earner household is equally explicable in terms of the changing structure and requirements of production. Deferred child-bearing can also be interpreted as a response to rapidly rising house prices. Thus, even in terms of Smith's own materialist frame of reference his analysis is both deficient and partial in that it entirely neglects two central material factors (see LeGates and Murphy, 1981). In consequence, Smith is only able to explain in general terms the occurrence of gentrification in certain areas of cities. He is entirely unable to explain why gentrification occurred in the type of cities it has at the time it has. As we have seen, Smith's analysis is confined solely to the mediating mechanism of ground rent, leaving the forces of differentiation unanalysed.

Not surprisingly this poses a problem for Smith given the existence of gentrification in many of the largest cities of advanced Western capitalist economies. As he observes: 'Only Ley's (1978) more general societal hypothesis about post-industrial cities is broad enough to account for the process internationally' (Smith, 1979a, p. 540). Such a perspective is clearly untenable for Smith who notes: 'the implications of accepting this view are somewhat drastic'. He therefore attempts to dispose of this unacceptable conclusion by arguing that:

If cultural choice and consumer preference really explain gentrification, this amounts either to the hypothesis that individual preferences change in unison not only nationally but internationally—a bleak view of human nature and cultural individuality—or that the over-riding constraints are strong enough to obliterate the individuality implied in consumer preferences. If the latter is the case, the concept of consumer preference is at least contradictory: a process first conceived in terms of individual consumption preference has now to be explained as resulting from cultural uni-dimensionality (Smith, 1979a, p. 540).

This is again an untenable argument. Leaving aside the irony that such a trenchant critic of choice and preference should be forced into arguing against such a 'bleak view of human nature and cultural individuality', Smith misrepresents Ley's thesis concerning the changing employment structure of 'post-industrial' cities. As we have seen, Ley's argument is marked more by its materialism than its idealism. Although Ley accords considerable importance to the role of consumer choice and preference, his stress on the role of the changing employment and occupational structure of 'post-industrial' cities is clearly far removed from saying that cultural choice and consumer preference explain gentrification. The real problem for Smith is that his analysis of gentrification focuses almost exclusively on the structure and operation of the urban land market under capitalism to the exclusion of other aspects of the capitalist mode of production, notably the changing form and relations of production and the changing social division of labour. Not surprisingly his analysis is consequently of only limited explanatory value.

Smith is correct when he asserts that a theory of gentrification must explain why some neighbourhoods are profitable to redevelop while others are not. As we have seen, however, this alone is inadequate. A satisfactory integrated theory of gentrification must also explain when and where gentrification has occurred. Not surprisingly Smith's theory fails to address these questions orientated as it is largely to the first question. As a consequence, Smith's explanation is, in essence, implicitly predicated upon the existence of the change in demographic and employment structure. Without the demand they have produced, the conditions for profitable reinvestment would not have existed and the old decaying nineteenth-century inner cities would have continued their decline. Gentrification is not an inevitable product of the depreciation of capital in nineteenth-century, inner-city neighbourhoods. It was and is contingent on underlying changes in employment and demographic structure. It is, therefore, only partly correct to conclude as Smith (1979a) does that 'gentrification is a structural product of the land and housing markets' (p. 546). That gentrification is largely a structural product there can be little doubt, but the structure of the land and housing market is but one, important, element of a far more complex process.

CONCLUSIONS: THE FUTURE OF GENTRIFICATION

If the approach to an integrated explanation of gentrification, outlined in the preceding section, is anywhere near correct then it should be possible to make some general predictions about the likely future of gentrification based on a consideration of the factors already discussed. In the conclusion to his most recent paper on the subject Ley (1981, p. 145) suggested that:

> Present social, economic, and political trends are redefining the morphology inherited from the industrial city. . . . If present trends accelerate, the social geography of the nineteenth century industrial city may even appear to urban scholars of the future as a temporary interlude to a more historically persistent pattern of higher-status segregation adjacent to the downtown core.

Whilst the preceding analysis of the impact of gentrification on the urban residential structure of certain large cities would certainly support this conclusion, the key phrase is, of course, 'if present trends accelerate'. Indeed, it can be argued that this may be to mis-state the question which should be 'if present trends continue'. Berry (1980) for one, is highly sceptical that they will. In answer to the question of whether private market renovation will be sustained, Berry says:

> A variety of factors suggest otherwise. First, the baby boom generation will age, and is followed by much smaller age cohorts. . . . Movement of the baby cohort along the scale of housing preferences will undoubtedly cause the demand for inner city living in revitalized neighbourhoods to subside rather than increase, at least until the early twenty-first century. Additions to the supporting job base may not be there either. There appears little likelihood that new post-industrial employment clusters will develop in inner city locations in the near future as they did in the 1960s; headquarters decentralization now appears the stronger force (Berry, 1980, p. 25).

Berry concludes this pessimistic assessment by arguing that:

> There is no reason to believe that ageing industrial cities will be able to revitalize unless they are able to develop a post-industrial high technology or service activity base. Neither is there any reason to believe that those metropolitan regions developing such a base will do so in a manner which recreated the inner cities of the past. Unless there is a prolonged recession there is little basis for believing that private market revitalization of inner city neighbourhoods will diffuse much further (Berry, 1980, p. 25).

Given the previous analysis it is difficult to disagree with Berry. The demographic basis for continuing large-scale gentrification will not be present from 1985 onwards when the size of the 20–30 year age cohorts will decline as a result of the decline in the birthrate from the mid-1960s onwards. Indeed, if the current generation of gentrifiers decide with increasing age, the arrival of children, and the possible (temporary) departure of one earner from the labour force, to move outwards towards the suburbs, there may even be a contraction of the existing gentrified areas if the first generation of gentrifiers are not replaced by younger age groups. This is an unlikely scenario, however, except in the more marginal and peripheral gentrified areas. The more gentrified areas are by now well established and are unlikely to decline spontaneously and the continuing demand for owner-occupation combined with the continuing of diminishing supply of inner-city privately rented housing is likely to result in a continuing tenurial transformation, even if the level of house prices begins to fall back somewhat from their current high levels relative to the suburban areas. In terms of Smith's analysis there is now too much capital locked up in the revitalized inner areas to allow for a rapid decline. Equally, however, the existence of declining inner-city areas and a rent gap is no guarantee of gentrification or a recipe for instant profitability. The extent to which areas can be profitably converted depends upon the demand base being present.

What can be said is that the continuing concentration of tertiary and quarternary jobs in a limited number of major office-based cities makes it unlikely that gentrification will spread much further down the urban hierarchy. If, however, the era of concentration of such jobs is at an end, and if they begin to decentralize on any major scale to smaller towns and cities following the well-documented outwards movement of population (see Barabba, 1980; Hamnett and Randolph 1982) in a process of counter-urbanization then not only the continuence of gentrification is at risk, so is the economic future of the large cities themselves. If, as has been argued, gentrification calls into question the general historical applicability of the classic ecological models of residential location, it should also be clear that gentrification is merely another stage in a continuing historically contingent sequence of residential-area evolution. There are no universally and temporally stable residential patterns.

REFERENCES

Abu-Lughod, J. (1961). A survey of city center residents In *Housing choice and housing constraints* (Ed. N. N. Foote) McGraw Hill, New York.

Ahlbrandt, R. S. and Brophy, P. C. (1975). *Neighbourhood Revitalization: Theory and Practice*, Heath, Lexington, Massachusetts.

Alonso, W. (1960). A theory of the urban land market, *Papers and Proceedings of the Regional Science Association*, **6**, 149–157.

Alonso, W. (1964). The historic and structural theories of urban form: Their implications for urban renewal, *Land Economics*, XL, 2, 227–231.

Alonso, W. (1977). *The Population Factor and Urban Structure*. Working Paper No. 102, Center for Population Studies, Harvard University, Cambridge, Massachusetts.

Auger, D. A. (1979). The politics and revitalization in gentrifying neighbourhoods, *American Planning Association Journal*, **45**, October, pp. 515–522.

Badcock, B. A. and Urlich Cloher, P. U. (1981). Neighbourhood change in inner Adelaide 1966–76, *Urban Studies*, **18**, 41–55.

Balchin, P. N. (1979). *Housing Improvement and Social Inequality*, Saxon House, Farnborough.

Ball, M. and Kirwan, R. (1977). Accessibility and supply constraints in the urban housing market, *Urban Studies*, **14**, 1, 11–32.

Barabba, V. P. (1980). The demographic future of the cities of America. In *Cities and Firms* (Ed. M. S. Bryce), Lexington Books, Lexington, Massachusetts.

Bassett, K. and Short, J. (1980). *Housing and Residential Structure: Alternative Approaches*, Routledge and Kegan Paul, London.

Bentham, G. and Moseley, M. J. (1980). Socio-economic change and disparities within the Paris agglomeration, *Regional Studies*, **14**, 55–70.

Berry, B. J. L. (1980). Inner city futures: An American dilemma revisited, *Transactions of the Institute of British Geographers*, New Series, **5**, 1, 1–28.

Berry, B. J. L. (1981). Forces re-shaping the settlement system. In *Cities and Firms*, (Ed. H. J. Bryce), D. C. Heath, Lexington, Massachusetts.

Birch, D. L. (1971). Toward a stage theory of urban growth. *Journal of the American Institute of Planners:* **37**, March, 78–87.

Black, J. T., Borut, A., and Dubinsky, R. (1977). *Private Market Housing Renovation in Older Urban Areas*, Research Report 26, The Urban Land Institute, Washington, DC.

Black, J. T. (1980). Private market housing renovation in central cities: An urban land institute survey. In *Back to the City: Issues in Neighbourhood Renovation* (Eds S. B. Laska and S. Spain), Pergamon, New York.

Boddy, M. (1975). Theories of residential location or castles in the air, *Environment and Planning A*, **7**, 109–111.

Boddy, M. and Gray, F. (1979). Filtering theory, housing policy and the legitimation of inequality, *Policy and Politics*, **7**, 39–54.

Braverman, H. (1974). *Labour and Monopoly Capital: The Degradation of Work in the Twentieth Century*, Monthly Review Press, New York and London.

Burgess, E. W. (1925). The growth of the city. In *The City*, (Eds R. E. Park, E. W. Burgess, and R. D. McKenzie), University of Chicago Press, Chicago.

Chambers, P. A. B. (1974). *The Process of Gentrification in Inner London*. Unpublished MPhil Thesis, School of Environmental Studies, University College, London.

Clay, P. L. (1979). *Neighbourhood Renewal*, Lexington Books, Lexington, Massachusetts.

Clay, P. L. (1980). The rediscovery of city neighbourhoods: Reinvestment by long-time residents and newcomers. In *Back to the City: Issues in Neighbourhood Renovation* (Eds S. B. Laska and D. Spain), Pergamon, New York.

Cybriwsky, R. A. (1978). Social aspects of neighbourhood change, *Annals of the Association of American Geographers*, **68**, 17–33.

Cybriwsky, R. A. and Meyer, J. T. (1977). *Geographical Aspects of the Housing Market in a Rejuvenating Neighbourhood*. Papers in Geography No. 16, Department of Geography, Penn State University.

Daniels, P. W. (1977). Office Location in British Conurbations: trends and strategies, *Urban Studies*, **14**, 261–274.

Davis, J. T. (1965). Middle class housing in the central city, *Economic Geography*, LXI, 238–251.

Dear, J. S. (1976). 'Abandoned housing'. In *Urban Policy Making and Metropolitan Dynamics: A Comparative Geographical Analysis* (Ed. J. S. Adams), Ballinger, Cambridge, Massachusetts.

Dynes, S. (1974). *The Spatial and Social Implications of White Painting*, Geographical Research Paper, Department of Geography, University of Toronto.

Evans, A. (1973). *The Economics of Residential Location*, MacMillan, London.

Firey, W. (1947). *Land Use in Central Boston*, Harvard University Press, Cambridge, Massachusetts.

Ford, L. and Fusch, R. (1976). Historic preservation and the inner city: The perception of German village by those just beyond, *Proceedings of the Association of American Geographers*, **8**, 110–114.

Form, W. M. (1954). The place of social structure in the determination of land use, *Social Forces*, **32**, 317–23.

Freedman, R. (1967). City migration, urban ecology and social theory. In *Urban Sociology* (Eds E. W. Burgess and D. J. Bogne), The University of Chicago Press, Chicago.

Fujii, G. T. (1981). The revitalization of the inner city: A case study of the Fairview Slopes neighbourhood, Vancouver, BC. Unpublished MA Thesis Department of Geography, University of British Columbia.

Fusch, R. (1980). A case of too many actors? Columbus. In *Back to the City: Issues in Neighbourhood Renovation* (Eds S. B. Laska and D. Spain), Pergamon, New York.

Gale, D. E. (1976). *The Back to the City Movement . . . or is it?* Occasional Paper, Department of Urban and Regional Planning, George Washington University, Washington, DC.

Gale, D. E. (1977). *The Back to the City Movement Revisited*, Occasional Paper, Department of Urban and Regional Planning, George Washington University, Washington, DC.

Gale, D. E. (1979). Middle class resettlement in older urban neighbourhoods, *Journal of the American Planning Association*, **45**, 3, 293–304.

Gilg, A. (1977). *All for a Roof Over Your Head*, The Guardian, 11 September 1973.

Glass, R. (1963). *Introduction to London: Aspects of Change*, Centre for Urban Studies, London.

Glass, R. (1973). The mood of London. In *London: Urban Patterns, Problems and Policies* (Eds D. Donnison and D. Eversley, Heinemann, London.

Gray, F. (1975). Non-explanation in urban geography, *Area*, **7**, 4, 228–235.

Grebler, L. and Mittelbach, F. (1979). *The Inflation of Housing Prices: Its Extent, Causes and Consequences*, Lexington Books, Lexington, Massachusetts.

Grier, G. and Grier, E. (1978). *Urban Displacement: A Reconnaissance*, US Department of Housing and Urban Development, Washington, DC.

Grigsby, W. (1963). *Housing Markets and Public Policy*, University of Pennsylvania Press, Philadelphia.

Hamnett, C. (1973). Improvement grants as an indicator of gentrification in inner London, *Area*, **5**, 4, 252–261.

Hamnett, C. (1976). Social change and social segregation in inner London 1961–71, *Urban Studies*, **13**, 3, 261–271.

Hamnett, C. and Randolph, W. (1981a). Flat break-ups, *Roof*, May/June, 18–24.

Hamnett, C. and Randolph, W. (1981b). Flat break-up and the decline of the private rented sector, *Estates Gazette*, **260**, 3 October, 31–33.

Hamnett, C. and Randolph, W. (1982). The changing population distribution of England and Wales, 1961–1981: clean break or consistent progression, *Built Environment*, **8**, 4, 272–280.

Hamnett, C. and Williams, P. (1979). *Gentrification in London 1961–71: An Empirical and Theoretical Analysis of Social Change*. Research Memorandum 71, Centre for Urban and Regional Studies, London.

Hamnett, C. and Williams, P. (1980). Social change in London: A study of gentrification, *The London Journal*, **6**, 1, 51–66.

Harris, S. R. (1976). *Gentrification in the Inner City*. Unpublished MA Thesis, Department of Geography, Ohio State University.

Hartman, C. (1979). Comment on neighbourhood revitalization and displacement: A review of the evidence, *Journal of the American Planning Association*, **45**, October, 417–427.

Hartshorn, T. (1971). Inner city residential structure and decline. *Annals of the Association of American Geographers*, **61**, 1.

Harvey, D. (1973). *Social Justice and the City*, Edward Arnold, London.

Hay, A. (1981). The economic basis of spontaneous home improvement: A graphical analysis, *Urban Studies*, **18**, 359–364.

Heinemeyer, W. F. (1966). The urban core as a centre of attraction. In (Eds) W. F. Heinemeyes, M. Von Hulten and H. D. de Vreis Reilingh, *Urban Core and Inner City*, E. J. Brill, Leiden.

Hodge, D. C. (1980). Inner-city revitalization as a challenge to diversity? Seattle. In *Back to the City: Issues in Neighbourhood Renovation* (Eds S. B. Laska and D. Spain), Pergamon, New York.

Hodge, D. C. (1981). Residential revitalization and displacement in a growth region, *Geographical Review*, **71**, 188–200.

Holcomb, H. B. and Beauregard, R. A. (1981). *Revitalizing Cities*. Association of American Geographers, Resource Publications in Geography.

Hoover, E. M. and Vernon, R. (1959). *Anatomy of a Metropolis*. Harvard University Press, Cambridge, Massachusetts.

Hoyt, H. (1939). *The Structure and Growth of Residential Neighbourhoods in American Cities*, Federal Housing Administration, Washington, DC.

Johnston, R. J. (1966). The location of high-status residential areas, *Geografiska Annaler*, **48B**, 1, 23–35.

Johnston, R. J. (1969). Population movements and metropolitan expansion: London 1960–1, *Transactions of the Institute of British Geographers*, **46**, 69–91.

Johnston, R. J. (1970). On spatial patterns in the residential structure of cities, *Canadian Geographer*, **14**, 361–377.

Johnston, R. J. (1971). *Urban Residential Patterns: An Introductory Review*, Bell, London.

Johnston, R. J. (1972). Towards a general model of intra-urban residential patterns: Some cross-cultural observations, *Progress in Human Geography*, **4**, 85–124.

Johnston, R. J. (1980). *City and Society: An Outline for Urban Geography*, Penguin, Harmondsworth.

Kirby, A. M. (1976). Housing market studies: A critical review, *Transactions of the Institute of British Geographers*, New Series, **1**, 1, 2–9.

Kumar, K. (1978). *Prophecy and Progress: The Sociology of Industrial Society*, Penguin, Harmondsworth.

Laska, S. B. and Spain D. (1980a). Anticipating renovators' demands: New Orleans. In *Back to the City: Issues in Neighbourhood Renovation* (Eds S. B. Laska and D. Spain), Pergamon, New York.

Laska, S. B. and Spain, D. (1980b). *Back to the City: Issues in Neighbourhood Renovation*, Pergamon, New York.

Lave, L. B. (1970). Congestion and urban location, *Papers of the Regional Science Association*, **25**, 133–152.

Legates, R. T. and Murphy, K. (1981). Austerity, shelter and conflict in the United States, *International Journal of Urban and Regional Research*, **5**, 255–75.

Ley, D. (1978). Inner city resurgence and its social context. Unpublished paper presented to Association of American Geographers, New Orleans conference.

Ley, D. (1980). *Inner-city Revitalization: Contexts, Effects and a Canadian Case Study*. Unpublished MS, Department of Geography, University of British Columbia.

Ley, D. (1981). Inner-city revitalization in Canada: A Vancouver case study, *Canadian Geographer*, XXV, 2, 124–148.

Lipton, S. G. (1977). Evidence of central city revival, *Journal of the American Institute of Planners*, **43**, 2, 136–147.

London, B. (1980). Gentrification as urban re-invasion: Some preliminary definitional and theoretical considerations. In *Back to the City: Issues in Neighbourhood Renovation* (Eds S. B. Laska and D. Spain), Pergamon, New York.

London, B., Bradley, D. S., and Hudson, J. R. (1980). The revitalization of inner city neighbourhoods, *Urban Affairs Quarterly*, **15**, 4.

Long, L. H. (1980). Back to the countryside and back to the countryside in the same decade. In *Back to the City: Issues in Neighbourhood Renovation* (Eds S. B. Laska and D. Spain), Pergamon, New York.

Maher, C. A. (1974). Spatial patterns in urban housing markets: Filtering in Toronto, 1953–71, *Canadian Geographer*, **18**, 2, 599–611.

Maher, C. A. (1979). The changing residential role of the inner city: The example of inner Melbourne, *Australian Geographer*, **14**, 112–22.

McCarthy, J. (1975). Some social implications of improvement policy in London. Unpublished paper, Sociological Research Department, Housing Development Directorate, Department of the Environment.

Milner-Holland Report (1965). *Report of the Committee Housing in Greater London*. Cmnd 2605, HMSO, London.

Moseley, M. (1980). Strategic planning and the Paris Agglomeration in the 1960s and 1970s: The quest for balance and structure, *Geography Forum*, **1**, 179–223.

Muth, R. (1969). *Cities and Housing*, University of Chicago Press, Chicago.

Neild, M. (1974). *Urban Residential Change in an Inner London General Improvement Area—Moore Park Estate, Fulham*. Unpublished BA Dissertation, Department of Geography, University of Liverpool.

O'Loughlin, J. and Munski, D. C. (1979). Housing rehabilitation in the inner city: A comparison of two neighbourhoods in New Orleans, *Econ. Geog.*, **55**, 1, 52–69.

Pattison, T. (1977). *The Process of Neighbourhood Upgrading and Gentrification*. Unpublished thesis, MIT, Cambridge, Massachusetts.

Raban, J. (1974). *Soft City*, Hamish Hamilton, London.

Ratcliff, R. U. (1949). *Urban Land Economics*, New York, McGraw-Hill.

Rapkin, C. and Grigsby, W. (1960). *Residential Renewal in the Urban Core*, University of Pennsylvania Press, Philadelphia.

Rebizant, R. and Whitaker, M. (1975). *New From Old: A Pilot Study of Rehabilitation and Neighbourhood Change*, Central Mortgage and Housing Corporation of Canada, Toronto Branch.

Richards, J. M. (1963). The significance of residential preferences in urban area. In *Human Resources in the Urban Economy*, Resources for the Future, (Ed. M. Perlman), Washington, DC.

Robson, B. T. (1969). *Urban Analysis: A Study of City Structure*, Cambridge University Press, Cambridge.

Rushton, G. (1969). Analysis of spatial behaviour by revealed space preference, *Annals of the Association of American Geographers*, **59**, 391–400.

Rushton, G. (1971). Behavioural correlates of urban spatial structure, *Economic Geography*, **47**, 1, 49–58.

Sayer, A. (1982). Explanation in economic geography: Abstraction versus generalization, *Progress in Human Geography*, No. 2, 68–88.

Schnore, L. F. (1965). On the spatial structure of cities in the two Americas. In *The Study of Urbanization* (Eds P. M. Houser and L. F. Schnore), pp. 347–398, Wiley, New York.

Simmonds, J. W. (1968). Changing residence in the city, *Geographical Review*, **58**, 622–651.

Smith, N. (1979a). Towards a theory of gentrification: A back to the city movement by capital not people, *American Planning Association Journal*, October, 538–548.

Smith, N. (1979b). Gentrification and capital: Practice and ideology in society, *Antipode*, **11**, 3, 24–35.

Smith, N. (1982). Gentrification and uneven development, *Economic Geography*, **58**, 2, 139–155.

Smith, W. F. (1964). *Filtering and Neighbourhood Change*. Research Report No. 24, Center for Real Estate and Urban Economics, University of California, Berkeley.

Spain, D. (1980). Indicators of urban revitalization: Racial and socio-economic changes in central-city housing. In *Back to the City: Issues in Neighbourhood Renovation* (Eds S. B. Laska and D. Spain), Pergamon, New York.

Stapleton, C. M. (1980). Reformulation of the family life-cycle concept: Implications for residential mobility, *Environment and Planning A*, **12**, 1103–1118.

Stobie, P. W. (1979). *Private Inner City Redevelopment in Vancouver: A Case Study of Kitsilano*. Unpublished MA Thesis, Department of Geography, University of British Columbia.

Sumka, H. (1979). Neighbourhood revitalization and displacement: A review of the evidence, *Journal of the American Planning Association*, **45**, October, 480–7.

Williams, P. (1976). The role of institutions in the inner London housing market: The case of Islington, *Transactions of the Institute of British Geographers*, New Series, **1**, 1, 72–82.

Winters, C. (1979). The geography of rejuvenation in an inner-city neighbourhood: The upper west side of Manhattan, 1950–1977. Paper presented at the Annual Meeting of the Association of American Geographers, Salt Lake City, Utah.

Zeitz, E. (1979). *Private Urban Renewal*, Lexington Books, Lexington, Massachusetts.

Geography and the Urban Environment
Progress in Research and Applications, Volume VI
Edited by D. T. Herbert and R. J. Johnston
© 1984 John Wiley & Sons Ltd.

Chapter 9

Demystifying Suburban Landscapes

David M. Evans

INTRODUCTION

We thank thee Lord, that by thy grace,
Thou hast led us to this lovely place,
And now, dear Lord, we humbly pray,
Thou wilt all others keep away.

Cotter's Prayer

That the above rhyme should appear as a suggestion for anti-growth lobbyists at the end of a review of the Los Angeles metropolitan area (Nelson and Clark, 1976) bears strong testimony to a trend in the residential environment to 'close the gates', to exclude those seen as a threat to the hard-won, single-family dwellings of the West Coast enclave. The recent development of anti-growth ideologies, in contra-distinction to the usual growth 'boosterism' of market society, marks the outcome of a long struggle to defend those middle and upper class residential spaces of the metropolis labelled variously 'suburban', 'elite', 'well-to-do', 'exclusive' and most recently 'exclusionary' (Molotch, 1976).

The impact of the development of 'defending our own' and the susceptibility to this sentiment are amply demonstrated by the speed with which Newman's (1972) concept of defensible space became an American household phrase in the mid-1970s. Within several months of its publication the term had become legitimated through Federal government financing of studies in this area. Primarily designed to monitor crime prevention at the micro-design scale through strong territorial control in buildings, the wider uses of this construct have been appreciated, and its enforcement by analogy at the neighbourhood and community scale are clear. Increasing evidence of the implementation of this ideology in the landscape through policing of territory, the building of gates and walls, and at least in one case in the Los Angeles area even moats, suggests that this exaggerated degree of social segregation warrants further study (Banham, 1971).

Possible ways by which such spaces have come about are discussed here, through what suburban has meant and means, both in theory (as an ideology) and in practice. The epistemological approach used is a relational one, which is well illustrated by Marx's comment that to begin with an all-embracing term (such as suburb) is to take 'a chaotic conception of the whole' (Marx, 1973, p. 100). Such a term has too many differing interpretations and must, therefore, be demystified by moving towards simpler concepts and determinations. Once these basic definitions have been established, the ladder can be reclimbed so that suburb now appears instead 'as a rich totality of many determinations and relations' (Marx, 1973, p. 100). Throughout the descent and reascent of the ladder consideration is given to the problem of the conflict between explanations that concentrate on the individual and those that stress society—what Giddens (1979) terms 'agency' versus 'structure'. It is suggested that the failure to reconcile approaches based on human action with those based on suprahuman structure has contributed to the mystification of the term suburbia in recent geographical research. The persistence of localism as an ideology amongst suburbanites is examined in conjunction with the wider material problems in which this is located: it is argued that this restricted outlook blinds this group to the structural problems in which they are bound up. Defensive action is seen to typify this limited awareness.

The first section of the paper examines some major themes of the contemporary suburb and reviews the associated difficulties. In this context changing ideas on the meaning of 'suburban' are judged to be most important. In particular consideration is given to the 'urbanization of the suburbs' stance and to the more recent position dealing with the promotion of suburban living space to benefit finance capital (Masotti and Hadden, 1973; Walker, 1978, 1981). Whilst welcoming these perspectives for the concern that they raise about suburban spaces in their own right, it will be argued that they do not alone achieve a demystified view of the suburban process. In the second section it is suggested that active ideologies of suburbia which are put into practice through institutional control are sustained through localism, although not without ensuing conflicts and social consequences. Of the various interpretations of localism that which is most appropriate to contemporary defensive actions, or attempts to create social and political independence for some suburban spaces from both the central city and other places labelled suburban, is chosen. Because such independence may remain little more than a belief, it is suggested that conflicts between jurisdictions ensue over 'fair' allocations of population and resources. Most attention is given to the North American suburb and a case study of a 'defended space' in Vancouver is developed. The applicability of suburban constructs to British experience is also discussed.

CONTEMPORARY APPROACHES TO THE SUBURB IN PERSPECTIVE

Usually 'suburb' brings to mind at least two definitions. Fischer (1976) argues that, taking 'suburban' to mean peripheral location in the metropolis, the ecological (deterministic) and compositional (sub-cultural) approaches to a theory of urbanism can be applied. The former, based on Wirth's (1938) axioms of increasing size, density and heterogeneity of social group within city life, logically implies that suburbanism reduces these effects through distance and dispersion, producing a quasi-primary or semi-rural society. Gans (1962) has modified this position by asking whether the differences between urbanism and suburbanism are as great as Wirth's contribution would suggest. The latter approach does not depend on any independent effects of distance but stresses the significance of the purposeful coming together of similar individuals in a common social network, linked through status, class or cohesive bonds such as a desire for a family environment. A variant of this approach (a life-style definition) does give more weight to distance in the sense that need for proximity allows individuals of similar outlook to 'concentrate' in a suburban neighbourhood. Selective migration is a key factor in the establishment of any suburban community in this latter approach, since it is voluntaristic in nature.

The ecological approach has been adopted by geographers as a morphological perspective in which the importance of adaptive processes is reduced and locational differences within urban form are emphasized so that variations in land-use mix, population density and land values are given more significance. Compositional approaches have been less eagerly adopted by geographers, although they remain of concern to sociologists. In practice most researchers have not regarded the two stances as mutually exclusive, but a debate has ensued as to which is the more convincing framework (Fischer, 1976; Schwartz, 1976).

Ideas of suburbia: An overview of theory and practice

Dominant ideologies of suburban expansion have found most expression in sub-cultural or life-style perspectives. Most common is the argument that some anti-urban bias exists in Western (particularly North American) society (Hadden and Barton, 1973). This can be clearly seen in early American attempts to create 'garden' or 'romantic' suburbs in the mid-nineteenth century. Care is needed, however, in the interpretation of the motivations behind these 'ideal' suburban environments. Hays (1964) has remarked in this context that there have been too many explanations of changes which have assumed that ideologies put forward succeed in practice without modification and opposition. This can be extended to explanations of suburbia at various time periods, with detailed consideration of views developed in the 1970s.

Olmsted (see Bender, 1975) for example advocated a 'romantic' ideal which aimed to create a metropolis of the *sub* and the *urb* which were to be united in a vision of the counter-force between dispersion for domestic purposes and concentration for business purposes. Even though Olmsted knew that this was not a totally egalitarian plan, in that some groups would be favoured over others for the *sub*, the ideal was challenged in the Progressive Era by a new view of the non-elite suburb. Lubove (1967) has documented how in the late 1920s the Regional Planning Association of America promoted new ideals of efficiency, order and low-density housing which were to create a middle-class homogeneous suburb. This is comparable in Britain to Howard's plea for a middle landscape blending town and country, for which a totally new start to Regional Planning would be needed. The aim of the new suburb was claimed to be anti-elitist because it assumed that the goals of a 'city efficient' could be applied equally to all people. By its later phases after the Second World War, continued class inequality and financial involvement (Checkoway, 1980) had eroded this ideal so that it became anti-unitary. Even if unintended, the ideal was found to be only fulfillable in general for middle-class groups, often associated with political segregation (itself an alternative definition of 'suburban').

During post-war regrowth an 'Organization Man' or 'lonely crowd' perspective became popular, very much associated with the belief that a new affluent society was emerging (Whyte, 1956; Reisman, 1957). Conforming members of a society based on strict adherence to familism as a norm were supposed to engage in frantic neighbouring in a neo-pastoral setting under single-family, ranch-home roofs. During the 1960s a protest was raised against such exaggeration by Berger (1960) and later Gans (1967). Earlier definitions were argued to be accurate to a point, representative of middle-class communities with particular life-styles and morphologies, such as the 'open' suburb. Here claims Dobriner (1963, p. 73): 'Everything is in its place and a man can see all the forces which shape his life.' This view, although seen by then as one of several, was still treated as an ideal, with little discussion of how such spaces were to be maintained through social control. By the late 1960s alternative one-dimensional viewpoints generated a '57 varieties' typology of suburbia. This is foreseen by Berger (1960) and exemplified by Thorns (1973).

Such definitions may have proved useful in detecting gross differences (for example retirement suburbs versus blue-collar suburbs), but inconsistency in the *a priori* use of the term 'suburb' is apparent. With such variety how meaningful is this label? Sternlieb (1974, p. 226) echoes this sentiment, in a summary of some of the main contributions to this literature:

> The crack in the picture window, the man in the grey flannel suit, the Levittown on the one hand and the Basking Ridge on the other, really require so much in the way of interpolation and modification as to make the term suburbia dangerously imprecise, hopelessly inadequate as a classifying mechanism.

Schwartz (1976) has claimed that the problem is that the suburban process is being interpreted too passively, so that some mysterious factor such as the inherent need in the potential suburbanite for familism in low-density land-scapes is postulated. This abstract ideology overlooks the institutional context of such needs, resulting in the suburbanization process as ecological difference being brought in to explain the political 'weeding-out' process that establishes precisely who can make it to the 'green pastures'. Again he feels that it is necessary to see that such landscapes are subject to social control. Whether *de facto* or *de jure* through political incorporation is not critical here—the point is that a meaningfully organized moral order is there to defend suburban territories against alternative plans for their development. Hence Schwartz places ecological factors, which to him are 'blind facts', as subordinate to sub-cultural considerations.

Some of these approaches did have an active side to them, however. Whyte (1956) suggested that perhaps the potential suburbanite would be attracted by a different physical landscape in which to live, rather than simply by class or life-style expressions unrelated to morphology. Suburbia would, therefore, create a 'classless' man. Although criticized by Gans (1967) for producing a 'cultureless' man, Whyte did raise the question as to what degree individuals internalize ideologies and react to them—ideologies which can have strongly ecological perspectives. What was not made clear, however, was the link between the production of living space and the internalization of ideologies. This is taken up below in discussion of institutional influences.

The Urbanization of the suburbs

Into this debate has come a stronger contender for a contemporary view of suburbanization, drawing largely on the ecological-morphological definition and employing the multivariate typology. Following Masotti and Hadden (1973), Muller (1976) has offered a view of the 1970s suburb as a place now economically, socially and politically independent of the central city. The American 'Outer City' represents the pivot point of a new diverse, multi-nodal metropolis, including a mosaic culture of specialized social districts. Older simplified models of a core-periphery metropolis dominated by a single central business district (CBD) are challenged. Increasing evidence of this decentraliza-tion of industrial, commercial, and, of course, retailing activities, as well as the deconcentration of population points to the central city as a 'sandbox', a residual dumping ground for the poor, ethnic minorities, and social sinkholes of crumbling infrastructure and homes (Sternlieb, 1971; Muller, 1976). At best the inner city is 'irrelevant', at worst a liability on state and federal government and an embarrassment to new life-styles based increasingly on consumption space.

Whether seen favourably or pejoratively, there does seem to be agreement that the loss of status of the central city is tied in with the gain of the suburbs. In the most favourable views of the suburbanization process the power of exclusionary political processes to maintain the suburban landscape is not discussed. On the other hand the most critical stances, such as that of the Suburban Action Institute (Davidoff and Davidoff, 1971) concentrate on the 'opening up' of these spaces to a wider variety of social groups.

This resistance to the in-migration of lower-income and ethnic minority groups is the main definition of 'defensive' or 'exclusionary' space as employed in the 'urbanization of the suburbs' stance. The exclusionary processes used here have been well documented (Saglyn and Sternlieb, 1973; Danielson, 1976; Newton, 1978) especially from political and economic viewpoints and further review is not necessary. From the point of view of anti-growth sentiment, however, this conception of 'defensive space' seems inadequate. As Frieden (1979) points out, exclusion in connection with growth controls in suburban communities is not aimed in particular at such groups (it is taken for granted that they are to be kept out) but at *all* middle-class groups wanting to follow in the footsteps of their predecessors by decentralizing. The continued lure of owner occupation, still usually a single-family home, is often seen as the explanation of this.

The temporal aspect of segregation here reinforces the need to consider the historical basis of contemporary suburbanization. For whilst mentioned in this recent perspective it is not followed through. Muller (1976) only briefly reviews the evolution of suburbia, pointing out correctly how the idea of the 'romantic' suburb grew up around middle to late nineteenth century from, for example, Olmsted's work. He then changes to the rather deterministic view of transportation technology in an outline of suburban development from the middle of the nineteenth century on. Whilst this is clearly relevant, it needs to be linked to the institutional context of the growth of urban form, for example, the contribution of Progressive Planning which was outlined earlier. Similarly, relatively little attention is paid to status mobility. To go back to the 'Organization Man' ideology, to what extent was he or was he not successful in his suburban space? More importantly, who else was influenced to become like him and *where* might they seek to achieve this emulation? In short, an embourgoisement thesis, which may well have significance, receives scant attention in Muller's analysis.

Social control of the potential suburbanite is also very much overlooked in recent perspectives. The Suburban Action Institute, for example, has paid little attention to social control and ways in which it might be linked to the solidarity of opposition to certain lower income and ethnic minority groups. Around Vancouver recent middle-class suburbanites have opposed subsidized homes for lower-income groups on the grounds that such subsidies would enable others to short-cut the struggle for status mobility that they themselves went through (Mercer, 1976). This resentment forms some of the basis for opposition to a varied social mix in suburbia. This illustration is intended to show that the complete context must be considered. Muller (1976) falls short of such an approach on several counts. He fails to recognize the complexities of socio-political processes at both institutional and individual levels. Moreover, by generally regarding social groups in terms of whether or not they 'choose' to live in suburbia, he grossly understates the role of social constraints and omits consideration of the local moral order. This is in spite of discussing exclusionary processes from a political viewpoint.

Furthermore, general ideals, well-legitimated in a market society, are also excluded in these recent positions. In particular the question of universal rights in a democratic society in practice, as opposed to in theory, is omitted. Many members of exclusionary social worlds claim a right to protective action which is opposed by 'opening up' lobbyists in the name of democracy, but which in fact the political basis of democracy has already legitimated. This is the right to individual determination and by extension to like-minded individuals. The American Constitution has been used equally by both 'anti-growth' and 'opening-up' lobbyists, often resulting in reversed decisions in Court Hearings as has happened at Petaluma, California. Frieden (1979) outlines the development of the controls. The reversals occurred as a result of action by the construction industry on behalf (it claimed) of potential residents who were being denied the right to travel under the American Constitution. Upheld in a district court, the decision in favour of the Construction Industry was reversed in the US Court of Appeals. Petaluma's growth controls have been widely discussed in other sources, but these rarely proceed beyond description (see for example Muller, 1976).

This reversal is not surprising: Macpherson (1964) has shown that the political theory of democracy was formulated at a time when not all individuals were considered equal (i.e. exclusion was built into its norms). It then becomes apparent why, when equality for all is claimed, that the same theory can guarantee legitimation for action which initially seems contrary to its code. Actual commentaries on these decisions present them as arbitrary, hinting at highly personal interpretations, sometimes with the suggestion that these are manipulative (see for example Johnston, 1981). This 'Manipulated City' view abstracts, however, from the logic behind the decision-making process in such cases (as in Gale and Moore, 1975, or the managerialist view of Pahl, 1975), in which structural factors are also important.

Different ideals may also survive side-by-side and be put into practice in different places. This point is not captured in the 'urbanization of the suburbs' stance, which concentrates on *in situ* change within spaces to the 'Outer City'. Muller's concept of specialized social districts is not sufficient to deal with this question of ideals either. Hughes (1975), however, avoids *in situ* change as the only relevant context when pointing out that recent anti-growth sentiment and controls could be interpreted as attempts to preserve older ideals of separate family-raising environments morphologically beyond the 'Outer City'. Frieden's (1979) study of Californian anti-growth communities bears this out in so far as the single-family, low-density development still stands the best chance of success in these places. Muller here seems to have missed a rather obvious point: if ecological and morphological changes to what were seen as 'suburbs' makes the label 'Outer City' more appropriate, then older ideas of 'suburb' may be abandoned, but the question of whether all (so named) suburban places are so affected is an empirical one. The new label cannot simply be applied *carte blanche* with places that fit the *a priori* definition poorly being termed specialized social districts. Ecological approaches by sociologists were never intended to be so mechanical in any case. Changes in land use and density are linked with social change also, even if in a deterministic (i.e. adaptive) manner.

The institutional shaping of suburbanization

The interaction of ideals with class and status differences has been taken-up in recent geographical work. As seen above, Macpherson shows that these differences are the Achilles Heel of all-embracing ideologies for 'man-in-general'. Harvey (1978) and Walker (1978) have stressed the need to consider active functional attempts to promote suburban landscapes. One main ideal is offered in this approach, dealing with the stable development of market society. This is seen as the continued reproduction of the finance-capital market (the secondary circuit of capital) by guaranteeing it investment in highly privatistic units, generally the single-family household, although the whole built environment is included. As Saunders (1980, p. 114) points out, Harvey draws directly on Baran and Sweezy's (1966) view that suburbanization absorbs the surplus product to guarantee adequate consumption. Walker has traced the main influences of this process, including links to business cycles, from the nineteenth century on and indicates the importance of the early stages of the development of residential living space. This perspective is incorporated into a specific theory of class segregation with the aesthetic bases of suburbanization ('anti-urban' and 'arcadian') seen as justification for the capitalist class to distance itself from the working class. Elsewhere Harvey (1975) has outlined a general theory of residential segregation consistent with this viewpoint, in which the working class is tempted into home ownership through suburbanization. This is part of a theory of residential living space as the basis of the reproduction of labour power.

Harvey is naturally aware of linked influences and reviews in some detail the contribution of Olmsted and Howard; Walker (1981) has extended the debate over suburbanization considerably, and in a more sophisticated manner. Whilst the core of the argument remains the hiving-off of surplus capital into the secondary circuit to prevent crises of capital overaccumulation, a considerable number of other factors are taken into account. Some of these may be compared with the theories reviewed here. For example, Walker (1981, p. 383) claims that 'suburbanisation is clearly a process of enormous complexity forming one part of the entire suburbanisation process, one aspect of the social whole'. The 'urbanization of the suburbs' stance is regarded as an 'essential truth' (Walker,

1981, p. 396) although exaggerated. A 'bourgeois hegemony' is also forwarded in the suburbanization process, made up of three parts (Walker, 1981, p. 398): first 'imitation', that is the bourgeois ideal of suburbia is offered as the ruling ideal; second 'no class alternative', that is it is considered rational to move into the American suburban middle-class; third 'conscious intervention' such as tax incentives for home ownership. Some of this framework is consistent with the embourgeoisement thesis, which Walker also reviews.

Although a good deal more eclecticism is evident in Walker's contribution (and to a lesser extent Harvey's), these visions of ideal living space are only considered in the final analysis in so far as they serve the ends of finance capital (the secondary circuit). Harvey (1978, p. 29) terms this a 'Faustian bargain' for labour. This is based on the bourgeoisie, and many workers also, seeking to banish the facts of production by choosing the (offered) suburban living space. In this argument Harvey in particular rapidly makes finance capital an end in itself, which gains the most at the expense of the alienation of the market and a false contentment for the capitalist. This personification of capital as a supra-human structure endowed with reason detracts from the importance of other ideals and images important to the suburban process and appears to contradict Marx's view which essentially critiques such thinking as Hegelian. It is true that Marx sometimes writes of capital as if it has a power of its own, but he is careful to link this to actual capital–worker relationships. The 'Afterword' to the Second German Edition of *Capital* (Marx, 1972) contains a scathing attack on Hegelian interpretations of his work.

Harvey seems to assume that the only ideals relevant are neopastoral ones, with a bourgeois bent. Workers may be bought off by these but cannot formulate any of their own. This view of false consciousness is too mechanical and loses touch with the links between structure and lived experience. A much more balanced perspective is offered by Sennett and Cobb (1973), who examine the social psychology of the worker faced with status mobility. They also show that this upward mobility is felt to be 'required' and that this causes the worker stress and problems with identity. Young and Willmott (1967) have applied very much the same idea in studies of suburbanization in London where workers become more middle class in their habits in the new landscape. Neither approach shows much inclination among workers to want to 'banish the facts of production' as such.

Walker, like Harvey, seems unwilling to ground the suburban process in actual practices, despite reviewing a considerable number of ideals. If this grounding were to occur, conflicts with the ideals of the capital market could be seen. Walker (1978) also argues for the suburbs as a place from which to banish the facts of production, but if the older suburbs in particular are now the 'Outer City' and have plenty of new production points, then to what places do such claims apply? Here the 'urbanization of the suburbs' stance is more accurate, although itself over-generalized. Walker could clarify this claim by actual empirical studies of changing suburban ideals and conflicting aims, as for example residents migrate out of older suburbs which have changed morphologically and socially. This consideration is linked to ideas of suburbia related to 'escape' for reasons other than from production and is taken up again later.

Summary discussion of the contemporary approaches

The preceding discussion has considered both the merits and pitfalls of recent approaches to the suburban process, whilst also implying that definitions of suburbia are infinitely more complex than the initial alternatives outlined. Although it appears that the less-documented functional approach is the more complete, this still suffers from overemphasizing the explication of ideologies, rather than the resulting practices. This is not to imply that the radical, institutional perspective used is ideological, but that it deals first and foremost with attempts to implement ideals, not the degree of success of these. Here, although different in content, is a strong similarity with the 'urbanization of the suburbs' stance. Both see some suprahuman structure, in the one case finance capital, in the other spatial form, which are viewed as exhaustive in explaining human action. Such an approach abstracts from the origin of these structures through human objectification, in conjunction with the material world. This produces structures which appear to be suprahuman and may then be given personification. When human input is forgotten, reification results and the structures are seen to 'act back' on human action. This view owes something to the position advocated by Berger and Luckmann (1967), although this is too idealist in that it fails to consider why individuals might not be able to follow norms objectified in structures through, for example, material circumstances.

Omitted in the two recent approaches is the reaction to this 'acting back' which in turn modifies the structures. This is what is meant by 'grounding structures' in everyday experience. Older approaches to suburbia in the lifestyle/sub-cultural mode have generally over-emphasized the 'agency side' (i.e. lived experience) but cannot relate this to the structural context, whilst recent approaches stress passive reaction to fixed structures. Harvey and Walker for example do not show the interaction and conflict between neo-pastoral ideals experienced in everyday reality and the modification of these which comes from the structural setting when cost-efficiency criteria lead to the land-development industry promoting cluster-home landscapes which are not viewed as 'neo-pastoral'. Thus the bourgeois ideal may not functionally support the capitalist motive indefinitely. Policy analysts such as Frieden (1979) tend to report the conflict but do not explore the structural constraints adequately.

The 'urbanization of the suburbs' stance tends to suffer more difficulties from proposing a mechanical interaction between agency and structure. This results for example in the treatment of the city as a 'residual' in urban form, which is as one-dimensional as the view of suburbanization prevalent in the 1950s. Muller's own example from Philadelphia seems particularly ironic in this respect since this is one of many American metropoli in which the city core is undergoing much change through, for example, gentrification (Cybriwsky, 1978). Second, there is generalization to all metropolitan experience in the US (Muller, 1976). This is a strange claim in the light of recent attempts to compare and contrast different metropolitan experience and there is other evidence to contradict such assertions (Morgan, 1971; Lineberry, 1975). Muller seems to forward a perspective most appropriate to the Eastern Seaboard. In any event such issues must be framed actively, not passively. Exclusionary practices (including for anti-growth purposes) in Canada for example have copied US experience, but with a different legal context which in fact may be more favourable to their achievement. In a study underway in Britain (Evans, forthcoming) similar sentiments are being found over anti-growth proposals in an urban fringe context, again with different structural factors to be considered in terms of the legal and planning framework.

Some unification of the structural setting is, of course, apparent, and this has been amply demonstrated by the radical, institutional perspective. This is its chief merit, given that other factors associated with the increasing rapidity of bureaucratic procedures may also be important. It has also shown the continued importance of ideologies in the emergence of urban form. But both this perspective and the 'urbanization of the suburbs' one are ultimately self-serving to their own biases, because they take for granted the success of the ideals discussed. Having now reached the bottom rung of the ladder, the localist basis of the interpretation of everyday reality and the way in which it interacts with the structural setting can be outlined.

LOCALISM AND THE FORMATION OF SUBURBAN SOCIAL WORLDS

Localism is a term open to different interpretations, often dependent on the context in which it is being used. No attempt is made here to define all contexts and moreover it is not implied that the term should only be applied to ideas of suburban social space. Indeed other definitions (Suttles, 1968) can relate to the inner-city context. It is suggested, however, that the concept is useful to an understanding of how suburban ideals work out in practice and that it represents the minimum building block of everyday experience needed to 'ground' structural settings. Its applicability to 'defensive space' will become apparent.

Definitions of localism in the suburban context

Localism is sometimes believed to involve 'limited horizons', that is there is no interest in, and usually no commitment to places far from one's own, and hence the social and political issues that dominate these spaces.* This can be made equivalent to a political expression, for example, through *de jure* territorial control, which is perhaps more evident in the American than the British case. 'External relations' beyond local commitment then become important and the question of to what extent outside control of, and influence over, local space takes place. This may be defined within the localist viewpoint.

Concepts of localism are present in the suburban literature, although they are rarely discussed at any length. Masotti (1973) sees it as an entrenched value in American government, producing a tendency for metropolitan political fragmentation. Fischer and Jackson (1976) define the term by surrogate measures of neighbourliness and the extent of social networks in suburbia. These are localized because increasing distance from the city centre inhibits interaction over a wider area. Hence an ecological bent is given to the term. Dunleavy (1980), using the term more broadly, views localism as a 'residual' feature of the political landscape, left over from times of greater spatial variation in institutions (this is formulated in the British context). He does, however, suggest that newer influences can be seen in the emergence of parochial electoral movements, such as ratepayers' groups, expressing local concern.

A rather different view of localism has been advanced by Bell and Newby (1978). This stresses its function, in an active sense, as a guide of social control in market society. They suggest that traditional local spheres of influence were broken down in the expanding capitalist economy, but that locally-orientated interest subsequently reappeared as an ideology of community. This they attribute largely to the concept of the 'neighbourhood' unit, which is linked to ideas of Howard and Perry in the inter-war period. Such units were supposed to promote local loyalties and a sense of identity which would guide social control. The same surrogate measures forwarded by Fischer and Jackson could be used to identify these.

This sense of identity can be related to the question of commitment to place. Property is frequently defined as the minimum commitment in this case. As Samuels (1979, p. 74) puts it:

> The ideology of place ... finds communal fulfilment in nationalities and various scales of parochial attachments, but it also finds social and individual manifestation in the doctrine of private property. This has, at minimum, its origins in attachments to and identities with particular places as one's own. Home, estate, land and the things within one's zone ... acquire legal, economic and political sanction to become a doctrine of privatism.

---

* This approach stems in fact from hermeneutics, without any explicit spatial connotation being applied. Gadamer (1976) states that 'A person who has no horizon is a man who does not see far enough and hence overvalues what is nearest to him. . . . A person who has a horizon knows the relative significance of everything within this horizon, as near or far, great or small'. The concept is akin to that of immanence, in which only thought relatable to experience is meaningful or possible.

Macpherson (1964) has formalized this view for relations in a market society. The individual is regarded as 'possessive', that is, the isolated proprietor of a set of unalienable rights most clearly manifested by ownership of property. To own land or goods is to be seen as fit to find a place in a clearly defined moral order, allowing a correct interpretation of societal organization. This can be linked back with an earlier claim by Schwartz (1976) that suburban ideals must be seen in this light. A local moral order is seen as necessary.

This view of property and place can be demonstrated in a number of political issues. Agnew (1981) has advanced the functional importance of this link to the maintenance of market society, in that it encourages privatized home ownership and consequently commits individuals to supporting a productive land industry. The mortgaging process holds the individual to this commitment and encourages defence of property values, commonly found in some suburban exclusionary tactics. Expression of this varies from one defensive space to another. In the case of strictly exclusionary tactics, loss of property values is often advanced as the effect of allowing in lower-income or ethnic groups. If anti-growth sentiments are involved, it is claimed that higher-density land-scapes, such as cluster homes, will produce lowered values, or the loss of open space and views may have this effect where environmental protection is claimed (Frieden, 1979).

Localism in its wider context: American examples

Two examples of localist sentiment and 'external relations' in places undergoing change illustrate the consequences of this belief. Gottdiener (1977), in the context of the expansion of the suburban environment in Long Island, examines the results of a public faith in the power of market forces to guarantee the political autonomy of these jurisdictions. It is assumed that direct control of the housing market is not needed. The idea of individual determination via freemarket expression is translated to the community level, and total detach-ment from the problems of other communities result. Nevertheless, this naive belief in localism is tied to a form of 'limited liability', where the local commitment to place only survives as long as certain ideals are fulfilled there, including this definite view of property (see Janowitz, 1952). Gottdiener shows that local suburban political parties are, however, only weakly formed, in keeping with the *laissez-faire* ethnic and this undermines the success of the ideals. 'Toy' governments result, created primarily for the defence of property values. In practice these governments are bought out by the private sector, especially the property industry and change is imposed on the landscape contrary to the ideals. This results in the 'limited liability' belief coming into play and if voice (protest) fails the exit options are chosen with ideals being fulfilled in newly-developed areas beyond the present zone of change.

This concept well illustrates the breakdown of a localist defensive space, by the failure to consider the power of external control, which can epistemologically be considered part of the structural setting. This process appears to be beyond comprehension at the level of everyday reality, unless it is suppressed. By no means can this automatically be regarded as the case for all defensive spaces. This will depend on the balance between *in situ* change and some tipping point beyond which conflict emerges overtly. Here another idea of the suburban process is of relevance, that of 'escape' but other than simply from the facts of production as suggested earlier. Gottdiener (1977) shows that this concept is not sufficient to show whether or not 'escape' actually succeeds. Rather there is evidence of 'disorientation avoidance' (Evans, 1978), where residents attempt to cope with submerged tensions and conflicts which re-emerge after the initial escape stage. These can in fact become overt whether or not threats to the landscape occur—the idea is hinted at in the 1950s view of suburbia and has been claimed more forcefully by Sennett (1970, 1978). Case studies of newly settled suburbs show a mismatch between claims that communities are peaceful and free of conflict and their actual reality, ridden with tensions, neuroses and stress.

Although this view of suburban communities is now unpopular as a general claim (except perhaps with Sennett and Schwartz), Kaplan (1976) has provided the basis for its relevance as well. Also working on Long Island, as a participant on a planning board, he suggests that Port Washington's development was handed over to external interests. The localist outlook of the planning board blinded most of its members to the type and degree of change being imposed. Fantasizing about the continued maintenance of former life-styles was rudely negated and became transformed into social instability as the taken-for-granted landscape disappeared. This leads Kaplan to draw a radically different conclusion to the 'urbanization of the suburbs' stance. Any suburban 'solution', a term also used by Walker, has been deferred and has itself become a problem.

The symbolic importance of localism in the landscape

Attempts to avoid *in situ* change are most clearly expressed in landscape identity. This may be as true for defensive actions aimed at exclusion of 'undesirable' groups as it is for anti-growth movements. The above discussion not withstanding, a more precise conceptualization of the minimum basis of 'turf' protection is needed. This arises because the assumption of certain values held is taken for granted and, even when linked to material considerations such as property, does not adequately explain the social psychology of such action.

In connection with valuation, frequent reference is made to Firey's (1945) work on sentiment and symbolism in Boston, but as Duncan (1973, 1976) has pointed out, a more subtle approach is required in terms of differentiation of landscape identity. He offers instead a symbolic interactionist perspective in which the individual invests a part of his/her social self in the residential landscape as an identity. This investment, based on being a part of a group undertaking social interaction, provides a means of image creation and a communication of status-expectation. In turn this results in a 'signification' process by which individuals, via landscape construction, communicate cues as to the socially-shared meaning of their tastes and identity. Duncan suggests that quite different symbolic landscapes can arise. There is no necessary consensus on the meaning and importance of objects across their boundaries. This gives a localist expression to social worlds.

Duncan's case study in Westchester County, New York, deals with social worlds where little change is occurring, *de facto* segregation between the established elite and the *nouveaux riches* is established. The identity obtained is by no means inviolate, however, Werthman (1968, pp. 152–154) has suggested some consequences when symbols are in danger of 'contamination'. He notes, following Gans, that to middle-class groups the area outside the home, the community landscape, matters much more than in the case of lower-income groups. Here the home is viewed more as a retreat from middle-class perspectives on orderliness; this recalls Dobriner's quote mentioned earlier. As also suggested by Duncan, these symbolic aspects of the landscape are widely defended and threats to them are viewed also as threats to personal identity, in a situation where class-consciousness is low. More importantly, he asserts, middle-class groups have not seen that self-esteem comes from themselves, rather than from the symbols, whereas lower-income groups have seen through these. Hence the question of identity preservation is translated into political action to preserve the symbols. These are in fact reified, robbing the middle-class of the means to act independently of them. There is also an economic basis to this linkage, but as Werthman points out, the value being defended is also a socially constructed one. Hence it might be added that irrespective of the way in which this value can serve finance capital, the social basis is more fundamental. Walker (1981, p. 391) makes some acknowledgement of a link through the 'collective regulation of private consumption and the search for mutually reinforcing homogeneity within communities (which) takes on greater import-ance as the mode of consumption assumes a more "public" display mode and as residents come to imbue residential landscapes with great significance'. Needless-to-say this is not furthered to the level of symbolic 'contamination'.

This view can now be extended into a theory of 'turf' defence, 'protecting our own', or 'defensive space'. However these actions are labelled, they are primarily based on a fear of symbolic presence. This symbolic avoidance behaviour, so named because money as wealth can temporarily buy exclusion of threatening objects, can be defined as follows. Social worlds with a certain consensus of status identity will aim to keep out of that identity, via landscape control, objects that are threatening to their esteem. These objects mediate between the social world and other status groups, so that particular symbols are associated with them. For example, cluster homes may be associated with lower-income 'undesirables'. This does not deny status mobility, but does imply that this must be accompanied by buying into the correct symbols. This point is of particular importance in anti-growth movements where persons of similar status may be excluded if it is felt that they will occupy unacceptable types of housing. This is now shown to be the case in one example studied.

A defensive space in Canada

The selected jurisdiction, West Vancouver, is a well-established community on the North Shore of the Burrard Inlet, facing the city of Vancouver and adjacent to the municipality of North Vancouver (Figure 9.1). Research was undertaken in 1977 and 1978 as part of a comparable study with anti-growth movements in the United States. More recent developments have not been investigated so the study should be regarded as a segment of an on-going process.

The municipality grew up as a series of disconnected villages, hemmed between mountain and water, which gradually coalesced. From its early stages

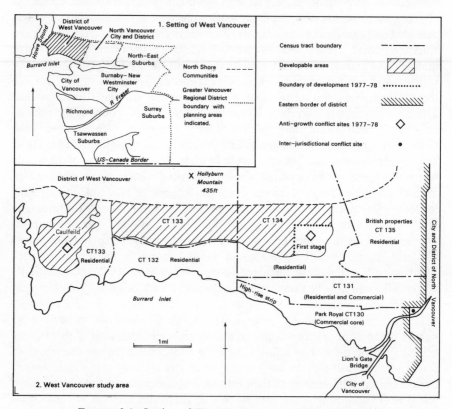

FIGURE 9.1. Setting of West Vancouver and the study area

of development West Vancouver Council has sought to keep out industrial activity, and until recently, large-scale commercial activity. Its recent residential development has resulted in it being viewed as middle to upper class, popular with the *nouveaux riches*, earning it the label of 'Martini Mountain', an image consistent with an exclusive suburb. With the exception of the commercial core and contiguous blocks along the waterfront, where high-rise development has occurred, nearly all residential areas are single-family dwellings at densities as low as one to the acre.

Exclusionary practices of more traditional kinds have been found in West Vancouver in the past, with 'restricted covenants' to exclude certain ethnic groups. These are now illegal, but since 1975 a new exclusionary sentiment has arisen, with the development as a consequence of anti-growth movements (West Vancouver Council, 1975). At the same time as the Council began to investigate growth schemes, developer pressure grew to construct higher-density cluster and townhouses in a belt above existing residential areas on the lower mountain slopes. These were to be started in the east of the municipality, moving gradually westwards, and not above the 1200 foot line, which for environmental reasons was considered the upper limit for residential development.

The various land developers were encouraged by the Greater Vancouver Regional District's policy proposal that West Vancouver should grow by about 500 persons per annum through the late 1970s to 1986 (Greater Vancouver Regional District, 1975). Overall growth targets for the North Shore were not in fact as high as for the Regional District as a whole, 15 per cent as against 25 per cent. The former figure, however, includes North Vancouver, the West Vancouver share being slightly lower. It could not be said, therefore, that the growth targets for the municipality were excessive when judged against the whole regional district.

The Municipal Council undertook a public relations exercise to monitor reactions to the concrete proposals from the developers which proceeded stage-by-stage.* Major concern was expressed at possible environmental damage to mountain slopes through increased run-off, in turn affecting properties on lower slopes. Social impact such as household mix and increased net densities of dwellings per acre also brought hostile reactions at public meetings. A number of local ratepayers' groups in the east and central sections of the municipality opposed any development beyond the existing areas. In the west new rate-payers' groups sprung up where none had previously existed, as townhouses and cluster homes were proposed in predominantly single-family dwelling areas.

A considerable amount of opposition was based on cost-sharing of new infrastructure and the amount to be contributed by developers, as distinct from

---

* Various public meetings were attended; other major sources include local newspapers such as the Vancouver Sun and North Shore News and several formal meetings were arranged with officers of the District Council.

the tax base. Confusion arose with the most vocal ratepayers' group, known as the British Properties and Area Homeowners Association, who would not accept that extensive expense would be necessary on the higher land, even if no new homes were built. This was due to erosional damage from streams threatening existing dwellings as well. The Council, as local state, were caught trying to mediate in this situation by arguing that the repair work could be spread across the new dwellings as well.

The question of landscape control and identity is really the most critical one, however, and dominated over environmental issues (except for some preservation of open space). This is evidently so since growth of population as such became something of a red-herring. From 1971 to 1976 the Canadian census shows that West Vancouver had zero population growth (remaining at about 36 400). Arguments used by residents groups that population growth had already occurred had little foundation, therefore. On the other hand with falling household size and a much reduced birth rate in the municipality in the 1970s, new household formation is very relevant. Most opposition was generated by the extension of the built environment to house smaller families including many younger, professional, and executive single people in up-market town-houses, often selling at higher prices than existing single-family dwellings (see for example the 'first stage' proposal in Figure 9.1). At public meetings, however, it was generally argued that such homes would encourage the in-migration of lower-income groups. It was then in these housing proposals that 'contamination' of symbols was most felt.

The preservation of landscape identity is well illustrated by one petition from a part of the municipality (Caulfeild) where no previous residents group had existed (Caulfeild Property Owners Association, 1978). This acknowledged that the municipal council would need to encourage some development to fulfil the Regional District's plans and to spread the load of unavoidable costs concerned with drainage improvements on the mountain slopes. To this extent the Association, predominantly middle-class in composition, was more realistic than the British Properties Homeowners' Association, a largely *nouveaux riches* group. The submission then, however, associated proposed new access roads with townhouse development and suggested adding only one such road which, it claimed, 'would not pass a single existing home'. On closer questioning one petitioner stated that: 'Well, townhouses and access roads go together, don't they? If these people will be living in townhouses, then they're supposed to put up with busy roads.' This is an excellent example of symbolic avoidance behaviour, illustrating the reification of a group who appear to be of a different status. It is assumed that there is a type of household right for a townhouse and to have, or perhaps suffer, access roads with that identity. When faced with the above-mentioned realities of housing price, a position made quite clear by the various developer groups, these property-owners associations sought compromise positions to preserve at least some part of the symbolic landscape.

Some attempt to retain a modicum of public open space was the most common tactic employed.

Localist sentiment is tied in with wider reactions and political action over West Vancouver, expressed in other ways than by the development industry. Although some developers were living in the community at the time, the great majority of the new housing proposals originated from outside companies or from trusts previously linked to ratepayers' groups such as the British Properties, but now divorced from them. The problem of labelling communities as a whole has been termed by Suttles (1972) the 'representative image' or 'average differences' that are used to identify one place from another. In the case of West Vancouver this has been very stereotyped, as already suggested. The 'Martini Mountain' label sums up the outsiders' typification of the community as inhabited by *nouveaux riches* groups who seek avid status expression at any cost. Examples include the purchase of large, single-family homes, but an inability to afford to furnish them, whilst gardens are kept meticulously in order. Abuse by outsiders of inhabitants of West Vancouver on mentioning place of residence has been found to be quite common.

A demystified view of West Vancouver, however, using a mixture of census information and qualitative investigation within the community produced a different picture. Only one census tract, with the most vocal *nouveaux riches* group (the British Properties and Area Homeowners' Association) showed any characteristics close to those of the typification (see Figure 9.1, and Table 9.1).

TABLE 9.1.   Census tract comparisons in West and North Vancouver

Variable	Parks Royal CT130 (Socially mixed)	British properties CT135 (*Nouveaux riches*)	North Vancouver census tract
Population	7865	6530	5100
Median value of homes	$33 840	$51 418	$34 544
Average cash rent	$184	$254	$231
Number of occupied dwellings with:	3750	1655	1365
One auto	2100 (56%)	335 (20%)	525 (38.5%)
Two or more autos	785 (21%)	1310 (79%)	825 (60.5%)
No autos	865 (23%)	10 (1%)	15 (1%)
Average total household income	$12 218	$22 880	$15 851
Highest range of household income (proportion)	$10 000 $15 000	$20 000+	$15 000 − $20 000

Source: Census of Canada 1971. Summary tables for Vancouver Region

Other census-tract information suggested socio-economic characteristics not unlike those found in parts of the adjacent North Vancouver. Table 9.1 compares the most socially mixed tract of West Vancouver with an 'average' tract of North Vancouver. Some of the latter municipality measures are closer to those of the British Properties tract in fact, although household income falls closer to the Park Royal figure. The typification of North Vancouver at this time, however, was of a pro-growth, 'open' middle-class community, favouring high-density development, quite at odds with that of West Vancouver.

Further liaison with the West Vancouver Council (1977a) turned up the observation that only the British Properties and Area Homeowners' Association were considered to be socially strong in the community. Nevertheless, whatever the external stereotype suggests this group is viewed as politically weak by older established elite groups (Caulfeild Property Owners' Association, 1978). The anti-growth sentiment tended to sweep the whole community, but not uniformly. For example the British Properties group was given first chance to oppose the new development, and then older groups took over later after initial failures to prevent release of land. At the time of the completion of the research in 1978, the final outcome of the conflict was uncertain, being a protracted process which had also begun to draw in provincial and municipal legislation. It was clear, however, that the strengthening of a common response to growth policies in West Vancouver had been the result of an active reaction to developer pressure, as Frieden (1979) has also reported in California.

No inherent 'suburban' viewpoint has been found in these landscape issues, although the response has been conditioned by overt feelings, expressed in the image of a conflict-free, peaceful community. This did not persist, however. Qualitative investigation revealed considerable ambivalence, however, towards the core area with its commercial centre (Park Royal) and high-rise development. There was a willingness to invest in these parts of the community for the function they serve, in particular their high tax revenue, but an acute sense of withdrawal if they were permitted to encroach too far into the adjacent lower-density areas. In the latter period of investigation lesser, but quite influential, opposition was expressed as well to continued high-rise development along the foreshore, which it was claimed would detract from views. It also became clear that the mixture of land uses found in the adjacent municipality was not favoured. One of the major inter-jurisdictional conflicts revealed (West Vancouver Council, 1977b) was a case where a twenty-storey high-rise had been constructed by North Vancouver right on the border with West Vancouver and overlooking two-storey luxury apartments with private pools.

Implications of localism and its general applicability

It is not intended that the above example should be regarded as typifying all anti-growth movements and 'defensible' spaces. Nevertheless, although only illustrative, characteristics common to American experience are apparent. In particular the institutional conflict over 'external control' is important. Using the terminology of the Harvey/Walker perspective, a contradiction is present in that the development industry is now attempting to take control over space reserved for localist defence, usually by businessmen and industrialists who have not viewed their 'turf' as vulnerable. Several company directors were known to be living in West Vancouver for example. There has been no Sierra Club involvement as in California (Frieden, 1979) but some similar consequences are apparent. In particular, institutions with the least local interest are seen to be the 'breakers' of defensive tactics: increasing Federal involvement in the United States is apparent with much court litigation (Rose and Rothman, 1977). Canadian action is more limited, although West Vancouver was the only municipality in British Columbia to be refused a special grant on grounds which politically may have been connected with anti-growth practices, although these were not formally admitted.*

In the case of Britain more recent research is tending to show the same effect in a situation where national control has been present much longer, through Town and Country Planning legislation, but where anti-growth movements are now springing up. A case study in North Leicestershire is showing that these are most predominant in urban fringe settlements pinpointed for possible growth, alongside others that will be restricted to little or no growth (a 'key' settlement policy). There is no exact equivalent to this in North America, although 'growth corridors' have been allocated in parts of California (Frieden, 1979). The question of landscape identity is more complicated because of traditionally higher-density developments in Britain but investigations do suggest opposition to all but detached (single-family) homes in certain villages or neighbourhoods. Defensive spaces may have been less common in Britain, although Young and Kramer (1978) have argued that this is true for London over the issue of decentralizing council housing. There is also the earlier example of the Cutteslowe Walls in Oxford (Collison, 1963), when middle-class residents built a wall in 1932 after lower-income groups were moved out of the central area. In general, however, it seems that the term may hold more applicability at the sub-regional scale, for example in relation to resistance to overspill developments in the Shire Counties from metropolitan centres such as Birmingham. The example of Wythall is well-documented here (Hall, 1973, Vol. 1). Most recently, however, it is probably in environmental factors such as the preservation of open space, views, and the separation of villages that similarities with the North American experience are evident.

* This grant, in the family-services programme, was paid to individuals in trouble in the schools, at home and with police and probation departments. The province had claimed that West Vancouver was paying this grant to individuals with adequate means. It is possible that the stereotype image was being enforced here (i.e. that all residents had adequate means).

The wider implications of localism and anti-growth movements have been largely examined to date in the context of equity in the housing market. Frieden (1979) considers that as an ideology anti-growth protest is elitist, and serves as a preservationist value that protects open space from development for a limited group of people. His analysis of the San Francisco Region suggests that anti-growth sentiment has cut housing starts, reduced choice of types of dwelling and in part escalated house prices. Anti-growth movements have done little to promote quality of life outside of the localist setting and cannot be said to have changed the decline of inner-city areas by discouraging outmovement. Indeed resistance to the development of unused plots for infilling is increasing there also, again with Sierra Club involvement (Frieden, 1979).

Diversion of growth elsewhere may be a consequence if there are regional goals for this. In the Greater Vancouver Regional District, for example, West Vancouver's rate of growth is linked to other targets in adjoining municipalities; resistance to growth in West Vancouver implies higher rates elsewhere. At the time of the research, however, the formerly pro-growth North Vancouver was contemplating resistance to excessive development that would be to West Vancouver's benefit. With controls on eastward expansion in the Greater Vancouver Region to protect agricultural land (Yeates, 1980) options for new development are further restricted. In the case of Leicestershire, 'shunting' effects are apparent which are largely due to the sequential nature of Local Plans working from Structure Plan targets which do not make precise allocations to any one community (with a few exceptions). The success of some anti-growth movements several years ago has resulted in a short-fall of housing plots in terms of Structure Plan allocation. Release of land is now suggested in settlements not previously targeted for any significant growth and some opposition is now appearing in these settlements, although in this case the local state is less ready to accede than in American examples. In these regional settings localism can be viewed as a belief in a closed system, not subject to external inputs (Clayton, 1978).

Distributive effects on access to housing and open space may be by no means the only ones, should localism become more widespread. If limited to a few spaces it would appear that a managerialist or more institutional 'manipulated city' perspective could epistemologically handle the explanation for its existence. But in fact localism is growing as an idealogy and is tied-in with societal trends. Most notable is the post-industrial ethic, which is now much more than the theory put forward by Bell (1973). It is being put into practice by social groups under quality-of-life beliefs and the previously mentioned 'preservationist' stance. In Vancouver, Ley (1980) has shown how a liberal 'liveability' ethic was promoted in the 1970s, very much in keeping with local-government policy (Greater Vancouver Regional District, 1975). This has not aided finance capital in investment opportunities and has in part contributed to the development industry turning to localist places such as West Vancouver, hoping to find less resistance there. For the American metropolis as a whole, however, Ashton

(1978) argues that such a process would undermine the advantages deliberately accrued through political fragmentation of the suburbs (such as low tax bases, cut-off from the central city).

Widespread development of localism as an ideology, a 'retreat' ethic from growth, could well undermine the logic of production in advanced market society, whilst satisfying new consumption tastes. Finance capital interests at a general level cannot come into conflict with other capital without effects on production and consumption, particularly of living space for those who see themselves as 'catching-up' with the established professional/managerial groups. Indeed, and contrary to, for example, Harvey (1978), it is precisely in the latter groups that a degree of false consciousness is the problem. The contradiction for those who control finance capital is that they must continually invest in suburban spaces for other groups to benefit and threaten their own living space which they appear to have regarded as not subject to the norms of market society. The only alternative is to withdraw from this branch of capital, or maintain only interests in other branches. Ashton (1978) argues that reinvestment in the central city may be a means out of this dilemma (for example gentrification), although at the cost of political independence of the suburbs. It is dubious, however, whether this alone could satisfy the land development industry.

In West Vancouver it appeared that most resident managers were more committed to industrial capital but their links with finance capital markets could also have been harmed if the latter industry became unprofitable. In California it appears that the land development industry has responded to a falling rate of profit by higher pricing of new housing (Frieden, 1979). This is inflationary because it is not backed up by a corresponding increase in value of production and economies of scale are also lost.

Manipulative action, elitist in nature, certainly occurs in localist space, but wider effects tend to offset it. It is interesting to note that in West Vancouver the only pro-growth group was an Indian organization which had a small area of land in one corner of the municipality, close to the core. Their own proposals included investment in commercial and residential development but this was strongly resisted by the established social groups and the District Council. Clearly local power and autonomy is significant, but the success of such proposals will also depend on societal questions, in which finance capital interests play a major part. This can also result in the wider state and the local State coming into conflict as managers of differing interpretations of the goals of advanced market society.

SUMMARY AND DISCUSSION

Now that the ladder has been reclimbed a different approach to 'suburban' can be offered. The term cannot relate simply to alternative, competing definitions, such as ecological and sub-cultural. Rather it represents a whole web of relations in market society which are concretized in particular places. These include characteristics as divergent as density of development, mix of land uses, forms of landscape identity and particular impacts of finance capital, not seen as a power apart from human action, but inexorably bound up in it. Over time these relations will change, though some less so than others. For example, density may remain unaltered whilst the wider net of capital relations undergoes change. In older suburbs industrialists were often concerned with creating living space, such as model communities (Port Sunlight, Bournville are clear examples). Now finance capital undertakes this role, although the extent to which this branch is truly separate from others has been disputed (Roweis and Scott, 1978). In this view landlords who were powerful along with industrialists in the nineteenth century housing market are now assimilated in the production of capital as a whole. If this is the case, then Harvey and Walker may be more historically accurate. However, contentious an issue this is, it remains the case that a development industry at a wider scale is a less localist form of control than that of industrialists solely concerned with providing living space close to factory sites. Hence as localism as an ideology strengthens, so do the objective relations in which this occurs become wider.

Walker (1981, p. 410) has said that: 'It is time that we advanced beyond merely listing the factors contributing to suburbanization—whether couched in Marxist theory or not—and approached the theory systematically, probing the various causal elements and establishing basic principles of analysis to link suburbanization to the structure of capitalism.' Needless to say the approaches reviewed only capture parts of this web of relations and cannot then synthesize the complexity of the process into an explanation that covers the wide application of the label 'suburban'. Alternatively new labels such as 'Outer City' are chosen, which generalize change over space termed 'suburban' when this is not valid. The survival of the label 'surburban', often as a shorthand term, is far less critical than the complete outlining of the interacting relations that it embraces. To do otherwise is to remain at a nominalist level, with definitions that reveal nothing, or satisfy contingent aims such as maintaining the same divisions of census names over time to analyse rates of change. Fischer (1976) is rightly suspicious of such approaches (which Muller uses) because of the restricted definition. It also appears that an unintended consequence of this fixed division is support of the claim that black suburbanization is increasing over time.

The critical difference in the position advocated here from recent structuralist perspectives is that the localist basis of defensive spaces and anti-growth movements is not forgotten, or simply determined by the wider structural setting. Some of the assertions of proponents of this view have been incorporated into the argument here, but are viewed in relation to agency as a force in market society. Structuralist views fall prey to the charge of scientism, because explanations are then *sui generis* (Duncan, 1980), that is teleological ultimately. They are also, as Rex (1974, p. 110) points out, remarkably 'quietistic' politically and survive on the sustenance of the very relations which they critique or see as producing contradictions. Ultimately they leave an explanation of human action purged of man. As Giddens (1979, p. 52) complains, whether starting with Parsons or Althusser they ultimately produce 'dopes'—cultural or economic ones. A more active view of ideology in both its conscious and unconscious forms can overcome this deficiency. Epistemologically the limits of awareness, or at least the suppression of this in individual consciousness, can be used to provide a meaningful empirical base to theoretical claims. Such a base does not represent a testing of these claims, but a grounding of them in the reality from which they spring. This constitutes the meaning of a demystified view of suburban space, which can then be brought together with the already demystified view of city space that is evident in recent work.

ACKNOWLEDGEMENT

I would like to thank David Ley for his interest and encouragement during the period the research was undertaken. The ideas in this paper sprang originally from doctoral coursework at the University of British Columbia.

REFERENCES

Agnew, J. A. (1981). Homeownership and the capitalist social order. In *Urbanization and Urban Planning in Capitalist Society* (Eds M. Dear and A. J. Scott), pp. 457–480, Methuen, London.
Ashton, P. J. (1978). The political economy of suburban development. In *Marxism and the Metropolis: New Perspectives in Urban Political Economy* (Eds W. Tabb and L. Sawers), pp. 64–89, Oxford University Press, New York.
Banham, R. (1971). *Los Angeles—The Architecture of Four Ecologies*, Penguin, London.
Baran, P. and Sweezy, P. (1966). *Monopoly Capital*, Monthly Review Press, New York.
Bell, D. (1973). *The Coming of Post-Industrial Society*, Basic Books, New York.
Bell, C. and Newby, H. (1978). Community, communion, class and community action: The social sources of the new urban politics. In *Social Areas in Cities* (Eds D. T. Herbert and R. J. Johnston), pp. 283–301, Wiley, Chichester.
Bender, T. (1975). *Toward an Urban Vision: Ideas and Institutions in Nineteenth Century America*, University Press of Kentucky, Lexington.
Berger, B. M. (1960). *Working Class Suburb—A Study of Auto Workers in Suburbia*, University of California Press, Berkeley.
Berger, P. L. and Luckmann, T. (1967). *The Social Construction of Reality*, Anchor Books, New York.
Caulfeild Property Owners Association (1978). *Submissions and Petitions to West Vancouver Council*, typed manuscripts.
Checkoway, B. (1980). Large builders, Federal housing programmes and post-war suburbanisation, *International Journal of Urban and Regional Research*, **4**, 21–45.

Clayton, C. (1978). *The Intended and Unintended Socio-Economic Consequence of Population Policies at the Community Level*, Paper presented to the Annual Meeting of the Association of Pacific Coast Geographers, Portland.

Collison, P. (1963). *The Cutteslowe Walls—A Study in Social Class*, Faber and Faber, London.

Cybriwsky, R. A. (1978). Social aspects of neighbourhood change, *Annals, Association of American Geographers*, **68**, 17–33.

Danielson, M. N. (1976). *The Politics of Exclusion*, Columbia University Press, New York.

Davidoff, P. and Davidoff, L. (1971). Opening up the suburbs: Toward inclusionary land controls, *Syracuse Law Review*, **22**.

Dobriner, W. M. (1963). *Class in Suburbia*, Prentice-Hall, Englewood Cliffs.

Duncan, J. S. (1973). Landscape identity as a symbol of group identity, *Geographical Review*, **63**, 334–355.

Duncan, J. S. (1976). Landscape and the communication of social identity. In *The Mutual Interaction of People and the Built Environment* (Ed. A. Rapaport), pp. 391–401, Mouton Press, The Hague.

Duncan, J. S. (1980). The superorganic in American cultural geography, *Annals, Association of American Geographers*, **70**, 181–198.

Dunleavy, P. (1980). *Urban Political Analysis—The Politics of Collective Consumption*, Macmillan, London.

Evans, D. M. (1978). Alienation, mental illness and the partitioning of space, *Antipode*, **10**, 13–23.

Evans, D. M. (Forthcoming). *Anti-Growth Movements on the Urban Fringe: A Cross-Cultural Comparison*, Doctoral Dissertation, University of Technology, Loughborough.

Firey, W. (1945). Sentiment and symbolism as ecological variables, *American Sociological Review*, **10**, 140–148.

Fischer, C. S. (1976). *The Urban Experience*, Harcourt Brace, New York.

Fischer, C. S. and Jackson, R. M. (1976). Suburbs, networks and attitudes. In *The Changing Face of the Suburbs* (Ed. B. Schwartz), pp. 279–307, University of Chicago Press, Chicago.

Frieden, B. J. (1979). *The Environmental Protection Hustle*, MIT Press, Cambridge, Massachusetts.

Gadamer, H. (1976). The historicity of understanding. In *Critical Sociology* (Ed. P. Connerton), pp. 117–133, Penguin, London.

Gale, S. and Moore, E. G. (1975). *The Manipulated City*, Maaroufa Press, Chicago.

Gans, H. J. (1962). Urbanism and suburbanism as ways of life: A re-evaluation of definitions. In *Human Behaviour and Social Processes* (Ed. A. M. Rose), pp. 625–648, Houghton Mifflin, Boston.

Gans, H. J. (1967). *The Levittowners*, Vintage Books, New York.

Giddens, A. (1979). *Central Problems in Social Theory*, Macmillan, London.

Gottdiener, M. (1977). *Planned Sprawl—Private and Public Interests in Suburbia*, Sage, Beverley Hills.

Greater Vancouver Regional District (1975). *The Liveable Region, 1976–1986*, Vancouver.

Hadden, J. K. and Barton, J. F. (1973). An image that will not die: Thoughts on the history of anti-urban ideology. In *The Urbanisation of the Suburbs* (Eds L. H. Masotti and J. K. Hadden), pp. 79–116, Urban Affairs Annual Review No. 7, Sage, Beverly Hills.

Hall, P., Thomas, R., Gracey, H., and Drewett, J. (1973). *The Containment of Urban England*, Vol. 1, George Allen and Unwin, London.

Harvey, D. W. (1975). Class structure in a capitalist society and the theory of residential differentiation. In *Processes in Physical and Human Geography* (Ed. M. Chisholm), pp 354–389, Heinemann, London.

Harvey, D. W. (1978). Labour, capital and class struggle around the built environment in advanced capitalist societies. In *Urbanization and Conflict in Market Societies* (Ed. K. R. Cox), pp. 9–37, Maaroufa Press, Chicago.

Hays, S. P. (1964). The politics of reform in municipal government in the progressive era, *Pacific Northwest Quarterly*, **55**, 157–169.

Hughes, J. W. (1975). Dilemmas of suburbanisation and growth controls, *Annals of the American Academy of Political and Social Science*, **422**, 61–76.

Janowitz, M. (1952). *The Community Press in the Urban Setting*, University of Chicago Press, Chicago.

Johnston, R. J. (1981). The management and autonomy of the local state: The role of the judiciary in the United States, *Environment and Planning A*, **13**, 1305–1315.

Kaplan, G. (1976). *The Dream Deferred—Politics and Planning in Suburbia*, Seabury Press, New York.

Ley, D. F. (1980). Liberal ideology and the post-industrial city, *Annals of the Association of American Geographers*, **70**, 238–258.

Lineberry, R. L. (1975). Suburbia and the metropolitan turf, *Annals of the American Academy of Political and Social Science*, **422**, 1–9.

Lubove, R. (1967). *The Urban Community—Housing and Planning in the Progressive Era*, Prentice-Hall, Englewood Cliffs.

Macpherson, C. B. (1964). *The Political Theory of Possessive Individualism: Hobbes to Locke*, Oxford University Press, Oxford.

Marx, K. (1972). Capital: selections. In *The Marx–Engels Reader* (Ed. R. C. Tucker), pp. 191–317, Norton, New York.

Marx, K. (1973). *Grundrisse: Foundations of the Critique of Political Economy*, Pelican, London.

Masotti, L. H. (1973). Epilogue. In *The Urbanisation of the Suburbs* (Eds L. H. Masotti and J. K. Hadden), pp. 533–542, Urban Affairs Annual Review No. 7, Sage, Beverly Hills.

Masotti, L. H. and Hadden, J. K. (Eds) (1973). *The Urbanisation of the Suburbs*, Urban Affairs Annual Review No. 7, Sage, Beverly Hills.

Mercer, J. (1976). *Subsidised Housing and Locational Conflict*, Paper presented to the Annual Meeting of the Association of American Geographers, New York.

Molotch, H. (1976). The city as a growth machine: Toward a political economy of place, *American Journal of Sociology*, **82**, 309–332.

Morgan, P. (1971). Community social rank and attitude, *Sociology and Social Research*, **55**, 401–411.

Muller, P. O. (1976). *The Outer City—Geographical Consequences of the Urbanisation of the Suburbs*, AAG Resource Paper No. 75–2, Association of American Geographers, Washington.

Nelson, H. J. and Clark, W. A. V. (1976). *Los Angeles—The Metropolitan Experience*, AAG Comparative Metropolitan Analysis Project, Ballinger, Cambridge, Massachusetts.

Newman, O. (1972). *Defensible Space*, Macmillan, New York.

Newton, K. (1978). Conflict avoidance and conflict suppression: The case of urban politics in the United States. In *Urbanization and Conflict in Market Societies* (Ed. K. R. Cox), pp. 76–93, Maaroufa Press, Chicago.

Pahl, R. E. (1975). *Whose City?* Penguin, London.

Reisman, D. (1957). The suburban dislocation, *Annals of the American Academy of Political and Social Science*, **314**, 123–146.

Rex, J. (1974). *Sociology and the Demystification of the Modern World*, Routledge and Kegan Paul, London.

Rose, J. G. and Rothman, R. E. (1977). *After Mount Laurel: The New Suburban Zoning*, The Centre for Urban Policy Research, Rutgers.

Roweis, S. T. and Scott, A. J. (1978). The urban land question. In *Urbanization and Conflict in Market Societies* (Ed. K. R. Cox), pp. 38–75, Maaroufa Press, Chicago.

Saglyn, L. B. and Sternlieb, G. (1973). *Zoning and Housing Costs: The Impact of Land Use Controls on Housing Price*, The Centre for Urban Policy Research, Rutgers.

Samuels, M. S. (1979). The biography of landscape. In *The Interpretation of Ordinary Landscapes* (Ed. D. W. Meinig), pp. 51–88, Oxford University Press, New York.

Saunders, P. (1980). *Urban Politics*, Penguin, London.

Schwartz, B. (1976). Images of suburbia: Some revisionist commentary and conclusions. In *The Changing Face of the Suburbs* (Ed. B. Schwartz), pp. 325–340, University of Chicago Press, Chicago.

Sennett, R. (1970). *The Uses of Disorder*, Pelican, London.

Sennett, R. (1978). *The Fall of Public Man*, Vintage, New York.

Sennett, R. and Cobb, J. (1973). *The Hidden Injuries of Class*, Vintage, New York.

Sternlieb, G. (1971). The city as sandbox, *Public Interest*, **25**, 14–21.

Sternlieb, G. (1974). The future of housing in New Jersey. In *Growth Controls—New Dimensions of Urban Planning Series*, Vol. 1 (Ed. J. W. Hughes), pp. 223–232, The Centre for Urban Policy Research, Rutgers.

Suttles, G. D. (1968). *The Social Order of the Slum*, University of Chicago Press, Chicago.

Suttles, G. D. (1972). *The Social Construction of Communities*, University of Chicago Press, Chicago.

Thorns, D. (1973). *Suburbia*, Paladin, St Albans.

Walker, R. (1978). 'The transformation of urban structure in the nineteenth century and the beginnings of suburbanization. In *Urbanization and Conflict in Market Societies* (Ed. K. R. Cox), pp. 165–212, Maaroufa Press, Chicago.

Walker, R. (1981). A theory of suburbanization: Capitalism and the construction of urban space in the United States. In *Urbanization and Urban Planning in Capitalist Society* (Eds M. Dear and A. J. Scott), pp. 383–429, Methuen, London.

Werthman, C. S. (1968). *The Social Meaning of the Physical Environment*. Doctoral Dissertation, University of California, Berkeley.

West Vancouver Council (1975). *Draft Report of the Task Force Appointed by Mayor Peter Jones to Examine the Implications of Policies Limiting Growth in West Vancouver*, Mimeo, West Vancouver.

Whyte, W. H. (1956). *The Organization Man*, Doubleday Anchor, Garden City, New York.

West Vancouver Council (1977a). *Communication with Director of Planning*.

West Vancouver Council (1977b). *Communication with Planning Officers*.

Wirth, L. (1938). Urbanism as a way of life, *American Journal of Sociology*, **44**, 1–24.

Yeates, M. (1980). *North American Urban Patterns*, Arnold, London.

Young, K. and Kramer, J. (1978). *Strategy and Conflict in Metropolitan Housing— Suburbia versus the Greater London Council*, 1965–1975, Heinemann, London.

Young, M. and Willmott, P. (1967). *Family and Kinship in East London*, Pelican, London.

Geography and the Urban Environment
Progress in Research and Applications, Volume VI
Edited by D. T. Herbert and R. J. Johnston
© 1984 John Wiley & Sons Ltd.

Chapter 10

Local Areas in the City

Michael Pacione

The definition and spatial delimitation of local areas in cities have occupied researchers ever since the classical ecologists' attempts to distinguish natural areas in the urban fabric of Chicago. Until recently efforts to identify urban sub-areas involved the plotting of objective social, economic and/or demographic data onto a small-scale base map, either directly or following statistical manipulation via social area analysis or factorial ecology. In terms of their relevance for patterns of daily urban life the correspondence between such physical areas and the activity patterns of individuals was poor. In order to resolve this dissidence between the physical neighbourhood and the social or behavioural neighbourhood, T. R. Lee and others turned to the subjective approach and set out to measure the local area through its representation in the minds of residents, and to relate this construct to observed activity patterns. The basic assumption behind this view—that overt spatial behaviour stems from individual preferences and perception of the environment rather than from more objective data—has been generally accepted as the organizing principle of the cognitive-behavioural approach to human geography.

Recognition of the significance of perceived home areas for urban life raises the question of whether they can have practical utility in addition to academic interest. Since the publication of the Skeffington Report (1969), planners have acknowledged the need to plan for people as opposed to places and yet the majority of urban plans are still based on areal subdivisions which pay only lip service to this ideal, usually being amalgamations of census enumeration districts or the creation of 'expert opinion'. With the growing importance of localism, particularly in urban United States (Hallman, 1974) there is a clear need for a thorough investigation of the potential utility of perceived local areas as a framework for the organization of the modern city. This objective may be approached from two perspectives. The first has its roots in urban-politics and the local-democracy movements, and concentrates on the city's political machinery. It is largely aspatial in emphasis (Bell and Newby, 1976). The second

349

approach may be termed 'geographical' in that its focus of concern is the spatial structure which underlies the urban political system.

Concentrating on the spatial dimension demands that some attention be given to the concepts of territory and territoriality. As Soja (1971, p. 19) points out, 'man is a territorial animal and territoriality affects human behaviour at all scales of social activity'. Territoriality may be defined as the propensity of people to define certain areas and defend them. The definition of territory is less straightforward, however, and despite the attentions of many writers (Lowenthal, 1961; Parr, 1965; Altman and Haythorn, 1967; Kuhn, 1968; Sommer, 1969; Lipman, 1970) no simple definition or explanation has been produced. Two definitions of relevance for the present investigation define this spatial translation of territoriality as:

the space, which may be continuous or discontinuous, used by an individual or group for most interactions and which, because of this, goes a long way towards satisfying the needs of identity, stimulation and security (Eyles, 1971, p. 2).

a behavioural phenomenon associated with the organization of space into spheres of influence or clearly demarcated territories which are made distinctive and considered at least partially exclusive by their occupants or definers (Soja, 1971, p. 19).

The interrelated concepts of territory and territoriality imply that, as Becker and Mayo (1971, p. 380) point out, 'some space is of more value than others . . . and that to give up this particular space is to incur a meaningful loss'. The idea of a 'valued environment' underlies all definitions of territory and this clearly assigns a central role to individuals' perception and evaluation of their surroundings. This view is supported by Uexkull's (1957, p. 54) claim that territory 'is an entirely subjective product', and Ardrey's (1972, p. 196) statement that a territory 'cannot exist in nature; it exists in the mind', while Suttles (1972, p. 22) considered cognitive maps as 'part of the social control apparatus of urban areas and of special importance in regulating spatial movement'.

Human territories vary in terms of their organization and a variety of taxonomies is available in the literature (Lyman and Scott, 1967; Goffman, 1972; Altman, 1975). Rapaport (1977) has presented a useful five-element ethological space model which describes an hierarchical arrangement of territories of increasing size. These range from the egocentric 'personal space', through 'jurisdiction', 'territory', and 'core area', to 'home range' defined as 'the usual limit of regular movements and activities'. Adopting this framework the core area (the space within the home range which is most commonly inhabited, used daily and best known) accords most closely with the notion of the urban neighbourhood.

Examining the place of these local or core areas in the modern city from a spatial or 'geographical' perspective raises a number of fundamental questions:

(i) Most basically, territories must be demarcated; and the boundaries may be physical or perceptual. The existence of distinctive spatial barriers in Belfast (Boal, 1969) and Philadelphia (Ley and Cybriwsky, 1974) raises the general question of neighbourhood boundary consensus. Specifically, to what extent are perceived local areas popularly acknowledged by residents?

(ii) The size of perceived local areas, in both areal and population terms, is important not least because this has clear implications for the economics of service provision. Apart from studies of the development of spatial cognition with age (Hart and Moore, 1973) and the effect of sex differences and length of residence on cognitive maps (Everitt and Cadwallader, 1977) little consideration has been given to the factors influencing the size of urban neighbourhoods. In particular the effects of environmental factors, such as population density, on neighbourhood size have proved resistant to formal investigation.

(iii) Attempts to incorporate space perceptions into a formal planning framework, as suggested by writers such as Saarinen (1976) and Golledge and Zannaras (1973), have been hampered by the idiosyncratic nature of individual mental maps and by the lack of information on the stability of subjectively defined local areas over time. The question of the temporal integrity of neighbourhoods is clearly of critical importance since there would be little practical merit in employing a spatial structure in which the basic framework changed over short time periods. Unfortunately few longitudinal studies have been undertaken and existing evidence on the subject is both scant and inconclusive.

(iv) Many researchers have stressed the importance of the urban neighbourhood (Mumford, 1954; Keller, 1968; Warren, 1978). Thomlinson (1969, p. 181), for example, considers that 'sociologically the most significant city segment having territorial aspect is the neighbourhood', while for Greely (1975, p. 100) neighbourhood loyalty is 'something quite primordial'. Others such as Webber (1963, 1964), however, have questioned the continued relevance of local areas and, despite recent attempts to synthesize the debate (Wellman and Leighton, 1979), contemporary researchers are still faced with contradictory assessments of the importance of the urban neighbourhood. Clearly, further empirical information on the extent to which local areas are perceived as meaningful socio-economic entities would be of great value.

(v) A suggestion that urban neighbourhoods should be made coterminous with administrative areas was made seventy years ago (Ward, 1913). Despite periodic restatements of this ideal (Perry, 1929; Dudley Report, 1944;

Young, 1970) it is still fair to state that in most urban areas any spatial coincidence between urban neighbourhoods and administrative areas is largely accidental. With the increasing pressures for devolution of power and increased local democracy (Hallman, 1974; Hambleton, 1978; Cohen, 1979) the question of the extent to which local-area boundaries coincide with existing political, administrative and service area boundaries assumes major importance.

The present investigation contributes to the debate on the significance of local areas in the city by employing empirical evidence from Glasgow to address each of these key questions.

STUDY AREA AND SAMPLE POPULATION

The selection of a study area within Glasgow was facilitated by examining two maps prepared at the city-wide scale; the first being a general land-use map, and the second depicting social areas based on a multivariate analysis of twenty-two census indicators. The study area selected satisfied the following criteria:

(i) An area of sufficient spatial extent to permit the definition and delimitation of home areas but not so large as to confound the data collecting exercise.
(ii) An area with a population of manageable size from the sampling viewpoint.
(iii) An area of mixed land uses and with a variety of housing types.
(iv) An area free from the temporary upheavals currently experienced in the large-scale redevelopment zones in the city.
(v) In addition to satisfying these basic criteria the study area had the additional advantage of being physically well defined by waterways on three sides and a major routeway on the other.

The area was in the west end of the city about three miles from the centre. It covered an area of approximately 550 hectares and enclosed a population of just over 50 000 (Figure, 10.1). A 5 per cent stratified random sample of households was taken based on the most recent electoral register. A total of 760 completed interviews was achieved representing 83.0 per cent of the target population.

THE DELIMITATION OF PERCEIVED NEIGHBOURHOODS

Methodological considerations

The most valid way to fulfil this objective is to ask people directly to indicate the extent of their home area. A survey of the existing literature suggested that, to date, six main methods have been used to achieve this. These are by asking

FIGURE 10.1. The study area

respondents to, (1) draw a boundary line onto a base map, (2) produce a free-recall sketch map on a blank sheet of paper, (3) draw a line on a large-scale photograph of the locality, (4) draw a line onto a stylized map of the locality, (5) describe verbally the extent of their home area, and (6) select from a prepared list of streets and places those within their home area. Each method has inherent advantages and disadvantages which must be borne in mind when considering which to employ. The above list of techniques can be divided into those which involve the respondent in some graphic test (1–4) and those which require verbal descriptions of the home area (5 and 6). The relative merits of each approach have generated considerable debate (Anderson and Tindall, 1972; Spencer, 1973; Mercer, 1975, Boyle and Robinson, 1979).

The direct approach to the delimitation of perceived neighbourhoods is to derive information in map form by means of a mapping exercise, responses either being structured by use of a base map (Lee, 1954) or unstructured by means of a free-recall sketch map of the type used by Lynch (1960) and others (De Jonge, 1962; Gulick, 1963; Pacione, 1976, 1978). Studies adopting the latter technique, however, have usually been more concerned with the details of the perceived internal structure of a study area and not simply with the areal extent of a home area. Free-recall sketch mapping, a more demanding task than drawing a linear boundary onto a base map, was considered unnecessarily complex for the objectives of the present investigation.

A frequently voiced criticism of the mapping procedure is that in general the overall correspondence between possessed information which forms the basis of the cognitive map and the elicited map is a function of graphicacy, defined by McFarlane-Smith (1964) as a general spatial ability to perceive and retain structure and proportion of forms as a whole together with cartographic skill to express possessed information. The distribution of such sophisticated abilities is unlikely to be random (Reiser, 1972). Nevertheless the weight of empirical evidence suggests that the majority of respondents faced with this task experienced little or no difficulty with the structured graphic method of representing perceived home areas. Lee (1968), for example, found that nearly 80 per cent of housewives in his Cambridge sample could delineate their neighbourhood on the map provided. In a similar investigation in East Kilbride, Henry and Cox (1970) found that 90 per cent of their respondents were able to draw the boundary of their home area on a piece of tracing paper placed over a street map of the whole town.

Other criticisms of the mapping method, as employed by Lee (1954), refer to the vagueness of the question put to respondents, i.e. to draw a line around their neighbourhood. Mercer (1975) for example reminds us that 11 per cent of Lee's own sample population experienced some difficulty in appreciating what was required of them. However, this can easily be overcome by the interviewer providing supplementary information when necessary to indicate exactly what is required. A related criticism concerns the actual phrasing of the task—the request to 'please draw a line round the part which you consider acts as your neighbourhood' implies that respondents do indeed perceive a bounded home area. To some extent this is a valid comment but much evidence exists to support the contention that people do organize space in this way. The fact that territorially based communities exist within cities has been amply demonstrated in the literature of urban social geography (Timms 1971, Herbert and Raine, 1976). Other supportive evidence ranges from the early work of McKenzie (1923) to the more recent conclusion of the Community Attitudes Survey (Royal Commission on Local Government, 1969) that four out of every five people claimed attachment to a home-community area; this home area being smaller than a local-authority area, with three-quarters defining it as no larger than a ward and many viewing it as a unit of a few streets.

On the other hand, in a direct evaluation of graphic and verbal techniques in the Selly Oak area of Birmingham, Spencer (1973) found that the difficulties seemed less when the neighbourhoods were verbally described than when a map was used. For those respondents who declined to draw a map Spencer judged lack of confidence, inability to map read, and concern for giving the 'correct answer' to be important explanatory factors.

Alternatives to the use of base maps or free-recall sketching which have been adopted include a method in which children were given large-scale photographs of their neighbourhood covered by a semi-transparent overlay on which they were asked to indicate their activity patterns (Anderson and Tindall, 1972). As the development of graphicacy is a learning process this could prove a valuable approach when dealing with younger age groups. A second related approach is to employ the type of stylized maps, constructed by the psychologist Fisher (1972), which transform the two-dimensional conventional map into a three-dimensional panorama of the city. Although Fisher has concentrated on the city-wide scale, similar maps could be constructed for urban sub-areas. However, while a photograph can be a reasonably faithful representation of reality the stylized map clearly involves highly subjective judgements in manipulating the elements of the real world. In addition the great deal of time and effort required to produce such base maps diminishes their usefulness.

The indirect or verbal means of constructing a cognitive map of the home area is a two-stage process; with the initial elicitation of places by verbal means being followed, after processing, by the drawing of a map. Abbott and Lee (1977) have used a structured verbal methodology in which they provided respondents with a list of places (names of shops, streets, cinemas etc.) in the area around their home and asked them to indicate which of the places were in their neighbourhood and which were outside. The selection of places, however, involves the subjective judgement of the researcher in selecting the important elements of the neighbourhood space.

The alternative unstructured verbal technique of delimiting perceived neighbourhoods is also not without its faults. One is the problem of bias-free recording of verbal descriptions of spatial images by the researcher, although a tape recorder could be employed. More significantly, as Bernstein (1965) has pointed out, verbal descriptions of the perceived environment may prove as difficult as map drawing for the less articulate members of society, whose images may consequently be under represented in the study.

The structured graphic technique, despite the criticisms discussed above, has in fact been employed with good effect in many studies since Lee's original presentation (Willmott, 1967; Eyles, 1968; Ladd, 1970; Sanoff, 1970; Orleans and Schmidt, 1972; Everitt and Cadwallader, 1972; Pacione, 1980). However, bearing in mind the reservations expressed concerning the utility and validity of both the graphic and verbal approaches it was considered most satisfactory in the present study to employ a dual method of eliciting home areas, employing the well-tested structured graphic technique supported by an unstructured verbal opportunity for respondents who find difficulty in defining their neighbourhood by such means.

Procedure

Respondents were provided with a simplified street map of the locality and were asked two questions designed to permit the delimitation of perceived neighbourhoods; (1) What is this part of Glasgow called? (2) If you had to draw a line around your neighbourhood or home area (the area which you feel most attached to) where would it go? These were placed at the beginning and end of the interview schedule respectively and were separated by a range of questions on personal and behavioural themes. The first question thus served to introduce the respondent to the subject area while the intervening questions enabled respondents to cognitively identify the concept before they were asked to put boundaries around it.

Results

Replies to the first question provided more than twenty local names for sub-areas which were within the study area. These ranged from area names employed by more than a hundred respondents to those identified by fewer than five persons. The boundaries of the perceived neighbourhoods depicted by each respondent in reply to the second question were superimposed upon a base map of the locality. Inspection of the aggregate map enabled a number of major and minor consensual boundaries to be identified. Nine major neighbourhoods were strongly depicted in the composite mental map in addition to five minor perceived neighbourhoods (identified by less than twenty respondents) whose boundaries tended to overlap those of one or more of the major neighbourhoods. These smaller areas reflected a finer spatial discrimination of parts of the study area by some residents. There were six 'unclaimed' areas in the composite map. These largely comprised areas of mixed industrial–residential–derelict land uses, and the grounds of institutions such as the Royal Mental Hospital (Figure 10.2). This may be compared with the findings of Smith, C. J. (1977) in Norman, Oklahoma where the State mental hospital emerged as a major 'fear zone' in students' mental maps. This structure of nine major and five minor perceived neighbourhoods included all of the neighbourhoods defined by 99 per cent of respondents. A second complementary map of the home locations of all respondents using the names of the fourteen neighbourhoods identified was also constructed as an additional test of the neighbourhood boundaries (Figure 10.3). Taken together the two maps provided a means of verifying the accuracy of the composite mapping procedure and of resolving areas of boundary uncertainty.

This procedure may be illustrated by a particular example (Figure 10.4). Superimposition of the revealed cognitive maps for Hyndland and Dowanhill suggested two possible lines for the boundary between these neighbourhoods; one following the main road through the area (Hyndland Road), and the other taking the line of the smaller Victoria Crescent Road a few hundred metres to the east (Figure 10.1 and Figure 10.4A). In an ambiguous situation of this kind reference was made to the complementary map which depicted the home locations of respondents claiming to live in each of the neighbourhoods. In the case of Hyndland–Dowanhill (Figure 10.4B) this clearly indicated the easternmost line as the more meaningful boundary. In practice this had the effect of slightly extending the area of Hyndland and reducing that of Dowanhill (cf. Figures 10.2 and 10.3). As a result of this kind of analysis of the aggregate and individual neighbourhood maps a number of minor boundary adjustments were made to those shown in Figure 10.2 and two of the five minor perceived neighbourhoods (Botanic Gardens and Partickhill) were not retained in the final structure (cf. Figures 10.2 and 10.3). As Table 10.1 indicates there was a generally high level of agreement between the spatial extent of each perceived neighbourhood in the final structure and the name assigned to their home locations by respondents. For example, of the ninety-six persons whose home was located within the Broomhill perceived neighbourhood, 91.7 per cent offered the 'correct' name for their neighbourhood.

It is important at this stage to underline the fact that the spatial and hierarchical distribution of perceived neighbourhoods in any urban area is complex and overlapping. The identification of discrete boundaries for neighbourhoods is a simplification of reality which is necessary for practical purposes. Public service agency areas and local administrative and electoral boundaries, for example, must be discrete in order to avoid duplication of effort and waste of resources.

In terms of the first objective of the research, the combined mapping procedure employed revealed the existence of a set of popularly acknowledged neighbourhoods with well-demarcated boundaries within the study area.

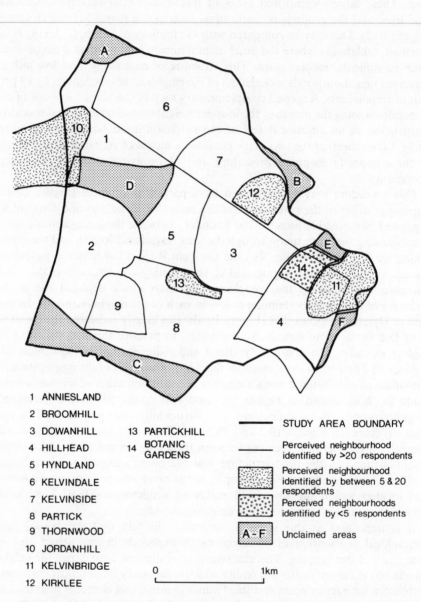

1 ANNIESLAND
2 BROOMHILL
3 DOWANHILL   13 PARTICKHILL
4 HILLHEAD   14 BOTANIC
5 HYNDLAND   GARDENS
6 KELVINDALE
7 KELVINSIDE
8 PARTICK
9 THORNWOOD
10 JORDANHILL
11 KELVINBRIDGE
12 KIRKLEE

───── STUDY AREA BOUNDARY

       Perceived neighbourhood
       identified by >20 respondents

       Perceived neighbourhood
       identified by between 5 & 20
       respondents

       Perceived neighbourhoods
       identified by <5 respondents

A - F Unclaimed areas

0   1km

FIGURE 10.2. Consensual neighbourhood boundaries: fourteen perceived
neighbourhoods

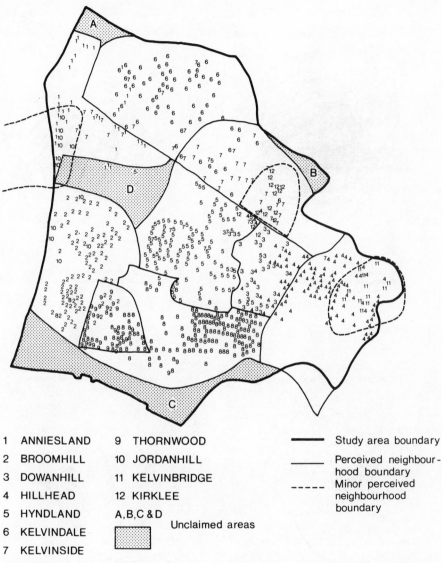

1	ANNIESLAND	9	THORNWOOD
2	BROOMHILL	10	JORDANHILL
3	DOWANHILL	11	KELVINBRIDGE
4	HILLHEAD	12	KIRKLEE
5	HYNDLAND		
6	KELVINDALE		
7	KELVINSIDE		
8	PARTICK		

A, B, C & D

Unclaimed areas

——— Study area boundary

——— Perceived neighbour-
hood boundary

- - - - Minor perceived
neighbourhood
boundary

FIGURE 10.3. Home locations of respondents using neighbourhood names, and final neighbourhood structure

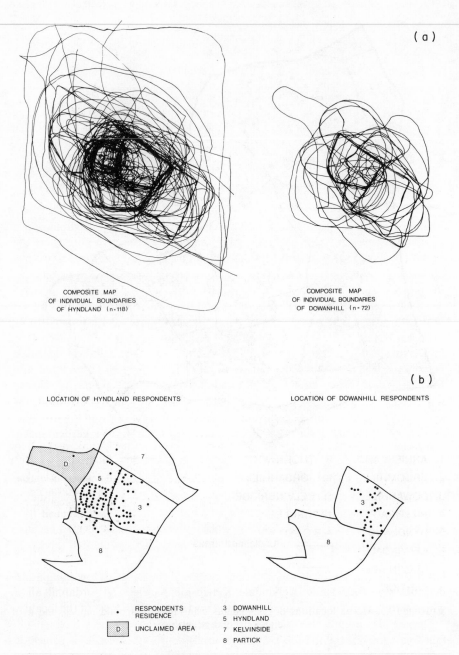

FIGURE 10.4. Perceived neighbourhood boundaries and home locations for Hyndland and Dowanhill

TABLE 10.1. Percentage of respondents citing correct*
name for their neighbourhood

Neighbourhood	%	Neighbourhood	%
Anniesland	80.0	Kelvindale	82.9
Broomhill	91.7	Kelvinside	54.5
Dowanhill	81.3	Partick	75.1
Hillhead	71.2	Thornwood	93.3
Hyndland	91.5		

* The name which corresponded to the areal extent of the
consensual neighbourhood structure of the study area.

NEIGHBOURHOOD SIZE

The most serious difficulty to be overcome in calculating neighbourhood
populations was that perceived neighbourhoods are cognitive constructs the
extent of which rarely coincides with the spatial bases of conventional sources of
population statistics, such as the census enumeration district. It was possible, in
the present study, to base population calculations on a combination of census
ward level data, the electoral roll and a population survey carried out by the
District Council. The population of the whole study area was estimated to be
51 758, with that of the nine major perceived neighbourhoods ranging from 3150
in Kelvinside to 12 000 in Partick (Table 10.2). Gross population densities,
persons per hectare (pph), ranged from very high ratios in Thornwood and
Partick to low values in Kelvinside and Kelvindale. These densities closely
reflected the housing and land use structure in the locality. Thornwood, for
example, contains within a dense street network both high-rise and low-rise flats
as well as tenement buildings with very little open ground or garden space.
Partick is also an area of closely packed tenements with traditionally high levels
of crowding. Broomhill, with a gross density of 97 pph, is mainly an area of
tenement and terraced housing which would have recorded a much lower
density but for the high-rise flats on the south-eastern edge of the neighbourhood. In contrast, Hillhead (87 pph), with a high proportion of tenement flats
and bed-sits, recorded a lower gross population density than expected because
the perceived neighbourhood enclosed the large non-residential areas of
Glasgow University campus and parts of Kelvingrove Park. The net population density for Hillhead was 130 pph. Neighbourhoods with low population
densities were Anniesland, Kelvindale, Kelvinside, Kirklee and Jordanhill all of
which were 'desirable' housing areas in the north and north-west of the locality.

Despite the popularity of neighbourhood studies researchers have so far
failed to agree on the influence of population density on the size of perceived
neighbourhoods. Two earlier studies which directly investigated the nature of
this relationship reached diametrically opposite conclusions. The Royal

TABLE 10.2.   Population characteristics of perceived neighbourhoods

Neighbourhood	Area			Gross population density		Net population density	
	hectares	acres	Population	pph	ppa	pph	ppa
Major							
Anniesland	49.87	123	3023	61	25	84	34
Broomhill	67.13	166	6501	97	39	117	47
Dowanhill	30.82	76	3649	118	48	118	48
Hillhead	80.38	199	7000	87	35	130	53
Hyndland	70.27	174	7015	100	40	117	47
Kelvindale	89.38	221	4050	45	18	67	27
Kelvinside	67.06	166	3150	47	19	60	24
Partick	72.12	178	12 000	166	67	191	77
Thornwood	22.81	56	5370	235	96	235	96
Minor							
Jordanhill	11.71	29	714	61	25	112	45
Kelvinbridge	24.84	61	3100	125	51	125	51
Kirklee	18.00	44	929	52	21	58	23

pph = persons per hectare; ppa = persons per acre.

Commission on Local Government (1969, p. 15) survey based on a sample of 2199 people drawn from a hundred local-authority areas of all sizes found that perceived neighbourhood size was inversely related to population density; the explanation being 'the closer clustering of social institutions in areas of greater population density—institutions (such as schools, clubs, churches and so on) which may be taken prima facie as components of community structure'. Lee (1968, p. 254), working with a sample of 219 Cambridge housewives, reached the opposite conclusion that territory and not population density is the major determinant of perceived neighbourhood size (i.e. people appear to conceptualize home areas based on distance from home). Specifically, 'it was found that housing density, which varies in the sample over a very wide range, has no effect on the area of schemata. This implies that size in this sense has been determined by delineating a territory and not a population aggregate' (Figure 10.5).

The absence of subsequent empirical contributions to this debate reflects the considerable input of time and resources required to measure perceived neighbourhood size for a statistically significant population sample. This information was collected in the present study. The area of each of the 760 perceived neighbourhood maps was measured three times and the mean value recorded for each. Histograms for individual neighbourhoods and for the study

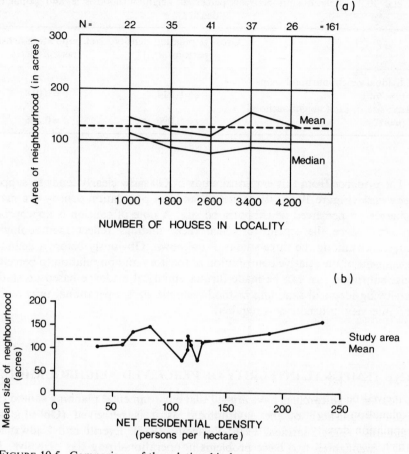

FIGURE 10.5. Comparison of the relationship between perceived neighbourhood size and population density according to (a) Lee 1968, (b) present study

area as a whole revealed a positively-skewed frequency distribution of neighbourhood sizes with a high proportion of values in the lower (<100 acres) size range and a tail extending to take in perceived neighbourhoods encompassing almost the entire study area. Correlation coefficients were calculated between individual respondents neighbourhood maps and both gross population density and net population density, as well as between these density variables and the mean size of perceived neighbourhood for each of the twelve neighbourhoods in the locality. As Table 10.3 and Figure 10.5b clearly indicate no significant relationships were found to exist between the variables at any level of analysis. The null hypothesis that there was no relationship between neighbourhood size and population density could not be rejected.

TABLE 10.3. Relationship between perceived neighbourhood size and population density

	Gross population density (persons/acre)	Net population density (persons/acre)
Individual neighbourhood maps (n = 760)	r = 0.014	r = 0.018
Mean size of each neighbourhood (n = 12)	r = 0.096	r = 0.126

The evidence from this empirical study in Glasgow clearly tends to support Lee's view (Figure 10.5a) that territory and not population density is a major influence on perceived neighbourhood size. A note of caution is appropriate, however, since the extent to which these findings reflect methodological differences among the three studies is unknown. Obviously before a definitive assessment of the relative contribution of territory and population to perceived neighbourhood size can be made further empirical evidence based on studies employing identical sampling methods, sample sizes, operational terminology and interview procedures is required.

THE TEMPORAL INTEGRITY OF PERCEIVED NEIGHBOURHOODS

A number of researchers have argued that environmental planning should take greater cognisance of the environment as it is perceived (Golledge and Zannaras, 1973; Saarinen, 1976; Porteous, 1977). Everitt and Cadwallader (1977) highlighted two basic problems in operationalizing this objective. The first raises the question of the environment as perceived by whom, since different people have different images of the real world. This difficulty can be overcome, however, by means of a well-designed sampling procedure since geographers and other spatial scientists are more concerned with the aggregate or group viewpoint than with individual mental maps. Most geographic studies of the perceived local area have aimed to identify an area with popularly acknowledged boundaries (Lee, 1976). Further a consensus definition of local area is essential in practical terms as no operational subdivision of an urban area can reflect the idiosyncratic cognitive maps of every individual.

The second problem concerns the stability of subjectively defined local areas over time. This presents a more fundamental obstacle to the use of these areas since there would be little practical merit in employing a spatial framework which changed over short time periods. Everitt and Cadwallader (1977, p. 176) considered that 'even if a satisfactory regionalisation of urban space could be made for one point in time, it would be unlikely to remain satisfactory over time'. Rapaport (1977) takes the more optimistic view that while the core areas of individuals may not be static, changing over time and varying with age, at the aggregate level most relevant for public decision-making neighbourhoods or community areas may be more durable. Neither of these studies, however, provided empirical evidence to support their assertions.

Although local area or neighbourhood studies form a major part of research into cognitive mapping this author is aware of no major studies which have been directly replicated over time either by the same investigator or by other researchers. This is unfortunate since it is only by gathering empirical evidence based on statistically respectable samples that the temporal integrity of perceived local areas can be tested in a scientific manner and the practical utility of subjectively defined urban areas be assessed.

The research reported in this section of the paper, therefore, was designed to provide information on the particular question of the temporal stability of perceived neighbourhood areas in a modern city. The prime objective was to compare the spatial characteristics of the networks of neighbourhood areas identified by two different random samples of residents in the same study area over a five-year period. Data on perceived local areas were collected for 1975 as part of a local-authority exercise to establish community councils in Glasgow and for 1980 by the procedure described earlier.

The 1975 survey

As part of local government reorganization Section 5 of the Local Government (Scotland) Act, 1973, required each new District Council to prepare in consultation with the public a scheme for the establishment of community councils wherever twenty or more local people demanded one. The procedures laid down by the Act provided for extensive public participation at all stages. The process of public involvement was pursued to the greatest degree in the city of Glasgow where the local authority employed an intensive publicity campaign with public meetings throughout the city, and established an advice and assistance team operating from city hall. As part of this process an open invitation was extended to all residents of the city to delimit the boundaries of their neighbourhoods or home areas on a base map. Responses took the form of submissions from individual citizens as well as group replies which were collated at a local level by over 100 *ad hoc* steering committees prior to formal submission to the District Council. It is important to note in this context that no pressure was put on respondents to employ existing administrative boundaries in considering their neighbourhoods. The end result of this procedure was a city map which displayed ninety-six popularly-agreed, subjectively defined, local areas representing a natural sub-division of the city 'from below'. Full details of the Glasgow scheme are provided elsewhere (Silk *et al.*, 1978).

Boundary comparison 1975–1980

The 1975 survey found that there were seven local areas wholly within the study area, in addition to a small part of the Templar area in the north-west, with three areas (Partick, Hillhead and Kelvinside) sub-divided internally (Figure 10.6). The 1980 survey identified nine major perceived neighbourhoods (Figure 10.7). In both cases over half of the boundaries employed followed main roads such as Great Western Road, Byres Road and Dumbarton Road (Figure 10.1), with the majority of the remainder related to railway lines and waterways.

Comparison of the two maps by simple cartographic superimposition was sufficient to indicate the high degree of correlation in the spatial extent of home

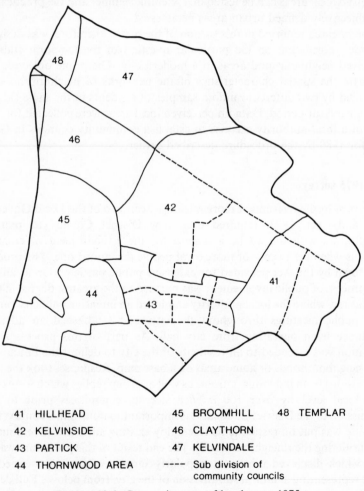

41	HILLHEAD	45	BROOMHILL	48	TEMPLAR
42	KELVINSIDE	46	CLAYTHORN		
43	PARTICK	47	KELVINDALE		
44	THORNWOOD AREA	----	Sub division of community councils		

FIGURE 10.6. Composite map of local areas 1975

areas over the five-year period. There was, for example, a very close relationship between the boundaries of Hillhead, Partick, Broomhill, and Kelvindale over time; with the same major boundary lines being employed by the populations sampled in 1975 and 1980. In addition, the Thornwood area of 1975 was clearly reflected in the 1980 neighbourhood of the same name; the only boundary

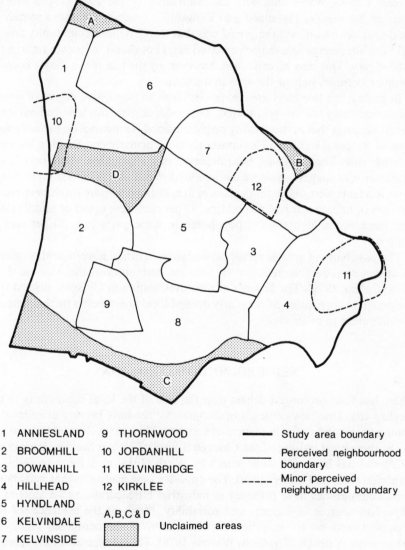

1	ANNIESLAND	9	THORNWOOD	———	Study area boundary
2	BROOMHILL	10	JORDANHILL	———	Perceived neighbourhood boundary
3	DOWANHILL	11	KELVINBRIDGE		
4	HILLHEAD	12	KIRKLEE	- - - -	Minor perceived neighbourhood boundary
5	HYNDLAND				
6	KELVINDALE		A,B,C & D		
7	KELVINSIDE			Unclaimed areas	
8	PARTICK				

FIGURE 10.7. Composite map of local areas 1980

difference being the south-westerly extension of the former area to include a zone of mixed residential–industrial–derelict land by the river Clyde. This zone has subsequently lost population and is in a state of decay, and it is not surprising that it was excluded from the later definition. Other evidence of the spatial correlation of home areas over the period is apparent in Figures 10.6 and 10.7. The 1975 boundary and internal division of Kelvinside, for example, reveals a close relationship with the boundaries of the 1980 neighbourhood areas of Kelvinside, Hyndland and Dowanhill. Overall, the sole anomaly in local-area definition over the period was that the Claythorn community area of 1975 did not emerge as a major perceived neighbourhood in its own right in the 1980 survey. This may be explained, however, by the fact that a major hospital complex occupies half of the area in question.

In general the two local-area maps displayed an impressive degree of spatial consistency over the five-year period. The evidence from this longitudinal study clearly suggests that in this locality neighbourhood boundaries do exhibit a high level of temporal stability. This constancy is particularly encouraging for work in other cities because it has been observed in a study area where population characteristics suggest an above-average level of mobility. (For example, one in three residents were under thirty years of age, 28 per cent were single persons, 82 per cent of households had no children, 47 per cent were upper or middle class, and there was a high student population in some parts (e.g. 20 per cent in Hillhead).)

The possibility of greater public participation in urban government continues to attract considerable attention in cities on both sides of the Atlantic (Hill, 1978; Cohen, 1979). The findings of this investigation in Glasgow suggest that the practical application of popularly defined local areas merits further detailed consideration in other cities.

NEIGHBOURHOOD COHESION

There has been prolonged debate over the role of the local community in the modern city. One view contends that communal ties have become attenuated in contemporary industrial bureaucratic societies. This perspective underlay much of the theoretical writing of the Chicago School of Urban Studies (Park et al., 1925) and has been well summarized by Wirth (1938) and, more recently, by Banfield (1968) and Slater (1970). The opposite view maintains that neighbourhood communities have persisted in industrial bureaucratic social systems as important sources of support and sociability. Much of the evidence for this argument rests on the empirical demonstration of the continued vitality of urban primary ties (Keller, 1968; Warren, 1978). These arguments have recently been reviewed by Wellman (1978) and Wellman and Leighton (1979) who have coined the terms 'Community lost' and 'Community saved' to describe the extreme viewpoints in the debate. Another perspective is provided by the 'community of limited liability' concept which recognizes the neighbourhood as one of a series of communities among which urbanites divide their membership (Janowitz, 1952; Kasarda and Janowitz, 1974). An extension of this model, which has appeared in the last two decades following improvements in personal mobility and telecommunications, contends that a variety of structural and technological developments has liberated communities from the confines of neighbourhoods and dispersed network ties from all-embracing solidary communities to more narrowly based ones. This model has been described as the 'Community transformed' (Wellman, 1978) or 'Community liberated' (Wellman and Leighton, 1979). It agrees both with the 'Lost' contention that neighbourhood communities have been weakened in modern societies, and also with the 'Saved' argument that primary ties have remained viable, useful and important. This 'community without propinquity' argument is based on McClenahan's (1929) earlier notion of communality, and was developed by Webber (1963) to account for the phenomenon which he later called the 'non-place urban realm' (Webber, 1964). A crucial difference between this and the other two models is that this maintains that modern urban communities are not necessarily organized on a neighbourhood basis.

Contemporary researchers are thus confronted by a series of contradictory assessments of the importance of the neighbourhood community in the modern urban setting. The present investigation set out to shed further light on this question by testing for the presence of meaningful neighbourhood communities in Glasgow.

Neighbourhood and community

Before commencing the search for neighbourhood communities it was necessary to clarify the meaning of the terms community and neighbourhood. Buttimer (1971, p. 168), in reviewing the concept of neighbourhood, considered that 'there are few concepts in the sociological literature which have been so variably and ambiguously defined'; while, for the term community, Hillery (1955) found 94 definitions in the literature up to 1953 and Sutton and Munsen (1976) 125 from 1954–1973. A major cause of the lack of consensus is the different emphases which have been placed upon the social and spatial aspects of each concept.

The Chicago human ecologists did not distinguish between the spatial and social dimensions underlying the community or neighbourhood (North, 1926; Carpenter, 1935). Since this classical position was stated, however, geographers and sociologists have followed divergent paths in their development of the community concept; one maintaining the spatial locus, the other emphasizing the aspatial nature of social networks. These different interpretations of community and neighbourhood together with the widespread use, in the post-war period, of the planners neighbourhood unit concept have all contributed to the confusion over the meaning of and relationship between the terms.

Two important points on which there is general agreement are that neighbourhood is smaller than community (Herbert, 1963; Golany, 1976) and that, while community may have lost some of its spatial sense, neighbourhood remains a word applied solely to a localized area (Gold, 1980). Blowers (1973) has attempted to relate the terms neighbourhood and community by suggesting a typology of neighbourhoods based on a continuum along which gradual change in the relative importance of the spatial and social components of the neighbourhood concept can be observed. In this scheme the neighbourhood community is defined as a close-knit, socially homogeneous, territorially defined group engaging in primary contacts. Underlying this are the concepts of *physical territory* and *social cohesion*.

Testing for the existence of neighbourhood communities in the modern city raises two major methodological problems. The first is to establish the boundaries of the neighbourhood communities. The second is to select measures of cohesion. The method of defining neighbourhood boundaries in the present study has been described above.

Measuring community cohesion

The concept of social cohesion has not been subjected to as rigorous an analysis as the concepts of community or neighbourhood and, consequently, there is less variation in its usage. It is, nevertheless, an awkward concept to define precisely (Theodorson and Theodorson, 1969; Schacter, 1963). We can accept Finsterbusch's (1980, p. 78) view that 'community cohesion refers to the amount and quality of social relations and interactions in rural communities or urban/suburban neighbourhoods and to the attraction to or identification with these units'.

Community cohesion is at least as difficult to measure as it is to define. Rossi (1972, p. 105) has observed that although the literature of community studies has been much concerned with the issue of the solidarity or strength of community cohesion 'it cannot be said that measures of the orientation of residents to their localities as collectivities have been developed beyond the most primitive level'. In small-group research cohesion is often measured by social interaction patterns or by sociometric choice. One measure of cohesion, therefore, is the proportion of friends and/or relatives that live within the local area. Traditionally neighbourhood cohesion is indicated by a neighbourhood interaction scale which uses a set of questions to score residents on their degree of intimacy with their neighbours (Bott, 1957). But neighbourhood cohesion also involves identification and satisfaction with the community. These have been measured by the desire to stay or the intentions to move and by questions about how satisfied the respondent is with the community or neighbourhood and with various aspects of it (Finsterbusch, 1980). Stone (1954) also emphasized the importance of use of local facilities as an indicator of neighbourhood solidarity.

Several attempts have been made to create a composite index of cohesion based on a number of different behavioural and perceptual variables. Rossi (1972) identified seven broad indicators of community solidarity together with a set of specific questions with which to tap each dimension. Buckhardt's (1971) index comprised a linear combination of scores on measures of, (1) neighbouring activity, (2) use of local facilities, (3) participation in neighbourhood organizations, (4) commitment to the area, and (5) neighbourhood evaluation. Smith, R. A. (1975) in the most complete review of measures of neighbourhood cohesion to date recommended a multivariate index based on the four factors of, (1) use of local facilities, (2) personal identification with the neighbourhood, (3) social interaction among neighbourhood residents, and (4) residents' consensus on certain values and forms of behaviour.

Based on a critical appraisal of these and other studies the present investigation selected a set of six measures to construct a composite index of neighbourhood cohesion for application in the study area. These related to, (1) personal attachment to the neighbourhood, (2) friendships, (3) participation in neighbourhood organizations, (4) residential commitment to the area, (5) use of neighbourhood facilities, and (6) resident satisfaction. Operational definitions of each are provided in Table 10.4.

TABLE 10.4.   Elements of composite index of neighbourhood cohesion

Dimension	Operational definition
1 Personal attachment	Responses on a 5-point semantic differential scale to the question: 'Suppose that for some reason you had to move away from this neighbourhood how sorry or pleased would you be to leave?'
2 Friendships	Proportion of residents with more than half of their adult friends and relatives within the neighbourhood.
3 Participation	Proportion of residents involved in neighbourhood organizations.
4 Residential commitment	Proportion of most recent house moves made within the neighbourhood.
5 Use of facilities	Proportion of household extra-domiciliary activities undertaken within the neighbourhood (for daily and durable shopping, church, school, employment and entertainment).
6 Satisfaction	Difference between the number of positive and negative attributes perceived for the neighbourhood, standardized by neighbourhood population size.

Analysis and results

Personal attachment to the neighbourhood

Residents were questioned on their feelings about leaving the neighbourhood. Eighty per cent expressed some degree of regret at the prospect of a move, 12 per cent were indifferent and only 8 per cent would have been pleased to move. Table 10.5 indicates the results for individual neighbourhoods; of those who would be 'very sorry' to leave their neighbourhood the strongest attachment was displayed by residents of Broomhill and the weakest by those in Anniesland, where one respondent in five was indifferent to the prospect of a move. Combining the two 'regret' categories of the scale revealed that only Anniesland scored below 75 per cent while the strongest score was recorded by Kelvinside (88.4 per cent).

TABLE 10.5. Feelings about leaving the neighbourhood (percentage of respondents by neighbourhood)

	Category				
	Very sorry	Quite sorry	Indifferent	Quite pleased	Very pleased
Anniesland	23.1	43.6	20.5	7.7	5.1
Broomhill	65.6	16.7	11.5	3.1	3.1
Dowanhill	46.9	31.2	15.6	6.2	0.0
Hillhead	39.8	40.7	13.6	3.4	2.5
Hyndland	44.9	37.6	11.9	3.4	2.5
Kelvindale	25.7	54.3	15.7	4.3	0.0
Kelvinside	37.2	51.2	4.7	2.3	4.7
Partick	48.0	32.4	9.2	6.9	3.5
Thornwood	34.5	41.4	10.3	10.3	3.4

Friendships

There is ample evidence to suggest that locally-based friendship patterns can be found most often in working-class areas of cities (Gans, 1962; Young and Willmott, 1962), while the level of local interaction tends to be lower in the case of more mobile upper- and middle-class populations. These general trends were supported in the study area where, as Table 10.6 indicates, the highest proportion of people with 50 per cent or more of their friends and relatives within their neighbourhood was recorded in the predominantly working-class areas of Partick (31 per cent) and Thornwood (30 per cent).

TABLE 10.6. Proportion of friends and relatives within the neighbourhood (percentage of respondents by neighbourhood)

	Category		
	More than half	Half	Less than half
Anniesland	7.5	15.0	77.5
Broomhill	9.4	13.5	77.1
Dowanhill	9.4	12.5	78.1
Hillhead	7.6	11.0	82.4
Hyndland	12.7	15.3	72.0
Kelvindale	11.4	10.0	78.6
Kelvinside	15.9	6.8	77.3
Partick	19.1	11.6	69.3
Thornwood	20.0	10.0	70.0

Participation in neighbourhood organizations

Within the study area as a whole one household in three held membership of a local organization. The nature of the organization varied to include residents associations which accounted for 73.4 per cent of responses, parent–teacher associations (18.3 per cent), community councils (3.3 per cent), church groups, political parties, conservation groups and youth groups. A comparative measure of the level of participation in each neighbourhood was obtained by relating the absolute number of organizational memberships to the local population. As Table 10.7 shows this produced a set of values ranging from a high of 0.86 in Broomhill to a low of 0.03 for Thornwood.

TABLE 10.7. Percentage of residents participating in neighbourhood organizations

	Type of organization					No. of responses
	Residents association	PTA	Church group	Community council	Other	No. of respondents
Anniesland	88.9	11.1	0.0	0.0	0.0	0.225
Broomhill	61.3	16.1	9.7	3.2	9.7	0.861
Dowanhill	75.0	0.0	12.5	12.5	0.0	0.250
Hillhead	66.7	13.9	0.0	2.8	16.6	0.305
Hyndland	77.8	11.1	0.0	0.0	11.1	0.458
Kelvindale	88.9	5.6	0.0	2.8	2.7	0.514
Kelvinside	58.8	35.3	0.0	5.9	0.0	0.386
Partick	68.9	11.1	2.2	4.4	13.4	0.260
Thornwood	100.0	0.0	0.0	0.0	0.0	0.033

Residential commitment to the area

One of the clearest indicators of any individual's affinity for an area of a city is his choice of home location. An analysis of recent house moves discovered that one-third of residents had migrated to their present house from within the study area; 29 per cent had moved into the area from outside Glasgow; and 37 per cent had previously lived in other parts of the city. Migration patterns within the Glasgow city region have been shown to consist of a number of independent systems with relatively weak connecting flows (Forbes and Robertson, 1981); one of which is centred on the Hillhead–Hyndland area. The present study found that within the locality as a whole more than half (53 per cent) of all house moves occurred within the Hillhead–Hyndland–Kelvindale triangle. While the mean proportion of intra-neighbourhood house moves was 9.8 per cent significantly higher levels of residential commitment were seen in Kelvindale where 20 per cent of households had moved within the neighbourhood, Hyndland (18.6 per cent) and Partick (16.8 per cent) (Table 10.8).

Use of neighbourhood facilities

Respondents were questioned on the spatial distribution of destinations, frequency of use and mode of travel employed for a comprehensive range of essential (such as food shopping) and discretionary (e.g. visiting friends) activities. Considering the study area as a whole, the proportion of activities performed entirely within the respondents neighbourhood ranged from a low of 6.2 per cent for visiting relatives to a maximum of 77.9 per cent for membership of local organizations, with an overall mean of 30.5 per cent of trips (Table 10.9). Activities with an above-average concentration at the neighbourhood level were related to involvement with local organizations, daily shopping, schooling and church attendance; while those with a weaker local focus included visits to relatives, durable goods shopping, work and entertainment trips for which the remainder of the city was of greater significance than the neighbourhood.

It was of interest to compare these activity patterns with evidence from other cities. None of the local-activity investigations uncovered by a review of the urban literature, however, examined the complete range of human activities examined in Glasgow. Direct comparisons were also complicated by socio-cultural, temporal, sampling, and definitional differences among studies. A summary of evidence from six studies is shown in Table 10.9.

The Royal Commission on Local Government (1969), in an analysis of activity patterns for a sample of urban and rural residents in England, found that activities with the greatest levels of local concentration included school trips, church attendance and membership of organizations, but that the home area did not coincide in any significant way with the pursuit of public

TABLE 10.8. Migration within the 'West-End' housing sub-system (percentage moves among the neighbourhoods)

Origin	Destination									Remainder of	
	Hillhead	Hyndland	Kelvindale	Kelvinside	Dowanhill	Partick	Thornwood	Anniesland	Broomhill	Glasgow	Elsewhere
Hillhead	9.3	7.6	0.8	3.4	2.5	3.4	0.0	1.7	1.7	29.7	39.9
Hyndland	9.3	18.6	3.4	2.5	0.8	3.4	0.0	0.0	2.5	22.9	36.6
Kelvindale	7.1	4.3	20.0	0.0	0.0	0.0	0.0	2.9	0.0	44.3	21.4
Kelvinside	13.6	6.8	4.5	9.1	4.5	0.0	0.0	0.0	2.3	20.5	38.7
Dowanhill	15.6	3.1	3.1	3.1	3.1	6.2	0.0	6.2	0.0	28.1	31.5
Partick	2.9	2.9	1.2	0.0	2.9	16.8	0.6	0.0	0.6	50.3	21.8
Thornwood	3.3	0.0	0.0	0.0	0.0	3.3	0.0	0.0	3.3	53.3	36.8
Anniesland	5.0	7.5	2.5	0.0	2.5	7.5	0.0	5.0	2.5	30.0	37.5
Broomhill	2.1	6.2	2.1	1.0	3.1	12.5	4.2	0.0	6.2	50.0	15.7

TABLE 10.9. Percentage of household extra-domiciliary activities undertaken within the local area

Activity	Pacione (1980) (n=760)	Royal Commission (1969) (n=2199)	Foley (1950) (n=400)	Ross (1962) (n=250)	Foley (1952) (n=446)	Hunter (1975) (n=154)
Daily shopping	51.9	47.0*	69.0	80.0	76.3**	48.0**
Durable shopping	11.8	—	5.0	7.0	—	—
School trips	45.9	61.0	68.0	—	—	—
Church visits	36.5	66.0	77.0	36.0	61.5	51.2
Employment	15.3	33.0†	18.0	22.0	17.0	11.4
Organization or club membership	77.9	58.0	—	—	—	—
Entertainment	20.7	55.5‡	58.0	22.0	44.5	9.1
Walks	23.9	41.0§	—	—	—	—
Health visits	27.8	—	30.0	—	46.7	19.3
Visiting friends	27.0	—	—	—	—	—
Visiting relatives	6.2	—	—	—	—	—
Other outings	21.2	56.0¶	10.0	—	25.6††	47.9
$\bar{x}$	30.5	52.2	41.9	33.4	45.3	31.2

* Weekly household shopping.
† Since some also usually travel outside the home area in the course of their work, only 14.0 per cent of all electors may be said to be employed entirely within their home area.
‡ Visit to public house or bingo hall.
§ Public park or garden.
¶ Visit public tennis court.
** Grocery shopping or small purchases.
†† Banking.

entertainment and recreational activities. Several urban sociological studies offered comparative data based on a sampling framework more directly relevant to the present investigation. Foley (1950, p. 246), working in a lower-middle-class area of St Louis, discovered that 47 per cent of trips were made within one mile of home and 30 per cent within half a mile, with 37 per cent of journeys made on foot. His results showed that

> a number of facilities is extensively used at the local level. Food and certain other types of shopping, childrens attendance at elementary school and use of play facilities, attendance at certain churches and patronage of certain small movie theatres take place to a great degree within a neighbourhood or local-community sphere.

Since he had hypothesized that metropolitan residents make relatively little use of local facilities he was forced to conclude that 'our large cities for all their urbanity, seem to contain an impressive degree of local community life (Foley, 1950, p. 246). Ross (1962, p. 83), working in a high-prestige, upper-income, area of central Boston, also found that 'local facilities usage in almost all categories appears greater than a chance model would predict, especially considering the absence of opportunities in the area'.

Two other empirical investigations provided data on local usage levels for some of the facilities studied in Glasgow. Both defined the local area as within five blocks of home. Foley's (1952) analysis of an inner-city neighbourhood in Rochester, New York, revealed a striking degree of local facility use, with 77 per cent of grocery shopping, 71 per cent of shopping for other small purchases, and 62 per cent of church visits being made in the local area. Hunter (1975), in a recent re-examination of the same neighbourhood, also found a significant level of local patronage of the facilities available.

The findings presented in Table 10.9 indicate that on average, in terms of overall human activity in the six studies covering the period 1950–1980, between one-third and one-half of extra-domiciliary trips were made within the local area. For individual activities, such as daily shopping, schooling, church attendance and membership of clubs and organizations the majority of trips were made within the neighbourhood. In Table 10.10 details are provided of the levels of local facility usage for individual neighbourhoods within the study area. Examination of these data confirms that for several types of activity a significant proportion of household trips are constrained within the boundaries of the perceived neighbourhood.

Given the lack of community attachment and the mobility of urban dwellers described by the 'non place urban realm' and 'community without propinquity' theses (Webber, 1963, 1964) it is perhaps surprising that such a high proportion of extra-domiciliary human activities are confined to what are very small local parts of the metropolis. The average area of one of the perceived neighbourhoods identified occupied less than 1 per cent of the metropolitan area and yet for certain household needs all nine major neighbourhoods displayed a high degree of local concentration of activity.

Resident satisfaction

Respondents were presented with an open-ended invitation to list the positive and negative attributes of their neighbourhoods. This produced a total of 2529 and 1460 responses respectively. These were grouped into six main categories related to transport and accessibility, services and facilities, leisure and recreation, physical environment, social environment, and personal safety. This classification procedure facilitated detailed analysis of both, (1) spatial variations in individual attributes throughout the study area, and (2) the position of individual neighbourhoods across the range of attributes (Figure 10.8). Analysis of the positive and negative attributes of neighbourhoods provides detailed

TABLE 10.10. Percentage of household extra-domiciliary activities undertaken within each of the nine main perceived neighbourhoods in the study area

Neighbourhood	Daily shopping	Durable shopping	School trips	Church visits	Employment	Organization or club membership	Entertainment	Walks	Health visits	Visiting friends	Visiting relatives	Other outings	Activity mean*
Anniesland	58.0	6.8	14.3	26.3	36.0	77.8	14.3	22.7	36.9	25.3	10.5	40.0	30.8
Broomhill	59.8	5.8	27.8	78.1	5.6	83.9	12.2	14.4	31.7	29.1	8.4	17.2	31.2
Dowanhill	66.2	17.9	33.3	27.3	13.0	100.0	28.8	28.6	23.8	32.6	7.1	40.0	34.9
Hillhead	71.7	14.8	70.8	53.7	17.1	88.9	32.3	31.8	37.2	30.6	4.1	47.6	41.7
Hyndland	53.3	8.6	63.0	44.0	13.5	90.7	17.9	19.7	33.5	34.9	9.7	35.8	35.4
Kelvindale	40.4	3.4	72.7	44.0	15.0	94.4	16.3	15.5	12.0	27.1	4.9	27.0	31.0
Kelvinside	36.1	4.8	75.0	26.1	16.7	76.5	11.0	36.7	11.1	23.0	7.5	5.7	27.5
Partick	68.8	32.6	60.9	86.4	20.0	88.9	38.9	26.4	58.1	33.9	10.4	40.7	47.3
Thornwood	55.7	26.9	33.3	26.7	21.4	100.0	29.5	16.7	44.6	22.9	5.5	0.0	32.9
Study-area mean	51.9	11.8	45.9	36.5	15.3	77.9	20.7	23.9	27.8	27.0	6.2	21.2	30.5

* Provides a broad comparative measure of neighbourhood 'self-sufficiency'.

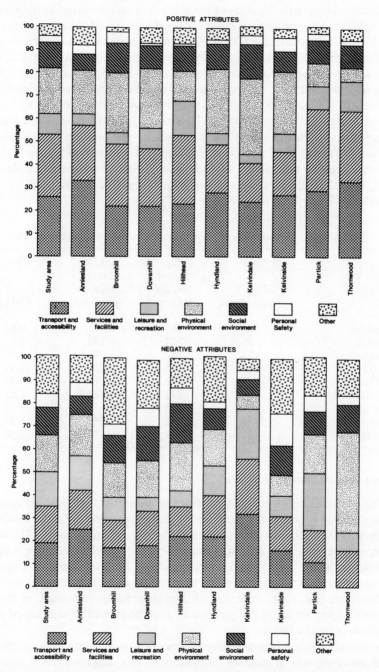

FIGURE 10.8. Perceived positive and negative attributes of neighbourhoods

insight into the perceived quality of life in the area and provides decision makers with valuable information on residents satisfactions and dissatisfactions with their local environment. Such findings could be incorporated in the process of plan formulation. Spatial concentrations of particular problems identified in the study area included the cost and shortage of parking space in Dowanhill and Hillhead, the nuisance arising from traffic noise and road congestion in Anniesland, the lack of local shopping facilities in Kelvindale and Kelvinside, environmental dereliction in parts of Thornwood, and the absence of parks and playgrounds in Partick. For the purposes of the present investigation a satisfaction score was calculated for each neighbourhood based on the difference between the number of positive and negative responses standardized by neighbourhood population—values ranged from 2.02 in Broomhill to 0.67 in Anniesland (Table 10.11).

TABLE 10.11.   Residents level of satisfaction with their neighbourhood

	(1) No. of respondents	(2) No. of positive citations	(3) No. of negative citations	(4) $\dfrac{\text{Col (2)} - \text{Col (3)}}{\text{Col (1)}}$
Anniesland	40	112	85	0.67
Broomhill	96	327	133	2.02
Dowanhill	32	112	61	1.59
Hillhead	118	425	225	1.44
Hyndland	118	388	213	1.48
Kelvindale	70	211	163	0.68
Kelvinside	44	155	79	1.72
Partick	173	582	341	1.39
Thornwood	30	89	50	1.30

A composite measure of cohesion

Having identified and measured six different socio-psychological indicators of neighbourhood cohesion it was necessary to decide on the optimum method of aggregating the individual components to form a composite index. The weight of empirical evidence to date suggested the use of a linear additive model, a formulation which has been used successfully in several major cognitive-behavioural studies (Campbell et al., 1976; Andrews and Withey, 1976). Table 10.12 reveals the rank ordering of neighbourhoods on each of the six components and indicates the position of each neighbourhood in terms of the composite cohesion index.

The neighbourhood which displayed greatest cohesion, with high rankings on all dimensions, was Hyndland. Significantly, this neighbourhood also had strongly demarcated boundaries in the composite mental map. The predomi-

TABLE 10.12. Rank ordering of neighbourhoods on a range of socio-psychological indicators of community cohesion

			Dimensions					
	(1)	(2)	(3)	(4)	(5)	(6)	ΣD1–6	Overall Neighbourhood rank
Anniesland	9	6	8	7	9	9	48	9.0
Broomhill	3	4	4	6	6	1	24	3.5
Dowanhill	7	7	7	8	7	3	39	7.5
Hillhead	4	9	5	4	2	5	29	5.0
Hyndland	2	3	1	2	3	4	15	1.0
Kelvindale	6	8	2	1	5	8	30	6.0
Kelvinside	1	5	3	5	8	2	24	3.5
Partick	5	1	6	3	1	6	22	2.0
Thornwood	8	2	9	9	4	7	39	7.5

nantly working-class neighbourhood of Partick was ranked second, followed by Broomhill and the middle-class residential neighbourhood of Kelvinside. The index revealed Anniesland to be the least cohesive neighbourhood with consistently low rankings recorded on all six dimensions.

The current consensus among urban sociologists would seem to be that city dwellers now have more choices about where and with whom to interact. They can choose whether to be rooted in a local area or to belong to an aspatial 'community of process' (Dunham, 1977). In some cases they can choose both possibilities. Acceptance of this 'liberated' interpretation of neighbourhood community requires that the spatial element of the neighbourhood definition be relaxed. There is no reason, however, why individuals cannot be simultaneous members of a (geographical) neighbourhood community as well as a more extensive (sociological) community without propinquity. This was well demonstrated in the present investigation by the analysis of individual activity patterns (Table 10.10) and the measurement of neighbourhood cohesion (Tables 10.5–10.12). These data also confirmed the view that while the majority of middle-class urbanites may have social networks which are not neighbourhood-based (Popenoe, 1977; Bender, 1978), for others including the elderly, children, lower class and housewives the neighbourhood is a significant territorial entity (Lee, 1982). Smith, C. J. (1980, p. 376) points out that 'traditionally a neighbourhood is thought of as a spatially defined unit that contains a population and a set of resources, while community refers to a perception about the existence of ties between members of a group'. The neighbourhood community can be envisaged as a fusion of these two concepts and the empirical evidence from the present research strongly supports the continued existence and vitality of such entities in the modern city.

NEIGHBOURHOODS AND PUBLIC SERVICE AREA BOUNDARIES

Over the last decade local democracy movements have grown up to argue the case for greater political power and more direct participation in decision-making by urban neighbourhood groups (Yates, 1973; Cohen, 1979). Although most governments have shown reluctance to delegate political and especially financial power, some urban local authorities in Britain and the United States have experimented with decentralization of certain administrative functions to the local level (Hambleton, 1978). It would clearly be of great practical advantage if the territories of neighbourhoods were coterminous with the boundaries of the administrative and service areas whose functions and responsibilities had been devolved.

This part of the research examined the particular question of the relationship between neighbourhood areas and the boundaries of public service, administrative and political divisions in the city.

The concept of boundary congruence

Seventy years ago Ward (1913) proposed that the urban neighbourhood should be based on two geographical areas, the school district and the voting precinct *which should be made coterminous.* The notion of a functional neighbourhood of this type was developed by Perry (1929) who recommended that the neighbourhood unit should coincide with the service area not only of the elementary school but of the other institutions for which it catered. The Dudley Report (1944) later proposed the coincidence of neighbourhood and ward boundaries in British new towns but, as Goss (1961) has illustrated, few complied with this suggestion. More recently, in the discussions preceding the reform of local government in Britain in the early 1970s a number of pressure groups argued for a new framework of local or community councils that had boundaries which correspond to the mental maps inside people's heads (Young, 1970).

In practice, however, very rarely do official political subdivisions coincide with people's home areas or neighbourhoods conceptualized on the basis of social attachment, local employment, or communality, reinforced by physical characteristics and boundaries. Rapaport (1977, p. 160) summarized the problem when he stated, 'subjective boundaries are important because they restrict movement and guide behaviour and ideally planned and subjective boundaries would be congruent (but) both official political units and standard planning neighbourhood units are too large'. It has now been generally recognized that neighbourhoods in the city are much smaller than most formal subdivisions, sometimes consisting of only a few streets around the home.

Empirical evidence for spatial congruence between neighbourhoods and other administrative areas is also weak (Hampton and Chapman, 1971; Hamble and Talbot, 1977; Hall, 1977). As Malmberg (1980, p. 130) explains:

there is a clear distinction between the natural area and the administrative area. The city is broken up into administrative units, such as the ward, the school district, the police precinct, and the health district, for the purposes of administrative convenience and the object is usually to apportion either the population or area of the city into equal units.

Nevertheless, because the political system emphasizes territorial representation, and because the expansion of governmental functions includes many welfare-state functions that are geographically based, the question of neighbourhood participation in urban government is of paramount importance. The recommendation of the Dudley Report (1944, p. 59) that 'it would obviously be sensible if the ward boundaries of a town followed the boundaries of neighbourhood units whenever these are strongly defined' is particularly relevant today given the growing pressures for open government and increased local democracy.

The present investigation identified a set of nine neighbourhoods with well-defined popularly acknowledged boundaries within the study area and it was clearly of interest to determine the extent to which these units corresponded with other spatial subdivisions of the city. The territories of thirteen services and agencies related to postal, police, fire, education, housing, political, and planning functions were examined. The length of each neighbourhood and service area boundary was measured and a summary index of boundary congruity was constructed:

$$Ic = k \cdot \frac{Cb}{Pb}$$

where Ic = the index of congruity
$\quad Cb$ = the length of common boundary (metres)
$\quad Pb$ = the length of neighbourhood boundary
$\quad$ k = a constant to scale the index values from 0–100.

This simple device indicated what proportion of the *neighbourhood* boundaries in the locality was used by each of the *service* areas. The value of the index was interpreted in conjunction with maps of the thirteen service areas. These indicated the number of territorial subdivisions employed by the various agencies as well as the nature of the boundaries adopted (Table 10.13).

The highest levels of agreement were found to exist between neighbourhoods and, (1) the estate agents' subdivision of the locality, (2) community council areas, (3) postal sectors, and (4) polling districts (Figure 10.9).

Estate agents' areas

Estate agents can be regarded as purveyors of a neighbourhood image. In order to examine the relationship between the neighbourhoods perceived by residents

TABLE 10.13.   Coincidence of neighbourhood and public service area boundaries

| Function | Sub-divisions | Ic | Index rank order | Type of coincident boundary (%) | | |
				Road	Rail	River/Canal
Community council areas	8	53.00	2	61.7	17.0	21.3
New district wards	6	26.23	8	41.9	20.5	37.5
Old district wards	3	24.92	9	33.0	18.5	48.5
Polling districts	16	41.92	4	59.6	16.9	23.5
Non-den. primary schools	10	38.46	5	74.4	11.4	14.2
RC primary schools	5	28.85	7	42.9	26.9	30.1
Postal districts	2	29.15	6	22.7	26.7	50.6
Postal sectors	7	52.67	3	33.2	13.4	53.4
Police districts	2	9.12	12	100.0	0.0	0.0
Fire areas	3	17.00	10	90.5	0.0	9.5
Local plan areas	2	16.15	11	18.6	14.3	67.1
Conservation areas	2	5.08	13	54.6	13.6	31.8
Estate agents areas	15	65.77	1	60.1	25.3	14.6

and those of the 'professionals', the managers of the five main estate agencies with offices in the area were asked to subdivide the locality into residential units. The results of the five independent exercises displayed a high level of consensus making it relatively easy to construct a composite estate-agency map of the area. This comprised fifteen residential neighbourhoods and the degree of agreement with the residents' neighbourhood map was striking (cf. Figures 10.7 and 10.9).

Community council areas

There were seven community-council areas wholly within the study area, with three of these (Partick, Hillhead, and Kelvinside) subdivided. A close spatial correspondence could be observed between the community council and neighbourhood boundaries of Hillhead, Partick, Broomhill, Kelvindale, and Thornwood. In addition the community council boundary and internal division of Kelvinside revealed a strong relationship with the neighbourhood boundaries of Kelvinside, Hyndland, and Dowanhill (Table 10.13 and Figures 10.7 and 10.9).

Postcode sectors

Postcode sectors are amalgamations of individual postcode units which comprise small groups of houses. Based on the index value alone the degree of congruence between postcode sectors and neighbourhood boundaries was particularly high for Hillhead and Kelvinside and for parts of Hyndland and Dowanhill. Examination of the map of postcode sectors (Figure 10.9), however, indicated that in this case the high index level reflected, in part, the common

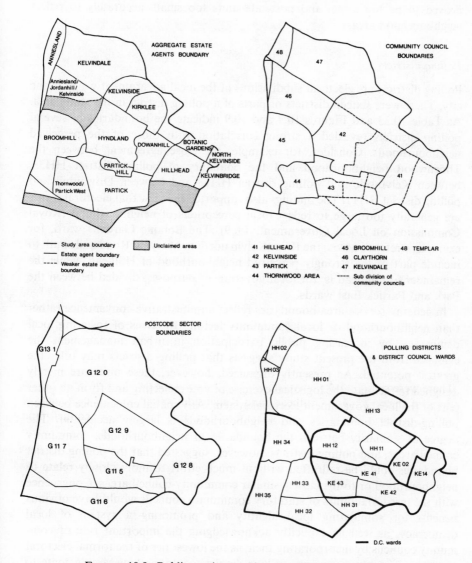

41 HILLHEAD   45 BROOMHILL   48 TEMPLAR
42 KELVINSIDE   46 CLAYTHORN
43 PARTICK   47 KELVINDALE
44 THORNWOOD AREA ---- Sub division of
                        community councils

FIGURE 10.9. Public-service area boundaries in the study area

boundary formed by the waterways delimiting the edge of the study area rather than close agreement on internal subdivisions. In general, postcode sectors proved to be too large, and postcode units too small, accurately to reflect neighbourhood areas.

Polling districts

Polling districts are electoral subdivisions of the local government wards in the city. There were sixteen districts or parts of a polling district in the study area. As Table 10.13 and Figures 10.7 and 10.9 indicate the boundaries of several polling districts revealed a strong correlation with those of the perceived neighbourhoods. Consider, for example, the close agreement between the Thornwood neighbourhood and the boundary of polling district HH33, between Kelvinside and polling district HH13 and between Dowanhill and polling district HH11. The findings also supported the view that electoral wards are generally too large to reflect local perceptions of neighbourhood (Royal Commission on Local Government, 1969). The Botanic Gardens ward, for example, stretched across the River Kelvin north to Maryhill Road and south to include part of the strongly perceived neighbourhood of Hillhead, while the remainder of Hillhead is, for local government purposes, divided between the Park and Partick East wards.

In general, service-area boundaries reflect administrative convenience rather than neighbourhood or local community feeling. In terms of fostering local democracy by increasing public participation in urban management the evidence from the present study suggests that polling districts may offer the greatest potential. As presently organized, however, these units are merely designed to facilitate the logistical exercise of vote collecting and form no other part of the local government electoral system. Any spatial coincidence between polling-district boundaries and neighbourhoods is largely accidental. The degree of similarity between the boundaries of neighbourhoods, community council areas, and polling districts, however, suggested that the polling district boundaries could be redrafted without much effort to more closely relate to neighbourhood or to the closely similar community-council areas. Congruence with the territorial limits of statutory community councils would have obvious benefits for stimulating local identity and promoting a system of local democracy, as well as explicitly acknowledging the important role of community councils by incorporating them as the lowest tier of the formal electoral structure. The new *community polling districts* could, as now, amalgamate to form city wards. The great advantage of this spatial reorganization would be that instead of wards being largely *ad hoc* groupings of polling districts which only occasionally correspond to natural areas, as at present, wards and ward councillors would be seen to be representatives of local neighbourhood communities.

CONCLUSION

The subdivision of urban space has received a good deal of attention ever since the concept of the natural area was first proposed by the classical human ecologists. A recurrent difficulty encountered by the objective approach to this question is that areas delineated by physical indices, such as rateable values, do not normally correspond with social areas (Glass, 1948). The subjective or cognitive-behavioural approach, which measures the neighbourhood as held in the residents' mind, offers a possible resolution of this misfit.

This perspective was employed in the present research to investigate the significance of the local area in the modern city. This issue has recently assumed importance in both the academic and applied field of enquiry. Within the academic context the theme has received attention because of the debate over the presence or absence of meaningful neighbourhood communities in the city (Wellman and Leighton, 1979) while in the applied sphere attention has been focused on the question as a consequence of the growing pressure for local democracy, more open government, and greater public participation in decision-making (Hunter, 1979; Cohen, 1979).

This chapter investigated five key questions with a bearing on the relevance of the local area in the modern city. The main conclusions were:

(i)   It is possible to extract individuals' cognitive representations of their home areas by employing a carefully designed mapping procedure. Use of the methodology described in the present investigation permitted the identification of a set of popularly acknowledged urban neighbourhoods with well-demarcated boundaries.

(ii)   The empirical evidence from this study tends to support the hypothesis that territory and not population density exerts an influence on the size of perceived neighbourhoods.

(iii) A longitudinal survey of two different random samples of residents in the same study area over a five-year period found a striking degree of consistency in the spatial extent and boundaries of neighbourhood areas over time. The strong level of temporal stability displayed in this locality suggested that the practical applications of popularly defined local areas merit detailed consideration in other cities.

(iv)   Political and service-area boundaries generally reflect administrative convenience rather than neighbourhood or local community feeling. Evidence from this study suggests that public participation in urban management may be fostered by judicious amendment of polling district boundaries so that they more closely relate to revealed neighbourhood community areas.

(v)   The levels of neighbourhood cohesion discovered in the study area supported the view that while the majority of middle-class urbanites may have social networks which are not neighbourhood-based, for a significant number of activities and for other groups of people, including the elderly, children, lower class and housewives, the neighbourhood remains an important territorial entity.

REFERENCES

Abbott, J. and Lee, T. (1977). Cited in D. Canter, *The Psychology of Place*, Architectural Press, London, pp. 27–30.

Altman, I. (1975). *The Environment and Social Behaviour*. Brooks Cole, Monterey, California.

Altman, I. and Haythorn, W. W. (1967). The ecology of isolated groups, *Behavioural Science*, **12**, 169–182.

Anderson, J. and Tindall, M. (1972). The concept of home range. In *Environmental Design: Research and Practice* (Ed. W. J. Mitchell). Proceedings of EDRA 3 Conference, Los Angeles.

Andrews, F. M. and Withey, S. B. (1976). *Social Indicators of Well Being: Americans Perceptions of Life Quality*, Plenum Press, New York.

Ardrey, R. (1972). *The Social Contract. A Personal Inquiry Into The Evolutionary Sources of Order and Disorder*, Collins, London.

Banfield, E. (1968). *The Unheavenly City*, Little, Brown, Boston.

Becker, F. D. and Mayo, C. (1971). Delineating personal distance and territoriality, *Environment and Behaviour*, **3**, 375–381.

Bender, T. (1978). *Community and Social Change in America*, Rutgers University Press, New Brunswick, New Jersey.

Bell, C. and Newby, H. (1976). Community, communion, class and community action: The social sources of the new urban politics. In *Social Areas in Cities*, Vol. 2 (Eds D. T. Herbert and R. J. Johnston), pp. 189–207, Wiley, London.

Bernstein, B. (1965). A socio-linguistic approach to social learning. In *Penguin Survey of the Social Sciences* (Ed. J. Gould), Penguin, Harmondsworth.

Blowers, A. (1973). The neighbourhood: Exploration of a concept. In *The City as a Social System* (Eds P. Sarre, H. Brown, A. Blowers, C. Hamnett, and D. Boswell), Open University Press, Milton Keynes.

Boal, F. W. (1969). Territoriality on the Shankill-Falls divide, Belfast, *Irish Geography*, **6**, 30–50.

Bott, E. (1957). *Family and Social Network, Roles, Norms, and External Relations in Ordinary Urban Families*, Tavistock Publications, London.

Boyle, M. J. and Robinson, M. E. (1979). Cognitive mapping and understanding. In *Geography and the Urban Environment*, Vol 2 (Eds D. T. Herbert and R. J. Johnston pp. 59–82, Wiley, London.

Burkhardt, J. D. (1971). Impact of highways on urban neighbourhoods: A model of social change, *Highway Research Record*, **356**, 85–94.

Buttimer, A. (1971). Sociology and planning, *Town Planning Review*, **42**, 145–180.

Campbell, A., Converse, P. E., and Rodgers, W. L. (1976). *The Quality of American Life*, Russell Sage Foundation, New York.

Carpenter, N. (1933). *Encyclopaedia of the Social Sciences*, Macmillan, New York.

Cohen, R. (1979). Neighbourhood planning and political capacity, *Urban Affairs Quarterly*, **14**(3), 337–362.

De Jonge, D. (1962). Images of urban areas, *Journal of the American Institute of Planners*, **28**, 266–276.

Dudley Report (1944). Design of dwellings, *Report of the Sub Committee of the Central Housing Advisory Committee*, HMSO, London.

Dunham, H. W. (1977). Community as process: Maintaining the delicate balance, *American Journal of Community Psychology*, **5**, 257–268.

Everitt, J. and Cadwallader, M. (1972). The home area concept in urban analysis. In *Environmental Design: Research and Practice* (Ed. W. J. Mitchell), Proceedings of EDRA 3 Conference, Los Angeles.

Everitt, J. and Cadwallader, M. (1977). Local area definition revisited, *Area*, **9**(3), 175–176.

Eyles, J. (1968). *The Inhabitants Image of Highgate Village*, Discussion Paper 15, LSE Graduate School of Geography, University of London.

Eyles, J. (1971). *Space, Territory and Conflict*, Geographical Paper 1, Department of Geography, University of Reading.

Finsterbusch, K. (1980). *Understanding Social Impacts*, Sage, London.

Fisher, G. H. (1972). *Perceptual Maps of Newcastle, Cardiff, Durham, York*, Department of Psychology, University of Newcastle.

Foley, D. L. (1950). The use of local facilities in a metropolis, *American Journal of Sociology*, **56**, 238–246.

Foley, D. L. (1952). *Neighbours and Urbanites*, University of Rochester Press, Rochester, New York.

Forbes, J. and Robertson, I. (1981). Patterns of residential movement in Greater Glasgow, *Scottish Geographical Magazine*, **97**(2), 85–97.

Gans, H. J. (1962). *The Urban Villagers*, The Free Press, New York.

Glass, R. (1948). *The Social Background of a Plan: A Study of Middlesborough*, Routledge and Kegan Paul, London.

Goffman, E. (1972). *Relations in Public: Microstudies of the Public Order*, Penguin Books, Harmondsworth.

Golany, G. (1976). *New Town Planning: Principles and Practice*, Wiley, New York.

Gold, J. R. (1980). *An Introduction to Behavioural Geography*, Oxford University Press, Oxford.

Golledge, R. G. and Zannaras, G. (1973). Cognitive approaches to the analysis of human spatial behaviour. In *Environment and Cognition* (Ed. W. H. Ittelson), Seminar Press, New York.

Goss, A. (1961). Neighbourhood units in British new towns, *Town Planning Review*, **32**, 66–82.

Greely, A. M. (1975). *Why Can't They Be Like Us?* Dutton, New York.

Gulick, J. (1963). Images of an Arab city, *Journal of the American Institute of Planners*, **29**, 179–198.

Hall, D. R. (1977). Applied social area analysis: Defining and evaluating areas for urban neighbourhood councils, *Geoforum*, **8**, 277–310.

Hallman, H. (1974). *Neighbourhood Government in a Metropolitan Setting*, Sage, London.

Hamble, S. and Talbot, J. (1977). Neighbourhood councils in England, *Research Report*, University of Birmingham.

Hambleton, R. (1978). *Policy Planning and Local Government*, Hutchinson, London.

Hampton, W. and Chapman, J. J. (1971). Towards neighbourhood councils II, *Political Quarterly*, **42**, 414–422.

Hart, R. A. and Moore, G. T. (1973). The development of spatial cognition: A review. In *Image and Environment* (Eds R. M. Downs and D. Stea), Aldine, Chicago.

Henry, L. and Cox, P. A. (1970). The neighbourhood concept in new town planning: A perception study in East Kilbride, *Horizon*, **19**, 37–45.

Herbert, G. (1963). The neighbourhood unit principle and organic theory, *Sociological Review*, **11**, 165–213.

Herbert, D. T. and Raine, J. W. (1976). Defining communities within urban areas, *Town Planning Review*, **47**(4), 325–338.

Hill, D. M. (1978). Neighbourhood councils, *Planning and Administration*, **5**(1), 27–40.

Hillery, G. A. (1955). Definitions of community: Areas of agreement, *Rural Sociology*, **20**, 111–123.

Hunter, A. (1975). The loss of community: An empirical test through replication, *American Sociological Review*, **40**, 537–552.

Hunter, A. (1979). The urban neighbourhood: Its analytical and social contexts, *Urban Affairs Quarterly*, **14**(3), 267–287.

Janowitz, M. (1952). *The Community Press in an Urban Setting*, University of Chicago Press, Chicago.

Kasarda, J. D. and Janowitz, M. (1974). Community attachment in mass society, *American Sociological Review*, **39**, 328–339.

Keller, S. (1968). *The Urban Neighbourhood: A Sociological Perspective*, Random House, New York.

Kuhn, M. (1968). Researchers in human space, *Ekistics*, **25**, 395–398.

Ladd, F. C. (1970). Black youths view their environment: Neighbourhood maps, *Environment and Behaviour*, **2**, 64–79.

Lee, S. A. (1982). The value of the local area, In *Valued Environments* (Eds J. Gold and J. Burgess), George Allen and Unwin, London.

Lee, T. R. (1954). *A Study of Urban Neighbourhood*. Unpublished PhD Dissertation, University of Cambridge, Cambridge.

Lee, T. R. (1968). Urban neighbourhood as a socio-spatial schema, *Human Relations*, **21**(3), 241–267.

Lee, T. R. (1976). Cities in the mind. In *Social Areas in Cities* Vol. 2, (Eds D. T. Herbert and R. J. Johnston), pp. 159–187. Wiley, London.

Ley, D. and Cybriwsky, R. A. (1974). Urban graffiti as territorial markers, *Annals of the Association of American Geographers*, **64**, 491–505.

Lipman, A. (1970). Territoriality: Useful architectural concept? *Royal Institute of British Architects Journal*, February 1970, 68–70.

Lowenthal, D. (1961). Geography, experience and imagination: Towards a geographical epistemology. *Annals of the Association of American Geographers*, **51**, 241–260.

Lyman, S. M. and Scott, M. B. (1967). Territoriality: A neglected sociological dimension, *Social Problems*, **15**, 236–249.

Lynch, K. (1960). *The Image of the City*, MIT Press, Cambridge, Massachusetts.

McClenahan, B. (1929). *The Changing Urban Neighbourhood*, University of Southern California, Los Angeles.

McKenzie, R. D. (1923). *Neighbourhood*, University of Chicago Press, Chicago.

McFarlane-Smith, I. (1964). *Spatial Ability: Its Educational and Social Significance*, University of London Press, London.

Malmberg, T. (1980). *Human Territoriality*, Mouton, Hague.

Mercer, C. (1975). *Living in Cities*, Penguin, Harmondsworth.

Mumford, L. (1954). The neighbourhood and the neighbourhood unit, *Town Planning Review*, **24**, 256–270.

North, C. C. (1926). The city as a community, In *The Urban Community* (Ed. E. W. Burgess), University of Chicago Press, Chicago.

Orleans, P. and Schmidt, S. (1972). Mapping the city. In *Environmental Design: Research and Practice* (Ed. W. J. Mitchell), Proceedings of EDRA 3 Conference, Los Angeles.

Pacione, M. (1976). Shape and structure in cognitive maps of Great Britain, *Regional Studies*, **10**, 275–283.

Pacione, M. (1978). Information and morphology in cognitive maps. *Transactions of the Institute of British Geographers*, New Series, **3**(4), 548–568.

Pacione, M. (1980). Differential quality of life in a metropolitan village. *Transactions of the Institute of British Geographers*, New Series, **5**(2), 185–206.

Park, R. E., Burgess, E. W., and McKenzie, R. D. (1925). *The City*, University of Chicago Press, Chicago.

Parr, A. E. (1965). In search of theory VI, *Art and Architecture*, **82**, 14–15.

Perry, C. (1929). The neighbourhood unit, *Regional Survey of New York and its Environs*, Vol. 7, Regional Plan Association, New York.

Popenoe, D. (1977). *The Suburban Environment*, University of Chicago Press, Chicago.

Porteous, J. D. (1977). *Environment and Behaviour: Planning and Everyday Urban Life*, Addison Wesley, Reading, Massachusetts.

Rapaport, A. (1977). *Human Aspects of Urban Form*, Pergamon, Oxford.

Reiser, R. L. (1972). *Urban Spatial Images*. Discussion Paper 42, LSE Graduate School of Geography, University of London, London.

Ross, H. L. (1962). The local community: A survey approach, *American Sociological Review*, **37**(1), 75–84.

Rossi, P. H. (1972). Community social indicators, In *The Human Meaning of Social Change* (Eds A. Campbell and P. E. Converse), Russell Sage Foundation, New York.

Royal Commission on Local Government (1969). *Research Studies 9: Community Attitudes Survey*, HMSO, London.

Saarinen, T. F. (1976). *Environmental Planning: Perception and Behaviour*, Houghton Mifflin, Boston.

Sanoff, H. (1970). Social perception of the ecological neighbourhood, *Ekistics*, **30**, 130–132.

Schacter, S. (1963). *International Encyclopaedia of the Social Sciences*, Vol. 2, Macmillan, New York.

Silk, P., Fyfe, A., and Gillon, S. (1978). *Community Councils in Glasgow*. Community Council Research Paper, Glasgow District Council, Glasgow.

Skeffington Report (1969). *People and Planning*, HMSO, London.

Slater, P. E. (1970). *The Pursuit of Lonliness*, Beacon, Boston.

Smith, C. J. (1977). *Geography and Mental Health*. Resource Paper No. 764, Association of American Geographers, Commission on College Geography, Washington, DC.

Smith, C. J. (1980). Neighbourhood effects on mental health. In *Geography and the Urban Environment* (Eds D. T. Herbert and R. J. Johnston), Vol. 3, pp. 363–415, Wiley, London.

Smith, R. A. (1975). Measuring neighbourhood cohesion: A review and some suggestions, *Human Ecology*, **3**(3), 143–160.

Sommer, R. (1969). *Personal Space. The Behavioural Basis of Design*, Prentice Hall, Englewood Cliffs, New Jersey.

Soja, E. J. (1971). *The Political Organisation of Space*. Resource Paper 8, Association of American Geographers, Commission on College Geography, Washington, DC.

Spencer, D. (1973). *An Evaluation of Three Techniques of Image Representation: A Study of Neighbourhood Perception in Selly Oak Birmingham*, MSocSci Thesis, Centre for Urban and Regional Studies, University of Birmingham, Birmingham.

Stone, G. P. (1954). City shoppers and urban identification, *American Journal of Sociology*, **60**, 35–45.

Suttles, G. D. (1972). *The Social Construction of Communities*, University of Chicago Press, Chicago.

Sutton, W. A. and Munsen, T. (1976). Definitions of community 1954 through 1973. Paper presented at the Annual Meeting of the American Sociological Association.

Theodorson, G. A. and Theodorson, A. G. (1969). *A Modern Dictionary of Sociology*, Crowell, New York.

Thomlinson, R. (1969). *Urban Structure. The Social and Spatial Character of Cities*, Random House, New York.

Timms, D. W. G. (1971). *The Urban Mosaic*, Cambridge University Press, Cambridge.

Uexkull, J. (1957). A stroll through the worlds of animals and men: A picture book of invisible worlds. In *Instinctive Behaviour: The Development of a Modern Concept* (Ed. C. H. Schiller), pp. 5–80, Methuen, London.

Ward, J. H. (1913). *The Social Center*, Appleton, New York.

Warren, R. (1978). *The Community in America*, Rand McNally, Chicago.

Webber, M. (1963). Order in diversity: Community without propinquity. In *Cities and Space: The Future Use of Urban Land* (Ed. L. Wingo), Johns Hopkins, Baltimore.

Webber, M. (1964). The urban place and the non-place urban realm. In *Explorations in Urban Structure* (Eds M. Webber, J. W. Dyckman, D. L. Foley, A. Z. Guttenberg, W. L. C. Wheaton, and C. B. Wurster), University of Pennsylvania Press, Philadelphia.

Wellman, B. (1978). *The Community Question: The Intimate Networks of East Yorkers*, Center for Urban and Community Studies, University of Toronto.

Wellman, B. and Leighton, B. (1979). Networks, neighbourhoods and communities: Approaches to the study of the community question, *Urban Affairs Quarterly*, **14**(3), 363–390.

Willmott, P. (1967). Social research and new communities, *Journal of the American Institute of Planners*, **33**(6), 387–398.

Wirth, L. (1938). Urbanism as a way of life, *American Journal of Sociology*, **44**, 3–24.

Yates, D. (1973). *Neighbourhood Democracy*, Lexington Books, Lexington, Massachusetts.

Young, M. (1970). Parish councils for cities? *New Society*, 29th January, 178–179.

Young, M. and Willmott, P. (1962). *Family and Kinship in East London*, Penguin, Harmondsworth.

Index